Minstrels and Minstrelsy
in Late Medieval England

Minstrels and Minstrelsy in Late Medieval England

Richard Rastall
with Andrew Taylor

THE BOYDELL PRESS

© Richard Rastall and Andrew Taylor 2023

All Rights Reserved. Except as permitted under current legislation no part of this work may be photocopied, stored in a retrieval system, published, performed in public, adapted, broadcast, transmitted, recorded or reproduced in any form or by any means, without the prior permission of the copyright owner

The rights of Richard Rastall and Andrew Taylor to be identified as the authors of this work have been asserted in accordance with sections 77 and 78 of the Copyright, Designs and Patents Act 1988

First published 2023
The Boydell Press, Woodbridge
Paperback edition 2025

ISBN 978 1 83765 039 2 (hardback)
ISBN 978 1 83765 255 6 (paperback)

The Boydell Press is an imprint of Boydell & Brewer Ltd
PO Box 9, Woodbridge, Suffolk IP12 3DF, UK
and of Boydell & Brewer Inc.
668 Mt Hope Avenue, Rochester, NY 14620-2731, USA
website: www.boydellandbrewer.com

Our Authorised Representative for product safety in the EU is Easy Access System Europe – Mustamäe tee 50, 10621 Tallinn, Estonia, gpsr.requests@easproject.com

A CIP catalogue record for this book is available
from the British Library

The publisher has no responsibility for the continued existence or accuracy of URLs for external or third-party internet websites referred to in this book, and does not guarantee that any content on such websites is, or will remain, accurate or appropriate

*To
Ian Bent
in gratitude and admiration*

Contents

List of illustrations   x

List of music examples   xiii

List of abbreviations   xiv

A note on references   xvi

A note on money   xvii

A note on dates   xix

Preface   xxii
    The myth, and the minstrel life • 'Minstrel' and 'minstrelsy': definitions and terminology • Minstrel-literature and the musical imperatives

Acknowledgments   xxix

Part I. Minstrels and Minstrelsy in the Elite Households
Introduction to Part I

1   The royal households and their minstrels   3
    The household and its operation • The accounts: Wardrobe and Chamber

2   The life of a royal minstrel   14
    Status and conditions of the minstrels • Residence: attendance and absences • Constitution and administration

3   Recruitment, training and retirement   49
    Recruitment • Training • Retirement

4   Minstrelsy at Court   73
    Duties of the royal minstrels • Domestic occasions for minstrelsy • Ceremonial occasions for minstrelsy

5   Minstrelsy in noble and ecclesiastical households   99
    The domestic context • Secular households • Ecclesiastical households

Part II. Urban Minstrelsy
Introduction to Part II

6   Minstrelsy in the towns   129
    The towns of late medieval England • Minstrelsy in civic life • Hiring minstrels • Hosting royalty and nobility

7   Civic minstrels   146

  Town minstrels in England and abroad • The institution of civic minstrels in England • The meaning of 'wait' • The appointment and conditions of civic minstrels • Status and standards

PART III. ON THE ROAD
  Introduction to Part III

8   Minstrels on the road   167

  The minstrel as traveller • The journey of Princess Eleanor, May 1332 • The journey of Margaret Tudor to Scotland, 1503

9   Minstrel itineraries   183

  Minstrel circuits? • Some venues and routes • Travel as a regular feature of the minstrel life

10 The regulation and protection of minstrels   198

  The control of minstrelsy: the minstrel courts • The control of minstrelsy: the kings of heralds and of minstrels • The protection of minstrelsy: the minstrel fraternities

PART IV. MINSTREL PERFORMANCE
  Introduction to Part IV

11 The enigma of the minstrels' songs   235

  ANDREW TAYLOR

  External evidence • Internal evidence • Modern nostalgia and the myth of the *séance épique*: the harper in the hall • The rogue at the door • Corruption, fragmentation and conversation

12 Professional recitation before the fourteenth century   269

  ANDREW TAYLOR

  The *joglars* as wanderers or travellers • Contact between the troubadours and *joglars* and the English court • Epic recitation before the fourteenth century • Taillefer at Hastings

13 Minstrels and heralds and chivalric fame   291

  ANDREW TAYLOR

  Fame and the *gestour* • Minstrels and heralds as chivalric memorialists • King Robert's judgment at the court of Edward II • Lawrence Minot and the Chandos Herald • Anonymous songs of praise and blame • Songs of shame • Knightly suspicion of professional chivalric memorialists • Minstrel performance and literary history

14 Instruments and performers   315

Wind instruments • Pipers in the royal households • Keyboards and percussion • Stringed instruments • Minstrelsy by those not known as 'minstrel' • Solo and concerted minstrelsy • Henry VII's reorganisation of his minstrels

15 The instrumental repertory in England   362

Literacy • Instrumental performance 1: dances in one and two voices • Notation-free composition • Instrumental performance 2: music in two and three voices • Minstrels' manuscripts? • Instrumental ensemble music in fifteenth-century England

Envoi   395

Bibliography   399

Index   427

Illustrations

Plates

1. J.F. Clemens (1748–1831), after Nicolai Abildgaard (1743–1809), *Ossian's Swan Song*. Statens Museum for Kunst, www.smk.dk, public domain. — xxiii

2. A bagpiper. Bench end in St Nonna's church, Altarnun, Cornwall, early 16th century. Photograph by Dr E.T. Fox, reproduced by permission. — 26

3. A fiddler. Bench end in St Nonna's church, Altarnun, Cornwall, early 16th century. Photograph by Dr E.T. Fox, reproduced by permission. — 27

4. The initial to Psalm 80, *Exultate Deo*, c. 1325. © Oxford, Bodleian Library, MS Douce 366 (the Ormesby Psalter), fol. 109r: reproduced by permission. — 33

5. Record of Master John's repair of the organ at Langley, February 1303. Kew, The National Archives, E101.363.18 (Household of the Prince of Wales, Controller's book, 31 Ed I), fol. 5v. — 35

6. A joust, with a trumpeter signalling and the herald's baton raised: from Christine de Pisan, *Le Duc des Vrais Amants*, early 15th century. © The British Library Board. London, British Library, MS Harley 4431, fol. 150r. — 82

7. The coronation of Charles VI, from Jean Froissart, *Chroniques*, fol. 215r: from Bruges, 1468 or 1469. Image © bpk-Bildagentur. Berlin, Staatsbibliothek Preussischer Kulturbesitz, Depot Breslau 1, MS Rehd. 2. — 89

8. The initial to Psalm 80, *Exultate Deo*, c. 1325. © Oxford, Bodleian Library, MS Ashmole 1523 (the Bromholm Psalter), fol. 99r: reproduced by permission. — 233

9. Adenet le Roi in the presence of Marie, Queen of France, Blanche of Castille, and Jean de Brabant. Paris, Arsenal MS 3142 (1275–1300), fol. 1r: reproduced by permission of the Bibliothèque Nationale de France. — 242

Illustrations

10	The seal of Richard Bottore, the king's gitterner, on a receipt for his robe, 2 August 4 Ed III (1330), kept with a livery list. Kew, The National Archives, E101.385.4.	318
11	King John of Portugal entertaining John of Gaunt in 1397: from Jean de Wavrin, *Chroniques d'Angleterre*. Bruges, late 15th century. © The British Library Board. London, British Library, Royal MS 14 E iv, fol. 244v.	324
12	*Quene Note* by Frank, with the tenors to *Anxce bon youre delabonestren* and *Eterne rex altissime*, late 15th or early 16th century. © Oxford, Bodleian Library: MS Digby 167, fol. 31v: reproduced by permission.	376

Tables

1	Royal minstrels c. 1344–7	6
2	Royal minstrels on the Agincourt campaign, 1415	7
3	Grants to minstrels confirmed during 43 and 44 Edward III	16
4	Annual fees to the royal minstrels, 1482–3	18
5	Marshals of the minstrels and trumpeters	45
6	Minstrels in the Chamber	52
7	Minstrels visiting the Warwick household, 1431/2	114
8	Minstrels visiting Durham cathedral priory, 1375/6	124
9	The Merchant Taylors of London: costs of minstrels at the feast of St John the Baptist, 1456	133
10	Minstrels rewarded at Barnstaple, 1470/1	140
11	Minstrels rewarded at Durham, 1375/6, by status	169
12	The king's minstrels at York, 1446–9	188
13	Minstrels at Durham cathedral priory, 1445–7	190
14	Minstrel itineraries in Kent	192
15	Minstrels at the relief of Rhuddlan	201
16	Minstrels' seals	317

Maps

Maps are schematic and show approximate straight-line distances between places. Actual distances travelled might be considerably greater.

1	The king's travels, April 1303	59
2	Princess Eleanor's journey, 1332: Westminster to Bruges	176
3	Princess Eleanor's journey, 1332: Bruges to Nijmegen	177
4	Margaret Tudor's journey to Scotland, 1503	180
5	Minstrel itineraries in Kent	191

All maps were supplied by Cath D'Alton.

The authors and publisher are grateful to all the institutions and individuals listed for permission to reproduce the materials in which they hold copyright. Every effort has been made to trace the copyright holders; apologies are offered for any omission, and the publisher will be pleased to add any necessary acknowledgement in subsequent editions.

Musical examples

These musical examples are transcriptions, not editions. All are presented in reduced note-values. For sources and dates, see the text (Chapter 15).

1	Openings of sections 1, 2 and 3 of the Bodleian *estampie*	367
2	Dance 1 from Harley 978, openings of sections 2 and 3	371
3	Dance 1 from Harley 978, openings of all sections	371
4	*Falla con misuras*, opening	375
5	*Quene note*	380
6	*Felix namque*, opening	383
7	*Anxce bon youre*, opening	385
8	Francisco de la Torre's *La Spagna*, opening	387
9	*Jeo hay en vos*, opening	388
10	*Go hert hurt with adversitie*, opening	390

Abbreviations

The following abbreviations are used throughout this book:

BL	The British Library, London
BnF	Bibliothèque Nationale de France
CPR	*Calendar of the Patent Rolls*. Public Record Office Calendars, 1891–
EETS e.s.	Early English Text Society, Extra Series
EETS o.s.	Early English Text Society, Original Series
EETS s.s.	Early English Text Society, Supplementary Series
MERH	Rastall, Richard, 'The Minstrels of the English Royal Households, 25 Ed I–1 Hen VIII: an Inventory'. Royal Musical Association *Research Chronicle* 4 (1967, for 1964), 1–41
NG	*The New Grove Dictionary of Music and Musicians*. London, 2001: available online
Ords & Regs	*A Collection of Ordinances and Regulations for the Government of the Royal Household*. Society of Antiquaries, London, 1790
REED	Records of Early English Drama. Cited here as *REED County* or *City*
SM	Rastall, G.R., 'Secular Musicians in Late Medieval England'. 2 vols. PhD. dissertation, Victoria University of Manchester, 1968
TNA	The National Archives, Kew, Surrey
c., circa	about (of date)
cal.	calendared
d.	died
d	pence
esp.	especially
f	following (of page or folio)
ff	following (plural)
fl.	flourished
fol.	folio

fols	folios
ibid. ibidem	in the same place (book or article)
m.	membrane (of a manuscript roll)
mm.	membranes
mk	mark (in sums of money)
mks	marks
p.	page
pp.	pages
s	shilling(s)

A note on references

The manuscript sources of Wardrobe and Chamber material come from a variety of libraries: references to them are here kept as short as reasonably possible. Those from the John Rylands University Library in Manchester and the library of the Society of Antiquaries in London are entered under the names 'Rylands' and 'Antiquaries' respectively, followed by the manuscript number; those formerly in the Public Record Office, London, and now in The National Archives (TNA) at Kew have call-numbers such as E101.363.11 or C34.15. Manuscripts in the British Library in London (BL) are from the Egerton, Harleian and Stowe collections (identified as such), and the Cotton collection, with press-marks beginning Galba, Nero or Vespasian. Additional Manuscripts from the British Library, Rylands Library or Society of Antiquaries library are further identified as 'Add'.

Most entries concerning minstrels in the Wardrobe and Chamber material are calendared in the second volume of G.R. Rastall, 'Secular Musicians in Late Medieval England', Appendix A. This work is accessible online, so any reference to a manuscript entry may be noted as calendared (cal.) in SM II. When an entry is not calendared there I have referred to any other work offering a calendar or the original text.

In the footnotes of this book, short bibliographic references relate to entries in the Bibliography, listed under the author or title shown.

Definitions and further explanations of musical instruments and performers will be found in the relevant sections of Chapter 14: for other references, the reader should consult the Index.

In discussions of instrumental ranges (Chapter 14) and the musical examples (Chapter 15) unspecified pitches are given in capital letters: so C is the note C (the octave will be obvious from the musical context if relevant). Specific pitches are referred to by the Helmholtz system, in which c'-b'-c" is the octave from Middle C upwards.

A note on money

Before decimalisation in 1971, and including the whole of the period covered by this book, the English pound (*libra -e*, £) was divided into 20 shillings (*solidus -i*, s), each of which consisted of 12 pence (*denarius -i*, d). The half-penny (ha'penny, *obolus -i*) was also used, and appears in the accounts as 'ob.'. The quarter-penny, which survived into the mid-twentieth century as the farthing (i.e. 'fourthing'), was also in use, but does not appear in any of the records discussed here. Most sums of money are given in full here – e.g. as £14 13s 10d – but a whole number of pounds is written in short form (e.g. £5). Sums could also be written as shillings and pence only – for instance, as 33s 4d (= £1 13s 4d).

Medieval transactions were frequently made in terms of the mark, which was worth 13s 4d (i.e. 160d, or two-thirds of a pound). Accounting scribes were equally at home with marks or £ s d,[1] although only the half-mark still circulated as a coin in the fourteenth and fifteenth centuries (at different times the angel or noble, valued at 80d = 6s 8d). This probably helped to retain not only the mark and half-mark but also the quarter-mark (3s 4d) and the one-eighth of a mark (20d, or 1s 8d) as normal accounting values, especially (for our purposes here) as gifts to minstrels and others.[2] For accounting purposes such sums had to be written as £ s d on the right-hand edge of the page, so that they could be included in the adding-up process, the sum of individual entries being written at the bottom of each page of the account. Where I have quoted a sum of money given in terms of marks I have also shown it as (£ s d). Conversely, apparently irrational sums of money in £ s d may have been conceived in marks. A very limited conversion-table will be useful in such cases:

1 mark	13s 4d	3 marks	£2 0s 0d	5 marks	£3 6s 8d
10 marks	£6 13s 4d	20 marks	£13 6s 8d	100 marks	£66 13s 4d

The value of a medieval sum of money in practical terms is always difficult to comprehend. It is tempting to multiply a medieval sum of money by a certain factor to reach the equivalent present-day value, but that process is always a failure. The first reason for this is obvious: continual inflation, which has devalued the currency since the early sixteenth century (and seriously so for much of the twentieth and into the twenty-first), makes any such attempt almost immediately outdated.

The second reason is more problematic. Values have a different significance in different circumstances. Someone with a very large income may think nothing

---

[1] See, for instance, the graduated rewards to minstrels at the 1306 Pentecost feast, given alternately in marks and £ s d (Chapter 4).

[2] The conservatism inherent in this situation will be obvious if we note that even into the twentieth century the normal fee for consultation with a solicitor was 6s 8d.

of buying a pot of jam for a sum that would keep a poor family alive for several days, or of decorating a room for what would seem a large fortune to others. It has always been thus in any developed society. In the late Middle Ages one penny was an acceptable gift to a beggar, whereas the king might reward a favoured entertainer with £30 or more. This differential is the main reason for the rule-of-thumb multiplication by 200 (say) being more or less useless: the true value of a gift, as opposed to its monetary face-value, depends on both the giver and the recipient; the true value of a service depends on both the supplier and the buyer.

On the other hand, the face-value of money remained fairly constant in the fourteenth and fifteenth centuries, because inflation was then low.[3] We can therefore treat these centuries as a single period when considering the value of goods, and some examples may help us to form an idea of what money was worth and what it would buy. In a rural area – and the rural/urban split is another reason for differentials – one might buy a sheep or a pig for a shilling or so, or a horse for two shillings.[4] This would be an ordinary working horse for a farm: a horse bought for work in a royal household would always cost more than that (usually between 10 and 20 shillings), and a war-horse more still (perhaps 40 shillings). Compared to the weekly income of a poor tenant farmer, probably measured in pence rather than shillings, the sums expended at Court must often have seemed to be in a different universe.

---

[3] For a summary of the complex story of prices and inflation/deflation, see J.L. Bolton, 'Prices and wages'. Paul Szarmach, M. Teresa Tavormina and Joel T. Rosenthal, eds, *Medieval England: An Encyclopedia* (New York NY and London, 1998), 609–11.

[4] See, for instance, H.J. Hewitt, *Mediaeval Cheshire: An Economic and Social History of Cheshire in the Reigns of the Three Edwards* (Manchester, 1929), 46, 62 and 163.

A note on dates

The medieval calendar year in England ran for some purposes from January to December, but the year-number normally changed on 25 March, the feast of the Annunciation. Thus 31 December 1300 was followed by 1 January 1300, and 24 March 1300 was followed by 25 March 1301. This method of dating was universal. Particular institutions had their own variants, however, especially for accounting years. A town or city might run its financial year from a major feast such as Michaelmas (29 September), or from the day on which a new mayor took office – a mayoral year – which might differ from one place to another.[1]

A special version of this was used in the royal households, and was normal in all national and royal administrative and governmental documentation. The regnal year normally began on the day of a king's accession, and so was different in each reign. The final regnal year of any reign was cut short by the king's death or deposition. The royal finances were accounted for by regnal years: I give the relevant ones here, all dates being new-style, with the year beginning on 1 January.

Edward I acceded 20 November 1272, died 7 July 1307

So 1 Ed I is	20 November 1272–19 November 1273
30 Ed I	20 November 1301–19 November 1302
35 Ed I	20 November 1306–7 July 1307

Edward II acc. 8 July 1307, deposed 20 January 1327

1 Ed II	8 July 1307–7 July 1308
10 Ed II	8 July 1316–7 July 1317
20 Ed II	8 July 1326–20 January 1327

Edward III acc. 25 January 1327, d. 21 June 1377

1 Ed III	25 January 1327–24 January 1328
50 Ed III	25 January 1376–24 January 1377
51 Ed III	25 January 1377–21 June 1377

---

[1] The town wardens' accounts at Dover, confusingly, worked to a year both starting and ending on 8 September. See *REED Kent: Diocese of Canterbury*, ed. James M. Gibson. 3 vols (2002), II, 309 and *passim*.

Richard II acc. 22 June 1377, deposed 29 September 1399

1 Ric II	22 June 1377–21 June 1378
20 Ric II	22 June 1396–21 June 1397
23 Ric II	22 June 1399–29 September 1399

Henry IV acc. 30 September 1399, died 20 March 1413

1 Hen IV	30 September 1399–29 September 1400
10 Hen IV	30 September 1408–29 September 1409
14 Hen IV	30 September 1412–20 March 1413

Henry V acc. 21 March 1413, died 31 August 1422

1 Hen V	21 March 1413–20 March 1414
10 Hen V	21 March 1422–31 August 1422

Henry VI acc. 1 September 1422, deposed 4 March 1461; reinstated 3 October 1470, deposed 11 April 1471

1 Hen VI	1 September 1422–31 August 1423
30 Hen VI	1 September 1451–31 August 1452
39 Hen VI	1 September 1460–4 March 1461

Henry was deposed and kept in captivity until his reinstatement: he then continued the regnal dates as if there had been no break in his reign. Edward IV did likewise.

49 Hen VI	September or October 1470–11 April 1471

Edward IV acc. 4 March 1461, died 9 April 1483

1 Ed IV	4 March 1461–3 March 1462
10 Ed IV	4 March 1470–3 March 1471
23 Ed IV	4 March 1483–9 April 1483

Edward V acc. 9 April 1483, deposed 25 June 1483

1 Ed V	9 April 1483–25 June 1483

Richard III acc. 26 June 1483, died 22 August 1485

1 Ric III	26 June 1483–25 June 1484
3 Ric III	26 June 1485–22 August 1485

Henry VII acc. 22 August 1485, died 21 April 1509

1 Hen VII	21 August (*sic*) 1485–21 August 1486[2]
20 Hen VII	22 August 1504–21 August 1505
24 Hen VII	22 August 1508–21 April 1509

Henry VIII acc. 22 April 1509, died 28 January 1547

1 Hen VIII	22 April 1509–21 April 1510

The Church had its own liturgical calendar, which changed the year on 25 March, the feast of the Annunciation (the conception of Christ), nine months before Christmas Day. The Church year incorporates two overlapping cycles: the fixed dates, which include all saints' days and certain other feast-days such as Christmas, and the feast-days that depend on Easter and are therefore movable, occurring on various dates within a range.

For further information on calendars and systems of dating, see C.R. Cheney, ed., *Handbook of Dates for Students of English History*. Corrected repr. (London, 1978); for historical events and persons, E.B. Fryde, D.E. Greenway, S. Porter and I. Roy, eds, *Handbook of British Chronology*. 3rd edn (London, 1986).

---

[2] Although Henry VII acceded to the throne on 22 August 1485, he dated his reign from 21 August so that those who fought for Richard III at Bosworth could be deemed traitors.

Preface

The myth, and the minstrel life

Who were the minstrels of medieval England? What did they do to earn a living, and what sort of lives did they lead? What music did they play, and what other sorts of entertainment could they offer? Medieval iconography shows that many instrumentalists lived comfortably as liveried servants of royalty and the aristocracy; records of court proceedings show that some of the lower-class independent minstrels had brushes with the law (and this is in fact the only type of evidence we have for most of them). Clearly, these are the two extremes of a wide range of social situations in which minstrels lived, and the picture in reality must be a much more complex one.

When it comes to vocal minstrelsy it is mainly literary evidence that provides information. But here a ready-made picture comes to mind: for everyone 'knows' that in medieval England minstrels wandered the countryside, singing love-songs and ballads to the accompaniment of a lute and earning a few pence, a meal or a night's lodging in any place where they were welcomed. While most such men were virtually stateless and included rogues and thieves among their ranks, some – like Robin Hood's Allan-a-Dale – were more respected and worked locally.

This popular myth, apparently confirmed by W.S. Gilbert (in *The Mikado*, 1885) and Hollywood, offers one version of the minstrel. Another was offered by eighteenth-century antiquaries, who saw the minstrel not as a ragamuffin but as a bard, a figure of great power. The age yearned for a primitive oral past, and found it when in 1760 James Macpherson published his *Fragments of Ancient Poetry*, the works he attributed to the legendary poet Ossian (Plate 1). These fragments, the 'words of the bards in the days of song: when the king heard the music of the harps, the tales of other times', were a literary sensation.[1] There was soon a ferocious debate over just how extensively Macpherson had reworked the materials he had collected from Gaelic oral tradition. Some, like Samuel Johnson, derided the Ossianic corpus as pure forgery. Nevertheless, Ossian was widely celebrated and many regarded the medieval minstrels as the inheritors of this bardic tradition.[2] Thomas Percy held

---

[1] James Macpherson, *The Poems of Ossian and Related Works*, ed. Howard Gaskill (Edinburgh, 2003), 170.

[2] Thomas M. Curley, *Samuel Johnson, the Ossian Fraud, and the Celtic Revival in Great Britain and Ireland* (Cambridge and New York NY, 2009); Howard Gaskell, ed., *The Reception of Ossian in Europe* (London, 2004). Most influentially, Thomas Percy referred to the minstrels as 'the genuine successors of the bards' in *Reliques of Ancient English Poetry Consisting of Old Heroic Ballads, Songs, and Other Pieces of Our Earlier Poets, Chiefly of the Lyric Kind*. 4 vols (Dublin, 1766), I, xv.

PLATE 1. J.F. Clemens (1748–1831), after Nicolai Abildgaard (1743–1809): *Ossian's Swan Song*. Statens Museum for Kunst.

that from the days of the Conquest, the minstrels 'entertained their hearers with chanting to the harp or other instruments, songs and tales of chivalry, or as they were called gests and romances in verse in the English language'.[3] Thomas Warton argued that the retinues 'of our Norman ancestors … abounded with minstrels and harpers, and … their chief entertainment was to listen to the recital of romantic and martial endeavours'.[4] Warton believed that the Middle English metrical romances were based on these lost oral performances, and offered what he called 'The Geste of King Horn' as the earliest surviving example.[5] Popular culture and scholarship continue to present a picture of minstrel activity that bears little relation to the historical evidence.

Clearly, the myths of the wandering minstrel and his bardic powers should be replaced by a truer picture of the social and artistic history of minstrelsy. Moreover, this picture must address the balance between vocal and instrumental minstrelsy, for the evidence – both iconographic and documentary – seems to refer almost exclusively to instrumental performance. It is therefore important to consider the literary evidence, which Andrew Taylor does in Chapters 11–13, exploring the lengthy vocal performances often attributed to minstrels (the recitation of *chansons de geste* and romances), and the kinds of shorter performance that were actually offered.

The overall picture, even so, is difficult to compile, and the medieval minstrel remains, for the most part, a shadowy figure whose life and music are difficult to discern. We have tried to piece together something of this picture, by collecting and interpreting much rather fragmentary and wide-ranging evidence that needs to be assessed very carefully. This material is introduced at the beginning of each part of the book.[6]

'Minstrel' and 'minstrelsy': definitions and terminology

A necessary beginning is to find usable definitions of 'minstrel' and 'minstrelsy' as they existed several centuries ago. There appear to be no medieval definitions of minstrelsy and no practical or eye-witness explanations of what a minstrel did. Nor is there any objective information on the scope or limits of minstrelsy: the nearest we can get is the list of accomplishments given in *Piers Plowman*, discussed in Chapter 11.[7]

It may be useful to think of minstrelsy as any entertainment in which music played a part, a definition that can be inferred from the evidence but not proved. The

---

[3] Percy, *Reliques*, I, 426–7.

[4] Thomas Warton, *The History of English Poetry*. 3 vols (London, 1774; edn of 1871), I, 39.

[5] Warton, *History of English Poetry*, I, 38–42. Warton's enthusiasm for minstrel performance may have led him to fabricate evidence for it (see Chapter 11).

[6] The various types of evidence are discussed more fully in G.R. Rastall, 'Secular Musicians in Late Medieval England'. 2 vols. PhD. diss. (Victoria University of Manchester, 1968), I, xvii–xxxv.

[7] See also Andrew Taylor, 'Were minstrels actors in waiting?'. ROMARD 55 (2016), 57–68; and Richard Rastall, 'Minstrels and players: functions and terminology'. ROMARD 55 (2016), 81–92.

singing of polyphonic songs would not normally be considered minstrelsy, however, and drama was not minstrelsy, although a dramatic performance often included minstrelsy as one of its elements. On the other hand, as the term could be applied to a bearward's presentation of a dancing bear, music may have been an ingredient in that performance. If this is correct, it is also true that music was rarely the kind of performance that we would think of as a musical recital: even when instrumental music was played apparently for its own sake it may have been the accompaniment to a dance or procession, or the background against which diplomatic discussion took place. The only situation that approached the modern-day concert was those occasions when a town's own minstrels or some travelling group performed in a public space for the entertainment of the citizens.

Any definition of minstrelsy is probably inadequate, and although the use of music is a helpful feature, even that is not certain. In particular, the minstrelsy of heralds, which must often have been verbal, may not always have included music, and the same goes for the minstrelsy of such as bearwards and waferers. If music was indeed not a part of such 'minstrelsy', it may still be helpful to regard this usage as an extension of the principal definition for which no other term would be appropriate.

With such a broad spectrum of what 'minstrelsy' could be, it is impossible to be precise about what sort of entertainer any particular minstrel was. Moreover, we have used only the English term so far, whereas the written records earlier than the late fifteenth century were in Latin or French. The Latin word normally used for a minstrel was *ministrallus*, although some account-books used *histrio* or *mimus*. The question arises whether these different terms imply any distinction of function. Another group of terms, which does seem to be distinct from the 'minstrel' words, includes *lusor*, *ludator* and the adjectival *ludens*: these refer to playing in the modern sense of acting or playing a game (such as dice), not to our modern use for 'playing' an instrument. The lack of clear definitions for these various terms has led the Records of Early English Drama project (REED) to translate all such words – and their French equivalents, *ministral* and *joueur* – as 'entertainer'. This is a practical and realistic solution, but it ignores the real distinctions that can sometimes be glimpsed through the various usages. It is certainly possible to reach some tentative conclusions about how these terms were used, and therefore to translate them more confidently. This matter is discussed in Chapters 6 and 8.

All these terms are masculine, but some feminine words were in use for a minstrel:[8] and although there is no evidence of women working as liveried minstrels they were occasionally rewarded for minstrelsy. Some of these women were the wives of known minstrels: Edward II's waferer Richard Pilke and his wife Helen were rewarded for minstrelsy, for instance, and it is possible that Margery, wife of Edward II's trumpeter William, was also a trumpeter.[9] Female minstrels did not excite particular comment. At a feast in 1317, a woman dressed as a minstrel and on horseback

---

[8] Charles du Fresne, Seigneur Du Cange, *Glossarium Mediae et Infimae Latinitatis*, ed. G.A.L. Henschel (Paris, 1882–7), offers 'ministrallissa' and others.

[9] TNA E101.374.19 (5–6 Ed II), fol. 8v (cal. SM II, 74); BL Cotton MS Nero C viii, fol. 42v (3 Ed II: cal. SM II, 71).

gained access to the king, the door-keepers letting her in on the grounds that minstrels were always allowed into the hall on such occasions.[10]

Women were evidently usual for certain types of minstrelsy, particularly dancing and singing. These were not confined to women, of course, nor to independent minstrels, but when women appear in the records that is usually the kind of minstrelsy concerned.[11]

Minstrel-literature and the musical imperatives

For all their riches, earlier minstrel-histories, such as those in Percy's *Reliques of Ancient English Poetry* (1764) and Chambers's *The Mediaeval Stage* (1903), had no real musical objectives, and the descriptions of minstrels' lives were based largely on what might be guessed from literary sources, together with isolated entries from relevant account-books and other records. This rather fragmentary evidence, relying heavily on the 'plums' that shed light mainly on special occasions, led to the construction of a rather fragile picture of medieval minstrelsy. Uncovering the day-to-day activity of minstrelsy requires the accumulation of large quantities of information from records of daily payments and other *minutiae* of everyday life, through which an overall picture can be drawn.

The first attempt at this, to my knowledge, was Rosalind Conklin's doctoral thesis of 1964.[12] This examined a wide range of materials, effectively opening up the subject of English minstrelsy in the late Middle Ages to serious historical study. My own thesis followed soon after.[13] Although we studied much the same evidence our aims were different. Conklin, as a professional historian, produced an excellent historical and social survey: Andrew Taylor and I are grateful to her for that and for many discussions over the years.

My own principal aim was to discover how minstrels performed in consort. The basic subject of this book is therefore the circumstances and conditions under which minstrels worked in England during the fourteenth and fifteenth centuries, and what those might tell us about minstrel performance. Part I examines the minstrels employed in royal and other elite households; Part II considers urban minstrelsy, including that of the civic minstrels employed by town governments; Part III is a discussion of the various ways in which both employed and self-employed minstrels interacted with the world around them; and Part IV attempts to uncover what we know and can infer of vocal and instrumental performance by minstrels.

The minstrels were never a separate department or sub-department in the royal households. When a scribe needed to list the minstrels specifically he certainly might do so under the heading of 'the minstrels' (or a sub-division such as 'trumpets' or

---

[10] Edmund K. Chambers, *The Mediaeval Stage*. 2 vols (Oxford, 1903), I, 44, n. 6; and below, p. 176.

[11] See below, pp. 176 and 350.

[12] Rosalind Conklin, 'Medieval English minstrels, 1216–1485'. PhD. diss. (University of Chicago, 1964).

[13] Rastall, 'Secular Musicians', hereafter SM. Working in different disciplines (History, Music), we did not know of each other's work for several years.

'*vigiles*') as a matter of description; but for general purposes such as livery-lists or the recording of wages due, the minstrels often appeared in the lists of *scutiferi* (squires) or *valetti* (yeomen) of the household without further distinction. Often the minstrels were grouped together, but not invariably so, and lists of household servants do not necessarily identify precisely those who were employed as minstrels. The minstrels were household servants in exactly the same way as many others, and the conditions under which they worked were largely those of other servants. In considering the daily lives and conditions of household minstrels, therefore, much of our discussion is not peculiar to the minstrels but more widely applicable.

The study of minstrels, their everyday lives and the conditions of their work were a means to an end, however, not the ultimate aim of my research. What was missing from all previous work was the *musical* history of the minstrels – how they played in consort, what exactly they did, musically speaking, in a performance, and what sort of relationship existed between minstrel performance and the surviving notated music. Of these, the question of minstrels playing in consort was partly explained, and the results have had some influence on the modern performance of late medieval instrumental music.[14] Groups performing late medieval music in the 1960s and early 70s tended to play a wide variety of instruments, because the instruments themselves (especially the louder and coarser ones) were seen to attract audiences. Thus a consort would typically include one each of several different types of instrument, often mixing 'loud' and 'still'.[15] The realisation that medieval practice included homogeneous pairings (such as two fiddles, or two trumpets and nakers) led to such groupings being used, with the further result that consorts were more consistently either 'loud' or 'still'.

The results, nevertheless, rely on evidence that is open to different interpretations, and for which confirmatory evidence is not available. For instance, there is almost no English iconography that has any bearing on the question, and no theoretical writing: and in both cases this is in strong contrast to the situation on the continent.

The equally problematic question of the relationship between minstrel performance and the notated music is discussed in Chapter 15. Minstrels are always depicted performing without notation, although some musical sources include notated pieces such as we might expect minstrels to have performed. Is it wrong, then, to think that minstrels were musically illiterate, working entirely in an aural tradition? Were there instrumentalists who could read notated music, and if so were they professional minstrels or highly-educated amateurs? If the latter, were they trained by (musically-illiterate) professional minstrels or by members of some other class of musician?

---

[14] SM I, 176–86, and more specifically Richard Rastall, 'Some English consort-groupings of the late Middle Ages'. *Music & Letters* 55/2 (April 1974), 179–202; repr. Timothy J. McGee, ed., *Instruments and their Music in the Middle Ages* (Farnham, 2009), 61–84.

[15] Groups could point to iconographical evidence for this (albeit misinterpreted). Medieval manuscript illustrations depicted as wide a variety of instruments as possible in praise of the Virgin Mary, but this was purely symbolic and bore no relation to real-life consorts.

The question of training is examined in Chapter 3, where those training others in instrumental and vocal minstrelsy are indeed found to be professional minstrels apparently working in a purely aural tradition. But since some of the music concerned survives in notated sources the old question remains: what is the relationship between the minstrels' performance and the notated sources? As in the similar case of recitation and the problems surrounding the *Chanson de Roland* and other literary works, there is a frustrating lack of evidence to connect performance and written remains. Hendrik van der Werf usefully discussed elements of medieval musical composition, including decoration (embellishment of existing music, whether notated or not), improvisation (the construction of musical materials 'on the hoof') and notationless composition (the use of improvisation to create musical structures and their constituent melodic, rhythmic and textural elements). While his work concerns vocal sacred music, it is used here (Chapter 15) to support a discussion of the notated English music that may be related to the minstrel repertory.

Acknowledgments

Much of this book is based on my research in the royal household Wardrobe and Chamber accounts. A notable gap in this work was the evidence of literature and of oral performance by minstrels, and these have been supplied in three chapters by Andrew Taylor. I am very grateful to him for these, and for much valuable advice on my own chapters. My debt to Professor Taylor relates to many years of his helpful exchange of ideas.

Of those who originally supported my research, and to all of whom I remain profoundly grateful,[1] I must single out Ian Bent, who suggested the subject to me and has remained a source of information and encouragement. The protracted visits to London needed for my initial exploration of the rich and extensive materials concerned were made possible by the generous hospitality of Ian and Margaret Bent and of the late Alan and Sheila Willmore. I am grateful to the staff of the various libraries and archives involved: The National Archives (formerly the Public Record Office), the British Library (for material formerly held at the British Museum), the College of Arms, the Bodleian Library, Oxford, the John Rylands University Library, Manchester, the Society of Antiquaries of London, the Warwick Libraries and the Warwickshire Record Office.

This book was initially discussed with Rosalind Conklin Hays, and I am grateful to Alexandra F. Johnston for suggesting collaboration with Andrew Taylor. Professor Hays' discussions with us were stimulating and enlightening, and her decision to bow out of the project for personal reasons was a great loss. I have also received valuable assistance from Alison Adams, Roger Bowers, Roger Brock, Alex Buckle, Martha Carlin, Wendy Childs, William Flynn, Ed Fox, Peter Greenfield, Leofranc Holford-Strevens, Fiona Jenkinson, David Klausner, John McKinnell, Keith Polk, Jane Tunesi of Liongam, Ronald Woodley, Christopher Woolgar, Diana Wyatt and Linda Marie Zaerr; and we are grateful for the advice of our anonymous readers. The section of Chapter 6 on Prince Edward's visit to Coventry in 1474 is adapted from an article published in *The Musical Times* in June 1977, and is used here by permission. I have benefitted throughout from the wise advice and continuous encouragement of Caroline Palmer and Elizabeth McDonald at Boydell and Brewer. Most of all I am deeply indebted to my wife, Jane Oakshott MBE, who has cheerfully accepted my mental absences, and whose constant encouragement has seen me through to the completion of this book.

Richard Rastall
Leeds, August 2022

---

[1] Acknowledged in SM I, xiv–xv.

Part I

Minstrels and Minstrelsy in the Elite Households

Introduction to Part I

These first five chapters consider minstrelsy in households, of which the king's was the most extensive as well as the best-documented. The principal sources of information about the king's household are the financial accounts of the Wardrobe and the Chamber. Not all of the records have survived, but even so there is an astonishing amount of material providing information on the day-to-day activities of household members, including the minstrels. These accounts contain the financial records of some special occasions, and the information these give is very important: but the accounts are also valuable in recording, in considerable quantity and detail, the kind of information that other sources do not – the wages, liveries, gifts, and reimbursements of expenses – and all in the context of often extensive and almost continuous travel as the court moved through the countryside. The information provided is basically objective: and although it is sometimes fragmentary, not easily interpreted, or inaccurate due to the errors of the accounting scribes, it is at least free of the deliberate hyperbole, allusion to symbolisms and other spin-related considerations that often make iconographic and literary sources problematic.

The records of dependent royal households – those of the queen, Prince of Wales and the king's younger sons – are equally detailed. Their survival is less extensive, however, and other secular households, even those of the great nobles, also yield much less documentation. Their recording systems were often robust, but unless the records were archived securely they could be lost or destroyed. Although there are some extensive survivals for short periods of time, most financial evidence consists at best only of a journal – the daily record of transactions – of an individual year or so. There are other types of record that can be useful, such as registers and household ordinances, and these help to build up a picture of life in a major household.

The domestic records of religious houses are likewise variable. At their best, they are the result of a meticulous accounting and archiving system, but in many cases water damage, accidental loss and deliberate destruction (especially at the dissolution of religious houses in the mid-sixteenth century) have ensured that little evidence remains of them. Unsurprisingly, the highest survival-rates are found in the archives of two cathedral priories that were refounded as secular cathedrals with minimum disruption of their lives: Durham and Worcester (although the latter's records are mainly of a later date than we consider here). For most houses, especially those that were dissolved in the 1530s, it is only by very good luck that any records have survived.

1

The royal households and their minstrels

The household and its operation

Minstrelsy could be a precarious way of making a living, but a permanent place in a large household offered considerable security. Of the many great households of late medieval England, the royal households provided the best positions available, with a good income and some security should a minstrel be unable to work through illness or old age. They offered the chance of lucrative work elsewhere, too, for the royal minstrels were not needed in Court all the year round. For much of the time they were free to work as independent minstrels, with the advantage of wearing the royal livery. We should expect the minstrels of the royal households to be among the most highly-skilled members of their profession, and therefore commanding higher rewards than others: rewards to liveried servants generally reflected the status of the noble whose livery they wore, so that gifts to the king's minstrels from towns and the nobility were more generous than those to other minstrels.

The word 'household' in this context was not a building but a group of people, the officers and servants forming a community around the principal. There were usually at least three royal households, being those of the king, the queen and the Prince of Wales. In some reigns there was an additional household for the king's younger sons (the daughters being brought up in the queen's household). These households tended to be peripatetic, partly to administer the various estates owned by the royal family, and partly because no one estate could feed and maintain a large household indefinitely. In times of war, too, the king and his household often travelled large distances very quickly. In such circumstances the household's structures and procedures had to be efficient and clearly defined.

The king's household

The king's household contained not only his domestic servants (of the privy chamber, kitchen, buttery, and so on), but also the gentlemen and household knights who acted as the king's daily companions and bodyguards, and the clerical and other staff of the Chamber, Wardrobe and other departments. Originally the Chamber and Wardrobe had been 'the place where the king slept, and the adjacent ante-room where he hung up his clothes':[1] but by the late thirteenth century the Chamber

---

[1] T.F. Tout, *The Place of the Reign of Edward II in English History*. 2nd edn (Manchester, 1936), 64. Tout's *Chapters in the Administrative History of Medieval England*. 6 vols

was a household department responsible for the running of the whole of the king's private apartments, while the Wardrobe had become his financial and secretarial department, also responsible for his jewels and treasures.[2] The household was a large institution, and running it was a hugely expensive operation. Not surprisingly, there were repeated attempts to understand exactly what the king's income was spent on and, if possible, to limit expenditure: this was part of the purpose of the household ordinances.

Household ranks

Household servants might hold any one of four principal ranks: in ascending order, page (*pagettus*), groom (*garcio*), yeoman (*valettus*) and squire (*scutifer*). Above these came the gentlemen, clerks and knights. The two ranks with which we shall be most concerned are those of yeoman and squire. A small household department, such as the Wafery, might be headed by a yeoman, and a larger department by a squire. Most minstrels were squires; waferers and *vigiles* were usually yeomen, although a senior waferer was sometimes a squire.[3] From the mid-fourteenth century onwards a *vigilis/vigilator* who was a regular performer of minstrelsy was sometimes admitted to the list of those called 'minstrels', with the rank of squire.

The household ordinances

The various ordinances of the king's household were drawn up to ensure the clarity and efficiency of the organisation and to control expenditure. The earliest are the *Constitutio Domus Regis*, drawn up in 1136 at the start of Stephen's reign, and the ordinance of Westminster, dated 13 November 1279, early in Edward I's reign. These provide information on the household's chief officers but do not mention the minstrels, *vigiles* or waferer, which were perhaps included among the servants of the Chamber.[4] It is therefore impossible to be sure how many minstrels there were in the king's household. Edward I seems to have employed about eighteen in 34 Ed I, although the question is complicated by the uncertainty of distinguishing minstrels *qui non sunt in rotulo marescalli* (those known to belong to this category being omitted from the total).[5]

(Manchester, 1920–33) remains the authority on royal administration in the fourteenth century, and is my source for much of this chapter. See also S.B. Chrimes, *An Introduction to the Administrative History of Medieval England* (Oxford, 1959), and Chris Given-Wilson, *The Royal Household and the King's Affinity* (New Haven CT and London, 1986) (the authority for a later but overlapping period).

[2] The Great Wardrobe eventually had a large storehouse for cloth in the City of London: see Maria Hayward, *The Great Wardrobe Accounts of Henry VII and Henry VIII* (London, 2012), esp. xi–xxii.

[3] For discussion of *vigiles* see Chapter 14.

[4] For the structure of the king's household in 1136, see Given-Wilson, *Royal Household*, 3: *vigiles* are included.

[5] Those temporarily in the household, and treated as guests, were not listed on the roll of the marshal of the hall, who allocated the seating for meals.

The ordinances of Edward II's reign, dated 6 December 1318, are the first to offer information about minstrels. They provide for two trumpeters and two other minstrels (or more, or fewer) to be in constant attendance on the king and to make their minstrelsy to him at his pleasure. These four were to eat in the chamber or in the hall, as required, and were to take wages and robes appropriate to the rank of each one (*chescun solonqe soun estate*), at the discretion of the steward and treasurer.[6] This selection of minstrels would provide what the king needed on a daily basis: ceremonial fanfares for meals and other events, and, if required, quiet music for the king's private entertainment. Loud and quiet (or 'still') minstrelsy constitute a basic distinction between types of minstrelsy appropriate for different functions: we shall return to this in Chapter 4. That these four minstrels might eat in the Chamber, rather than the hall, underlines the possibility of private entertainment in the king's own apartments.

The king employed other minstrels too, who were required for the major feasts of the church year and for various special occasions.[7] These principal feasts were (until St George's day was added in 1348) Christmas (25 December), Easter (variable), Pentecost (= Whitsuntide, seven weeks after Easter) and All Saints (1 November) or perhaps Michaelmas (29 September).[8] The ordinances of 1318 do not name the minstrels, nor say how many there were in total. The financial records show, however, that around the ninth year of Edward II's reign (1315/16) the king employed four trumpeters (Richard de Blyda, Roger, John Scot and Arnold), together with a nakerer (John), at least two harpers (William de Morle and Hugo de Naunton), five other minstrels (Thomas, fiddler, Ivo Vala, citoler, Nicholas de Renty, Reymund Arnald de Rycan and John Mauprine), three or four *vigiles* (not identifiable) and a waferer (Richard Pilke) who was capable of minstrelsy. This totals at least fifteen minstrels, counting the *vigiles* but not the waferer.[9]

The ordinances of 18–21 Ed III list sixteen minstrels, without naming them, but the livery-rolls of that reign show that Edward III actually employed more than that. A summary list of the peace-time establishment in 21 Ed III shows nineteen minstrels and three waits; another list of household members in the period 21 April 18 Ed III (1344) to 24 November 21 Ed III (1347) confirms that number and shows what

---

[6] Tout, *Place of the Reign*, 303–4, from BL Add MS 32097 and BL Cotton MS Tiberius E.viii.

[7] Richard Rastall, 'The minstrels of the English royal households, 25 Ed I–1 Hen VIII: an inventory'. Royal Musical Association *Research Chronicle* 4 (1964), 1–41 (hereafter MERH), gives a summary list of royal minstrels for the period c. 1297–1509, but needs revision.

[8] If this arrangement was in place in Edward I's reign, no direct evidence of it survives: but the very varied periods of residence of the minstrels certainly suggest that it was. A fifth principal feast was celebrated at Court after 1348, when St George's Day (23 April) was added following the Black Prince's victory at Poitiers and the subsequent creation of the Order of the Garter.

[9] MERH, 12–14. The king's *vigiles* constituted a band of pipers and were usually counted as minstrels; the waferer headed his own sub-department. At this time the queen's household also contained two psaltery-players (Janotus and William), a gitterner (Dominic), two *vigiles* (Robert Chaunceler and Robert de Baumburgh) and a waferer (John de Bria).

instruments were involved.[10] The minstrels are not named, but from other records we can guess at their identities, shown in Table 1: some alternatives are offered here because the list is not firmly datable.[11] Clarioners are rarely recorded separately from other trumpeters, and the second one remains unidentified: he would have been one of the six trumpeters whose names we know. The three waits were pipers whose primary duty was as household watchmen. The word 'wait' occurs rarely in the royal accounts before the fifteenth century because the documents are mainly in Latin: the term for a household watchman is *vigilis* until the mid-fourteenth century and *vigilator* thereafter.[12]

Table 1. Royal Minstrels c. 1344–7.

5	trumpets	from Roger, John de Hampton, Egidius, Nicholas, Robert Barber, Richard
1	citoler	Thomas
5	pipers	Ralph, Godscalk, Libkin, Hankin fitzLibkin, Arnold
1	tabrett	Lambert
2	clarioners	Peter and one other from the trumpeters, above
1	nakerer	John (or perhaps George)
1	fiddler	probably Henry
3	waits	William Harding, Ralph, and either William de Hedele or Richard

Of the nineteen minstrels in this list only two (the citoler and the fiddler) represent quiet indoor music, with a third (the taborer) joining them in dance-music. This may indicate a war-time establishment, although the king's minstrels always included a majority of loud ceremonial instruments.

A list of Henry V's household dated 29 May 3 Hen V (1415) shows who was expected to travel overseas, and is certainly for war-time: this campaign ended with the victory at Agincourt. In addition to the fifteen minstrels shown in Table 2,[13] the list names 'the king's guides by night' – his household *vigilatores* – as Guy Middleton and John Melton, men whom we know from other sources to be pipers and capable of minstrelsy.

---

[10] *A Collection of Ordinances and Regulations for the Government of the Royal Household* (London, 1790) (hereafter *Ords & Regs*), 11 and 4, printed from BL MS Harley 782, p. 62. The latter list also shows a single waferer.

[11] MERH, 15–20.

[12] The word 'wait' is discussed in Chapter 6: in a household context it signifies the shawm-playing watchman who was sometimes also a minstrel.

[13] Thomas Rymer, *Foedera conventiones, literae et cujuscunque generis acta publica*. 20 vols (London, 1704–35), IX, 255; repr. in Sir Nicholas Harris Nicolas, *History of the Battle of Agincourt* (London, 1832), 98 and 101, and Christopher Hibbert, *Agincourt* (London, 1964), 147 and 149. Indentures were later written for John Cliff and another 17 (un-named) minstrels: Rymer, *Foedera*, IX, 260. The English army landed in France on 14 August 1415 and returned to England on 17 November.

Table 2. Royal Minstrels on the Agincourt campaign, 1415.

John Cliff	
Thomas Norys tromper	
William Baldwin	
John Michel	
[John] Panel trumper	
[John] Peut trumper	Payte or Peyte
Richard piper	Richard Geffrey?
Thomas Haliday	known as a still minstrel in other sources
Walter Haliday	known as a still minstrel in other sources
[William] Meysham piper	known as a still minstrel in other sources
[John] Broune piper	
[Conute] Snayth fiddler	
William Langton	
Thomas Hardiberd	
William Halliday	

These seventeen minstrels and *vigilatores* were part of a reduced war-time household, and at least two minstrels were among the household servants left behind in England. The inclusion of William Maysham as a piper suggests that in wartime a 'still' minstrel who could play a loud instrument might be transferred to the more useful occupation. Some minstrels were no doubt competent on two or more types of instrument: so while a man may have been known as 'harper', 'piper' or 'trumpeter', for instance, he was not debarred from making minstrelsy in some other capacity.

Henry VI probably inherited all of his father's minstrels, but he was less than a year old when he became king in 1422 and later showed little taste for regal pomp. The ordinances of 1445 are part of an attempt to limit the cost of his household: they offer only 'xij menistrealx, one le gaite' for his entertainment and security, a definite reduction compared to his father's establishment.[14] Ten years later, the ordinances of 1455 (33 Hen VI), also designed to reduce the financial burden of the household, show thirteen minstrels including the wait, although the actual numbers fluctuated between fourteen and seventeen later in the reign. The ordinances of 1455 again specify a nucleus of four minstrels, with the other nine coming at the principal feasts.[15] The four minstrels are named as Thomas Ratclyff, William Wykes, John Clyff and

---

[14] A.R. Myers, *The Household of Edward IV* (Manchester, 1959), 71.

[15] *Ords & Regs*, 18, printed from BL Cotton MS Cleopatra F v, ff. 170–4. The single *vigilator* was presumably indispensable and therefore one of the four minstrels always available. There were now five principal feasts celebrated at Court (see n. 8, above, and n. 17, below).

Robert More, 'wayte'. This gives a rather different picture of day-to-day minstrelsy, perhaps reflecting the saintly Henry VI's less ceremonial tastes: for Ratclyff, Wykes and Clyff are all known to have been still minstrels, performers of quieter entertainments suitable to the private chamber. Robert More was the household wait, so his main function was as a watchman, patrolling the buildings at night. As a piper, he was the one loud minstrel at Court for much of the time.

The latest set of household ordinances in our period is the *Liber Niger* ('Black Book') of Edward IV's reign, compiled probably between June 1471 and September 1472: this states that there are thirteen minstrels.[16] The ordinances require that at all times there shall be two of them in Court. These would be loud minstrels, 'beyng present to warn at the King's rydinges, when he goeth to horse-backe, … and by theyre blowinges the houshold meny may follow in the countries'. Their function of keeping the whole retinue – the household 'meny' – together would be particularly important when the Court was travelling, the 'blowings' keeping the slower-moving parts of the household train informed of the king's progress. Like earlier ordinances, the Black Book provides that there shall also be two string-minstrels in attendance if the king wishes: this would allow for 'still' music for private entertainment. The ordinances also require the other royal minstrels to come to Court for the five principal feasts and to leave Court the day after each feast was finished.[17]

The item immediately following the minstrels deals with a single wait and his groom assistant.[18] The wait was charged with the household's security at night, keeping a watch for fire and other dangers. Every night between Michaelmas (29 September) and 'Shere Thursday' (the Thursday of Holy Week, or Maundy Thursday) he was to pipe the watch four times, except in summer, when he was to pipe three times.[19] An occasional duty was to watch in the chapel during the vigil of those to be made knights of the Bath. The wait ate in hall with the minstrels; he ranked as a yeoman, taking a daily wage of 4½d or 3d 'aftyr the coning that he can'. This last can hardly refer to his competence as a watchman, and may mean that he took a higher wage if he could perform as a minstrel.[20]

The waferer also ranked as a yeoman, according to the Black Book.[21] It is noted, however, that the waferer was of higher rank in Edward III's time because then 'his

---

[16] Myers, *Household of Edward IV*, 131–2. Myers discusses the dating of the book on pp. 29–33. He also included fragmentary draft ordinances dated 1478, but these give no specific information about minstrels, waits or waferers.

[17] *Ibid.*, 243, n. 151, names the feasts as probably All Hallows (i.e. All Saints' Day), Christmas Day, Easter Day, St George's Day, and Whitsunday.

[18] *Ibid.*, 132–3.

[19] Michaelmas was the start of the winter season, the feast of The Annunciation (Lady Day, 25 March) the start of summer. The latest possible date for Shere Thursday was 22 April (which occurred in 1451), four weeks after Lady Day.

[20] 'He … taketh … dayly, if he be present in the courte by the chekker rolle, 4½d or 3d by the discression of the Steward and Thesaurer, and aftyr the cunnyng that he can, and good deservyng; also cloathing with the houshold yomen or minstrelles, according to the wages that he taketh'. *Ords & Regs*, 48.

[21] Myers, *Household of Edward IV*, 172.

busynes was much more'. It is true that the celebrations in that reign were relatively frequent and lavish, that John Drake was given the style of 'Master', and that waferers of that time were probably expected to be entertainers in ways that could include 'minstrelsy' – all circumstances that confirm the Black Book's statement.

Lack of documentary evidence makes the minstrel-body largely unknown in Richard III's reign (1483–5): but Richard certainly inherited eight or nine trumpeters and four other minstrels from Edward, and in turn passed on perhaps as many as five trumpeters and four other minstrels to Henry VII. On 23 July 1486 Henry, noting that he had paid his minstrels nothing since his accession the previous August, ordered a payment of 80 marks (£53 6s 8d) against the wages owing to them, naming them as Alexander Mason (Marshal of the Minstrels), Robert Grene, John Hawkyns, Thomas Mayho, William Grene, Thomas a Spence, Henry Swan and William Davy. The following month payment was made to a different group of king's minstrels, named as Marquis, Jaket and William Elder: by late 1486 these were known as the queen's minstrels. The first two may be Marcus Lorydon and Marcus Jaket.[22]

There are problems of identity here, for Jaket, John Hawkins, Henry Swan and William Davy are known to have been trumpeters and/or taborers. The others appear as still minstrels in subsequent documentation, and we can reasonably assume that the queen's three minstrels were still minstrels, too. As always, any minstrel might have played both still and loud instruments; and, perhaps more importantly at the start of the reign, the scribes may not have been able to identify the minstrels accurately. The picture clarifies somewhat from 1495 onwards, when wages were regularly paid to three groups: nine trumpets, four sackbuts and three string-minstrels.[23] The numbers of trumpets and sackbuts fluctuated slightly thereafter, but from June 12 Hen VII (1497) settled at nine trumpets, three sackbuts and three string-minstrels.[24] The situation is still not wholly clear, however, for the king's New Year gifts in 1497 included not only items to the trumpets, sackbuts, string-minstrels and the queen's minstrels, but also to 'the stilmynstrelx' – three or four of them at least, judging by the size of the gifts.[25] These still minstrels may be the group later known as the 'still shawms':[26] the thirteen minstrels specified in the Black Book were mentioned as playing trumpets, shawms, small pipes and stringed instruments, so that 'small pipes' and 'still shawms' could be identical. What the instruments were is another matter: perhaps crumhorns, small indoor bagpipes, *dulcinas* or recorders?

---

[22] Andrew Ashbee, ed., *Records of English Court Music*. 9 vols (Aldershot, 1986–97), VII, 2, 3 and *passim*.

[23] BL Add 7099 (7–10 Hen VII), fol. 24r, and TNA E101.414.6 (11–13 Hen VII), fols 6r, 10r, 13v and *passim* (cal. SM II, 133 and *passim*). See Ashbee *Court Records*, VII, 153–6, *passim*.

[24] E101.414.6 (11–13 Hen VII), fol. 77r ff, printed in Ashbee, *Court Records*, VII, 159 ff (cal. SM II, 138 ff).

[25] E101.414.6 (11–13 Hen VII), fol. 57v, and following, printed in Ashbee, *Court Records*, VII, 158 ff (cal. SM II, 133, 135, 137 and 140). The gifts made were 100s 0d (£5) to the trumpets, 50s 0d (£2 10s 0d) to the sackbuts and string-minstrels, 40s 0d (£2) to the queen's minstrels, and £4 to the still minstrels.

[26] See H.C. de Lafontaine, *The King's Musick* (London, 1909), 4.

The dependent households

The other royal households are known as dependent households because of their financial dependence on the king's. They kept their own accounts, but the survival-rate of their documentation is less than for the king's household. To a large extent they maintained their own personnel, although there was sometimes a necessary borrowing between households, resulting in the temporary appearance of a minstrel in the accounts of the 'wrong' household. Dependent households did employ minstrels independently of the king's, but there was a general understanding that the minstrels were ultimately his. Thus the queen's harper was described in 1449 as '[the king's] servant, ... harper to the queen'; and the king continued to pay wages to Gilbert his trumpeter in January 1301, when Gilbert was out of Court in the company of Prince Edward.[27]

The queen's minstrels were nevertheless generally distinct from the king's, because her needs were different. The queen did not normally require trumpets, or any loud minstrelsy,[28] since she would be with the king on state occasions: but she might need a trumpet if she were travelling on her own, as Lady Talbot did in 1432.[29] A special case concerns the queen's minstrels at the marriage celebrations of Princess Philippa on 26 October 1406 (8 Hen IV). The minstrels given livery for the occasion included a trumpeter and two pipers: William Byngeley (a piper), Walter Lynne, William Algode (piper), John Trumpyngton, Walter Aleyn, Richard, trumpeter, John Beauchamp and John, harper.[30] These are elsewhere described as the king's minstrels. Evidently they were on loan for the occasion, probably because part of the ceremonies did not include the king and were headed by the queen.

The queen's still minstrels numbered between one and three performers. It seems that a single psaltery-player or harper could be sufficient for her needs, although she might also have both a fiddler and a psaltery-player, with perhaps a gitterner as well. One cannot be sure, but the evidence suggests that the psaltery, and perhaps the gittern, was more in favour in the ladies' households, while the citole was favoured by the king.

Although the king's children had to be financed by the king when they were young, as they grew older there was a need for them to become independent. The sons, when old enough, could be granted estates that would provide enough income to live on: and if they could marry an heiress that was all to the good. John of Gaunt (1340–99), Edward III's third surviving son, became one of the wealthiest men in

---

[27] *Calendar of the Patent Rolls.* Public Record Office Calendars (London, 1891–) (hereafter CPR), Henry VI, vol. 5 (1446–52), 250; Add 7966A (29 Ed I), fol. 178r (cal. SM II, 25).

[28] This does not contradict my earlier remarks: the queen's minstrels did make minstrelsy in the king's presence, although not often.

[29] See Table 7, p. 114.

[30] Philippa married Erik IX of Denmark: the expenses of the marriage are listed in E101.406.10 (cal. SM II, 122). See also MERH, *passim*.

England, mainly due to his first marriage (1359), to Blanche of Lancaster, through whom he obtained the earldom of Lancaster.[31]

The household of an adult Prince of Wales was in many respects like the king's, with trumpeters, nakerer, still minstrels and so on probably in the same proportions. The Black Prince was independent enough to employ minstrels *qui non sunt*, and this was probably true of other adult princes: but more often there was considerable interchange of minstrels between the households of the king and the Prince of Wales, with the prince's minstrels even being paid through the king's household.[32]

The king's daughters, on the other hand, were brought up in the queen's household. They did not need to be a charge on the king's purse once they had reached marriageable age, and early marriage was common. Of the nine daughters of the first three Edwards who married, all but two were married before the end of their 'teens: the youngest was just seven (and presumably did not cohabit with her husband until she was of child-bearing age), four were aged 13, 14 or 15, one married shortly before her 17th birthday, and one was just 18 at the time of her marriage'.[33] Any unmarried daughter remained in the queen's household and was supported by the king unless she entered a convent.

The accounts: Wardrobe and Chamber

The king's household comprised a number of departments, each with its own staff. Each department kept its own accounts, which were submitted at the end of each regnal year to the keeper of the Wardrobe.[34] In the Wardrobe these various accounts were made up into two books, one for each of the two senior officers of the Wardrobe who could check the year's summary accounts before submission to the Exchequer: the Keeper, sometimes known as the king's Treasurer, who had overall charge of the Wardrobe, and his deputy the Controller (*Contrarotulator*, or keeper of the counter-roll), who was responsible for the secretarial functions of the Wardrobe, with control of the Privy Seal. In theory, therefore, the archived records of the household for each regnal year should include two Wardrobe books (the Keeper's and the Controller's) and one book for the Chamber. The departmental records from which the Keeper's and Controller's books were made up were also retained: so the archived material might include the journals (the record of daily expenses in gifts and small payments for many different purposes) and such materi-

---

[31] For the households of John of Gaunt and his elder brother the Black Prince, see Chapter 5.

[32] For payment of wages to Prince Arthur's organ-player, see E101.414.16 (13–15 Hen VII), fols 46r, 50v and 60r, printed in Ashbee, *Court Records*, VII, 164, 165 and 166 (cal. SM II, 139 (two items) and 140).

[33] See the information on these princesses (under the heading 'Issue') in E.B. Fryde, D.E. Greenway, S. Porter and I. Roy, eds, *Handbook of British Chronology*. 3rd edn (London, 1986), 38–40. Of the princesses who survived infancy, only one who lived well beyond marriageable age remained single, while another was unmarried at her death aged 14 or 15.

[34] For regnal years see the Note on Dates, above.

als as receipts – small pieces of parchment recording the delivery of wages or robes, bearing the seal of the man concerned as his signature.

The audit was supposed to happen soon after the end of each accounting year, but there was sometimes a considerable delay. In the final years of Edward I's reign, when the figures could not be balanced because of the king's huge military expenditure in Wales and Scotland, the accounts were so chaotic that they went for audit very late, or even not at all. It is a feature of such a situation that it affects the finances of individuals: members of the household were often paid considerably in arrears, and not a few (including minstrels) helped their sovereign with substantial loans, as we shall see.

The survival of all these types of record is patchy. They were normally archived at Westminster, and then in the Tower of London, but the audit sometimes took place several years late and one suspects that not all records were archived after audit. The records were eventually transferred to the Public Record Office, now the National Archives (TNA) at Kew. But during antiquarian activity in the eighteenth and nineteenth centuries it was not unusual for records to be borrowed by scholars, and inevitably some were not returned: so royal household accounts found their way to the British Museum (some of the most visually-attractive specimens, now transferred to the British Library), the Bodleian Library in Oxford, the John Rylands Library in Manchester, and the Society of Antiquaries library in London.

While the Wardrobe was originally responsible for the king's clothing, and for the cloth and furs required for liveries to his servants, it became the office through which he normally made a much wider range of payments for the household, while payments on behalf of the government were made through the Exchequer. By the end of Edward I's reign the Wardrobe was used to make many types of payment that would normally have gone through the Exchequer. Later kings also found this convenient, and Edward II also used the finances of the Chamber to make certain payments of the kind that his father had made through the Wardrobe. Among these are payments and rewards to minstrels.

Wardrobe and Chamber accounts were written in Latin and French, respectively, until English began to be used in the late fifteenth century. The scribes were responsible for recording financial transactions: they did not necessarily know the people involved, nor what they did, and were not usually concerned to identify them definitively. Identification of individuals is sometimes difficult for modern readers of the accounts, therefore, and one cannot always establish precisely who was among the royal minstrels and what instruments they played. Livery lists are useful in identifying minstrels by name and as a group, but individual payments often cause difficulty.

Socii

When a payment was made, a note was entered of the person who received the money and signed the receipt by means of his seal. Payment to an individual was usually 'by his own hands' (*per manus proprias*) or by the hands of another named individual (*per manus N*). When a large sum was to be distributed among several minstrels it was usually by the hands of the senior person involved (minstrel or king of heralds, for example). Some royal minstrels were well known at the Wardrobe, where the clerks also recognised that certain minstrels lived and worked in pairs as *socii* (fellows, work-partners). The system of *socii* was official, for some lists of servants are divided into those *cum sociis* and those *sine sociis* (with and without *socii*), but there is no mention of it in household ordinances. It was useful in bestowing authority on a minstrel to act for his *socius* in receiving payments. *Socii* were apparently of the same rank (*valettus* or *scutifer*), sometimes players of the same instrument, and often of instruments that were likely to have performed together. The implication is that *socii* lodged together, and probably performed together as well.

2
The life of a royal minstrel

Status and conditions of the minstrels

Fees and Wages

Payment to royal servants came in two ways, both probably in operation throughout the period covered by this book. Edward I paid a daily wage that applied when a servant was resident in Court, generally 7½d for a squire (*scutifer*) and 4½d for a yeoman (*valettus*). The other method of payment was as fees in the form of grants out of the income from property or by the gift of a particular post. This method is not always visible in the surviving records. Among royal minstrels paid in this way by Edward I was Gilbert the harper, who in 32 Ed I (1303/4) held lands in Chesterton (Warwickshire) by grand serjeanty, with the task of keeping Tiddersley Hay, in the Forest of Cannock, at his own cost.[1] Income from the land held would more than pay for the costs of looking after Tiddersley Hay, if Gilbert had a good head for finance. Other fourteenth-century examples are William de Morley, who was granted property in Pontefract on 28 October 1322, Peter le fitheler and Peter le crouder.[2] In 1405 the piper William Bingley was granted the office of bailiff of the town and lordship of Flint, with the due fees, wages, profits and other commodities, and with two cottages in Oundle and the reversion of a cottage in Fotheringay; and in 1413 William Haliday received a grant of £20 13s 4d *per annum* from the issues of properties.[3] This was the method often used to pay non-royal servants, too: examples include William Wolston, trumpeter of the Earl of Northumberland, and Hugh Cook, trumpeter of Lord Beaumont.[4]

The list of peace-time fees for 21 Ed III (1347/8), noted in Chapter 1, includes 19 minstrels and three 'waytes' (i.e. *vigilatores*), each at 20s 0d *per annum*. The items

---

[1] See Thomas Blount, *Ancient Tenures of Land* (London, 1679), 36.

[2] For William de Morley, see CPR, Edward II, vol. 4 (1321–4), 210; for Peter le fitheler and Peter le crouder (these two were not certainly minstrels), see CPR, Edward III, vol. 10 (1354–8), 41 and 102.

[3] Calendared in Gratton Flood, 'Entries', under these dates. For Bingley, see CPR, Hen IV, vol. 3 (1405–8), 55 (7 September 1405); for Haliday, CPR, Hen V, vol. 1 (1413–16), 130 (28 August 1413). Haliday's grant, of 31 marks, seems a strange sum.

[4] CPR, Henry IV, vol. 3 (1405–8), 117 (Wolston) and CPR, Henry V, vol. 1 (1413–16), 137 (Cook). Robert II of Scotland paid Thomas the harper this way: H.G. Farmer, *A History of Music in Scotland* (London, 1947), 42.

surrounding this are for five clerks of the chapel at 40s 0d each and, below the minstrels and waits, launderers at 26s 8d (i.e. two marks), messengers at 13s 4d (1 mark) and archers at 10s 0d. A later list of fees, confirmed during 43 and 44 Ed III (1369/70 and 1370/1), shows grants for life to members of the household 'for good service to the king' which, unlike the earlier fees, were at various levels: those to minstrels are shown in Table 3.[5]

In the fourteenth century such grants were perhaps not made to all royal minstrels,[6] but under Henry VI they were standardised and fixed at 100s 0d (£5) *per annum*, in accordance with a verbal grant of Henry V.[7] At first these annual grants were made only during the king's pleasure: Thomas Radcliff and William Paynell received theirs in 1437 and 1438, respectively.[8] Later, between 1439 and 1447, the same sum was granted to each of the minstrels for life.[9] Almost immediately, the grants were raised to 10 marks (£6 13s 4d) per year, and by 1452 all the minstrels were receiving the increased grant.[10] In the struggles between the king and the Duke of York, the grants to some of the minstrels reverted for a time to their former value of 100s 0d (£5) per year.[11] The reason for this is not apparent: but under Edward IV, 10 marks (£6 13s 4d) became again the grant payable to each minstrel.[12] Alexander Mason was evidently especially favoured, for in addition to the 10 marks that he received as a king's minstrel, from 1471 he received another 10 marks for his reward;[13] and in 1477 he was granted the reversion of the office of Marshal of the Minstrels.[14]

At the end of Edward IV's reign and at the beginning of Richard III's these grants had the same value, except that William Clifton received only 50s 0d (£2 10s 0d) per year. Mason's grant had become a single sum of 20 marks, which suggests that he was

---

5 Frederick Devon, ed., *Issue Roll of Thomas de Brantingham, Bishop of Exeter* (London, 1835), under relevant dates.

6 The number is not known, but a search of all relevant CPR volumes might produce that information.

7 CPR, Henry VI, vol. 1 (1422–9), 102 (14 May 1423) and 234 (26 October 1424). Guy Middleton was not included in this grant, and he seems at this time to have been regarded as a *vigilator* rather than as a minstrel: see SM II, 125.

8 CPR, Henry VI, vol. 3 (1436–41), 129 and 141.

9 CPR, Henry VI, vol. 3 (1436–41), 303; CPR, Henry VI, vol. 4 (1441–6), 71; CPR, Henry VI, vol. 5 (1446–52), 42 and 72 f.

10 CPR, Henry VI, vol. 5 (1446–52), 49, 130, 200, 250, 505 and 512.

11 CPR, Henry VI, vol. 6 (1452–61), 458 and 507.

12 CPR, Edward IV (1461–7), 221, 293 and 297 (the grant to William Christian was payable out of the fee-farm of Cambridge: see C.H. Cooper, *Annals of Cambridge*. 5 vols (Cambridge, 1842–1908), I, 213); CPR, Edward IV and Henry VI (1467–77), 424, 44, 61, 481, 482, 549, 565, 588 and 589; CPR, Edward IV, Edward V and Richard III (1476–85), 14, 89, 95, 198, 310, 389, 439, 470 and 473. For grants to other minstrels, see CPR, Edward IV (1461–7), 109 (10 marks to Thomas Draper, formerly granted by Humphrey, late Duke of Gloucester) and 297 (grant, to Robert Grey, of the 'Lamb' in Distaff Lane, London, to the value of 40.0d *per annum*); CPR, Edward IV, Edward V and Richard III (1476–85), 100 (5 marks *per annum* to William Barley, late a minstrel of George, late Duke of Clarence).

13 In 1471: CPR, Edward IV and Henry VI (1467–77), 261.

14 In 1477: CPR, Edward IV, Edward V and Richard III (1476–85), 22.

Table 3. Grants to minstrels confirmed during 43 and 44 Edward III.

Receiving 10 marks (£6 13s 4d) *per annum* for life:	
	Nicholas de Praga, valet of the king's household
Receiving 100s 0d (£5) *per annum* for life:	
	Walter Wayte of the king's household
	Hugh Joye, 'one of the king's watchers'[a]
	Thomas Merlyn, valet
Receiving 60s 0d (£3) *per annum* for life:	
	Hanekin Fitz Lybkyn, king's minstrel[b]
	Richard Pigeon
	John Francis
Receiving 12d *per diem* for life:	
	Ralph le Wayte, valet[c]
Receiving 7½d *per diem* for life:	
	Arnald le Pyper, king's minstrel
	William Harding, king's watchman
	Lambekin Taborer, king's minstrel
	John de Hampton, king's minstrel
	Nicholas Hanneye, king's minstrel
	Richard Baath, king's minstrel
	John Prat, king's minstrel
	John Absolon, king's minstrel
	John de Middelton, king's minstrel
	John de Bukyngham, king's minstrel
	Nicholas de Prage, one of the king's minstrels[d]
	Nicholas Trompour, one of the king's minstrels (Hanneye? Praga?)
Receiving 4½d *per diem* for life:	
	William Lamport, one of the king's watchmen

Notes:
[a] Presumably not the Hugo Joye who was a royal *vigilator* in 35–6 Hen VI (1456–8), but perhaps his grandfather.
[b] Devon, *Issue Roll of Thomas de Brantingham*, 55, transcribed the name as 'Havekin'. Pigeon and Francis may not be minstrels.
[c] Perhaps not a *vigilator*.
[d] This grant was in addition to that of 10 marks *per annum* already made. Later the two grants were confirmed together: Devon, *Issue Roll of Thomas de Brantingham*, 380.

already Marshal of the Minstrels. The grants made to minstrels, with the sources of revenue, are given in Table 4: they are not all adjacent in the lists.[15] The second list is dated only two days after Richard acceded to the throne, so it is likely that all these items were the confirmation of grants made in the previous reign.

It is difficult to know how comprehensive these lists are. Certainly the first one (22 Ed IV) includes all the trumpeters known from the end of Edward's reign (Paynell, Crowland, Hatche, Hills, Prior, Paynter, Clifton and William Ducheman) except for John de Peler, who started in royal service that year. The second list names only five of the eight (Crowland, Hatche, Hills, Prior and Paynter), but adds John de Peler. John Paynell and William Ducheman had presumably retired or died.

Of the other minstrels, the first list names Alexander Mason (apparently already Marshal), Robert Grene, Thomas Cawthorn, Thomas Hawking and Thomas Mayhue: this is Cawthorn's last appearance in the records. John Hawkins and William Barley, both known to have been royal minstrels from before 1480 and into the next reign, are missing. Only Grene and Hawkins appear in the list of 1 Ric III, but as Mason, Mayhue and Barley are known to have continued into the next reign, the list is clearly incomplete. Possibly the other confirmations of grants were added at a later date. These lists do however show a continuity of income-source for individual minstrels: it was evidently simpler and neater to continue taking a royal servant's annual grant from the existing sources of revenue.

The records of payments out of the revenues from land and property were usually entered in the Patent Rolls, and so did not appear in the Wardrobe records. The annual fee presumably obliged the minstrel concerned to appear at Court as required, but it also provided a financial cushion against possible lean times when he was out of Court on his travels.

Daily wages, on the other hand, were paid from the general revenues of the Wardrobe and so entered into the Wardrobe's journals, the running account of daily expenses. Consequently they appear under the heading of *Dona*, *Necessaria* or *Vadia* (wages) in the Wardrobe books made up for audit, according to the particular circumstances of the payment. These records show that the fee was payable (as the ordinances prescribe) when the minstrel was resident in Court.

The name of a resident minstrel would be entered *in rotulo marescalli* – that is, on the roll kept by the marshal of the hall, whose task it was to allot seating at meals according to the rank and status of those eating. It was being entered on this roll that showed a minstrel's status as a member of the household and his eligibility for the daily wage of 7½d or 4½d, and it was the marshal's check-list of those present in Court on any particular day.[16] According to the ordinances of Edward II's household the Steward and Treasurer of the household decided the amount paid to the

---

[15] BL MS Harley 433, fols 45v, 46r, 78r, 96r, 104r and 311v–315r (cal. SM II, 131 f), transcribed in Rosemary Horrox and P.W. Hammond, *British Library Harleian Manuscript 433* (Stroud, 1979). There is no reason to think that there was any connection between the minstrels and the properties involved.

[16] There were two serjeant marshals of the hall, one of whom had to be on duty in the hall at any mealtime. See Tout, *Place of the Reign*, 284, for the household ordinance of 1318.

Table 4. Annual fees to the royal minstrels, 1482/3.

Name	Annual fee	from the issues of
Grants made 22 Ed IV (1482–3)		
Alexander Mason, *geyster*	20 marks	Cumberland
Robert Grene, minstrel	10 marks	Norwich
John Haich, trumpet	10 marks	Devonshire
Thomas Cawthorn, minstrel	10 marks	Dudeston (Duddlestone, Somerset?)[a]
John Crowland, minstrel	10 marks	(Dudeston Hundred)
Thomas Hawking, minstrel	10 marks	Manor of Berkeley, Gloucestershire
William Ducheman, trumpeter	10 marks	Winchcombe
John Paynell, trumpet	10 marks	County of Hereford
Richard Hills, trumpet	10 marks	Assert between the bridge of Stamford and the bridge of Oxford
Thomas Payntour, trumpet	10 marks	Oxfordshire and Berkshire
William Clifton, trumpet	50s 0d	Patricksbourne (Kent)
Thomas Mayow, minstrel	10 marks	(Port of Gloucester)
John Priour, trumpet	10 marks	(City of Winchester)
Grants made for life, 28 June 1 Ric III (1483)		
John Crowland (confirmation)	10 marks	5 marks each from Dindeston and the manor of Berton
John Priour	10 marks	£4 from Winchester, 53/4d from the manor of Lokerle
Thomas Paynter, trumpet	10 marks	Forest of Cornbury
Robert Grene, minstrel	10 marks	Norwich
John Hawkyns, minstrel	10 marks	Lordship of Barton
John de Peler, trumpeter (conf.)	10 marks	Hundreds of Kystesgate, Holford and Creston, by the hands of the abbot and convent of Winchecombe
Richard Hills, trumpeter	10 marks	The forest between the bridges of Stamford and Oxford
John Hache, trumpeter (conf.)	10 marks	County of Devon

Note:
[a] This and the next three entries are in a section devoted to issues from Gloucestershire.

four minstrels in permanent attendance.[17] Probably they decided the wages to be paid to all minstrels, 'soun estate' (his status as *scutifer* or *valettus*) being the main consideration for each man. Another group whose wages were presumably decided according to status and ability was those *qui non sunt in rotulo marescalli* – that is, those who were not on the roll of the marshal of the hall and so treated as visitors. Earl Warenne's trumpeters Nicholas de Doncaster and John Crakestreng, who were at Court for a time in 32 Ed I, were each paid 9d per day, for the livery that they wore commanded much respect and they were probably very skilled minstrels; the Welsh trumpeters Yven and Ithel, on the other hand, received only 2d per day each during their stay in Court in 1 Ed II.[18]

For the regular household minstrels, seniority alone does not always explain fluctuations in their wages. The accounts for 33–4 Ed III, for example, show that Elias the piper was paid 7½d per day between 19 May and 5 August 1360, but only 4½d per day between 6 August and 12 December.[19] These sums reflect war-time and peace-time wages, respectively. The king had returned to England on 18 May, ten days after the preparation of a treaty with France. Elias was no doubt in attendance on the king, but was evidently stood down on 6 August.[20]

Pay-scales dating from 18 to 21 Ed III show what was considered the norm, or perhaps the desired norm, at that time.[21] They list the daily wages in war-time, and include the king's chaplains and esquires, the apothecary, the minstrels and others, all at 12d. The items surrounding it are for knights, cofferer, controller and various clerks at 2s od, and archers, messengers, cross-bowmen, etc. at 6d. The list does not include the *vigilatores*, who were normally of lower status than the minstrels and paid accordingly. This was true even when a *vigilator* was rewarded for minstrelsy and occasionally described as 'minstrel' in the records. In 33–4 Ed III the peace-time daily wages of William Harding, minstrel, and Gerard le Wayte (both *vigilatores* and occasionally known as minstrels) were 6½d and 6d respectively, compared with 7½d to other minstrels.[22]

In practice, the war-time wage sometimes depended on the value of the servant's horse. Some minstrels who normally received 4½d had their wage increased only to 9d in war-time because they did not possess horses *ad arma*. In 8 Ed III (1334/5)

---

[17] Tout, *Place of the Reign*, 303.
[18] For Doncaster and Crakestreng see BL Add MS 8835 (32 Ed I), fol. 39r (cal. SM II, 40): they had the expense of two grooms and two horses. For Yven and Ithel see TNA E101.373.15 (1 Ed II), fols 14v, 15v, 17v and 19r (cal. SM II, 64–5).
[19] E101.393.11, fol. 117 (cal. SM II, 111).
[20] *The Oxford Dictionary of National Biography* (hereafter ODNB), online article 'Edward III (1312–77), king of England' (accessed 2 June 2019). Available online at <https://www.oxforddnb.com>. The king returned to France on 9 October to ratify the treaty.
[21] *Ords & Regs*, 9 and 11, from BL Harley MS 782, fols 62r–71v.
[22] See E101.393.11 (33–4 Ed III), fols 117r f. (cal. SM II, 111): these were higher payments than the norm for *valetti*, however.

Northleigh, Marchis and Wycombe did not have suitable horses; and the same was true of Marchis, William Harding, John Harding and Wycombe in 9 Ed III.[23]

This is one of several factors that make it difficult to interpret the records of wages, which in any case are often fragmentary. Another is the existence of 'split' wages in the fourteenth century when the king was travelling, usually in war-time. Sometimes part of the wage was allocated *in rotulo marescalli* and the rest due to the minstrel *hic* (wherever the king was). The former portion, not available to the minstrel during a campaign, must have accumulated as a Wardrobe debt to be paid when the minstrel returned to Westminster or elsewhere. Possibly the portion allocated *in rotulo marescalli* was available to his wife, who would otherwise have no financial support while her husband was abroad.[24]

The king's almost constant travelling during the fourteenth century must sometimes have caused difficulty in paying his retinue; and in war-time his extra expenses would have exacerbated the problem. For this and other reasons members of the household usually received their wages in the form of prests, or part-payments. These were sometimes an advance on wages, but were usually in arrears, with large Wardrobe debts to royal servants being paid off gradually.[25] At some time in the period 11–15 Ed III the minstrel Henry Whissh was paid £82 of the astonishing £152 owed to him. Accumulated Wardrobe debts to sixteen minstrels, *vigiles* and waferers in a long list of royal servants in 35 Ed I totalled £110 13s 10d: of this sum, £30 2s 1½d was owed to Master John Drake, the senior waferer (who had squire's rank), and £21 14s 6½d to the *vigilis* Robert de Finchesle. Such debts must represent unpaid fees, wages and other expenses over considerable periods of time.

The king's substantial debts to his servants were sometimes due to cash loans. The almost constant warfare of the fourteenth century – against the Welsh, the Scots, the Irish and, most of all, the French – undoubtedly stretched the royal finances, a situation inherited by Richard II in 1377 and by the Lancastrians in 1399. In Henry IV's reign (1399–1413) the war-time daily wage of a minstrel of the Prince of Wales was 8d, although their leader, John Cliff, received 12d per day.[26] This John Cliff was the second royal minstrel of that name: John Cliff I was the Black Prince's minstrel in 18 Ed III (1344/5); John Cliff II served Henry of Monmouth as both Prince of Wales and Henry V, being chief minstrel during the Agincourt campaign; and John Cliff III served both Henry VI and Edward IV, being Marshal of the Minstrels in 1477.[27]

Henry V paid all his minstrels the more usual war-time wage of 12d per day, and the huge costs of the military campaign in France were responsible for a major fund-raising early in 1415. The king used his jewels and plate as securities for loans, a normal way of raising funds. Among those providing loans was the king's chief

---

[23] 8, 9 and 10 Ed III: see BL Cotton MS Nero C viii, fols 235v, 239v and 244r (cal. SM II, 91 f).

[24] I have found no direct evidence for this, but wives sometimes visited the Court on occasions when such an arrangement may have been operative.

[25] See SM II, 60, 103 and elsewhere. On the nature of prests, see E.B. Fryde, ed., *A Book of Prests, 23 Ed I* (Oxford, 1962), xviii.

[26] 4 and 5 Hen IV: E101.404.24 (cal. SM II, 121).

[27] These men are discussed further in Chapter 5.

minstrel, John Cliff, who accepted the king's securities against future payment of his wages:[28]

> To John Clyff, one of the King's minstrels. Security by indenture, for his wages, 3 Hen V in the war against France: a reading desk of silver, over gilt, the foot of it in the fashion of a tabernacle, standing on four feet; two ewers of silver gilt, one enamelled with the arms of England and France, the other with harts; a table with various relics in it, standing on two lions – weighing together, 26lb 6oz. Value the lb, 40s.
>
> One great bowl, three candlesticks, with three pikes, a great silver spoon, a skummer, and other plate – weighing together 19lb. Value the lb, 30s.

This has a total value of £81 5s 0d, and the entry notes that everything was redeemed from Cliff's executors in 12 Hen VI (1433/4). By this time Cliff and his wife had both died, as the record of repayment shows:[29]

> 13 February [1434]. To Henry Jolipas, clerk, executor of the will of Joan, late wife of John Clyff, a minstrel, executrix of the will of the said John Clyff, deceased, with whom an account was made at the Exchequer of Accounts of the receipts of the said John Clyff, who was lately ordered and appointed to go in person with Lord Henry, late King of England, father of the present King, in a certain voyage to France, or elsewhere, which was performed in the 3rd year of his reign, with 17 minstrels his companions, each receiving 12d *per diem*: viz. from the 8 July in the said 3rd year of the said late King, unto the 24 November then next following; at which time there was due to the said John Clyff upon the account aforesaid £33 6s 0d, as appeared by the said account, etc., for security of the payment of which the said John Clyff had the underwritten jewels delivered to him, viz., [listed as above, with minor variants] delivered to the Treasurer and Chamberlains to the King's use, etc., £10 0s 0d.

This implies that Cliff was responsible for the payment of all eighteen minstrels, which for 140 days' service at 12d per day would have cost the king £126.[30] It is a measure of the king's financial problems that full repayment was not made for almost nineteen years. It appears an extraordinary situation, but perhaps it was quite usual: the loans from Whissh, Drake and Finchesle, too, must have been secured with jewels and plate.

It is small wonder that the English monarchy had been in such financial difficulty ever since Edward I waged war on the Scots. Henry VI's advisers certainly saw a need to retrench, including the revision of wages in the royal households. By 1439

---

[28] For the full list of loans and securities see Nicolas, *History of the Battle of Aginourt*, xliii–liii; the entry concerning Cliff is on p. liii. I have slightly modernised Nicolas's translation.

[29] Frederick Devon, *Issues of the Exchequer, Henry III–Henry VI* (London, 1837), 423: account made from Michaelmas 12 Hen VI (1433–4). Cliff had probably retired or died around the end of Henry V's reign, as he does not appear in the grants to minstrels confirmed in the Patent Rolls on 14 May 1423 and 26 October 1424.

[30] This is £44 15s 0d more than the £81 5s 0d of the original valuation, but since Cliff was owed only £33 6s 0d at the end of the campaign, some of this must already have been repaid.

the king's minstrels were all paid 4½d per day in peace-time, rather than 7½d, and the payment for robes also decreased at about that time.[31] The lower wage of 4½d per day was also paid to all the minstrels of Edward IV (reigned 1461–83); and the *wayte* might be paid only 3d, according to his ability.[32]

In Henry VII's reign the minstrels' wages were organised quite differently: the amounts were fixed according to the type of minstrel, and the system of payment by the day was superseded by monthly or quarterly accounting. Henry's trumpets, sackbuts and string-minstrels were paid monthly, as was the minstrel Bonetemps (of whom more in Chapter 14).[33] The trumpeters received £2 each per month: the sackbuts received £7 between the four of them until Trinity Sunday, 11 Hen VII (29 May 1496), after which date the number of the sackbuts (actually the sackbuts and shawms) fluctuated and they invariably received £2 each per month.[34] The three string-minstrels were paid 100s (£5) every month, but this was not divided equally: when there were only two of them the wage was 60s 0d (that is, 30s 0d each), while a payment of 40s 0d (£2) to a single string-minstrel shows him to have been the leader of the three.[35] Bonetemps received only 20s 0d per month.

The accounts searched do not include records of payments to Henry VII's still minstrels, nor to the queen's minstrels. The wages paid to the French minstrels, too, seem usually to have been recorded elsewhere, and the two items which appear in the accounts do not show how many French minstrels there were.[36] Records of two payments to Arnold Jeffrey, Prince Arthur's organ-player, show that he was paid 10s 0d per quarter.[37]

Liveries

The word 'livery' covers several categories of things delivered to household servants. These include the daily allowances of ale, bread, candles and fuel necessary for their welfare, as well as bedding and whatever was needed for their horses.[38] These daily liveries, which were standardised and given each evening in kind, are specified in Edward IV's *Liber Niger* for all members of the household, including the thirteen minstrels and their two servants, the yeoman wait and his groom assistant, and the yeoman waferer and his groom assistant. To some extent these liveries reflect the

---

[31] CPR, Henry VI, vol. 3 (1436–41), 303.

[32] *Ords & Regs*, 48. The Exchequer roll evidently fulfilled the function of the former marshal's roll.

[33] SM II, 133–41, *passim*. On the question of the wait's ability, see p. 8.

[34] SM II, 134 ff. For the 'sackbuts' see MERH, 36 and 40; for Guillam, presumably William Burgh (also known as Guyllam Borrow), see Andrew Ashbee and David Lasocki, assisted by Peter Holman and Fiona Kisby, *A Biographical Dictionary of English Court Musicians, 1485–1714*. 2 vols (Aldershot, 1998), I, 216 f, and E101.414.6, fol. 36v (cal. SM II, 134).

[35] E101.414.16, fol. 38v (cal. SM II, 139): this was payment of wages for the month of August, which his companions had already received.

[36] SM II, 138: they were paid quarterly, at a wage of 66s 8d (five minstrels at a mark each?).

[37] SM II, 139.

[38] C.M. Woolgar, *The Great Household in Late Medieval England* (New Haven and London, 1999), 31–2.

particular requirements of the office: the wait, for instance, who ate in the hall with the minstrels, had both a bread-allowance and more ale (half a gallon, as opposed to just under a third of a gallon to each minstrel) to sustain him during the night watch.[39] The allowance of candles varied between summer and winter. As for all household servants, provision was made for an allowance of bread in case of a minstrel's or wait's illness, when meals in hall would be missed.[40]

The second kind of livery, recorded in the livery rolls of the households, was the regular allowance for cloth and furs to make robes. An allowance for shoes was recorded separately.[41] The minstrels normally received liveries of two robes per year, for winter and summer. In the fourteenth century the usual allowance to squires was 20s 0d (£1) per robe, although some senior squires received slightly more cloth for their winter livery, with a correspondingly increased allowance. In 32 and 34 Ed I the waferer John Drake received 2 marks (£1 6s 8d) for each winter robe; and the same allowance was made to Andrew Norreys, King of Heralds, in 12 and 13 Ed III.[42] The usual minstrel's allowance of 20s 0d was for 6 ells of narrow cloth and one lamb-skin: counting an ell as 45 inches, this gives 22'6" or 7½ yards of cloth. By the middle of Henry VI's reign, however, the allowance to minstrels had decreased to 10s 0d per robe, and this smaller allowance continued under Edward IV.[43]

Those *vigiles* who were also regarded as minstrels sometimes received a minstrel's allowance (20s 0d per robe, reduced to 10s 0d per robe in Henry VI's reign).[44] Most, however, received only one robe per year,[45] the allowance for which was 20s 0d or, more usually, 2 marks (£1 6s 8d). This latter payment allowed for a warmer robe if the garment had to last for a whole year. The *vigiles*, of course, were more in need of warm clothes than most servants, for they had to patrol the royal lodgings during the night throughout the year. As a protection against the cold, they were sometimes given a tunic or a cloak with a hood as an additional winter livery: the allowance for this was usually 6s 8d, which was enough for 2 or 3 ells of cloth and a lamb-skin.[46] By the middle of Henry VI's reign this extra livery had been discontinued, the *vigilatores* receiving 6 ells of cloth in two colours.[47]

The waferer, if he were a squire of the household, also received liveries like those of the minstrels, being allowed 40s 0d for two robes, or 2 marks (£1 6s 8d) or 20s 0d for a robe for the whole year. A waferer who was a *valettus* received only 13s 4d (1

---

[39] Quantities also varied between households: Woolgar, *Great Household*, 127.
[40] Myers, *Household of Edward IV*, 132–3.
[41] On liveries generally see Given-Wilson, *Royal Household*, 236–7.
[42] For Drake: see BL Add 8835, fols 112 and 117 (cal. SM II, 42); E101.369.11, fols 156 and 163 (cal. SM II, 47). For Norreys, see E36.203, fol. 122v (cal. SM II, 101).
[43] E101.409.9 (20–1 Hen VI), fols 37 f (cal. SM II, 125); *Ords & Regs*, 48; Myers, *Household of Edward IV*, 132.
[44] William Harding, for instance: see E36.204 (16–18 Ed III), fol. 90v (cal. SM II, 104), and E101.393.11 (33–4 Ed III), fol. 77 (cal. SM II, 101).
[45] SM II, 76 and 78.
[46] SM II, 44, 82, 87, 108 and 113. The Black Prince gave his *vigiles* an extra fur: see SM II, 99.
[47] See the liveries *annis* 17–18, 19–20 and 22–3 (cal. SM II, 125 f).

mark) for a robe for the whole year, and a groom waferer received 10s 0d. Valets and grooms also received an allowance for winter and summer shoes, usually 2s 4d per season. This 4s 8d brought a valet's total annual allowance for liveries to 18s 0d: this, like the minstrels' robes-allowance, was halved at some time during the period 22–5 Hen VI, in the mid-1440s.[48]

The winter and summer robes were delivered in time for the major feasts of Christmas and Pentecost, so that the new liveries could be worn during the festivities. A servant who was absent from Court on one of these feasts was not entitled to his allowance for the new robe,[49] but if he was away on the king's business, or for other good reason, he would be given his livery-allowance later, usually as a gift.[50]

Exceptionally, special robes might be given to certain servants, or the robes-livery might be increased. At Pentecost 13 Ed II (18 May 1320), King Robert was given a robe containing 9 ells of cloth and two furs, at a cost of 33s 2½d; and on the same occasion robes were given to Tussetus and Trumellus, minstrels of the King of France, each containing 7 ells of cloth and one lamb-skin, at a cost of 24s 9d each.[51] This was probably during preparations for the king's visit to Amiens in June and July, when he did homage to Charles IV of France for the provinces of Ponthieu and Gascony. King Robert and the French minstrels were therefore members of diplomatic missions, and special liveries would be appropriate. At Christmas 4 Ed III (1330) the robes delivered to the queen's minstrels each contained 7 ells of cloth:[52] this may reflect the special nature of the festivities that year, the first Christmas of Edward III's real kingship, following the execution of Roger Mortimer the previous month. Another reason for increased liveries was the presence of a distinguished guest whom the king wished to impress. In the run-up to the Agincourt campaign, at Pentecost 3 Hen V (19 May 1415), which the king celebrated in the presence of the Emperor, the Duke of Holland and other lords, the sixteen minstrels received lined gowns of three colours.[53]

Pentecost, the feast of the coming of the Holy Spirit, was regarded as a suitable occasion for initiating important projects, as suggested by the Pentecost celebrations of 1306, 1320 and 1415. Lesser feasts than Christmas and Pentecost are unlikely to have occasioned special liveries, however, and we should look for other reasons. For instance, in 4 Ed III Queen Philippa's *vigilis* received a tunic for the feast of St Mary Magdalene (22 July 1330), in addition to the robe and winter tunic already delivered to him at Christmas that year.[54] This is unlikely to be a substitute for a

---

[48] See E101.409.16 (25–6 Hen VI), fol. 35v (cal. SM II, 127): the livery-list in E101.409.11 (22 Hen VI), fol. 39v (cal. SM II, 126), still gives 18s 0d as a yeoman's allowance.

[49] SM II, 42, 47 and 76.

[50] Richard de Blida received his winter allowance for 9 Ed II even though he must have been out of Court at Christmas: see SM II, 76.

[51] Add 17362, fol. 33v (cal. SM II, 78). The king's livery was not given exclusively to his own household: see SM II, 96 for Edward III's livery given to Welsh minstrels.

[52] Rylands 234, fol. 27r (cal. SM II, 87).

[53] Stowe 1043, fol. 227v (cal. SM II, 123). For the livery of the harper William Corff, see Stowe 1043, fol. 220v (cal. SM II, 123).

[54] Rylands 234, fols 3r and 18r (cal. SM II, 87): the tunic contained 3 ells of cloth.

Pentecost robe, to which he was apparently not entitled, but it may relate to the ceremonies attending Philippa's *relevacio* after the birth of her first child, Edward of Woodstock (the Black Prince) on 15 June that year.[55]

Liveries were especially impressive at coronations and royal weddings. For the wedding of Princess Philippa in 1406, the queen's household received liveries of scarlet and green robes: those delivered to the minstrels each contained 8 ells of cloth.[56] Scarlet was a colour apparently reserved for these occasional celebrations: liveries for the queen's coronation in 9 Hen V were again scarlet.[57]

Nothing in the records of liveries suggests that the minstrels' dress distinguished them from other servants, and this would be unnecessary in the household context. But there are a few indications that minstrels could generally be identified from what they wore. The story of a woman riding into Westminster Hall to confront Edward II depends on the porters allowing her in because she was dressed as a minstrel.[58] What might this distinctive clothing be? An episode in *La Tour Landry* (1371–2) relates that a squire wearing a coat in German style was jokingly taken for a minstrel by one of the knights at a feast, so it was a question of style rather than of colour or attachments.[59]

Any sort of uniform style would no doubt vary with place and time, so it would be difficult to pin down exactly what distinguished a minstrel's dress. Iconographic evidence is considerably limited by the fact that so many minstrels depicted are angels – wearing what the artist regarded as angels' attire – or grotesque. Real minstrels are depicted in the late thirteenth and early fourteenth centuries wearing long robes without a coat, while from the early fifteenth century a knee-length coat is more usual, appearing as a sort of uniform by the early sixteenth century. A bagpiper and a fiddler on bench-ends in St Nonna's church at Altarnun, Cornwall, wear coats with full skirt and sleeves (see Plates 2 and 3), seen again on the minstrels on the famous pillar (1524) in St Mary's church at Beverley, where the minstrels depicted are certainly wearing uniform clothing.[60] The coats are mostly of knee-length, but the presumed senior minstrel, in the centre of the group, wears a slightly longer coat, to just below the knee. There is confirmation of the leader of a professional group wearing a longer coat in the livery-list for the coronation of Henry VIII in 1509. Here the marshals of the trumpets (Peter de Casa Nova) and of the minstrels (John Chamber) are allowed five yards of cloth, while all other trumpeters and minstrels received four and a half yards.[61]

---

[55] Whit Sunday 1330 was on 27 May.

[56] E101.406.10, fol. 3r (cal. SM II, 122).

[57] E101.407.4, fol. 37v (cal. SM II, 124).

[58] At Pentecost 1317. For similar cases of a minstrel bearing an unwelcome message, see below, pp. 307–8.

[59] Mary Remnant, *English Bowed Instruments from Anglo-Saxon to Tudor Times* (Oxford, 1986), 81.

[60] Remnant, *English Bowed Instruments*, 81, and Plate 145 for the Beverley pillar; and Plate 146 for the fiddler; also E.T. Fox, 'Tudor bench ends of the West Country': <https://benchends.wordpress.com> (accessed 14 January 2020).

[61] Ashbee, *Records*, VII, 28, 29.

PLATE 2. A bagpiper. Bench end in St Nonna's church, Altarnun, Cornwall, early 16th century.

PLATE 3. A fiddler. Bench end in St Nonna's church, Altarnun, Cornwall, early 16th century.

Another form of livery in the king's household was the collar (that is, something worn round the neck, *col*), which took the form of a metal scutcheon on a chain. Edward IV's *Liber Niger* shows that the lords, knights and squires of the household were required to 'weare collers of the kinges liuerie about their neckes'. Failure to do so would cost a squire a month's wages.[62] This would include the minstrels, who held squire's rank. There is no mention of collars in the Wardrobe books, however, a situation distinct from that of civic minstrels, where the scutcheons were retrieved and weighed each year (see Chapter 7).

Rewards: gifts and grants

The *Dona* (Gifts) sections of the Wardrobe books of Edward I's reign are large and shed considerable light on the subject of minstrelsy at Court. Those of the following reigns are smaller, but remain very revealing until the end of Edward III's reign (1377). Thereafter, coverage is more patchy and interpretation of the evidence commensurately more difficult.

Gifts to many minstrels are recorded in the *Dona* sections of the accounts. Some were royal minstrels, some attached to other nobles, and some independent: but most entries are for minstrelsy in the presence of the king or other members of the royal family. When the gift is not for minstrelsy it was usually bestowed for a specific purpose: to enable an independent minstrel to return to his own district, or to help a royal minstrel to buy himself a horse, for instance. These and other gifts not specifically for minstrelsy sometimes seem to take the place of payments that could have been recorded elsewhere in the accounts. Thus royal servants carrying messages sometimes received their expenses as a direct gift from the king rather than as a payment which would be recorded in the *Nuncii* (Messengers) section of the Wardrobe accounts. The expediency of such a course is obvious: the payment was made with the maximum of speed and administrative simplicity.

In many cases there may have been no alternative. The Wardrobe was not responsible for paying the expenses of messengers or minstrels who came to the king from other nobles,[63] nor could payments easily be made for horses or other necessaries for a non-household minstrel who travelled for a while with the Court.[64] Sometimes, too, the king's own minstrels were ordered to remain in a certain place while the king moved on, or a minstrel was taken ill and was left behind: in these cases a gift was the most practical way of paying his expenses in advance, or at least without a long delay.[65] The king's gifts might extend beyond the minstrel's professional life at Court,

---

[62] Myers, *Household of Edward IV*, 205.

[63] For examples, see BL Add 7965 (25 Ed I), fol. 52r (Gillotus, harper of Sir Hugo de Cressingham: cal. SM II, 16); and *ibid.*, fol. 54r (Miemus de Mantzt, minstrel, coming to the king on a mission from Gascony: cal. SM II, 17).

[64] For examples see SM II, 24, 41, 88 and 93.

[65] E101.363.18 (31 Ed I), fol. 23r (Bestruche, minstrel of Geneva, ordered to remain in London); E101.369.11 (31 Ed I), fol. 96r (Bestulphus and Bertuchus, minstrels of Geneva); and E101.373.15 (1 Ed II), fols 21r (Little Andrew, John Scot, Roger the trumpeter and Francekinus the nakerer) and 21v (Lambyn Clay, ill at London). These are cal. SM II, 40, 45 and 65 (two items), respectively. See also the case of King Robert (Chapter 10).

helping a minstrel to set up a home or to visit his own district: and money might be given to a minstrel who was poor, or who wished to go on a pilgrimage.[66]

Early in the reign of Richard II (1377-99) the rewards of some junior royal servants seem to have been standardised.[67] Towards the end of the reign the household grooms received a fixed annual reward of 20s 0d: this was temporarily decreased to 16s 8d (one and a quarter marks) in 27 or 28 Hen VI, and reduced again in 19-20 Ed IV to 13s 4d (one mark).[68] Only in the Tudor period, in the reign of Henry VII (1485-1509), do we find individual gifts again recorded in the account-books.

Comparison of these accounts with the Wardrobe books of Edward I's reign shows that the amount of the king's disbursements in gifts to minstrels had altered very little in the intervening two centuries. In the years 25, 29, 32 and 34 Ed I the king's gifts to minstrels totalled £71 9s 2d, £25 9s 6d, £21 9s 11d and £224 14s 8d, respectively. Of the total for 25 Ed I, £41.10.0d was due to the wedding of the Princess Elizabeth to John, Count of Holland, in December 1296. 34 Ed I was an expensive year by any standard, but £170.10.8d of the total was accounted for by three special events: the Pentecost feast (22 May 1306) at which the future Edward II was knighted, and the weddings of two favoured nobles. Earl Warenne married Joan, daughter of the Count of Bar, on 25 May 1306, and the following day the younger Hugo le Despenser married Eleanor, daughter of the Earl of Gloucester. But if we disregard the occasional expense of the royal wedding in 25 Ed I, the years 25, 29 and 32 Ed I average just over £25 disbursed in eleven or thirteen gifts.[69] The accounts for four years of Henry VII's reign, *annis* 11-14, inclusive, show an average of £41 16s 3d per year spent in gifts to minstrels, in an average of twenty-two gifts per year.[70] £64 13s 4d of this expenditure, however, was given to the royal minstrels for their New Year largess, which was not a feature of earlier reigns: and if we omit this from our total, the average total per year shrinks to just over £25, within a few pence of the average just noted in Edward I's reign.[71] Henry VII gave money more frequently than Edward I, but his gifts were smaller on average.

Instruments

Some royal persons owned musical instruments. A harp was bought for Henry IV's second wife, Joan of Navarre, at a cost of 6s 8d (half a mark) in 7 or 8 Hen V; Henry V played the harp, as did his wife Katherine of Valois; members of Henry VII's family owned and played musical instruments; and the extensive instrument collection of

---

[66] See, for instance, items cal. SM II, 40, 62, 65, 66, 68, 82, 93, 104 and 119.

[67] See Devon, *Issues*, 159, 171, 247, 318, 413 and 452 (ranging in date from 27 Ed III to 23 Hen VI).

[68] See the various accounts calendared in SM II, 119-31, *passim*. The relationship between these rewards and the annual fee is unclear.

[69] See the various accounts cal. SM II, 16 f, 23 f, 40 ff and 45 f. For more on these weddings and the Pentecost feast, see Chapter 4.

[70] See the accounts cal. SM II, 133-41. I exclude gifts to players and the poet here.

[71] The effect of inflation in Henry VII's reign is probably negligible. The influx of gold from South America to Spain caused little inflation in England until well into the sixteenth century.

Henry VIII is well known.⁷² These relate to amateur domestic music-making, and are an important adjunct to political and social activities as well as overlapping with the music-making of some household servants. This love of amateur music-making filtered down to other educated people, judging by the ownership of instruments by some Oxford academics in the fifteenth century.⁷³

The minstrels, however, seem normally to have possessed their own instruments. When the king's trumpeters John de London and John de Depe had new trumpets made in 25 Ed I, the king reimbursed them with 40s 0d (£2).⁷⁴ Compared to the 4s 0d paid for only part of a latten trumpet, these may be the full cost (£1 for each trumpet).⁷⁵ On 7 November 1303 Prince Edward gave his trumpeter Janin de Cateloyne 13s 4d (1 mark) to buy himself a copper trumpet.⁷⁶

Only very valuable items such as silver trumpets seem to have belonged to their employer. These were for ceremonial purposes – civic, military or religious – and were a sign of considerable wealth and power. Gretchen Peters cites several instances of them being used by civic trumpeters in French towns: and although they may have been played during religious processions, the purposes that she specifies were civic and diplomatic.⁷⁷ Two silver trumpets bought in 32 Ed I and given to Prince Edward's trumpeter Janin (or Januche) appear in the Wardrobe inventory of jewels and plate,⁷⁸ so they were apparently kept in a secure place when not in use. They were perhaps replacements, for two silver trumpets appear in earlier inventories of jewels and plate, in 28, 29 and 33 Ed I.⁷⁹

Indirect confirmation of the use of silver trumpets is found in the York mystery plays. The Mercers staged the Last Judgment, in which angel trumpeters sound the Last Trump, effectively a signal for the dead to arise and pay attention before the Judgment begins. The Mercers' records for the play in 1433 include an inventory in which 'ij trumpes of White plate' appear.⁸⁰ This is effectively the dramati-

---

72 E101.406.30, fol. 11r (cal. SM II, 124); Devon, *Issues of the Exchequer*, 363 and 367; for the inventory of Henry VIII's instruments, see David Starkey, Maria Hayward and Philip Ward, *The Inventory of King Henry VIII* (London, 1998).

73 *REED Oxford* (ed. John R. Elliott Jr, Alan H. Nelson, Alexandra F. Johnston and Diana Wyatt). 2 vols (2004), I, 15–20, *passim* (1427–69).

74 BL Add MS 7965 (25 Ed I), fol. 56v (cal. SM II, 17).

75 For the tube of a latten trumpet, see p. 101.

76 E101.363.18 (Household of the Prince of Wales, 31 Ed I), fol. 22v (cal. SM II, 39–40). It is unlikely that Janin's trumpet *de cupro* was of pure copper: an alloy such as latten or brass (these include zinc, lead and tin) is more likely. See Catherine E. Karkov's article 'Metalwork, gothic', in Szarmach *et al.*, *Medieval England*, especially 510.

77 Gretchen Peters, *The Musical Sounds of Medieval French Cities: Players, Patrons, and Politics* (Cambridge, 2012), 49, 50, 55, 58, 110 and 187. See also M. Olivier Langeron, 'La Trompette d'argent'. *Mémoires de la Commission des antiquités de la Côte d'Or*, 2nd ser. 14 (1851), 91–102.

78 BL Add MS 8835 (32 Ed I), fol. 130v: the inventory entry is on fol. 127v (cal. SM II, 42). These trumpets were again inventoried in 33 Ed I: E101.369.11, fol. 177v (cal. SM II, 47).

79 BL Add MS 35291, fol. 140v; Add 7966A, fol. 151v (cal. SM II, 20 and 25, respectively).

80 *REED York* (ed. Alexandra F. Johnston and Margaret Rogerson). 2 vols. (1979), 55. For the use of these trumpets in the play, see Richard Rastall, *Minstrels Playing*. Music in Early

sation of an heraldic function, though in a religious context. Trumpets – no doubt including silver ones – had ceremonial uses also in actual liturgical contexts. There is no English evidence for this, but Bowles cites an occasion on which a trumpet was sounded at the Elevation of the Host during Mass in Florence cathedral;[81] and in *Le songe du vieil pèlerin* (1389), Philippe de Mézières warned Charles VI of France against the excessive use of musicians, making an exception for the playing of 'great trumpets' at the Elevation of the Host on special occasions. Philippe was apparently referring to a known practice, as the evidence from Florence would suggest, so it is possible that the silver trumpets in the Wardrobe inventory were used in liturgical ceremonial as well as secular celebrations.[82]

Although the minstrels were generally responsible for their own instruments, it was not unusual for the king to make a gift to a minstrel who needed a new instrument, or who required materials for repairs, as just noted in the case of John de London and John de Depe. A similar gift made on 29 January 32 Ed I (1304) included travelling-expenses in the 50s 0d given, for the Court was at Newcastle upon Tyne, and it was necessary for Robert de York to travel to London for suitable instruments for himself and his *socius* Richard de Blida.[83] Probably the majority of reputable instrument-makers in England – or at least, those that the Court dealt with – were in London.[84] But the 13s 4d, also noted above, given at Dunfermline by the Prince of Wales to his trumpeter Janinus de Cateloyn for the same purpose in 1303 included no travelling-expenses:[85] possibly the instrument was bought from the maker who supplied trumpets to the Scottish Court. A gift to the king's *vigilis* John de Staunton on 8 February 1306 to buy *diversa instrumenta* may not refer to musical instruments, although it is hard to imagine what else it could be for.[86] Perhaps new pipes were being bought for the *vigiles* against the forthcoming Pentecost celebrations.

A curious story emerges from the accounts for the summer of 1336, when the 23-year-old Edward III travelled north from Pontefract to St Johnstone. On the journey he was entertained by one Robert de Farebourn, the *tympanistra* of the constable of Pontefract castle, Robert de Dosenill. On arrival at St Johnstone the king took Robert's instrument and gave it to his own *tympanistra*, compensating Robert on 3 July with a gift of 20s 0d. A month later, on 5 August, the king made a gift of 20s 0d to John Perot, *cornemuser de montvalour*, in compensation for his *tympanum*, which the

---

English Religious Drama, II (Cambridge, 2001), 43–6.

[81] Edmund A. Bowles, 'Were musical instruments used in the liturgical service during the Middle Ages?'. *Galpin Society Journal* 10 (1957), 40–56, especially 52, citing Franz Xaver Haberl, 'Die römische Schola Cantorum und die papstlichen Kapellsänger' (1888), 36. I have been unable to consult Haberl's work, and do not know if he gave a date.

[82] André Pirro, *La Musique à Paris sous le regne de Charles VI* (Paris, 1930), 14, cited in Bowles, 'Were musical instruments used', 52. For silver trumpets in the household of the Black Prince, see pp. 101–2.

[83] BL Add MS 8835 (32 Ed I), fol. 44r (cal. SM II, 41).

[84] See SM II, Appendix F.

[85] TNA E101.363.18 (Household of the Prince of Wales, 31 Ed I), fol. 22v (cal. SM II, 39 f).

[86] E101.369.11 (34 Ed I), fol. 100r (cal. SM II, 46).

king had broken.[87] The royal minstrel John Perrot (or Perot) played the cornemuse, a small bagpipe, and is not otherwise known as the player of a *tympanum*: he perhaps played pipe-and-tabor.[88] This may not seem promising for entertainment on a journey of well over 200 miles, but Robert de Farebourn, too, may have played pipe and tabor: and other minstrels must have been involved, so that Robert was not necessarily playing *solo*.

Perrot may be the man who later, in 1360, presented an *eschequier* of his own making to Jean II of France as a gift from Edward III (see p. 336–7, below). Although there are records of minstrels repairing instruments, Perrot must have been unusual as a maker and new instruments seem to have been bought from professional makers out of Court. The various instruments provided by the Black Prince for his minstrels and those of the Count of Eu in 1352 and 1358 would be outside the financial reach of the minstrels as performers, and as makers.[89]

For these portable instruments there is scattered and fragmentary evidence for protective cover. Damage from the weather would be a constant concern of any minstrel travelling or accompanying his master in the hunt, for the sun can be as damaging as rain, especially to wooden pipes and stringed instruments. A bag or pouch would both protect an instrument and make it easier to carry on horseback. Manuscript illuminations seem to show that harpers kept their instruments in bags, which made a firmer base in the lap for holding the instrument during performance (Plate 4). This is not the sort of expense that we could expect to find recorded in the Wardrobe books, and the accounts provide no definite information: but it is possible that prests made to Nicholas de Eland, John de London and John de Depe on the price of ten ells of canvas for each of them refer to cloth for instrument-bags:[90]

> The king's harper: to Nicholas the king's harper, as a part-payment on the price
>   of 10 ells of canvas delivered to him through the same [Ralph de Stok'] 3s 4d
> The king's trumpeters: to John de London and John de Depe the king's
>   trumpeters, as a part-payment on the price of 20 ells of canvas delivered
>   to them through the same Sir Ralph 6s 8d

---

[87] BL Cotton MS Nero C viii, fols 278v and 279r (10 Ed III) (cal. SM II, 94).

[88] See Christopher Page, 'German musicians and their instruments: a 14th-century account by Konrad of Megenberg'. *Early Music* 10/2 (1982), 192–200; repr. McGee, *Instruments and their Music*, 29–37, especially 33–4. Perrot may have played the cornemuse with one hand and the drum with the other.

[89] E.C. Lodge and Sir Robert Somerville, eds, *John of Gaunt's Register, 1379–1383*. 2 vols. Camden Society, third series 56 and 57 (1937), IV, 73: also MERH, 21.

[90] Ed I: BL Add 7966A, fol. 167r (cal. SM II, 25): 'Citharista Regis: Nicholao cithariste Regis de prestito in precio x ulnarum canabi sibi liberatarum per eundem iij s iv d'. 'Trumpatores Regis: Johanni de London' et Johanni de Depe trumpatoribus Regis de prestito in precio xx ulnarum canabi sibi liberatarum per eundem dominum Radulphum vj s viij d'. In quotations using a hanging indent in this book the first words, up to the colon, are a marginal heading in the original.

Plate 4. The initial to Psalm 80, *Exultate Deo*, c. 1325. The Ormesby Psalter: Oxford, Bodleian Library, MS Douce 366, fol. 109r.

This however remains speculative. In 1352 the Black Prince gave pouches to two of his pipers to put their pipes in,[91] but the record does not specify either the type or the amount of material.

Whatever the level of protection, the minstrels' instruments must have needed constant maintenance and occasional repair. Minor repairs could probably be handled by the minstrels themselves. The prince's nakerer Janinus was reimbursed 3s od for the cost of skins when he repaired his nakers in April 31 Ed I (1302); and Martinettus the taborer was paid 11d on 18 November 34 Ed I (1306) for repairing drums of the young princes Thomas and Edmund and for the cost of parchment for the drum-heads.[92] The princes were 6 and 5 years old, respectively, at the time.

Major repairs would usually be the work of a professional instrument-maker,[93] and any minstrel who could undertake them must have been exceptional. John Perrot was apparently one such; another was Master John, Earl Warenne's organist, who was employed by the Prince of Wales for nine days in February 31 Ed I (1303) to overhaul the organ in the royal manor of Langley (Plate 5):[94]

---

[91] Lodge and Somerville, *John of Gaunt*, IV, 72.

[92] TNA E101.363.18 (31 Ed I), fol. 21v (cal. SM II, 39); E101.368.12 (Household of Thomas and Edmund, 34 Ed I), fol. 3r (cal. SM II, 52).

[93] A minstrel would not be expected to provide a new section for a trumpet, for instance.

[94] TNA E101.363.18, fol. 5v (cal. SM II, 38): 'Reperacio organorum: magistro Johanni organiste comitis Warenn' pro xv libris stagni per ipsum emptis pro organis principis

Repair of the organs: to Master John, organist of Earl Warenne, for 15 lb of tin
    bought by the same in respect of the prince's organs made and repaired
    in his manor of Langley against the coming of the king and queen there
    in the month of February in the present year [31 Ed I], together with
    various other items bought by him there for the same, 7s 6d. To the
    same for his expenses of his horse and groom for 9 days during which
    they stayed at Langley that month for the preparation of the said organs
    as aforesaid, taking 9d per day: 6s 9d by his own hands.
        Total 14s 3d

Master John was evidently a skilled organ-builder, for the 15 lbs of tin required were presumably needed for repairs to the pipe-work, and perhaps for replacements.

A category of instrument not owned by the minstrels (apart from the expensive instruments noted above) were for noise-making rather than musical purposes – the tabors and horns used for hunting, fowling and hawking. An item in the accounts for 31 Ed I, dated 10 December [1303] suggests that the provision of these could be a considerable operation:[95]

Tabors and horns bought for fowling: to John Dengaigne, yeoman of the
    Chamber of the lord Edward the king's son, Prince of Wales, for two
    tabors for fowling, bought by the same at London on the orders of the
    same lord and sent thence to Marlborough to the same Prince, the price
    of the one being 7s 0d and of the other 4s 0d: 11s 0d.
To the same, for 90 small horns, similarly bought by him and sent in the same
    way, with the same tabors, to the said Prince for fowling: 23s 0d, by his
    own hands, 10 December of the present year. Total 34s 0d

Ninety horns at a total of £1 3s 0d makes them just over 3d each. Such a large number of horns (as opposed to only two tabors) suggests that they were regarded as con-

---

inde faciendis et reparandis in manerio suo de Langele contra adventum Regis et Regine ibidem, mense Februarii anno presente, una cum aliis diversis minutis per ipsum emptis ibidem pro eisdem vij s vj d. Eidem pro expensis suis equi et garcionis sui per ix dies per quos morabant apud Langele eodem mense pro dictis organis preparandis ut predicitur percipiendo per diem ix d vj s ix d per manus proprias. Summa xiiij s. iijd'. *Stagnum* can mean pewter as well as tin, so the metal concerned may have been an alloy. The plural *organa* does not indicate more than one instrument.

[95] TNA E101.363.18 (31 Ed I), fol. 5r (cal. SM II, 38): 'Tabores et cornua empta pro ripariatione: Johanni Dengaigne valletto camere domini Edwardi filij Regis Principis Wallie pro duobus taboris de ripariatione emptis per eundem apud London per preceptum eiusdem domini et missis abinde usque Marleberge ad eundem principem, precium unius vij s et alterius iv s xj s'. 'Eidem pro xc minutis cornibus similiter emptis per eundem et missis eodem modo ad dictum Principem pro ripariatione simul cum eisdem taboris xxiij s per manus proprias x die Decembris anno presenti. Summa xxxiiij s'. *Ripariatio* can mean fowling, hawking or hunting: it is not clear which is intended here. For further examples, see BL Add 7965 (25 Ed I), fol. 3r (24s 0d paid for six tabors bought for the king's falconers); Add 35292 (31–4 Ed I), fol. 27r (15s 0d for five tabors bought for fowling); and Add 8835 (32 Ed I), fol. 69r and 69v (15s 0d for five tabors bought for fowling, and 36s 0d for six tabors for fowling, with covering for the tabors and carriage from London to York): (cal. SM II, 16, 32 and 42, respectively). 'Small' horns were perhaps the short noise-makers, as opposed to those with a longer, coiled, tube (see p. 323).

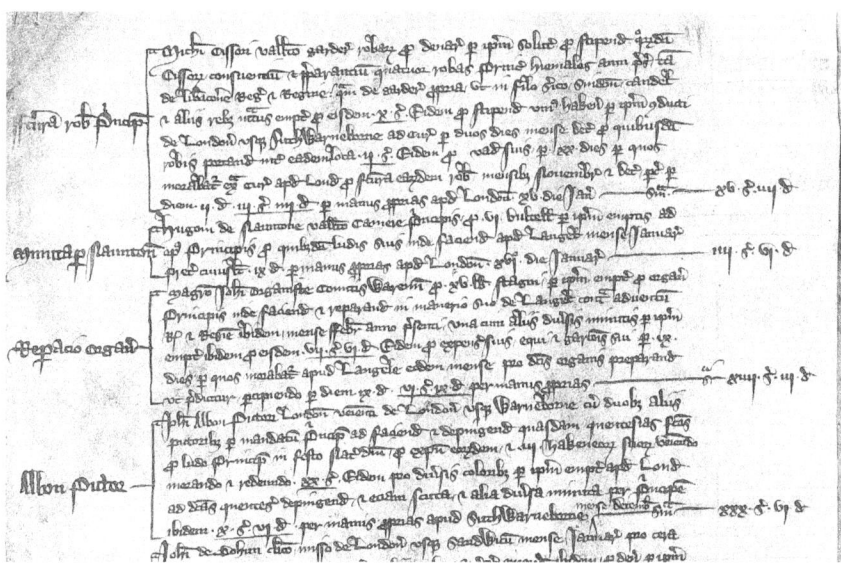

PLATE 5. Record of Master John's repair of the organ at Langley, February 1303. Kew, The National Archives, E101.363.18 (Household of the Prince of Wales, Controller's book, 31 Ed I), fol. 5v.

sumables – breakable and expendable. We think of horns in the late Middle Ages as coming from slaughtered cattle, and indeed many of them must have been of this kind. Natural horn is very durable, so the rate of breakage of such horns should have been small. What proportion of them was available for hunting is another matter. Horn was widely used in windows as a cheaper alternative to glass, so the availability for hunting-horns (or drinking horns) may have been limited. Of the alternatives, we can immediately discount the oliphant, the large horn made from elephant tusk, as too expensive for day-to-day use: it was, indeed a ceremonial instrument, which is why so many have survived. We can also discount glass horns as impractical. Those made in metal and wood were no doubt durable enough for the purpose, but not inexpensive. The cheapest alternative was the ceramic horn, for which there was a large market: and we should probably assume that the great majority of horns used in hunting, for making noise in battle, and so on, were of this type. Crane comments that 'in Germany, at least, pottery horns may have been the commonest type for everyday signaling purposes in the Middle Ages'; but Jean Le Patourel showed that they were common also in England, where they were manufactured as well as being imported from the Low Countries in small quantities.[96]

---

[96] Frederick Crane, *Extant Medieval Musical Instruments: A Provisional Catalogue by Types* (Iowa City IA, 1972), 60 f; Jean Le Patourel, 'Ceramic horns'. David Gaimster and Mark Redknap, eds, *Everyday and Exotic Pottery from Europe, c. 650–1900* (Oxford, 1992), 157–66, *passim*.

These ninety horns bought for hawking or hunting would be used by the beaters, simply for making noise. More durable and expensive instruments made from natural horn would be needed for the chief huntsmen who signalled the progress of the hunt.[97] They were not minstrel instruments and could not be used for making music. However, minstrelsy might well have been called for on hunting expeditions, and it is possible that some falconers and huntsmen could produce acceptable minstrelsy, which they would perform on proper minstrel instruments: musical names amongst royal falconers indicate this as a possibility. As we have also seen, in the time of Edward IV the two loud minstrels in constant attendance were required on such expeditions.

Horses

In war-time, royal servants had their own horses valued, and their wages were fixed accordingly. If a horse died in the king's service a payment was made in compensation, and at other times the king might make a gift for the purchase or replacement of a horse. These payments and gifts were usually recorded in the *Restaurum Equorum* and *Dona* sections, respectively, of the Wardrobe books.[98]

A payment often made to squires, including minstrels, was 40s 0d, which seems to have been the cost of a good average hackney: but payments varied widely according to the status of the recipient and the kind of horse required. King Capiny, for instance, received 73s 4d (£3 13s 4d, or 5½ marks) to replace a horse; Roger de Porchester, waferer, and Nicholas de Wycombe, *vigilis*, were given only 24s 0d and 20s 0d, respectively; and the piper Godscalk was given 40s 0d. Much later, in September 1499 (15 Hen VII), an un-named royal trumpeter received 26s 8d (two marks) to buy a horse.[99]

With the Court often travelling, the king sometimes found it necessary to enable visiting servants and those *qui non sunt* to buy themselves horses. A lower-quality animal was probably considered adequate for the purpose, and the gift was only 20s 0d or 13s 4d. On 14 May 32 Ed I (1304) Earl Warenne's trumpeters Nicholas de Doncaster and John Crakestreng were given 26s 8d (a mark each) to buy horses at Stirling; John, messenger and minstrel of the Count of Savoy, was also given 13s 4d to buy a hackney that year; and Bernard de Burdegala, minstrel of Lord Ufford, received 20s 0d at Canterbury on 16 April 9 Ed III (1335) to replace a horse, his mount having perhaps died on the road while Bernard was riding to Canterbury with

---

[97] The signals used during hunting are noted in two manuals, but the descriptions are not easy to interpret. See Edith Rickert, ed., *Chaucer's World* (New York NY and London, 1948), 218–25, for the treatise by Edward, Duke of York; and William Twiti, *The Middle English Text of The Art of Hunting*, ed. David Scott-Macnab (Universitätsverlag Winter, 2009).

[98] For Wardrobe book entries concerning horses, see SM II, Appendix A, *passim*.

[99] TNA E101.369.11 (34 Ed I), fol. 103v; E101.383.8 (1–2 Ed III), fol. 9r; BL Cotton MS Nero C viii (section for 10 Ed III), fol. 276v; E101.414.16 (13–15 Hen VII), fol. 77v: cal. SM II, 47, 84, 94 and 141, respectively.

the king.¹⁰⁰ The Wardrobe books also record gifts of saddles to minstrels *qui non sunt*: the German *gigatores* Henry and Gunradus were given 6s 8d for a sumpter-saddle at Eston on 19 January 29 Ed I (1301); and when John Perrot, acting on the queen's orders, bought a saddle for the German *gigator* Hanekin de Cologne at Melton, the queen later reimbursed him in the sum of 4s 0d (at Windsor, 22 October).¹⁰¹

Most royal minstrels probably had at least one horse in Court whenever they were resident there, both for travelling with the Court and for going home or elsewhere between feasts. Prests on the price of hay and corn are not uncommon in the Wardrobe books, and the *Liber Niger* of Edward IV required that lodgings be found near to the Court for the minstrels and their horses. No numbers are stated, although the assumption seems to be that all thirteen minstrels were mounted.¹⁰² Some had more than one horse, perhaps partly in order that their servants and apprentices could ride. The three horses given to Guillotus the queen's psaltery-player in 28 Ed I were an exceptional gift.¹⁰³ Other minstrels may have done without a horse whenever possible, the cost of stabling and feeding a horse being considerable. Richard de Blida perhaps did not have a horse when he was sent out of Court on the king's business in November 1315 (9 Ed II), since one was bought for him.¹⁰⁴ He was absent from 2 November until 31 January following. As he had already required assistance in setting up a home, he was probably not well-off. The situation was different in wartime, when it was vital for all members of the force to have horses sufficient for themselves, their men and their baggage. On the return from France beginning in January 1320 (13 Ed II) most of the minstrels had two horses each; but Francekinus, Bisshop and Polidod had three each, Purchaceour had six, and Whissh had nine.¹⁰⁵ The larger numbers may be due to horses captured from the enemy, part of the spoils of war.

The Wardrobe books give little indication that minstrels who visited Court were mounted: nor do they show that royal minstrels were mounted when they worked as itinerant performers away from Court. Ivo Vala and Thomas Denys were apparently not mounted when they came to Court in 6 Ed II, since the king had to equip them with both horses and saddles in order to take them to France as his own minstrels.¹⁰⁶ On the other hand, it was probably not uncommon for the best minstrels, royal and otherwise, to be on horseback, especially if they intended to travel large distances: in

---

¹⁰⁰ For Doncaster, Crakestreng and John, see BL Add MS 8835 (32 Ed I), fol. 42v, 43v (cal. SM II, 41); for Bernard de Burdegala, see Nero C viii, fol. 270r (9 Ed III) (cal. SM II, 93).

¹⁰¹ BL Add MS 7966A (29 Ed I), fol. 67r, and Rylands 235 (5 Ed III), fol. 20r (cal. SM II, 24 and 88). This latter entry says that Hankin was from Hanover.

¹⁰² Lodging 'nygh the court': see Myers, *Household of Edward IV*, 132. For prests on the price of hay and corn see SM II, 37 and n. 28, and 84, for instance.

¹⁰³ BL Add MS 35291 (28 Ed I), fol. 43r (cal. SM II, 20).

¹⁰⁴ TNA E101.376.7, fol. 83r (cal. SM II, 75 f): for the assistance in setting up a home, see E101.373.15 (1 Ed II), fol. 20r (cal. SM II, 65).

¹⁰⁵ TNA E36.203, fol. 154v (cal. SM II, 102).

¹⁰⁶ TNA E101.375.8 (6 Ed II), fol. 29v (cal. SM II, 73).

the time of Henry VI the fraternity of the Holy Cross at Abingdon paid for the 'dyet and horsemeat' of the minstrels who performed at their annual feast.[107]

The accounts of certain towns in Kent show that liveried minstrels sometimes, but not invariably, travelled on horseback. A mounted minstrel of the Archbishop of Canterbury who was rewarded at New Romney in 1453/4 may have been in his master's company,[108] and the same applies to the mounted minstrels of the Earl of Arundel who received gifts at Dover in 1470/1.[109] When the Earl's minstrels were again rewarded in 1494/5, however, the gifts for wine and horsemeat suggest that they were travelling independently of the Earl.[110] Payments for expenses or costs of visiting minstrels are common in the Kentish accounts, and especially in the Dover records. While most items are unspecific, many are for wine and bread, which was presumably unnecessary if the town were extending hospitality to the noble whose livery the minstrels wore. For the same reason, the king's minstrels who visited Lydd in 1458/9, and who received 22d for the expenses of 'them and ther horse', were probably not travelling with the Court.[111]

In this last entry, 'horse' might be either singular or plural. In any case, we cannot assume that royal or other liveried minstrels were always mounted. The payment to the *histriones equestres* of the queen in the Canterbury accounts for 1477/8 seems by implication to distinguish these minstrels from the other *histriones* paid at Canterbury that year. It is possible that the term relates to minstrels who made a point of *performing* on horseback: but in that case one might expect them to be rewarded generously, whereas the 20d that they received compares unfavourably with payments to other minstrels. Perhaps there were fewer of them.[112]

Residence: attendance and absences

The system by which some minstrels were on duty at all times, presumably in rotation, was general in the king's household. Edward IV's *Liber Niger* shows that it had long been the custom for some servants to be on duty, with others available to replace or supplement them as need arose. This is stated most clearly in the case of the 40 squires of the household, only 20 of whom were required at any one time, though at the discretion of the king.[113]

As we have seen, apart from the small group required to be in attendance at all times the royal minstrels were expected in Court only for the major feasts, primarily those of Christmas and Pentecost. At other times they were expected to live

---

[107] Thomas Hearne, *Liber Niger Scaccarii* (London, 1728; 2/1771), II, 598: 'horsemeat' in this context refers to food for the horses.

[108] REED Kent: *Diocese of Canterbury*, 736.

[109] *Ibid.*, 347: at this time the earl was Warden of the Cinque Ports, and so may have been a regular traveller along the south coast.

[110] *Ibid.*, 380.

[111] *Ibid.*, 662.

[112] *Ibid.*, 80.

[113] Myers *Household of Edward IV*, 127.

independently, although apparently on call should the need arise: but the small permanent group, together with the liveried and independent minstrels who visited Court, were normally enough to provide all the minstrelsy required.

If this system had been strictly adhered to, we should find that about four of the king's minstrels were in Court for the whole of any one year, the others being present for perhaps twenty days or so. In fact, the resident minstrels probably worked to a rota with a tour of duty of much less than a year. Sometimes, too, they were no doubt unavailable through illness or because they had temporarily left Court for some reason, with replacements being needed; and in this case one or more would have to be recalled to Court for a period. Residence would also look very different in war-time – and the king was often at war, particularly in Scotland and France – when all available men were needed at any potential conflict and the minstrels became fighting men.

The accounts give comprehensive information on the residence of some minstrels in certain years. The longest periods of residence of the minstrels are those of the king's harpers during the reigns of Edward I and Edward II: in 31 Ed I, Adam de Cliderhou and William de Morley were resident for 150 days and 114 days respectively; in 34 Ed I, Hugo de la Rose and Adam de Cliderhou were resident for 187 days and 207 days respectively, although William de Morley spent only 38 days in Court; in 5 Ed II, Elias de Garsynton was in Court for 134 days out of the 163 days between 27 January and 7 July (1312), but Robert de Clough was in residence for only 30 days in the whole year (a leap year), and was probably out of Court at Pentecost, when he was not given money for a summer robe.[114]

We might guess from this that the two minstrels remaining in Court as the 1318 ordinances require were harpers: but the evidence is far from conclusive, and there is no evidence that the same number of trumpeters also remained. William the trumpeter was in Court for 122 days in 4 Ed II, but in 3 Ed II he spent only 20 days in Court, and two years later a mere 8 days.[115] In these latter two years he was no doubt required only at the major feasts and special occasions; but 122 days does suggest his permanent attendance for much of 4 Ed II.

One reason for leaving Court would be when a minstrel needed to visit his home. With the Court travelling all over the country, royal servants were sometimes great distances from home, and gifts to enable them to return there are occasionally recorded in the Wardrobe books.[116] A visit was also possible when the king's itinerary happened to pass close to a minstrel's home and the man concerned could take the opportunity – with permission – to check that all was well with his family and property. Visits at other times may have been for a variety of reasons, such as illness in the family, but there is no information on these.

---

[114] BL Cotton MS Nero C viii, fol. 118v (cal. SM II, 72). For these various harpers, see TNA E101.364.13 (31 Ed I), fols 25v and 26r (cal. SM II, 35); E101.368.27 (34 Ed I), fols 20v, 21r and 22r (cal. SM II, 49); and E101.373.26 (4–5 Ed II), fols 24r and 24v (cal. SM II, 70).

[115] E101.374.5, fol. 34v; E101.373.26, fol. 26r; Nero C viii, fol. 42v: (cal. SM II, 69, 70 and 71, respectively).

[116] TNA E101.373.30 (4 Ed II), fol. 5v, and BL Nero C viii (8–11 Ed III), fol. 273r: (cal. SM II, 68 and 93).

Probably some minstrels went home anyway when they were not needed at Court, and perhaps led a normal life as local minstrels until required at Court again. It may have been considered important for a royal servant to have a personal and family base, and there are records of the king helping a minstrel to set up his home. In 31 Ed I John the luter set up a home in London, and in 1 Ed II the trumpeter Richard de Blida set up a home in Blida (Blyth in Nottinghamshire) where he had presumably spent his earlier life.[117] John spent 50 days at Court in 31 Ed I: he was absent at Pentecost the following year and in 34 Ed I spent only 16 days in Court, when he was absent at Christmas.[118]

Financially, many minstrels probably found it worth their while not to spend too much time in Court. When the Court was travelling a minstrel, like other royal servants, often lived in lodgings near to the Court. On 13 January 17 Ed II (1324) Henry de Neusom (harper) and Richardyn (fiddler) were reimbursed for this.[119] Away from Court a royal minstrel could earn 3s 4d for a day's work without difficulty: two or three of them travelling together could earn 6s 8d or more. This was several days' wages, and if audiences and town officials were generous a minstrel could do without the robes-money which he normally forfeited if he were absent from Court at Christmas or Pentecost. The queen's minstrel William Sautreour was one of twelve of the queen's squires who received nothing for winter robes in 9 Ed II because they were out of Court at Christmas; and in fact William spent only 7 days of 4 Ed II in Court.[120]

On the other hand, during the fourteenth century, at least, minstrelsy was required at many feasts other than the major ones. The gifts at these times must often have tempted minstrels back to Court, as must other, more occasional, celebrations.[121] The result was probably a more or less constant coming and going of minstrels at Court. There were occasions, it seems, when the minstrels available were too few for the work to be done: in 34 Ed I the king recalled the trumpeters John de London and his son John, and in ?17 Ed III the minstrel Ranulphus Taillour was paid for his expenses in returning to his own district after coming to the king at

---

[117] E101.363.18 (31 Ed I), fol. 23r, and E101.373.15 (1 Ed II), fol. 20r (cal. SM II, 40 and 65, respectively).

[118] TNA E101.364.13 (31 Ed I), fol. 22v; BL Add 8835 (32 Ed I), fol. 119r; E101.368.27 (34 Ed I), fol. 19r: (cal. SM II, 35, 42 and 49). An intriguing absence was recorded on 18 August 5 Ed III (1331) in the accounts for Queen Philippa's household, when a gift of 60s 0d was made for the expenses of her string-player Merlin, to whom she had given leave to travel to France: 'Merlin, fiddler: to Merlin, fiddler, going to parts of France by leave of the queen, by gift of the lady queen to help with his expenses in going there, by his own hands at the same place [Rockingham] and on the same day [18 August], 60s 0d' (Rylands 235 (5 Ed III), fol. 19r (cal. SM II, 88)). No reason is given for Merlin's absence. If it was on royal business it was of a secret nature, but this seems unlikely: what business can the queen have had in France, and why were the expenses not paid by the king? This must remain a puzzle unless more information comes to light.

[119] TNA E101.380.4 (17–18 Ed II), fol. 22v (cal. SM II, 83).

[120] Ed II: TNA E101.374.5 (4 Ed II), fol. 33v, and E101.376.7 (9 Ed II), fol. 93r (cal. SM II, 68 and 76).

[121] See Chapter 4.

Oswestry ('Ostrye') and making his minstrelsy there. These payments were made in mid-August and mid-September, respectively, when there were probably few minstrels in Court. The summer weeks between Corpus Christi and Michaelmas would offer favourable conditions for itinerant minstrelsy, and the minstrels would make as much money as possible. While the recall of minstrels was sometimes necessary, however,[122] it does not seem to have occurred frequently.

The *vigiles*, as opposed to the minstrels, spent most of their time in Court, for their work required them to be present every night throughout the year. Adam Skirewith was in Court for all 365 days of the years 31 Ed I and 34 Ed I; Robert de Finchesle, likewise, was present throughout 34 Ed I; Robert Chaunceler was in Court for the whole of 4 Ed II; John de Staunton was absent for only 11 days of 5 Ed II (a leap year), when Chaunceler was absent for only 22 days.[123] This record is in stark contrast to that of the minstrels, and suggests that two *vigiles* were permanently required.

The waferers were also required at all times, since the king and his immediate family might end any dinner with wafers: but they were clearly busiest at the major feasts, when wafers were offered also to senior household officials and any guests present. As the Wafery was a small department (often staffed by only one senior waferer – squire or valet – and a groom), any celebration caused considerable extra work for the department. Master John Drake, whose responsibilities almost certainly extended beyond the Wafery, did not absent himself in 31 Ed I, and was in Court for 334 days in 34 Ed I.[124] In contrast to this, his successor Richard Pilke spent only 12 days in Court in 4 Ed II, although he was in residence for 91 days the following year.[125]

Under Henry VII, some minstrels seem to have been in residence far more than in previous reigns. The king's trumpets, sackbuts and string-minstrels received wages every month, as did Bonetemps:[126] the French minstrels, on the other hand, were paid quarterly. The reason for this is unclear: they may have been only temporary members of the household (i.e., *qui non sunt*, although the term was no longer in use), and they were absent at Christmas, 1499.[127]

---

[122] TNA E101.369.11 (34 Ed I), fol. 202v and E101.368.27 (34 Ed I), fol. 63r (cal. SM II, 48 and 50).

[123] See TNA E101.364.13 (31 Ed I), fol. 24v; E101.368.27 (34 Ed I), fols 20r and 21v; E101.374.5 (4 Ed II), fol. 33v; E101.373.26 (4–5 Ed II), fol. 27r; and BL Nero C viii (3–5 Ed II), fol. 132v. (Cal. SM II, 35, 49, 68, 70 and 72).

[124] TNA E101.364.13 (31 Ed I), fol. 24v, and E101.368.27 (34 Ed I), fol. 20r (cal. SM II, 35 and 49).

[125] TNA E101.374.5 (4 Ed II), fol. 34r, and E101.373.26 (4–5 Ed II), fol. 26v (cal. SM II, 69 and 70).

[126] See SM II, 133–41, *passim*.

[127] See TNA E101.414.16 (13–15 Hen VII), fols 7r and 17r (printed in Ashbee, *Court Records*, VII, 160–7; cal. SM II, 137–41). The accounts searched for the present work unfortunately do not include wages to either the still minstrels or the queen's minstrels (these categories are distinct from the string-minstrels and from each other: see the New Year's gifts in these accounts). We cannot, therefore, estimate the periods of residence of these minstrels.

Constitution and administration

Loud and still minstrelsy

Music was a largely functional art during the Middle Ages, and instruments were classified according to their function and social status. Trumpeters and harpers were regarded more highly than other minstrels, but the variety of instrumental music available made a rigid classification difficult. Of prime importance was the broad division into *haut* and *bas*, first found in fourteenth-century French sources. These terms refer to 'loud' and 'quiet' or 'soft' music, not to high- and low-pitched sounds. Examination of the instruments used on specific occasions shows that this division was normally adhered to, at least in France. Some occasions required loud minstrelsy, some quiet, while others (such as banquets) might need both: but there was never any doubt as to which was required, and which instruments were therefore suitable.

The terms *haut* and *bas* appear to have been used to distinguish different instrumental groupings only from the late fourteenth century, but Edmund A. Bowles showed that the distinction itself obtained as early as the thirteenth. The grouping of instruments in contemporary French literature shows a consistent division between noisy instruments (trumpets, nakers and shawms) and quiet ones (such as portative organs, flutes and all the stringed instruments, both plucked and bowed).[128] A few instruments could belong to either division: the bagpipe, because it took many forms, some louder than others, and the pipe-and-tabor, which could accompany either loud or quiet groups.

In England, as on the Continent, the distinction between loud and soft minstrelsy seems general in the late Middle Ages. The terms *haut* and *bas*, however, are not found in English sources, the equivalent English terms being 'loud' and 'still'. Both are found rather later than their French counterparts – 'still-minstrel' in Henry V's reign and 'loud minstrel' perhaps no earlier than the sixteenth century.

The distinction between *haut* and *bas* had its roots in purely practical considerations. There is the simple matter of balance when instruments are used together in performance: a harp cannot compete with a shawm, so there is no point in playing them simultaneously. Equally, an instrument, or a combination of instruments, must be appropriate for the venue and for the occasion. Playing trumpets outside a noble's apartment door as a *reveillé* on New Year's Day is one thing;[129] playing them in the queen's private sitting-room would be quite another. The distinction between *haut* and *bas* is nevertheless a coarse-grained one, and in the area of *bas* minstrelsy, at least, some further classification may have been at work. Questions surround the citole, for instance: why was it not used in the queen's private apartments? Why was it not played, apparently, in consort with other instruments?

---

[128] Edmund A. Bowles, '*Haut* and *Bas*: the grouping of musical instruments in the Middle Ages'. *Musica Disciplina* 8 (1954), 115–40; repr. McGee, *Instruments and their Music*, 3–28, especially at 119.

[129] See Chapter 5 concerning the Northumberland household.

These and other questions will arise again in Chapter 14, where discussion of the instruments themselves will lead to a consideration of how instruments were used in consort together.

The minstrel body: personnel

The king always had trumpets, nakers, pipes of various sorts (especially shawms, but at times including bagpipes), tabors and at least one harp: but at different times the king's minstrels also included players of the lute, citole, psaltery, gittern, crowd, fiddle (which came in various sizes) and organ, besides such entertainers as rymers, *gestours* and fools.[130]

The actual number of the king's minstrels fluctuated, as we saw in Chapter 1, and for some of the same reasons it is difficult to decide on the relative numbers of 'loud' and 'still' minstrels. Edward I was fond of indoor minstrelsy, judging by the number of harpers he employed, and his still instrumentalists were probably the more numerous. But neither then nor in the reign of Edward II – who appears to have employed loud and still musicians in roughly equal numbers – can we be precise.

The same problem exists in Edward III's reign: but so many of that king's minstrels are known to have played still instruments that the minstrels listed in the wartime ordinances of 18–21 Ed III (Table 1) cannot have been typical. Edward was in Flanders during July 1345, and in France from July 1346 until October 1347, and the minstrels are those of a military expeditionary force of the period. Of those listed, only a fiddler and a citoler would make still minstrelsy: any other still minstrels perhaps went to France as archers or men-at-arms.

With the use of the designation 'still minstrel' in Issue Warrants from Henry V's reign onwards,[131] it sometimes becomes possible to decide the exact numbers of loud and still instrumentalists in certain livery-lists. Those of the reign of Henry VI divide into equal numbers of loud and still minstrels. Those of Edward IV's reign apparently do the same to start with, but the ratio of loud to still instrumentalists may have been increased later. Edward seems to have employed eight or nine trumpeters by the end of his reign, so that of the thirteen minstrels mentioned in the *Liber Niger* as playing trumpets, shawms, small pipes and stringed instruments, very few can have made still minstrelsy. The question arises, certainly, how far the *Liber Niger* or any other household ordinances reflected the actual state of the king's household. While ordinances were a blueprint from which the organisation of the household might deviate for whatever reason, the differences were probably not very great.

The rather clearer picture of Henry VII's court shows that loud minstrels were in the majority. Henry had eighteen or nineteen minstrels, of whom only six or seven (the three string-minstrels and three or four still minstrels) played still instruments. Perhaps it is due only to a new clarity in the accounts, but Henry does

---

[130] For the variety of instruments played at Court, see the inventory of royal minstrels, MERH, *passim*.

[131] *List and Index of Warrants for Issues, 1399–1485*. Public Record Office Lists and Indexes, no. 9, vol. II (repr. New York NY, 1964).

seem to have reorganised the minstrels along functional lines. This is explored further in Chapter 14.

The marshals

What was the command structure for the royal household minstrels? The first clear indication of a leader amongst the royal minstrels is a grant of 1448, in which William Langton is described as 'Marshal of the king's minstrels'.[132] 'Marshal' was a term used in several departments of the king's household to denote an official with responsibility for ensuring the smooth running of a particular function by its personnel: we have met it already in the marshals of the hall. The Marshal of the Heralds of Brabant was apparently of lower status than the King of Heralds of Sprus, although presumably in charge of a group of heralds: on 1 September 12 Ed III (1338) these two were rewarded with 10s 0d and 26s 8d (2 marks) respectively for bringing news of their districts to the king.[133] It is perhaps not surprising that a senior English royal minstrel, nominally in charge of his colleagues, should eventually be given the title of marshal when the need arose. The known and possible marshals of the minstrels and trumpeters are listed in Table 5.[134]

The post of Marshal of the Minstrels is not known to have entitled its holder to any special privileges, but marshals certainly received higher wages than their colleagues. These wages suggest that John Cliff and another were the leaders of the future Henry V's band and of Henry VII's string-minstrels, respectively. This assumption may turn out to be untenable, but the Marshal's duties did demand considerable responsibility, at least by Edward IV's time. Precisely what this responsibility was is hinted at in a rather puzzling reference in the *Liber Niger*,[135] which mentions a

> veriger that directeth [the minstrels] all in festivall dayes to theyre stacions, to blowinges and pipinges, to suche offices as must be warned to prepare for the king and his housholde at metes and soupers, to be the more redy in all servyces, ...

This seems to mean that the 'veriger' (that is, verger, one who carries a rod or staff of office) ran the day-to-day work of the minstrels at the major feasts and special occasions, and was responsible for the efficient working of the minstrelsy directly connected to the king's movements. Perhaps this was principally an administrative responsibility, co-ordinating the minstrels' work in the household. It seems likely that 'veriger' was another name for the Marshal of the Minstrels, in which case he presumably had some musical responsibility as well. The matter must remain speculative unless more evidence comes to light.

The Wardrobe books of the mid-fourteenth century contain some hints that the office of Marshal of the Minstrels predated 1448. In a livery-roll of 37–8 Ed III (25 January 1363 to 24 January 1365) Hankin fitzLibkin is entered as 'Hankin

---

[132] CPR, Henry VI, vol. 5 (1446–52), 200.

[133] TNA E36.203, fol. 100v (cal. SM II, 100).

[134] Table 5 is based on records calendared in SM II, Appendix A, *passim*, and Ashbee, *Records*, VII, *passim*.

[135] Myers, *Household of Edward IV*, 131.

Table 5. Marshals of the minstrels and trumpeters.

Date	Minstrels	Trumpeters	Comments
37–8 Ed III	Hankin FitzLybkin		until 49 Ed III
Temp. Ric II	Henry, piper		in E101.403.25
1447		? John Paynell	serjeant: see below
1448	William Langton		dead by May 1449
1464–9	Walter Haliday		
1467		Richard Paten	
1477	John Cliff III		dead by 24 July 1482
?1482–94	Alexander Mason		
1483		John Crowland	M of the Minstrels
1486–1514		Peter de Casanova	
1495–1506	Henry Glasebury		
1506–?	Hugh Woodhouse		
1509–18	John Chamber		

Mareschall'.[136] Although Hankin is not at the head of this list, he had headed all the minstrel-lists for four years or so previously,[137] which may indicate that he had held the post of Marshal since 33 or 34 Ed III (25 January 1359 to 24 January 1361). He is entered on a robes-list for 49 Ed III as 'Hankin lodder': this word usually carries the meaning of a beggar or rogue, but here may be derived from 'lode', in the sense of a guide or leader. Hankin does not appear at the head of such lists again.[138] The title of 'Marshal' reappears in the following reign, a list of Richard II's minstrels being headed by 'Henri Marchal'.[139]

Hankin and Henry were both pipers, if I have identified the latter correctly: comparison of minstrel-lists between the last years of Edward III's reign and the early years of Henry IV's shows that Henry was almost certainly the man otherwise known as Henry Piper.[140] His name *Marshal* was not, then, a 'fixed' surname, as it must have been in the case of Robert Marshal (*c.* 1441–69), who cannot have been Marshal of the Minstrels after 1448. After Henry there is a gap of fifty years or more before the next known Marshal, William Langton (Marshal by 1448 until his death or retirement, apparently in 1449). Langton was probably a still minstrel, as was the next known holder of the post, Walter Haliday. At some stage during Haliday's

---

[136] E101.394.16 (37–8 Ed III), m. 8 (cal. SM II, 113). This is for robes at Christmas, 1364 or 1365.

[137] E101.393.11 (33–4 Ed III), fols 76v and 107v; and E101.393.15 (34–5 Ed II), m. 4: (cal. SM II, 110, 111 and 112).

[138] E101.397.20 (48 Ed III–1 Ric II), m. 25 (cal. SM II, 116).

[139] E101.403.25 (*temp.* Ric II) (cal. SM II, 117).

[140] MERH, 23.

tenure of the post (1464–9), the administration of the minstrels was divided, with Richard Paten holding the post of Marshal of the Trumpeters (from 1467) and Haliday that of Marshal of the Minstrels.[141] This division continued, with the Marshal of the Minstrels always being a still minstrel. This may mean that the loud minstrels were administered with the trumpets, or perhaps that the king chose his marshal from among those minstrels who were closest to him by reason of their private performances in the Chamber – usually 'still' minstrels. The *Liber Niger*, unfortunately, does not say whether the *veriger* who directed the minstrels was a loud or a still minstrel. But as the 'blowings and pipings' that the *veriger* oversaw were the province of trumpeters and pipers, a loud minstrel seems more likely.

The Marshal of the Trumpeters was probably more important than his colleague. In the list of minstrels at Richard III's coronation the trumpeter John Crowland is described as Marshal of the *Minstrels* although Saunder Marshall (i.e. the *gestour* Alexander Mason) was also present. Mason had been granted the reversion of the office of Marshal of the Still Minstrels in 1477, and he presumably took up that post on the death of John Cliff III in or before 1482. Evidently the Marshal of the Trumpeters could take charge of the still minstrels as well in matters which involved all the minstrels.[142] This probably reflects the higher status of the loud minstrel, and explains why the Marshal of the Minstrels was a loud minstrel in the days before the trumpeters had their own Marshal.

Serjeanties

In a Patent Roll of 1447 John Panell is described as 'the king's serjeant': he had then been in royal service longer than any other trumpeter except for Thomas Chatterton, and heads the list of the king's trumpeters, although he is not known to have held the position of Marshal.[143]

A serjeanty was a feudal tenure, held in return for some service to the king, and included some held by those who were not otherwise royal servants.[144] Within the royal household the serjeants-at-arms were part of the military presence guarding the king, but other household serjeants held offices in various departments and sub-departments: it is the latter that concern us here.[145]

---

[141] For Paten, see CPR, Edward IV–Henry VI (1467–77), 42 (10 November 1467). For other dates of tenure of the two Marshals' posts, see MERH, 30–40, *passim*. See CPR, Henry VI, vol. 5 (1446–52), 250 (Langton); CPR, Edward IV (1461–7), 293 (Haliday); CPR, Edward IV, Edward V and Richard III (1476–85), 22 and 310 (Cliff); Lafontaine, *King's Musick*, 1 (Crowland and Mason); Collier, *History*, I, 46 (Glasebury); Lafontaine, *King's Musick*, 3 (Chamber); *ibid.*, 4 (Chamber and Peter de Casa Nova). See also Richard Rastall, 'The minstrels and trumpeters of Edward IV: some further thoughts'. *Plainsong & Medieval Music* 13/2 (2004), 163–9.

[142] MERH, 34, taken from Lafontaine, *King's Musick*, 1.

[143] May 1447: CPR, Henry VI, vol. 5 (1446–52), 72 f.

[144] J.H. Round, *The King's Serjeants* (London, 1911): Round defines serjeanty on p. 1.

[145] For the serjeants of the royal households, see Given-Wilson, *Royal Household*, 11–12 and 58.

A household serjeant usually held the rank of clerk or squire. The *Liber Niger* does not define them, but it is clear that they had authority over other members of their office. While a serjeant was not necessarily head of an office or sub-department – the larger sub-departments might have two or even three serjeants – the head of a sub-department was usually a serjeant. Like John Panell, William Wykes and John Cliff were serjeants in 1447, so the title of serjeant was not the same as that of Marshal of the Minstrels. Wykes and Cliff were two of the minstrels later named as being in constant attendance on the king, which provides a possible reason for their serjeanty.[146] William Maisham, serjeant in 1452,[147] may have been another in constant attendance on the king.

If John Panell's serjeanty was for duties as Marshal of the Trumpets, we must ask why Richard Paten was promoted to that position during Panell's life-time. The answer would have been Panell's age: since he had been a minstrel of Henry V, he must have been around sixty years old in 1467. This was not too old to be a king's minstrel, and Panell held that position for another sixteen years: but it was perhaps considered wise to give the Marshal's duties to a younger man, while Panell retained the title of serjeant.

The style 'Master'

Another title held by some minstrels (and other household servants) was that of 'Master', found in the thirteenth and fourteenth centuries. The precise significance of this too is not explained: it does not indicate a university degree, but probably something closer to a master in a trade guild. Sometimes it distinguishes the head of a household department, like Edward I's waferer John Drake (who was capable of minstrelsy), or Edward III's waferer John.[148] Others were senior members of a group, such as Edward I's trumpeter John de London, Edward II's trumpeter John Garsie, or the harpers Elias de Garsynton and Robert de Clough. In some cases, such as that of Edward II's string-player Richard Dorre, there is no obvious reason.

The term was not peculiar to the king's household. The organist of Earl Warenne was referred to as 'Master John' in 31 Ed I, and in Richard II's reign the style was given to John, nakerer of the Earl of Derby (later Henry IV). The style had an even wider usage, since Adam le Boscu and Adam de Reve are referred to as 'Master' in the list of minstrels at the 1306 Pentecost celebrations.[149]

In the royal households the style 'Master' seems to imply some sort of authority which is not necessarily inherent in the departmental organisation. One possibility is that those men were responsible for training boys as if they were trade-guild apprentices. These do not often appear in the accounts, but when they do it is clear that there were considerable numbers of them – the five boy trumpeters of the 1306 Pentecost list are probably a case in point (see Chapter 3). In 31 Ed I the harper John

---

[146] CPR, Henry VI, vol. 5 (1446–52), 42 and 49.

[147] CPR, Henry VI, vol. 5 (1446–52), 512.

[148] MERH, 7–20, *passim*.

[149] TNA E101.369.6 (34 Ed I), French list at 20s 0d each (Master Adam le Boscu) and at 2 marks (Master Adam le Reve): cal. SM II, 53 and 54, respectively.

de Newenton was paid for the maintenance (*pro putur[a]*) of three groom *gigatores* and two groom harpers: and while Newenton was never given the style of 'Master' he may have been acting during the temporary absence of the harper Master Elias de Garsynton.[150] The trumpeter son of John de London was probably the trumpeter referred to as John Garceon in 31 Ed I: whether this was the senior trumpeter's son or not, John de London was clearly the most likely trumpeter to teach the boy. Also in 31 Ed I, Master John [Drake], the king's waferer, was paid for shoes for his grooms; and Master John the prince's organist had a groom with him when he made repairs to the organ at Langley.[151] On balance, the case for those addressed as 'Master' being in charge of the training of young royal servants seems plausible. The matter of training will be considered further in Chapter 3.

---

[150] BL Add MS 35292 (31 Ed I), fol. 14v (cal. SM II, 31).

[151] BL Add MS 35292 (31 Ed I), fol. 7v (12 August [1303]); and TNA E101.363.18 (31 Ed I), fol. 5v: cal. SM II, 30 and 38.

3
Recruitment, training and retirement

Recruitment

A minstrel might obtain a position in the king's household, or in any elite household, in various ways. Most of these involve transfer from one household to another, or from one department to another within a household, but there are examples of transfer from civic to domestic employment. There are hints, too, of independent minstrels gaining employment in royal service, although this is unprovable. These all involve established professional minstrels obtaining promotion. The question arises as to how a young minstrel could get a foot on the employment ladder, and therefore how boys were trained for service as minstrels.

Transfers between households

Perhaps the most obvious way by which a minstrel could gain permanent employment in the king's household was from a dependent household. It was not unusual for vacancies in the king's household to be filled by minstrels from the household of the queen or the Prince of Wales,[1] though we must remember that the minstrel was, technically, already an employee of the king. Even when a household was no longer strictly dependent, transfer from there to the king's household was probably an obvious possibility. Edward IV found a place for William Barley, formerly a minstrel of his brother the Duke of Clarence, who apparently joined Edward's minstrels on Clarence's death in 1478.[2] This was presumably a matter of expediency – even of charity – although one assumes that Barley was a highly competent minstrel. A case of transfer in the opposite direction, however, was clearly a matter of career promotion, when Edward III's trumpeter John Buckingham was promoted to be chief minstrel to John of Gaunt in 1379/80.[3]

John of Gaunt, Duke of Lancaster, and George Duke of Clarence were close relatives of the king (son of Edward III and brother of Edward IV, respectively), so that their minstrels were no doubt well known in the households to which they transferred. A minstrel in the household of a non-royal magnate could become known to the king through his performance when the magnate was a guest of the king, or sometimes the host. Possible examples rely on the similarity of names: this is never

---

[1] See MERH, *passim*.
[2] CPR, Edward IV, Edward V and Richard III (1476–85), 100; also MERH, 33 and n. 8.
[3] See pp. 105–6.

conclusive evidence, but in the relatively small world of the liveried minstrel it shows high probability. Robert Polydod, who was a king's minstrel by 1 or 2 Ed III, had previously visited Court as a minstrel of the Bishop of Ely, John Hotham; John Bisshop, another minstrel of that same prelate, may be the man of that name who became a royal servant at about the same time;[4] and the minstrel Lubkin, a piper of the earl of Northampton who was rewarded for minstrelsy at Court on 22 June 1342, was probably the piper Libekin who was a king's minstrel by 14 August the same year.[5] Edward III, like most monarchs, was not slow to obtain what he wanted.

A special case of multiple transfer occurred in Richard II's reign. In 1399, between the death of John of Gaunt and Bolingbroke's return from exile, many Lancastrian minstrels and other servants were given employment at Court, another case of royal care for those who would otherwise be unemployed. Some Lancastrian minstrels were thus already in the king's service when the new duke of Lancaster came to the throne as Henry IV.[6]

It was not unknown for minstrels to join an elite household from civic employment, since town waits sometimes performed before royalty and the nobility. As we shall see in Chapter 7, several London waits were employed by Henry VII, one of them on a permanent basis, and a civic minstrel of Canterbury transferred to the archbishop's household. In such cases the new employer will have been able to assess the quality of his new employee in advance.

Minstrels in the Chamber and other departments

Those described as 'the king's minstrels' were not a sub-department of the household, but only one of several loose groupings under the governance of the Keeper.[7] They therefore had a certain flexibility in their operations, which particularly concerned the Chamber, the king's private apartments, where the king could enjoy various entertainments in relatively intimate and informal conditions. According to the household ordinances of 1318 the minstrels in permanent attendance would eat in the hall or in the Chamber, as required, which reflects the king's option to have private minstrelsy in his own apartments.[8]

---

[4] BL MS Stowe 553 (15–17 Ed II), fol. 67r; TNA E101.379.19 (17 Ed II), fol. 4v; E101.383.8 (1–2 Ed III), fol. 10r; and E101.384.1 (2–3 Ed III), fols 11v and 35v (cal. SM II, 80, 81, 84 and 85, respectively). While these identifications are tenuous, the world of minstrelsy at this high level was a relatively small one.

[5] TNA E36.204 (16–18 Ed III), fol. 85r (two items, cal. SM II, 104).

[6] For Lancastrian minstrels at Richard II's court, see CPR, Richard II, vol. 6 (1396–9), 525, 538 and 558, for instance: also MERH, 23, n. l, and Brian Trowell's article on Henry V in *Die Musik in Geschichte und Gegenwarte* (Kassel, 1949–; 2nd edn 1994–), VI, col. 63–6. The future Henry V had also lived at Court for several years before his father's accession in 1399.

[7] Given-Wilson, *Royal Household*, 13.

[8] '... Et mangerount en chambre ou en la sale solonqe qils serrount comaundez': Tout, *Place of the Reign*, 303. Gifts for minstrelsy in the Chamber were usually to visiting minstrels, perhaps because performing before the king was normally routine for his own minstrels. See BL Add MS 17362 (13 Ed II), fol. 31r; Add 9951 (14 Ed II), fols 20r and 21r;

The Wardrobe books record some gifts to minstrels who performed in the Chamber, but these are invariably to visiting minstrels: any king's minstrels performing there apparently did so as part of their regular duties, without extra reward. Payments made to such people occasionally describe them as grooms, valets or squires 'of the Chamber and household' or 'of the Chamber and other offices', which suggests some flexibility in where servants worked. Relevant payments listed in Table 6 apparently show three different categories of recipient.[9] First, there are men whose names suggest minstrels but who cannot be identified as such. Men named Wayte and Harper probably were capable of minstrelsy, but these are surnames that did not necessarily indicate a musical profession: by the middle of the fifteenth century most surnames were fixed, and it was relatively rare for people to be known by what they did for a living. Thomas Trumpeter almost certainly was a trumpeter, for that name is rare except as an indication of a minstrel, but he is not recorded as a royal trumpeter in the reign of Edward III. These men may have been Chamber servants who, although capable of minstrelsy and valued as such, did not make the move into 'the king's minstrels'.

A royal servant of any department who could entertain his colleagues at work was perhaps encouraged to do so,[10] taking the appropriate surname. John le Taburer, servant of the Almonry in 32 and 34 Ed I, was certainly not primarily a minstrel.[11] Certain senior officers at Court had their own minstrels, and such a minstrel might work in the department headed by his master.[12]

Second, there were known members of the royal minstrels evidently working in the Chamber for a limited period. William Clifton may be the trumpeter of that name, who had already been in royal service for many years (although it might be his son or other relative). Nicholas Praga, Richard Wafrer and Peter Roos are listed among the 'scutiferi Camere Regis' c. 45 Ed III:[13] I have not found Richard Wafrer rewarded for minstrelsy, but Nicholas was a fiddler and Peter a trumpeter, both of several years' standing as royal minstrels and receiving liveries, etc., with other minstrels of the king's household. Another case is that of Bartram Brewer, described as 'minstrel of the Chamber' in the list of minstrels at Henry VII's funeral in 1509, although early in the following reign he appears – with other still minstrels – under

---

TNA E101.380.4 (17–18 Ed II), fol. 26r; BL Nero C viii (8 Ed III), fol. 268r; and TNA E36.204 (16–18 Ed III), fol. 85r (cal. SM II, 78, 79 (two items), 83, 92 and 104).

[9] These items cal. SM II, 97, 127 (two items), 128 (two items), 129 (two items) and 131. I added '?Thomas' among the king's trumpeters in MERH, p. 15, on the basis of this item, but there is no other evidence.

[10] Cf. the 'fool of the kitchen' in the Norfolk household: SM II, Appendix C, *passim*, and Anne Crawford, ed., *The Household Books of John Howard, Duke of Norfolk, 1462–1471, 1481–1483* (Stroud, 1992), *passim*.

[11] BL Add 8835 (32 Ed I), fol. 40v; TNA E101.369.11 (34 Ed I), fol. 93v: (cal. SM II, 40 (and n. 30) and 45).

[12] It is possible that Henry Glasebury was a groom of the Chamberlain rather than of the Chamber.

[13] E101.397.5 (45–7 Ed III), fol. 43r (cal. SM II, 114).

Table 6. Musicians in the Chamber.

- Thomas the trumpeter (recorded under Debts to Servants of the Chamber), in 11 or 12 Ed III (E101.388.9, fol. 62v).
- A groom of the Chamber called John Wayte, in 26 or 27 Hen VI (E101.410.1, fol. 28r).
- Grooms of the Chamber or other offices called Thomas Harper and John Wilde (the latter also listed as a minstrel of the household) in 26, 27 or 28 Hen VI (E101.410.3, fol. 29v).
- John Wayte, in a list of grooms of the household in 29 or 30 Hen VI (E101.410.6, fol. 38r).
- Thomas Harper, valet of the king's Chamber, in the same period (E101.410.6, fol. 41r) and in 30 or 31 Hen VI (E101.410.9, fol. 43v).
- William Marshall, John Goodyere, John Wayte and others, grooms of the Chamber and other offices, in 30 or 31 Hen VI (E101.410.9, fol. 40v). This item reads *garc' Cam'ar'* (for *Camerarii*, or 'Chamberlain') rather than *Camere* (for 'Chamber'), however: we cannot assume a scribal error.
- Thomas Wilde, Robert Grene, John Harper and others, squires of the king's Chamber and household, in 3 or 4 Ed IV (E101.411.13, fol. 36v). The surnames of Wilde and Grene may be relevant (though they are common names), and perhaps that of Harper.
- William Clifton, Henry Glasebury and others, grooms of the Chamberlain (or Chamber?) of the king and queen, 19 or 20 Ed IV (E101.412.11, fol. 35r).

the heading of 'the still shawms'.[14] These seem to be cases of temporary secondment to special duties in the Chamber, being either among the four minstrels always on duty or subject to a more flexible arrangement.

Third, the Chamber employed young minstrels apparently still in training: some later joined the royal minstrels, but some perhaps remained as Chamber servants. The accounts for 3–4 Ed IV name Thomas Wilde, Robert Green and John Harper in a list of squires of the king's Chamber and household.[15] Robert Green became a king's minstrel by Michaelmas 13 Ed IV (1473):[16] and while it cannot be shown that Wilde and Harper also became king's minstrels, both names are strongly connected with minstrelsy – Harper for obvious reasons, and Wilde as the name of a family of minstrels.[17] While it is difficult to define precisely the relationship between 'the minstrels' and those servants of the Chamber capable of minstrelsy, the evident connections probably made the musical Chamber servants possible recruits to the minstrel body proper. More definitely, Henry Glasebury, a groom of the Chamberlain (or Chamber) in 19–20 Ed IV (1479–81) is no doubt the man who became Marshal of the Minstrels in 1494.

The grooms of the household under Henry VI and Edward IV include a surprising number of family names suggesting the sons of royal minstrels – Marshall,

---

[14] Lafontaine, *King's Musick*, 3 f.
[15] TNA E101.411.13 (3–4 Ed IV), fol. 36v (cal. SM II, 129).
[16] CPR, Edward IV and Henry VI (1467–77), 482.
[17] MERH, 29 f.

Goodyere, Clifton, Wilde and Green, for instance.[18] The role of family groupings and the incidence of young minstrels in training are discussed below.[19]

Music-making in the king's household

We should bear in mind that minstrelsy was not confined to those employed to entertain royalty and their guests: self-entertainment was important. The *Liber Niger* provides for the squires of the household during afternoons and evenings to entertain themselves and any visitors in an appropriate manner:[20]

> Thes esquiers of houshold of old be acustumed, wynter and somer, in after nonys and in euenynges, to drawe to lordez chambrez within courte, there to kepe honest company aftyr theyre cunyng, in talkyng of cronycles of kinges and of other polycyez, or in pypyng, or harpyng, syngyng, other actez marciablez, to help ocupy the court and acompany straungers, tyll the tym require of departing.

Thus minstrelsy in its broadest sense was encouraged at Court among all who had the ability ('cunning'). The kind of material considered suitable should be compared to that listed in William of Wykeham's statutes for Winchester College in the 1390s. These state that after dinner on winter nights when the fire was lit in hall the scholars and fellows may remain in hall and entertain themselves with 'songs and other honest pastimes', such as the recitation of poems and the chronicles of kings.[21] Wykeham almost certainly derived such statutes from ideas and procedures that he knew from his time as a courtier and royal administrator, and they surely reflect a situation at Court during the later fourteenth century, if not earlier.

This self-entertainment was not left to chance. The *Liber Niger* made provision for the henchmen, six or more young men kept close to the monarch, to be taught some necessary skills, including riding and languages. The Master of the Henchmen was also required 'to teche them … to herping, to pype, sing, daunce, …'. Thus as each henchman left this particular post and became a squire of the household, the Master's teaching of music and dancing filtered down to the rest of the household.[22]

---

[18] TNA E101.410.9 (30–1 Hen VI), fol. 40v; E101.411.13 (3–4 Ed IV), fol. 36v; E101.412.11 (19–20 Ed IV), fol. 35r: cal. SM II, 128, 129 and 131. The cases of Green and Clifton are discussed above.

[19] TNA E101.412.11 (19–20 Ed IV), fol. 35r (cal. SM II, 131). Glasebury was Marshal at Easter, 1495: E403.2558, fol. 53v (printed in Ashbee, *Court Records*, VII, 10).

[20] Myers, *Household of Edward IV*, 129.

[21] See T.F. Kirby, *Annals of Winchester College* (London, 1892), 489. Similar statutes existed in various Oxford and Cambridge colleges; see Nan Cooke Carpenter, *Music in the Medieval and Renaissance Universities* (Norman OK, 1958; repr. New York NY, 1972), 81 and 91. Richard Rastall, *Two Fifteenth-Century Song Books* (Aberystwyth, 1990), x–xi, discusses Wykeham's statutes in relation to the contents of Cambridge University Library Add MS 5943.

[22] Myers, *Household of Edward IV*, 126–7.

Young minstrels in the household

Some professional minstrels came to Court relatively late in their careers, but others were undoubtedly royal minstrels at an early age. John Paynell, who was one of Henry V's trumpeters probably earlier than *anno* 9 (1421/2), played at the coronation of Richard III, and was therefore a king's minstrel for over sixty years if the records all refer to the same man: Walter Haliday held his post for over forty years, and several minstrels served at Court for thirty years or more.[23]

Some royal minstrels were recruited young enough to be given their training at Court. The list of gifts to minstrels at the Pentecost feast of 1306 (34 Ed I) includes an item:[24]

> v Trumpatoribus Principis, pueris, cuilibet ij s. x s. in toto

'Pueri' could perhaps be translated 'apprentices': certainly they were all young and in training. Constance Bullock-Davies was probably right to identify them with the Prince's five boy-minstrels, elsewhere named as John Scot and Roger, trumpeters, Franceskinus, nakerer, Richard, rymour, and Andrew.[25] Their description as trumpeters in the 1306 account was probably a matter of convenience to the accounting scribe concerned, who knew three of them as a trumpets-and-nakers group. All five became king's minstrels in the following reign.

Such apprentices perhaps ranked as grooms of the household. In 31 Ed I John de Newenton had the care of three groom *gigatores* and two groom harpers.[26] John Garceon, trumpeter, was presumably a groom (*garcio*) also. He can probably be identified with John, son of John de London, in which case he was no doubt promoted from the rank of groom in either 32 or 33 Ed I.[27] A more difficult case is that of Thomas Harper, groom of the king's Chamber in around 30 Hen VI (1451/2) and promoted to yeoman that year. If he did in fact play the harp (not necessarily implied by his surname), it is not clear that he became one of 'the minstrels': a possible identification is with Thomas Green, still minstrel, who became a king's minstrel at Michaelmas 1458.[28]

Certain minstrels had their own grooms as servants, but these were not necessarily minstrels themselves. John de Newenton's groom, Simon de Hills, is not known as a minstrel, and neither is Walter, groom of Hugo de Naunton.[29] The organist and trumpeters of Earl Warenne each had a groom in 31 and 32 Ed I, respectively.[30]

---

[23] MERH, *passim*.

[24] TNA E101.369.6 (34 Ed I: cal. SM II, 57).

[25] Constance Bullock-Davies, *Menestrellorum Multitudo* (Cardiff, 1978), 148–9, citing Harley 5001, fol. 32v. She is surely wrong, however, to identify them with the five choristers elsewhere rewarded, who would have been specialist chapel singers.

[26] BL Add MS 35292 (31–4 Ed I), fol. 14v (cal. SM II, 31).

[27] MERH, 7.

[28] TNA E101.410.3 (26–8 Hen VI), 29v (cal. SM II, 127 f); also MERH, 31, and CPR, Henry VI, vol. 6 (1452–61), 507.

[29] TNA E101.367.16 (33 Ed I), fol. 19r, and E101.374.5 (4 Ed II), fol. 87v (cal. SM II, 44 and 69, respectively).

[30] TNA E101.363.18 (31 Ed I), fol. 5v, and BL Add MS 8835 (32 Ed I), fol. 39r (calendared in SM II, 38 and 40). Doncaster and Crakestreng were reimbursed for (among other things)

The grooms undergoing training in minstrelsy do not seem usually to have been described as 'minstrel of the king' or 'of the prince'. The case of the prince's boy-trumpeters would be exceptional in this regard if they ranked as grooms, but their very presence on the occasion of the 1306 Pentecost celebrations seems exceptional anyway. The phrases 'young minstrel' and 'small minstrel' may refer, therefore, to minstrels who had been promoted from groom – perhaps to yeoman – but who were not yet full 'king's minstrels' with the rank of squire; or the term might refer to a more senior minstrel who was of small stature.

One such would be Little William, organist of the Countess of Hereford: he was rewarded with 5s 0d at the 1306 Pentecost celebrations, which compares very well with the 2s 0d each to the prince's boy-minstrels.[31] While 'Parvus' could be a fixed surname, the wording for Little William is unambiguous, 'Parvo Willelmo organiste Comitisse Herefordie'. He was clearly not a junior minstrel, but a man of small stature, perhaps a dwarf. As such, he would usually be a general entertainer, but there was nothing to prevent such a man being a royal minstrel, or even, as we shall see, a King of Minstrels (Chapter 10).

Of the prince's five 'boy' minstrels, four remained with him when he acceded to the throne in 1307: Little Andrew, John Scot, Roger the trumpeter and Francekinus the nakerer are named as 'young minstrels of the king's household' ('iuvenes menestralli de hospicio Regis') in 1 Ed II, while a reference to 'Little Alein' in the accounts of 17 Ed II may indicate the same status; William Cardinal appears in accounts of 6 Ed III as 'the small minstrel of the lord king of England' ('parvus menestrallus domini Regis Anglie').[32] The name of Walter Cardinal amongst the minstrels on a livery-roll of 4 Ed III must be a clerical error for William: and so the other minstrels on this list – Richard the gitterner, John Malhard and Roger de Braybrok – may also have been 'small' or 'young' minstrels in 4 Ed III.[33]

It is apparent from the list of royal minstrels that minstrelsy could be a family business. The recurrence of certain surnames points to this, although one cannot usually prove a relationship. In Edward I's reign, John de London and John his son were both royal trumpeters; in Edward III's reign, Libkin and his son Hankin FitzLibkin ('son of Libkin') were both royal pipers, while Andrew the organist had a son, John, who was also a minstrel. In the same reign the minstrels Robert and John Polydod were surely related.[34] It is also striking that various minstrels shared a surname with someone employed at Court in a non-minstrel capacity: the situation is too common to be mere coincidence. Of visiting minstrels, two at the wedding

---

the expenses of two horses and two grooms.

[31] TNA E101.369.6 (34 Ed I), list of gifts in Latin (cal. SM II, 57): and see Bullock-Davies, *Menestrellorum Multitudo*, 1.

[32] TNA E101.373.15 (1 Ed II), fol. 21r; E101.380.4 (17–18 Ed II), fol. 22v; and E101.386.7, fol. 7v, and Add 38006, fol. 8v (both of these 6 Ed III): cal. SM II, 65, 82 and 89.

[33] TNA E101.385.4 (livery roll of 4 Ed III) (cal. SM II, 86). Walter Cardinall was a messenger, possibly William's father. These four minstrels appear after lists of messengers and yeomen, so 'Walter' may be due to a simple mental error.

[34] TNA E101.368.6 (33 Ed I), fol. 21r; E36.204 (16–18 Ed III), fol. 129r; and E101.394.16 (37–8 Ed III), m. 8: cal. SM II, 43, 105 and 113, respectively.

of Princess Elizabeth in 1296 – perhaps in the Count of Holland's entourage – were John *vidulator* (fiddler) and Conute his son.[35]

Perhaps the child of any royal household servant could be trained as a minstrel if he showed ability. Those who were sons of minstrels were probably trained by their fathers and, in every certain case we know of, the son played the same instrument as his father. Other sons of royal servants may have been employed as grooms in an appropriate department such as the Chamber or the Wafery. The latter might be considered appropriate because it was desirable, if not strictly necessary, that a waferer be a capable entertainer. Employment in the Chamber might be a good training for a servant who would work close to the king's person, as the minstrels often did, and we have already noted servants of the Chamber with relevant family names. The question demands more investigation of Chamber servants.

Recruitment of independent minstrels?

Occasionally an independent minstrel who visited Court might be of sufficient quality to become a royal minstrel in regular pay. Henry de Neusom, if it was the man who was later a king's harper, is not stated to have been a liveried minstrel when he visited Court at the 1306 Pentecost feast and again in 13 Ed II.[36] A more difficult case of identity is that of the harper John de Shareshull, who took liveries for the king's household in 1338. Edward III's harpers, throughout his reign, were called John, causing insuperable problems of identifying them.[37] At some time in the 10th, 11th or 12th year of Edward III's reign the duke of Cornwall (Edward of Woodstock, later known as the Black Prince) gave livery to a minstrel of Shareshill who was with him in his illness. The record reads:[38]

> Also, a tunic and tan cloth furred appropriately, given to a minstrel of Shareshill being with my lord the duke in his illness.

This item cannot have been recorded earlier than 3 March 1337 (11 Ed III), when the prince was made duke of Cornwall, nor later than 24 January 1339, the last day of 12 Ed III. The minstrel was apparently not a royal minstrel, and presumably described himself as coming from Shareshill, in Staffordshire.

The harper John de Schareshull is in a list of liveries for the king's household dated 11 July 1338: although he may not be the same man, the coincidence of name and date is striking.[39] There is no evidence that he was paid wages as a regular member of the king's household, but the accounts for the relevant period are incomplete. On the other hand, Edward III left England only five days later for a protracted stay in Antwerp, and John

---

35 Cal. SM II, 16. For toponyms, indicating a place of origin, see below.

36 TNA E101.369.6 (34 Ed I), penultimate entry in the French list of those paid 1 mark; and BL Add MS 17362 (13 Ed II), fol. 32r (cal. SM II, 55 and 78, and n. 45).

37 See MERH, 16, and the calendars for the relevant dates in SM II, Appendix A.

38 'Item j cote et cloth de drape de Tanne furr' de mannier. Done a j menestral de Schareshall esteant ovesq' monsieur le Duk' en sa maladie'. TNA E101.387.25 (roll): accounts for 10, 11 and 12 Ed III (cal. SM II, 96).

39 TNA E101.388.5 (12 Ed III), m. 11 (cal. SM II, 97).

de Schareshull does not appear in the king's household records during that time. The giving of liveries to minstrels on 11 July that year was presumably part of the administrative tidying-up that happened before the king went abroad, therefore, and need only imply that Schareshull was rewarded for services previously rendered. The eleven-year-old Prince Edward was regent during his father's absence, and could have honoured any outstanding commitments: but John de Schareshull does not appear again in the records. He cannot be identified with the royal harper called John who appears just in front of him in the livery-list of 11 July 1338. Even though he had been admitted to the king's livery, John de Schareshull was apparently being paid off that day.

It would be interesting to know if the prince was ill in south Staffordshire at some time between 3 March 1337 and 11 July 1338: but the only sense to be made of these two records, it seems, is that the prince employed a local harper while he was unwell somewhere in the area of Shareshill, rewarding him with a livery; that he later recommended the harper to his father, or brought him in his own household to Court; and that the harper remained in royal service until the king's departure for the Low Countries. The prince certainly had some connection with south Staffordshire, for several other servants named 'of Shareshill' appear in his household records.

John de Schareshull was probably not unusual in being recruited on his own territory during a magnate's travels. Among Edward I's minstrels,[40] the harpers Nicholas de Eland and Adam de Cliderhou were recruited closely together and associated closely in their work. Here one suspects that they joined the household during one of the king's journeys in the north, Elland (in Yorkshire) and Clitheroe (Lancashire) being about 30 miles apart. The trumpeters John de Depe (i.e. Dieppe) and Master John de London, who were *socii*, were apparently recruited in the same year, 22 Ed I, and probably as a pair. Similarly, the harper Walter de Sturton and the still minstrel Michael de Sturton, both probably recruited in 18 Ed I, perhaps came from one of several Sturtons in Lincolnshire and Nottinghamshire and were recruited in that area.

The toponym 'de Sturton' obviously suggests that Walter and Michael came from the same village. None of the Sturtons is, or was, a large enough place to support many minstrels or minstrel-families. Walter and Michael were probably related – perhaps brothers, or father and son – as it is likely that any two minstrels coming from the same small place would be. Other minstrels for whom this supposition may be true are three of Edward I's *vigiles*, John, Alexander and Geoffrey de Windsor, probably part of a family group, local to a major royal residence and by no means the only royal servants called Windsor. Judging by the dates of employment, John and Alexander de Windsor seem to be of the same generation, probably brothers, while Geoffrey was younger.[41] In general, we can perhaps say that a shared toponym may indicate family relationship if two minstrels were taken on together *or* one took over from the other at a generation's distance *and* they played the same instrument.

A toponym may indicate local recruitment, then, but other factors should be present. The trumpeters Nicholas de Doncaster and John Crakestring, borrowed by

---

[40] MERH, 7.
[41] See MERH, 8–9. The periods of employment are 23–32 Ed I (John), 25–33 Ed I (Alexander) and 31–5 Ed I (Geoffrey).

Edward I from Earl Warenne in the 32nd year of the reign, offer a case in point. Earl Warenne's main residence in the north was at Sandal, near Wakefield, only 20 miles or so from Doncaster: so it is reasonable to suppose that Nicholas was recruited locally to the earl's service.

A toponym may be useful as an indication of provenance, at least until the late fourteenth century. A pair of minstrels recruited in 31 Ed I provide the first of two illustrations. The trumpeters Richard de Blida and Robert de York appear for the first time together in a Wardrobe book entry dated 9 July 1303 (31 Ed I), and seem to have been *socii* until Robert disappears from the records in June 1304.[42] Richard continues in the records (somewhat irregularly) until about Christmas 1315, although he seems still to have been in Court in 1318. The particular interest of these is that they may have been independent minstrels who travelled to meet the Court in order to present themselves for royal employment.[43]

Robert presumably came from York; Richard certainly came from Blyth, Nottinghamshire, for a gift dated 17 September 1 Ed II (1307) shows him returning there to build a home.[44] The king was then at his manor of Clipstone, near Mansfield, so Richard's home was the Nottinghamshire Blyth, some 20 miles away. The king had been at Doncaster on 14 August, on his way back from Scotland, probably passing through Blyth (as his baggage-train certainly did) on the way to Clipstone.[45] Richard had no doubt made his plans while he was at Blyth on that occasion.

The entry of 9 July 1303 does not mean that Richard and Robert joined the king's service on that day, for Edward I paid wages in arrears and usually in part-payments. The two men were paid 1 mark (13s 4d) each, which would represent 40 days at 4d, a yeoman's wage of 4½d for about 35 days, or a squire's wage of 7½d for about 21 days. The king had been in Scotland since 16 May, however,[46] so unless the two trumpeters had joined the king in Scotland they must have been recruited earlier than mid-May. The next payment to them, on 8 August 1303, is of 10s od each on their wages. This is 30 days later, so that the payment could represent a full accounting for the period since 9 July at 4d per day or a part-payment at a higher rate.[47] That being so, the 40 days of service before 9 July are a likely minimum period of service, and it would be wise to look for a recruitment-date at least a month earlier still, in early May or late April.

The month of April 1303 offers possible circumstances for the two trumpeters to be recruited on or near their own territory (Map 1). The king was at Lenton priory

---

[42] BL Add MS 35292 (31 Ed I), fol. 7v (cal. SM II, 29).

[43] Had they been in liveried employment they would probably have described themselves to the accounting clerk as 'trumpeter of Lord X' – unless they were playing truant in order to change posts without their current employer(s) finding out. Otherwise, the toponym suggests a preference for their place of origin as the distinguishing information.

[44] TNA E101.373.15 (1 Ed II), fol. 20r (cal. SM II, 65).

[45] Elizabeth M. Hallam, *Itinerary of Edward II and His Household, 1307–28* (London, 1984), 23.

[46] Henry Gough, *Itinerary of King Edward the First* (Paisley, 1900, and London, 1976), II, 225–7.

[47] One might expect a trumpeter in royal employment to receive a squire's wage of 7½d, but these men were presumably on probation (and in any case being maintained at royal expense).

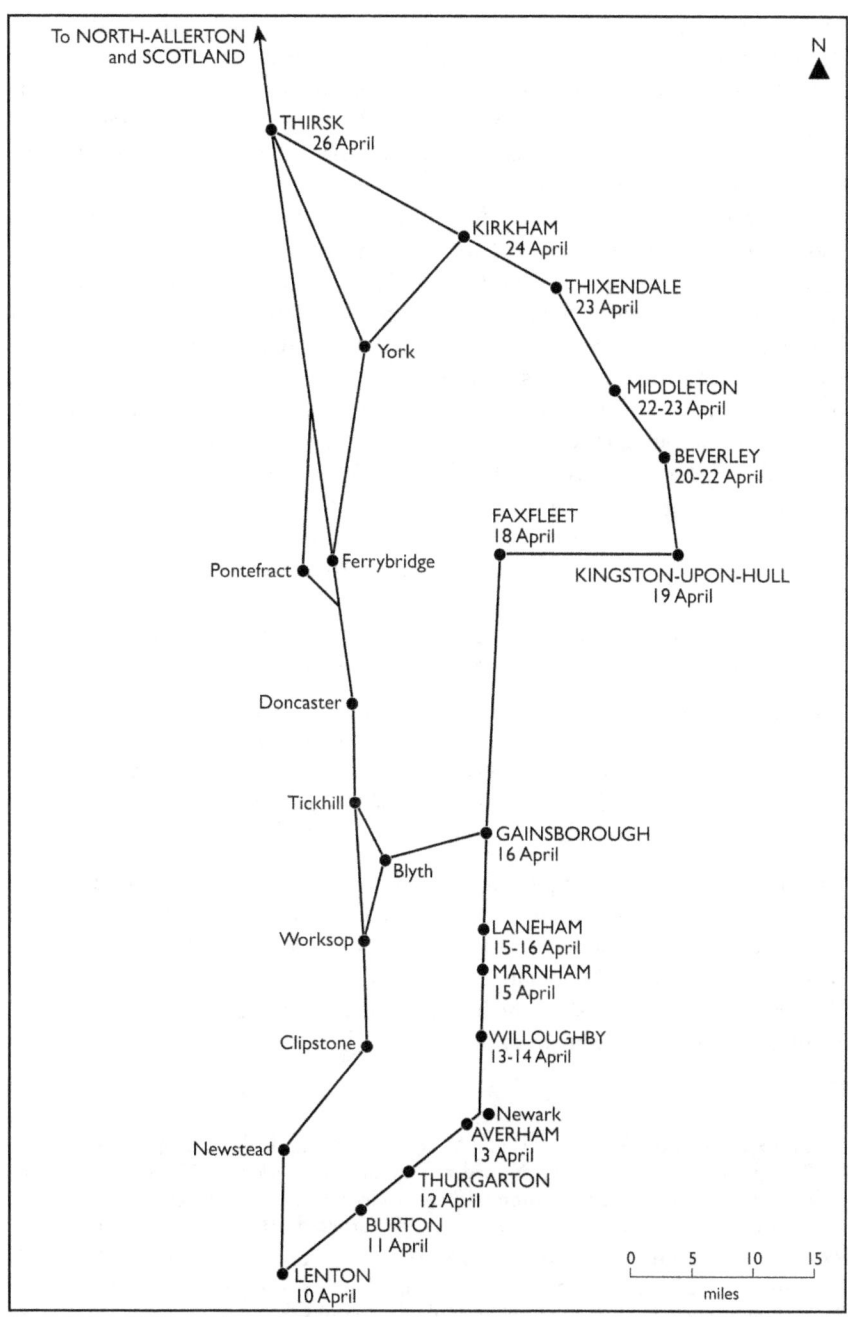

MAP 1. The king's travels, April 1303 (after Gough, *Itinerary*)

for Easter (7 April), leaving there probably on the 11th and following the Trent downstream, probably travelling by water. The king was at Gainsborough on the 16th, at Faxfleet, on the north bank of the Humber, on the 18th, and at Kingston-on-Hull the following day. He was at Beverley on the 20th until the 22nd, and then cut across country to Middleton, Thixendale and Kirkham. He was at Thirsk on the 26th, where he turned north, and so to Scotland.

The period between the king's departure from Lenton and his arrival at Thirsk was just over two weeks. The first week was spent in travelling down the Trent; then, after a day travelling to Kingston-on-Hull, the second week was spent in cutting across above York to the main road north. If the two trumpeters came to the king from Blyth and York the most convenient places to join him would have been Gainsborough and Kirkham, respectively. These are journeys of around fifteen miles or so, allowing several days to monitor the king's progress beforehand. In this case Richard de Blida joined the king on about 16 April, and Robert de York a week later. For both minstrels, however, the king's itinerary offered alternative joining-places with quite manageable distances to travel, and the payments suggest that the two men aimed for joint employment and probably met the king together.

Richard de Blida seems to have enjoyed a flexible relationship with the king's household. He perhaps took wages and liveries as one of those *qui non sunt*, for an entry recording an agreement made on 3 April 11 Ed II (1318) states that Richard was first taken onto the king's wages on 2 November 9 Ed II (1315):[48]

> Richard the trumpeter: Richard the trumpeter of Blyth, first received into the wages of the lord the king on 2 November of the present, ninth, year, of the gift of the same lord the king made to him [Richard] at Tickhill in the same month, for the sustenance of the horse bought for him, by account made at Stratford, 3 April *anno* 11 [1318] 40s 0d

Richard had in fact been employed at Court in the previous reign, and was returning to royal service after a long absence. He came to the king at Tickhill, a frequent stopping-place for the king on the road north, about 5 miles from Blyth. He had been commissioned to obtain cranes and other birds in parts of Yorkshire and Lincolnshire: Blyth is close to the borders of those counties, and the commission seems to require a man who knew the area.[49]

---

[48] E101.376.7 (9 Ed II), fol. 43v (cal. SM II, 75–6): 'Ricardus le Trumpour: Ricardo le Trumpour de Blida recento primo ad vad' domini Regis secundo die Novembris anno presenti nono de dono ipsius domini Regis facto eidem apud Tykhill eodem mense ad vitio' equ' sibi emendum per comp' factum apud Stretteford tercio die Aprilis anno xj xl s'.

[49] E101.376.7 (9 Ed II), fol. 83r (cal. SM II, 76): 'Ricardus le Trumpour: Ricardo le Trumpour de Blida misso per Regem extra Curia ad diversas partes Comitiis Eboraci et Lincolnie ad capiendum Grues et alia volatilia ad opus dicti domini Regis pro expensis oris' [?] sui per xxxvij dies per quos fuit extra Curia circa negacia predicta vicissini inter secundum diem Novembris quo die retentus fuit cum Rege tanquam anceps et ultimum diem Januarie percipiendo per diem iiij d ob. hic quia in rotulo marescalli per idem tempus per compotum factum apud Stratford tercio die Aprilis anno undecimo xiij s x d ob'. '*Tanquam anceps*' is presumably a joke shared between Richard and the accounting scribe.

> Richard the trumpeter: To Richard the trumpeter of Blyth, sent by the king out of Court to various parts of the counties of York and Lincoln to capture cranes and other birds for maintenance of the said lord the king, for the expenses of his work in the 37 days during which he was out of Court about the aforesaid purchases in the neighbourhood, between 2 November (on which day he was retained with the king as if he were a hawk) and the last day of January, taking 4½d per day here because [he was] on the marshal's roll for that time, by account made at Stratford, 3 April *anno* 11 [1318] 13s 10½d

It is possible that Richard de Blida had been introduced to Edward I's court by the then Prince of Wales. On 28 March 1303, some three months before Richard's first appearance in the records of the king's household, the prince had rewarded a trumpeter called Richard de Tykhill, who had made minstrelsy before him for three days at Clipstone.[50] It is tempting to identify Richard de Tykhill with Richard de Blida, taken into the king's service on the prince's recommendation and eventually serving his first royal employer again when he came to the throne as Edward II. One should certainly be even more careful about non-identical names than identical ones, but there are possible reasons for Richard's appearance under those two names. A Wardrobe scribe might well identify him as 'of Tickhill' because that was where he joined the Court.[51]

A factor in the process of recruiting minstrels must always have been the visits of one noble to another. When two nobles conferred, and their various minstrels performed, discussion of the minstrels must sometimes have followed.[52] The number of foreign minstrels visiting the king's household as members *qui non sunt* is an indication of this, and we have also seen probable examples of permanent transfer from a noble's or prelate's household to the king's. Three pipers employed by the Black Prince were possibly those of John of Aragon (see Chapter 5). The minstrels themselves must sometimes have had a hand in these processes, through their contacts made at the minstrel-schools.

These various recruiting methods seem to have produced an adequate supply of minstrels at Court until Henry VI's reign. Then, on 10 March 1456, the king commissioned four of his minstrels to find suitable boys, instructed in the art of minstrelsy, to take the place of certain of his minstrels who had died.[53]

> Commission during pleasure to Walter Halyday Robert Marshall William Wykes and John Cliffe appointing them to take boys elegant in their natural members and instructed in the art of minstrelsy and to put them in the king's service at the king's wages to supply the place of certain of the king's minstrels deceased.

---

[50] E101.363.18 (31 Ed I), fol. 21v (cal. SM II, 39).

[51] Blyth is about 5 miles south-south-east of Tickhill; Clipstone is about 20 miles due south of Tickhill.

[52] See Maricarmen Gómez, 'Minstrel schools in the late Middle Ages'. *Early Music* 18/2 (May 1989), 213–16, at p. 214.

[53] CPR, Henry VI, vol. 6 (1452–61), 278. William Wykes may have been related to three London waits named Wikes in 1442/3: see Rastall, 'Civic Minstrels', 205–6.

This was a special measure arising from unusual circumstances. The trumpeter John Payte and the still minstrel William Langton had died some years earlier, and William Maisham and Thomas Radcliff were probably dead or retired as well. Other minstrels disappear from the records at about this time, too: the trumpeters Bradstrete, Chaterton, Gildesburgh and William Paynell, and the still minstrels Thomas Haliday and John Wilde. Of those remaining by March 1456, the four named in the commission were probably the only still minstrels (a term not by then in use), the other minstrels being the trumpeters John Paynell and William Goodyere and the wait, Robert More. While the loss of records may partly account for the apparently serious decline of the minstrel-establishment, there is no doubt that numbers had not been maintained for several years past.[54]

The commission implies that 'talent-spotting' was not normally one of the duties of the royal minstrels as they travelled around the country. Just possibly this had been one task of the minstrel-kings: if so, the need for this commission is explained by the fact that by 1456 the office of *Rex ministrallorum* was ineffectual, if not extinct.[55] The four minstrels sent out to find suitable recruits had between them more than enough expertise to do so, but while those four were away fulfilling the commission, the minstrels we know to be available to the Court were the absolute minimum required to cater for the king's needs: the wait Robert More, whose services could not be dispensed with; the trumpeters John Paynell and William Goodyere; and the queen's harper, John Turges, the only still minstrel remaining if the situation was really as bad as it seems.

The running-down of the minstrel-establishment was only one symptom of a more wide-ranging malaise at Court, hinted at in the preamble to the household ordinances of 1454.[56] Henry VI was at this time mentally unwell, and the enmity between Queen Margaret and the Duke of York had already precipitated the first battle of the civil war, at St Albans, in the previous year. It is difficult to know how successful Halyday, Marshall, Wykes and Cliffe were in the task of bringing the minstrel-establishment up to strength. The surviving records do not indicate substantial recruitment in the last few turbulent years of Henry VI's reign, nor in the early years of Edward IV's. Probably a stable regime in the royal administration took some time to achieve even when the situation was less volatile.

---

[54] Chatterton had apparently stopped acting as 'fixer' for the city of London in 1452/3: see pp. 141–2. The household ordinances of 1454 name Thomas Ratclyff, William Wykes, John Clyff and Robert More, wait, as the 'Mynstrall to entende upon the kyng', but do not name the '9 Mynstralles comyng at the principall festes in the yere' (*Ords & Regs*, 18: the document is printed from BL Cotton MS Cleopatra F v, fols 170–4). The implication is that nine was the desirable number but there were not then nine of them.

[55] See pp. 216–17.

[56] On 12 July 1440 the king issued a commission to the Dean of the Chapel Royal to take suitable choristers from other choirs in the kingdom: CPR, Henry VI, vol. 3, 452. St Paul's cathedral was exempted on 9 July 1453: CPR, Henry VI, vol. 3, 90. For the circumstances of the 1454 ordinances, see *Ords & Regs*, 15.

Training

Personal instruction

The training of the royal minstrels, and by implication of other liveried minstrels, must have encompassed several necessary competencies. Any royal servant needed some training in how to behave in the presence of royalty, members of the nobility, and their seniors in the household. There would be protocols, of which we now know little, regulating all the minstrel's interactions with others, from the king downwards. In small household departments it might be the senior member who was responsible for this. The king's waferer, for instance, if he were a squire, like Edward I's waferer Master John Drake, would presumably be mentor to his groom assistant; but if he were of lower rank or less experienced as a royal servant, perhaps that task would fall to a senior member of the larger unit to which the department belonged, in this case the Pantry and Buttery. This part of a servant's training might be a matter of mentoring rather than education as such, and a servant who had come from another post, or whose father was already a royal servant, must already have known much of what was required of him.

Secondly, there were the necessary techniques of the particular work concerned. Any royal minstrel, however young, was already a competent instrumental (and probably vocal) performer, having received training from his father, another family member or a local professional. We are fortunate in having the records of two agreements for the training of a young minstrel by a professional. The first is a draft indenture concerning Thomas Lorymer, a harper from Bury St Edmunds who took an apprentice named William Stevenson in around 1461. The boy was the son of Thomas Stevenson of Braburne in Northumberland, beginning a seven-year apprenticeship. In his final year William was to receive from Lorymer a pair of shoes, a harp, a loud pipe (presumably a shawm) and a still pipe (a recorder? *dulcina*?); and at the end of the term, 20d. The indenture does not mention any specific music, but these three instruments imply that Lorymer both knew and could teach a variety of instruments and the kind of music and improvisation appropriate to each. Singing is not specified.[57]

The second agreement is found in the records of John Howard, Lord Howard and later Duke of Norfolk: it is an indenture, dated 18 October 1482, for the teaching of a boy, himself the son of a harper, to harp and sing:[58]

> William Wastell harper, for a chylde: Item, the same day my Lord [Howard] made couenaunte with William Wastell of London, harper, that he shall have the sone of John Colet of Colchester, harper, for a yere, to teche hym

---

[57] Cambridge, University Library Add MS 7318, fol. 28v. See A.E.B. Owen, 'A scrivener's notebook from Bury St Edmunds'. *Archives* (The Journal of the British Records Association) 14, no. 61 (Spring 1979), 16–22, cited in Nigel Wilkins, 'Music and poetry at court: England and France in the late Middle Ages'. V.J. Scattergood and J.W. Sherborne, eds, *English Court Culture in the Later Middle Ages* (London, 1983), 183–204, at 190.

[58] J. Payne Collier, ed., *Household Books of John, Duke of Norfolk, and Thomas, Earl of Surrey.* Roxburghe Club (London, 1844), 300.

to harpe and to synge, for the whiche techynge my Lord shall geve hym
xiij s iiij d and a gown; whereof my Lord toke hym in erneste vj s viij d.
And at the ende of the yere he shall have the remnaunt and is gown;
and he is bound be endentur to my Lord to performe this couenauntes
before wretyn.

One might expect John Colet's son to be trained by Colet himself, and probably he had been: but Howard may have decided that a year's training in London was needed in addition. Wastell must have given the boy technical help in both harping and singing, and the program of work no doubt followed an older tradition of professional training in a specific repertory. There is no evidence that Wastell, Colet or the boy was ever Lord Howard's minstrel, but the arrangement implies that Colet was Howard's servant.

A third example of professional teaching concerns a middle-class amateur, the merchant George Cely, who took tuition from the harper Thomas Rede at Calais in 1473–5. Cely himself noted that he received instruction – which would include technical instruction – in playing the harp and lute. Most of what he learned, however, was to do with repertory: he states that Rede gave him instruction in playing forty dances, which would be very important to him socially, and seven songs. Among the latter were 'O rosa bella' and 'Go hert, hurt with adversitie'.[59] We shall discuss these songs further in Chapter 15.

The differences in these three cases are probably due to differences in need. William Stevenson was at an early stage of his training, so that a full seven-year apprenticeship was required: and for so long a period it was worth transplanting him from his northern home to Suffolk, where he would live as a member of Lorymer's household. His training was to be in at least three of the main branches of instrumental performance – harping, loud wind music and still wind music – and the first of these may well have included song or recitation to the harp.[60] One might expect him to be instructed also in performance on the fiddle: but he would be entirely employable as a harper and wind-player. Young Colet, on the other hand, was to be in training for only a year, so this was probably a finishing-off period when he would consolidate extensive previous training. As a harper and singer he, too, would be employable at the end of the year. Cely's need was that of a gentleman amateur, who would be able to entertain himself and perhaps his friends with still music and, if required, to play for dancing. This would be an entirely social accomplishment, not a professional one.[61]

---

[59] Alison Hanham, 'The musical studies of a fifteenth-century wool merchant'. *Review of English Studies*, n.s. 8 (1957), 270–4. For a similar agreement between master and pupil, made at Avignon in 1449, see Daniel Heartz, 'A 15th-Century Ballo: *Rôti Bouilli Joyeux*'. Jan LaRue, ed., *Aspects of Medieval and Renaissance Music: A Birthday Offering to Gustav Reese* (New York NY, 1966; repr. 1978), 359–75, at 359.

[60] Instruction on the trumpet was apparently not offered, being a specialism in general mutually exclusive with other forms of instrumental minstrelsy.

[61] This book is very little concerned with amateur music-making, but see above, pp. 29–30, for examples. George Cely is our first recognisably serious amateur musician of the rising merchant class, learning to play and sing for reasons of social position and advancement.

A quite different case is that of a royal *rhymer* being taught to play the crowd, presumably in order to accompany his own recitation or singing. Edward II, as Prince of Wales, apparently had no crowder in his household when he wrote to the Abbot of Shrewsbury on 12 September 1305. His *rymour* Richard, who was probably the king's fiddler of that name, 23–9 Ed I (1294–1301), wished to learn to play the crowd, or perhaps Edward required him to. Edward knew that the abbot employed a fine crowder, and therefore made two specific requests of him: to ask his crowder to teach Richard his skill, and to maintain Richard in the abbey for the period of this instruction.[62] It is not known whether the abbot's crowder plucked his instrument or bowed it, but the latter is probable. A fiddler with skill as a *rhymer* might well wish to take up another bowed instrument associated with the *rhymer*'s work, but would hardly want to transfer to a plucked instrument: also, the seal of Roger Wade shows that a bowed crowd was normal in aristocratic circles before *c*. 1316 (see Table 16). The end-result, in any case, would be that Richard extended his performance-options.

In none of these cases is there any hint that written music was part of the training. As John Stevens pointed out, even Cely, whom one might expect to be literate, seems to have learned everything by ear: there is no record that he ever bought a songbook or paid a music copyist.[63] The repertory was apparently transmitted aurally from teacher to pupil.

The minstrel-schools

The repertory learned by Cely was extensive, but we can be sure that learning a large repertory was even more important for a professional minstrel, who would need to keep up with both current trends in repertory and the assimilation of new playing styles. For a royal minstrel this would happen anyway to some extent, through interaction with his household colleagues; and both young and experienced minstrels could always learn from visiting minstrels, especially the foreigners who would bring new repertory and playing styles from abroad. Another way of gaining useful knowledge and new repertory was through attendance at the minstrel schools: and there is no doubt that royal and noble masters from all over Europe sent their minstrels to the schools for this purpose.

The minstrel schools of late medieval Europe were held in Lent, when minstrelsy was not usually heard in noble households. Rob Wegman notes that they occurred around the fourth Sunday in Lent, *Letare* Sunday, which was a special time of mid-Lent rejoicing, and that this allowed maximum time for minstrels to travel, both before and after the school.[64] A list of the schools compiled by Wegman and Keith

---

Below the level of the liveried minstrel, however, the boundary between 'professional' and 'amateur' was generally far from firm, and further exploration is needed.

[62] E163.5.2, m. 14: see *REED Shropshire* (ed. J. Alan B. Somerset). 2 vols. (1994), I, 126, translated II, 562.

[63] John Stevens, *Music and Poetry in the Early Tudor Court* (London, 1961), 284.

[64] Rob C. Wegman, 'The minstrel school in the late Middle Ages'. *Historic Brass Society Journal* 14 (2002), 11–30, at 12. This article is the most comprehensive discussion of the minstrel schools.

Polk starts at 1313 (when a school was held at Ypres) and ends at 1447 (at Damme):[65] but, as we shall see, there were schools held in the late thirteenth century, and there is some evidence for them in the late fifteenth century. The schools were held in various locations in the Low Countries and northern France,[66] and some were held in un-named locations in Germany.[67]

There was also a southern operation, based on Bourg-en-Bresse and Geneva, between at least 1359 and 1417. It is at present impossible to know whether this was a separate organisation or part of the same series as the northern schools. Discussions of the minstrel schools have so far been centred on particular geographical areas, in relation to surviving documentation that happens to mention them: but they were a pan-European phenomenon, and they need to be investigated in relation to minstrel mobility across at least western Europe.

Many royal and noble masters regularly provided financial backing for their minstrels to travel to the schools. Those attending included some of the finest liveried minstrels, and the schools were clearly high-powered meetings at which very experienced performers could meet, exchange ideas, buy instruments, learn the newest songs, styles and techniques, and test the job-market. It was to their masters' advantage that they should attend, for many nobles evidently enjoyed, and so demanded, the latest pieces in the minstrel-repertory.[68]

English minstrels probably went overseas to the schools more often than the surviving records show. France and the Low Countries were easily accessible from southern England: Bruges is closer to London than York is as the crow flies, and Paris not much further. France is a short sea-journey from Dover, and there was regular traffic by land and sea along the trade routes between the Low Countries and eastern England. From a mid-Lent visit to a minstrel school in Bruges, Brussels or even further east or south, an English minstrel could still be back at Court in southern England by Easter.

---

[65] Wegman, 'Minstrel School', 18–24, gives a list of dates and locations. Damme is c. 4 miles NE of Bruges.

[66] These were Beauvais, Bruges, Brussels, Cambrai, Deventer, Ghent, Mechlin, Mons, Namur, Saint-Omer, Valenciennes and Ypres.

[67] In a Facebook posting dated 6 June 2015, Wegman added five more schools, citing *Mémoires de la Societe des Antiquaires de Picardie* (Amiens, 1845–) for 1 January 1854: at Namur (1364), Mons (1378), Soissons (1390 and again in 1402) and again Mons (1419–20).

[68] In addition to Wegman's article, there is a brief overview of the minstrel schools in Lawrence Gushee's article 'Minstrel' in *The New Grove Dictionary of Music and Musicians*, ed. Stanley Sadie. 2nd edn (London, 2001) (hereafter NG): and see also Maricarmen Gómez, 'Minstrel schools in the late Middle Ages'. *Early Music* 18/2 (1989), 213–16 (with special reference to Spain); Peters, *Musical Sounds*, 214–17 (France); Justin de Pas, 'Les Ménestrels et écoles de ménestrels a Saint-Omer (XVe et XVIe siècles)'. *La vie musicale dans les provinces françaises*, II (1937; repr. Geneva, 1972), 173–84; and Andrew Wathey, 'The peace of 1360–1369 and Anglo-French musical relations'. *Early Music History* 9 (1990), 129–74, especially at 133–6. I have been unable to consult the work of Justin de Pas.

The first examples I have found of minstrels going to the schools date probably from 17 Ed I (1288/9), but a search of earlier records could be fruitful. Perhaps in early 1289, gifts were made by John of Brabant, at that time betrothed to Princess Margaret (they married in 1290), to two minstrels to help them attend the schools in Paris: 2s 0d to a fiddler of the Lord Edward (the future Edward II, soon to become John's brother-in-law) and 5s 0d to a minstrel of Edmund, Earl of Lancaster (the king's brother).[69] These items are not dated, but judging from the dates of nearby items the first was probably paid at some time between Epiphany (6 January) and the first Saturday in Lent, which in 1289 fell on 26 February.

An item dated 14 February [8 Ed III] records gifts to Merlin, a fiddler, Barberus the bagpiper and Morlanus, another bagpiper, so that they could attend the minstrel schools:[70]

> To Merlin, fiddler, [and] Barber, bagpiper, given leave to go to the schools of minstrelsy overseas, by gift of the king himself to help with their expenses, 30s 0d each by the hands of Thomas Cary at the same place [Newcastle] and on the same day (14 February 1334), 60s 0d.
> To Morlanus the bagpiper, similarly given leave by the king to go to the schools of minstrelsy, by a gift of the king's ?council, 40s 0d.

14 February 1334 was the first Monday in Lent, six days after Shrove Tuesday. The minstrels probably had two weeks or so before the schools began.

Here, as in many cases, the record does not say where the schools were held. In 1377 the pipers Henry and Peterkin, and the nakerer Master John, were given 9s 0s to go to the schools overseas during Lent, but again the record does not say where.[71] There was an event at Bourg-en-Bresse that year, which would be a long journey from England.

Minstrel schools were held in England on at least three occasions (1358, 1365 and 1385). Edward Bond noted that in Lent 1358 the dowager Queen Isabella gave Walter Hert, one of her *vigiles*, 13s 4d to visit London (from Hertford castle) in order to learn minstrelsy; and that she made him another gift on his return from London 'de scola ministralcie' ('from the school of minstrelsy'). Bond would have

---

[69] TNA E101.352.6 (14–17 Ed I), m. 3, printed in Byerly and Byerly, *Records 1286–1289*, 409. Edward's *vidulator* is elsewhere named Thomas: see SM II, Appendix A, under dates 31 Ed I–5 Ed II, *passim*.

[70] BL Cotton MS Nero C viii (8–11 Ed III), fol. 269v (cal. SM II, 92): 'Merlino vidulatori Barbero Baggepiper licenc' adeund' scolas menistralc' in partibus transmar' de dono ipsius Regis in subsid' expensarum suarum utrique xxx s. per manus Thome Cary ibidem [Newcastle] eodem die [14 February 1334] lx s'. 'Morlano Baggepiper scil'ct' licenc' per Regem adeundi scolas ministr' de consili' dono Regis xl s'. This item is sometimes dated 1335, but it appears in the section of *Dona* for 8 Ed III, and therefore dates from 1334. (14 February 1335 fell two weeks before Shrove Tuesday and was therefore too early for such a payment to be made.)

[71] Nagel, *Geschichte*, I, 149, n. 20, quotes from BL Add MS 24511 (1 Ric II): the entry is on fol. 69r. This source is not the original, however, but an antiquary's transcription of items from a variety of sources.

had great difficulty in reading these items, which he did not publish *verbatim*, but Roger Bowers has transcribed them:[72]

> To Walter Hert, going to London in order to stay there and to teach minstrelsy in the time of Lent, of the Queen's gift, 13s 4d [22 February]
> To Walter Hert, returning to Court from London, from the school of minstrelsy, of the Queen's gift, 13s 4d [31 March]

22 February 1358 fell on the Thursday eight days after Ash Wednesday; and 31 March was Holy Saturday, the day before Easter Day. Walter was away for five weeks and two days, therefore, and back just in time for the major feast.

Dr Bowers notes that the term *erudiendi* shows that Walter attended the school not to learn minstrelsy, as Bond stated, but to teach.[73] This is our first indication that the minstrel schools may have offered more than simply an informal gathering for exchange of information, although it is impossible to know how formal or extensive Walter's teaching was, nor the extent to which it was centrally organised.

There is also a report that two court minstrels of Brabant were sent to the schools in England in 1365, which would be in the early part of 39 Ed III.[74] Andrew Wathey believes, too, that schools were held in England in February 1385 (the latter part of 8 Ric II) and October 1390 (in 14 Ric II).[75] The first of these was recorded on 23 February 1385 (the Friday nine days after Ash Wednesday) and allows two minstrels of the queen, Anne of Bohemia, 'to go to the school in various parts of our kingdom' ('daler a lescole en diverses parties de nostre roialme'). This may suggest that the event took place in more than one location, but it is more likely that the Chamber scribe did not know where it was to take place.

The second piece of evidence, dated 5 October 1390, records a gift by Louis, Duke of Touraine, for the expenses (including those of being suitably dressed and equipped) of his minstrels going to England 'a la feste'. This was not a minstrel school, however, for it is at the wrong time of year, *feste* is the wrong word, and suitable attire would hardly be relevant: but the occasion is not in doubt. In October 1390, as the most important of a series of events demonstrating his kingship, Richard II staged a magnificent tournament at Smithfield attended by several foreign rulers, including his brother-in-law Waleran of Luxembourg. Richard himself took part in

---

72 Bond, 'Notices of Isabella', 468; BL Cotton MS Galba E xiv (household of dowager Queen Isabella, 30 Sept 31 Ed III (1357) to 4 Dec 32 Ed III (1358), fol. 51v). The MS was badly damaged in the Cotton library fire of 1731. When I went to consult it in 2015, Galba E xiv was withdrawn for conservation: a microfilm showed nothing legible for relevant entries. I am grateful to Dr Bowers for sharing his transcription of the items concerning Walter Hert, to Professor Martha Carlin for showing me her transcription of the MS's heading, and to both of them for allowing me to use their work here. 'Waltero heret eunti london' causa morandi ibidem et erudiendi Minestralc' tempore quadragesimali de dono Regine xiij s iiij d' [22 February]. 'Waltero hert revertenti ad curiam de london' de scola menestralc' de dono Regine xiijs iiijd ' [31 March].

73 Private communications, July 2016.

74 TNA E101.395.4 and E101.396.2. See Sleiderink, 'Pykini's Parrot', 382.

75 Wathey, 'The peace of 1360–1369', 136, n. 11, quotes from TNA C.81.1355.35 (1385) and Paris BN MS fonds fr. 26954 (p.o. 470), dossier 'Bourgeois' (10443), no. 1.

the tournament, which was timed to finish on 12 October, the eve of the Translation of St Edward the Confessor, his patron saint. It was on this occasion that Richard's new badge of the white hart was first seen. Later events included a crown-wearing at High Mass, a feast at his palace of Kennington, and the investiture of William of Bavaria, Count of Ostrevant, as a Garter knight. A *feste* indeed: but while it provided much opportunity for minstrel activity, a minstrel school was not part of it.[76]

The information just set out allows some speculation about the dating of the minstrel-schools during Lent. Lent is six and a half weeks long. Where we have exact dates, the English minstrels did not leave Court until a week or so after Lent started, and one would expect to travel for a week or more in either direction if crossing the Channel or the North Sea. The minstrel-schools may have begun in the week before *Letare* Sunday, the 4th Sunday in Lent, and must have finished by two weeks before Easter Day at the latest. Since we do not know for how long the schools ran we can only guess at the timetable of a minstrel travelling from England to anywhere on the Continent; but it seems unlikely that the schools ran for more than 10 days or so.

The date-range for minstrel schools can now be extended back from the period 1318–1447 into the late thirteenth century. A minstrel school was held at Paris in or before 1289, with no indication that this was an innovation, and we may find minstrel schools in earlier years as more records are searched. Extending the period forward into the late fifteenth century is more problematic: the only evidence, which is from the household records of the King of Scots, relates to the wrong time of year. This may have resulted from moving the minstrel-schools from Lent to the autumn, but it may also mean that the schools as they were known in the fourteenth and early fifteenth centuries no longer existed. The evidence is not easily interpreted.

On 3 September 1473 the King of Scots made a gift of £5 to his luter John Brown 'at his passage oure sey to lere his craft'.[77] Seeking instruction abroad does suggest a minstrel school, but September is not the expected time of year, and it was a very late payment if it was for the previous Lent. The following year, on 4 September 1474, 'the Kingis littill lutare that he send to Bruges' was the subject of a payment of 24s od so that suitable clothes could be bought for him.[78] There are several possible reasons for the king to send his 'little luter' to Bruges, but instruction is perhaps the most obvious. The dates early in September 1473 and 1474 seem too close to be entirely coincidental, and suggest an annual event.

Returning to 1473, a clerk of the royal chapel named Heroune was given 40s od 'to his passage to the scolis' some time between 11 August and 4 December.[79] This could be for attendance at a minstrel school, for chapel singers did perform in secular entertainments: but the smaller payment than that given to John Brown suggests a less distant destination. Perhaps there were 'schools' held in Scotland

---

[76] Bennett, *Richard II and the Revolution of 1399*, 42. According to Wegman's Facebook posting, a minstrel school was held that year at Soissons, presumably in Lent as usual.

[77] Dickson and Paul, *Accounts of the Lord High Treasurer*, I, 43. Dickson glosses 'lere' as 'to learn': *ibid.*, I, 423.

[78] *Ibid.*, 60.

[79] *Ibid.*, 67.

for liturgical singers, possibly in conjunction with one of the regular song-schools situated in Perth, St Andrews and Aberdeen. Perhaps, too, Heroune was there to teach, not to learn.

Retirement

Gifts, annuities and corrodies

The fourteenth-century Wardrobe books record a few gifts made to minstrels when they left the service of a royal household. In 34 Ed I the dependent household of the king's younger sons Thomas de Brotherton and Edmund de Woodstock lost a *vigilis* and a waferer. Stephen de Northampton, the *vigilis*, was transferred from the boys' household at Windsor to the queen's household at Kingston in Dorset, on the orders of the queen: the young lords gave him 6s 8d as a parting gift in recognition of his service to them. If not an actual promotion, Stephen's transfer signified some royal recognition. The other loss was less happy: the boys' waferer, William de Salisbury, was given 3s 4d on 6 December 1305, when he left their service to return to his own district because of infirmity. Another servant who left Court for that reason was a falconer of the king, Patrick the trumpeter, who received 40s 0d on 21 February 25 Ed I (1297), when he left the king's service to go to his own district because he was too infirm to carry out his duties adequately. A rather different case, perhaps, was that of Richard II's minstrel Richard Guildford, described as 'impoverished' (*pauper*) when he left the king's service in 16 or 17 Ric II with a gift of 6s 8d.[80] Such gifts were made not only to minstrels but to other royal servants in these circumstances.

This gift cannot have provided much financial support for a man no longer working, but the king had means of ensuring that his former employees did not starve. The first of these was the kind of annuity already discussed, in which a fixed income was granted, sometimes from the revenues of a specified property or properties; or the property itself might be granted, with the whole of the income given to the man concerned. If such a grant were for life, rather than 'during pleasure', it would ensure a living income for the rest of his days.

A second kind of provision made for some royal servants was maintenance by a religious house. According to Warton, a harper named Jeffrey received a corrody in 1180 from Hyde Abbey, near Winchester, in return for his minstrelsy on public occasions.[81] In 1328 Edward III required the abbot and convent of Ramsey to house and maintain Queen Isabella's psaltery-player Janettus.[82] During the late thirteenth century, and for the whole of the fourteenth, these corrodies appear to have been

---

[80] BL Add MS 7965 (25 Ed I), fol. 54r; TNA C47.4.6 (25 Ed I), fol. 3r; E101.368.12 (34 Ed I), fols 4v (two entries); and E101.403.22 (16–17 Ric II), fol. 29r: (cal. SM II, 17, 18 fol. 52 (two items) and 119).

[81] Warton, *History*, II, 98.

[82] Rymer, *Foedera*, II (2), 738.

residential: the retired servant went to live in a religious house and was entirely maintained by the community.[83]

This kind of arrangement was not used only for retirement. John Mauprine was maintained by the abbey at Bury St Edmund's in the 1330s, together with his horse and a groom, at a time when he was still employed at Court.[84] Another case is shown by a letter dated 25 October 1364 from the Black Prince to the prior and convent of St Michael's Mount in Cornwall. The prince had sent to them his trumpeter Gilbert Stakford, asking them to take him in and to provide him with such sustenance as was formerly given to Roland Trewennard, deceased. They were to decide on the provision to be made for Gilbert, to give him letters patent under the house's seal specifying what this provision was to be, and to reply in writing, by the bearer of the prince's letter, to let the prince know their decision. Trewennard had presumably retired, his death making available a place for Gilbert.[85]

Gilbert was not retiring, in fact, and the arrangement was to be for a limited time. On 5 February 1365 the prince ordered a payment of 2d per day for Gilbert, to run from 1 May last (i.e. 1364) until the Michaelmas to come, a 17-month period in which Gilbert was expected to need support. But the prior dragged his feet, and on 26 May 1365 the prince wrote to the steward of Cornwall with an order that his request of 25 October 1364 be put into effect as soon as possible. This was presumably done, and Gilbert lived to serve the prince's son, Richard II, being awarded a pension of 6d a day for his service to the two monarchs.[86]

Although heads of religious houses cannot have welcomed such an arrangement, especially if the man concerned were infirm, there were occasions for minstrelsy in a religious house. In some cases, too, the minstrel had skills that made him useful in other ways: the harper named Thomas who lived in Durham cathedral priory in the mid-1330s worked as a carpenter.[87] Nevertheless, such royal demands could be interpreted by abbots and priors as stretching the requirements of charitable hospitality.

In the early Tudor period corrodies were usually non-resident, and appear to have worked much like grants from the issues of any other lands. Henry VII used them to reward his Chapel Royal clerks and other servants.[88] This may indicate a shift in the perception of a monastery's place in society, from an institution dedicated to

---

[83] Conklin, 'Medieval English Minstrels', 72–3, gives further examples of royal minstrel-corrodians: John de Trentham, king's harper (d. 1335) at Muchelney and Bath, John le Trumpour (1329) at St Alban's and later at Durham, John Maupryne, king's piper (1330s) at Bury St Edmund's, Peter Giles (1384) at St Mary's (presumably York) and (1385) Carlisle; Edward III awarded corrodies to John le Nakerer and Thomas Purchaseour at Burton on Trent.

[84] Conklin, 'Medieval English Minstrels', 72, citing CPR, Edward III, vol. 3 (1334–8), 573.

[85] *Black Prince*, II, 208–9.

[86] *Ibid.*, II, 210–11, and CPR, Richard II (1385–9), 413. Southworth, *English Medieval Minstrel*, 107, suggests that Gilbert had been wounded in the Poitiers campaign and needed recovery time: but so long after the battle (1356) and the Peace of Bretigny (1360) this seems unlikely.

[87] For minstrels living in religious houses see below, Chapter 5.

[88] See Ashbee, *Court Records*, VII, 1, 2 and *passim*.

prayer, the liturgy, charity and hospitality to a going commercial concern that could afford to help the king with his financial obligations. The system had been in danger of abuse for some time. In 1440 a charge was made by a monk of Humberston to the bishop's visitation that the abbot had sold a corrody to a harper, John Harden, to the disadvantage of the abbey. There is no indication of whether Harden was resident or not, and no suggestion that he performed for the abbey: but he was certainly not in need of charitable support, as he had paid ten marks (£6 13s 4d) for the corrody. The monk's complaint was that the corrody was worth 40s 0d per year and the harper had held it for eight years – a good bargain for the harper, but a loss of £9 6s 8d to the abbey.[89]

---

[89] *REED Lincolnshire*, 347, translation 723.

4
Minstrelsy at Court

Duties of the royal minstrels

The royal household minstrels fulfilled a wide spectrum of requirements, ranging from the most official ceremonial duties to the most nearly private entertainment for the king or other personage. Since almost the whole of a monarch's life was 'official', minstrelsy of various sorts must have been needed every day: and while there would be plenty of warning of any occasion needing large resources (such as a major feast or the arrival of a foreign ruler), some solo or small concerted minstrelsy might be demanded at any time. The four minstrels required at all times would have been enough for normal day-to-day requirements, with the rest of the minstrels coming to Court for the major feasts of the year. In theory this arrangement cut the costs of minstrelsy to a minimum; in practice, the year was full of minor celebrations and occasions for which more than the minimum minstrelsy was needed.

The only substantial extant account of the minstrels' duties is in the *Liber Niger* of 1471–2. While this is late in our period, the 'Black Book' was based on earlier ordinances, and the basic outlines of a royal minstrel's work cannot have changed greatly for a long time.[1] The minstrels played to announce meals. Outside the feast-times when all the minstrels were present, this function was presumably carried out by the two trumpeters on permanent duty. Their other main function was to signal the king's position in the countryside when he went riding, so that the household could follow.

If the king wished it, the two trumpeters could be supplemented by two string-minstrels, bringing the resident minstrels to the four (two loud and two 'still') specified in previous ordinances. The still minstrels would be able to provide intimate entertainment: and if other still minstrels were present in Court there would be a wider range of possible minstrelsy.

The other nine minstrels specified by the Black Book were to come to Court

> at v festes of the yere, and than to make theyre wages of houshold after iiijd. ob. a day if they be present in court; and than they to auoyde the next day after the festes be don.

This is a very simple arrangement in theory, and we saw in Chapter 2 that some minstrels did indeed remain in Court for a large part of the year. Most, however, were in

---

[1] Myers, *Household of Edward IV*, 131–2.

Court for only limited periods, from which it seems that the minstrels took turns in providing the four on stand-by.

The household ordinances sought to regulate the household in peace time. In war-time other arrangements were made according to circumstances, when the minstrels became mounted men-at-arms. On 23 April 1303 (31 Ed I) the king's trumpeter John de Depe received 100s 0d (£5) to pay for his equipment for the war in Scotland. He was then at York, on his way north, one of many royal servants going to war, including not only trumpeters and *vigiles* but also Nicholas de Eland, the king's harper.[2] The sum is large enough to suggest a considerable kitting-out. In May that year (1303), at Roxborough, the Prince of Wales made a gift of 33s 0d to his trumpeters and nakerer, Master John Garsie, John de Cateloyne and Janotus, to pay for three hauberks and three iron gorgets.[3] A year later, on 14 July 1304 (32 Ed I) the prince paid 63s 0d (£3 3s 0d) for items for his two trumpeters: two tunics of his livery, two hauberks and two helmets.[4] It is unlikely that John Garsie and John de Cateloyne would need new hauberks after only fourteen months, so these men were probably additional or replacement trumpeters, perhaps Januche and Lambyn Clay.[5] On 25 July 1352, in a much later war, the Black Prince bought two habergeons for his minstrels Hans and Soz. There is no indication of what instruments they played, but they are likely to be two of the four pipers sent to the prince that year by the Count of Eu.[6]

A hauberk is a chain-mail tunic, and a gorget a piece of armour to protect the throat; an habergeon is a sleeveless chain-mail tunic, usually shorter than a hauberk, although the two terms were sometimes used interchangeably. There is no doubt that these men were going to fight, even if they had special duties as minstrels. Most of these are loud minstrels, who would have gone partly to make military music, a visual and aural show necessary to a military campaign. An inventory of the royal armoury dated 20 May 1455 includes five trumpet-banners, which had been delivered to the trumpeters when the Duke of Gloucester went to the rescue of Calais.[7]

Domestic occasions for minstrelsy

Private entertainment

The main duties and functions of the loud minstrels, especially of the trumpeters, seem clear, but what of the 'still' minstrels on permanent duty, there to entertain the

---

[2] TNA E101.364.13 (31 Ed I), fol. 81r (cal. SM II, 36). Rewards in war-time show that still-minstrels took their instruments and performed as usual.

[3] TNA E101.363.18 (31 Ed I), fol. 23r (cal. SM II, 40).

[4] BL Add MS 35292 (31–4 Ed I), fol. 53r (cal. SM II, 34).

[5] Both are mentioned as trumpeters within the next year or two: see SM II, 40 and 34. 'Januche' may be the Janotus referred to earlier: some minstrels were known as both nakerer and trumpeter.

[6] Lodge and Somerville, *Black Prince*, IV, 71.

[7] CPR, Henry VI, vol. 6 (1452–61), 247; and see SM II, 154 and 164.

king at his pleasure? They had the relatively informal task of making minstrelsy for the king's relaxation – 'relatively' because it is unlikely that any occasion on which minstrelsy was made *coram Rege* was informal by modern standards.[8] Any royal person was constantly surrounded by at least the closest body-servants: and while it is true that a favoured harper might be deemed to fulfill that function, the apparently intimate occasions when king and harper were alone together almost certainly included other servants.

The least formal of such occasions was perhaps when the king was having his blood let. Blood-letting was a normal treatment when the patient had a fever, but in moderation it was considered beneficial at any time. Edward I rewarded a harper who played to him during his blood-letting in late April 25 Ed I (1297):[9]

> A certain harper: To Meliorus, a harper who was formerly with Sir John
> Mautravers, making his minstrelsy before the King for several days
> at the time of the King's blood-letting at Plumpton in the month of
> April, of the gift of the same King, by the hands of Walter de Sturton at
> Plympton, 23 April 20s od.

Clearly there was a period of several days when the king needed to be soothed by music and his own minstrels were perhaps not available. Quite how long this period was, and whether the king's blood was let every day, it is impossible to know, but the reward of £1 is generous. The king may have been ill, requiring blood-letting at regular intervals. He was certainly under considerable stress, with a growing crisis caused by opposition to his foreign policy and his attempts to raise more taxes, which in itself may have suggested that blood-letting would be helpful.[10]

Some forty years later, probably in 1337, a harper was rewarded for being with Edward of Woodstock when he was ill (see Chapter 3).[11] Although we do not know what Edward's illness was, we can assume that the minstrel's service to the 6- or 7-year-old prince was to keep him entertained and in good spirits.

Another relatively informal occasion for minstrelsy was during a journey. Payments for this service indicate that a minstrel would play to the king or other royal person while the household was actually travelling. The records do not say whether the minstrel rode on horseback or in a carriage with his patron, but this probably depended on how the patron was travelling and whether vocal, loud or still

---

[8] That is, 'before the king', in the king's presence. See Stevens, *Music and Poetry*, 269; and Myers, *England in the Late Middle Ages*, 92 f: 'Even in the largest households privacy did not exist …'.

[9] BL Add MS 7965 (25 Ed I), fol. 54v (cal. SM II, 17): 'Quidam cithariste: Melioro cithariste qui fuit quondam cum domino Johanne mautravers facienti menestralciam suam coram Rege per dies aliquos tempore flenbotoniaconis eiusdem Regis apud Plumpton' mense Aprilis de dono ipsius Regis per manus Walteri de Sturton' apud Plympton' xxiij die Aprilis xx s.'.

[10] See the article on Edward I in the ODNB.

[11] Cal. SM II, 96.

music was involved. When the patron was a lady, still minstrelsy in a closed carriage seems most likely. We return to this subject in Chapter 8.[12]

Conferences

A more formal occasion for minstrelsy was during meetings with visiting nobles. At such times not only the noble but some or all of his retinue would be in attendance. The minstrelsy was supplied by the king's minstrels, by those of the visiting noble, or both. As John Stevens noted in relation to the first meeting in 1503 of Margaret Tudor and her prospective bridegroom, James IV of Scotland, 'It is easy to underestimate the formality of such occasions'.[13] Stevens was discussing the use of music as a means of 'conversation' between individuals who had to get to know each other in the terms of the society in which they lived. Minstrelsy at a business meeting fulfilled rather different functions, since the immediate objectives were political rather than social. The meeting of Edward III and the Archbishop of Cologne on 25 August 12 Ed III (1338) was probably typical of many such, although descriptions are rarely so clear:[14]

> To Conrad and Ancelinus, minstrels of the Archbishop of Cologne, making their minstrelsy in the hall in the presence of the king, where the said bishop consulted the lord King at ?Bonn, of the King's gift, 25 August. 100s 0d.

Probably magnates took the opportunity to discuss issues of common interest on any occasion when they met socially, so that a banquet or other meal – always a formal occasion – might be part social, part business.[15] In any case, minstrelsy would tend to cover the sound of conversation, so that a quiet discussion would not be overheard. The boundary between a purely social occasion and a business meeting was probably not rigid.

Alms-giving

Whenever a royal personage entered a church he or she made an offering: and if the church were a place of pilgrimage offerings might be made at two or more places of special veneration. On 6 October 1351 Queen Philippa visited Canterbury cathedral and made offerings at the image of the Blessed Virgin Mary in the crypt (20s 0d), at the tomb of St Thomas (60s 0d), and at the head of St Thomas (3s 4d).[16] While St Thomas's tomb was the goal of pilgrimages throughout the later Middle Ages, it was

---

[12] Relevant entries are calendared in SM II, 32, 41, 75, 89, 94, 95 and 126. See also Chapter 2 for the story of Edward III and the tympanum.

[13] Stevens, *Music and Poetry*, 269.

[14] 'Conrodo et Ancelino menestrallis archiepiscopi colonie facientibus menestralciam suam in aula in presencia Regis ubi dictus Episcopus convinavit dominum Regem apud Bu'ne de dono domine Regis xxv die Augusti c s.'. Edward's visit to the Low Countries included many such occasions, as is shown by the gifts to minstrels: see TNA E36.203 (12–14 Ed III), fol. 99v (cal. SM II, 99–100).

[15] However, this meeting was apparently not over a meal. 'Banquet' is here used in its modern sense of a lavish dinner given for special social purposes.

[16] Society of Antiquaries MS 208 (queen's household, 25/6 Ed III), fol. 3v.

at the image of the Blessed Virgin that the queen's alms-giving was accompanied by minstrelsy:[17]

> Henry, fiddler: to Henry, fiddler, a minstrel making his minstrelsy before the image of the blessed [Virgin] Mary in the crypt in Christ Church Canterbury, of the gift of the lady queen, by his own hands the same day [6 October] 3s 4d.

The Wardrobe books record another eleven occasions in the reigns of Edward I and Edward III when rewards were made to minstrels, verifiably or by implication during the offering of gifts.[18] The principals were, variously, Edward I, Edward III, Queen Philippa and the princess Eleanor, Edward III's sister; and the locations were the tomb of St Richard in Chichester cathedral (once), the image of the Virgin in the crypt of Canterbury cathedral (seven times), St Augustine's church, Canterbury (twice, one specifying the saint's tomb), and the cross at the north door of St Paul's cathedral in London (twice). A possible thirteenth example occurred in 1358, when the dowager Queen Isabella went on pilgrimage to Canterbury. According to Bond, on 10 or 11 June the queen made oblations at the tomb of St Thomas, at the crown of his head and at the point of the sword, making gifts to minstrels in the crypt (*in volta*). This was probably during alms-giving before the image of the Blessed Virgin, but it may now be impossible to verify the entry in the 'Alms' section of the accounts.[19]

It appears that minstrelsy did not occur at all of the places where oblations were offered. In any of these churches the high altar could be a place of offering, as could the saint's tombs at Chichester and St Augustine's Canterbury; and at both St Paul's and Canterbury cathedral there were several places of veneration where offerings were made. The cross at the north door was the most important place of veneration in St Paul's, and the image of the Blessed Virgin in the crypt at Canterbury cathedral. The latter apparently took precedence even over the tomb of the most important English saint, Thomas Becket, and the places where he was wounded in the head and killed with a sword-thrust. When Princess Eleanor visited St Paul's cathedral on 30 April 1332 she made offerings at five places, rewarding minstrels at the cross by the

---

[17] Society of Antiquaries MS 208, fol. 5r: 'Henricus Fitheler: Henrico Fitheler ministrallo facienti ministralciam suam coram ymagine beate Marie in volta in ecclesia Christi Cantuarie de dono domine Regine per manus proprias eodem die [6 October] iij s. iiij d.'.

[18] Rastall, 'Minstrelsy, church and clergy', 87–8 (entries cal. SM II, *passim*), and Antiquaries MS 208 (25/6 Ed III), fol. 5r. The earliest example known to me was on 26 May 25 Ed I (1297), but Nagel, *Geschichte der Musik*, 107, quoted an entry from 23 Ed I, and on p. 146, n. 8, cited PRO Exchequer QR 25, no. 7/5. This records a gift to three hurdy-gurdy players, two harpists and a fiddler, 'minstrels of Canterbury', performing before the Virgin's image in the vault: 'Johanni Simphoniste Seniori & Johanni Simphoniste Juniori, Roberto cithariste, Waltero cithariste, Thome vidulatori & Thome Simphoniste, menestrallis cantuar', facientibus ministralciam suam coram ymagine beate marie in [vouta] in ecclesia …'. This is an old call-number, and despite generous help from TNA staff I am unable to locate the manuscript and so to confirm the reference and the entry.

[19] Bond, 'Notices of Isabella', 461–2, citing BL Cotton MS Galba E xiv (for which see Chapter 3, n. 72).

north door; and a few days later, on 4 May, she made offerings at several places of veneration in Canterbury cathedral, rewarding minstrels at the image of the Blessed Virgin Mary in the crypt.[20]

There was undoubtedly a tradition of making minstrelsy before an image of the Blessed Virgin. A statute of the dean of St Paul's, dated c. 1263, orders that prostitutes, market porters and beggars 'who lay claim to certain parts of the church' (*qui certa sibi loca uendicant in ecclesia*), presumably for business purposes, are to be excluded from the building, as are minstrels who perform before the altars of the Virgin and at the Cross.[21] Elsewhere, there is the evidence of one of the *cantigas de Santa Maria* that tells of a minstrel who regularly played before the image of the Virgin as his way of worshipping her.[22]

Most of these records show that the minstrels performed in the presence of the royal personage, but three of them state specifically that the performance took place while the offerings were being made. The minstrels were sometimes soloists, sometimes a group of up to fourteen, and they seem to have been local in each case. When Edward I made offerings at the tomb of St Richard in Chichester cathedral on 26 May 1297, the record states that the king 'found' or 'came upon' (*invenit*) the harper Walter Lund of Chichester playing before the tomb. The use of *invenio* here means that the king was not expecting Walter to be there (although Walter may have been expecting the king, and a reward in consequence), and the item-heading 'Quid*am* cithar*ista*' ('a certain harper') confirms that Walter was previously unknown to the royal party. It is notable, in fact, that in none of these cases were royal minstrels involved.

Whatever the extent to which such minstrelsy-as-worship was normal in these churches, it cannot have been entirely unusual, and perhaps did not occur only when a royal personage was visiting. One suspects that such minstrelsy was not uncommon, and that performing at a place of special veneration, and therefore of regular pilgrimage, was a lucrative activity. Clearly, it was accepted as normal in royal circles.

Ceremonial occasions for minstrelsy

The distinction between 'household' and 'ceremonial' occasions is not clear-cut: almost any occasion involving royalty was 'ceremonial' in being subject to formal protocols. Nor is the proper distinction quite that between 'private' and 'public' occasions, no performance for the king or queen being 'private' by modern standards. Nevertheless, some celebrations involved the general public, or at least large numbers of the privileged public, rather than being exclusive to the household and a restricted circle around it: it is such events that are considered here.

---

[20] The princess's journey is discussed in Chapter 8.

[21] *REED Ecclesiastical London*, 16 and 324.

[22] The fiddler Pedro de Sigrar in Cantiga 8, *A Virgen Santa Maria*. The story is depicted in late thirteenth-century illustrations from Madrid, El Escorial Palace, códice rico T.I.1, f. 15v: see Lovillo, *Cantigas*, Plate 11.

Principal elements

A celebratory occasion at Court often included one or more of three principal constituent elements: processions, a banquet,[23] and a joust or tournament; some occasions also included a liturgical ceremony. Minstrelsy was normally required in a procession, and likewise at a banquet, although the evidence does not provide the kind of detail that we should like; a joust or a more extensive tournament required trumpets and perhaps shawms.

Processions

Processions varied from the civic to the domestic. At one end of the scale, a royal personage entering the City of London was met by the mayor and other civic dignitaries at Blackheath and escorted to the Tower of London (the royal residence in the capital).[24] The actual entry was at the gatehouse on London Bridge, and from there to the Tower there might be 'sights' with singing and minstrelsy. A princess coming to be married to the king, or a queen coming to be crowned, was also met at Blackheath, unless she came by barge from Greenwich directly to the Tower: she would spend a night at the Tower before travelling to the palace and abbey of Westminster. It was usual before a coronation for the king to create several knights of the Bath, who formed part of the escort the following day. The royal *vigilatores* were present at the overnight vigil.

Processions through the city *en route* to Westminster again included 'sights', speeches and music. These were largely civic events, but they also involved the royal households, for the royal minstrels and trumpeters were present, as were heralds and other household members.

At the other end of the scale of processions were those between the palace of Westminster and the abbey, on the occasions of coronations and weddings. Westminster Hall, the great hall of the palace where banquets took place, was also the hub where processions assembled and from where they dispersed. The royal minstrels and trumpeters came with the royal party from the palace, and then formed part of the main procession to the abbey. Exactly who played and when is mainly unknown, as such processions were subject to unchanging protocols that did not need to be written down. It is likely that the trumpets announced the advent of royalty and that the other minstrels played for processions on the move.

Banquets

Minstrels also played a large part in banquets, providing periods of varied entertainment as well as music for dancing and musical items that underscored the structure of the event. Documentary evidence about this is limited – the main statement in the Black Book (1471–2) concerning the minstrels' duties before and during mealtimes gives no detail – but some information about the precise functions of the

---

[23] I use 'banquet' in its modern sense of a special celebratory meal.

[24] It is at Shooter's Hill, Blackheath, that a traveller from the Kent road has his or her first sight of the city.

minstrels can be found in literary and iconographical evidence. In the romance *Sir Eglamour* (c. 1440) the minstrels concerned are waits – that is, shawmists:[25]

> Grete lordys were at the Assent;
> Waytys blewe, to mete they wente. (lines 1066–7)

Evidently in the fourteenth and fifteenth centuries it was shawms that warned the company to go to the hall in readiness for a meal.[26] Of course, the integrity of this passage as evidence depends on the assumption that such literary evidence was recognisably true to life for the noble audience that read or heard it.

This may all suggest different functions for different groups of minstrels when all are available: loud wind music for warnings and for the serving of courses, and trumpets specifically for heraldic announcements. This is seen during a five-day festival of jousts and tournaments held by Sir Rhys ap Thomas to celebrate St George's day in 1507.[27] While everyone stood before the serving of the evening meal, the trumpets sounded and the herald called for the king to be served (although the king was in fact not present); while the food was brought to the king's table, and before Grace was said, 'the Cornetts, Haultbois and other winde Instruments' were played; and during the service of the king, while conversation was carried on, various sorts of music were performed.[28] This may have been all instrumental, but later, when Sir Rhys was served with his meal, the bards and poets sang songs of the deeds of the ancestors of those present.[29]

This is a late description, and it may be that procedures had changed since the early fourteenth century. The use of trumpets, shawms or trumpets and shawms together seems partly interchangeable: it may be that trumpets were used when royalty was present, the higher-status instruments reflecting the status of the senior person present. The other distinction, the division into loud ceremonial music for the serving of a course and still music or vocal minstrelsy for its consumption, seems more standard. Stevens cites the coronation banquet of Henry VIII for this,[30] but other occasions also support it. The distinction is confirmed by iconographical evidence.[31] These illustrations do not firmly assign these types of minstrelsy to specific sections of a meal, however, mainly because it is more interesting to show servants

---

[25] Cook, *Sir Eglamour*.
[26] One might expect this to be one of the duties of the *vigilatores*: but it is not specified in the Black Book, and it would be possible only at times when the *vigilatores* were capable of minstrelsy.
[27] *REED Wales*, 256–67.
[28] *REED Wales*, 261. See also *REED Oxford*, I, 6, for a clarion being used to announce meals in the Queen's College, 1340. 'Haultbois' are the loud (*haut*) woodwind instruments – i.e. shawms.
[29] *REED Wales*, 262. On praise songs, see Chapter 13, *passim*.
[30] Stevens, *Music and Poetry*, 238 ff.
[31] See, for example, Bowles, *Musikgeschichte in Bildern* III/8, Plates 27–35; Salmen, *Der Spielmann*, Plates 94, 96, 98, 99 and 101–4; Remnant, *English Bowed Instruments*, Plates 41, 67 and 133.

bringing on the dishes and the diners talking than the diners eating. For detailed information the documentary evidence is more helpful.

Tournaments and jousts

Military exercises of various kinds were normal for any young man of good family, for landowners and their sons were expected to fight for their lord whenever necessary. For most of our period tournaments and jousts were used for training and entertainment, with a strong element of competition. 'Tournament' is commonly used as a generic term for various types of martial exercise: but strictly its specific meaning is a contest between two groups of knights fighting as if on a battlefield. An alternative word for this is *melée*. The other main type of exercise was the joust, in which two knights rode against one another with lances, the object being to break one's lance against one's opponent,[32] or to unseat him.[33] Jousting ideally took place along a straight line: at the end of the fourteenth century it developed a central barrier, which separated the combatants and thus eliminated the risk of collision.[34] These entertainments, usually in conjunction with feasting and dancing, might be arranged in the form of a festival lasting two or three days, known as a 'round table'.

Tournaments and jousts involved the trumpeters almost exclusively,[35] and in a close working relationship with heralds. The heralds were responsible for the practical arrangements of the fighting, for proclaiming the rules of the event, and for starting and stopping each part of the event's program. For all of this, at least one trumpeter was needed, to blow for silence so that the herald could make himself heard (Plate 6). It seems also that, once the main actions of the event had been set out, some of them could be started by means of a trumpet-call without further announcement from the heralds.

In the *Canterbury Tales* the trumpets are sounded after the announcement of the rules at a tournament, as a signal to start the contest, and to announce the victory.[36] In real life, this was seen in the abortive contest between the dukes of Hereford and Norfolk in 1398, set up at Coventry to decide the quarrel between them before the king himself.[37] The proclamation of the contest was made by a king at arms, who also announced the rules; another herald announced the presence of the duke of Hereford (Henry of Bolingbroke) and his reason for being there. The Duke of Norfolk was also announced, after which the weapons of the contestants were examined. The herald then ordered the two dukes to mount and prepare for the contest. A trumpet-call signalled the start of the joust. The king stopped the contest, however,

---

[32] Barber and Barker, *Tournaments*, 6 f.
[33] Barber and Barker, *Tournaments*, 2.
[34] Barber and Barker, *Tournaments*, 4.
[35] While trumpets and shawms are often shown in continental iconography, English sources seem to show trumpets only.
[36] See Manly and Rickert, *Text* III, 105 f and 108: also Douce, 'Peaceable jousts', 4 f.
[37] This account is printed in full in *REED Coventry*, 3–5.

PLATE 6. A joust, with a trumpeter signalling and the herald's baton raised: from Christine de Pisan, *Le Duc des Vrais Amants*, early 15th century. London, British Library, MS Harley 4431, fol. 150r.

the heralds crying 'Ho, ho' for this purpose.[38] Eventually the heralds 'cried silence' for the announcement of the king's decision after a two-hour wait while the king consulted his advisors.

The various announcements by the heralds (except perhaps for 'Ho, ho') were probably preceded by trumpet-calls: this is not stated, although the trumpet signal for the start of the contest is noted. Corroborative information is again found in the jousts and tournaments held by Sir Rhys ap Thomas of Carew in 1507.[39] On the third day, which was St George's Day, drums and trumpets signalled the start of the formal proceedings. In the procession to the bishop's palace, two miles away, Sir Rhys was mounted, with two pages and a herald on horseback before him. The procession was accomplished in silence, but the company then 'bidd good morrow to the Bishop in the language of Souldiers with Arquebusses, Musketts and Calivers …'.[40] Sir Rhys was later admitted to the palace having approached on foot, with a trumpeter before him and a herald with him. The trumpeter sounded his instrument to give notice of Sir Rhys's arrival, and the gates were opened. On the return to Carew Castle, 'the Captains Saluted the Castle with a brave volley of Shott, and the like was returned from the walles'. Sir Rhys led his followers into the castle to the sound of drums, trumpets, fifes 'and other warlike Musicke'.[41] The following morning a trumpeter again started the day's proceedings by calling Sir Rhys to judge the jousting, to which he went on horseback with a herald and two trumpeters before him. The trumpets sounded to announce the arrival of the appellants, the first of whom, the challenger, had a trumpeter before him. The first contest was started by the trumpets. On the remaining two days of the occasion, also, the trumpets gave the signal to start the contest.[42]

This confirms much of what was already noted about the relationship between heralds and trumpeters. Any noble or other person of consequence might have a herald with him or her to make announcements on his or her behalf and to negotiate (for example) for permission to enter a town or castle. A herald also made announcements and enforced discipline at tournaments and military musters. To do this he needed trumpet-calls to demand silence or to alert those responsible of his arrival, and so was normally accompanied by one or more trumpeters. On the occasion just mentioned when the heralds intervened vocally, crying 'Ho, ho' to stop the contest, it was a non-routine event, initiated by the king for immediate action. Here there was no time for routine protocol: one imagines that the heralds rode between the combatants, raising a hand or a baton of authority as a signal to stop.

---

[38] In hunting the cry 'ho(w)' was 'normally used to calm or restrain the hounds': Twiti, *Middle English Text*, 64. It was evidently more widely used to call attention to oneself, often with the specific intention of stopping someone doing something. Another variant, 'Woa', is still in use as the instruction to a walking horse to stand still.

[39] See above, and *REED Wales*, 256–67.

[40] *REED Wales*, 259. The firing of guns was probably more common than the evidence suggests: see Chapter 8, concerning Margaret Tudor's arrival at Newcastle.

[41] *REED Wales*, 260–1.

[42] *REED Wales*, 263–6.

There are some indications that a herald might be his own trumpeter, or rather, that a trumpeter might be raised to the status of herald in appropriate circumstances. In this case he would be acting as what later became known as a pursuivant, a word that was used only in the late fifteenth century, when the position itself was regularised: it signifies an assistant herald, a position that could then have been occupied by any trumpeter who had worked with heralds and understood how they functioned.[43]

There is apparently no information about what sort of fanfare, trumpet-call or signal might have been sounded by one or more trumpeters attending a herald. Their various functions probably required specific and distinct signals for starting the various elements of a pre-arranged tournament or joust, calling for silence before a herald's announcement, and so on.[44] Similarly, the call to draw attention to some royal or noble person's arrival at a town or castle gate must have been different from the celebratory fanfares at their actual entry. This diversity is also implicit in the roles of trumpeters on the field of battle.

Liturgical ceremony

Ceremonial events might include a liturgical element, for worship and celebration often went together. Weddings and coronations included the celebration of Mass: but any secular celebration, too, might include a church service of thanksgiving, as when Henry V returned to London from his victory at Agincourt in 1415, breaking his procession to Westminster by entering St Paul's cathedral for the singing of *Te Deum*. The ceremony of alms-giving almost certainly included liturgical ceremony, although there is no record of it. Some liturgical events, on the other hand, had one or more important secular elements. Baptism and the ceremony of purification – thanksgiving after childbirth – were liturgical events, but when royalty or nobility were involved there were usually processions and a banquet. The same was true of the ceremony of installing a bishop, abbot or prior.

The extent to which minstrels participated in these ceremonies varied considerably, depending on the nature and importance of the occasion. The banquet following the installation of a prelate need not have involved minstrelsy at all, as trained singers were available to provide the entertainment: but we know that minstrels were sometimes in attendance. The banquet following the *purificatio* ceremony probably involved only *bas* minstrelsy, that being virtually a ladies-only occasion. The evidence is incomplete, but some broad outlines can be deduced.

The major feasts

The festivals of the Church year

The four major feasts celebrated at Court early in the fourteenth century were Christmas (25 December), Easter, Pentecost (i.e. Whitsuntide) and, probably, All Saints (1 November). There is some doubt about All Saints, and it is possible

---

[43] Or possibly by other minstrels: see Chapter 8 for the case of John Taysaunt in Princess Eleanor's temporary household.

[44] This situation must have been parallel to that concerned in hunting, where specific signals were made for sighting the quarry, the kill, and so on. Hunting treatises do not describe these precisely, however.

that the last of these feasts was Michaelmas (29 September). Following the Black Prince's victory at Crécy in 1346 and Edward III's subsequent completion of the Round Tower at Windsor and founding of the Order of the Garter, St George's Day (23 April) was added as a fifth major feast from 1348 onwards.

Christmas and Pentecost were the feasts celebrated most lavishly, with liveries given in the royal households. The festivities for Christmas included New Year's Day (1 January), the day on which presents were given, and Epiphany (6 January, also Twelfth Night). This period usually required more minstrelsy than any other part of the Court's yearly life, and perhaps a greater variety of entertainments. Many Christmas payments to minstrels are near items concerned with disguisings, and the minstrels certainly took part in spectacular entertainments at Court, as we shall see.

Pentecost was seen as a time when new initiatives should be undertaken. One of the most lavishly-celebrated occasions in our period was Pentecost 1306, when the Prince of Wales was knighted and Edward I rallied his knights to fight against the Scots. The heralds and minstrels on that occasion were rewarded with a total of 200 marks (£133.6.8d), and they are listed, and mostly named, with the rewards to be given to each. Yet despite this wealth of financial information, we have no information about their performances at the banquet. This, unfortunately, is typical of the surviving evidence.[45]

Clearly, the major feasts were occasions of great ceremonial. St George's Day (23 April) was celebrated with tournaments, for which banners were supplied to the king's minstrels;[46] and at the meeting of the Order of the Garter in 1358 the Black Prince spent £100 in gifts to minstrels and heralds at Windsor.[47] This sum was of the order of those made at weddings late in Edward I's reign and at the knighting of the Black Prince's grandfather in 1306.

The anniversary of the king's accession should be added to the major feasts as an occasion on which minstrelsy was required, probably, again, at the banquet. On 8 July 14 Ed II (1320), Edward's accession day, the king gave £20 to King Robert and other minstrels, including those of the King of France.[48] Such accession-day celebrations sometimes included a crown-wearing: Edward III wore his second-best crown (redeemed from a money-lender just in time) at his accession-day celebrations at Windsor in 1344.[49]

Coronation

The ritual of coronation has developed over many centuries in England, and although there have been additions and modifications 'the Coronation rite has

---

[45] For an extended discussion of the events at Pentecost 1306, see Bullock-Davies, *Menestrellorum Multitudo*; also Rastall, SM II, 53–8, for some amendments.
[46] SM II, 112, 116 and perhaps 136: also Devon, *Issues*, 169, 413 and perhaps 171 and 207.
[47] Paid on 18 May 1358: *Black Prince*, IV, 252.
[48] BL Add MS 5591 (14 Ed II), fol. 19r (cal. SM II, 79). Edward was at Amiens to do homage to the French king for Gascony.
[49] Munby, Barber and Brown, *Edward III's Round Table*, 42–3.

been essentially a conservative one'.[50] The king usually made a formal entry into the city of London in order to spend one or more nights at the Tower, his London residence.[51] There it was traditional for him to create several new knights of the Bath. The following day he would process from the Tower to Westminster, where the evening was spent in relatively informal entertainments.[52] The day of the coronation itself began with a procession to Westminster Hall, where the processions assembled and dispersed, the coronation regalia were brought from the Abbey, and the coronation feast was held.[53] A procession on foot into the abbey was followed by the coronation service; and after a recession to Westminster Hall the principals could relax in their private apartments and prepare for the evening banquet. This relaxation sometimes included private entertainment. On the day following the coronation there might be a tournament to end the official ceremonies.

The coronation of the queen followed much the same pattern, the various events calling for minstrelsy from royal and civic minstrels and also, at the banquet, from the minstrels of the nobles present. At any such celebration the minstrels' role depended on the precise nature of the events, but the chroniclers tended not to give detail on matters that they could take for granted. It was important for any coronation to be celebrated according to custom, however, and it is probably safe to assume that information is likely to be of general relevance. We learn from the ordinance for Henry VII's coronation in 1485, for instance, that the king was to ride in state from the Tower to Westminster Hall in a procession that included the mayor of London, aldermen, heralds, serjeants at arms, trumpets, minstrels and other officers: but specifically that the heralds and minstrels were placed just before the king in the procession, with only certain officers and symbols of the king's state between them.[54] This disposition of minstrels before the king was no doubt a matter of accepted protocol.

Processions to and from the Tower of London involved a passage through the city, requiring the escort of the mayor and city dignitaries: there were usually 'sights' mounted along the route, with speeches, singing choirs, and minstrelsy. Edward IV's queen, Elizabeth Woodville, was received in 1465 by the mayor and aldermen on Shooter's Hill, and escorted over London Bridge to the Tower. Her entertainment *en route* included much spectacle, speech-making and singing, but apparently little

---

[50] Hughes (Anselm), 'Music of the Coronation', 82. Hughes was mainly concerned with the liturgical element of the ceremony, but included a section on minstrelsy, pp. 85–7. See also Hughes (Andrew), 'Antiphons and Acclamations'; Mitchell, *Medieval Feast*; and Epstein, 'Eating their words'.

[51] London and Westminster were (and still are) separate cities: the Tower of London was the king's London palace, but monarchs preferred to live at Westminster or elsewhere.

[52] Richard II retired to his chamber for dances, dance-tunes and solemn minstrelsies ('tripudiis coreis et solempnibus ministralciis'), probably on the evening before his coronation in 1377: Taylor (Arthur), *Glory of Regality*, 257, quoting Rymer. 'Solemn' here signifies intellectually uplifting, as opposed to the physical activity of the dance.

[53] Further on Westminster Hall and the table and seat used at banquets, see Collins *et al.*, 'King's high table', *passim*.

[54] Ives, *Select papers*, 93–170.

or no minstrelsy.[55] Her procession the following day, through the city and on to the palace of Westminster, included the mayor and other civic dignitaries, who continued with her to Westminster: it also included the knights of the Bath created in her honour the day before her arrival at the Tower.[56] The presence of these knights implies that heralds and trumpeters were also present, as well as the *vigilatores* who would have attended the newly-created knights at their vigil.

Henry VII's queen, Elizabeth of York, came for her coronation in 1487 from the palace of Greenwich, travelling to the Tower by barge. She was accompanied by the mayor, sheriffs and aldermen of the city of London, with many liveried guildsmen. It was a festive event, and the spectacular entertainments started on the barges themselves. The queen was also[57]

> furnished in every Behalf with Trumpettes. Claryons, and other Mynstrelleys, as apperteynid and was fitting to her Estate roiall.

The queen's procession from the Tower to Westminster the following day again passed many spectacular displays, with professional singers at several places. In the procession, riding immediately after the new knights as in the king's procession two years earlier, were the 'Kings of Armes, Harolds, and Pursuyvaunts'. It may be that the term 'pursuivants' subsumes trumpeters.[58]

On the day of the coronation there were two types of procession between the palace of Westminster and the abbey, very different from those through the city. From the royal apartments to Westminster Hall was a private procession of the household, but including any guests staying in the palace. In the hall, however, this group was joined by non-household participants, such as civic and clerical personnel, who formed part of a larger and essentially public procession to the abbey. The minstrels certainly played in this procession.

Henry VII's procession in 1485 entered the abbey by the west door and proceeded to the *pulpitum*, where the king was presented to the people and his coronation agreed to by acclamation.[59] The procession then went to the high altar for the coronation itself, after which the clergy and nobles paid homage to the king and Mass was celebrated. Afterwards the king returned to the palace, where the assembly of bishops, nobles and knights, 'with Harawlds, Officers of Armes, Trumpetts and Mynstrells, shall attende uppon him throughout Westminster Hall'.[60] The king then withdrew to his private apartments, returning to the hall later for the coronation banquet.

---

[55] MacGibbon, *Elizabeth Woodville*, 46–7: see also p. 143, below.
[56] MacGibbon, *Elizabeth Woodville*, 48. The queen was carried in a horse litter.
[57] Ives, *Select Papers*, 127, cited in Taylor, *Glory of Regality*, 275.
[58] Ives, *Select Papers*, 130. For pursuivants and trumpeters, see below.
[59] The procession of Edward IV's queen, Elizabeth Woodville, on Sunday 26 May 1465, however, entered the Abbey by the north door and proceeded straight to the high altar. Elizabeth was crowned separately from her husband, and acclamation in the nave was not required.
[60] Ives, *Select Papers*, 119.

The minstrels must have played in procession to the abbey, and there seems no reason why they should be silent on entering: but they would stop playing at the *pulpitum*, where the king was to be acclaimed by the congregation. Did they then join the procession through the screen into the choir for the coronation and the celebration of Mass, and did the trumpets and other minstrels play any part in the proceedings?

Grafton tells us that trumpeters preceded the heralds in the coronation procession of Richard III in 1483.[61] This is entirely expected, but in this case the list of trumpets is unusually long, which may be Grafton's reason for mentioning it. In addition to the king's nine trumpeters there were 23 'taborets and trumpets' who seem to have been brought together for the occasion.[62] Modern perception suggests that these trumpets would be used to play fanfares during the coronation ceremony, but the documentary evidence is lacking.

There is however some iconographical evidence, all continental, that offers clues on the use of loud music. An illustration of the coronation of Louis XII of France in 1498, painted at Amiens *c.* 1501, shows the moment before the crown is placed on the king's head.[63] In galleries high on either side of the chancel are two pairs of *buisines*, one pair on each side. This would seem a sensible arrangement for celebratory fanfares, and could depict late medieval practice. The symmetrical arrangement of pairs of *buisines* is also seen in manuscript illustrations of the Last Judgment, however, with the same symbolism of authority: this argues for both mutual influence and a common practice at coronations.

Two illustrations from a copy of Jean Froissart's chronicle, produced at Bruges *c.* 1468–9, show wind bands performing from balconies during the coronation ceremonies of Richard II of England (1377) and Charles VI of France (1380).[64] In these the monarchs have already been crowned and are accepting homage, Richard from a kneeling lord and Charles from a senior cleric (Plate 7). Both illustrations show a three-man loud group in which a folded (?slide-) trumpet is identifiable. The other two instruments in Plate 7 are probably a treble shawm and a bombard (tenor shawm), but the treble seems to have a covered joint like a *buisine* and the bombard has no fontenelle; nor are the hand-positions of the players identifiable as those expected for shawms.

Medieval pictures often amalgamate the images of separate but proximate events, but there is no indication of that here. We can therefore come to certain tentative conclusions: that, at least in Flanders at the end of the fifteenth century, a small group of trumpets (apparently without nakers) might provide fanfares at the coronation itself; that a loud wind band might play during the acts of homage; and that these performances were probably given from small galleries above the main arcades. It is possible, presumably, that either group might perform at both occasions – that is,

---

[61] Taylor (Arthur), *Glory of Regality*, 272.
[62] The trumpeters are listed in MERH, 34–5 (taken from Lafontaine, *King's Musicke*, 1) and discussed in Sutton and Hammond, *Coronation*. For Richard's forces from York, see Davies, *Extracts*, 149, and Gairdner, *History of the Life*, 59–60.
[63] Paris, Musée de Cluny, Inv. Nr. 822b, reproduced in Bowles, *Musikgeschichte*, Plate 4.
[64] Berlin, Staatsbibliothek Preussische Kulturbesitz, Depot Breslau 1, MS Rehd. 2, fols 112v and 215r: reproduced in Bowles, *Musikgeschichte*, Plates 1 and 2.

Plate 7. The coronation of Charles VI, from Jean Froissart, *Chroniques*: Bruges, 1468 or 1469. Berlin, Staatsbibliothek Preussischer Kulturbesitz, Depot Breslau 1, MS Rehd. 2, fol. 215r.

that the two groups were alternatives. If a large group of trumpets and tabors did play during Richard III's coronation service (rather than only in processions and the coronation banquet), and such a small gallery could not accommodate the musicians present, the obvious place for them would be the *pulpitum* or main screen and loft separating the chancel from the nave.

The evening after a coronation was the occasion of a banquet in Westminster Hall. We have accounts of the banquets for Elizabeth Woodville in 1465 and Elizabeth of York in 1487. Both of these were essentially ladies' occasions at which the king was not officially present, his place being taken by a senior noble. At Elizabeth Woodville's banquet the trumpets were sounded 'solemnly' before and during the service of each course, and between courses there was instrumental music from 'the king's minstrals and the minstrals of other lords'. For their part in the day's celebrations the heralds were given £20, and the same sum was delivered to Walter Halyday, the marshal of the still minstrels, to distribute amongst the minstrels involved. There were more than a hundred of these, for in addition to the royal minstrels, many others had come in the retinues of the various lords and gentlemen who had taken part in the ceremonies.

Like that for Elizabeth Woodville, Elizabeth of York's banquet was largely a ladies' occasion. The king did not preside (the Archbishop of Canterbury was his proxy), but sat with his mother to witness the occasion from a special stage constructed in a window embrasure. At one end of the Hall,[65]

> before the Wyndowe, there was made a Stage for the Trumpetts and Mynstrells; which, when the first Course was set forward, began to blowe; the Sergeaunt of Armes before them.

This was loud wind music announcing the serving of the course, as stated in the *Liber Niger*, perhaps with both trumpets and shawms. At one end of the queen's table there was another dais made for the kings of arms, heralds, pursuivants and certain visitors to the Court.

When the first course was finished, 'the Trumpetts blewe to the seconde Course', but this time, 'as the high Bourde was servid, the Kings Mynstrells played a Song before the Queene', and the kings of arms, heralds and pursuivants did obeisance to her and afterwards cried 'Largesse' through the hall.[66] Then the heralds received a drink, and 'the Queenes Mynstrells [played], and after them the Mynstrells of other Estates' (presumably in order of precedence of their masters). Finally, the queen was served with fruit and wafers.

What sort of minstrelsy was performed while the queen was served with the second course? 'Song' can signify an instrumental piece, as may be the case here, but was it played on 'loud' or 'still' instruments? As the minstrels played it 'before the queen' they perhaps took up positions nearer to her table, which suggests 'still' minstrelsy: and similarly, the minstrelsy performed between the second course and the serving of fruit and wafers may well have been 'still' minstrelsy.

The day following Elizabeth Woodville's coronation, Monday 27 May 1465, a tournament was held at Westminster, and this completed the formal celebrations of the coronation.[67] In 1487, however, there was no tournament because Parliament was about to meet, 'or els the Feast had dured lenger'.[68] Instead, the queen took some relaxation, for after dinner 'the Queene and the Ladies daunced', which would have required the attendance of minstrels. The next day she returned to Greenwich.

Weddings

A royal wedding always called for minstrelsy on a large scale, mainly at the feast after the wedding ceremony. According to the royal household ordinances of 1494, the minstrels should play at the second or third course of the banquet following the marriage of a princess,[69] which suggests that, as at a coronation banquet, the first course was normally reserved for serious eating and social conversation.

---

[65] Ives, *Select Papers*, 140.

[66] The crying of 'Largesse' by the heralds was to thank patrons for their reward.

[67] For Richard III's coronation, see Sutton and Hammond, *Coronation*.

[68] Ives, *Select Papers*, 145.

[69] *Ords & Regs*, 129 (pr. from BL MS Harley 642, fols 198–217). For illustrations, see the Marriage-feast of the Lamb in the thirteenth-century Trinity Apocalypse (Trinity College, Cambridge, MS R.16.2) reproduced in Remnant, *English Bowed Instruments*, Plate 41; the fourteenth-century Braunche brass at King's Lynn, reproduced *ibid.*, Plate 101; and BL Royal MS 14 E iv, fol. 244v, reproduced here as Plate 11.

Edward I's gifts to minstrels at the wedding of his daughter Elizabeth, who married the Count of Holland in December 1296 (25 Ed I), were typically generous, totalling £52:[70]

> King Page, John *vidulator* and Conute his son, making their minstrelsy, 50s 0d each. 8 January [1297] Total £7 10s 0d
> Grisecote, Visage and Magote, similarly making their minstrelsy before the lady, 20s 0d each. Total 60s 0d [£3]
> Ruardinus *vidulator*, King Morellus, Guillotus de Ros, Janinus le Leutor and Thomas *le Fole*, 50s 0d each. Total £12 10s 0d
> Two harpers, two of the king's trumpets, John Drake the waferer, Dunrine, Baudettus, Thomelmus *vidulator*, two harpers of the Bishop of Durham, two minstrels of the Earl Marshal, Hamon Lestivour, Lambyn Clay and John de Cressin, 20.0d each. Total £15
> A harper of Dns John Comyn, 1 mark 13s 4d
> Druettus, Monthaut and Jakettus de Scocia, kings, 40s 0d each. Total £6
> The waferer of the king's son, four *vigiles* of the king and the king's son, two harpers of the Earl of Oxford and Dns Thomas de Mylton, Henry the harper, Laurence the harper and Martinettus the taborer, 10s 0d each. Total 100s 0d [£5]
> Various other minstrels, between them, 46s 8d £2 6s 8d[71]
> Sum total £52

The date of the first payment, and presumably of the rest, is two days after Epiphany (Twelfth Night). These payments were not for a single day, therefore, but for wedding celebrations that continued, apparently, for the whole of the Christmas season. The kings of arms in this list would be well known at Court, and many of the rest were royal minstrels, including two trumpeters, the waferer of the Prince of Wales (perhaps Reginald, or his predecessor) and four royal *vigiles*. John or Janinus the luter was at that time in the household of the Prince, as were Lambyn Clay (a trumpeter) and John de Cressy; John Drake was the king's waferer, Baudettus a royal taborer, and Hamon Lestivour (bagpiper), a minstrel of the Keeper of the Wardrobe;[72] Martinettus was taborer to the king's younger sons, Thomas and Edmund. Several other minstrels in the list may have been royal minstrels but identification is uncertain. One would expect the Count of Holland's own minstrels to appear in this list, too, and this may be the reason for the high rewards given to the unidentified John and Conute, Grisecote, Visage and Magote near the top of the list. Other minstrels came from the household of various named nobles, and the 'various minstrels' at the bottom of the list were probably employed by less important nobles and gentlemen.

---

[70] BL Add MS 7965 (25 Ed I), fol. 52r (cal. SM II, 16–17). The count's alliance with the French had recently made the ports of Holland, especially Middleburgh, unavailable to English wool merchants: see Tout, *Place of the Reign*, 244 and 260.

[71] These various unnamed minstrels were presumably rewarded with less money than the others, i.e. less than 10s 0d each. The sum of 46s 8d represents seven minstrels at 6s 8d (half a mark) or, less probably, 14 minstrels at 3s 4d.

[72] Bullock-Davies, *Register*, 92–3. The Keeper was Master John de Drokensford.

All the nobles and others whose minstrels were rewarded would have been present at the celebrations.

The naming of entertainers called Grisecote, Visage and Magote gives a rare window onto a dramatic performance, for they were evidently actors or mimes. Southworth identifies them as Greycoat, Face or Mask, and Maggot: the elderly cuckold figure, the girl, and her young lover.[73] The performance presumably included instrumental and/or vocal music, as it is described as 'minstrelsy'. Indeed, they may have been three of the count's minstrels, identified here by their dramatic roles and evidently not known to the accounting clerk.

It would not be surprising to find minstrels performing drama – they were, after all, professional performers – and it may be that 'minstrelsy' covers dramatic performance more often than we could know. A rare record of acting by the royal minstrels uses unequivocal terminology:[74]

> To King Capiny, John de Cressy and other minstrels performing miracle plays and making their minstrelsies before the queen, of the queen's gift, by the hands of Guillotus de Psalterio, 29 May (35 Ed I) [1307] 40s 0d

Ludens is the word for a player of games or an actor, so there is no doubt that the minstrels were acting in a dramatic event. The phrase 'facientibus menestralcias suas' suggests that there was instrumental or vocal minstrelsy as well, either in the drama or as a separate part of the entertainment.[75] The term *miracula* could refer to almost any kind of religious drama. The date does not help us, for Monday 29 May 1307 was not a special occasion, merely the day following the first Sunday after Trinity. The play was probably what we should now call a 'saint play', showing the life and works of a particular saint during his or her lifetime.[76]

Edward III's sister Eleanor gave £20 to minstrels who played to her on the day of her wedding to the Count of Guelderland on (probably) 20 May 6 Ed III (1332).[77] The king and queen were not present on that occasion, but they were at the Tower of London on 14 August 1342 when their son Lionel of Antwerp married Elizabeth de Burgh, daughter of the Earl of Ulster. Lionel was not quite four years old at the time, but even so the celebrations must have been quite extensive: Libkin the piper and his companions – presumably all royal minstrels, but we do not know how many – were

---

[73] Southworth, *English Medieval Minstrel*, 81–2.

[74] TNA E101.370.16 (35 Ed I–1 Ed II), fol. 13v (cal. SM II, 63): 'Regi Capiny, Johanni de Cressy et aliis menestrallis ludentibus miracula et facientibus menestralcias suas coram Regina de dono Regine per manus Guilloti de Psalterio xl s.'.

[75] For the use of music in vernacular saint plays and miracle plays, see Rastall, *Minstrels Playing*, especially Part 2. This payment was made less than six weeks before the death of Edward I, who was by then very ill although still pursuing his Scottish campaign.

[76] This was a matter of historical fact for the medieval man or woman. A biblical play is also a possibility, but perhaps less likely. For discussion of medieval dramatic *genres*, see Alan Knight, *Aspects of Genre* (1983) and Rastall, *The Heaven Singing*, 2–10.

[77] TNA E101.386.7, fol. 7v, and BL Add MS 38006, 8v (both 6 Ed III) (cal. SM II, 89). Further on Princess Eleanor's journey to Guelderland, and Margaret Tudor's journey to Scotland, see Chapter 8.

rewarded with the sum of 20 marks (£13 6s 8d).[78] Later weddings in that reign saw similar sums paid to the minstrels and heralds: John, Duke of Brittany, disbursed £20 to minstrels on the day of his marriage to the king's daughter Mary in the summer of 1361 (35 Ed III), and a few years later the king paid out £100 to minstrels present at the marriage of his daughter Isabella to Enguerrand de Coucy.[79]

Henry IV's daughter Blanche gave £26 13s 4d (40 marks) to minstrels who played at the celebrations of her wedding to Ludwig, son of Ruprecht, King of the Romans and Count Palatine of the Rhine, on 6 July 1402 (2 Hen IV). The heralds and minstrels concerned are named as those of the King of the Romans, the Archbishop of Cologne, and other nobles.[80]

These are large sums of money. Moreover, it is likely that the bridegroom in each case also rewarded entertainers, so that the total given to minstrels and others was a small fortune. Of course, it had to be shared out among many individuals, but even so the individual shares would be considerable.

Another of Henry IV's daughters, Philippa, married King Erik IX of Denmark on 26 October 1406 (8 Hen IV). No record of rewards survives, but the accounts show that new liveries were given to the queen's minstrels for the occasion: William Bingley (a piper), Walter Lynne, William Algode (piper), John Trumpington, Walter Aleyn, Richard (trumpeter), John Beauchamp and another John, who was a harper.[81] Although we do not know what most of these played, the identification of a trumpeter, two pipers and a harper shows that both loud and still minstrelsy were heard. As a queen's household would not normally include loud minstrels, and not as many as eight minstrels in all, the king apparently transferred some from his own household to hers for the occasion. William Bingley, Walter Lynne and Richard the trumpeter are all known to have been in the king's household previously.

Similar resources might be put towards the celebration of the wedding of a favoured noble. 34 Ed I was an unusually expensive year, not least because of three notable events in late May 1306, which between them caused a total of £170 10s 8d to be given in rewards. The first of these was the Pentecost feast on 22 May, when the future Edward II was knighted. A total of 200 marks (£133 6s 8d) was distributed on that occasion. This event was followed by the weddings of two favoured nobles. On 25 May 1306 Earl Warenne married Joan, daughter of the Count of Bar; and the following day, 26 May 1306, the younger Hugh le Despenser married Eleanor, daughter of the Earl of Gloucester, in the king's chapel at Westminster.[82] Gifts to minstrels on these two occasions are combined in a single item in the accounts, which show that £37 4s 0d was given to Richard de Whiteacre, harper, Richard de Leyland, harper, and other minstrels. These harpers are known from the Pentecost list, but do not

---

[78] TNA E36.204 (16–18 Ed III), fol. 85r (cal. SM II, 104). Lionel's marriage is usually dated to 9 September 1342.

[79] Devon, *Issues*, 175 and 188. Devon lists the latter payment under 40 Ed III, which would be 1366, but Fryde, *Handbook*, 39, gives 27 July 1365 as the date of the wedding.

[80] TNA E101.404.11 (2 Hen IV), m. 1 (cal. SM II, 120).

[81] TNA E101.406.10 (8 Hen IV), fol. 3 (cal. SM II, 122).

[82] TNA E101.369.11 (34 Ed I), fol. 96r (cal. SM II, 45).

appear to have been royal servants: probably they were servants of Earl Warenne and Lord Despenser, or perhaps of the Count of Bar and the Earl of Gloucester. The named minstrels were probably those to whom the money was given for distribution, one on each day. The gifts are rather smaller than for the royal weddings discussed above, but still substantial – an average of £18 12s od per wedding.

Although more might be given for minstrelsy at a royal wedding, then, £20 or so seems to be the sum suitable for the wedding of a noble. Edward II gave £20 when his favourite Piers Gaveston, newly created Earl of Cornwall, was married at Berkhamstead on 1 November 1307 (All Saints' Day, 1 Ed II). All Saints' was a feast-day anyway, so the celebration of Gaveston's marriage did not stand alone. The record seems careful not to give the wedding primacy, mentioning the feast of All Saints first; and it also seems careful to mention that the gift was not only from the king but from his council as well. This is apparently a unique wording:[83]

> Minstrels: In money given on the third of November by the king himself and his Council to various minstrels making their minstrelsy before the same king on the feast of All Saints, that is, on the day of the wedding of the Earl of Cornwall, by the hand of William of Balliol, received at Berkhamstead on the aforesaid third day of November, at the meeting of the same, on behalf of the said king £20.

At a more domestic level, the king's minstrels played at the wedding of one of the queen's damsels. The queen gave 26s 8d (two marks) to [John] Mauprine and his companions, minstrels of the king, for making their minstrelsy on the day that Robert de Maule married Helen, a damsel of the queen's chamber, at Barlings on 14 July 5 Ed III (1331).[84]

Financial records of weddings and other celebratory events do not always say how many constituent events took place. Some marriages were celebrated not only with a banquet but a tournament or joust as well. Edward III celebrated his marriage to Philippa of Hainault in January 1328 with a three-week festival, an unusually extended celebration that reflected Edward's enthusiasm for martial exercise. Philippa herself patronised tournaments of all sorts, and attended. Barker and Barber note that it was[85]

> no coincidence that there was a remarkable growth in pageantry in Edward's reign; colourful costumes, processions of participants, fantastic themes, role-playing and play-acting became part and parcel of the fourteenth-century joust and tournament.

---

[83] TNA E101.373.15 (1 Ed II), fol. 21r (cal. SM II, 65): 'Menestralli: Tercio die Novembris in denariis datis per ipsum Regem et consilium suum diversis menestrallis facientibus menestralciam suam coram eodem Rege in festo Omnium Sanctorum videlicet die nupciarum Comitis Cornubie per manus Willelmi de Baillol recipient' apud Berkhamstede predicto tertio die Novembris ad conferend' eisdem ex parte dicti Regis xx li.'.

[84] Rylands 235 (5 Ed III), fol. 18v (cal. SM II, 87).

[85] Barber and Barker, *Tournaments*, 32.

With this increased pageantry, theatricalism and attendant expenditure there was obviously an increased demand for and use of minstrelsy, especially of trumpets but also of other instruments.

In his later years Edward III was forced to retrench because of the cost of war, but for much of his reign he invested lavishly on jousts, probably considering the expenditure to be money well spent for the political prestige. When Edward held a round table at Windsor in 1358 it cost him £32 to have the event proclaimed by his heralds in Scotland, the Low Countries, Germany and France.[86] It is therefore not surprising that, even after he had to cut down this expenditure, he mounted an important jousting for the marriage on 19 May 1359 of his son John of Gaunt to the heiress Blanche of Lancaster.[87] In the following reign Richard II held jousts at Westminster to celebrate his marriage to Anne of Bohemia and her coronation (1382).

Lancastrian monarchs used jousts less, although some of them thought such events politically useful. Henry IV held jousts; Henry V thought them a waste of money that he badly needed for other purposes, and did not hold a tournament even for his marriage to Katherine of Valois in 1420; and Henry VI had no taste for it. Edward IV, as an athletic young man, enjoyed jousting. But he, like his brother Richard, was embroiled in civil war; and Henry VII, too, had other matters to deal with. Only with the more settled reign of the sport-loving Henry VIII did the pageantry and athleticism of tournaments re-emerge fully in England.

Purification

Another occasional and semi-domestic celebration at which the royal minstrels performed was that of purification, the *relevatio* after childbirth. The main event of the day was the service of thanksgiving, which derived from the Jewish rite of purification set out in Leviticus 12/1–8. In this, offerings were made in the Temple on the fortieth day after childbirth. The Christian version showed some important differences, with the emphasis on thanksgiving rather than purification.[88] There is no direct evidence that music other than plainsong psalms and antiphons was heard, but any polyphony would be sung by the chapel clerks. Nor is there any evidence of minstrelsy during the service, but there was always minstrelsy at the banquet that followed.

When Queen Eleanor of Castile celebrated her *relevatio* at Rhuddlan castle after the birth of Princess Elizabeth in August 1282 (10 Ed I), she gave £10 to various minstrels (*diversis menestrallis*) and 12d to an actor (or perhaps storyteller – *histrio*).[89] The banquet was a relatively quiet affair, principally for the lady herself and her attendant women: etiquette required the king not to be present. The minstrels' reward

---

[86] Barber and Barker, *Tournaments*, 35.

[87] Edward held a round table at Windsor to launch the Calais campaign, and several more (in 1344) to celebrate his victory, with special liveries for the minstrels, among others. See Barber and Barker, *Tournaments*, 34 f.

[88] The medieval service is in the *Manuale ad usum ecclesie Sarisburiensis*, 43–4. For a brief history of the service, see Rastall, *The Heaven Singing*, 258–60.

[89] TNA C47.3.18, m. 4, printed in *REED Wales*, 288.

is large enough to suggest that they attended her in the procession to and from the service of purification, as well as providing entertainment at the banquet.

Two celebrations of the *relevatio* of Philippa of Hainault are recorded. After the birth of William of Hatfield, Roger the trumpeter and other minstrels performed at the feast on 10 March 1337 (11 Ed III) and were rewarded with £10. This was probably one of the royal trumpeters named Roger, coming to Hatfield with the king. Although the king was probably not present in the same room as the queen, any noble standing in for him would require a trumpet for his entry to the feast. On a later occasion, the queen's *relevatio* feast at Antwerp on 6 January 1339 (12 Ed III) after the birth of Lionel of Antwerp, the king rewarded Ludkin the piper and other minstrels of the Emperor and the dukes of Brabant and Guelderland with £13 10s. 0d. Apparently there were no trumpets on this occasion.[90]

For the purification celebrations of Elizabeth Woodville following the birth of Princess Elizabeth of York on 11 February 1466 (5 Ed IV) there is an eye-witness account.[91] This states that in the processions to and from the Abbey – that is, starting and finishing in Westminster Hall – twenty-four heralds and pursuivants were preceded by the trumpeters, pipers and string-minstrels.[92] The loud winds probably announced the queen's presence while the still minstrels performed as the procession moved forward.

At the dinner, the queen sat by herself in state, attended by the ladies of her family and various noblewomen. The king was represented by a senior lord, probably the earl of Warwick. This lord, sitting in a different room from the queen, was served as if he were the king, and it was in this room that the normal minstrelsy of trumpets, other loud wind and still entertainment-music was performed. Whether there was any minstrelsy in the queen's room during the dinner we are not told: but afterwards there was dancing, probably some other instrumental music, and singing by the king's choir.[93]

There was minstrelsy at the purification of certain noblewomen, too. On 20 February 1312 (5 Ed II) occurred the churching of the Countess of Cornwall:[94]

---

[90] Calendars in SM II, 95 and 101. According to Fryde *et al.*, *Handbook*, 39, William of Hatfield (who died in boyhood) was born in 1336: but 40 days before 10 March 1337 would be 29 January, so he was probably born in January 1337, new style. Lionel of Antwerp was born on 29 November 1338 (Fryde *et al.*, *Handbook*, 39): if that is correct, the *relevatio* on 6 January 1339 (perhaps chosen because it was Epiphany?) was only 37 days after the birth.

[91] The date of these celebrations is unknown, but it was apparently in late March.

[92] There were also 42 singers of the king's chapel, which suggests the possibility of polyphony: Leo of Rozmital, *Travels*, 45–6; MacGibbon, *Elizabeth Woodville*, 56.

[93] Leo of Rozmital, *Travels*, 46–7; MacGibbon, *Elizabeth Woodville*, 57.

[94] BL Cotton MS Nero C viii (3–5 Ed II), fol. 84v (cal. SM II, 71): 'Rex Robertus et alii menestralli: Regi Roberto et aliis menestrallis diversis facientibus menestralcias suas coram Rege et aliis magnatibus in dominiis fratrum minorum Eboraci existentibus die purificationis domine Margarete Comitisse Cornubie de dono ipsius Regis per manus dicti Regis Roberti recipientis denarios ad participandum inter eosdem apud Eboracum xx die Februarii xl marc'.'.

> King Robert and other minstrels: To King Robert and various other minstrels making their minstrelsies before the king and other nobles in the house of the Friars Minor of York, being there on the day of the purification of the Lady Margaret, Countess of Cornwall, of the gift of the same king by the hands of the said King Robert, receiving money to divide between them at York, 20 February [1312]
> 40 marks

Forty marks (£26 13s 4d) is a large gift, but then the countess was the wife of Piers Gaveston, the king's favourite. On a day in April 1335 (9 Ed III) the king gave 10 marks (£6 13s 4d) to various minstrels on the occasion of the purification of the countess of Oxford, almost certainly at Canterbury.[95]

The installation of a prelate

There is evidence for a tradition of minstrelsy at the installation-feasts of senior churchmen: but much of this comes from Thomas Warton and, as Andrew Taylor notes in Chapter 11, his evidence must be viewed with caution. The occasions Warton noted are:

> 1309 The installation-feast of abbot Ralph of St Augustine's, Canterbury. The sum of 70s 0d was given to minstrels, although the number is not stated;[96]

> 1374 The feast of bishop Alwyn at St Swithin's, Winchester:[97]

> 'At the feast of Bishop Alwyn ... And during the celebrations in the hall of the priory six minstrels, together with four harpers, made their minstrelsies ...';

> 1432 The consecration of prior John of Maxstoke. Two minstrels had come from Coventry, some 10 miles away, and were rewarded with 12d.[98]

Information on two later enthronement feasts comes from other sources and can probably be taken at face value:

> 1465 Music was to be supplied by church singers at the enthronement feast of archbishop Nevill of York. At the first course 'The ministers of the Churche doth after the old custome, in syngyng of some proper or godly Caroll', and they were to sing again, 'solemnly', at the serving of the second course, and also after the saying of Grace.[99] Here is an element, supplied by devotional or other improving texts, that could be expected at a celebration for a prince of the Church. No minstrelsy is mentioned.

---

[95] BL Cotton MS Nero C viii (8–11 Ed III), fol. 270v (cal. SM II, 93).

[96] Warton, *History*, II, 96.

[97] Warton, *History*, III, 118: 'In festo Alwyni episcopi ... Et durante pietancia in aula conventus sex ministralli, cum quatuor citharisatoribus, faciebant ministralcias suas'.

[98] Warton, *History*, II, 98: 'Dat' duobus mimis de Coventry in die consecrationis prioris xij d.'.

[99] Leland, *Collectanea*, VI, 9, 11 and 13. This description is set out as directions for the proper ordering of the feast.

1505 The enthronement feast of archbishop Warham of Canterbury on 9 March 1505 featured 'subtelties' at each course, and one of these included a choir with singing-men in surplices: here too the texts sung were presumably devotional in character.[100] On this occasion we know that the king's minstrels were rewarded, presumably for their entertainment at the feast:[101]

> Item paid to the kyng*is* mynstrell*es* at the enstallyng of the lorde archiebisshop of Caunte*r*bury vj s. viij d [half a mark]

The royal minstrels were involved in a wide range of domestic, civic and national activities, and at various lower levels they and other minstrels performed for a similar range of occasions. Some of these – the installation of a prelate, or the civic entry of a great magnate, for instance – can be seen as a close reflection of life at the highest level; others, such as the civic minstrels' street performances for the entertainment of the citizens, is a less obvious parallel to the royal life-style.[102] The full range of entertainment and its purpose certainly encompasses everything between the most informal minstrelsy for relaxation and dancing to music-making of the most formal and ceremonial nature. Likewise, a wide range of expenditure on minstrelsy is shown, from the royal occasions to the civic ceremonial of the smaller and less wealthy communities (see the case of Barnstaple, for instance, in Chapter 6). It is also clear that, however affluent or otherwise a community might be, minstrelsy was indispensable to all levels of society.

---

[100] Leland, *Collectanea*, VI, 24.

[101] *REED Kent: Diocese of Canterbury*, I, 99: accounts of the chamberlains of Canterbury, 1504/5.

[102] For the town waits' public performances, see p. 156.

5
Minstrelsy in noble and ecclesiastical households

The domestic context

Any householder is the head of a household, whatever its size. A small household may have little or no structure, but it will have financial or bartering transactions, and the building must be maintained. If a household employs servants there are wages to be paid, and at a certain size of the household some records are needed. Records may be secretarial or financial, and they depend on someone in the household (or someone brought in from outside) being literate and numerate.

The households that concern us here are all of a considerable size. The king's household usually comprised around four hundred people, and some noble households approached the king's in size.[1] In 4 Ed III the king gave liveries to a total of 669 persons,[2] who would include members of dependent households and some servants who were not permanent members of any household. Many noble households supported minstrels – this livery-list named nineteen, as well as a waferer and three *vigiles* – and these roughly divide into three categories. First, the minstrels regularly employed by the head of the household, taking wages and annual fees, and normally being granted a livery in exchange for their allegiance to the principal; and some local minstrels employed, perhaps regularly, on an *ad hoc* basis. Second, the minstrels of important visitors, treated as honoured members of the visiting household: they normally performed during their visit, and would be rewarded accordingly. Third, some independent minstrels, or liveried minstrels not travelling with their patron or employer, would seek hospitality. These might be sent away without performing, perhaps receiving a small sum in compensation; or they might be allowed to perform, in which case they would be rewarded with money and a meal. All three categories of minstrel appear in the household accounts, although one cannot always identify the category to which a particular minstrel belonged.

We have so far discussed only royal households, but both the secular and the ecclesiastical nobility maintained households that included minstrels. Some bishops and abbots kept at least one still minstrel as a personal household servant, and many

---

[1] Given-Wilson, *Royal Household*, 278–9.
[2] TNA E101.385.4 (Keeper's livery roll, 4 Ed III), cal. SM II, 86. Cited in Tout, *Chapters*, II, 414, n. 1, as EA385.4.

gave rewards to visiting minstrels. Religious houses also gave rewards to various kinds of entertainer: not only was entertainment often welcome, especially at the major feasts and patronal festivals, but abbeys and priories formed a different type of household, that had a duty of hospitality even greater than that of secular households. Like the secular households, ecclesiastical households supported minstrels of all the three categories just identified.

Some comment is needed here about terminology. In the royal households minstrels were normally recorded as *ministralli* unless a more precise word was used, such as *trumpator* or *citharista* (harper). In records generally this is one end of a spectrum comprising *ministrallus* – *histrio* – *mimus*, with secular households and towns commonly using *ministrallus*, but with *histrio* and to some extent *mimus* appearing.[3] The precise use depends on the particular institution, however, and both *histrio* and *mimus* could be used for a singer or instrumentalist making minstrelsy. In records of conventual houses, on the other hand, *mimus* is more common than elsewhere, while *histrio* is probably the word most often used for a minstrel, *ministrallus* rather less so.

Although usage varied between institutions, it is clear that within any one institution the tradition of using particular terms could be strong. The case of Beverley, with its use of *spiculator*, is particularly telling (see Chapter 7), but the records of selected towns in Kent, for instance, show that some used *ministrallus*, some *histrio* and some *mimus* as the norm. Dover and Hythe used *ministrallus/ministrellus* in the Latin accounts, Sandwich used *histrio* in some years and *ministrallus* in others, and Lydd used *mimus* (but 'minstrell' in English, as elsewhere). Several towns used two or more terms, sometimes in discrete years and sometimes within the records for a particular year. This almost certainly indicates the work of different individual scribes, and future work on minstrels in the records must take account of this possibility in working out the Latin equivalents to 'minstrel'.[4]

Secular households

The household of the Black Prince, c. 1337–67

Edward of Woodstock, the Black Prince, was Edward III's eldest son, born in June 1330. During his childhood, his household cannot have been large. Information is mainly lacking for the first few years of the prince's life, and is not plentiful for any of it. There are some accounts for his household, and the prince's registers survive for

---

3   Rastall, 'Minstrels and players', 87–9. The last two might suggest story-telling and gesture, respectively, but players in the dramatic sense are normally signified by *lusor, ludator* or *ludens*. Story-tellers and reciters appear in the records as *jestour/gestour/geyster, rymour* or *disour*.

4   For examples of scribal individuality in this respect, see Chapter 6, Table 11 (on Barnstaple), and Chapter 7 concerning Beverley. Further on this problem see Meredith, 'Professional travelling players', *passim*, and Rastall, 'Minstrels and players', esp. 85–9.

the periods 1346–8 and 1351–65.[5] These latter record the prince's written instructions to his officers, and are therefore some of the records of the household, so it is possible to piece together part of the prince's minstrel-establishment. The prince employed a bagpiper named Morlanus in his household from 8 Ed III until 12 Ed III, probably the king's cornemuser John de Morleyns, temporarily transferred.[6] In 12 Ed III (1338–9) his household also included a *vigilis* named Roger and a waferer named Thomas; and in 13 or 14 Ed III these were joined by a fiddler (Thomas) and an organist (Nicholas).[7] By the age of fourteen or fifteen at the latest, in the mid-1340s, the prince employed two trumpeters – John Cliff and Ralph Dexestre in 18 Ed III (1344–5), Dexestre and John Martin thereafter.[8] By 1352 the prince's household was large enough to sustain servants *qui non sunt*, and he was employing four pipers of the Count of Eu.[9] He also employed two still minstrels (and sometimes a *gestour*), two *vigilatores* and a waferer (who is not known for minstrelsy).

Several very expensive instruments were provided by the Black Prince for his minstrels.[10] Two silver trumpets paid for on 8 November 1346 were to be played by Dexestre and Martin. The payment was ordered in early November 1346, but the instruments may have been delivered before the campaign that ended with the battle of Crécy on 26 August that year. The cost of these trumpets, 19 marks (£12 13s 4d), is in marked contrast to that of the latten trumpet that was repaired at the same time (4s 0d)[11] or the trumpet of copper (*de cuprio*) for which John de Cateloyne was given a mark (13s 4d) in 31 Ed I.[12]

---

[5] The Wardrobe accounts for the prince's household are calendared in SM II, 96–109, *passim*; the prince's registers are transcribed in *Black Prince*.

[6] E101.388.12 (12 Ed III). As already noted in Chapter 3, the prince was probably without a 'still' minstrel when he rewarded a minstrel of Schareshull.

[7] E101.388.12 (Keeper's roll of winter liveries, household of the Black Prince, 12 Ed III, cal. SM II, 98); E101.389.6 (roll of expenses, household of the Black Prince, 14 Ed III, cal. SM II, 99). There is no evidence of the *vigilis* or waferer making minstrelsy.

[8] E101.390.3 (16–18 Ed I), m. 3, and BL Harley MS 4304 (13–18 Ed III), both cal. SM II, 106. See also MERH, 21 (where regnal years refer to Wardrobe-book entries, other dates to the prince's register). It was not unusual for a royal teenager to employ trumpeters. Thomas of Brotherton was just six years old when his two trumpeters played at the Pentecost feast of 1306: and Thomas was not even the king's eldest son, as Edward of Woodstock was.

[9] *Black Prince*, IV, 73. Eu was a Norman county, owing allegiance to England until the loss of Normandy in the thirteenth century. John of Artois, Count of Eu 1352–87, seems to have been a friend of the Black Prince: after the count's capture at the battle of Poitiers (1356) the prince bought his ransom.

[10] In the accounts of the Black Prince searched for the present work, no records were found of gifts for the buying of instruments: this does not, of course, mean that the prince did not make such gifts.

[11] *Black Prince*, I, 30. The trumpets were paid for by the prince's wardrobe, so they were effectively part of the prince's jewels and plate. Latten is an alloy of copper, tin and zinc, typically beaten into thin sheets for manufacturing purposes.

[12] E101.363.18, fol. 22v, cited by Bullock-Davies, *Menestrellorum Multitudo*, 119. Janinus's trumpet was presumably not of pure copper but an alloy – probably brass, containing zinc, lead or tin. For copper alloys see Szarmach, *Medieval England*, 510.

Nine years after their purchase in 1346 the silver trumpets were still in use, and the prince had bought some other very expensive instruments:[13]

> Order ... to discharge ... of two silver trumpets given to Ralph Dexestre and John Martyn respectively, and of four pipes, silver-gilt and enamelled, which the prince has given to the four minstrels sent to him by the Count of Eu, and of a cornemuse, a pipe, and a tabor, silver-gilt and enamelled, which the prince has given to his own minstrels ... [7 September 1355]

'Has given to' probably means 'delivered into the keeping of' rather than 'given into the ownership of'. Such instruments would be well outside the financial reach of the minstrels and presumably remained the prince's property. This order was made at Plymouth when the prince was *en route* for his duchy of Aquitaine, no doubt part of a 'conspicuous consumption' intended to demonstrate his magnificence as a powerful ruling prince.

A gift of £6 13s 4d (10 marks) from the prince to Jakelyn the piper on 18 May 1358 was to help towards making him a new pipe. Again, the sum is much larger than seems necessary, suggesting a fine set of bagpipes at least, with expensive decorations.[14] Other payments for instruments suggest more routine dealings. On 12 August 1352 a drum was bought for the prince's minstrel John, and on 13 November that year two pouches for keeping pipes in were delivered to two of his minstrels.

The gift to Jakelyn and a gift to Zevlyn the piper towards buying a hackney were recorded shortly before the prince's payment of £100 to heralds and minstrels at the jousts at Windsor, so the gifts may have been intended to prepare them for their duties on that occasion.[15] The payment to Zevlyn is only one of several recording the prince's provision of horses for his servants: like all such employers, the prince was concerned that his household be appropriately mounted and that adequate transport be available for travelling. On 19 April 1352 he gave two horses to four French minstrels (probably those of the Count of Eu), three cart-horses to two German minstrels, two cart-horses to four minstrels of Bruges (*Burgilensibus*), and a cart-horse each to several servants, including Ralph, trumpeter, and Thomas, waferer;[16] on 5 November that year he gave saddles to three of his minstrels;[17] on 14 March 1353 he made a gift of 40s 0d (3 marks) to enable Ralph, trumpeter, to buy himself a horse;[18] and the gift to Zevlyn on 18 May 1358 was of 66s 8d (5 marks) towards the purchase of a hackney.[19]

Some of these horses may have been needed in time of war. Although the records for equipping his minstrels as soldiers are mainly missing, in addition to those

---

[13] *Black Prince*, IV, 73 and 157.

[14] *Black Prince*, IV, 251.

[15] This last name is spelled Zeulyn, but the man's likely identity suggests that the U is consonantal.

[16] *Black Prince*, IV, 71.

[17] *Ibid.*, 72.

[18] *Ibid.*, 101.

[19] *Ibid.*, 251.

already discussed we can note that Hans and Soz, described as the prince's minstrels, were given three-quarters of a rayed cloth on 11 May 1352 in order to make robes for themselves, and on 25 July that year were equipped with two habergeons; and that on 6 March 1358 the items given out at the Wardrobe on the prince's orders included a 'ketilhat' to Jakelot, piper.[20]

Gifts of money made by the prince to his own minstrels could be very generous.[21] Those for specific purposes (in addition to those already noted) include the huge sum of £26 13s 4d (40 marks) given to the pipers Jakelyn and Ulyn on 5 November 1361 'to clear their debt for a time'.[22] The size of these debts is reminiscent of the sums owed to minstrels by Edward I and Edward III, and perhaps their debts – and the expectation that they would soon be in debt again – were due to the prince's failure to keep up with their wages and fees.

Most money gifts from the prince were for unspecified purposes. They are listed briefly here in order to provide the names, with their variants, of the prince's minstrels:

24 September 1353: 20s 0d to Hankyn, piper.
7 September 1355: 20s 0d to Ralph, trumpeter (while waiting to set sail for Aquitaine, as already noted).
?17 June 1355: 13s 4d (1 mark) to Hankyn, piper.
1 July 1355: 20s 0d to John, waferer; 40s 0d (£2) each to two of the prince's minstrels (unnamed).
Post-Michaelmas 1355: 100s 0d (£5) to Jakelyn, piper.
14 September 1358: 40s 0d (£2) to John Alisaundre, *rymour*, and 20s 0d (£1) to the minstrel Adam Unton. (Alisaundre was the king's rymer, 31–8 Ed III.)
10 March 1359: 66s 8d (5 marks) to Ulyn, piper.
22 October 1359: 66s 8d (5 marks) to Jakelyn, piper.
7 July 1361: £11 13s 4d to Willyn, piper; £16 13s 4d (25 marks) to Jakelyn, piper; and £9 6s 8d (14 marks, presumably 2 marks each) to seven of the prince's minstrels (not named).
18 March 1362 (payment recorded 8 November 1362): £6 13s 4d (10 marks) to Jakelyn, piper, Yevelyn, piper, and Conutz, piper.
26 March 1362: 66s 8d (5 marks) to Ulyn and Jakelyn.
7 February 1363: 10 marks to Jevelyn, the prince's piper.

Jakelyn seems distinct from Ulyn and Willyn (who were perhaps the same man), and from Yevelyn, Jevelyn and Zeulyn/Zevlyn (also probably one man).[23]

Some or all of these gifts were for minstrelsy on special occasions, and the prince's gifts to visiting minstrels were probably for the same purpose. In 1358 he gave £10 (15

---

[20] Ibid., 245. The kettle-hat was the wide-brimmed helmet, made of steel or leather, worn by archers and men-at-arms.

[21] For the years for which the prince's register includes instructions to the auditors of his accounts, the register presumably contains records of all his gifts.

[22] For gifts to the prince's minstrels, see *Black Prince*, III, 317; and *Black Prince*, IV, 101, 158, 161, 163, 167 (two items), 283, 326, 388 f (three items), 402, 428, 475 and 486.

[23] It is just possible that at least one of these three was later employed by John of Aragon and named in 1388 as Everlin (a shawmist) and his two companions. See Gómez, 'Minstrel schools', 214.

marks) to Cremeryak and his nine companions, minstrels of Duke William; £6 13s 4d (10 marks) to the minstrels of Queen Philippa; and, as previously noted, £100 (150 marks) to the heralds and minstrels at the jousts at Windsor.[24] The following year he gave 60s od (£3) to three pipers of the duke of Lancaster (Henry of Grosmont, a great-grandson of Henry III).[25] The first and last of these work out at £1 per minstrel, a generous reward.

These sums must reflect in each case the importance of the occasion and the level of service given, as well as the status of the patrons involved. The jousts at Windsor were a special Round Table celebration to mark the king's successes in Scotland and France, the captured French king (Jean II) and the previously captured King of Scots (David II, the king's brother-in-law) both being present. William, Duke of Bavaria, Count of Holland and Count of Hainault, was married to Matilda of Lancaster, daughter and co-heir of Henry of Grosmont, Earl of Lancaster. John of Gaunt married her younger sister Blanche on 19 May that year.

Finally, as we saw in Chapter 3, the prince made provision for his servants on retirement or during incapacity, the trumpeter Gilbert Stakford being admitted in 1364 to the convent of St Michael's Mount.

The Lancaster households, 1372–99

John of Gaunt, earl of Lancaster from 1361 and created duke the following year, was one of the most powerful men of his time. After the death of the Black Prince in 1376 his position was second only to that of the king.[26] As the son and (after the death of Edward III the following year) uncle of kings, Gaunt had the position to emulate the king's household, which he did in both size and expenditure: and this can be seen in the records of the Lancaster household, as it can in those of the Black Prince.

The surviving registers of John of Gaunt date from 1371–5 and 1379–83, when he was already at his most powerful.[27] Like those of his eldest brother, they do not give a complete picture of minstrelsy in the household, although they provide some useful detail. No daily or classified accounts have survived from John of Gaunt's household, so it is not possible to supplement information derived from the registers.

Gaunt's minstrel-establishment can be pieced together, although not completely. One trumpeter can be identified in an instruction to the duke's receiver in Yorkshire not to pay any fee or wage to John Tyas, one of the duke's minstrels (20 May 1373). Payments to Tyas were renewed, with arrears, on 16 September 1374, presumably on his return to the household after an absence on the duke's

---

[24] *Black Prince*, IV, 251 f; Barber and Barker, *Tournaments*, 34–5.

[25] *Black Prince*, IV, 283.

[26] John of Gaunt succeeded to the earldom of Lancaster in 1361 in right of his wife, Blanche of Lancaster, whom he married in 1359; he was created duke on 13 November 1362.

[27] Armitage-Smith, *John of Gaunt's Register* (for 1372–6) and Lodge and Somerville, *John of Gaunt's Register* (for 1379–83): relevant entries are edited and translated in *REED Staffordshire* (online, accessed November 2019).

business. A record dated 13 January 1380 shows that John Tyas and Piers Cook were then the duke's trumpeters.[28]

Information about pipers is more plentiful. Two of them, named Henry and Roger, were with the duke in Gascony some time before 28 February 1372, when they received arrears of their war-time wages. A series of indentures dated 13 June 1373 concern various servants, including three pipers and a clarioner: they set out, in standard form, the terms of employment of Hans Gough, piper, Smelltes, piper, Henry Hultescrane, piper, and James Sauthe, clarioner.[29] Gough is employed for life, serving the duke in peace and in war and working for him wherever the duke pleases, properly arrayed. He takes the same liveries for his horses as others of his rank, and a penny a day as wages for his groom. He takes 100s 0d (£5) per year from the receipts of the Honour of Leicester as his fee, at Michaelmas and Easter in equal portions. The indentures for the other three are in short form, referring to the same conditions as set out in Gough's.[30] Hultescrane could be the Henry, piper, who was in Gascony in 1372; Smelltes, if that was his surname, could be the Roger, piper, of that time, although this seems less likely.

The three pipers no doubt made up a shawm band, and the clarioner was a specialist military trumpeter. The high-pitched clarion was not a likely instrument to join with the pipers in a shawms-and-trumpet ensemble, but the clarioner may well have played a lower-pitched trumpet as well. Buckingham had been the king's trumpeter during the 1370s, and was not then named as a clarioner.

In June of (probably) 1374 the duke's receiver for the Honour of Leicester was instructed to raise the fees of Gough, Smelltes, Hultescrane and Sauthe from 100s 0d *per annum* to 200s 0d (£10).[31] This was probably to provide a war-time fee, as specified later for John Buckingham. The next year, 1375, apparently on 26 January, payments were made to the band of pipers, named as Henry, Hans, Hankyn and Smelts.[32] Assuming that Henry is Hultescrane and Hans is Gough, Hankyn seems to be a new recruit, perhaps hired to take James Sauthe's place. Hankyn was not a clarioner, however, for a later record describes him as 'piper'. Later records seem to show that four pipers were now usual, even when a clarioner was also present in the household.

There is a gap in the registers between 1376 and 1379. Records resume with a series of indentures for knights and squires, including one, recorded probably on 1 November 1379, for the clarioner John of Buckingham. It is more informative than the earlier indentures, and specifies his 'proper array' in war-time as that of a man-at-arms. Buckingham is required to be in court for the four principal feasts of the year:[33] when he is in court he takes a daily wage of 7½d for himself, his servants and

---

[28] Armitage-Smith, *John of Gaunt's Register*, II, 153–4 and 244.
[29] *Ibid.*, 1 and 859.
[30] The order to the receiver of Leicester to pay these annual sums is in *ibid.*, 219.
[31] *Ibid.*, 219.
[32] *Ibid.*, 298.
[33] These are not named, but the missing one may be St George's day. 'In court' refers to John of Gaunt's court.

his horses, and 12d per day when he is out of court on the duke's business. His annual fee in peace-time is to be 100s 0d (£5) for life, which he takes from the duke's receiver general in equal portions at Michaelmas and Easter; in time of war he takes £10 per annum and such wages as others of his rank take.

By 1379/80 Buckingham was quite a senior royal minstrel. He had served Edward III since 1370, joining the household of Richard II after the old king's death in 1377.[34] His subsequent transfer to John of Gaunt's household was probably a promotion, for the indenture shows that he was to be leader of the minstrels:[35]

> And the said John will commence [sit at the head of] the table of the minstrels of the said king and duke.

Buckingham may have become one of the duke's two trumpeters, although he is described only as 'clarioner'; it is possible that he took James Sauthe's place in a shawm-and-trumpet band (Sauthe having died or retired), although that band now apparently consisted of four pipers and there is no firm evidence that Sauthe was part of that ensemble; it is more likely that he acted only as a clarioner, in a military and heraldic capacity. As the record of him in the king's household in 1 Ric II (1377/8) does not describe him as a clarioner, the question remains open.

The arrangement that gave royal servants both an annual fee and a daily wage was clearly in operation at John of Gaunt's court, and this confirms what appeared to be the case in the king's household earlier. Buckingham's fee was paid by the receiver-general, confirmed by an entry dated 3 January 1380.[36] For many Lancastrian servants the annual fee came from a specific source and was paid by the relevant officer: those for most minstrels were from the Honour of Leicester and were provided by the receiver of that Honour directly. The duke ordered fees for Hans Gough, Smeltes, Henry Hultescrane and James Sauthe in 1373; on 6 November 1379 for Rollekyn, Petrekyn, Henri and Hankyn (the piper previously known: a payment made on 2 January 1380 names him as Hankyn piper); for John Cliff of Coventry on 1 August 1381; for Hankyn Frysh (whose fee was for some reason only 5 marks) on 14 December 1382; and for Claus, nakerer, in 1389.[37] The duke's trumpeters took their fees from the issues of Yorkshire: John Tyes from the Honour of Pickering in

---

[34] Devon, *Issues of Thomas de Brantingham*, 56. Buckingham appears in livery lists from 48 Edward III to 1 Ric I: see E101.397.20 (Keeper's livery roll), m. 23 (28 November 1374), m. 25 (11 December 1375), m. 27 (6 December 1376) and m. 32 (1377/8, probably before Christmas 1377) (All cal. SM II, 116–17).

[35] Lodge and Somerville, *John of Gaunt's Register*, I, 15 (undated, but between 1 November 1379 and 23 June 1380): 'Et comencera le dit Johan la table des ministralx le dit roy et duc'.

[36] Lodge and Somerville, *John of Gaunt's Register*, I, 90.

[37] For Gough, Smeltes, Hultescrane and Sauthe, see Armitage-Smith, *John of Gaunt's Register*, II, 1 and 219; for Rollekyn, Petrekyn, Henry and Hankyn, Lodge and Somerville, *John of Gaunt's Register*, I, 33; for Cliff, *ibid.*, I, 197; for Frysh, *ibid.*, II, 255 and 311; for Claus, CPR, Ric II, vol. 6 (1396–9), 558. Rollekyn and Petrekyn were no doubt two pipers or a piper and a clarioner, but are otherwise unidentifiable; Frysh is probably the Hankyn of earlier records; Claus was presumably retained in the king's service in 1399; Tyes/Tyas is spelled either way in the register.

1373 and 1374, and Tyes and Piers Cook from the Honour of Pontefract in 1379/80, ordered on 3 January 1380.³⁸

Wages, payable by the day, varied according to whether the minstrel was in or out of court and whether it was peace-time or war-time. The register does not record the level of wages of other minstrels, nor their payment except for a few payments in arrears. These last include war-time wages to Henry Piper (£8 0s 1d) and Roger Piper (£6 13s 2d) for their service during the duke's expedition to Gascony in 1372.³⁹ Allowance was made for the servants and horses of the duke's minstrels: the terms of employment of Hans Gough, Smeltes, Henry Hultescrane and James Sauthe in 1373 allow each minstrel such livery for his horses as others of his estate took, and 1d per day as wages for his groom.⁴⁰

The day following the pipers' annuities, 7 November 1379, John of Buckingham's annuity of 100s 0d was confirmed; on the 13th arrears were paid to the trumpeters Tyas and Cook, as already noticed; and on 20 January (1380) an annuity of 100s 0d was recorded for Jacob Bumbepiper. This annuity was also from the revenues of the Honour of Leicester, as was that made on 14 December 1382 to the duke's piper Hankyn Fryssh, who was awarded 5 marks *per annum*.⁴¹ Jacob presumably played the bombard or tenor shawm. Whether he replaced one of the other pipers or not is unknown. These records seem to show that annuities were reviewed and confirmed around the beginning of each calendar year.

Records of liveries are rare, and there is none for cloth-livery to any minstrel. An interesting record appears at the end of a series of commands to the treasurer of the duke's household for the delivery of wine and reimbursement of expenses. The duke had been in Scotland, and was now back at Fulham, apparently preparing for the coming Christmas season:⁴²

> And also deliver to our well-beloved minstrel John Cliff of Coventry a silver scutcheon with a collar [chain] for a minstrel, and a pair of nakers with two chains and a belt, and two silver sticks made for the same nakers.

This item is dated 4 December 1381, the items probably being delivered in time for the Christmas celebrations. A 'coler for a minstrel' was no doubt a less expensive and prestigious neck-chain than those worn by higher-ranking servants and officials; but the scutcheon was of silver, and the nakers, with their silver sticks, were evidently high-quality items, suspended from a belt (*ceyntoure*) by means of two chains.⁴³

---

38 For Tyas, see Armitage-Smith, *John of Gaunt's Register*, II, 153 and 244; for Tyas and Cook, Lodge and Somerville, *John of Gaunt's Register*, I, 49.

39 Armitage-Smith, *John of Gaunt's Register*, II, 21.

40 *Ibid.*, 1.

41 Lodge and Somerville, *John of Gaunt's Register*, II, 255 and 311.

42 Lodge and Somerville, *John of Gaunt's Register*, I, 209: 'Et auxint facez liverer a nostre bien ame ministralle Johan Cliff de Coventre un eschucon dargent ovesque un coler pur un ministral, et un peir de nakers ovesque deux colers et un ceyntoure et deux stykkes dargent faitz pur meismes les nakers'.

43 Evidently *coler* or *colerium* could mean a chain, even when not suspended from the neck (*col*).

John Cliff may have been new to the duke's household: 'well-beloved' (*bien ame*) means only that he was in good standing. In fact, Cliff first appears in the records on 1 August that year, when he was granted an annuity of 100s 0d (£5) per year from the seigneury of Leicester, as paid to others of the duke's minstrels of his rank. There had been a John Cliff among the Black Prince's trumpeters in 18 Ed III (1344/5),[44] but nothing more was heard of him in the existing records. It is unlikely that Gaunt's nakerer was the same man, but perhaps their careers overlapped and the epithet 'of Coventry' distinguished the nakerer from the earlier trumpeter. It is possible that the nakerer was the son of the first John Cliff, working also in a trumpets-and-nakers ensemble.[45] For the sake of clarity we might designate this man John Cliff II.

It is presumably John Cliff II who had joined the king's household by 17 Ric II (1393/4), although he is not listed among the trumpeters nor named as a nakerer.[46] The name appears again in 4 Hen IV among the minstrels of the Prince of Wales (the future Henry V), and John Cliff II remained a royal minstrel to the end of Henry V's reign. He had died or retired by 14 May 1423, as he was not included in the Patent Roll grants to minstrels of that date. If he was born in the early 1360s, becoming John of Gaunt's minstrel as a young man, John Cliff of Coventry would have been aged around 60 at his death or retirement. A third John Cliff was a still minstrel in the king's household from 25 or 26 Hen VI (i.e. around 1447) until well into the following reign: he became Marshal of the Minstrels in 1477, but was dead by 24 July 1482.[47] Thus there were at least three royal minstrels named John Cliff, of whom John of Gaunt's nakerer was the second. They were probably all related.

Like other royal persons, John of Gaunt occasionally provided horses for his servants. Only one record of this has survived in the registers, but it is interesting that the hackney bought for a groom falconer on 26 January 1375 at a cost of 35s 2d was sold to the duke by an unnamed trumpeter – whether his own or another's is not stated.

The register records several gifts from the duke to minstrels, made on occasions which are familiar from the royal Wardrobe books.[48] The major feasts and other celebrations were evidently family affairs. At Candlemas 1375 a gift of £16 13s 4d (25 marks) was made to the minstrels of 'our very dear cousin the Count of Flanders', and also £65 to various heralds, minstrels and other officers of the king, and to the squires and valets of various lords and ladies bringing New Year gifts ('apportants a nous novelles douns'). These sums, which are a small fortune in modern terms,

---

[44] Harley 4304 (13–18 Ed III), fol. 20v (cal. SM II, 106).

[45] Minstrels may have been described as trumpeter or nakerer indiscriminately. The group of two trumpeters and a nakerer being standard, accounting scribes who did not know which member of the group played what instrument perhaps used these terms generically for any member of the group.

[46] E101.403.25 (*temp*. Ric II) (cal. SM II, 117).

[47] E101.404.24 (4–5 Hen IV), *passim* (cal. SM II, 121); CPR, Henry VI (1422–9), I, 102; E101.409.16 (25–6 Hen VI), fol. 35r (cal. SM II, 127); CPR, Edw IV, Edw V, Ric III (1476–85), 22 and 301.

[48] Armitage-Smith, *John of Gaunt's Register*, II, 299 (1375); Lodge and Somerville, *John of Gaunt's Register*, I, 113, 151 and 152 (1380); *ibid*., I, 179 f (1381) and 230 (1382); *ibid*., II, 239 (1382) and 259 (1383).

were evidently normal in the generous and competitive social world of gift-giving in royal circles.

New Year 1380 was celebrated at Kenilworth: the register records gifts to heralds, and then to the minstrels of the duke and his guests:[49]

> And to Hankyn, piper, and his seven companions, our minstrels, and [to] four minstrels of our very dear brother the earl of Cambridge, to each of them, of our gift the same day at Kenilworth, 6s 8d, [total] £4; and to the said Hankyn and eleven minstrels, by the gift of our very dear cousin the earl of Nottingham at Kenilworth the same day, 20s od; and to three minstrels of Sir Baldwyn Freville, of our gift the same day, 20s od; and to a foreign minstrel, being without a *socius*, of our gift the same day at Kenilworth, 3s 4d.

These were substantial, but not exceptional, gifts: 6s 8d (half a mark) each to the duke's eight minstrels and the Earl of Cambridge's four minstrels, and an extra 1s 8d each from the Earl of Nottingham; 6s 8d each to the three minstrels of Sir Baldwin Freville; and 3s 4d (a quarter-mark) to a solo stranger. Presumably it was more convenient for the duke to pay for the gift from the Earl of Nottingham, who presumably repaid him later.

The duke gave 33s 4d (five half-marks) to the minstrels of Sir Robert Beaumanoir of Brittany, who performed before him at the Savoy palace on 20 February 1380. The number of minstrels is not given, but this could represent 6s 8d (half a mark) for each of five minstrels.[50] An occasion of considerable expense for the duke was his daughter Elizabeth's marriage to the Earl of Pembroke at Kenilworth in 1380, when the 'various minstrels making their minstrelsies' received £13 6s 8d (20 marks) between them. This would be an average of half a mark (6s 8d) to each of forty minstrels, although that was probably not how the money was distributed: but clearly it was a large gathering of minstrels.[51]

A series of gifts recorded on 6 March 1381 go back to the New Year, when a mark was given to each of the duke's six minstrels and 'Johan Gybeson le vij^{me}', a curious wording perhaps indicating that Gibson was a newcomer, that he was a minstrel only second to another post in the household, or that he had been absent when the

---

[49] Lodge and Somerville, *John of Gaunt's Register*, I, 113: 'Et a Hankyn piper et sept ses compaignons noz ministralx et quatre ministralx nostre trescher frere le conte de Cantebrig a chescun de eux de nostre doun meisme le jour a Kenilleworth vj.s. viij.d, quatre livres; Et as ditz Hanekyn et unsze ministralx de doun nostre trescher cousin le conte de Notyngham a Kenilleworth meisme le jour vynt soldz; Et a troys ministralx monsire Baudewyn Freville de nostre doun meisme le jour vynt soldz; Et a un estrange ministralle esteant sanz compaignon de nostre doun meisme le jour a Kenileworth troys soldz et quatre deniers'. The earl of Cambridge was Gaunt's younger brother Edmund of Langley (born ?1342), created duke of York in 1385; the earl of Nottingham was John de Mowbray (born c. 1363–5). A 'strange' minstrel is a foreigner – that is, not local and unknown to the company.

[50] Lodge and Somerville, *John of Gaunt's Register*, I, 151.

[51] Ibid., 152.

money was distributed to the others.⁵² Gifts made on 2 January 1381 included payments to a pursuivant of the Earl of Douglas and to 'another minstrel of his' (40s), suggesting that the pursuivant performed as a minstrel.⁵³ At Epiphany the duke rewarded some heralds (100s 0d) and then gave five marks to 'various minstrels of our very dear brother of Cambridge, being with us the same day'.⁵⁴ On 6 February 1381 the earl of Derby (the future Henry IV) married Mary Bohun, daughter of the earl of Hereford: gifts on that occasion included 10 marks to ten minstrels of the king and two marks to four minstrels of the earl of Cambridge.

In 1382, on 7 February, the duke rewarded a minstrel of the King of Scots with 40s (£2). Later that month he rewarded minstrels of the King of the Romans (Richard II's brother-in-law Wenceslas of Bohemia) with £20, and three minstrels of the King of Scots with 60s (£1 each). This is a little over the normal year's expenditure on gifts to minstrels, which was about £20,⁵⁵ but it was in the aftermath of Richard II's marriage to Anne of Bohemia on 20 January, and the total expenditure for that year came to more than four times the normal amount. On the day of the wedding the duke gave £20 to various heralds and 20 marks (£13 6s 8d) to various minstrels; at the jousts at Smithfield that followed the wedding he gave another 20 marks to heralds and £10 to minstrels. The wedding, together with the associated celebrations and hospitality, cost the duke a total of £81 13s 4d in gifts to heralds and minstrels alone.

1383, the last year covered by the registers, was less expensive but still unusually so. The duke gave £10 to heralds and 10 marks to minstrels at the St George's Day celebrations at Windsor, 10 marks to heralds and the same to minstrels at the jousts held at Hertford on May Day, and the same again to heralds and minstrels at jousts held at Chelmsford. In all, this totals £43 6s 8d.

To summarise our knowledge of John of Gaunt's minstrel-establishment, there may have been eight of them in 1380 and seven in 1381.⁵⁶ If we can assume that the duke's need of minstrels remained stable in the period 1371–83, the personnel can tentatively be listed as follows:

Two trumpeters, and a nakerer who may have performed with them;
Three or four pipers, perhaps the group attending a minstrel-school overseas in early 1379;⁵⁷
A clarioner, available for military/heraldic duties, and who perhaps also played
    a larger instrument in joining the pipers to form a shawm-and-trumpet band.

This does indeed number seven or eight minstrels, but it can hardly have been the sum total. It includes no waferer or *vigilis* capable of minstrelsy, but more importantly there are no *bas* minstrels, nor even a taborer to fulfill a need for dance-music. While dances

---

⁵² Ibid., 179–80. Gibson may be the man of that name given some brushwood for fuel on 25 September 1382: Lodge and Somerville, *John of Gaunt's Register*, II, 239.

⁵³ Lodge and Somerville, *John of Gaunt's Register*, I, 180.

⁵⁴ Ibid., 180.

⁵⁵ The duke gave £21 3s 4d in 1380, £18 in 1381, and £20 in 1383.

⁵⁶ Ibid., 113 and 179.

⁵⁷ Safe-conducts were issued on 17 January 1379 for four of the Lancaster minstrels, their three servants and seven horses: Wathey, 'Peace of 1360–1369', 134–5.

might be covered by *haut* instrumentalists, it would be highly unusual if a noble in Gaunt's position in society were to employ so incomplete a minstrel-establishment.

The administration of his lands obliged Gaunt to control minstrelsy and other sections of society, and the fair-time courts by which he regulated minstrelsy at Tutbury and Newcastle under Lyme are discussed in Chapter 10. Later information on the household minstrels of the Lancasters comes from the accounts for the expeditions to Prussia in 1390/1 and 1392/3 made by Henry, earl of Derby, son of John of Gaunt and later king as Henry IV. The earl's household was independent of his father's, and none of his minstrels on these expeditions seems to have come from John of Gaunt's household. In 1390/1 Henry took with him John Brothir and his *socius* Robert Crakill, trumpeters; William Bingley, William de York and William Algood, pipers; and Master John, nakerer. The minstrels on the second expedition were John (?Brothir), Robert Crakill, Thomas Aleyn and Thomas, trumpeters; and John Algood, John Smith and John Aleyn, pipers. At the end of September 1392 all except Thomas returned to England. These minstrels ranked as valets, taking 4d per day, except for the period from 18 August to 22 October 1390, when they took 6d as war-time wages.[58]

Henry therefore had no still minstrelsy at his court, a lack which he made good with many gifts to local minstrels. Most items in the accounts do not record the type of minstrelsy concerned, but on three occasions he was entertained by fiddlers. Three of them received 12s 8d for making their minstrelsy before the earl on Christmas Day, 1390; two fiddlers received three Prussian marks for attending him for six days in February 1391;[59] and Henry gave 13s 4d to three fiddlers who entertained him during Lent in the same year.[60]

The earl's own minstrels were mounted, having seven horses between the six of them in January 1391.[61] The extra horse was probably to transport their baggage, either in panniers or on a cart. On the second expedition they certainly had a cart, for in August 1392 the earl bought a horse from John Aleyn 'pro carrecta'.[62]

The Derby accounts do not describe the minstrels' duties. From a payment of a ducat (3s 3d) for a fringe for his banner made to Thomas, trumpeter, after his companions had returned to England, it would appear that a solo trumpeter was not too small a minstrel-force for ceremonial occasions.[63] Nor do the accounts give information about the minstrels' instruments, although a payment of 60s od made to the minstrels in 1391 for six fustian bags may refer to instrument-bags.[64]

---

[58] See Smith (L.T.), *Expeditions to Prussia*, 132 f, 137, 141 f and 269 ff. Thomas 'Trumpet' is distinguished from Thomas Aleyn in the list of wages (*ibid.*, 269): no other name is given for him.

[59] Three Prussian marks were worth approximately 10s od in English money: Spufford, *Handbook*, 255.

[60] Smith (L.T.), *Expeditions to Prussia*, 109, 110 and 113. The first and third of these sums cannot be divided equally by the number of minstrels concerned: presumably the leading minstrel took a larger share, for his organisation.

[61] Smith (L.T.), *Expeditions to Prussia*, 112 and 199.

[62] *Ibid.*, 262.

[63] *Ibid.*, 287. Thomas may have acted as a pursuivant.

[64] '... pro vj sackes de fostyon': *Ibid.*, 112.

The Warwick Household, 1420–1 and 1431–2

Two account-books survive from the household of Elizabeth Berkeley, the countess of Richard Beauchamp (1382–1439), Earl of Warwick. Both are journals, and both for periods when the earl was away in France with the king (Henry V and Henry VI). The countess was resident mainly at her castle of Berkeley, between Gloucester and Bristol. The information provided on minstrels is very limited, but it concerns the household's hospitality to visitors, an aspect of domestic life that complements material found elsewhere.

The earlier book is for the year 1420/1.[65] Miscellaneous items show that the household was visited by a minstrel of the earl of Stafford (6 November 1420), three trumpeters and two harpers (23 December), two Welsh harpers (10 January 1421) and two minstrels of Lady Abergavenny, Warwick's aunt by marriage (12 February). An item earlier in 1420 shows that 8d was expended on two minstrels *domini de Wallia* who came to Berkeley for talks with Lady Warwick, presumably acting on behalf of her absent husband. They stayed for six nights, not in the castle but at the house of John Shepherd, apparently a trusted Warwick official. In view of the anonymity of the *dominus de Wallia* – there was no Prince of Wales until the birth of the future Henry VI on 6 December 1421 – one wonders about the secrecy of these talks over a five-day period. The designation 'minstrels' may be a cover for more important negotiators: being lodged outside the castle would release them from any need to perform, besides offering a more private venue for the talks.

An entry for the Christmas period, 24 December 1420 to 6 January 1421, shows something of the entertainments in the household at that time, which included various players. A minstrel of the duke of Clarence stayed for a day and a night, receiving 6s 8d; and two minstrels of Lady Abergavenny who were in the household at Epiphany also received 6s 8d. Clarence was Henry V's brother Thomas of Lancaster; Lady Abergavenny, Warwick's aunt by marriage, was the widow of William Beauchamp, first Lord Abergavenny, who had died in 1411.[66]

The second Beauchamp Household Book covers the period from 14 March 1431 to 18 March 1432.[67] It is rather roughly written and heavily abbreviated, often in ways that now obscure the meaning. The entries are formulaic, however, and the overall meaning is rarely in doubt. Like the earlier accounts, these are largely concerned with hospitality: they list those who came for the mid-day meal (*ad prandium*) or for dinner (*ad cenam*) and state whether they stayed the night or not. The general form of entries is

Ven' [one or more persons] ad prand*ium* [*or* ad cen*am*) et mane't [*or* et ret'].

(There came [...] to the mid-day meal [*or* to dinner] and stayed [*or* went away].)

---

[65] Longleat House, MS Misc. IX. An edition of relevant entries is in *REED Cumberland, Westmorland, Gloucestershire*, 347–8.
[66] ODNB under 'Beauchamp, Richard'.
[67] Warwickshire County Record Office, CR1618/W19/5R1618/W19/5

Maneo is to remain or stay, but the abbreviated form *ret'* is more difficult: probably it comes from *returno*, I return, or perhaps from *retrocessio*, I retreat or retire. The phrase *cum 1 pa* sometimes appears, positioned between the visitor and his horse, which suggests an associated person such as a servant. In the entry for 23 January 1432 it is spelled out as *pag'*, so it stands for *pagus*, a page. One would expect *pa* to stand for the ablative of *pagetta*: but it is unlikely that the servant was female, so the abbreviation probably stands for the masculine ablative *pago*. The accounts show another consistent error: the use of the abbreviation *d'n's* (for *dominus*, lord) where the genitive *d'n'i* (for *domini*) is required.

It is simplest to show these formulaic entries in tabular form (Table 7). 'Lunch' is not entirely appropriate for the meal that they called *prandium* and we should regard as a late breakfast or early lunch[eon]; nor is 'dinner' quite right for *cena*, a main meal taken in the late afternoon or early evening. 'Lunch' and 'dinner' are however the nearest equivalents.

The entries dated 23 January and 13 February 1432 show that the travelling household of the Talbots included over ninety people and enough horses for their needs. While the size of this entourage is not surprising, it is a useful reminder that such a large body of people and horses could be accommodated overnight. In fact this was a quite normal pattern of hospitality for any large house, including a monastic house. These accounts also show minstrels, and especially trumpeters, apparently travelling on their own. There might be all sorts of reasons for this, some of which are noted in Part III: but the main reason was certainly the private postal services by which landowners transacted business and kept in touch with their families, friends and estates. Reading through the accounts of Elizabeth de Burgh, for example, one discovers the huge volume of traffic for this purpose, and the wide range of servants – including minstrels and heralds – who were used as messengers. We might guess that the most important letters were carried by heralds, the less important by trumpeters and the least important routine ones by servants of lower rank, including minstrels.[68]

The Howard household, 1462–85

Sir John Howard (*c.* 1425–85), a wealthy Suffolk landowner, became Lord Howard in late 1469 or early 1470 and Duke of Norfolk in 1483. He died fighting for Richard III at Bosworth. The surviving accounts of his household are found in a journal: they rarely record wages or liveries, and certain other payments were detailed in a separate volume, now lost.[69] Most of Howard's gifts are recorded, however, and the accounts probably give an accurate picture of the minstrelsy made in his presence.

Sir John Howard employed a pair of trumpeters, a taboret and a harper: the trumpeters are named as Robert Dunwich and Cole, and the taboret as John Symond.[70] Of these, the taboret appears most prominently in the accounts, and the impression

---

[68] For the carrying of Elizabeth de Burgh's letters, see Ward (Jennifer), *Elizabeth de Burgh*, 41–51.

[69] The surviving accounts are edited in Botfield, *Manners* (1462–7) and Collier, *Household Books* (1481–5), repr. in Crawford, *Household Books*. Items concerning minstrels are calendared in SM II, Appendix C. The lost accounts are mentioned in those that survive.

[70] See SM II, 150–3, *passim*.

Table 7. Minstrels visiting the Warwick household, 1431/2.

Date	Person(s) and horses	meal	stayed/left
1431			
Thurs 19 Apr	one of the king's trumpeters	lunch	left
Tues 22 May	Wild, trumpeter, with one page and two horses	dinner	stayed
Mon 11 June	two trumpeters	dinner	left
Thurs 5 July	one of the king's trumpeters	dinner	left
Thurs 12 July	four trumpeters with one page of Lord Clinton	dinner	left
Weds 15 Aug	one trumpet of Lord Lovell	dinner	left
Thurs 16 Aug	four of the king's trumpeters with three pages, and two yeomen of the king	dinner	left
Fri 24 Aug	one trumpeter of the count of Perche, with one page	lunch	left
Thurs 27 Sept	Blache (?), trumpeter, with one page	both	left
Tues 18 Dec	one waferer	lunch	left
Thurs 20 Dec	four minstrels	lunch	left
1432			
Tues 1 Jan	three trumpeters of the earl of Arundel	both	left
Sun 6 Jan	five minstrels	both	left
Weds 9 Jan	three trumpeters of the earl of Stafford, with three pages	dinner	left
Weds 23 Jan	At Calais, at lunch: Lord and Lady Talbot, 8 damsels, 3 chaplains, 12 squires, 3 trumpeters, 1 pursuivant, 20 yeomen, 44 grooms and pages, 69 horses	lunch (both?)	stayed
Tues 29 Jan	2 pursuivants of the earl of Stafford and the earl of Arundel, 2 trumpeters of the earl of Salisbury	both	left
Weds 13 Feb	Countess Talbot, 7 damsels, 2 chaplains, 8 squires, 1 trumpeter, 11 yeomen, 16 grooms, 18 pages and 27 horses	dinner	Stayed

given is that Howard preferred to be attended by his taboret at all times rather than by a still minstrel.

This impression is not altered after Howard's elevation to the rank of baron. Thomas the harper, who was a trusted servant of the household,[71] may have been primarily Lady Howard's minstrel: when Howard was in London in 1481, preparing for an expedition to Scotland, Thomas remained at the Howards' main residence at Stoke by Nayland. Howard did take harpers on the expedition of 1481, however, in addition to five trumpeters and a total of eleven taborets. How many of these were regular members of his household, it is impossible to tell: but even after his elevation to the Dukedom of Norfolk, he seems to have kept only one taboret in his household.[72] Of the five trumpeters, Edmund Frente received lower payments and gifts than the other four, and he may have been a temporary war-time addition to Howard's household trumpeters.[73]

A minstrel called James, mentioned in the accounts for 1482, may also have been a household minstrel. If so, he probably played the lute, for the minstrels had to mend a lute in that year. Other payments for repairing instruments are for a cord for a tabor (1464), for the mending of a harp (1465), for parchment to repair a tabor (1481), and for the repairing of the chapel organ (1482). A payment of 1d for the purchase of a pipe for the fool suggests that the instrument was greatly inferior to a minstrel's pipe.[74]

Howard evidently enjoyed minstrelsy: often his rewards to minstrels were large sums, of the order of those given in the royal households, although many were only a matter of pence. If he spent Christmas at home, he rewarded certain local minstrels and players who came to entertain him, and when he entered or left a city such as Lincoln, Colchester or London, the town waits often earned a reward from him.[75]

The Northumberland household, c. 1511

The ordinances of the household of the Earl of Northumberland were drawn up at Michaelmas 1511.[76] On certain subjects, such as the constitution of the earl's chapel, they are very informative, but they can also be remarkable for their silence. For instance, no mention is made of cloth-liveries: nor is there any information about the earl's trumpeters, of which there were six.[77]

The household minstrels were a taboret, a luter and a rebec-player. The latter two could probably supply all the still minstrelsy that the earl might require, while the taboret would play for dances and probably martial exercises. Perhaps all three of them played when they serenaded the earl on New Year's Day. The taboret

---

[71] A payment was made by his hands in 1481: SM II, 157.
[72] SM II, 160. A single taboret was sufficient for all but military purposes.
[73] SM II, 153 ff, 155, and 156, under the dates 22 April and 28 July.
[74] SM II, 158.
[75] 478 SM II, 150, 153, 156, 157, 159 (two items) and 160.
[76] Transcribed in Percy (Thomas), *Regulations and Establishment*.
[77] It is possible that the trumpeters' wages are detailed with those of other servants of the same rank: but the ordinances do not state the rank of the trumpeters.

received four marks (£2 13s 4d) *per annum* for his fee, while the luter and rebec-player received 33s 4d each.[78] The minstrels' status was not high, even amongst the household yeomen, with whom they ranked, and at meals they made up a *meas* with the footman.[79]

The earl's gifts to minstrels, players and other entertainers were on the scale that we have noted in other households. He was accustomed to give 3s 4d (a quarter-mark) to the minstrels of an earl if they came annually, and 6s 8d (half a mark) if they came only every two or three years: a single minstrel of an earl who was a special friend or kinsman received the same reward. The trumpeters of an earl or duke received either 6s 8d or 10s 0d in the same circumstances if they came all six together. Three of the king's shawms who had been accustomed to come every year were given 10s 0d.[80]

The earl also made regular gifts to his own servants. The three household (still) minstrels serenaded the whole Percy family on the morning of New Year's Day, perhaps as part of the ceremonies when gifts were exchanged. On this occasion they received 20s 0d between them for playing at the earl's chamber door (13s 4d from the earl, 6s 8d from the countess), 2s 0d for playing at Lord Percy's door, and 8d for playing at the door of each of the two younger sons. The six trumpeters, similarly, played outside the earl's door, for which they received 20s 0d.[81]

Ecclesiastical households

Minstrelsy and its relations with the Church

The Church officially held minstrels in some suspicion, as being associated with prostitutes, thieves and other undesirables, and injunctions were occasionally sent out to clergy and religious forbidding them to consort with minstrels and other entertainers.[82] Theoretical polemic had little to do with practical reality, however, and it is clear that the better class of minstrelsy was entirely acceptable to churchmen. Music symbolized Divine Order and the music of the angels around the throne of God, *musica celestis*; and, by extension, using psalms and other scriptural passages as authority, mankind could make music in the worship of God. This included

---

[78] Percy (Thomas), *Regulations and Establishment*, 46 and 253. The first of these gives the taboret's wages as £4, which must be a mistake: the Dean of the Chapel received £4 *per annum*, while 33s 4d was the wage of a yeoman.

[79] *Ibid.*, 80 and 88.

[80] *Ibid.*, 339, specifies the gifts to visiting minstrels. The sum given to the minstrel of a friend or kinsman coming yearly is left blank, but 3s 4d was probably intended: 6s 8d is laid down for such a minstrel coming once every two or three years.

[81] *Ibid.*, 342.

[82] Chambers, *Mediaeval Stage*, I, 55–62; Rastall, 'Minstrelsy, Church and Clergy'. This situation is explored in Dobozy, *Re-membering*, 33–84, for which see also p. 251, below.

instrumental minstrelsy, about which some of the psalms were very specific. As Psalm 150 has it, in a vernacular verse paraphrase by Robert Manning de Brunne:[83]

> Yn harpe yn thabour and symphan gle
> Wurschepe god yn troumpes and sautre
> Yn cordes and organes and bellys ryngyng
> Yn al these wurschepe the heuene kyng.

For this reason King David, the supposed author of the Psalms, was often depicted playing the harp.[84]

One result of this acceptance of minstrelsy was the depiction of angelic and other minstrels and singers in church carvings and manuscript illuminations. The latter was for the wealthy, but the former might be seen by anyone entering a church: the man or woman in the street could look up at the roof of Lincoln or Manchester cathedral, or even of his own parish church (such as St Wendreda's in March, Cambridgeshire), and see heavenly minstrels playing their instruments. There are even all-too-human instrumentalists as well, although those tend to be nearer the ground and on the north side of the church (traditionally the devil's side), as in Beverley minster.[85] Like many depictions of minstrelsy in manuscript illuminations, misericords and other iconographic forms, these are not always complimentary to minstrels and often deliberately subvert or reverse Christian values. Such depictions are not subject to a simple good/bad dichotomy, but reflect a more complex matrix of spiritual and social values that have to be negotiated in real life.

Those most closely concerned with minstrelsy and other types of entertainment were anxious to treat their livelihoods as acceptable to the Church and to society as a whole. Thus it is in stories written by authors in favour of minstrelsy that we find those who worship the Blessed Virgin by performing before her statue.[86] Acceptance of this view by lay and church authorities led to such events as minstrelsy during alms-giving, religious processions and performances of religious drama.[87]

This made it possible to use a church building as a venue for minstrelsy, drama and dancing, as apparently happened at Rye. The duchess of York's minstrels performed 'in the chirche here' in early 1486, when the town gave them 3s 4d, and other rewards for minstrelsy may be for performance in the church. An item dating from the period Christmas 1483 to mid-April 1484 started as a record of minstrelsy 'in the Chirche' but was changed to one for dramatic performance ('Pleyeres' rather

---

[83] Robert Manning de Brunne, *Handlyng Synne*, ed. F.J. Furnivall. 2 vols. EETS o.s. 119, 123 (London, 1901 and 1903), I, 158 ff, lines 4769–72.

[84] Mainly in the Beatus pages of psalters (Psalm 1). Even so, Manning felt it necessary to justify Bishop Grossteste's employment of a harper: the harp, being stretched strings on a wooden frame, symbolised Christ's sinews stretched on the cross. See Manning, *Handlyng Synne*, I, 158, lines 4755–6.

[85] The bibliography for this subject is extensive: but see, for instance, Gardner, *English Medieval Sculpture*, 116–25 (Lincoln); Hudson, *Medieval Woodwork*, 149–74 (Manchester); and Montague, 'Beverley minster' (Beverley).

[86] On almsgiving see above, pp. 76–8.

[87] Rastall, *The Heaven Singing*, passim.

than 'Myn[strelles]'); and several items record occasions between 1474/5 and 1492 when players performed in the church. Possibly it was the best, or the only suitable, indoor venue in the town.[88] Some of the latter occasions were associated with the Christmas season, but the players were not necessarily performing sacred dramas. The duchess's minstrels, too, may have been with their patron while she was making an offering, but the record does not say so.

Drama was associated with dancing, and on 3 February 1504 a group of disguisers 'of Edinburgh' danced in the abbey there. Dancing could also be a ceremonial civic action. When Queen Isabella announced the birth of her son, the future Edward III, on 13 November 1312, the mayor, aldermen and people of London danced in the Guildhall in his honour; and the next day they went to St Paul's cathedral, where the bishop of London celebrated Mass, offerings were made, and then there was dancing in St Paul's, with trumpets. Six days later, after dining in the Guildhall, the mayor and aldermen danced through the city for the rest of that day and into the night.

Such events remind us of important facts: that the modern distinction between sacred and secular did not present itself in the same way in the late Middle Ages; that notions of propriety and impropriety were therefore quite different; that the social act of dancing could be ceremonial; and that in consequence a bishop might well look kindly on dancing (and minstrelsy) in a church building in appropriate circumstances.

This is not to say that instruments were normally or even frequently used in the liturgy. There were however occasions of special rejoicing when wind instruments were heard in church services: at coronations, at the reception of senior clerics into church buildings and during thanksgivings of various kinds when *Te Deum* was sung. In sum, whatever the hard-line divines might have said, many clerics, both secular and religious, allowed minstrelsy both in their personal domestic lives and in the social lives of their religious communities. As we saw in Chapter 3, minstrels were among those provided with accommodation in religious houses after retirement, as part of the charitable and hospitable functions of the religious orders.

Personal minstrels of the clergy

A prelate's household was in most ways similar to a secular magnate's, and many of the higher clergy employed their own personal minstrels.[89] At the marriage of Edward I's daughter Elizabeth, payment was made to two harpers of the Bishop of Durham, and a few years later John de Greyndon, minstrel of the Bishop of Durham, and Guillotus the bishop's harper were rewarded at Court: the latter was in residence for 'some time' while the king travelled from Alverton (Nottinghamshire) to Beverley (Yorkshire), a distance of around 70 miles.[90] In the records of the Pentecost feast

---

[88] REED Sussex, 57; 57–61, passim.

[89] REED volumes have shown the extent of minstrel-employment by clerics. Rosalind Conklin noted that at various times minstrels were employed by the Archbishop of Canterbury, the bishops of Norwich, Winchester and Dublin, the cardinals Wolsey and Beaufort, and the Abbot of Reading: 'Medieval English Minstrels', 150 and 153.

[90] BL Add MS 7965 (25 Ed I), fol. 52r, and Add 8835 (32 Ed I), fol. 44r (cal. SM II, 16 and 41).

of 1306 Guillotus appears as 'Guilaume le Harpour qui est ove le Patriarke':[91] the harper of the Bishop of Durham (the same man) and Robert, harper of the Abbot of Abingdon, appear on a separate list on that occasion. Another on this list, John, the crowder of Shrewsbury, was probably the Abbot of Shrewsbury's minstrel, as Hayes suggested, who appears to have taught the Prince of Wales's rhymer to play the instrument.[92]

With the exception of John the crowder, all these are harpers: we have seen that there was a symbolic reason for this (n. 84, above), but we should expect it anyway from the situation in secular households. The Durham Priory accounts for 1362 show that at that date the Bishop of Norwich, too, had a harper; and at the end of our period, when the lute had largely taken the place of the harp as the courtly instrument, two Scottish prelates – the Prior of Whithern and the Bishop of Moray – kept their luters.[93]

Judging by the size of the payments made to them, the minstrels of the Bishop of Durham were skilled players:[94] a prelate's household could no doubt attract and foster good minstrels just as a secular magnate's could. In May 15 Ed II Roger the harper and John Bisshop, minstrels of the Bishop of Ely, were rewarded for minstrelsy at Court: a John Bisshop was a servant of the king's Chamber in 2 or 3 Ed III, so the bishop's minstrel may have become a royal minstrel. In 17 Ed II Robert Polydod and Thomas le Barber, minstrels of the same bishop, were rewarded at Court: Polydod was a king's minstrel in the following reign.[95] Of course, these identifications depend primarily on the names, and must be treated with caution: but Polydod was not a common name, and a William Bisshop (perhaps a relative of John?) was a royal minstrel in 14 Ed III, so there is other circumstantial evidence for them.

There is no evidence for clerics employing trumpeters or pipers, which for other reasons would seem unlikely: the men concerned appear always to have been *bas* minstrels. One or two seems to have been the usual number for a bishop, but the accounts of Winchester College show that four minstrels of the Bishop of Winchester

---

[91] TNA E101.369.6 (34 Ed I): Anthony Bek, Bishop of Durham (1284–1311), was also titular Patriarch of Jerusalem; he had two minstrels present, therefore; see SM II, 54 and 57 f.

[92] Hayes, *King's Music*, 31; E163.5.2 (33 Ed I), m. 14 (letter of Edward Prince of Wales to the abbot of Shrewsbury, 12 September 1304, printed in REED Shropshire, I, 126, with translation in II, 562). See p. 65, above.

[93] In 1501 and 1504, respectively (cal. SM II, 144, 173 and 183).

[94] At the marriage of Elizabeth and at the Pentecost celebrations of 34 Ed I they are placed among payments to royal minstrels, the rewards being comparable. John de Greyndon received the considerable sum of 40s od for his minstrelsy.

[95] BL Stowe MS 553 (15 Ed II), fol. 67r, and TNA E101.379.19 (17 Ed II), fol. 4v (cal. SM II, 80 and 81); also (for Bisshop) E101.384.1 (2–3 Ed III), fol. 35v (cal. SM II, 85); and (for Polydod) E101.383.8 (1 Ed III), fol. 10r; E101.385.4 (4 Ed III); Nero C viii (8–11 Ed III), fols 226r, 228r, 229v, 231r, 235v, 239v, 244r and 284v; E101.388.5 (11–12 Ed III), m. 11; E36.203 (12–14 Ed III), fol. 123r, 129v and 155r; E36.204 (16–18 Ed III), fol. 90r: (cal. SM II, 84, 86, 91–2 *passim*, 95, 97, 101, 102 and 104). See also E101.390.3 (keeper's roll, household of the Black Prince, 16–18 Ed III), m. 3, for the prince's minstrel John Polidod (cal. SM II, 106).

were rewarded there in Easter week 1412.[96] Fifteenth-century records show that the minstrels of the Archbishop of Canterbury visited Dover, Lydd and New Romney.[97]

Minstrelsy in religious houses

The rather relaxed attitude that welcomed entertainers to ecclesiastical establishments led to statutes forbidding the clergy even to consort with minstrels, let alone employ them.[98] While this may seem a direct contradiction of the situation so far outlined, the real purpose of these statutes was to ban contact with the most disreputable sections of society, not the respectable liveried minstrels whose work symbolized Divine Order; and it was sometimes to protect the sanctity of the most holy places. The statute of St Paul's cathedral of *c.* 1263, for instance (see p. 78, above), orders the clergy to keep certain classes of person out of the church building; and the clergy were also to ban minstrels making an 'unholy dance' before the altars of the Blessed Virgin and the Cross (presumably the famous cross at the north door).[99] The 1437 constitution of Bishop Thomas Spofford for the convent of Limebrook, Herefordshire, expressly forbade any form of minstrelsy, interludes, dancing or revelling within the 'holy place'.[100] The annals of the abbey of Burton-on-Trent for 1259 state that minstrels were to be given food not because they were minstrels but because they were paupers. Their performances were not to be seen, heard or permitted before the abbot and monks,[101] which perhaps leaves open the possibility of minstrels performing before the lay servants.

Two sets of accounts from religious houses make clear the distinction between respectable liveried minstrels and the disreputable entertainers who should be shunned. The account-rolls of Durham cathedral priory, a wonderful series running from the 1280s onwards,[102] show that minstrels and players were regularly rewarded. Durham was one of the largest and wealthiest monasteries, and its rewards were more generous than elsewhere: but they were not unregulated. When the cathedral priory underwent a visitation on 9 July 1442, the commission investigated a

---

[96] REED pre-publication collections: <http://reedprepub.org/> (accessed 3 March 2015). The evidence for prelates not having trumpeters is negative, but probably conclusive. In the various accounts and other records searched for the present work, the trumpeters of secular magnates frequently appear but there is no reference to any trumpeter of a prelate. For Walter le Cornour, minstrel of the Bishop of Exeter, see BL Add MS 9951 (14 Ed II), fol. 20r (cal. SM II, 79).

[97] *REED Kent: Diocese of Canterbury*, II, 337 (Dover, 1452/3); 656–64 *passim* (Lydd, 1450–2, 1453/4, 1454/5, 1459–61 and 1465/6); and 735–6 *passim* (New Romney, 1449/50, 1453/4 and 1454/5). Only Richard Barton is named.

[98] Bowles, *Liturgical*, 45 f. He specifically mentions the Synod of Chartres (1358).

[99] *REED Civic London*, I, 3. The statute did not ban minstrelsy *per se.*

[100] *REED Herefordshire*, 188.

[101] BL Cotton MS Vespasian E iii: *REED Staffordshire* (online, accessed November 2019).

[102] The Durham accounts are published in shortened form in Fowler, *Durham*: these are calendared in SM II, 142–9. A full edition by John McKinnell is in progress for REED, and I am grateful to Professor McKinnell for letting me use his transcriptions. The surviving accounts are departmental summaries and so do not give much detail: but the picture is one of regular in-house activity by minstrels and players.

complaint *quod dominus Prior excessiue dat dona Histrionibus mimis et Joculatoribus* (that the lord Prior gives rewards too generously to *histriones*, *mimi* and *joculatores*). The prior and his advisory committee replied[103]

> that the lord prior does not give to *joculatores* nor admit them, but that he gives to the minstrels of the king, dukes, earls, barons and others as his predecessors have done, and by submitting in this way hopes to be exonerated. They mean, then, that he gives moderately and not excessively.

This is a very careful reply – the draft of this response survives, too, and shows the modifications made in the final version – in which the prior and his advisors shift the terms of the complaint. In place of *histriones* and *mimi*, both words that could imply forms of acting rather more questionable than that of *lusores*, the response introduces the terms *joculatores* and *ministralli*. Of these, the former are placed in the same category as *histriones* and *mimi*, whereas *ministralli* are an acceptable category. The response is also careful to specify that these are not just any minstrels but those of the king, nobles and others – by implication, other magnates and landowners. This was probably true during the priorate of the then incumbent, John Wessington, although a more miscellaneous range of entertainers had been admitted to the priory in earlier times: indeed, the priory had even employed a fool, Thomas *fatuus*, in the period 1330–57.

The terminology is variable, then, according to the institution concerned and sometimes, perhaps, to the individual scribe: for example, an entertainer named as 'pratt *Jugulator*' in 1401/2 appears as 'pratt *ministrallus*' the following year.[104] Without knowing precisely what these terms mean in any one instance it is impossible to be sure of the speciality of each entertainer. Some writers set out their own terminology: Thomas Chobham, writing *c.* 1216, castigated minstrels who dealt in nudity, lascivious gestures, scandal and backbiting, but approved of those *joculatores* who sing of 'the deeds of princes' and the lives of saints.[105] Here *joculator* is apparently used in contradistinction to the *histriones* of whom he does not approve. Thomas Docking, writing a little later but clearly influenced by Chobham, made a distinction between *histriones*, whom he defines as story-tellers using gesticulation and telling obscene stories, and those *mimi* who give comfort by playing the harp or fiddle (although not all *mimi* do so). What these commentators have in common is their approbation of string-players who perform morally uplifting songs.[106]

---

[103] Information from John McKinnell: '... quod dominus prior non dat joculatoribus nec admittit eos sed quod dat ministrallis Regis Ducum Comitum et Baronum et aliorum sicut predecessores sui fecerunt et ab huiusmodi dacione vellet libentissime exonerari Volunt tum quod det moderate et non excessiue'.

[104] Information from John McKinnell.

[105] Page, *Owl and Nightingale*, 23–4; and see below, p. 293.

[106] Page, *Owl and Nightingale*, 24–6. It is tempting to think that a *gestour* was a teller of *gestes* (the deeds of princes and saints), *rymour* a poet and *disour* a teller of jokes, aphorisms or *bon mots*: but we do not have the information to confirm this, and such a simple solution is perhaps unlikely.

Another set of accounts making this kind of distinction is from the household of William Worsley, Dean of St Paul's, between 1480/1 and 1489/90.[107] The summary accounts for each year give the total sum expended on various minstrels (*mimi, ministralli*, or *mimi seu/sive ministralli*) of the king and other lords. In other words, no riff-raff. In the seven years concerned Worsley expended, respectively, 57s 6d, 75s 2d, £7 1s 7d, 52s 8d, 57s 6d, 56s 8d and 28s 8d. This averages at £3 7s 1d – more than enough for ten visits from the king's minstrels at 6s 8d a visit – which is a lot of money to spend on minstrels. The average does not give a true picture, however, as there was a very high expenditure in 1482/3, perhaps due to the costs of entertaining associated with the accession and coronation of Richard III. Expenditure of between £2 10s 0d and £3 seems the norm: but even at this level it is clear that minstrels were rewarded frequently and generously in the dean's private household.

There were many occasions for minstrelsy in medieval religious houses. The main feasts of the Church's calendar always drew minstrels, and these included the patronal festival of each individual church. Thus the Durham accounts show that more money was paid in reward to minstrels at the two feasts of St Cuthbert than at other times.[108] According to Warton, the Augustinian priory of Bicester paid minstrels for six separate feasts in a single year, 1431, while the contemporary accounts of Maxstoke priory suggest a similar number of occasions for minstrel activity.[109]

Some celebrations of a more occasional nature must have been attractive to minstrels, who would have fulfilled a useful function in providing entertainment for the clergy and their guests, both lay and clerical. As already noticed, the installation-feast of a senior cleric was an event at which minstrelsy might be required. These events included important guests, both lay and clerical, some of whom brought their own minstrels. At any time when a religious house extended hospitality to a nobleman, as Durham did to Lord Percy at Christmas 1376, the guest's minstrels might be asked to perform.[110]

Religious houses could, in fact, be especially favoured as places for minstrels to work. In 1467 the Coventry waits were so much in demand that the Corporation had to proscribe their activities outside the city, although allowing them to perform for abbots and priors within ten miles of Coventry.[111] Waits were as welcome at religious houses as any other minstrels, and the accounts of Thetford priory show visits by the Norwich waits as well as other minstrels between 1498 and 1510.[112]

Details of the performances are rare, but harpers are easily the minstrels most commonly specified: indeed, harpers are sometimes distinguished from other,

---

[107] *REED Ecclesiastical London*, 33–6.

[108] SM II, 142–9, *passim*. The main feast-day was on 20 March and the feast of the Translation on 4 September.

[109] Warton, *History*, II, 97 f. In the Maxstoke accounts 'mimus' is the word used for a minstrel, as was usual in monastic records. On Warton's reliability, see pp. 237–8, below.

[110] Fowler, *Durham*, 585, cal. SM II, 146.

[111] Mary Dormer Harris, *The Coventry Leet Book*. EETS o.s. 134, 135, 138, 146 (London, 1907–13), p. 335. The ten-mile radius encompassed several religious houses, including Maxstoke.

[112] Harvey, 'Last Years of Thetford', *passim*.

unspecified minstrels. An example of this in the accounts of St Swithin's priory led Warton to believe that the distinction was a common one. He pointed out, however, that the minstrels sang on this occasion, and suggested that the distinction was made because it was the harpers who sang to their own accompaniment.[113] Other visiting *bas* instrumentalists appear in the Durham accounts[114] – a fiddler (*c*. 1336), a crowder (*c*. 1360), a luter (1361), a minstrel of the duke of Lancaster who performed with a dancer in the prior's chamber (1381/2), and a Scottish *roter* (hurdy-gurdy player, 1394/5). *Haut* instruments were also welcome, and the priory rewarded two trumpeters of the earl of Northampton (?*c*. 1357), a piper 'and other minstrels' (at Christmas 1360), a trumpeter called Robert (at the feast of St Cuthbert, 1368 or 1369) and a trumpeter of the king (1394/5).

The Durham accounts for 1375/6 are particularly rich in records of visiting minstrels and their rewards from the prior: relevant items are listed in Table 8.[115] A total outlay of £3 16s 10d for occasional minstrelsy during the year is probably more than most abbeys and priories would pay out. At Worcester, however, where the annual sum was normally much lower, rewards went out of control between 1471/2 and 1481/2, with annual expenditure on minstrels, *mimi*, etc. of £12 19s 9d, £11 8s 6d, £24 18s 8d and £29 7s 0d; and again in 1486/7 with £50 10s 4d, and in 1490/1 with £37 5s 0d.[116] Even taking some inflation into account, these sums make the complaints at Durham in 1442 seem nugatory (the average expenditure there on minstrels in the previous three years being £5 4s 8d).[117]

It is very rare for such accounts to say what *gestes* were sung on these occasions. Of the information available, much comes from Thomas Warton's *History of English Poetry* (1871), a source that must be treated with caution. According to Warton, the visit of Adam Orleton, Bishop of Winchester, to St Swithun's priory in 1338 included entertainment in the prior's hall during which the 'Song of Colbrond' (a Danish giant) and 'Queen Emma delivered from the ploughshares' were sung by a minstrel named Herebert.[118] Warton also reported that during the Epiphany celebrations at Bicester priory in 1432 six minstrels of Buckingham, performing in the refectory, sang the story of the Seven Martyred Sleepers.[119] These songs are such as might be considered morally improving, as they fall into the category of songs suitable for after-dinner

---

[113] Warton, *History*, III, 119.

[114] SM II, 142–9 under relevant dates.

[115] Calendared in SM II, 146.

[116] REED *Herefordshire and Worcestershire*, 405 and 411.

[117] This is calculated from Professor McKinnell's transcription: the figures are not given in the calendar (SM II, 148). The Durham accounts also contain a payment to a minstrel 'jestour' named Jawdewyne at Christmas (?)1362, perhaps a type of entertainment particularly suited to a monastery.

[118] Warton, *History*, I, 97, apparently quoting the priory's register: 'Et cantabat Joculator quidam nomine Herebertus canticum Colbrondi necnon Gestum Emme regine a judicio ignis liberate in aula prioris'.

[119] Warton, *History*, III, 119, apparently quoting the priory's accounts: 'Dat' sex Ministrallis de Bokyngham cantantibus in refectorio Martyrium septem dormientium in Festo epiphanie iv s.'.

Table 8. Minstrels visiting Durham Cathedral Priory, 1375/6.

To minstrels on St Cuthbert's day in March	13s 4d
To a certain minstrel playing before the lord prior in his chamber	18d
To three minstrels of the earl of March, playing before the lord prior	6s 8d
To a certain minstrel of the lord the king, coming with Lord Nevill	5s 0d
To twelve minstrels at the feast of St Cuthbert in September	20s 0d
To four minstrels of the lord the prince on the feast of the Holy Cross	13s 4d
To a certain minstrel on the feast of St Matthew	20d
To minstrels at the feast of St Cuthbert in March 1375	13s 4d
To two minstrels on Easter Day	2s 0d

entertainment in a specifically religious and educational context.[120] However, there is some doubt about the status of these entries, which scholars working on the REED project were unable to find. The matter is considered further in Chapter 11.

Payments for less purely musical types of minstrelsy are also rare. The Maxstoke accounts record several payments to players (*lusores*), who probably acted out biblical stories or other narratives with a moral bias: there is also a payment to a *joculator*, which probably means the same as *gestour*. On one occasion (in 1381 or 1382) the prior of Durham was entertained by a minstrel of the Duke (presumably Northumberland) with a tumbler or dancer (*saltans*), an entertainment which took place in the prior's own chamber. Dancing did sometimes have a religious significance, as we have seen. There is good biblical precedent for this, such as Miriam's celebration after the destruction of the Egyptian army in the Red Sea, the rejoicing of Jephtha's daughter, and David's dancing before the Ark.[121] Some actual instances were noted earlier.

Some abbeys and priories kept musicians in permanent employment. Warton mentions that Jeffrey the harper received a corrody in 1180 from the Benedictine abbey of Hyde, near Winchester, in payment for his minstrelsy on public occasions, and Warton considered that the abbeys of Conway and Stratfleur, too, probably had their own harpers at this time.

If we can trust this information, Jeffrey's employment was no doubt occasional and part-time: in the life of an abbey there was little work for a minstrel, and there would be no apprentices to teach. In that situation it seems obvious that any minstrel would be expected to make himself useful in other ways. At Durham, where the records show gifts being made to harpers and other minstrels (including trumpeters) over a long period, Thomas Harper was certainly employed as a minstrel, for a harp was bought for him in 1335 or 1336. This was probably not his main employment at the priory, however, since he carried out repairs and other works as a carpenter between 1339 and 1341.

---

[120] As in the case of the Winchester College statutes.
[121] Exodus 15, 20–1; Judges 11, 34; II Samuel 6, 14–15. Nevertheless, this is the second instance of dancers performing in the prior's private apartments, not before the monks.

Thomas and four companions, all carpenters, were paid for repairs to the buildings in 1339 or 1340, and in the following accounting year they made a hearse for the prior.[122] For some reason Thomas was imprisoned at Carlisle by the Sheriff of Durham in 1341 or 1342, when Robert Scot was sent to plead with the sheriff. The outcome of this affair is not known: a Thomas Harper appears in the accounts for 1364, but it may not be the same man. About that time he seems to have injured his leg, for a physician was paid to attend to him.[123] By around 1362 a certain Barry Harper appears in the records: he was given a tunic, and so was probably in permanent employment at the priory. In around 1365/6 Barry Harper was among those receiving Christmas gifts. There is no evidence that he was a minstrel, however.

A Thomas Harper reappears in the records for 1377, and again in the accounts for 1380–1, when the prior made him the substantial gift of 6s 8d. This looks like a reward for minstrelsy, but need not be such. One gift that was probably for entertainment was made in 1374/5 to William Harpour in the prior's manor of Beaurepaire (now Bearpark) during a *ludus* (a holiday from normal monastic life) there.[124]

Other men named Harper carried out repairs at Durham:[125] Heliseus Harper between 1412 and 1422, and William Harper – a labourer working in the infirmary – in 1442–3. Surnames like Harper mainly became fixed during the fifteenth century, no longer indicating the profession of the men bearing them. The dates for Heliseus and William are perhaps a little early for this, and they were probably both minstrels. Whether they were *primarily* minstrels, or artisans who had minstrelsy as a sideline, is another matter. A harper who had been used to making and repairing instruments might well take up carpentry if the need arose, but in general the alternative seems more likely. One John le Harper was employed as a mason on the king's works in 43 Hen III (1258/9),[126] a career that a minstrel was unlikely to take up in later life; but a John Harper who supplied various provisions to the household of the duchess of Buckingham in 1465/6 may have done so as a way of supplementing his main income, as musicians have often done.[127]

As we saw in Chapter 3, the granting of corrodies was a way by which a household servant could be provided for in his old age. Such a man would soon lose his identity as a former member of a secular household. Jeffrey, the harper corrodian at Hyde abbey, may have been in retirement and making himself useful in his new home by performing as needed, and Queen Isabella's psaltery-player Janettus, similarly, could have made himself useful to the Abbot and convent of Ramsey.[128] Some of the harpers known to have worked at Durham and elsewhere may well have been corrodians in retirement.

---

[122] Fowler, *Durham*, 538, 539: cal. SM II, 143.

[123] 'Cuidam medico sananti tibiam Thome Harpour' (To a certain physician healing Thomas Harper's shin): Fowler, *Durham*, 568 (cal. SM II, 145).

[124] Fowler, *Durham*, 180: cal. SM II, 146.

[125] Fowler, *Durham, passim*: cal. SM II, 143–8.

[126] Devon, *Issues*, 46 and 49.

[127] BL Add MS 34213, fols 8r, 15v, 40v and 57v (new foliation).

[128] See Rymer, *Foedera*, II (2), 738.

Part II

Urban Minstrelsy

Introduction to Part II

Urban minstrelsy in England has been little studied. From the eighteenth century, writers have treated minstrelsy as a minor aspect of the history of individual towns: colourful and illustrative, but ultimately of little importance. Urban history at first relied on the researches of individual scholars, not usually professional historians, who delved into a mass of civic records and, where minstrelsy was concerned, pulled out such 'plums' as would be immediately interesting to the reader. This strategy was not unuseful, and in some cases did indicate a comprehensive picture of ceremonial and entertainment. Thomas Sharp's work on Coventry is especially important (and Sharp actually focused on civic drama, ceremonial and their attendant minstrelsy),[1] and there are other examples. The serious and only recently recognised difficulty, for us, was that these historians did not explain what they had omitted from their published transcriptions. This left the reader in the dark as to the extent and precise nature of the surviving records, and additionally gave the impression that the transcriptions were complete.

This situation is largely changed by the Records of Early English Drama (REED) project, which has published the records of drama and minstrelsy in many towns, secular households and religious houses, with volumes still in preparation. For all urban entertainment two types of record are particularly important: those of the civic authorities, and those of the religious and trade guilds. These two types partly overlap, since in many places the trade guilds effectively made up the civic government; but they are also complementary, because the guilds took direct financial and practical responsibility for a large proportion of civic ceremonial and entertainment. The immediate result of the REED project, even with more material to be presented, is that we have a much fuller and more accurate view of entertainments, including minstrelsy, in the towns and villages of late medieval England. In the chapters that follow I have usually been able to refer to REED volumes, and have cited the earlier sources only where REED material is unavailable.

---

[1] Thomas Sharp, *A Dissertation on the Pageants ... at Coventry* (Coventry, 1825; repr. with a new foreword by A.C. Cawley, East Ardsley, 1973).

6

Minstrelsy in the towns

The towns of late medieval England

To modern minds, medieval towns were surprisingly small. Most of them held fewer than 1,500 people, and at the lower end of the scale there was little to distinguish towns from the larger villages. Those that grew prosperous through trade, especially through the textile trade with continental outlets, formed a select group of towns with populations of perhaps 5–10,000.[1] At a high point in 1348 London may have numbered as many as 80,000 people, most of whom lived within the city walls, but the Black Death of 1348–9 was devastating. The plague revisited London and other cities several times in the 1360s and early 1370s, and the Poll Tax of 1377 assessed just over 23,000 people in London. It is estimated that the total population of London, Southwark and Westminster at this time could hardly have been more than 45–50,000. Although the population increased through the fifteenth century, London did not return to its former size until the sixteenth.[2]

York, the country's second city, was created a county corporate in 1386. It probably had a population of around 15,000 by 1348, reduced to 50–70% by 1350.[3] Bristol, widely regarded as the third city of the country and created a separate county in 1373, was rather smaller than York; and Norwich, also claiming to be third only to London and York for much of the Middle Ages, had a population that 'may have reached 20,000', much reduced by the Black Death and estimated at 6,600 from the Poll Tax returns of 1377.[4] Coventry, which 'recovered quickly from the Black Death (1348–50) and remained prosperous for roughly a century thereafter', paid 'the fourth-highest poll-tax in the kingdom' in 1377.[5] These very prosperous trading towns were highly influential in the fourteenth and fifteenth centuries, with far more power than the old county towns such as Exeter (with a population of around 3,000

---

[1] Tittler, 'Towns and urban life', 736–7.
[2] Harding, 'London', especially 458.
[3] Dobson, 'York', 829.
[4] Virgoe, 'Norwich', 549; Mortimer, *Time Traveller's Guide*, 10. According to Barker (*England Arise*, 333), Norwich came fifth in the country in 1377, with just under 4,000 taxpayers.
[5] Tittler, 'Coventry', 239.

after the Black Death), Lincoln (between 5,000 and 10,000 before the Black Death, fewer than 4,000 in 1377),[6] Nottingham and Leicester.[7]

Most towns were governed by a two-tier system of ruling bodies: typically, there was a large advisory group of perhaps twenty-four citizens and a smaller group of twelve aldermen from whom the mayor was elected each year. London, because of its size, had around 24 aldermen, each with judicial responsibility for one of the city's wards; and York had a third group, of forty-eight, from about the time it became a county in 1386.[8] In some cases members of these councils were elected directly from the trade guilds, which therefore had a very close relationship with the town's governance. In discussing the use of minstrelsy in civic affairs, therefore, the financial records of the trade guilds will be considered as well as those of the town itself.

The men who governed the town, its wealth and its guilds also controlled the town's charitable institutions. This was itself a charitable activity, and one that influential men took seriously for the best of altruistic motives, but it was not wholly free of self-interest. Poverty and deprivation were not good for a town in any respect, including the financial: poor citizens made for a poor town. But more importantly, charitable acts – which many guildsmen could easily afford – were good for the soul, reducing the time that the donor would spend in Purgatory after death. The trade guilds therefore took on many charitable duties for their members and their families, including paying for a member's burial and supporting his widow and children. The wealthier citizens also founded and supported charitable institutions such as hospitals, alms-houses and religious guilds.

The religious guilds were normally attached to a particular church and might have specific aims such as the organisation of a procession at Corpus Christi or Trinity. Their charitable functions, like those of the trade guilds, included looking after their members and their families, and they might also support a chantry priest or a priest in charge of a bridge chapel to pray for travellers. They sometimes took part in the same kinds of celebration as trade guilds, although they generally spent less money on minstrelsy, and on fewer occasions.

The wealth of the most successful towns brought both the ability and the will to patronise musicians and to use music as a spectacular and sonic resource to enhance the town's prestige. From the late thirteenth century onwards the major towns spent considerable sums on minstrels at their various ceremonies and civic functions. From the late fourteenth century, as they grew in wealth and influence during recovery from the Black Death, they found it convenient and prestigious to employ minstrels on a permanent basis and to give them livery as if they were household servants. By the early sixteenth century even some relatively small towns had their own liveried minstrels, which they called 'pipers' or 'waits'. The employment of civic

[6] Kermode, 'Lincoln', 420.
[7] Mortimer, *Time Traveller's Guide*, 10, shows the numbers of taxpayers and estimated populations of the thirty largest towns and cities in 1377.
[8] REED Civic London, I, xiv; REED York, I, x.

minstrels did not add a new dimension to civic life, but partly regularised the existing situation. The early history of the town waits is explored in Chapter 7.[9]

Minstrelsy in civic life

Daily life

A town dweller could hardly avoid minstrelsy in daily life, although not all of it was of high quality. Indeed, one regular type of minstrelsy heard in the larger towns on a daily basis was 'rough music', the raucous, noisy music that accompanied criminals to their punishment. There are few records of this in the medieval period, and the function may be hidden in payments to minstrels for unspecified purposes. The records of London include several instances for which specific information is given. All are for punishment at the pillory or the ducking-stool – none, as it happens, for the death sentence – and show that minstrels accompanied the miscreant from prison to the place of punishment, and again on the return journey. The procession was a public humiliation of the criminal: the music drew attention to this, often in a parody of the processional music used to accompany nobility and royalty. The instruments played are variously described as trumpets, trumpets and pipes, loud minstrelsy, bagpipe or hornpipe,[10] and there are hints that such processions were accompanied by at least drummers. It is not possible to say what the norm might have been, and probably there were considerable variations from place to place.[11]

Other day-by-day uses of minstrelsy at the lower levels of society, where the evidence is most likely to be destroyed (supposing that it was generated in the first place), are even more difficult to track down. One such is minstrelsy in the stews, the bath-houses where men could have a hot bath, meet friends and enjoy female company. While there is iconographic evidence of the stews, including minstrelsy, there seem to be no records of payments surviving, so that it is not possible to say who the minstrels were. The assumption must be that the stews employed local independent minstrels,[12] perhaps the less respectable performers who could not command large rewards elsewhere. We do not know the likely remuneration available, however, and we may never have that information.

The guilds and minstrelsy

The interconnections of town and guilds meant that many events in the civic calendar were jointly organised and financed. In these various events minstrels had two functions. The first was to contribute to the public spectacle of colourful pageantry

---

[9] For a survey of towns employing civic minstrels by 1509, see Rastall, 'Civic minstrels'.
[10] *REED Civic London*, 7 (1336/7), 19–21 (1381/2), 23 (1381/2), 112 (1423/4), and 176 (?1453/4).
[11] The continental illustrations in Bowles, *Musikgeschichte*, 144–7, show trumpets and bagpipes, but these are rather special examples and may not be typical.
[12] For the stews see Mortimer, *Time Traveller's Guide*, 21 and 197. An illustration is in Bowles, *Musikgeschichte*, 151 (Plate 145).

and dramatic presentation, through both the vision of minstrelsy – often including banners and bright livery – and the symbolism of music and instruments. The sound of minstrelsy acted to draw attention to the total spectacle as well as to itself, enhancing the overall effect of the processions and 'sights' of the events. The second function was entertainment at the private celebrations, and especially at the feasts, of the institutions of civic government and individual guilds. At the feasts, payment was often to a single minstrel, sometimes identified as a harper: one may guess that he was usually a *gestour*, able to sing songs and to recite the deeds of heroes and other worthies.

The relationships between towns and guilds also meant that the town minstrels were able to perform at the annual dinners of certain guilds and to take part in the Corpus Christi pageants. In effect, the civic minstrels were hardly full-time employees of the town, even if the civic authorities had first call on their services. At Norwich, the guild of St George decided in 1408 to give a yearly fee to the city waits, presumably for services to be rendered.[13] The Coventry Smiths made the town waits and their wives members of the guild in 1481 on condition that they 'serve the crafte on corpus Christi day' by performing.[14]

A much later example of such collaboration, although apparently not including membership, is found in some early sixteenth-century records of the Jesus Guild in London. An order was made around 1506, and implemented from at least 1514/15 until 1534/5, for six waits to give notice to members that the Guild would celebrate the feasts of the Transfiguration (6 August) and the Name of Jesus (7 August). The waits would display painted banners and wear embroidered badges of the guild (the 'garlands') sewn onto the pipers' coats.[15] This seems an expensive way of telling the guildsmen of the approaching celebrations, and clearly the guild did not do things by halves: presumably someone with a loud voice went with the pipers to make the actual announcement at various points along the route, but the procession must have been a considerable spectacle. The waits also performed at dinner, another spectacular event, both literally and metaphorically, with their banners and badges.

These waits may have been the civic minstrels of London, who numbered six at the time, but the guild's order does not say so, and their wearing of the guild's 'garlands' suggests otherwise. They may have been an *ad hoc* group of pipers:[16] certainly there was no shortage of independent pipers in London.

In London, then, the institution of civic minstrels may have made relatively little difference to the general availability of minstrels. We know, for instance, that the Merchant Taylors hired the waits for their feast on the Nativity of St John the Baptist

---

[13] Stephen, 'Waits of Norwich', 5.

[14] Sharp, *Dissertation*, 213, repr. in *REED Coventry*, 64.

[15] 'Also to vj way*tes* with ban*er*s payn*ted* cognisau*nces* embrowdred with Iesus goyng all the Stre*tes* and Suburbs of london playing with their Instrume*ntes* to yif warnyng & knowlegge to the people of the said Fraternitie of the said Festes of T*ra*nsfigura*cion* & name of Iesu accordyng to the aforsaid ordena*nces* x s. in rewarde by cause of their attenda*un*ce at the dyner & for their garlo*n*des iiij s. in all … xiiij s.'. *REED Ecclesiastical London*, 49 and *passim*.

[16] The meanings of 'wait' are discussed below.

in 1454, 1455 and 1456,[17] but it is clear that they were not the most important musical force there, as they were in many other towns. The Merchant Taylors' costs for the feast in 1456, for instance, included the minstrels listed in Table 9.[18] The payment to the waits is hardly more than a fifth of that to the trumpeters. Without the waits this would still have been an event in which minstrelsy played a very conspicuous part.

Table 9. The Merchant Tailors of London: cost of minstrels at the feast of St John the Baptist, 1456.

Trumpeters	30s 0d
The Waits of London	6s 10d
Wine for he said trumpeters	10d
Ale consumed by [the trumpeters]	6d
Henry Luter and his boys	3s 8d
A minstrel of the Earl of Oxford	20d
A tumbler	3s 4d
John Piper, minstrel	8d

Civic ceremonies

Civic records rarely name the minstrels, so that their employment tends to look casual: but hiring a competent minstrel was not left to chance, as is clear from records that do name them, sometimes the same man over several years. Any town had resident minstrels who were well known and respected by their fellow-citizens and by the civic authorities, who could easily secure their services for specific occasions. At York, the Chamberlains paid out 13s 4d to local minstrels and £7 7s 4d to those of the king and other nobles when Richard II attended the Corpus Christi festivities in 1397.[19] This kind of annual expenditure could be a serious drain on resources, but it was not until 1490 that York imposed a limit of 45s 0d on the city's expenses for Corpus Christi Day.[20]

The high standing of some of these local independent minstrels is shown by their entry into the guilds. At Leicester, William le Tauborer appears in a Guild Roll of 1313/14; John Sturmyn, trumpeter, bought his freedom in the city of Norwich in 1346/7; and Roger Wait, piper, became a freeman of York in 1363. At Coventry, the Carpenters' Guild employed various minstrels in the mid-fifteenth century, and in some cases made them brothers of the guild: the harper Robert Crudworth and his wife Alice in 1453, William Barnebroke in 1454, and William Metcalf in 1463.[21]

---

[17] REED Civic London, I, 176–7.
[18] REED Civic London, I, 179.
[19] Davies, York, 230.
[20] Raine, York, II, 55.
[21] Bateson, Leicester, I, 356; Stephen, 'Waits of Norwich', 5; Langwill, 'Waits', 171 (there is however no reason to think that Roger was employed by the city as a town minstrel); REED Coventry, 26, 547 and 552.

Liveried minstrels, too, could become members of guilds: Hugo the trumpeter, who entered the Merchants' Guild at Leicester in 1343/4, was probably a minstrel of the Earl of Derby, at whose request the entrance-fee of a gold florin was remitted to him. John Brothir, trumpeter of a later earl of Derby, may have been a guild-member, as may the John Broder who was a minstrel of Edward IV.[22]

A very important part of any civic ceremonial was the procession, among which were the marching watches at Midsummer (St John the Baptist's day, 24 June) and the feast of St Peter in Chains (1 August). These were largely military: the marchers were armed, marched in military fashion, and were accompanied by military music. The accounts of the mayor of Leicester for 1338/9 show that minstrels were paid 3d for playing trumpets (*tubant'*) before the community, who had been mustered on the earl's orders before the feast of St Peter in Chains.[23] Since the marching watch on that day was a militaristic procession anyway, the earl presumably found it a convenient occasion to convene all the local militia at a time when armed conflict with France was at a serious level.[24]

In Coventry the minstrelsy on St John's night and St Peter's night gave employment to fewer minstrels than one might expect, and often minstrels were paid for the two occasions together: it is also unclear what payments are for the procession and what for the dinner. The Smiths employed a harper, in 1449 and 1451, and two harpers in the intervening year. In 1469 they paid one minstrel for each occasion, but in 1471, 1474 and 1477 they paid two. The number of minstrels supplied by the Carpenters also fluctuated between one and two on these occasions,[25] and after 1453 they had Robert Crudworth as their own harper. A payment to 'metcalf and banbreke' in 1467 suggests that those two minstrels were regularly employed by the company: but although more than one minstrel was paid in 1478, the Carpenters had only one minstrel apart from the waits at the annual dinner in the previous year – and that at a fee of a mere 2d. It seems unlikely that the company employed two minstrels regularly, and the payment in 1485 is again to a single minstrel.

The Dyers, too, were not big spenders on minstrels. They made an unspecified payment to minstrels for Midsummer night and St Peter's night in 1463; paid two minstrels 8d for the Midsummer celebrations in 1482; and 16d to an unknown number – but more than one – for both Midsummer and St Peter's nights in 1494. Rather intriguingly, the Dyers gave 4d to 'journeyman minstrels' on an unspecified occasion in 1480 and 20d 'to the Jernamen' on Midsummer night 1504: could these be the Dyers' own journeymen, journeymen of other trades who were capable of minstrelsy, or professional minstrels under training?

In contrast to the marching watches, most civic processions were religious events in which the clergy joined with the civic authority. Some of these saints' days were

---

[22] Bateson, *Leicester*, II, 58 f, and Kelly, *Notices*, 128 and 131; MERH, 26, n. 1.
[23] Bateson, *Leicester*, II, 45.
[24] Bevan, *Edward III*, 46–7.
[25] The entry for 1451 gives only 'mynstrelles': but the payment was only 6d, which compares unfavourably with other payments even if only two minstrels were concerned. If more than two were involved then 6d was a poor reward.

celebrated universally, others mainly locally. At York, minstrels were paid by the minster for performing at the feast of the Translation of St William (the Sunday after Epiphany) and at Pentecost, and by St Leonard's Hospital at the celebration of St Leonard's day (6 November).[26] We should expect that any guild organising a procession would wish to make a fine display, and therefore to have as much minstrelsy as possible. This was probably the intention when it was ordained that the Guild of St Helen and St Mary at Beverley should process to the church of the Minorites on the feast of St Helen 'with much music'.[27]

Such celebrations were spectacular events that did honour to the town. Some, like the patronal feasts of the individual companies, fostered business connections and trade with the guilds concerned; others demonstrated loyalty to a wealthy patron, a local magnate or the king. London, which had a close but not always happy relationship with the Crown, saw more royal processions than other towns did, as we have seen.[28] The London companies were also much involved in wholly civic occasions such as the ridings of the mayor and sheriffs after their election, and the Goldsmiths, Grocers, Mercers and Merchant Tailors all paid for minstrels on these occasions. The existing records are sparse and irregular, and in many years only one company's accounts survive to show that minstrels were hired. Those for 1402/3 are unusual in showing that the Grocers, the Mercers and the Merchant Tailors all hired minstrels for the mayor's riding. Some companies simply made a financial contribution to another company, which would arrange the minstrels for the occasion. In 1420/1 the Grocers received 20s 0d from the Ironmongers as their contribution to the cost of minstrels at the mayor's riding.[29]

London was unique in its participation in royal processions, when the guilds formed part of the civic presence. The Grocers, and presumably other companies too, went with the mayor and aldermen to Blackheath in 1422, first to meet the king and then, a week later, to meet the queen, Katherine of Valois, and accompany her to the Tower. The following day they processed with her from the Tower to Westminster ahead of her coronation. These two events cost the Grocers £10 for the hire of minstrels, with another 10s 0d for the minstrels' expenses.[30] This sum could perhaps account for other companies involved, if the Grocers were acting as their agent: but if so they were not the only ones, for in the same year, and apparently for the same occasions, the Merchant Tailors paid £8 1s 0d for minstrels meeting the king and queen, and for their livery.[31] Similarly, the Grocers and the Merchant Tailors both provided minstrels on the occasion of Henry IV's coronation in 1399: the Grocers paid 48s 4d in fees for seven minstrels (unspecified), 8s 6d for their

---

[26] REED York, passim. Some of the minster payments may be for the other feast of St William, on 8 June.

[27] Smith, Gilds, 148 f. The feast is on 3 September.

[28] REED Civic London, I, passim.

[29] Ibid., I, 88.

[30] 562 Ibid., I, 89. The costs are unspecified, but would probably be for food, drink, and fodder for the horses.

[31] Ibid., I, 89.

hoods, and 6s 8d for their food. Participation in royal events was a very costly business: and on top of the fees, hoods and food, the guild also paid 20d for the repair of 'our banners'.[32]

Several companies owned banners for the minstrels' instruments. In 1369/70 the Goldsmiths paid a painter for materials including fringes; and in 1399/1400 the Merchant Tailors' banners were painted at a cost of 23s 0d (not demonstrably for Henry IV's coronation, although that is possible).[33] Professional minstrels normally provided their own instruments, but some companies also held a considerable capital in musical instruments. In the 1380s the Goldsmiths owned two silver trumpets, presumably to be played by hired trumpeters and returned to the company afterwards. These may be the trumpets mended in 1380-2 and perhaps replaced in 1390/1.[34] On this latter occasion a list of newly-made instruments delivered to the Goldsmiths includes trumpets (two of them, to judge by the weight recorded), clarions, a small shawm, a bombard, a large shawm and a cornemuse. The last four appear to be the 'four pipes for the minstrels', valued at 25s 4d.[35]

In 1396-8 the Goldsmiths paid 4s 0d for a chest for the 'minstrelsy' (i.e. the musical instruments). At about the same time (1397/8) the Grocers also bought a chest (*cista*) and twenty banners for the minstrels (which argues for an unusually large body of minstrels).[36] This chest may have been for storing and protecting the banners to be used on the minstrels' own instruments: there is no evidence that the Grocers owned any instruments.

Of all the saints' days celebrated with a procession through the town the feast of Corpus Christi was the most important, with a procession involving minstrels, a feast and, in some places, dramatic entertainments.[37] Corpus Christi (the Body of Christ) was a movable feast, celebrated on the Thursday after Trinity Sunday (therefore between 21 May and 24 June), when the Sacrament was carried through the town in a procession that included both *haut* and *bas* minstrelsy. In general, the *haut* consort (usually trumpets, sometimes with shawms) led the procession, while the *bas* instruments (almost invariably stringed instruments) accompanied the Sacrament, as we should expect.[38]

At Coventry, as in other towns, the guilds employed more minstrels for the Corpus Christi procession than for other processions. The earliest of the Smiths' accounts do not specify the number of minstrels hired in 1450 and 1451, but their

---

[32] *Ibid.*, I, 35, 36.

[33] *Ibid.*, I, 10 and 37.

[34] *Ibid.*, I, 25, 27 and 30; 15, 31.

[35] The two silver trumpets noted in 1389/90 weighed 10 marks and half an ounce; the newly-made trumpets in 1390/1 weighed 10 marks 8½ ounces. See *REED Civic London*, I, 30 and 31. The weights shown for the individual instruments must refer to the shawms, bombard and cornemuse that were intended for the minstrels.

[36] *REED Civic London*, I, 34.

[37] Bowles, 'Corpus Christi procession', and see *REED York, passim*. Corpus Christi is the Thursday after Trinity Sunday, itself a feast.

[38] Bowles, 'Corpus Christi procession', *passim*. Most of Bowles' examples are continental, but they are sometimes paralleled by English examples, as the REED volumes show.

payment of 8s 0d is comparable to those made to four minstrels in 1463 and to the civic waits from 1467 onwards: the minstrels hired in 1450, 1451 and 1463 may in fact have been the town waits. By 1498 the Smiths employed their own minstrel,[39] but he does not appear in the accounts, just as the waits do not appear for Corpus Christi payments after their admission to the Smiths' company in 1481. The luter who played at the Smiths' annual dinner in 1452 was perhaps in the company's regular employment, therefore.[40]

The Coventry Smiths' expenditure on minstrels at Corpus Christi each year was far in excess of payments made by other guilds. In 1450 they spent a total of 10s 6d on the hire and food of an unspecified number of minstrels in the two days of the Corpus Christi celebrations, compared with only 13d paid by the Carpenters for one minstrel.[41] The payment for 1456 shows that their minstrel was a harper, perhaps in addition to Robert Crudworth, the company's own harper.[42]

The Smiths made another large payment the following year, but in 1454 they seem only to have hired a single minstrel for the occasion (see below). The larger payments continued in 1463 with 9s 0d to four minstrels for playing in the pageant and procession (that is, again on both days). These minstrels may have been the city waits, who numbered four at this time, and who had been hired by the Smiths for their annual dinner in 1452. The accounts for 1467, 1471 and 1477 specify that the Smiths hired the city waits for the Corpus Christi celebrations, and in 1481 the four waits and their wives were admitted to the guild (see above).[43]

The admission of the waits indicates that in the late fifteenth century they provided the music for the Smiths' pageant when the famous Coventry plays were performed. Payment to the waits in 1477 was for 'pypyng': but it seems to have been normal at Coventry for one of the waits to be a trumpeter,[44] and they probably formed a shawms-and-trumpet band of the type known elsewhere. The Smiths performed the Passion sequence in the mystery plays, probably from the agony in the Garden up to the death of Christ, perhaps including the burial of Christ and

---

39 See the payment for St Peter's night under this date.
40 Note, too, that the payment for the minstrel in 1454 was for expenses, not a fee: it reads more like an account for food (cf. 1450, 'Payd ... for their hyr', but 'spend on their bord': also 1451). These expenses were probably for the company's own minstrel.
41 The Carpenters employed a single minstrel in 1450, 1453, 1456 and 1487, although there may have been more in 1452. The mention of 'menstrells' may indicate only that the company did not employ the same minstrel for all three occasions.
42 Crudworth had been admitted to the Carpenters' company in 1453: I say 'in addition to' only because of the discrepancy between the 14d given to Crudworth for Midsummer and St Peter's night and the 3d given to 'j harp' for Corpus Christi. However, the Carpenters' own minstrel received only 3d at the annual dinner in 1461, so the payment at Corpus Christi, 1456, could have been to Crudworth.
43 REED Coventry, 64. The waits are named as Thomas West, Adam West, John Blewet and Brese: their wives are not named.
44 Harris, Coventry Leet Book, 59 (1423), 189 (1439) and 200 (1442).

certainly taking in the dream of Pilate's wife and the hanging of Judas.[45] Loud ceremonial music would be in order at the entrances of Herod and Pilate.[46]

The Church required only a procession for the feast of Corpus Christi, first celebrated in England in 1318, but to this were added the individual guilds' feasts and, in some places, the civic plays. The minstrels who performed in the Coventry processions were the waits (apparently three shawms and a trumpet: see Chapter 7), plus perhaps a luter or other *bas* instrumentalist (Smiths); one, and sometimes two, harpers (Carpenters). A payment to a single minstrel by another company dates from the sixteenth century (Cappers). This evidence is not conclusive, but it does agree with Bowles' continental findings on the Corpus Christi procession in general.[47] Minstrelsy was also required at the guild dinners, not always distinguishable in the records from that of the procession. Ingram noted that the Coventry waits 'were busy throughout Corpus Christi day ... : they played first in the procession, then as they were contracted for the plays (at different times as a group or as individuals), and finally for the official feasts that closed the day'.[48] Music in the plays was used to fulfill two different functions: first, to characterise certain persons and locations in the presentation (as we shall see in the case of the 'sights' at Prince Edward's entry to Coventry, below); and second, to mark certain important boundaries in the dramatic structure.[49]

Levels of expenditure

The major towns and cities were perhaps less extravagant than London in celebrating the annual civic events, but all towns tended to display the pomp and ceremony of processions, church services and feasts. There were certainly great differences in the finances and other resources available to the various towns, however, and the records illustrate this in two ways: through the buildings available to the civic and guild organisations, and in direct comparisons of the expenditure on the kind of event discussed above.

The wealthiest London guilds, and some of the wealthier cities, built themselves magnificent guildhalls to meet in, and it is tempting to think that all guild celebrations took place in these buildings and with lavish entertainment. But whatever the situation with the large-scale civic occasions, the private internal celebrations probably involved only one or two minstrels. Various civic accounts show that some events took place in private houses and not in the guildhall at all, even if the guild had

---

[45] King and Davidson, *Coventry Plays*, 29–33.

[46] The Crucifixion itself would not include music. Still minstrelsy was a frequent feature of heavenly scenes, but Heaven did not intervene at the Crucifixion: Stevens, 'Music in mediaeval drama', 83.

[47] It also agrees with the 'mynstrallcy of the Wayts of the Cite' and 'mynstralcy of harpe and lute' at the entry of Prince Edward in 1474, as noted below.

[48] *REED Coventry*, xxi.

[49] Rastall, *The Heaven Singing*, 175–249 (Chapters 5 and 6). Music was not used as background music or to underline emotional content. For Coventry especially, see Rastall, *Minstrels Playing*, 179–221. Relevant Coventry accounts in *REED Coventry* supersede those printed by Sharp and others.

one. It is difficult to see any pattern in these private occasions, but an inquest held in Oxford on 21 August 1306 is informative. One Gilbert Foxlee, a clerk, had caused an affray in the early hours of 24 June that year, receiving a wound from which he died eight weeks later. It is the circumstances of the affray that concern us here, for Gilbert had objected to celebrations held by the Tailors of Oxford. This celebration was held not on guild property but in the tailors' shops – effectively in private houses, since a tradesman normally lived above his workshop.[50]

On the eve of the Nativity of St John the Baptist 1306 the Tailors of Oxford and others with them were keeping watch in their shops through the night, 'singing and making merry with harps and fiddles and various other instruments' (*cantantes et facientes solatia sua cum Cytharis viellis et alijs diuersis instrumentis*) according to custom. Some time after midnight, believing that the streets were empty of people, they all left the shops and danced in the High Street. As they were playing (*ludebant*), Gilbert Foxlee appeared with an unsheathed sword in his hand and started a quarrel with them.[51] The affair ended in Gilbert's fatal wounding, but that is not our present concern. Here we should note that the guild's entertainment included singing and the playing of various musical instruments, perhaps by some of the guildsmen but almost certainly led by professional minstrels. The guildsmen may have danced indoors as well as making music, but evidently they preferred to go outside to dance, presumably to give themselves a better space. The night's entertainment was intended to be indoors, however, the street being a bonus that presented itself to them. Guild records of payment to minstrels at such feasts were perhaps not unusually for celebrations in private houses, although they only occasionally say so.

Secondly, a direct comparison of expenditure in a wealthy town and a less wealthy one will show very clearly how the scale of rewards to minstrels varied. In this chapter it has been convenient to concentrate on the wealthiest towns: not only did they spend most generously on minstrelsy but their records, in general, survive better than in smaller places. The major centres were in the minority, however, and there were many smaller towns that paid for minstrelsy on various occasions, so cities like London, York and Coventry were not the norm.

We can take York as a place that spent generously on minstrelsy. Among the visiting minstrels each year were those of the king, who received the highest rewards: to begin with these were normally 6s 8d, occasionally 13s 4d and once, in 1486, 20s 0d. The cost to the city was greater than just the rewards, however, because visiting minstrels were often given food and wine as well. Looking at the costs of rewarding minstrels and other entertainers in 1446–9, for which the detailed expense-accounts survive, we can see that occasional rewards alone cost an average of about £7 each year, with another £3 or so for the Corpus Christi celebrations: and all this in addition to the costs of maintaining three civic minstrels.[52]

---

[50] *REED Oxford*, I, 5–6; translation by Patrick Gregory (here slightly modified), *ibid.*, II, 905–6.

[51] The use of *ludere* ('to play') here relates to the guildsmen's dancing, not to the modern usage of playing an instrument.

[52] *REED York*, I, 65–77.

In the second half of the century the city probably tried to limit gifts to royal minstrels, but even those to the king's, the queen's and the prince's might come to £1 or more when food and wine were included. It is perhaps not surprising, therefore, that in 1489 the city decided that only the king's minstrels should be rewarded each year, and that the expenses of the Corpus Christi celebrations should be limited to £2, the chamberlains being made responsible for paying any sum above that. These limitations were evidently unworkable, however: in 1499 the city gave 10s 0d to six minstrels of the prince (Arthur) and spent £3 13s 11d on various expenses for Corpus Christi, with another 3s 4d paid to the doctor of theology who preached the sermon.[53] In 1506 the city rewarded the minstrels of the prince (Henry) with 10s 0d 'as in previous years', those of the king with 20s 0d 'as in previous years' and two minstrels of Lord Darcy with 20d.[54] The annual expenditure on minstrels and other entertainers must have come close by then to the average of £11 or more in the late 1440s.

Table 10. Minstrels rewarded at Barnstaple, 1470/1.

Given to a minstrel	4d
William Grevyll [minstrel]	12d
A bearward	2s 0d
In wine given to Philip Beaumunt [minstrel], the same time	4d
Given to a minstrel of Lord Denham	8d
a minstrel called Nytherton	4d
a minstrel	4d
Thomas Luter	4d
a piper (*ffustulator*)	4d
a minstrel of Exeter	4d
the minstrel William Grevyll	8d
a/the bearward, by the mayor	12d
(a) minstrel(s) of the Duke of Gloucester	12d
(a) minstrel(s) of the Duke of Buckingham	16d

Many of the same occasions were celebrated in smaller boroughs such as Barnstaple in north Devon, a flourishing port that regularly rewarded minstrels and other entertainers. In the surviving records of 21 years from 1435/6 to 1483/4 the annual sums disbursed range from 2s 10d in 1474/5 to 15s 6d in 1467/8, with an average of 8s 10d.[55] The sums paid in 1470/1, shown in Table 10, are typical (the original is in Latin). These entries show the usual spectrum of named and un-named minstrels

---

53 Ibid., I, 181.
54 Ibid., I, 203.
55 REED Devon, 30–6.

and bearwards (the names recurring through the years), together with the servants of local and other magnates. In other years there are also heralds, trumpeters and actors. In some years (although not in this one) there are payments to entertainers during the Christmas period, at the vigil of the nativity of St John the Baptist (24 June), and on Hock Day (the second Tuesday after Easter). It seems that 4d was the standard gift to a minstrel, or some multiple of 4d for a well-known local minstrel or the servant of a great lord. The 2s od given to the first bearward seems exceptional, but in general, as one would expect, the rewards are small compared with those given at York and by other major cities and households. Nothing here compares with the 6s 8d regularly provided by those institutions, and the total annual expenditure is a small fraction (under 4%) of that paid by the major centres.

Hiring minstrels

The occasional employment of musicians for civic events required the existence of 'fixers' on both sides – someone deputed by the town authorities or the guild concerned to negotiate for performers, and someone who was in touch with performers and could gather the necessary group together. A guild needing a small group of singing-men for a mystery play, for instance, would approach the precentor or some other singing-man of the local cathedral or large church; if they needed boy singers, then they contacted the Master of the Choristers.[56] For minstrels, similar points of contact were needed. The London Grocers rewarded a member (or perhaps a servant) called Thomas Bourne who was deputed to 'ride for minstrels' – that is, going to find minstrels to hire – several times between 1412/13 and 1419–21. This could be a lengthy process involving considerable travel: he was reimbursed for the costs of his horse, and payments for his meals show that he was sometimes away for more than twenty-four hours. Occasionally he had to treat minstrels to meals during the negotiations.[57]

The London Mercers paid a man named Thomas to procure minstrels between 1429/30 and 1452/3. He is shown as 'Thomas Trumpere' in the accounts for 1429/30 and 'Thomas with the trumpet' (*ouesque le trompe*) in those for 1452/3. It is not certain that these are the same man, but he or they invite further investigation. The records for 1436/7 name him as Thomas Chatirton, minstrel; and in 1444/5 a payment 'pur bryan & Chaterton Trumpettis pur son labour pur lez mynstrelx suisditz' concerns the engagement of minstrels for the mayor's swearing-in. The Thomas Chalkton who arranged seventeen trumpeters for the mayor's riding in 1449/50 is

---

[56] Some relevant records published by REED are analysed and discussed in Rastall, *Minstrels Playing*, 198–217, 292–9 and *passim*. Although these are for performances in the late sixteenth century, London records for earlier royal entries hint at a similar pattern. See *REED Civic London*, I, 103, for payment to Lionel (?Power) and his singing boys in 1425/6; *ibid.*, 119–27, for choristers singing at the reception of the king in 1432, probably under the direction of John Steynour, clerk of St Dunstan, who apparently composed the music.

[57] *REED Civic London*, I, 60–77, *passim*. Bourne's work is reminiscent of the costs of civic officers looking to hire minstrels as town waits for Canterbury: see p. 153.

clearly the same man.[58] The trumpeter Bryan is not yet identifiable, but Thomas Chaterton is surely the royal trumpeter of that name, first heard of in 1416 (he was not in the Agincourt campaign) and serving the monarch until 30 or 31 Henry VI, about the time of the Mercers' last payment to him. The Mercers' employment of Chaterton as fixer makes it likely that some of the trumpeters engaged by him were also royal minstrels.

Other companies employed entertainers named Thomas, possibly in some cases as a fixer. The Merchant Tailors made regular payments to minstrels for the St John's day feast, Thomas and a waferer between 1421/2 and 1435/6. In both of those years Thomas is named as Tom Fool, but in the years between only as Thomas. There is no direct evidence that he worked as a fixer, and perhaps he was paid simply for his entertainment as a fool: but there is a problem of identity. The Grocers paid one Thomas 'with the staffis' in 1431/2 (twice) and Thomas 'with the trumpe' in 1448/9, probably as a fixer on both occasions; the Drapers made two payments to 'Thomas' in 1433/4, the second to Thomas 'with the trumpet', in both cases apparently for arranging for minstrels; and the Brewers paid Thomas Gestour for his work at their feast in 1434/5, and both 'Thome' and 'Thomas Iestour' for unspecified work in 1436/7. In 1454/5 the Merchant Tailors rewarded Thomas Reymer 'with þe trumpe' for performing at the feast of St John the Baptist. Thomas Gestour and Thomas Jestour are likely to be the same man: if he was also 'Thomas Reymer with the trumpe', his use of the instrument suggests that his entertainment was like that of a herald rather than a story-teller using a *bas* instrument.[59] It is unclear how many men were involved here, and how many of them were fixers for the hiring of minstrels: Thomas 'with the trumpe' was certainly working as a fixer, and so, probably, were all of the others except Tom Fool. How many of them, one wonders, were Thomas Chaterton?

Hosting royalty and nobility

The visit of a royal or noble personage placed responsibilities on the civic authority of both security and the requirement to do honour to the visitor. A local lord who regularly visited would be met at the town gate and escorted through the town with suitable music. A royal person making an occasional visit and staying in the town for a night or two would have a full program of events for which the town was responsible: and the celebrations not only honoured the visitor but also demonstrated the town's loyalty and capabilities. In the case of the king or other noble in a position to patronise the town, the civic authority would have a message to give, lauding the visitor for his or her lineage and good deeds, and incidentally soliciting his or her favour towards the town. To this end, the visitor was usually treated to a series of 'sights', with written mottoes or live speeches. Progress through the town took a considerable time, and it is clear that this entertainment was appreciated by the recipient – and, no doubt, by the townsfolk.

---

[58] *REED Civic London*, I, 115, 140, 162, 170 and 173.

[59] *REED Civic London*, I, 92–140, *passim*, and 135 and 169.

As we noted in Chapter 4, the reception of any royal person into London, or their passage through the city to Westminster, was usually accompanied by 'sights', speeches of welcome and singing. It is the verbal texts and the symbolic significance of the music that mattered, not the musical content *per se*. For this reason eye-witnesses may describe the visual and verbal content of the procession and sometimes described what instruments were used: but the music itself, unless it was vocal, carrying a text, is never mentioned.

Henry V's reception into the capital after his victory at Agincourt in 1415 was carefully thought out and executed at considerable financial cost.[60] The king was met by the civic authorities at Blackheath, as was customary, and on London Bridge and on the processional route to St Paul's cathedral were many tableaux, or 'sights'. The music included the singing of the Agincourt carol ('Owre Kynge went forth to Normandy') by boys dressed as angels and accompanied by an organ, and the psalm *Cantate domino canticum novum* sung by a group of prophets. At St Paul's, a group of young girls sang a welcome to the king. Thomas of Elmham wrote that the conduits ran with wine.[61]

Elizabeth Woodville was also met at Blackheath before her coronation in 1465, entering the city at London Bridge, where the sights and music were concentrated because she was going only to the Tower.[62] The queen was met on the south side by a clerk representing St Paul, followed by a group of clerks singing to her. The main pageant was further along the bridge, where a stage was set up and twenty-six singers greeted her. The pageant included ballads, the words of which were painted on six boards, and St Elizabeth greeted the queen with a speech.[63] At St Thomas's chapel, near the centre of the bridge, choirboys and their master sang to her, and at the north end of the bridge more vocal music was made by the master and choristers of St Magnus' church.

In all this pageantry detailed information is very sparingly given: those describing it wished to give an impression of the quality and extent of the entertainments, but did not feel the need to give details. The importance of the speeches is made clear in the account of Queen Margaret's visit to Coventry in 1456, when the city thought the speeches worth recording in full:[64] but here, rather surprisingly, no mention is made of any singing.

There is however one description of a royal entry that provides more information on the music. When the future Edward V entered Coventry on 28 April 1474 he was only three years old, and the brevity of the speeches made to him were a concession to his youth: but the sights and their symbolisms were all there, just as if the visitor

---

[60] A brief account of these is in Hibbert, *Agincourt*, 131–4.
[61] Elmham, *Vita et Gesta*, 72.
[62] MacGibbon, *Elizabeth Woodville*, 46–8.
[63] This was presumably Elizabeth of Hungary, who is known to have been venerated in England at this time.
[64] *REED Coventry*, 29–34.

were a well-educated adult.⁶⁵ The prince probably understood little or nothing of the entertainment displayed for him, but those responsible for his education no doubt understood it completely and would make sure that the prince did so at a later stage of his life.

Edward approached Coventry from the west and was met by the mayor and corporation outside the city. After a speech of welcome, the prince was given a gilt cup containing 100 marks (£66 13s 4d).⁶⁶ The procession entered the city at Bablake, and from here on the prince was entertained with 'sights', each with its own speech and music:

1. At the gate, the prince was addressed by Richard II, surrounded by peers.⁶⁷ The city waits performed, a loud band to accompany royalty, helping to identify Richard and his companions.
2. Once in the city, the prince was met by three patriarchs standing on the conduit, together with the twelve sons of Jacob. One of the patriarchs addressed the prince, likening his arrival at Coventry to the advent of Christ. Wine ran in one place. The music was that of harp and dulcimer. This still minstrelsy symbolised Divine Order and therefore Heaven itself, appropriately for the forerunners of the Kingdom of Christ. The harp specifically symbolised Christ's body on the Cross.⁶⁸
3. In Broadgate the prince was addressed by St Edward (the Confessor) from a pageant, accompanied by ten estates, representatives of the Heavenly Kingdom. The minstrelsy was that of harp and lute (symbolism as above).
4. At the cross in the Cross Cheaping were three prophets, censing, with Children of Israel above them singing and throwing out wafers and flowers: four pipes ran with wine. The text is not specified. The singing was probably unaccompanied: no instruments are mentioned.
5. At the Panyer inn was a pageant with the three kings of Cologne (i.e. the Magi) and two armed knights, one of whom addressed the prince. The minstrelsy was of 'small pypis', which might be recorders or small bagpipes: the latter, often associated with pilgrims, would be appropriate for the Magi.

---

⁶⁵ Ibid., 53–5, gives the city's record of the sights and the texts of all the speeches except for the opening welcome; for the instruments and their symbolism see Rastall, 'Music for a Royal Entry'.

⁶⁶ This was a standard type of gift, although the money in this case was twice that given to Margaret Tudor at York in 1503: see *REED York*, I, 194. This is probably because the city of Coventry was thought of as 'the prince's chamber' and is referred to thus in the Leet Book account of this visit: London was thought of as 'the king's chamber' and York as 'the queen's chamber'.

⁶⁷ Richard II was associated with the house of York, descendants of his uncle Edmund of Langley, because Richard had been deposed by the Duke of Lancaster (Henry IV). Prince Edward was the Yorkist heir.

⁶⁸ This music was probably inaudible except to those standing close to the minstrels: but the symbolism of the instruments was transmitted visually in the first place.

6. On the conduit in Cross Cheaping was St George, rescuing a king's daughter from the dragon, the girl's parents looking on from a tower. The conduit ran wine in four places. The music was from an organ: organs, associated with the Heavenly Kingdom, were appropriate to the saving of a Christian soul from the devil. St George directly addressed this question in his speech, asking God to defend the prince as he, George, had defended the princess.

Some of the same elements of these sights were shown again when the twelve-year-old Prince Arthur visited Coventry on 17 October 1498.[69] At the cross in the Cross Cheaping, which was the third of four stations, there was running wine and 'Angels sensyng & syngyng with Orgayns and othere melody'. 'Other melody' would be a still consort.[70]

Although such events had to be organised centrally, a town with flourishing trade-guilds could delegate specific responsibility for parts of the entertainment to individual guilds. For Prince Edward's visit, the Smiths' guild spent 7d on 'bryngyng furth the pagent' that day.[71] A pageant (pageant-waggon) was a convenient movable platform on which the actors and singers could stand at stations where there was no high place such as a city gate, cross or conduit.[72] There were two such places: Broadgate and in front of the Panyer inn. The Smiths' pageant was presumably at one of these.

Welcoming royalty to a town was an onerous enough task for most civic governments, and if the personage were staying for one or more nights a longer program of events and entertainments had to be devised. Some towns evidently used the resources available to them through the guilds, and especially those that presented plays. Towns with the resources to mount large dramatic events could provide the singers and minstrels needed for a royal reception, through the guilds or centrally.[73]

---

[69] *REED Coventry*, 89–91; Sharp, *Dissertation*, 155–7.

[70] *REED Coventry*, 91. The text of the song begins 'Ryall prince Arthur / welcomme nowe tresure / with all oure hole Cure / to þis your Cite'. The music is lost.

[71] *Ibid.*, 56.

[72] The alternative was to build a wooden platform, or scaffold, for the purpose, a more cumbersome, expensive and inflexible solution to the problem.

[73] The use of minstrelsy in the plays is discussed briefly above, but see also Rastall, *The Heaven Singing*, and REED volumes for relevant towns.

7

Civic minstrels

Town minstrels in England and abroad

The position of town minstrels, the reasons for their employment and the way in which they were developed varied widely in Europe, and to some extent in England and Scotland.[1] For historical reasons it is useful to consider their position in late medieval Flanders and France before considering the situation in England. While no two towns worked in exactly the same way, the broad outlines of civic security and musical entertainment can be seen.[2]

Many towns in France and Flanders had a bell-tower from which the surrounding countryside could be viewed, and this enabled the performance of several duties. First, because bells could be heard all over the town they could be rung to signal the opening and closing of the town gates at the beginning and end of the day. Second, a watchman could give warning of the approach of an enemy force against which the gates must be closed or of the train of an important personage who must be welcomed; he could also look out for fires at night, very necessary in an age when buildings were largely made of timber and candles or rush lights were the normal lighting. Third, it would be possible to mark certain hours of the day, an important function that could be combined with that of entertaining the citizens with music. Towns therefore employed a watchman – *guet* in French – who could fulfill, or initiate action towards, these various functions.[3]

This *guet* did not have to play a musical instrument if bells were used for signalling purposes, but almost everywhere he played some lip-reed instrument. This was at least an animal horn: but easily the most common was a trumpet, occasionally an inexpensive one, sometimes even a valuable silver one, with the *guet* being known as the city trumpeter. If he were competent as a musician there were also ceremonial functions for which he could be employed. During the fourteenth and fifteenth centuries some of the more wealthy northern towns in the Flemish orbit added

---

[1] No civic minstrels are known in Wales until the sixteenth century.
[2] See Peters, *Musical Sounds*, passim.
[3] In St Omer and Lille the term was *wette/wete*, which appears to be cognate: Peters, *Musical Sounds*, 128, 142–3. Further north (in Bruges, Ghent, Mechelen and Antwerp) the term was *wachter*, but this corresponds to a different, primarily watch-keeping, function: Polk, 'English Instrumental Music', 665, and personal correspondence.

shawmists (usually three) to the trumpeter, forming a standard four-man band.[4] Their principal employment remained that of watching from the tower and playing for the citizens' entertainment at the opening and closing of the gates and at other specified hours during the day: but they were also available, as the trumpeter had been, for various routine and occasional duties such as playing at civic ceremonies and welcoming nobility to the town.

In England, some of these functions of the civic minstrels can be seen in the town records. The purely musical duties in which they performed as the mayor's minstrels in processions and other ceremonial events were the main reason for their existence; and, as on the Continent, in many places they were allowed to entertain the citizens and presumably to accept rewards from the audience. In some places, too, they walked through the town at night, marking the hours and performing at specified places and times, and for specific citizens, as a sort of musical time-piece. On these occasions they also kept their eyes and ears open for security problems such as affrays and fires.

There are also some considerable differences between the various continental arrangements and those in English towns. In England the civic minstrels were rarely, if ever, part of the official watch, which was organised ward by ward with a rota of citizens.[5] Nowhere in England was there a civic bell-tower built on the pattern of the Flemish and French ones from which a professional watch could be kept. The separate belfries that we know of in England were associated with a church in each case, and were smaller than the continental civic belfries: a watchman on such a tower would not see over the adjacent church. This would not affect the playing of music from a tower, but the only evidence for this in England is found in Grenade's account of the Exchange in London, which had two galleries around the bell-tower. Writing in 1578, Grenade explained that the bell not only gave the time through the day but was sounded for the end of trading at noon and again at 6 pm; and that the city's waits entertained those below by playing music from these galleries at 4 pm on Sundays in summer time.[6] This was not a long-standing tradition, however, for the Exchange had been built in 1566 on a continental model.[7]

Some French towns used a church tower for the purposes of keeping watch and providing the musical entertainment described above. There are suitable church towers in England – a watchman on the central tower of Lincoln cathedral or Beverley minster would have an excellent view of the town and the countryside around – but there is no evidence that they were so used.

---

[4] Peters, *Musical Sounds*, 141–3.
[5] See Rastall, 'Secular Musicians', I, 215–16, and *REED Civic London*, I, *passim*. The question of possible watch-duties in ports is addressed below.
[6] Grenade, *Singularities*, 112–18, especially 117.
[7] Grenade, *Singularities*, 172–3 (n. 134), and Stow, *Survey*, 104 and 173.

The institution of civic minstrels in England

With a general growth of civic wealth in the second half of the fourteenth century, towns began to employ minstrels as if they were household servants. The main purpose was to provide the music needed for civic ceremonies: and since the minstrels were attendant on the person of the mayor on these occasions they were sometimes known as 'the mayor's minstrels', as at Lincoln in 1422 and at Bristol later in that century.[8] The Bristol mayor's register for 1479–1503, which often refers to established custom, records an annual payment of 5 marks to the mayor 'for his mynstralles'.[9] At Norwich, the minstrels' liveries were paid for out of the mayor's funds and the city treasury in equal portions c. 1440.[10] Records such as these provide our first certain evidence of the regular employment of civic minstrels.

The minstrels might be referred to as pipers or 'waits'. Some towns, such as Norwich and Coventry, called their minstrels 'waits' almost from the start, but elsewhere the term took some time to emerge. The accounts of the bailiffs of Shrewsbury, for instance, referred to 'the minstrels called the waits' (*ministralli vocati Wayts*) in 1479 and 'the common minstrels called the waits of the town' (*Com' histriones vocati le Wayts ville*) in 1483, which suggests that the term was not firmly established even then. There is, indeed, no reason why the terminology should have been standard, but this lack of standardisation is largely responsible for us not knowing when civic bands were first appointed in different places. In many towns it is only with the records of salaries, liveries or the annual administration of an oath that the employment of civic minstrels is certain.

Civic minstrels appeared first in the 1360s (Exeter, Dover), with other towns following slowly in the 1380s (perhaps Cambridge and Colchester, both doubtful) and 1390s (Bristol, Grimsby, Winchester); there was a steady increase in civic bands through the fifteenth century, with an average of three towns per decade, but ending with a larger increase in the 1490s, when no fewer than nine towns set up civic minstrels. By 1500 most major towns and cities had established their civic minstrels, and many smaller towns followed suit during the sixteenth.[11]

Among the seven towns that probably established civic minstrels by 1400, at least four were ports (Exeter, Dover, Bristol, Grimsby and perhaps Colchester). It seems that some ports (including inland ports on navigable rivers) engaged men to pipe the watch and announce the state of the tide and wind: and some places used horns to make occasional public announcements. These functions are not always separate (or at least not easily separable by us) from the musical matters that concern us here. The rather fragmentary evidence suggests that the town minstrels were not the same men as those who made announcements that were prefaced with a horn-call, but it is also fairly clear that minstrels were sometimes closely associated with this work.

---

[8] Lambert, *Lincoln*, 205. See also Rastall, 'Civic minstrels' under those towns.
[9] Smith, *Gilds*, 423.
[10] Stephen, 'Waits of Norwich', 44.
[11] Rastall, 'Civic minstrels', especially the tables.

The relationship between heralds and trumpeters may or may not be a useful parallel to consider.[12]

Although the terms of employment might vary in different places, there is no doubt that some exchange of information and practices took place at both civic and group levels. The London waits' request for livery in 1442, for instance, was sparked off by their knowledge of what was happening elsewhere. Perhaps because of this, too, there was some movement of civic minstrels from one place to another, a job-mobility that has not previously been recognised. Before these matters are considered, however, there is an important diversion to be followed.

The meaning of 'wait'

It has long been thought that the civic minstrels, or town waits, were originally the civic watchmen, who at some stage in their history replaced the horn with the shawm or 'wait-pipe' as their instrument, turned themselves into musicians and gradually lost most of their watchmen's functions. This theory seems untenable for many reasons: and even after the publication of a great deal of relevant record material by Records of Early English Drama (REED) there is no evidence that it could be true.[13] The town waits were apparently instituted as a group of minstrels attendant on the mayor and charged with supplying the ceremonial music needed for civic ceremonies.

The REED project has however uncovered evidence that in certain places the town waits' early history was more complex than was formerly realised. This evidence concerns the night-time patrols in certain towns, which appear sometimes to be connected with watchmen although there is no firm evidence that the town waits and the watchmen were the same people.[14] The nature of this co-operation is not radically changed by the new evidence: we have long known that the waits of some towns patrolled the streets at night in order to call the hours, and that they kept a lookout for fires and thieves. But it was always acknowledged that a band of musicians walking the streets at night were hardly front-line security: and in fact we still do not know whether calling the hours was a requirement of the town or an opportunity that the waits took to make some income by performing a service to certain wealthy citizens. The new evidence suggests some co-operation between waits and watch that must be explored in future research.

One of the biggest impediments to helpful discussion of the town waits has been the indiscriminate way in which the word 'wait' itself has been used. It did not refer exclusively to the town minstrel, but bore several meanings at different periods. The failure to distinguish between the various meanings has helped to obscure the early history of civic musicians and, especially, to support the myth of

---

[12] See above, pp. 81–4.

[13] The most influential statement of this theory is in Woodfill, *Musicians in English Society*, 33, refuted in Rastall, 'Secular Musicians', I, 214–17, and more fully in Rastall, 'Origin of the Town Waits'.

[14] See my comments on the town minstrels' duties in Rastall, 'Civic minstrels', and especially the sections on Canterbury, the Cinque Ports, Dover, New Romney and Sandwich.

the watchman-turned-town-minstrel. At this stage, therefore, we should explore the various meanings of the word 'wait'.

The term derives from Old French *guet*, a watchman, noted earlier in this chapter.[15] 'Wayte' as a description or surname is found in the English royal households only in 1357,[16] but a Wardrobe book for 15 Ed I (1286–7) records a gift to two local *Gweyte vigilatores* in Gascony.[17] This use of the vernacular term is rare because the royal accounts are in Latin, a domestic watchman being a *vigilis* or *vigilator*. *Vigilis* apparently denoted a civic watchman too: Alexander Neckam (1157–1217), wrote in the late twelfth century,[18]

> Assint etiam excubie vigiles, cornibus suis strepitum et clangorem et sonitum facientes.
>
> (Let the night watches be at hand with their horns making harsh, ringing and loud noise.)

The manuscript concerned dates from the second half of the thirteenth century. It includes interlinear glosses in Anglo-Norman, and here the word *excubie* ('those keeping watch') is glossed as 'veytes'.

This is not the only use of 'wayte' in the late thirteenth century. London's Letter Book A under date 1286/7 records an order requiring each of the city's gates to be guarded by two armed men during the day and closed at night by the servants living there. Each of these servants was to have a wait (*vnum woyte*) at his own expense.[19] If *veyte* and *woyte* are indeed versions of the English for *guet* it is easy to see why this order was made. While the gates would be opened, closed and guarded by men at ground level, those keeping a lookout for travellers to be admitted or refused entrance would be at the top of a town or castle gate, two floors or more higher. Communication from the lookout to the gate-keeper had to be by recognisable signal, and the instrument normally used for that (as the Neckam quotation shows) was the horn.[20] This instrument was normally without finger-holes and could sound only one note, although there was a limited possibility of lipping it up or down to provide others.

---

[15] The change from initial G(u) to W is common in transfers from French to English: guard/ward and guarantee/warranty are two of many examples.

[16] See MERH, 16 and 17.

[17] TNA E36.201 (15 Ed I), f. 31v: printed in Byerly and Byerly, *Records (1286–9)*, 109 (19 August 1287). The spelling suggests that *gweyte* was the Gascons' own description of themselves, in which case it may then have been a new term at the English court.

[18] From *De nominibus utensilium* ('On the Names of Things'), in Wright, *Volume of Vocabularies*, 106: the comma is presumably Wright's. I am grateful to William Flynn for his suggested translation.

[19] REED *Civic London*, I, under that date. I assume that one servant and one wait were employed at each of the city gates, or at least that only one wait was on duty at any time. The possibility of 'wait' being an instrument is ignored here: I have found no instance of that usage, nor any example of the term 'wait-pipe', which may be a fiction.

[20] The horn was also used to raise the hue and cry when a criminal had to be apprehended: see, for instance, SM I, 215.

Late in Edward I's reign (1272–1307) the royal household accounts show that the king's four *vigiles* were occasionally rewarded for minstrelsy as a group, presumably forming a shawm band.[21] This gives us two distinct uses of the word *vigilis* for two different types of watchman: the horn-blowing lookout on the gate of a town or castle, whose function was not musical, and the shawm-playing domestic watchman, who could have been musical and clearly sometimes was. These two types coexisted: there is no question of one turning into the other. There is however a question to be asked: was the domestic shawm-player at this time only an indoor watchman, as the Black Book of 1471–2 describes, or did he also have outdoor responsibilities? There is no real evidence of an outdoor responsibility. Henry V's *vigilatores* on the Agincourt campaign were called his 'guides by night', which may mean only that, as watchmen used to moving around in relative darkness (albeit indoors) they were the best people to attend the king in his encampment. At present the distinction between the use of the horn out of doors and that of the shawm indoors otherwise seems safe, and as far as I know the horn-blower was not known as a 'wait' after the thirteenth-century examples just noted.

To return to the shawm band, Edward II reduced the number of *vigiles*, so that the balance of *vigiles* in the band of pipers was changed. There is no doubt that all these *vigiles* were pipers – probably shawmists, as there is little evidence of bagpipers – with a decreasing number of pipers being *vigiles*.[22] By the end of Edward III's reign (1327–77) it is not certain that any of the *vigilatores* were minstrels: as far as one can see the conditions of employment and payment of a *vigilator* might depend on his capacity to perform minstrelsy, but minstrelsy was not a requirement.[23]

It is in the later part of Edward III's reign that some pipers were given the description of 'wait' ('wayte'), sometimes apparently as a surname. The term was probably applied to any piper from the start and not just to civic minstrels: 'waits' could refer to any band of pipers, often attached to named aristocratic patrons but probably including *ad hoc* bands of independent minstrels.

Current knowledge of the use of the word 'wait' is fragmentary, but clearly the term should be treated with circumspection, as by itself it does not distinguish between town minstrels and other types of piper. With that warning in mind we can explore the early history of the civic minstrels.

The appointment and conditions of civic minstrels

The publication of record material by REED since 1979 has greatly increased the available information about civic minstrels in various places,[24] and this chapter

---

[21] SM II, 17 and 57. This phenomenon was not confined to the Court, nor to England. In 15 Ed I a visiting 'minstrel and *vigilator*' was rewarded in Gascony: TNA E36.201 (15 Ed I), f. 33v: printed in Byerly and Byerly, *Records (1286–9)*, 117 (2 November 1287).

[22] Rastall, 'Pipers and waits', under those reigns.

[23] This may be reflected in the Black Book's section on the wait. In the English Court the term *vigilis* gave way to *vigilator* in the second half of the fourteenth century.

[24] The Malone Society started this kind of work, but with the emphasis on dramatic activity. The very useful collection Dawson, *Kent*, is now superseded by the REED volumes for that county.

offers only a summary of current knowledge of town minstrels in those places where they were established by 1509.[25] Many of the earlier antiquarian publications of town records are now seen to have been very selective, but not always saying precisely what was omitted. The REED volumes are now the standard source of information on early drama and minstrelsy in England, Scotland and Wales, and are cited here. Where a town's records are not yet covered by REED, the older antiquarian publications have been consulted, but in the knowledge that the information they give may be incomplete.[26]

Appointment and pay

Some records of the appointment of town minstrels (the usual term for employment is 'retained') show that an oath was administered. It seems obvious that any employee serving a town or city should swear to do the job efficiently and honestly – or, as the Beverley governors required in 1452, 'well and faithfully' (*bene et fideliter*).[27] Town minstrels would have to be available for any civic function requiring their services, but the post offered many professional advantages, and some continued in their employment for 40 years or more. It is unlikely that they were appointed for life, however, and there is plenty of evidence for an annual review, when the minstrels were named and sworn in. Renewal was perhaps usual as long as the minstrel behaved himself and did his job satisfactorily. Towns varied in the stability of their minstrel group: many show the same men as waits over long periods, others a less regular pattern of employment. Beverley maintained a fairly regular turnover of its civic minstrels, which may have been a matter of policy.[28]

There was also competition for places, although we have no statistics for this. In 1484 or 1485, on the death of the Chester wait William Smethley, several minstrels applied for 'the Rowme and charge of the waitmen of the said city'.[29] Probably a minstrels' network passed around the news of a vacancy very quickly, resulting in several minstrels making their interest known. The serving minstrels would have had a view, and perhaps the mayor and council asked their opinion: certainly the London waits made their choice known in 1517/18, when they nominated John Frith to replace a deceased colleague called Blewet, and Frith was appointed.[30] There are also many cases where relatives were concerned – brothers, fathers and sons – and here a range of considerations no doubt came into play. While the mayor and council would make the final decision, they would not be short of advice.

---

[25] For detail concerning individual towns see Rastall, 'Civic minstrels'.

[26] See <http://reed.utoronto.ca/> for REED publications and work in progress. More information has also been published on the website of the International Guild of Town Pipers: <http://www.townwaits.org.uk/>.

[27] Diana Wyatt, private communication. I am grateful to Dr Wyatt for letting me see her Beverley transcripts for the forthcoming *REED East Riding of Yorkshire* volume.

[28] See the lists of minstrels for various towns in Rastall, 'Civic minstrels'.

[29] BL MS Harley 2091, fol. 21r.

[30] *REED Civic London*, I, 348.

Nevertheless, some towns did have difficulty recruiting suitable minstrels for permanent employment, as is shown by the fluctuating numbers of minstrels in certain towns. Occasionally, too, towns were short of minstrels for specific occasions, such as the major celebration of St Thomas's day in Canterbury. In 1505/6, when Canterbury had no waits, a man was sent to hire the Cambridge waits, apparently for St Thomas's day. He was evidently unsuccessful, but the London waits came and performed as required, as they did in several subsequent years; sometimes (perhaps when the London waits were unavailable) a group of royal minstrels came instead. This arrangement operated until Canterbury could recruit a new band of three waits, employed from 1513/14 onwards.[31]

In general, however, a town wait's post was not difficult to fill satisfactorily, and civic minstrels could sometimes make a career move. Precise information is needed on wages and the opportunities for rewards before this can be proved, but there are several examples of town minstrels moving from one place to another. In most cases the places concerned were close together, and usually with good road communications, such as Sandwich, Canterbury and London, or Hull, Beverley and York. Hull was also connected to the ports of York and Beverley by navigable rivers. Other movements, some at greater distances, suggest easy travel by sea, such as between Hull, Lynn and Sandwich. One assumes that such moves were usually with the consent of both towns concerned, but this was not the case when Southampton apparently poached the civic minstrels of Winchester in 1434, paying them £1 6s 8d each *per annum* (records of the Winchester fees have not survived). The minstrels – Richard March, John Goddislond and William Goldfynch – evidently transferred from Winchester without obtaining permission, and the mayor of Winchester had all three of them arrested. Southampton's steward attended the assizes at Winchester to stand surety for them, and Winchester eventually released the minstrels to Southampton.

Town minstrels had various sources of income, including the rewards that they could earn from the city or elsewhere for particular performances. Their regular payments as civic minstrels varied from place to place, although they no doubt made sure if possible that their emoluments were comparable to those in other towns.[32] The payments came in several forms: as an annual fee payable directly by the town, or sometimes by one or more of the guilds; as a payment for cloth-liveries, either once or twice a year; and as a tax levied directly by the minstrels on individual households. In many cases we do not have all of the figures available (including the number of minstrels), so that it is difficult to compare their incomes in different towns. Income also tended to increase slightly in any one town, at some time in the course of the fifteenth century. It is probably an accident of survival that the picture looks so irregular: further information may show that there was more uniformity amongst towns in how they paid their minstrels, and how much. The figures for various towns suggest

---

[31] See the Canterbury section of Rastall, 'Civic minstrels'. Civic minstrels most commonly (but far from invariably) consisted of three pipers, a grouping frequently shown in continental iconography and documents: see Polk, *German Instrumental Music*, 53 and *passim*.

[32] See Rastall, 'Civic minstrels', for the London waits' petition concerning liveries.

a normal income for each man of between 7s 0d and 10s 0d for the annual fee, and much the same for cloth liveries.[33]

Some towns imposed a tax for the upkeep of their minstrels. If it formed part of the general taxation levied by the town, it was simply revenue out of which the minstrels' fees would be paid, along with other civic costs. Norwich and York operated a means test, so that citizens were charged different sums according to their rank and income, and this would need to be kept separate from the general taxes. In some places the collection of this specific tax was delegated to the minstrels themselves, as at York in the reign of Richard III (1483–5). At Coventry, the quarterly tax imposed on householders in 1423 was 1d for every 'hall place' and ½d for every cottage: two men from each ward were to help the waits to collect the money. The waits might accept larger sums if the citizens thought them deserving of an extra gift.[34] The waits had problems collecting this tax: perhaps the helpers were unwilling to collect money from their neighbours, and they may also have lined their own pockets. In 1460 the waits successfully petitioned the mayor to assign an honest man in every ward to go with them to gather the tax. This does not seem an improvement, but perhaps these 'honest' men were more efficient enforcers than the previous helpers.

The numbers of householders falling into the categories of 'hall place' and 'cottage' are not known, so the minstrels' income from this tax is unknown. We do know the sum in the case of Leicester, however, for there the tax was imposed only on the forty-eight aldermen of the borough.[35] Each alderman paid 2d per quarter, so the minstrels' income from the tax was £1 12s 0d *per annum*, which – even divided between three or four of them – was a useful addition to the fixed annual fee. Even so, this highlights the differences in payment from one town to another. At Coventry, where there were about four thousand tax-payers,[36] the contributions ought to have totalled far more. Assuming around two thousand households and an (admittedly arbitrary) distribution of 4:1 between cottages and 'hall places', the tax would bring in around £20 *per annum*, or £5 to each of the four waits. Granted that the assumptions cannot be accurate, this is still a very substantial annual income: but the sheer labour of collecting from so many households, even if they could do so, must have been a serious charge on the minstrels' time and energies. No wonder they needed help.

Liveries

The civic minstrels could be given liveries of two kinds: cloth liveries once or twice per year (or the monetary allowance in cash) and some sort of cognizance – a badge to be sewn on the sleeve, or a metal 'coler' in the form of a chain and scutcheon. Liveries had been made *ad hoc* to minstrels on special occasions, such as the reception of a monarch, but the institution of civic waits introduced a class of servant

---

[33] Fees for various towns are given in SM I, 228–30.
[34] Harris, *Coventry*, 59, quoted in SM I, 228, n. 53.
[35] Bateson, *Leicester*, 355.
[36] Mortimer, *Time Traveller's Guide*, 10, offers 4,817 as the number of tax-payers in Coventry in 1377.

which, in providing entertainment, needed to be spectacular and therefore required livery at all times. Some towns perhaps continued to give liveries only on special occasions for some years after the establishment of their waits, but annual liveries became normal everywhere, sooner or later, to demonstrate the town's prestige by aural and visual means.

The records mainly show that gowns were the earlier livery, scutcheons and chains coming later, although some records show the opposite. Any livery was a visible sign of the waits' status and advantageous to the minstrel who wore it. It is surprising that as late as 1442 the London waits had to petition for livery. Lincoln, Lynn and Norwich had all given liveries to their waits by this time, and our first record of liveries at Coventry also dates from 1442.[37]

At Coventry liveries were provided in time for Corpus Christi (late May or June), but at Norwich and York they were given at Christmas. While most towns gave liveries once a year, in the late fifteenth century Norwich made liveries both in winter and summer.[38] The money provided for this varied, but the 5s od per wait given at Nottingham and Shrewsbury may have been fairly typical. The intrinsic value of these silver badges was perhaps the reason for scutcheons being generally a later development than cloth-liveries. Scutcheons were the property of the town, and security was required for them: they were taken back each year and weighed, to ensure that the silver had not been clipped. Scutcheons are known to have been provided at Beverley, Norwich, Coventry, Nottingham, Exeter, Lincoln, Hull and perhaps Leicester.[39]

Few medieval scutcheons survive. When the Municipal Corporations Act abolished town waits in 1835, surviving scutcheons were either melted down or put to use as the badge of another civic officer. Of the scutcheons in existence by 1509, those from Hull (1436/7) and Coventry (1441) are known to be lost. The Exeter waits' shields and chains (1456/7) are probably those worn by the serjeants-at-arms from 1895 and still part of the city's regalia. The slightly later scutcheons and chains of the Lincoln town minstrels (1514) also survive, and are in the regalia room in the Lincoln guildhall. The oval sleeve-badges of the Cambridge waits, probably dating from the early to mid- sixteenth century, are in the Cambridge guildhall. The three scutcheons surviving at Beverley originated in the early fifteenth century, but they were remade several times and are presumably no longer in their original state.[40]

Duties

The waits' principal duties were to attend the mayor whenever he required loud minstrelsy: principally in procession, where the waits could draw attention to the spectacle of the mayor and other civic officers, and at civic and guild feasts, announcing the mayor and playing for the service of the first course. Some occasions of civic

---

37 SM I, 232.
38 Stephen, 'Waits', 49 ff; Davies, *Extracts*, 12; SM I, 233.
39 SM I, 234–6.
40 For photographs of surviving scutcheons, see <http://www.townwaits.org.uk/cognizances.shtml> (accessed 9 June 2019).

ceremonial warranted extra gifts to the minstrels. In 1420/1 Norwich gave its waits 13s 0d in rewards and expenses for the Mayor's riding and the Corpus Christi celebrations, and 10s 4d in rewards and expenses at the visit of the king; in 1423 Beverley gave its waits 20d for riding with the banns of the Corpus Christi play; and in 1460, when the same town sent men to Northampton to fight for the king, the waits were given 6d for playing when the men departed.[41] This last brings the waits closer to the military functions that loud minstrels normally had in war-time, although the performance was on behalf of the town.

The waits normally had other duties or expected activities, too. In some places they marched through the town at night, sounding the hours. The town of Lynn employed its waits in 1432 on condition that they play their instruments through the town on winter nights, and a similar arrangement obtained at Norwich in 1440.[42] This appears to have been a privilege for the waits rather than an imposed duty, and presumably brought the waits some extra income. In at least some places influential citizens could obtain a performance outside their house as a sort of musical alarm-clock for which the waits were paid. The waits' perambulations were in any case regarded as an entertainment for the populace: in 1454 the London council made it clear that the waits' nightly marches were primarily for the entertainment of the citizens.[43]

The relative importance of entertainment and information probably depended on the location. In the port of Sandwich there is evidence from the mid-1460s that players of stringed instruments and trumpets went through the town at night announcing the state of the wind. This would be an important function in a sea-port, and even in an inland port, and it may be the reason for town minstrels in several towns being called *vigiles* or *speculatores*. In some places the minstrels may have been associated with watchmen who fulfilled this function, rather than undertaking it themselves, but the evidence is unclear. There are some hints (at Newcastle upon Tyne in 1511 and at Poole in 1512/13) that the minstrels were associated with a serjeant at arms, perhaps for their personal safety at night.[44]

Several towns employed a man to blow a horn in order to call the citizens to a general assembly or to issue a proclamation. The horn-blower was usually separate from the minstrels, but in some cases there was apparently a working relationship between them. In Dover the minstrels were certainly responsible for blowing the horn(s) and for delivering proclamations, but if they called the time and weather they did so as *fistulatores*, pipers or waits, not as the horn-blowers who were paid

---

[41] SM II, 133–41 and 150–61, *passim*. For Norwich, 1420/1, see Stephen, 'Waits', 6; for Beverley, 1423, HMC 54, 160; and for Beverley in 1460, Poulson, *Beverlac*, 228.

[42] SM I, 222–6. Norwich, like York and Beverley, was an inland port on a navigable river. The Lynn waits were to patrol from Michaelmas (29 September) until the Purification (Candlemas, 2 February); the start date was changed to All Saints (1 November) in 1433: Green, *Town Life*, 145; Janssen, 'The waytes of Norwich', 12.

[43] Woodfill, *Musicians in English Society*, 45.

[44] See under Newcastle and Poole in Rastall, 'Civic minstrels': the Dover records associate the minstrels with a serjeant in livery-payments. Following such leads will demand the use of record items not published by REED.

separately for each sounding.⁴⁵ The town of Dover bought two horns in 1370, as did New Romney in 1486/7.⁴⁶

Clearly there is circumstantial evidence to be explored here: but evidence of what? Horns were used for out-door noise-making, such as raising the hue-and-cry⁴⁷ or calling the citizens together: they had nothing to do with music. At Dover the pipers were not paid separately for calling the time and weather, although they may have done this as part of their normal duties; whereas at Sandwich in the 1460s (if Leo of Rozmital's secretary is to be trusted), *fidicines* and *tubicines* were used in announcing the state of the wind every night. The leggings provided for Walter Wayte at Grimsby in 1396/7 indicate a harsh environment for his nightly work: in the docks, perhaps, rather than just in the town?

The town minstrels potentially had three separate duties, then: the minstrels' work, making music for mayoral and civic events, including playing for (presumably influential and wealthy) individual citizens; a non-musical duty of calling the hours and the weather; and the giving of information concerning announcements and meetings. Quite who did what and when varied from place to place: the issue must be followed up in individual towns through evidence still to be assembled.

The waits were also allowed to perform purely for the entertainment of the citizens at large, separately from any civic events. Typically this music-making took place on a raised public space, such as the top of a conduit or a suitable roof of the guildhall. This was a privilege granted to the waits, and they presumably made a collection from the audience.

Independent work

No town could give its civic minstrels enough work to keep them fully occupied, and the waits' fees were modest, even if supplemented by rewards. Town waits therefore accepted other work in their own towns, making good use of their status as liveried retainers. The anomaly of this position inevitably caused friction. As liveried minstrels, they offered serious competition to other local minstrels; but as they were not 'foreign' in their own towns, they could neither be prevented from playing nor fined in the usual way by a minstrels' fraternity.⁴⁸ It was sensible for the waits to belong to a fraternity where there was one, or individually to buy their freedom through one of the trade-guilds, as any other minstrel could.⁴⁹

Town waits did not have to be restricted to working only in their own towns. They could compete with other liveried minstrels elsewhere on equal terms, and would always have an advantage over independent minstrels. The Norwich waits

---

45 The Dover accounts show up to a dozen or so payments for soundings and proclamations each year – far fewer on average – so these do not relate to the daily updating of weather and time information.

46 HMC 5, Appendix, 547. New Romney had no civic minstrels at that time.

47 SM I, 215–16.

48 For the disagreement between the London fraternity and the City waits, see Rastall, 'Civic minstrels', *sub* London.

49 Thus Thomas Wylkyns, 'wayte' (but not necessarily a civic minstrel), was admitted to the Merchants' Guild at Leicester in 1499: Kelly, *Notices*, 131.

visited Thetford Priory in 1498/9, and again in 1509/10, earning 1s 4d in each case;[50] the four waits of Bristol were at the Duke of Buckingham's Epiphany celebrations in 1508;[51] and the three Cambridge waits performed for a drama at Bassingbourn, Cambridgeshire, in 1511.[52]

These visits did not take the waits far from home. The minstrels of a noble could be away from the household for several months between major feasts, but it seems that town waits were expected to be near at hand in case they were needed. The Norwich waits could easily have visited Thetford within two days, while Bassingbourn and Thornbury were one-day excursions from Cambridge and Bristol respectively.[53] On the other hand, the Leicester waits' visit to Nottingham at Pentecost 1500 was a different matter, since the distance between the two towns, around twenty-seven miles, would have required an overnight stay. Other visits involved even greater distances, as lists of visiting waits at York demonstrate: in the years 1446–9 the city rewarded civic minstrels from Lincoln, Leicester and Nottingham, and perhaps from Durham and Newcastle upon Tyne (these two groups were not certainly town waits), in addition to civic minstrels from elsewhere in Yorkshire. These groups presumably travelled with permission from their employers, but it would be awkward if the minstrels were needed at short notice – on the unexpected visit of a noble, for instance. The town minstrels could easily neglect their civic duties, too, in seeking work further afield, and towns would be anxious to avoid this. When Coventry in 1467 limited the travelling of its waits to religious houses within 10 miles of the city, it effectively prohibited work that would keep the waits away overnight.[54]

Employment mobility

The records show that town waits sometimes moved from one town to another. A similarity of names alone is not enough to prove this: but the profession of minstrelsy, and specifically that of town piper, was restricted. An uncommon name increases the possibility of identity, although it may indicate two related men. There are examples of brothers working together, and also fathers and sons. Where dates of the two employments seem to match, however, it is more likely that the names relate to the same person, and identity seems certain when two or more men are involved.[55]

There are several apparently certain cases of relocation. Three waits migrated from Winchester to Southampton in 1434; Thomas Williamson moved from Lynn to Beverley in 1456/7; John Wardlow left Beverley around 1447 and became a wait

---

[50] Harvey, 'Last years', 18 and 20.
[51] Gage, 'Extracts', 311 f.
[52] Westlake, *Parish Gilds*, 64; Bridge, 'Town Waits', 81.
[53] Journeys further afield certainly did happen, such as the Bristol waits' attendance at the drama festival at Chelmsford in 1562: see Coldewey, 'Digby Plays', and Rastall, *The Heaven Singing*, 170–2. Earlier examples may come to light.
[54] REED Coventry, 45.
[55] The evidence for all relocations is set out in Rastall, 'Civic minstrels' under the towns concerned.

of Hull by 1454; Robert Speke moved from Hull to Beverley around 1460–4. The relocation of William Watson and John Watson from Beverley to Sandwich between 1467 and 1476 seems certain from the coincidence of names, despite the time-lag concerned. William Scarlett apparently moved from Sandwich to Canterbury around 1476/7: two men of that name (the elder, the younger) were among the 'taborets and trumpets' at Richard III's coronation in 1483. A colleague on that occasion, John Bulson, was probably the Beverley wait of that name (1467–70).

Apparent movements between Canterbury and London involve three men, two of whom were related. William Palling and Nicholas Ryppes, London waits in 1501/2, had apparently been waits of Canterbury until 1498/9. The 'Ryppis' listed as a Canterbury wait in 1504/5 was not Nicholas, therefore, but probably his son or other relative. A John Ryppys ended his career as a London wait in 1517/18, having presumably followed an older relative to London some time after 1505. An undoubted father-and-son relationship is that in 1498 of John and William Blewit of Coventry. One of these, or a relative, may be the London wait of that name who died in 1517/18.

William Raumpayn, a London wait in 1442, was perhaps the Canterbury wait of the period 1446/7 to 1461/2. Brese, a wait of Coventry in 1481, could be the William Breese who was a Shrewsbury wait in 1505/6, but the chronological gap invites investigation of the intervening period: how would a town wait earn a living between civic appointments? Perhaps two related men are involved, but we cannot always assume so.

A difficult problem of this sort concerns two Yorkshire town waits. Robert Schene was a Beverley *spiculator* from 1433 to 1436, and the York wait Robert Sheyne retired in 1486 after more than forty years' service. If these were the same man, there is a gap in his biography between 1436 and the mid-1440s. Assuming that he embarked on his first post at the age of sixteen, he was probably born not later than 1417, retiring at the age of 69 or so. If the Beverley and York waits were two different (but presumably related) men, the York wait was born probably not later than 1430, retiring at around 56. Either of these is possible, although the record makes much of Sheyne's great age and incapacity.[56]

There is another side to this story, however. Sheyne was replaced at York by one Robert Comgilton, who then disappears from the records. Comgilton shares his name with the Beverley *spiculator* Robert Congilton, appointed there in 1440 but leaving that post by 1443. A gap of 43 years (1443–86) casts doubt on Congilton and Comgilton being the same man. Quite apart from the question of Congilton's career in that period, there is the problem of his age: even if he was only sixteen on appointment at Beverley, he would be 62 or so on taking Sheyne's place as a York wait, which one might think too old to be appointed to such a post. The alternative is that the York wait Comgilton was a different (again, presumably related) man, born no later than 1470 or so.

How many men were involved? Another story seems to link the two York waits in their careers. On Sheyne's retirement the city of York made much of his long service,

---

56 REED *York*, I, 143. I choose 16 as the age to start a professional career on the basis of 7 years' apprenticeship or training from the age of 9, which is arbitrary but perhaps a reasonable rough estimate.

providing him with two complementary retirement provisions.⁵⁷ First, they came to an agreement with his successor, Robert Comgilton, that during Sheyne's lifetime and while Comgilton held the wait's post, Comgilton would pay Sheyne an annuity of 13s 4d (one mark); and, second, that the city would provide Sheyne with a house for the rest of his life, free of charge.

The second part of this arrangement is unusual, but the first is truly extraordinary. It argues for Comgilton being in some way indebted to Sheyne, for his post or for other reasons. Certainly the arrangement suggests a long-standing link. The obvious one is that Sheyne had been Congilton's master, but that works only if the age-gap between them was larger than the seven years suggested by their dates of first employment at Beverley: hence my suggestion that the York Comgilton was the Beverley Congilton's son.⁵⁸ A possible reason for the financial arrangement would be that Sheyne had recommended Comgilton for the York post. There is no known evidence for these possibilities, but they invite further exploration of the Beverley and York records.

The relocations so far noted are between towns, but there are some examples of town waits moving to a non-civic post. The Canterbury wait John Raffe (1496–8) was perhaps the man of that name who joined the king's still minstrels in 1503.⁵⁹ Another Canterbury wait, Richard Barton or Burton, left the town's service in 1430 and was working for the archbishop by 1446. Some civic minstrels were temporarily employed at Court: William Scarlett of Canterbury may be one of the men of that name (the elder, the younger) listed among the 'taborets and trumpets' at Richard III's coronation in 1483; another on that occasion, John Bulson, was probably the Beverley wait of that name.⁶⁰

Instruments

There is surprisingly little information about the instruments played by town minstrels before the sixteenth century. Where a designation is given – and this is in the minority of places – individuals are named as pipers, except in those rare instances where a trumpeter is mentioned. Civic minstrels were often a band of three shawms, to which a trumpeter (as at Coventry) or a fourth shawm might be added. In the first case this resulted in a band of three shawms and a trumpet, as on the Continent,

---

57 REED York, I, 143: order of 4 October 1486.

58 The same applies to my suggestion, in Rastall, 'Civic minstrels', that Comgilton might have been named Robert because he was Schene's godson.

59 The possibility of waits becoming still minstrels has yet to be addressed: Richard Barton of Canterbury presumably played a 'still' instrument professionally. In general, though, a specialist still minstrel was employed: the Coventry guilds employed a separate harper even when the waits played for them, and the waits were associated with harpers at Beverley and Shrewsbury (see those sections of Rastall, 'Civic minstrels'). None of these still minstrels is known to have been in regular civic employment.

60 See MERH, 35; Ashbee, Records, VII, 21. William may have joined relatives in royal service: Edmund Scarlett was also among those taborers and trumpeters in 1483; John Scarlett was a trumpeter of the Duke of York, attending at his coronation as Henry VIII, in 1509. Richard III brought to his coronation many supporters from his power-base in the north.

Pensions

In 1423 the city of Coventry gave a lifetime annuity to Richard Waite (presumably a civic minstrel), who was retiring: the provision of £2 per annum was divided between the Trinity Guild (which gave 13s 4d, or one mark), the Corpus Christi Guild (6s 8d, or half a mark) and the city wardens (20s 0d, or £1).[61] Another instance of a pension was that granted to Robert Sheyne by the city of York in 1486, discussed above: 13s 4d *per annum* and a house to live in.[62]

Two Norwich waits are known to have received pensions. Thomas Barwyck, who was removed from office in 1505 on account of his age and infirmity, received an annual pension of 6s 8d (half a mark) until his death in 1508. John Reynolds retired in 1519 with an annual pension of 20s – three times as much as Barwyck.[63]

Two London waits, John Wykes in 1495/6 and John Ryppys in 1517/18, were provided for on retirement. Wykes was given clothing and Ryppys an annuity, presumably reflecting their particular needs. Both were to be provided with accommodation in the premises of a local charity, Philpot's Alms, when a room became available.[64]

Such pensions were not automatic, or more records of them would have survived. Money and other facilities given to retired waits seem to have been an *ad hominem* support, presumably calculated after such factors as length of service, wealth and property at retirement, the man's health, etc., were taken into account. Further investigation of this aspect of the civic minstrels' lives could put the pensions into perspective by investigating the retirement provisions made by towns for other categories of civic servant.

Status and Standards

As the case of Chester showed, there could be competition for a position as town wait: such a post offered many of the advantages of liveried employment, but without the more or less constant travel attached to employment in a noble household. We should therefore expect town waits generally to be the best minstrels in their

---

[61] Harris, *Coventry Leet Book*, 59: 'Allso [the city authorities] orden that Ric. Waite for his good service he hathe doone to ye Cite of Coventre and for his long contynuance in the same shall have of the Trinitie gylde whill he lyvythe xiij s. iiij d. of CorpusXpi yeld vj s. viij d. and of the wardens of the said Cite xxs.'. This item appears in neither Sharp, *Dissertation*, nor REED *Coventry*, perhaps because there is no proof that Richard was a minstrel. This item is immediately followed by the Leet Book's first reference to the four town minstrels, however, so it seems likely that he was.

[62] See the Coventry and York sections of Rastall, 'Civic minstrels'.

[63] Janssen, 'The waytes of Norwich', 16 f and 26.

[64] See the London section of Rastall, 'Civic minstrels'.

district: and as the scale of gifts and payments to waits is comparable to that of other liveried minstrels,[65] it seems that local opinion generally estimated waits highly.

There is good reason to believe, however, that the best of the town waits were to be considered good players by any standards. The Norwich waits – perhaps the finest band of civic minstrels throughout the fifteenth and sixteenth centuries – accompanied Edward IV to France in 1475.[66] As this was at the express wish of the king, we must assume that the waits compared favourably with the king's own minstrels. Two men who appear in the list of trumpeters and taborers at Richard III's coronation may have been waits: John Bulson, who was at Beverley in 1467, and William Scarlett, at Canterbury in 1478/9 and 1489/90.[67] If these identifications are correct, they say much for the Beverley and Canterbury waits.

In view of the pre-eminence of the Norwich waits, an item in the Norwich chamberlains' accounts for 1533/4 is especially interesting:

> And to the waytes at commandement forsed For studyeng to playe upon the pryksong iij s iiij d.

The civic authorities, then, were giving financial encouragement to the waits to read mensural notation. This may indicate that they could already play from plainsong notation, or perhaps from stroke notation, but it is not possible to tell how many other minstrels had learned or were learning the same techniques. If they were not the first to do so, the Norwich waits were not far behind in the process of adapting themselves to the changing role of minstrelsy in the sixteenth century.

Since the Norwich waits, unable to read mensural notation, could take the place of the king's minstrels in 1475, it may be that the royal minstrels, too, did not then need that technique. This is a subject that needs more exploration, however: it is discussed briefly in Chapter 15.

---

[65] The Coventry accounts for 1477 (Carpenters' Company) and 1492 are typical of the difference in payments to waits and to independent minstrels: see SM II, 190 f.
[66] Stephen, 'Waits', 7.
[67] MERH, 35, taken from Lafontaine, *Musick*, 1.

Part III

On the Road

Introduction to Part III

Although we must reject the romantic concept of the wandering minstrel, it is true that minstrels travelled frequently and in many cases long distances. Liveried household minstrels were often in the company of their employers, who travelled widely between their own properties and on military or political business. Chapter 8 examines two specific cases in which minstrels accompanied a princess going to her wedding, examples of a temporary household travelling a considerable distance. These are an uncommon occurrence, but they shed light on the circumstances surrounding the journey of a noble and her household, and by implication give some information about the planning of such an event.

Planning must certainly have been an important element in minstrel travel, whatever the circumstances. Even when liveried household minstrels took to the road independently (Chapter 9) it was along pre-planned routes, on a time-bounded itinerary, and with the specific purpose of obtaining financial reward as efficiently as possible. Independent minstrels almost certainly travelled much shorter distances, for in general they had no need to do otherwise: their financial rewards tended to be local, and attending events further away carried the risk of earning too little to make it worthwhile. For them too, travelling haphazardly and arriving at a venue unexpectedly was poor practice and unlikely to be rewarded. Minstrels, like anyone else, were entirely serious about earning a living.

Only one type of occasion made it financially sensible for a minstrel to travel to a venue 'on spec': fairs. There the potential rewards were considerable and available to all, depending only on the minstrel's ability to entertain. For this purpose, it was worthwhile for an independent minstrel to travel rather further than usual. This meant that for several days, while the fair continued, there would be both known and unknown entertainers present, making what money they could. It was a situation where criminals would be active, particularly pickpockets and cut-purses but also charlatans posing as entertainers, and it demanded some regulation (Chapter 10). In the first place this was provided by the owner of the land (or of the fair, if different). While some policing was necessary to keep order at the fair, eventually exercised through minstrel-courts, most of the evidence for this control arose because of financial arrangements: landowners exacted fees from minstrels and others in return for licence to perform or trade.

These controls were of course local, although some of them were operated by the kings of heralds, who added the regulation of minstrelsy to their normal duties of controlling the bearing of arms. This situation seems to have obtained for only a relatively short period, perhaps from *c*. 1300 until the 1380s, when the kings of heralds were occasionally known as kings of minstrels, or as both. None of the fair-time controls was a nation-wide organisation, but there is some evidence of control being exercised over relatively large areas, and eventually not just at fair-times. To what extent this change was due to the kings of heralds is unknown, but it seems likely that they were influential in the setting-up of more wide-ranging organisations.

To some extent this regulation of minstrelsy may have protected the livelihood of non-liveried minstrels, by guarding against competition by strangers and charlatans: but minstrels also needed insurance against old age and inability to work, the costs of their funeral expenses, and the later welfare of their widows and families. In the days when there were no national welfare services, and no insurance as such, this need was filled by the social and charitable functions of religious and trade guilds. Minstrels are known to have joined both, but they also formed local associations that showed some of the charitable features of the existing guilds, as well as some of the protectionist features of the trade guilds.

The evidence for these chapters is generally fragmentary. We are fortunate to have the accounts for Princess Eleanor's temporary household, showing the finances of her journey from Westminster to Guelderland in 1332. In the case of Margaret Tudor's journey to Edinburgh in 1503, the royal household accounts provide information about the household personnel, the records of certain towns show the arrangements for her visit, and the Scottish royal accounts give information about the post-nuptial celebrations and the return of her temporary servants to England. Evidence of liveried minstrels travelling independently along well-known routes in the summer months comes from the records of various towns.

Documentary evidence for the fair-time controls and other regulatory arrangements comes from a variety of sources, for there is no one place where such material would be stored. The royal household accounts are the main source of information about the kings of heralds and minstrels, most of whom were squires of the king's household. Evidence of the fraternities comes partly from documents generated by the organisations themselves and partly from civic records. On these matters we are more than usually reliant on the chance survival of documentation.

8
Minstrels on the road

The minstrel as traveller

The romantic myth is that the medieval minstrel was a wanderer, going from place to place as the whim took him, welcomed everywhere but constantly moving on. Minstrels did travel, certainly: but it was a purposeful travelling, always in search of reward and usually on a well-beaten path. Independent minstrels often found frequent working of a relatively small area to be fruitful, especially if there were local institutions that needed entertainers on particular occasions. Towns and religious houses celebrated certain events annually, for instance, and multiple saints' days gave multiple opportunities for work.

For the minstrels of the great lords, travelling was often an annual event, undertaken in the summer months when they were not required in the household, and the distances travelled might be two hundred miles or more.[1] A liveried minstrel might also travel for another reason. In any major household the administration of often widely-separated estates, the processes of government and the maintenance of social networks demanded a large traffic of correspondence. Some messages could be carried in the memory, others in the form of sealed letters. Apart from the heralds, who were used for occasional diplomatic and chivalric announcements, the king employed full-time messengers: the mounted *nuncii*, and the *cokini* (*cursores* from Edward II's reign), who travelled on foot.[2]

The sheer quantity of traffic in these constant communications between households often required other household servants to carry both written and verbal messages: clerks, chaplains and others, including minstrels, depending on the nature of the task and who was available. John the trumpeter was described as *cokinus* when he was paid his expenses on 31 March 29 Ed I (1301), and appears amongst *nuncii* when reimbursed for carrying the king's letters at an unknown date in the same regnal year.[3] This was probably John de Depe, who is known to have carried letters at

---

[1] Further on this matter, see Chapter 9.
[2] See Hill, *King's Messengers*, 1–9 for their duties, conditions of work, etc.
[3] TNA E101.359.5 (29 Ed I), fol. 1v, cal. SM II, 22; BL Add MS 7966A (29 Ed I), fol. 123r, cal. SM II, 24.

about this time, or perhaps a man employed primarily as a messenger and who was competent at blowing the necessary signals on a trumpet.[4]

In lesser households the task of carrying letters might fall to any suitable servant who could be spared. Some idea of the volume of correspondence can be gained from the published letters of the Paston family or of Lord Lisle, and from the accounts of the Lady Elizabeth de Burgh, where the servants are named.[5] Such a regular and extensive traffic may explain many of the visits and overnight stays of minstrels and others recorded in such accounts as those of the Warwick household and others discussed in Chapter 5. Some of the visiting minstrels appearing in the Wardrobe books may also have arrived at Court for that purpose. Whether they made minstrelsy during their visit or not, there were many minstrels purposefully travelling the roads of England and abroad at any given time.

One of these purposes might be the collection of information, and there are records of minstrels being asked to report back. Occasionally it is clearly a secret assignment of some sensitivity, a matter of spying, for which minstrelsy was always an excellent 'cover':[6]

> To Gerard, *vigilis* of queen Philippa, sent to Paris on the king's business to investigate secretly the activities of the lord Philip de Valois for 40 days in the months of September and October *anno* 12 [Ed III, i.e. 1338], taking 18d per day 60s 0d [£3]

This payment is high, perhaps reflecting exceptional expenses and the difficult nature of his covert operations. When minstrels visited a household, for whatever reason, the host's reward depended on the status of the livery or the personal respect in which the individual minstrel was held. Royal minstrels could always be sure of a reward wherever they went, and when they travelled independently it was worthwhile visiting the largest and wealthiest towns and institutions along the main road network. When the city of York decided, on 5 February 1489, to make no more automatic annual gifts to visiting entertainers they nevertheless made an exception for the king's minstrels:[7]

> Item it is agreed that þer be no Rewardes yeven by yere from this day forwerd to eny minstralles bot to the kinges ...

This suggests that the king's minstrels were regular annual visitors, a question to which we shall return in the next chapter.

---

4 Hill, *King's Messengers*, lists several otherwise unidentified *cokini* and *cursores* named John, one of them in the year 1300/1 (p. 153).

5 Gairdner, *Paston Letters*; Ward (J), *Elizabeth de Burgh*, 41–51, *passim*.

6 TNA E346.203 (12–14 Ed III), fol. 94v (cal. SM II, 99): 'Gerardo vigili Regine Philippe misso in negotio Regis usque Paris ad explorandum secrete de gestibus domini Philippi de Valois per xl dies mensibus Septembris et Octobris anno xij percipiente xviij d. per diem lx s.'. Further on the taking of letters, see Wathey, 'Peace of 1360–1369', 133 and 136; and below, under the Warwick household.

7 *REED York*, I, 158.

If the royal minstrels were unlikely to be sent away empty-handed, the same was normally true of the servants of the great lords, and of the lesser nobility and gentry who were local landowners. Any town would wish to show respect to the livery of a local magnate, and although civic records do not show this specifically their attitude was no doubt similar to that of the Earl of Northumberland, c. 1511, to the minstrels of his peers. The size of his gifts to minstrels of other lords depended on the rank of the lord concerned and whether he was a friend of the earl.[8]

This system for deciding the relative values of rewards was in widespread operation, as almost any set of accounts will show. Consider, for instance, the rewards given by the cathedral priory of Durham in the year 1375/6, shown in Table 8, above. If we list the minstrels' patrons and work out the reward per minstrel (ignoring unknown numbers of minstrels) the distinctions of rank become clear, as Table 11 shows. We do not know precisely how much work the minstrels did on these occasions, although it is reasonable to assume that it was normally one evening's work, based on entertainment at dinner. Some of these rewards – a mark, half a mark – are standard sums: but the hosts clearly took account of this, so that the individual rewards work out in rank order. At the top is the king (60d to his minstrel), followed by the prince, that is, Richard (40d),[9] and an earl (just under 27d). Un-named minstrels, who were perhaps fairly local but not necessarily already known to the priory, were given lower but generous sums: 20d, 18d or 12d.

Table 11. Minstrels visiting Durham Cathedral Priory, 1375/6, by rank.

Minstrel(s)	Reward	Each
To a certain minstrel of the lord the king, coming with Lord Nevill	5s 0d	60d
To four minstrels of the lord the prince on the feast of the Holy Cross	13s 4d	40d
To three minstrels of the earl of March, playing before the lord prior	6s 8d	c. 27d
To twelve minstrels at the feast of St Cuthbert in September	20s 0d	20d
To a certain minstrel on the feast of St Matthew	20d	20d
To a certain minstrel playing before the lord prior in his chamber	18d	18d
To two minstrels on Easter Day	2s 0d	12d

I suggest that the un-named minstrels were fairly local because there was no reason for independent minstrels to travel very far. The better-known they were, the more they were likely to earn as long as they were competent and respected. A minstrel could make money most easily in his home town or village, therefore, as long as work was available. When necessary, he could travel to nearby villages if he did not compete seriously with minstrels living there. He could also travel further abroad if the prospects of employment were good – that is, if the money was likely to be

---

[8] See above, p. 116.

[9] The Black Prince was too ill to travel far at this time, and died on 8 April 1376; Richard's uncles, Edmund duke of York and Thomas duke of Gloucester, would have been known by their ducal titles.

available. It would be worth his while to visit a fairly distant religious house, for instance, at a major festival such as Easter or Christmas, or at the patronal festival or other saint's day. The Durham payments just examined show independent minstrels at the two patronal festivals (St Cuthbert's day in March – see Table 8 – and September), the feast of St Matthew, Easter and the Holy Cross.

A minstrel who appeared regularly on such occasions, even if not frequently, might be recognised and welcomed as a regular visitor. It is important to notice, however, that when an accounting clerk recorded a payment to such a minstrel his method of identification was not usually what we might now assume. The minstrel's name, which we would think of as the defining information, would be the least important from the scribe's point of view: probably no-one used or remembered it at first, and in any case with a limited range of names in use they were rarely a precise identification. A performer would be identified first as a minstrel or the player of a particular instrument; then, by what he did ('that sang to the king') or by some other attribute ('the blind minstrel'); by the town that he came from or the patron that he worked for; and at some stage, when he was well enough known to the household or community for it to be convenient, by his name.[10]

These different types of recognition can be seen in the accounts of places like Durham priory, which gives rather more information than the Beauchamp household books, for example.[11] Even so, the different ways in which a minstrel might be identified on any particular occasion, no doubt adequate for the scribe's immediate accounting purposes, do not help the present-day reader but are more likely to cause confusion. We can reasonably assume that William the blind harper and William the blind harper of Newcastle (?1357) are both to be identified with William the Kakeharpour (?1362), *cecus* meaning 'blind': but is William Harpour, rewarded in 1374–5, also the same man, now so well known that he need not be identified by his blindness? Only the relatively large chronological gap would suggest that this is a different man.[12]

Following the career of a particular minstrel is normally impossible, therefore, unless he were employed over several years in a household for which adequate records survive. Even in the royal households, information on the household minstrels is sparse and names often confusing.[13] For visiting minstrels the situation is even more difficult. When a royal or noble personage was met by minstrels during a journey, one can often not tell even if they were independent minstrels or the liveried retainers of a noble or a town. For example, when three Scottish trumpeters accompanied Edward I from Stirling to Yetham on 22 August 1293, one assumes that they were in royal or at least noble employment, because the association of

---

[10] See, for example, Greville and Netherton in the Barnstaple records, Table 10. Much depends on the individual scribe: note, for instance, the variant spellings even of civic minstrels' names (Chapter 7, *passim*).

[11] Compare the entries given for these two households in Chapter 5.

[12] See SM II, 144–6.

[13] Bullock-Davies, *Menestrellorum Multitudo* and *Register* are brave attempts, largely successful, to create biographies for royal and other minstrels, but some of the identifications are doubtful or demonstrably incorrect.

three trumpeters was otherwise unlikely, and free-lance trumpeters were rare. On this occasion, too, the trumpeters are named, which means that they were of high status – confirmed by the reward of half a mark (6s 8d) each – and had probably already performed before Edward. The circumstantial evidence suggests that they were some of the trumpeters of John Balliol, King of Scots, whose residence Stirling Castle was.[14]

Shortly before this event, in May 1293, Edward was entertained by an apparently miscellaneous collection of free-lance minstrels. The king had been at St Johnstone, and when he left he was entertained by a group of fiddlers, *timphaniste* and other minstrels of the town of Perth. These could not have been employed by the town at so early a date, although they may have been among those regularly hired for civic occasions. They must have known each other, and perhaps the town arranged for them to perform for the king. This they did, and the king rewarded them:[15]

> Minstrels of Perth: Various fiddlers, drummers and other minstrels coming before the king at his departure from St John's town and making their minstrelsies, of the gift of the same king 4s 0d

Since each class of minstrel is in the plural there were at least six minstrels present, which makes this a much smaller gift than that to the three trumpeters a few days later. These were probably local independent minstrels, therefore, rather than liveried minstrels.

A more puzzling event occurred on 6 March 32 Ed I (1304), when the king was met by five harpers on the road above *Sabulones* or *Sabulum*, between Dovayn and Sanford.[16] The gift of 5s 0d (12d each) is just large enough to suggest that these were liveried minstrels who all knew each other and arranged together to perform before the king. Did they stop the king's train and perform while stationary, or did the king hear them while still travelling? It would be useful to know what sort of arrangements were considered suitable for such an occasion, what was demanded by etiquette, what sort of security checks were in place, and how long the performance was expected to last. Above all, one would like to know what sort of performance it was. The size of the reward suggests that the performance was pre-arranged.

A guess might be made at these circumstances if we knew what were the distances involved: but it is not clear where Dovayn, Sanford and Sabulones are. All we know is that the payment was made six days later, on 12 March, at St Andrews, so that these places are within six days' journey of that town.

How far might a minstrel be prepared to travel to his work? Richard Sheale rode about 30 miles on the first day of his ill-fated journey from Tamworth to London in 1556 or 1557, a ten-hour journey travelling at an average of 3 miles per hour. Although

---

[14] BL Add MS 8835, fol. 43v, cal. SM II, 41. They are named as Nigel Beymer, Andrew de Clidesdale and Gilbert Bride.

[15] BL Add MS 8835 fol. 42v, cal. SM II, 41: 'Menestralli de Perth: Diversis vidulatoribus Timphanistis et aliis menestrallis euntibus coram Rege in recessu suo de villa sancti Johannis et facientibus menestralcias suas de dono ipsius Regis iv s.'.

[16] BL Add MS 35292, fol. 32v, and Add MS 8835, fol. 42r, cal. SM II, 32 and 41.

he intended to go a little further before stopping for the night,[17] this would have made an unusually long day, and in normal circumstances 35 miles must have been the absolute maximum for a day's riding: more than enough, perhaps, when the horse needed to be rested and the animal had several days' work to do. Thirty miles constituted a full day's riding for a king's messenger (and, rather surprisingly, for a messenger on foot), with a maximum of 35 miles.[18]

A minstrel intending to perform at dinner in the early evening would want to arrive at his destination by mid-afternoon: so perhaps 20 miles was the furthest distance he could travel if he were to stay the night, or about 10 miles if he were to return home the same day.[19] Even so, in this last case it might be dark before he returned home, depending on the time of year. If he were on foot, he would hardly travel more than 7 or 8 miles away from home, and at that distance he might need to spend the night somewhere on his return journey. The distance he could travel would depend also on the terrain: no minstrel would want to rely on a barn or haystack for his night's rest in winter on the Pennines. Any lone minstrel, too, with a valuable instrument and (if he were lucky) a certain amount of money in his purse, would not risk being out after dark, even if he were mounted. The fear of being robbed was a good reason for travelling in groups, a precaution that Richard Sheale disregarded to his great cost.

Minstrels must have weighed the likely reward against the number of days that they would have to be away and the possible sources of income and accommodation *en route*. If one were to travel a considerable distance to a potentially lucrative patronal festival, it would be worthwhile making a small detour to perform at a nearby village. We shall return to this question in the next chapter.

Royal minstrels on the road

While the royal minstrels were in Court, their attendance often involved travel as their royal master moved from one residence to another. Minstrelsy was required whether the household was staying in its accommodation for one night or for several weeks. Travelling with the king was the norm for many royal servants, who followed the Court – that is, where the king was – wherever it went. The king's itinerary was curiously wayward to modern eyes, rarely going in straight lines, often leaving the main roads and visiting small villages as stopping-places. This is because he stayed wherever he could: at his own palace or manor if there was one conveniently placed, with local aristocracy, or at a monastic house. The latter was a good option that the king frequently used. A large and wealthy religious establishment was by its constitution the provider of hospitality and had the space and financial resources to entertain a royal household. There was rarely room for the whole household, however, and usually many non-vital members were lodged somewhere close by.

---

[17] Taylor, *Songs and Travels*, 1–2.

[18] Hill, *King's Messengers*, 3.

[19] Concerning the 10-mile limit imposed by Coventry on its waits, preventing them from staying away overnight, see p. 158.

There were three categories of minstrel who might appear in the accounts for a journey made by royalty or nobility: the principal's own minstrels (and those of senior members of his entourage), the minstrels of the host where the principal spent the night, and any local minstrels allowed to perform before the visitor. The second of these might also be sub-divided into the minstrels of the host person or institution, and those of the host's town (the town pipers). The third category might include local liveried minstrels or independent entertainers. All these categories can be found throughout the royal account books, although it is not always possible to decide in which category a particular minstrel belonged.

Many of the circumstances of minstrelsy made during a journey occurred when a royal princess travelled to her wedding, a one-way journey in which the ceremonial of visiting towns was observed. One such journey was that of Princess Eleanor in 1332, for which the Wardrobe books give very full financial accounts.

The journey of Princess Eleanor, May 1332

Eleanor, sister of the young Edward III and soon to be Countess of Guelders, set out from Westminster at the end of April 6 Ed III (1332) for Nijmegen, the capital of Reginald II, Count of Guelders. From Westminster to Nijmegen is about 250 miles as the crow flies, but in practice considerably further: the journey was accomplished in 18 days, at least three of which were rest-days for her, although not necessarily for the baggage-train. Eleanor reached Nijmegen on 17 May and the marriage took place on the 20th. She was a month short of her 14th birthday.[20]

The household

A royal princess normally lived in her mother's household, but for a long journey made independently of her family she needed a travelling household of her own. After her marriage a few of these servants would remain with her in the permanent household created for her new position. The royal accounts show that during April 1332 the members of a temporary household were appointed, while officials prepared for the transport of over a hundred people with their horses and baggage on a three-week journey by land and sea.[21]

About ninety people are named or identified by their position in this household. Some travelled with her for diplomatic purposes rather than as household officials, but in effect all were part of her retinue. More than twenty others travelled at least part of the way as additional personnel: the king and the queen mother, Isabella, both sent favourite servants to assist for some of the journey, and after the sea crossing the count sent some of his own officials to her. The safety of the retinue demanded a

---

[20] The *Handbook of British Chronology* gives her birth date as 18 June 1318; Safford, 'Account of the Expenses', gives 8 June. My account of Eleanor's life is a summary of Safford's, his material being taken largely from M.A.E. Green, *Lives of the Princesses of England* (London, 1849).

[21] The accounts are those of her Treasurer and Controller, covering the months of April, May and June 1332: TNA E101.386.7 and BL Add MS 38006 (both 6 Ed III), cal. SM II, 88–90.

sizable military force (although this is not apparent from the records), and for both military and haulage reasons horses would outnumber humans.

Among Eleanor's household were three clerics who formed her private chapel: Dns Nicholas Touk (the 'dominus' and style 'Sir' being clerical, for one in priest's orders), and two clerks of the chapel, Soerus of Valencenis and John of Tong. Sir Nicholas was Eleanor's almoner and probably also her confessor; Soerus, from Valenciennes, was presumably from the queen's household;[22] John of Tong was clerk of the almonry, and therefore Sir Nicholas's assistant in that office. All three clerics, being responsible for the worship in her private chapel, must have been singers. There is no evidence that they performed polyphony, but it is possible.

Another cleric in Eleanor's retinue was a Carmelite friar, Brother Richard de Blyton, who had formerly been almoner to Edward II. He too could have been Eleanor's confessor. The Abbot of Langedon was in the retinue, but in a private capacity, in order to undertake negotiations for the king.

In the realm of secular music, the resources of Eleanor's household were much as one would expect: no trumpeters or other loud music and only a few still minstrels.[23] The senior minstrel was John Taysaunt, a royal minstrel between 4 Ed III (1330/1) and 11 July 12 Ed III (1339), inclusive, described as 'the king's minstrel' (*ministrallus regis*) in the records for 9 Ed III (1335/6). He was in Eleanor's household as a herald, however, a position that he relinquished on his return to England.[24] There are no records of him making minstrelsy before the princess, but he must surely have done so.

Private music in Eleanor's chamber was supplied by a *vidulator* named Richard, probably Master Richard Dore, who had been a royal minstrel since at least the summer of 1324.[25] Dore disappears from the royal records after this, so he perhaps stayed to serve the new Countess of Guelders. Eleanor's entourage also included two minstrels of Holland who travelled with her all the way from England to Nijmegen, from where they presumably turned west for the last stage of their journey home. They would have been known beforehand and had perhaps been at Court for some time before the journey started. There are no identifiable gifts to them for performing, so we do not know what instruments they played. There is in fact no evidence that they performed at all; but then, we have almost no such evidence for Richard, either. Eleanor paid their expenses, however, and they were presumably lodged and boarded at the household's expense, so they surely performed for her as part of the

---

[22] The queen, Philippa of Hainault, had brought several Hainaulters with her when she married Edward III on 24 January 1328.

[23] The household of a royal lady would not include trumpeters. When ceremonial music was needed it was usually in the company of her husband. Eleanor's herald, however, John Taysaunt, may have been a trumpeter at least to the extent that he could blow for his own announcements.

[24] The name 'Taisant', meaning quiet or silent, may seem inappropriate for a herald, but perhaps it implied an associated meaning of 'discreet'. A secondary modern meaning, optimistic or cheerful, was probably not in use.

[25] TNA E101.380.4, fol. 11r, cal. SM II, 82.

arrangement. In effect, they must have acted as household minstrels, presumably *bas* minstrels supplementing Richard Dore's work.

The household was joined by another royal minstrel for the last leg of the journey, from 'sHertogenbosch to Nijmegen: William Cardinall, the king's 'small minstrel'. He, too, disappears from the royal records after the 6th year of the reign and may have remained in Eleanor's household.

Eleanor's in-house entertainment was supplemented locally, as always happened when a royal personage travelled. In addition to entertainment on the road, wherever Eleanor stayed the night her hosts provided entertainment for her, resulting in gifts to the minstrels concerned. Following the journey, day by day, we see the variety of musical entertainments available to her during her journey through southern England and the Low Countries.

Minstrelsy on the road

Eleanor left Westminster after visiting the Abbey and making oblations there on Thursday 30 April 1332. The first leg of her journey was to London,[26] where she visited St Paul's cathedral and made oblations at the various sites of veneration: the high altar, the cross at the north door, the Annunciation in the New Work (the extended east end, only recently completed), the image of the Blessed Virgin in the lady-chapel, and the shrine of St Erkenwald. Of these, the miraculous Rood at the north door was probably the most important – tradition said that it was carved by Joseph of Arimathea – and there she gave 12d to various *vidulatores* making their minstrelsy before the cross. These were presumably local minstrels, as they are not named and 12d is a small reward.

Eleanor apparently stayed that night in London,[27] but on 2 May she was in Rochester and the next day, Sunday 3 May, travelled to Canterbury (see Map 2). At Ospring (near Faversham) she was joined by a minstrel who entertained her until Canterbury, a ten-mile stretch that would have taken three hours or so. She also visited St Nicholas's hospital in Harbledown, just outside Canterbury, where she made a donation. At Canterbury she made offerings in the cathedral. The following day, 4 May, she again made offerings at various places in the cathedral, at one of which – the image of the Blessed Virgin in the crypt (*in volta*) – she rewarded minstrels who performed there. These too would seem to be local minstrels, since they are not named. She travelled to Dover that same day, and on Tuesday 5 May made offerings in the conventual church there, where she heard Mass.

At this point various servants of Queen Philippa and of Eleanor's mother, Queen Isabella, left Eleanor's company to return to their principals. The considerable flotilla needed to transport Eleanor's household across the Channel apparently spent the night of 5 May at sea. At least one of the ships landed at Boulogne, since some of the horses later had to be fetched from there, and others apparently landed at

---

[26] At least some of the household did not travel by road along the north bank but took boats across the Thames to Lambeth, and on into Kent.

[27] A servant who had been in Rochester looking for a bed for her returned to London the following day, 1 May.

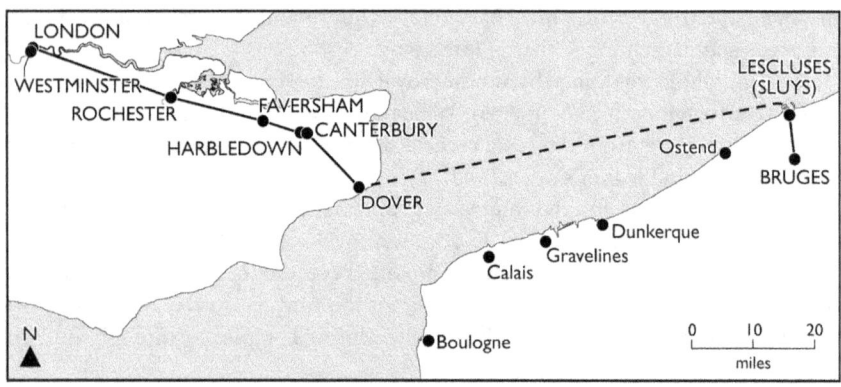

MAP 2. Princess Eleanor's journey, 1332: Westminster to Bruges

Calais, Dunkirk or Gravelines. Probably the horses and heaviest baggage-carts took the shorter sea routes in order to minimise the time spent at sea. Eleanor, and presumably several officials and enough servants for the purpose, made a longer sea crossing to Lescluses (that is, Sluys), the sea-port for Bruges (see Map 3). Eleanor was entertained between the sea and Lescluses by four presumably local minstrels – perhaps, but not necessarily, a loud band of shawms and trumpet. This was certainly not a piece of private initiative: the minstrels were surely sent by the authorities at Lescluses, and perhaps also performed at Eleanor's formal reception in the town when she disembarked.

She spent the nights of 6 and 7 May in Lescluses. Thursday 7 May was spent in preparing the carriages and horses for the onward journey and in paying off the ships that had brought the retinue from Dover. That evening Eleanor was entertained by two groups of musicians: four Aragonese minstrels, and four women of Lescluses who sang to her. Each of these groups was paid a mark (13s 4d), or the substantial sum of 3s 4d to each person.

On Friday 8 May an interim payment for expenses was made to the two minstrels from Holland. The same day, liveries were given to fourteen squires taken into Eleanor's household temporarily from other establishments: they included John Taysaunt, her herald, and several officers and servants of the Count of Guelders.[28] The same day Eleanor travelled up the river from Lescluses to Bruges, where she remained until Monday 11 May.[29] At some stage on 10 May she rewarded thirteen minstrels who

---

[28] Another, who would have helped in negotiating the geography, customs and languages of the Low Countries, was a young Hainaulter, Paon de Roet, who had come to England in the service of Queen Philippa. Paon's youngest daughter, Philippa, later married Geoffrey Chaucer; his daughter Katherine became the mother of the Beaufort family and John of Gaunt's third duchess. Paon thus became an ancestor of every English monarch from Edward IV onwards.

[29] Part of the Wardrobe was left behind and was fetched from Lescluses the next day, Saturday 9 May. On 10 May two cart-loads of cloth and other goods were sent forward to

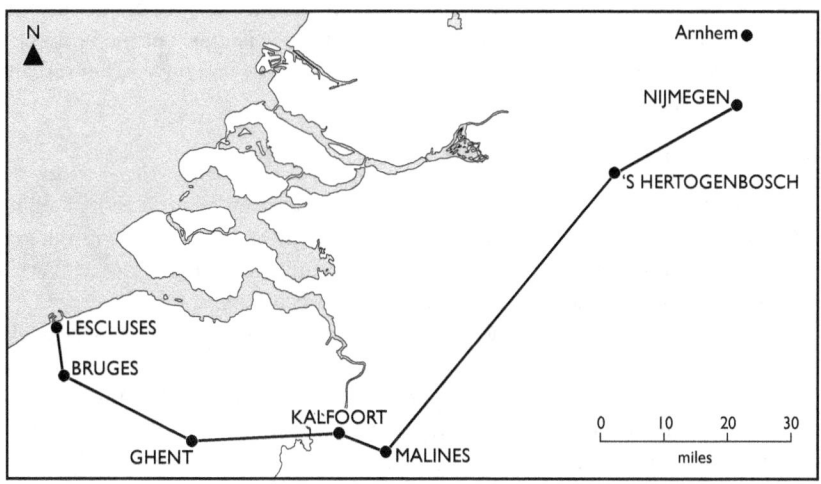

MAP 3. Princess Eleanor's journey, 1332: Bruges to Nijmegen

danced and made their minstrelsies before her. There is no indication of who they were: they may have included local people, but as she was lodged in the Bruges house of the Count of Flanders they probably included some of the count's minstrels.

Eleanor travelled to Ghent on Monday 11 May, and by Friday 15 May she had arrived at Malines. On the way she stopped at the nuns' church at Kalfoort (about ten miles west of Malines), where she made offerings. She later rewarded a bagpiper who had met her on the journey and performed for her, either at a stopping-point (such as Kalfoort) or while Eleanor was actually travelling. Another four minstrels were rewarded that day for dancing and making their minstrelsies before her, presumably at Malines that evening.

Eleanor's retinue then travelled to 'sHertogenbosch (where William Cardinall joined the household) and Nijmegen: this last leg of the journey apparently ended on Sunday 17 May. Eleanor was married to the Count of Guelderland three days later, on Wednesday 20 May in the 'great church of the town of Nijmegen', after which she distributed money in the parish church and made offerings in the chapel of the count's castle. To various minstrels who performed for her, presumably at the wedding feast, she distributed the very considerable sum of £20 by the hands of her herald, John Taysaunt.

Eleanor spent the following day at Nijmegen, but by the 23rd had visited both Arnhem and Rosendaal, perhaps as part of a progress that would introduce the new countess to her people. At Rosendaal she rewarded Richard the *vidulator* for his minstrelsy. She was back in Nijmegen by the 25th, when the king's bearward Philip de Windsor began the long journey home to England with the bear which was a present to Edward from the count. From then onwards Eleanor's household soon

Ghent and Malines, but it was almost certainly not a travelling day for Eleanor.

dispersed and returned to England. She probably retained a few English servants, perhaps including William Cardinall and Richard the *vidulator*, but the household of the Countess of Guelders was dependent on the count's, and most of her servants from then onwards would be Guelderlanders.

Professional minstrels in Eleanor's service

Minstrels appearing in Eleanor's accounts must have been of professional ability, and we can be sure that none of them came before her by accident or without very careful vetting. The circumstances in which they came to perform before her varied, however, and it may be helpful to categorise them accordingly.

The first category comprises those minstrels who were in Eleanor's service or else travelling under her protection. Among these is the royal *vidulator* Richard, who was in her household for the whole journey; and the king's minstrel William Cardinall, who joined the household for the last leg of the journey, presumably to assist at the wedding celebrations. Neither of these, apparently, returned to England. The herald John Taysaunt may also have provided minstrelsy: after the wedding he returned to England and resumed his post as a royal minstrel. As noted earlier, the two minstrels of Holland may have worked at Court before joining Eleanor's retinue.

The second category comprises several unknown minstrels who performed for Eleanor on the journey. One minstrel earned 12d for performing between Ospring and Canterbury on 3 May, presumably a *bas* minstrel travelling in her carriage. This is a reasonable sum for a ten-mile journey, and it could have included playing during her visit to the hospital at Harbledown. The four minstrels rewarded on 6 May for entertaining her between the sea and Lescluses were probably sent by the town authorities. They were probably four loud minstrels – a shawm band – with or without a trumpet.[30]

Another minstrel rewarded with 12d was the bagpiper who joined the retinue somewhere on the road from Ghent to Malines. 'Meeting the lady Eleanor on her journey' (*obvianti domine Alianore in itinere*) rather suggests that he was resident in or near Malines and had ridden out to entertain her for the last few miles of that day's travel. Again, 12d is a good reward, and perhaps he had performed for the ten miles or so from Kalfoort, much the same distance as between Ospring and Canterbury (from Ghent to Malines is a little over thirty miles).

In the third and last category, minstrels performed for Eleanor at various stopping-places along the route. In the case of those playing in St Paul's and Canterbury cathedrals while Eleanor made her offerings it is likely that the church authorities and probably the relevant mayor had set that up.[31] The minstrels were probably local performers well known to the authorities. Local minstrels were also involved

---

[30] At a later date, payments to 'four minstrels' seem to refer to the standard loud band of shawms, with or without a trumpet.

[31] Other minstrels rewarded along the way may have performed during the making of offerings: the unknown minstrel at Harbledown and Canterbury on 3 May, the bagpiper between Ghent and Malines (which could have included Kalfoort), and the various minstrels rewarded on the day of her wedding (20 May) when she made offerings in the count's chapel.

when Eleanor stopped for the night and her host arranged an evening entertainment. One might wonder about the status of the women who sang at Lescluses, since professional female minstrels were rare: but they were paid the same as the four minstrels of Aragon – undoubtedly professionals – so their performance was certainly of professional quality. About the minstrels of Aragon there are different questions to be asked: how did they come to be so far from home, and was it coincidence that they were at Lescluses for Eleanor's visit? They were surely liveried minstrels, perhaps attached to a royal or noble Aragonese household; they were presumably following an extended independent tour rather than travelling with their principal (who is not mentioned in the accounts); and they surely timed their attendance in Lescluses to coincide with Eleanor's visit, even if they did not originally come there for the purpose. Possibly they had been sent on from Bruges, where a good deal of minstrelsy awaited the princess, to Lescluses, where the evening's entertainment was considerably thinner.

As already noted, the thirteen minstrels who danced and played for Eleanor in the Count of Flanders's town house in Bruges probably included locals, but perhaps also some of the count's own minstrels. Eleanor's arduous journey from England to Guelderland – over three hundred miles in a mere eighteen days – nevertheless allowed her many of the comforts of a properly-constituted travelling royal household, including minstrelsy of various kinds.[32]

The journey of Margaret Tudor to Scotland, 1503

Margaret Tudor, a sister of Prince Arthur and the duke of York (the future Henry VIII), travelled to Scotland in the summer of 1503 to marry James IV, King of Scots. Like Eleanor, she took a travelling household on the journey, including minstrels and heralds, but there were differences. Eleanor effectively travelled as the future wife of a count, and under his protection, once she had made the sea-crossing to the Low Countries; Margaret, who was recognised as the Queen of Scots from the time of her betrothal in January 1502, travelled entirely on land, entering towns along the way in her own right as a queen. This may be why there were trumpeters in her entourage; it also explains the great pains taken by certain towns where she stayed to know exactly how the queen had been received elsewhere and when she was expected to arrive and depart (see Map 4).[33]

Following the queen's visit to York, 14–16 July, a detailed memorandum of the procedures involved was entered into the House Book: the purpose was probably partly to show that everything was done properly and partly as a reference that could be consulted in the event of any future royal visit.[34] It is stated, for instance, that Margaret was met at the west door of the minster, and that after she had kissed certain relics she processed to the high altar while the ministers of the church sang an

---

[32] Since there were at least three rest-days, allowing a maximum of 15 days for travelling, Eleanor's retinue must have averaged around 20 miles per travelling day.

[33] Records of the preparations are in *REED York*, I, 193–4; the accounts of the visits are in *REED York*, I, 194–9 and *REED Newcastle upon Tyne*, 9–11.

[34] *REED York*, I, 194–8.

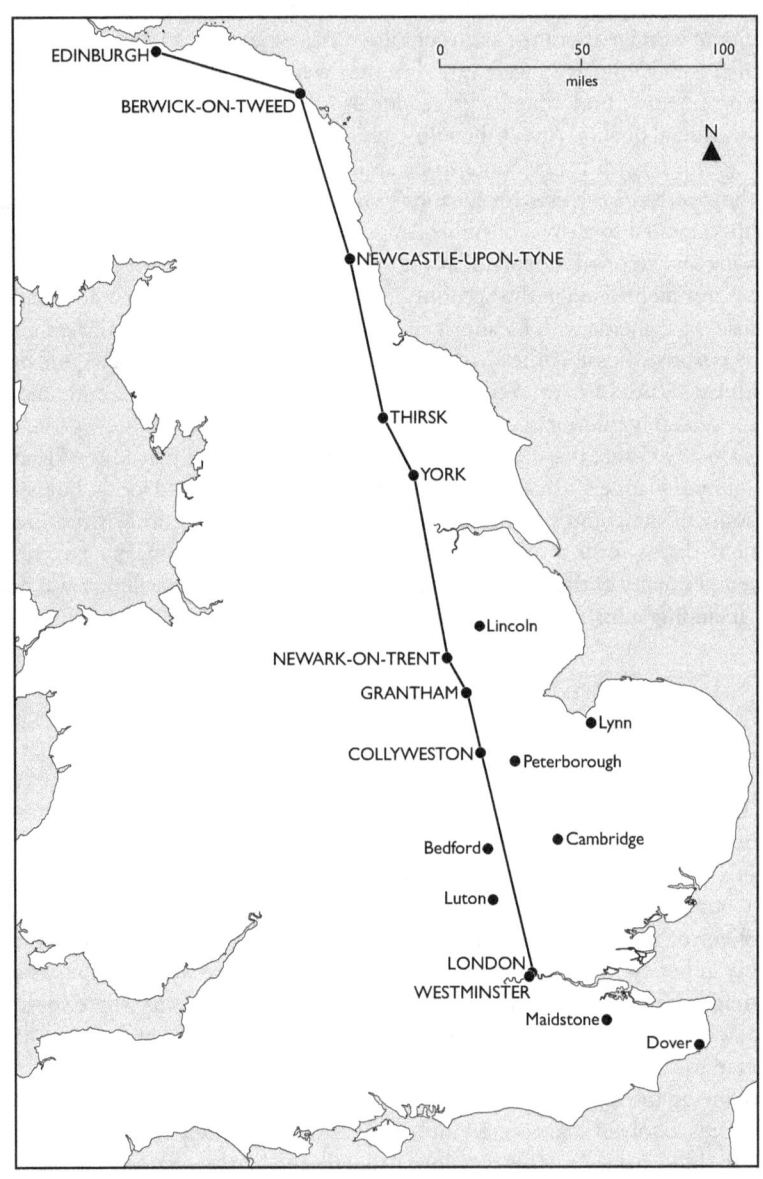

MAP 4. Margaret Tudor's journey to Scotland, 1503

antiphon ('antheym'); and that prayers were said before the high altar, after which the princess made offerings there and at St William's head. But there is no mention of any singing in the procession that met her at the west door, or of any musical performance while she made her offerings; and there is a blank space where the name of the 'antheym' should have been entered. While we can see occasions on which minstrelsy might well have been performed, therefore, it seems that it would have been considered unimportant, and there is no evidence that any minstrelsy took place.[35]

There is also no mention of ceremonial music during her reception into the city. On the other hand, since towns consulted one another on the proper reception of the princess, we can assume a certain consistency of practice, so it may be helpful to discuss Margaret's reception at Newcastle upon Tyne. This account is considerably shorter than the York one, and probably in draft form. Like the York account, it says where the princess was met and by how many men and horses, with the names and offices of those involved. The account does say that certain things happened 'as in the man*ere* of the entryng of York', however, so the town had conferred with the authorities at York, just as York had consulted towns further south.[36]

Margaret arrived at Newcastle on 24 July. She was met three miles out of the town and escorted to the bridge over the Tyne, where the mayor and civic authorities received her. At the town end of the bridge, on the gate, were

> Many children Revested of surpeliz syngynge mellodyously hympnes. & oþers instrume*n*tes of many sortez ...

This is very much the kind of music-making that one would expect at the entrance of a royal personage to the town, and it would be surprising if this had not happened also at Margaret's entrance to York at Micklegate. It is interesting that the writer also expected the 'sound of artyllery & ordonnaunce', although this was missing 'for fawte of powder' (for lack of gunpowder, or perhaps because the powder was damp).[37] Again, one wonders whether a salute of various guns was undertaken at York. The princess was lodged at the Augustinian friary, and went to hear Mass the following morning, St James's day. She would have made offerings there, although the account does not mention them. That evening the earl of Northumberland gave a banquet, with entertainments of 'games dauncers sport*es* & song*es*' continuing until midnight. The evening would certainly have included minstrelsy, if only for the dancing.

Although the events differed in detail in the various towns the civic authorities apparently had a common understanding of what was required in receiving and lodging a royal lady. It is therefore fair to some extent to amalgamate the types of

---

[35] Some of this kind of information is available in the descriptions of the visits of Edward IV in 1478 and of Richard III and his family in 1483: see *REED York*, I, 120 and 132–3, with translations *ibid.*, II, 781–2 and 786–7. The account of Richard's visit describes much of what happened in the minster and names liturgical pieces sung. It mentions neither offerings nor minstrelsy, but may provide a template for occasions when a monarch heard *Te deum*, and perhaps for other visits when offerings were made.

[36] *REED Newcastle upon Tyne*, 9–10.

[37] See Stevens, *Music and Poetry*, 240, for guns fired at the reception of Anne Boleyn.

event that occurred to build a picture of the possible range of activity and events that were considered appropriate. Certainly both devotional singing and minstrelsy could be involved, although it was so much taken for granted that the civic records do not bother to mention it. It is fairly certain that at both York and Newcastle at least three groups of musicians performed at some stage: the singers of the local church, the princess's own minstrels, and the town waits. An eye-witness account of the journey in fact states clearly that the royal minstrels played in procession as the princess and her retinue entered and left each town.[38]

There were two 'Mynstrells to the Quene of Scottes', Gabriell and Kenner, both presumably 'still' minstrels. Kenner – 'the queen's luter' – travelled to Edinburgh with the queen, but Gabriell is not named in connection with the journey, and apparently remained behind.[39] Other royal minstrels who travelled with the princess from Westminster to Edinburgh were on loan from the king's household: Bountas the cornettist, five named trumpeters, two named sackbut-players, two heralds (Somerset Herald and Bluemantle Pursuivant, who may or may not have made minstrelsy) and the un-named 'four minstrels' who may be identical with the 'four Italian minstrels'. The eye-witness is helpfully precise in noting the order of procession on entering or leaving a town:

- Johannes and his company. 'Company' here must mean 'companion', i.e. *socius*. Johannes de Peler was the leader of the Sackbuts and Shawms, and he and his son, Edward de Peler, were both sackbut-players.[40] The other three members presumably stayed behind to serve the king. It is possible that the 'four minstrels', if they were shawmists, as seems likely, may have joined the sackbuts in a larger loud group.
- The minstrels of music: presumably Kenner, Bountas and the 'four minstrels' (if not with the sackbuts).
- The trumpets, with their banners displayed. The five were Peter de Casa Nova (Marshal of the Trumpets), Thomas Freman, Adrian, Dominic Justinian and Frannc Bocard.

The heralds are not mentioned, but probably followed the trumpeters and were in turn followed by the queen with her guard and nobles. The officials of the town, with the waits, will have preceded the queen's part of the procession.

Of the various minstrels, heralds and trumpeters who came to Scotland with the queen, all but Kenner returned to England.

At this point we return to the matter of royal and other liveried minstrels travelling away from their usual workplace and independently of their principal. The next chapter is concerned with their travels during the summer months when household minstrels were normally free from their usual duties.

---

[38] Stevens, *Music and Poetry*, 236, citing John Leland, *De Rebus Britannicis Collectanea* (ed. Thomas Hearne, 2/1770), IV, 267.

[39] Ashbee, *Records*, VII, 20; SM II, 179–87. Kenner is named as the queen's luter in Dickson and Paul, *Accounts*, II, 337 (cal. SM II, 182).

[40] Ashbee, *Biographical Dictionary*, II, 875–6. The warrant for banners, naming all the heralds, trumpeters and sackbut-players, is in Ashbee, *Records*, VII, 22.

9
Minstrel itineraries

Minstrel circuits?

Since the 1960s and 70s, when scholars have been editing records of drama and other entertainments in a concentrated fashion, it has been suggested occasionally that players followed 'circuits' – well-known itineraries that could be repeated year after year and which presumably offered more or less assured rewards. Giles Dawson made the claim in 1965,[1] and subsequently several REED editors have proposed the same: but on the whole they have shown some caution, because the records do not provide firm proof. But the accumulation of hints has been enough to give the editors the feeling that known circuits must have existed. Not surprisingly, but to be treated with equal caution, the records of itinerant minstrelsy, too, have given the impression that regular itineraries might have been followed.

There are good reasons for this provisional conclusion. If a minstrel travelled a large distance – say, to York from the Court at Westminster – the necessity for speed might demand the best road: in this case, the main road north. The journey would almost certainly not be entirely along the main road, however, for several circumstances would require a detour. The first would be the need for an evening meal and lodging for the night, which might be obtained in either a secular or a religious household. The Warwick household books (discussed in Chapter 5) show hospitality being offered to minstrels travelling independently, and such hospitality was also an obligation of conventual houses. The accommodation might be a small, bare guest-room in a priory, but more likely a straw palliasse in a dormitory or a pile of hay in a barn. In a secular household it could mean dossing down in a corner of the hall. The standard of accommodation might depend on the status of the minstrel's employer. What we can be sure of is that the minstrel would take the opportunity to earn some money by performing for his host if he could.

Another reason for leaving the highway would be the occasion of a fair, or of a patronal or other festival at a religious house. If the minstrels were in no particular hurry any lucrative detour would be an attractive proposition. One therefore looks for evidence of minstrel activity in groups of small places connected by relatively minor roads. This kind of evidence, if it exists at all, needs to be firmly dated and from various places along a route if it is to be really useful.

---

[1] Dawson, *Kent*, xxviii.

The word 'circuit', too, should be used with caution, because it implies a specific type of itinerary. Strictly, a circuit would be a route of which at least a considerable portion is circular in nature – that is, returning to a point of departure without retracing steps over any part of the route. The records of minstrel activity in Kent will show that such circuits almost certainly did exist: but it is probable that longer journeys, necessarily using major roads for reasons both of speed and maximising income, made use of the same road for outward and return travel, even if various detours were made in each direction. It is probably best, therefore, to discuss the routes in terms of itineraries rather than circuits.[2]

The *prima facie* evidence for regular itineraries is something of a rag-bag, consisting of apparently unconnected items. First, there is Henry VI's commission to his household minstrels, dated 17 June 1449:[3]

> Whereas many uncultured husbandmen and craftsmen (*rudi agricole et artifices*) ..., pretending to be minstrels and some of them wearing our livery and so pretending to be our own minstrels, fraudulently collect in certain parts of our said realm great exactions of money from our subjects by virtue of their livery and art, and although they are unskilled in it and follow various crafts and trades on working days and receive enough money from them, they go from place to place on festival days and take all those profits from which our minstrels and others should live, being skilled in the art [of minstrelsy] and using no other trades or crafts ... we have appointed our beloved William Langton, Walter Haliday, William Maysham, Thomas Radeclyf, Robert Marshall, William Wykes and John Clyf, our minstrels, jointly and severally, to enquire, by all ways and means, through our whole realm, except the county of Chester, concerning all such persons pretending to be minstrels and wearing the said livery and to punish them, to hold the same inquisition themselves or by deputies during good behaviour.
>
> At Winchester, 17 June [1449] under the private seal

This commission set up a sort of minstrel court, to which we shall return in Chapter 10, but its immediate purpose was evidently to deal with a specific complaint by the royal minstrels that money that was theirs by right was being appropriated by imposters. The implications of this are immediately relevant to the question of itineraries, because the imposters were able to pick up money that was earmarked for the king's minstrels. The royal minstrels being regular visitors at these places, although not necessarily specific men known to the authorities, no questions would be asked when minstrels in royal livery turned up. The loss of such rewards would be considerable. In the mid-fifteenth century the city of York allocated certain sums to minstrels coming regularly each year. The usual reward to the king's minstrels was 20s 0d (£1), which one would think a large enough reward to draw the royal

---

[2] Richard Sheale and his wife seem to have followed a regular itinerary in the mid-sixteenth century, to customers in Lichfield and Atherstone, starting and finishing at the home base of Tamworth: see Taylor, *Songs and Travels*, 17–18. These towns are in a straight line on and to the north of the Roman Watling Street (now the A5), but the Sheales were not, of course, restricted to customers on the roads between them.

[3] CPR, Henry VI, vol. 5 (1446–52), 262, slightly modified, from TNA C66/468.

minstrels each year.[4] The money was always limited, however, and at York more specifically so from 1489 onwards. As we have seen, that city decided to dispense with rewards to all minstrels but the king's (presumably with the exception of the city waits). When the money was thus limited, the city would not happily find such a sum for the real king's minstrels if it were once paid to the imposters.

We shall return to the York records, but it is worth noting that the Northumberland Household Book, a formulary dating from the second decade of the sixteenth century, also supports the notion of regular visits (see Chapter 5). Specific sums were to be given to visiting minstrels and trumpeters of earls and dukes, dependent on whether they came every year or only once in two or three years, whether their employer was a special friend or kinsman of Northumberland, and whether a noble's trumpeters came all six together or as a smaller group; a special case was made for three of the king's shawms who came annually.[5]

This is a clear indication, if a late one, of regular annual visits with regular but less frequent visits as an alternative. Henry VI's commission to his minstrels falls into the category of overkill if the problem was simply a general one that the king's minstrels occasionally found no money available for a reward: but the use of the king's livery suggests an organised, premeditated appropriation of rewards on which the king's minstrels depended during the summer months. That would be a serious situation. How did the imposters obtain the king's livery? If they were somehow able to pick up last year's discarded gowns, this might be a starting-point for investigation; if the imposters made counterfeit gowns anew, the investigation would have to begin on the road, in the places where the impostures took place.

From all this evidence it seems likely that the royal minstrels visited most places only once a year during the summer touring season. This means that if they did return through a place they had already visited they expected neither to perform nor to be rewarded a second time. It is probably safe to assume that the royal minstrels toured independently of the king in the period between Pentecost and All Saints.[6] They might also travel between Twelfth Night and Easter, between Easter and Pentecost, and between All Saints and Christmas. We shall see that this was indeed the case, even though the winter was more difficult for travellers, the time available much less, and the period before Easter largely taken up by Lent. When towns rewarded groups of royal minstrels outside of the main summer touring period the minstrels were sometimes attending their principal – king, queen or prince – but it is often difficult to know if their employer was present or not, at least from the records selected for a REED volume. This problem is particularly difficult when the noble concerned was local to the place of reward, and this is a good reason for concentrating on the royal minstrels for the time being.

The main purpose of searching the original records of towns and institutions again would be to improve the dating of entries, for the lack of trustworthy chronology is a

---

[4] That they apparently did not come every year may be due to particular circumstances in the royal household, or simply to gaps in the accounts during the 1470s and 80s.

[5] Percy, *Regulations and Establishment*, 339: see Chapter 5. At this time it was usual for earls and dukes to employ a group of six trumpeters (see Chapter 14).

[6] For evidence that All Saints was the autumn feast by which the minstrels returned to Court, see below.

major impediment to research on minstrel itineraries. The precise date on which minstrels were rewarded is always helpful, for several reasons: we can identify a possible reason for celebration, the stage of the Pentecost-All Saints or other period involved, and – where two or more institutions or towns are concerned – the order in which visits occurred. This type of examination relies on certain record-keeping procedures. Expenditure was recorded on the day concerned, in order of payments: these might then be enrolled, or entered into a journal (a book of day-to-day accounts). In such records the first item for each day would be clearly dated, succeeding entries being marked as 'the same day': the order of those entries for each day would normally be retained when the daily records were copied to classified lists – for example, of gifts (*Dona*) or necessary payments (*Necessaria*) – for audit. Transfer to a classified list, however, could cause the loss of dating, so when a journal is available it should be used as a check for dating against the Keeper's or Controller's book.

The same uncertainties of dating occur in town records. Here too, any item recorded as 'the same day' needs to be dated by reference to an item that may be far ahead in the list. Finding the relevant item is often a very time-consuming procedure, and one that REED editors generally could not follow. For this reason, working out the precise chronology of a minstrel-group's travel will usually demand another and more detailed examination of the relevant town records. There are however a few years of records of rewards to entertainers by the city of York where this problem is reduced, although not eliminated.

Some venues and routes

Minstrels at York, 1446–50

The city of York's records of rewards to heralds, messengers and minstrels for the years 1446–50 are relatively detailed, a classified list of payments made up for auditing purposes.[7] The items were presumably extracted from a journal in which all payments for each day were entered. If items were copied in date order it should be possible to assign a date to all of them. Not all dates were retained during the transfer to the final accounts, however, and some entries are certainly out of order. One can assign rough datings on the basis of the few precise ones that survived the transfer, if caution is used: an entry appearing between payments of 9 February and 16 February may be as early as the 9th and is probably not later than the 15th. Moreover, where two or more items appear between specified dates, those items are probably in chronological order. But these are assumptions.

Many of the minstrels listed are anonymous: of those that are named, some can be further identified by place or employer. Most are identified only as the minstrels of a particular patron, which allows one to see the same minstrels – or at least, the same liveries – returning year after year. Some of the patrons were local landowners, and any visit made by their minstrels could be when they were travelling in company

---

[7] REED *York*, I, 65–77. The civic records used the year starting on the feast of the Annunciation, 25 March, but in this volume all dates are given as new-style dates, with the year starting on 1 January.

with their employer: but some minstrels appear so often that they must sometimes have worked independently of their masters. Visiting civic minstrels were certainly working on their own behalf: those of Beverley were relatively frequent visitors, as was their colleague the harper John Whetlay.[8]

The civic minstrels of York do not seem prominent in these lists, but they appear on key occasions. In all four years they apparently head the list of rewards on Easter Day, as they do at Corpus Christi, the Nativity of St John the Baptist (24 June, Midsummer Day), and Christmas (25 December). They also head the rewards for the feast of the Translation of St William of York, the first Sunday after Epiphany, in 1446 and 1449, when the dating of following items shows that several other minstrels were also rewarded. They are absent from the list for 1447, when only a harper called Simon was rewarded. The list for 1448 is headed by eight minstrels of the earl of Salisbury, who was a local magnate (Richard Nevill, whose son would become known as the Kingmaker); and they are followed by four minstrels of Lord FitzHugh and Thomas Buxnell, the minstrels of York, and a waferer called Robert. All of these were frequent visitors rewarded by the city at various times of year. In the list for 1449 the city waits are followed by seven minstrels of the earl of Salisbury and, probably on the same day, Lord Clifford's minstrels Christopher (a harper) and John Somerset, both known in other years. On this occasion they were in the company of their employer. A minstrel of Lord Egremont was also rewarded, possibly on the same day. The variation in numbers of minstrels is not easily explicable: but it is clear that the city waits were normally expected, with other known minstrels welcomed if they were available, or if the noble concerned were visiting.

In contrast to these and other frequent visitors, the king's minstrels were rewarded only once in each of these years. Their timing is worth examining, since they evidently came according to a plan confirming their summer season between the feasts of Pentecost and All Saints (Table 12a). Although the composition of the group is variable, these payments are fairly consistent in providing each minstrel with 3s 4d (a quarter-mark) on each occasion. The more generous gift in 1446 may be a set sum for the group, reduced from 1448 onwards and calculated according to the number of minstrels coming. As already noted, the city eventually reduced the sum still further in theory (though not in practice), to 6s 8d to the group.

Fortuitously, these entries are precisely dated. The first, on 3 October 1446, is quite late in the season for royal minstrels to be so far from home, and shows that the first major feast of the winter, for which they returned to Court, was probably All Saints (1 November) and not Michaelmas (29 September). That gave them exactly four weeks to return – ample time if the king was in the south-east, and still allowing them to make some visits en route.

Only the 1448 visit coincided with an important feast. Perhaps there is not much to be read into this, although the minstrels would surely have arranged to be in York then, rather than on any day close by. Putting together the dates on which the minstrels would have left Court the day after Pentecost, their visit to York, their return to Court on the day before All Saints, and the number of days between these events, we find that a vague pattern emerges (Table 12b). Taking the close dates of Pentecost in 1447 and

---

[8] See Rastall, 'Civic minstrels' in the Beverley section.

Table 12. The king's minstrels at York, 1446–9.

(a)			
1446	Item iiij Ministrallis domini Regis iij die Octobris	xx s.	[5s 0d each]
1447	Et vj Ministrallis domini Regis xxvj die Iulij	xx s.	[3s 4d each]
1448	Et iiij^{or} Ministrallis domini regis in vigilia Nativitatis Sancti Iohannis Baptiste [i.e. 23 June]	xiij s. iiij d.	[3s 4d each]
1449	Et vij Ministrallis domini Regis quinto die Augusti	xxiij s. iiij d.	[3s 4d each]

(b)					
Year	Pentecost + 1 day	(days)	York	(days)	All Saints less 1 day
1446	6 June	119	3 Oct	28	31 October
1447	29 May	59	27 Jul	96	31 October
1448	13 May	41	23 Jun	130	31 October
1449	2 June	64	5 Aug	94	31 October

1449, it seems that the minstrels probably followed much the same path, in the same order and at the same rate of travel in those years: only five days' difference before York and two days' after, and in a space of five months, suggests a fairly precise schedule. In 1448, when Pentecost was earliest and the total time available correspondingly long, it seems likely that the minstrels made fewer visits before York and more visits after. Whether these were rescheduled visits to regular venues or to different ones we cannot know: nor is there any way of telling how long the minstrels stayed at any other venue, a factor that could easily move the schedule back or forward several days. From these figures it appears that in the three years concerned the minstrels visited York on their way north to a further destination – perhaps Durham or Newcastle upon Tyne – and did not revisit York on the return journey. Conversely, the dates for 1446 suggest that the visit to York took place on the way home: perhaps this was one of various adjustments to the schedule because Pentecost was relatively late and the time available consequently less. (The boundary dates for Pentecost are 10 May and 13 June.)

It would be helpful to find records from other places – towns, monasteries or households – that might shed light on these minstrels as they travelled up and down the Great North Road. Such records are not necessarily from places that are important now, but it is a question of survival. Of extant records from places north of York, those of Newcastle upon Tyne begin only in the sixteenth century. Those of the cathedral priory of Durham survive in quantity, and here the royal minstrels were welcome and assured of a reward and accommodation.

Minstrels at Durham cathedral priory

Few monastic accounts are as informative as those of Durham.[9] Like most of York's records, they are largely classified accounts produced for audit, and as such share

---

9   Cal. SM II, 142–9: Fowler's edition only summarises accounts for the 1440s.

the limitations concerning precise dating. Table 13 is a calendar of payments to minstrels in the Durham accounts for the years 1446–9: these are typical of the Durham accounts in general, and they can be compared with the York records of the same period.[10] As in the York accounts, the list for 1445/6 is extracted from a journal: the last item (not shown here) also dates from Christmas 1445, so that the chronology of all these items is doubtful. Even assuming that the payments to minstrels are in chronological order there are still too few dates to help us very much. Put in a simpler form, the payments might be expressed as follows:

> Dorchester, Northumberland (1), Salisbury, Westmoreland (Christmas), Salisbury, Westmoreland (3), Bishop of Durham (Hugh), king.

If these are in chronological order then only those after Christmas could relate to the York accounts for 1446, where the list of rewards to minstrels and heralds belongs to the accounting year starting on 3 February. Relevant payments in the York accounts, expressed in the same way, are:

> Bishop of Durham (Hugo Loyter [luter?]), Westmoreland (2), [3rd Sunday in Lent, 20 March], [Easter Day, 17 April], Salisbury (one waferer), Salisbury (10 May), Westmoreland (1 fool, 23 May), [Sunday after Ascension, 29 May], king (3 October)

Putting these two sets of accounts together shows possible connections between them. Disappointingly, the payments to the king's minstrels do not match up: if the minstrels were at Durham before 5 June 1446, when they would have been required at Court, this entry does not relate to the group who were at York on 3 October that year. Possibly the Durham entry is out of chronological order. There is a Salisbury-Westmoreland parallel, but even this is confusing: Lord Salisbury's minstrels were at York in early May (the waferer perhaps in late April), but seem to have been at Durham soon after Christmas; and only one of Lord Westmoreland's three minstrels was at York after Salisbury's, the other two being there earlier. Either the chronology of the accounts is in fact defective, or – as is quite likely anyway – the Westmoreland minstrels had followed two different itineraries. In any case, the earls of Westmoreland and Salisbury could be regarded as local for these purposes.[11]

The study of minstrel mobility in a 'strung-out' itinerary involving large distances clearly does not provide firm answers. Nevertheless, such work may eventually bring some results: and the chances of success can be increased by bringing other centres into the study and going through the same processes. For the main north-south route, Doncaster, Pontefract and Selby are obvious candidates if relevant and matching records exist.

Minstrels on the south coast of Kent

A very different kind of route, along the south coast of Kent, almost certainly did not involve any return over the same ground east of Rochester. This itinerary, or

---

[10] I am very grateful to John McKinnell for allowing me to use his transcriptions.

[11] Westmoreland was a Neville who had married a Percy; Salisbury was also a Neville. Payments to their minstrels could be due to their own presence in the north-east. The bishop's minstrel, Hugh, was of course local to Durham, so the chronology of his visits can tell us nothing helpful.

Table 13. Minstrels at Durham cathedral priory, 1445–7.

11 November 1445–5 June 1446	
Gifts	
To minstrels of the earl of Dorchester (i.e. the marquess of Dorset and earl of Somerset)	40d (i.e. 3.4d)
To a minstrel of the earl of Northumberland	20d
To minstrels [or a minstrel] of the earl of Salisbury	20d
...	
To minstrels [or a minstrel] of the earl of Westmoreland at Christmas	3s 0d
To minstrels [or a minstrel] of the earl of Salisbury	3s 4d
To three other minstrels of the earl of Westmoreland	2s 0d
And to Hugh, the minstrel of the bishop [of Durham]	20d
And to minstrels [or a minstrel] of the lord the king	6s 8d
	[Total 23.4d]
...	
5 June 1446–28 May 1447	
Gifts made to minstrels and messengers ... and other payments ...	55s 3d
[28 May 1447–1 June 1449 *absunt*]	

itineraries, took in the towns of Sandwich, Dover, Hythe, New Romney and Lydd, together with Canterbury, the hub from which the ports of Sandwich and Dover were accessed.[12] These towns are shown in Map 5: all have records surviving from the fifteenth century, enabling us to see something of the minstrel activity in that area. No records survive so early from Folkstone, where there was dramatic activity and no doubt money for minstrels too, nor from Ashford, from where minstrels might have travelled to the coast at Folkstone, Hythe or New Romney.

The coastal towns' records show some regular features. Minstrels of the king, queen and Prince of Wales made annual visits and received rewards that match the annual sums normally available elsewhere for royal minstrels travelling independently.[13] Canterbury, Sandwich and Dover gave the king's minstrels 6s 8d (80d), with perhaps 5s 0d (60d) to the queen's and 3s 4d (40d) or 1s 8d (20d) to the prince's. Other towns gave 5s 0d or 3s 4d to the king's minstrels, with commensurately lower sums to other groups, including in Yorkist times the minstrels of Edward IV's brothers, the dukes of Clarence and Gloucester (these, too, were frequent visitors). Although these sums were normally available only once in the year, there were

---

[12] The major route to the coast was Watling Street, the Roman road from London to Rochester, Faversham and Canterbury, with extensions to Sandwich and Dover. There are no relevant records pre-1509 from other towns on the south coast, nor from Rochester or Faversham. No doubt there was minstrel-traffic to the north coast, too, which cannot now be followed in this period.

[13] From the evidence of the York and Northumberland records: see Chapter 5.

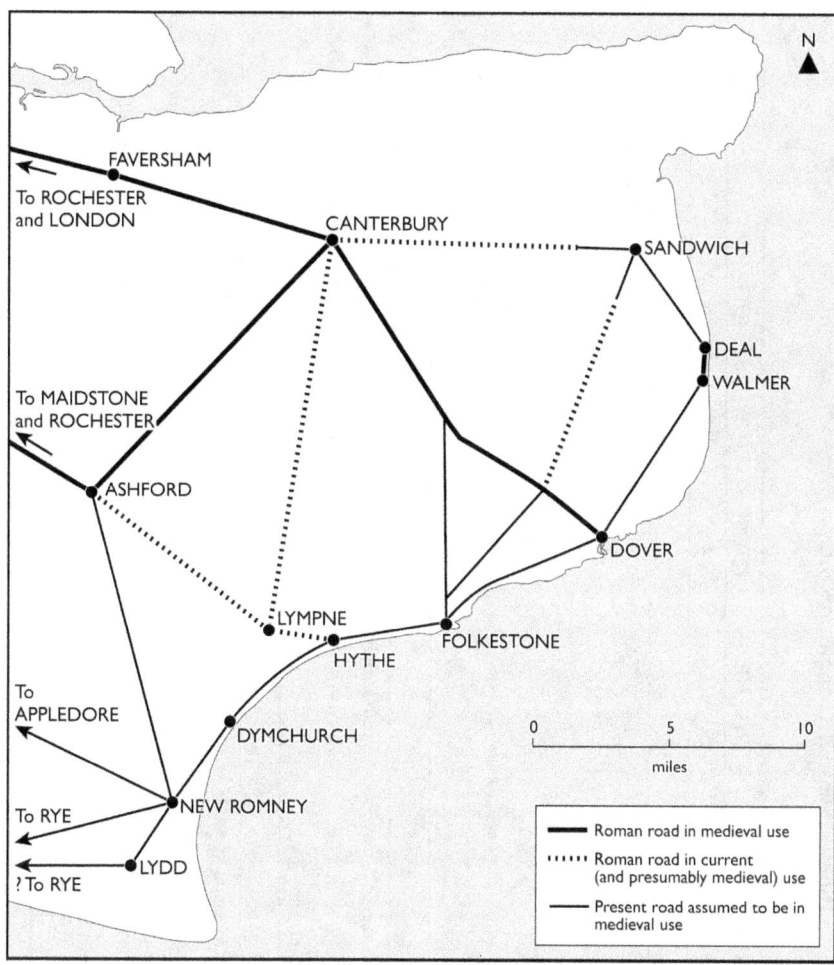

MAP 5. Minstrel itineraries in Kent

obvious exceptions, such as when the minstrels were in the train of their principal and were rewarded as part of the hospitality involved. Also, a lone minstrel, such as the king's bearward, might be rewarded in addition to the usual sum given to the main group. The coastal towns were also generous to minstrels of the local magnates, the earl of Arundel and the current Warden of the Cinque Ports. These groups seem to have worked the coastal roads only, as they do not appear in the Canterbury records: they sometimes appear more than once in the accounting year.

Table 14 shows the rewards to identifiable minstrels in the period 1487–91. Players (i.e. actors) and unidentified minstrels are omitted unless their entries offer help with dating. Most of the extant financial records of these towns are those copied for the annual audit, in which dating is usually lost: only a few entries retain exact dates or the occasion concerned (saints' days are here translated into calendar dates).

Table 14. Minstrel itineraries in Kent.

CANTERBURY	SANDWICH	DOVER	HYTHE	NEW ROMNEY	RYE
29–28 September	Dec–Dec variable	8–8 September	2–2 February	25–25 March	variable
1487–8					
mm K (PdeC) 6.8d		mm Ld Arun' 3.4d	mm K 3.4d	mm Q 20d	mm dss York [26 Aug–25 Dec 87] 2.0d
mm Q 5.0d		mm dss of York 20d			m Ld Arun' [6 Apr–24 Jun 88] 12d
		mm of Sandwich 20d			mm K [6 Apr–24 June 88] 5.0d
		mm K 18 Apr [88]			mm Q [24 Jun–24 Aug 88] 3.4d
		6.8d			bw e of Derby [24 Jun–24 Aug 88] 2.0d
					m Ld Arun' [24 Jun–24 Aug 88] 12d
1488–9					
mm K 6.8d		mm K 6.8d	mm K 3.4d	m[m] K ? 2.0d+5d	bw e Derby [19 Apr–24 Jun 89] 3.4d
		mm e of Arun' 5.0d		m[m] Ld Arun' 12d	mm Ld Oxford [24 Jun–24 Aug 89] 3.4d
		bw Ld Derby 3.4d		mm Q 2.0d	
1489–90					
mm K August [90]	mm K 6.8d	waits of Sandwich 20d		m(m) Ld Arun' 4d	mm K [late Aug 1489] 6.8d
[6.8d]/	2 mm Ld Arun' 12d	mm Ld Arundel 2.8d			mm Ld Arun' [late Aug] 2.0d
w wine 7.2d	mm Pr 20d	mm Pr 20d			hpr Ld Arun' [25 Dec–11 Apr] 12d
		2 mm 12d			m Pr [11 Apr–24 Jun 1490] 2.0d
		mm K 6.8d			mm K 10 Aug 1490 3.4d

1490–1

mm K 6.8d	mm Pr 20d	mm Ld Arun'	m(m) Pr 8d
mm Q 5.0d	bw Ld Oxfd 20d	12d	m(m) Ld Arun' 4d
mm Pr 3.4d	mm Ld Arun' 5.0d	mm K 3.4d	
	mm Q 12 Jun 91 5.0d		
	mm K 21 Jul 91 6.8d		
	mm Ld Daubeney 20d		
	2 tabs Regent 20d		
	3 trpts K of Romayns		
	12d		

mm d Bedfd 14 Sept 1490 2.0d
mm Pr [29 Aug–25 Dec 1490] 2.0d

mm e Arun' [25 Dec–3 Apr 1491] 12d
bw e of Oxford [25 Dec–3 Apr 1491] 3.4d
bw e of Derby [25 Dec–3 Apr 1491] 20d
m Ld Wells [25 Dec–3 Apr 1491] 12d
m Ld Derby [3 Apr–24 Jun 1491] 12d
4 mm Ld Arun' [3 Apr–24 Jun 1491] 3.4d
mm Q [3 Apr–24 Jun 1491] 2.0d
4 mm K *c.* 20 July 5.0d

Key:

m / mm / m[m] = minstrel(s)
K = king   Q = queen
PdeC = Peter de Casanova

bw = bearward
Pr = Prince (of Wales)
Ld Arun' = Lord Arundel

tabs = taborers
e = earl

trpts = trumpets
d = duke

hpr = harper
dss = duchess

Since the towns have individual accounting years, stated under the name of each town in Table 14, it is rarely possible to trace the progress of any group along its likely route. Sandwich has records surviving for only one of these accounting years; Lydd has none, and does not appear in Table 14.

To these records are added those of Rye, over the border in Sussex. These are lists of daily expenses, collected in rather shorter periods of time and sometimes dated precisely. This means that items can be assigned to within a period of a few months, rather than to a whole accounting year, and sometimes to a particular date. Rye was clearly a point of entry to or exit from the coastal route in Kent, from where minstrels could travel to and from Rochester and London via Tunbridge Wells or, further west, through Battle, Lewes and East Grinstead. Scattered records from the abbeys of Robertsbridge and Battle on these two routes, respectively, show rewards to royal minstrels and other groups named at Rye, providing *prima facie* evidence that they shared itineraries with Rye and towns further east.[14]

Looking first at the entries for 1487/8, we see that the king's minstrels were in Dover on 18 April 1488. This is earlier in the year than the expected Pentecost-All Saints period, being between Easter (6 April that year) and Pentecost (25 May). The king's minstrels – presumably the same group – were at Rye between 6 April and 24 June that year. It is not possible to tell in which direction they were travelling: but assuming that they left Court the day after Easter (i.e. on 7 April), their presence in Dover eleven days later would suggest that this was the start of their coastal journey rather than the end (although a visit to Sandwich would have been possible). The rewards to the king's minstrels at Canterbury and Hythe during that accounting year may relate to the same visit. At Canterbury the reward was handed to Peter de Casanova, presumably the leader of the group. He was a king's trumpeter by 1483, and Marshal of the Trumpets at Henry VIII's coronation in 1509.

After Dover the group had another 36 days before returning to Court by the day before Pentecost (i.e. on 24 May).[15] Five weeks would be plenty of time for the return journey, whichever way they went. There is no evidence that they returned through Canterbury, however, and it seems sensible to suppose that they travelled clockwise from Canterbury, perhaps taking in Sandwich *en route* to Dover, Hythe and New Romney (and perhaps Lydd), and thence to Rye and back to the London area via one of the westerly routes. If this is correct, they would have arrived in Canterbury around 12–15 April and in Dover, as we know, by the 18th; working along the coast road to Hythe, they would be in New Romney around 25 April, leaving a month for their return in time for Pentecost on 25 May. This allowed time to follow the coast road into Sussex before turning north for London. An obvious visit to make on the way would be Robertsbridge or Battle, both abbeys known to have rewarded the

---

[14] REED Kent: *Diocese of Canterbury*, under Rye, Robertsbridge Abbey and Battle Abbey for relevant dates. It is possible that groups travelling in Sussex were not the same as those working the Kent coast, but it seems likely that they were.

[15] Westminster to Dover via Canterbury is about 75 miles.

king's minstrels in other years, and where they could earn money at the celebrations for Ascension Day, 15 May that year.[16]

In the accounts of Canterbury and Rye the king's minstrels are followed by those of the queen: at Rye the king's minstrels visited before 24 June, the queen's minstrels after that date. A relatively rare visit by the minstrels of the duchess of York to Dover and Rye earlier in that accounting year can be dated to late 1487, as the Rye entry was in the period 26 August to Christmas day.[17]

Another visitor to Rye in 1487/8 was the earl of Derby's bearward, some time between 24 June and 24 August 1488. There is no matching entry for other towns, so Rye may have been his starting-point for a journey through Sussex. The following year, however, he was at Rye between 19 April and 24 June 1489 and at Dover on an undated but probably matching visit.[18] The Rye accounts also record minstrels of the earl of Oxford at some time between 24 June and 24 August 1489: again, as there are no matching entries for them elsewhere, they may have arrived at Rye and turned westwards into Sussex.

The king's minstrels' undated visits to Canterbury, Dover, Hythe and New Romney in 1488/9 were probably summer visits that match their presence in Rye in late August 1489. Their visit to Rye on 10 August 1490 matches their visit to Canterbury in August 1490 and probably their visits to Sandwich and Dover during 1489/90. As usual, it is not possible to see whether they travelled clockwise or anti-clockwise. That accounting year also saw visits to Sandwich, Dover, New Romney and Rye by the minstrels of the Prince of Wales. At Sandwich the prince's group followed the king's, but at Dover and Rye they were there earlier. There is no matching record of a visit by the prince's minstrels to Canterbury, and again it is not possible to tell which way round the groups were travelling: but the reversal of order at Sandwich suggests that the prince's minstrels (and indeed those of Lord Arundel) were not going in the same direction as the king's.

The accounts of Dover and Rye for 1490/1 show a year in which more minstrels than usual were rewarded. The mismatches of personnel suggest that Dover rewarded minstrels attending those travelling to and from the continent (the Regent, the King of the Romans), while Rye was one end of an itinerary in Sussex (the duke of Bedford, bearwards of the earls of Derby and Oxford, a minstrel of Lord Wells). Others seem to be following the route along the Kent coast. Minstrels of the Prince of Wales were at Rye in late 1490 (between 29 August and Christmas day, but later than the duke of Bedford's minstrels on Holy Rood day, 14 September), probably on the same occasion as the visits to Dover and Canterbury; the visit to New Romney must date from 1491. The queen's minstrels were rewarded at Rye between 3 April and 24 June 1491, which matches their visit to Dover on 12 June that year; and the king's minstrels were rewarded at Rye within a few days either side of 20 July 1491,

---

[16] The records of Battle and Robertsbridge abbeys do not survive for 1488, but royal minstrels were rewarded in various other years: see *REED Sussex*, 182–7.

[17] The duchess of York was Cecily Neville, widow of Richard, duke of York, and mother of Edward IV and Richard III. She was *persona grata* with the Tudors as grandmother of the queen, Elizabeth of York.

[18] The earl of Derby was Thomas Stanley, Henry VII's step-father.

which matches their presence at Dover on 21 July.[19] Again, it is impossible to tell in which direction these groups were travelling. In 1491 Easter day was on 3 April and Pentecost on 22 May.

The record of payment at Rye to 'iiij of the kynges Mynstrelles' suggests a shawm band, with or without trumpet, as does the payment to 'iiij of the lorde of Arundelles mynstrellis'. The records occasionally specify six minstrels, more often two or three. The latter, one feels, may have been regarded as a small group by the scribe concerned, sometimes reflected in the reward given.

How much money might a group of minstrels make in the course of a tour? The rewards of such independent travel were certainly substantial. For the king's minstrels, the sum of 6s 8d, which was normally offered by several towns and institutions, when multiplied by the number of visits concerned and added to the lesser gifts from other places, guaranteed a very considerable income over the course of any particular itinerary. It is hardly possible to calculate what the total income might be: but if we assume that the tour through Kent would assure the group of 6s 8d from the towns of, say, Rochester, Canterbury, Sandwich and Dover, with an average of two or three shillings from Folkestone, Hythe, New Romney, Lydd, Ashford and other places along the route, they could expect to bring several pounds home in their saddlebags, with very little paid out by way of expenses. Shared between three or four, or even six, this was an income worth travelling for: and the same was evidently true for groups – from the queen's minstrels downwards – whose level of reward was lower. Even a single minstrel, earning between 4d and 12d in any one location, would return home with several shillings. But this, of course, raised a question of security: a lone minstrel might well be robbed, and travelling in a group was certainly safer.

Travel as a regular feature of the minstrel life

What information can be gained from this consideration of minstrel itineraries? Two distinct types of itinerary seem certain on the balance of probabilities. The first involved long distances with venues strung out on and near to a major highway. There is no reason to suppose that the Great North Road was the only one of these that the minstrels followed. Such distances would probably best be covered in the period between Pentecost and All Saints, but almost certainly other times were available too and were used by minstrels for independent touring. The second kind of itinerary was on a roughly circular route that did not involve much duplication. This sort of itinerary, that we could reasonably call a 'circuit', was suitable for the main summer season but could also be undertaken in the shorter periods between major feasts: and there is evidence that minstrels might absent themselves from the major feasts at the home base – with permission, one assumes – in order to continue performing elsewhere.

Concerning the royal minstrels, there were evidently several groups, touring at different times and on different itineraries. As each group could not expect more

---

[19] The date at Rye is given as 'in the weke of Saynt margett'. This is presumably St Margaret, virgin and martyr, whose festival day is 20 July, rather than the Queen of Scotland, feast-day 8 July. In 1491 St Margaret's day was a Wednesday, which makes her week 17–23 July.

than one reward in any one place per year, the groups evidently did not compete with one another but came to an agreement as to which group should work which itinerary and when. The allocation of rewards was according to the liveries, however, so the minstrels of the queen or Prince of Wales could expect a reward in places where the king's minstrels had been or were expected. Regular annual rewards were allocated for non-royal minstrels too: this is clear from the pattern of rewards in various towns and is clearly stated in the Northumberland ordinances.

There is almost no information about the constitution of the groups travelling. The occasional reference to 'four minstrels' suggests a shawm band, with or without a trumpet, and the group headed by the trumpeter Peter de Casanova must have been such a consort, or perhaps a group of trumpeters. The records give little hint of still minstrels, although it seems unlikely that there could be no work for them in the private chambers of a mayor or abbot. It is true that some entries in the accounts imply indoor performance, at the house of the mayor or other civic personage or in the private chamber of an abbot, but this does not necessarily imply still minstrelsy. In the records summarised in Table 14, a harper at Rye in 1489/90 is the only still minstrel specified, and this proportion is probably normal throughout the records available. The proportion of still minstrels would probably increase, however, if there were more records surviving from religious houses.

There is indeed much more record material to be searched and analysed, and other geographical areas to be considered. Such work would certainly be fruitful, for it is already obvious that independent travel by individual minstrels such as bearwards and by groups of four to six minstrels was a rather larger and more important part of the minstrels' life than could be recognised before the publication of REED volumes. And this, let us remind ourselves once more, was organised, regular travel with a clear financial purpose. But, as Henry VI's commission to his minstrels shows, the circumstances of this travel could be abused, so that effective policing of minstrelsy was required. This will be considered in the next chapter.

10

The regulation and protection of minstrels

It has been a common view that itinerant minstrels were at the lowest level of society, reviled as immoral and criminal, cast out by the Church and severely circumscribed by the secular and civic authorities. Writers on minstrelsy in Germany, England and France have held this view, citing examples from various places throughout the late Middle Ages to show minstrels committing crimes, supporting immorality, and being excluded and punished by ecclesiastical and secular authority. As John Southworth expressed it,[1]

> It is not just that the [social] status of the minstrel was low; for very many of his contemporaries, he was altogether beyond the pale of social acceptance. ... Not only was he excluded ... from the normal web of ties and responsibilities that constituted medieval society, but even his membership of the universal church, the fellowship of baptised Christians, was at one time in serious dispute.

This is a view that I have accepted in the past, but is it really justified? Does enough evidence exist to demonstrate the case for itinerant minstrels being abhorred as 'beyond the pale'? On further reflection, perhaps not.

The Church was certainly suspicious of those who performed music that resulted in sensual enjoyment and might encourage illicit sexual behaviour and other immorality. It is hardly surprising that the Church as an institution should play safe by taking a conservative view, recognising the potential dangers to the Christian soul and acting accordingly. Civic authorities, too, were wary of an itinerant trade that could cause disturbance of various kinds, such as loud noises at night, drunken brawls in ale houses, and enjoyable distraction while pickpockets and other thieves were at work. But there is also much to be said on the other side. As noted in Chapter 5, individual clerics were more practical in their approach to minstrelsy, enjoying the entertainment of minstrels on appropriate occasions and extending to them the hospitality that was part of the Church's charitable obligation. The heads of secular households took the same course; and towns saw no harm in minstrelsy *per se*, only a need to exercise crime prevention and administer punishment when necessary.

Nor is there a case for saying that minstrels were particularly guilty of crime and immorality. Commentators have tended to offer a few cases, usually from a wide range of places and dates, but the evidence against minstrels is notable less for its

---

[1] Southworth, *English Medieval Minstrel*, 4–5. See, for example, Chambers, *Medieval Stage*, II, 262–3; Woodfill, *Musicians*, 109; and Peters, *Musical Sounds*, 218–27. Dobozy, *Re-Membering*, Chapter 2 ('Minstrels as Pariah'), gives a full and carefully considered assessment, mainly concerning minstrels in Germany.

pervasiveness than for its paucity. A few plums do not make a fruit harvest, and minstrels were not demonstrably more criminal than other trades and groups, either itinerant or resident. How do the few examples of minstrels committing crimes and assorted misdemeanours compare with those committed by others? They certainly do not support a case for itinerant minstrels being the dregs of society. A thorough examination of crimes and their punishments would settle this question, but meanwhile we should accept the *prima facie* evidence that minstrels were sometimes involved in criminal activity, but no more so than other trades and groups.

This chapter examines various kinds of control concerning minstrels: the courts that regulated minstrels at fairs and licensed them to perform over a wide geographical area, together with the royal ordinances that sought to prevent subversive performances; the minstrel-kings who were responsible for enforcing the conditions of the licences; and the guilds and fraternities that offered charitable benefits and professional protection from 'foreign' competition.

The control of minstrelsy: the minstrel courts

The nature of the minstrel courts has not been generally understood, although Chambers and Woodfill both realised that the administrations at Chester and Tutbury could not originally have been fraternities.[2] Whatever their later manifestations, these organisations certainly started out as a landowner's way of exacting a fee for a licence to perform at the fair, or for a whole year in a wider geographical area, with the control over minstrels that this implies.[3]

The earliest administration, at Chester, was the longest-lived and the most successful. The story of its origin c. 1199–1211 was first told briefly by William Smith in 1588, and then in more detail by Sir Peter Leycester. Leycester's original account, which remains in manuscript, was apparently written in 1642 and revised in 1666; in the published text of 1673 some details are changed.[4] The story goes that Randal, Earl of Chester, being besieged in Rhuddlan Castle by the Welsh, sent for help to Roger Lacy, constable of Chester. The midsummer fair was under way, and Chester was full of the crowds that the fair always attracted: the implication of this, not stated anywhere, is that Lacy had too small a force available both to raise the siege and to leave the town adequately policed. He solved the problem by taking with him the whole noisy crowd to the earl's rescue. The Welsh withdrew in the face of an apparently powerful military force. As a reward to the constable, the earl conferred on him the right to control certain trades in the city and county of Chester. The constable

---

[2] Chambers, *Mediaeval Stage*, I, 42–3 and 59; Woodfill, *Musicians in English Society*, Chapter 5, especially 117–19.

[3] The characteristics of minstrel courts and guilds were distinguished in SM I, 20, and more fully in Rastall (G.R.), 'Minstrel court'. Later commentators still discuss these organisations only as fraternities: but for a probable fair-time licensing in France see Peters, *Musical Sounds*, 181.

[4] See *REED Cheshire*, I, 36–44, superseding items in *REED Chester*, 461–6, 486–9, 503 and 505–6; Leyster's account in Sir Peter Leycester, *Historical Antiquities* (London, 1673), 141, is repeated in Thomas Blount, *Antient Tenures of Land* (London, 1679), 156–8.

retained the rights over some, but others he later conferred on his steward, Hugh de Dutton.

The three accounts give different versions of the classes marched to Rhuddlan and over whom rights were conferred. Smith says that the constable took 'all ye players & musicians in the Cittie' to Rhuddlan, and that the Duttons received rights over 'all the musicians, within the Countie'. Leycester's earlier account states that the constable[5]

> gathered forthwith all the merry persons hee could meete with in the Citty of Chester. As Coblers, ffidlers, merry Companions, Whores, & such routish Company, ... both of men and weomen ...

According to this account, the earl handed over to the constable 'power ouer all kind of such Loose persons residinge within the County of Chesshire', and that these rights were passed to Hugh Dutton. Leycester's published account states that Lacy 'gathered a tumultuous Rout of Fidlers, Players, Coblers, debauched persons, both Men and Women, out of the City of Chester' to march to Rhuddlan; that the earl bestowed 'Power over all the Fidlers and Shoemakers in Chester' on the constable; and that the latter retained the rights over the shoemakers, giving authority over the 'Fidlers and Players' to Dutton.[6] The earliest original document that we have, an inquisition *post mortem* for Sir Hugh de Dutton dated 6 June 23 Ed I (1295), says that Sir Hugh had the right to payment from all minstrels and prostitutes in the county of Cheshire.[7]

It is impossible to know, from these accounts, quite what the documents in front of Smith and Leycester actually said. One may suspect that these authors preferred not to publish the details concerning prostitutes, and also that some assumptions were made equating those taken to Rhuddlan with those over whom the rights were given away. The inquisition *post mortem* of 1295 is perhaps the only document that can be taken at face value, with Leycester's first version being more trustworthy than Smith's account or Leycester's own published version. This information is set out in Table 15: those listed in the 'Taken to Rhuddlan' column are 'in/of the city' because they were there at the time of the fair; the rights given away are mostly 'in the county' because that was the nature of the licences.

The original grant to Hugh Dutton, as quoted by Leycester in both versions of his account, gave Dutton authority over lechers and prostitutes throughout Cheshire ('magistratum omnium Leccatorum et meretricum totius Cestershiriae'). This corresponds to the 'loose persons' of Leycester's first account and to the 'debauched persons' of his publication, but not specifically to cobblers, fiddlers, players or

---

5 REED Cheshire, I, 37.
6 Ibid., I, 37 and 41.
7 'Et idem hugo habuit aduocariam omnium Menestrallorum & meretricium in Cestrisiria'. See REED Cheshire, I, 44–5. The document is actually dated the Monday following the feast of St Boniface ('die lune proxima post festum sancti Bonefacij anno regni Regis Edwardi vicesimo tercio'). The feast is on 5 June, which in 1295 fell on the first Sunday after Trinity. As Andrew Taylor notes below (p. 272), Charlemagne ceded Provence to minstrels and lechers, and it would be interesting to know why.

Table 15. Minstrels at the relief of Rhuddlan

Source	Taken to Rhuddlan	Rights to Constable	to Dutton
Inquisition p.m. 1295			minstrels and prostitutes in the county
Smith 1588	players and musicians in the city		musicians in the county
Leycester 1 1642/66	Merry persons: cobblers, fiddlers, whores	loose persons in the county	loose persons in the county
Leycester 2 1673	Fiddlers, players, cobblers, debauched persons of the city	fiddlers, shoemakers	fiddlers, players in the city

musicians. On the other hand, the rights given by the earl to the constable (and thence partly to his steward) need not refer to the crowd actually taken to Rhuddlan. What the earl did was to make a financial settlement on the constable of the income from one class of stall-holder at the fair (the shoemakers) and at least one class of those doing business without renting a stall. The constable kept the stall-holders to himself because it was easy to levy the fees; from the lechers and prostitutes, who were ambulatory, the fees were more difficult to claim.

It is clear that non-stall-holders were looked down on as people of a much lower social and moral order: fiddlers or musicians (a newer name for minstrels), players, cobblers and whores are classed together as 'loose' or 'debauched' persons with very little attempt to distinguish between them. 'Players' would not necessarily be actors using any form of staging, but here could include those, such as clowns and fools, dealing in any sort of mimetic entertainment; cobblers were the mere menders of old shoes, a very different matter from the shoemakers, who were craftsmen.[8]

On the basis of later documentation it is clear that only minstrels and prostitutes came under the Duttons' jurisdiction. This agrees with the 1295 inquisition, so it is likely that these were indeed the classes of person concerned. When Laurence Dutton responded to a writ of *Quo warranto* (By what right?) in 14 Hen VII (1499/1500), his reply stated that he exercised authority over the minstrels of Chester and Cheshire; that the minstrels were required to meet him or his deputy annually on the feast of the Nativity of St John the Baptist (24 June); that he claimed four gallons of wine, a lance and a fee of 4½d from each minstrel on that occasion; and that he also took a fee of 4d from each prostitute.[9] The fee paid by the minstrels was for a licence to perform, which, Leycester reported, exempted the 'Fidlers of Cheshire' from the Elizabethan vagrancy laws.

---

[8] L.F. Salzman, *English Industries of the Middle Ages* (London, 1970), 254.

[9] *REED Cheshire*, I, 40. In the margin against '*Quatuor Lagenas vini*' is a note 'fowre bottles of wine'. This is Leycester's translation, which he incorporated into the body of the text for publication. 'Gallons' or 'flagons' is the more likely meaning of *lagena* in the late fifteenth century.

Earl Randal did not create the rights which later fell to the Duttons: he already exercised control over the shoemakers and minstrels in his territory, and indeed over all those who did business at the St John's Day fair. Those who marched to Rhuddlan were – primarily or entirely – the traders who worked 'on the hoof' rather than from a stall: minstrels, players, prostitutes and cobblers. Stall-holders would pay stallage on the day, but the non-stall-holders would have to be charged a fee to work on the fair-ground or in the town. This may be an annual licensing that simply made use of the main fair as an occasion when all traders would be present; but it could equally be a fair-time control that took the opportunity to sell licences for the whole year. Lacy was able to take the crowd with him on the 25-mile march to Rhuddlan because he could otherwise withhold licences and therefore the right to ply a trade both at the fair and in the year to come.

The Chester court died out in the eighteenth century, but it never lost the basic characteristics of a court:

1. control by a feudal authority;
2. over all minstrels and other entertainers in a wide area;
3. through licences to perform, for which fees were exacted;
4. during annual attendance at a fair.

Leycester's description of the court on 24 June 1642 shows that at the east gate of the city a proclamation was read, requiring all musicians and minstrels in the county and city of Chester to attend the Lord of Dutton (usually represented by a deputy) and to render such 'Hommages, duties, and services' as were due to him.[10] A procession to the courthouse stopped *en route* at St John's Church, where 'A sett of the Lowd Musique vpon their Knees playeth A solemne Lesson or Two'. At the courthouse, a jury was empanelled to enquire into three matters:

1. Whether anyone present knew of any treason against the king or prince (of Wales, and earl of Chester);
2. Whether any minstrel was known to have performed without the court's licence, or on the Sabbath Day without the court's permission, or while drunk; and
3. Whether anyone had heard any 'scandalous words' prejudicial to the heir of Dutton.

The enquiries concluded, the lord went to dinner, after which he was presented with a new lance, to which was fixed the banner always displayed on this occasion. The minstrels then paid the fee for their licences, which was 2s 2d in 1642 and 2s 6d in 1666.[11]

Although there was a nod towards the church-going side of charitable organisations, this procedure formalised the distribution of licences in return for fees, essentially perpetuating the purpose and character of the minstrel court. The procedure was a relatively simple one that could have been used by other landowners controlling minstrels on their land and levying fees in return for a licence to work. One such landowner was John of Gaunt, who exercised control in at least one town

[10] REED Cheshire, I, 38–9.
[11] Ibid., I, 40.

owned by him, Newcastle under Lyme.¹² As in the Chester case, the right to exact fees had been passed on, in this case to an ancestor of the wife of a burgess.¹³ In a document dated from his palace of the Savoy on 26 November 46 Ed III (1372) Gaunt wrote to his steward of Newcastle under Lyme concerning an enquiry undertaken by the steward. It had been found that William de Brompton, a burgess of the town, and his wife Margery and all Margery's ancestors 'from time beyond memory' (*de temps dont memoire ne court*) had taken fees at the feast of St Giles (1 September): of 4½d from minstrels coming to perform (*pur faire leur ministralcie*) and bears coming to be baited (*pur estre chace*). These rights and privileges (*les choses et liberteez avantditz*) were to be given to William and Margery as formerly.

This was again a fair-time control with purely financial implications. No administration on the part of William and Margery is mentioned, nor any licensing, so it may be that this was a simple toll-taking for the fair itself. But the fee payable, 4½d, was the same as at Chester, so the licence may have covered performance in the area for a whole year.

Gaunt was also lord of the Honour of Tutbury, a multiple estate that covered parts of Staffordshire and Derbyshire. Tutbury castle, on the river Dove that formed the boundary between the two counties, was the administrative centre of the honour. By 1314, if not earlier, there was a minstrel administration at Tutbury when entertainers (*histriones*) came to the fair there. This was held at the feast of the Assumption of the Blessed Virgin (15 August), the patronal festival of the Benedictine priory. In 1314 the minstrels paid the earl of Lancaster 20d, perhaps as rent for pasturing their horses,¹⁴ but it may be that a fee was also being paid for a licence to perform. John of Gaunt, duke from 1362, was at Tutbury for the festivities on 15–16 August 1374, and again in 1375.¹⁵ The arrangements concerning the minstrels may have been in operation then, but five years later they apparently were not. On 22 August 1380, following that year's festivities, the duke issued a mandate that sought to set them in motion again.¹⁶ Orders sent to the administration at Tutbury gave notice that the duke's king of minstrels in the Honour of Tutbury had authority to arrest any minstrels in the honour and related lands that refused to fulfill the obligations and attendance (*leurs services et ministralcies*) required of them 'from ancient times' (*dauncien temps*) each year on the days of the Assumption of Our Lady (evidently the fair was held on more than the one day).

---

[12] John of Gaunt, duke of Lancaster and earl of Leicester, was the favourite son of Edward III. His lands and properties included the palace of the Savoy in the Strand (Westminster) and the castles of Leicester, Tutbury, Pontefract, Bolingbroke and Kenilworth. See Sir Oswald Mosley, *The History of the Castle, Priory, and Town of Tutbury, in the County of Stafford* (London, 1832), 73.

[13] Armitage-Smith, *John of Gaunt's Register*, II, 98.

[14] Nigel Tringham, 'Honor of Tutbury'. *A History of the County of Stafford, X: Tutbury and Needwood Forest* (Woodbridge and Rochester NY, 2007). See TNA DL 29/1/3, m. 5 (Rolleston section).

[15] Tringham, 'Honor of Tutbury', citing *John of Gaunt's Register*, 324–5.

[16] Lodge and Somerville, *John of Gaunt's Register*, 341: translated in Robert Plot, *The Natural History of Stafford-shire* (Oxford, 1686), 435–6, and Mosley, *History of Tutbury*, 77.

This administration had the main elements of the Chester system. The lord of the Honour of Tutbury required all minstrels working anywhere in the honour to attend the fair and give him their *services et ministralcies*. As at Newcastle under Lyme, the exact age of the administration is in doubt: *de temps dont memoire ne court* (from time out of memory) and *dauncien temps* (from ancient times) date the Newcastle and Tutbury administrations equally vaguely. The earliest reference to the Tutbury minstrel administration dates from 1314, but the Tutbury fair was in operation at least as early as 1252 and the minstrel administration could have started between those dates.

The minstrels' *services et ministralcies* are not specified, but perhaps the payment of a fee was included, as elsewhere. A description of the event in 1415 shows that the woodmaster of Needwood Forest was acting as deputy to the lord of the honour. The woodmaster and other keepers of the forest, who brought a buck from the forest as a gift to the prior, processed into Tutbury on 15 August accompanied by the minstrels. The procession went to the market cross, and then to the priory church, where the buck's head was offered while the minstrels performed; the keepers then heard Mass, and dined at the castle. The next day, 16 August, the minstrels' court was held before the woodmaster. When the proceedings ended, a bull that was the gift of the prior was set loose: if the minstrels could catch it, the bull was theirs.[17] The bull was presented annually by the prior until the dissolution of the priory, and thereafter was the gift of the earl of Devonshire.[18] There is no evidence that the bull-running dated from the time of John of Gaunt.[19] It may however have originated as an encouragement to minstrels to support a weakened institution following Gaunt's death in 1399 and the subsequent merging of the dukedom of Lancaster with the crown.[20]

Like the Chester administration, the Tutbury court claimed authority over a wide area, and the lordship of the duke of Lancaster made the Honour of Tutbury largely autonomous for much of the fourteenth century. The fact that Gaunt administered the minstrel court through his own minstrel-king shows that his authority over-rode that of the crown in the Honour. As a son and uncle of kings who was also the wealthiest man in England, Gaunt was one of very few who could make such a statement. Only one other English minstrel-king known to me was not the king's officer and a member of the king's household: that is Druet, minstrel-king of Gilbert de Clare, earl of Gloucester, Edward II's cousin.[21] Gaunt may have felt that employing a minstrel-king was appropriate to his own status as King of Castile and Leon, a claim made through his second wife, Constance of Castile, but renounced in 1387;

---

[17] Tringham, 'Honor of Tutbury'.

[18] Plot, *Natural History of Stafford-shire*, 437; Henry Kirke, 'The Ancient Court of Minstrels at Tutbury'. *Journal of the Derbyshire Archaeological Society* (1910), 105–13, at 109 f.

[19] [ ] Pegge, 'The bull-running, at Tutbury, in Staffordshire, considered. By the Reverend Mr Pegge'. *Archaeologia* 2 (1773), 86–91, showed (at 86) that the bull-running was not part of the original organisation.

[20] The duchy of Lancaster has been held by the monarch since Henry Bolingbroke's accession as Henry IV in 1399. (The dukedom, as opposed to the duchy, was held by Prince Henry until his accession as Henry V in 1413, and by the monarch from then on.)

[21] TNA E101.374.19 (household of Thomas and Edmund, the king's brothers, 5–6 Ed II), fol. 8r (cal. SM II, 74).

and he would certainly have known of the provincial minstrel-kings in France, where the land-owning nobility tended to rule autonomously over larger tracts of land than in England.[22] One imagines that Richard II was not pleased by this show of regality, and in fact Gaunt's minstrel-king is not heard of again.

The third minstrel-court that controlled minstrels over a wide area was that at Beverley, which turned itself into a fraternity by the mid-sixteenth century. The renewed statutes of 1555 describe a fairly typical charitable and protective trade organisation: but the preamble to the statutes shows that it was originally a minstrel court, with minstrels from a wide area coming annually to a specified place:[23]

> Whereas it is and hath been a very aunciente custome aute of the memorie of dyvers aiges of men heretofore contynually frequented from the tyme of King Athelstone, ... as may appear by olde bookes of antiquities. That all or the most part of the mynstrell playing of any musicall instruments, and thereby occupying there honest lyving inhabytyng dwelling or servyng any man or woman of honour, and worshype of any citie or towne corporate or otherwise, between the rivers of Trent and Tweed, have accustomed yerely to resort unto this towne and borough of Beverley, at the Rogation days, and then and there to chose yerely one Alderman of the Mynstrells, with stewards and deputies authorized to take names, and receive customable duties of the said Mynstrells' Fraternitie; and the Alderman to correcte, amend, execute and continue all such laudable ordynances and statutes as they have hitherto ever used for the honestee and profit of their science and art musicall, to be only exercised to the honour of God, and to the comfort of man.

The statement of the organisation's antiquity is intended to claim long custom, but it is precise in pointing to the reign of Athelstan, King of Wessex and Mercia from 924 and King of England 927–39. The accuracy of this statement is another matter: but control over a wide area and the annual gathering at a festival time are features of the minstrel courts. The election of officers belongs to a guild organisation, as at the Chester and Tutbury courts in their later forms: so, probably, does the exclusion of independent minstrels from the organisation. They would surely have been included in the original court.

The Rogation days are the Monday, Tuesday and Wednesday immediately before Ascension Day (always a Thursday), five weeks after Easter. They can occur anywhere between late April and early June, effectively at or near the beginning of the summer touring season for both liveried and independent minstrels. The Archbishop of York held markets and fairs at Beverley at least as early as 21 Ed I (1292/3), including a fair on the eve and day of the Ascension and the seven days following.[24] If the minstrels met at Beverley on the three Rogation days they could all be licensed by the end of the first day of the fair.

---

[22] Peters, *Musical Sounds*, passim.
[23] BL MS Lansdowne 896, fols 153r–56v, printed in Poulson, *Beverlac*, 303, and Lambert (J.M.), *Two Thousand Years*, 134.
[24] Poulson, *Beverlac*, 150.

The large area over which this fraternity claimed to operate indicates an original court administration, because charitable and trade fraternities work best in small localities. The area between Trent and Tweed – that is, the whole of northern England – is so large that if guild-protection had been the original purpose many separate organisations would have sprung up in various towns. It is precisely the element of control that marks this area out as appropriate. It is, in fact, the area almost certainly administered by a king of heralds and minstrels, a matter to which we shall return.

In all of these organisations for which we have any detail, the element of control (beyond the obvious need for crime-prevention) was a secondary consideration to that of financial gain for a landowner or fair-owner. There were occasions, however, when for political reasons or simply to protect his own interests, the king was moved to take action against a group of minstrels or the minstrel-class as a whole. On 6 August 9 Ed II (1315) Edward II issued an ordinance that sought to limit expenditure, and so to prevent extravagance, among his nobles, and to curtail the activities of those who would sponge off them. He specifically mentions that 'many idle persons, under colour of minstrelsy, and going in messages, and other feigned business, have been and yet be received in other men's houses to meat and drink', who 'be not therewith contented if they be not largely considered with gifts of the lords of the houses'. All this, the king wrote, was greatly detrimental to his realm. He proceeded to limit the number of meat courses and dishes to be served at table, and similarly with fish on the fish-days, under pain of punishment. He continued:[25]

> And lykewyse that to the houses of Prelates, Earles, and Barons, none resort to meate and drynke, unlesse he be a mynstrel, and of these minstrels, that there come none except it be three or foure minstrels of honour at the most in one day, unlesse he be desired of the lorde of the house. And to the houses of meaner men, that none come unlesse he be desired, and that such as shall come so, holde themselves contented with meate and drynke, and with such curtesie as the maister of the house wyl shewe unto them of his owne good wyll, without their askyng of any thyng. And yf any one do agaynst this ordinaunce, at the firste tyme he to lose his minstrelsie, and at the seconde tyme to foresweare his craft, and never to be receaved for a minstrel in any house.

The ordinance goes on to deal with messengers, runners, archers 'and other idle men' in a similar fashion.[26] 'Minstrels of honour' must have included all liveried minstrels and, perhaps, certain well-known and skilful minstrels in any area. Edward probably issued a corresponding ordinance to his own minstrels, warning them not to ask too much from casual patrons during their travels.

---

[25] John Leland, *Joannis Lelandi antiquarii De rebus britannicis collectanea*, ed. Thomas Hearne (London, 1774), VI, 36 f, and a shortened version in William Chappell, *Popular Music of the Olden Time* (London, 1859; repr. 2 vols, with an introduction by Frederick W. Sternfeld. New York NY, 1965), 30. Leland printed the message as sent to the sheriffs of Kent, but copies would be sent to sheriffs in every county.

[26] This does not mean that messengers, runners and archers were considered 'idle': the 'other, idle', men would have included minstrels not considered to be 'of honour'.

This ordinance was directed against minstrels and other travellers, but it also curtailed the free activity of the nobility. The precise reason for it is hard to gather from the document itself: but Edward's unpopularity had almost certainly led to scurrilous and subversive songs being circulated widely by the itinerant minstrel community, a real problem for the king that could be dealt with only by curtailing the mobility of minstrels and other itinerants. There is no evidence that this ordinance had any effect, and it can hardly have increased Edward's popularity: but Edward IV quoted such an ordinance in the *Liber Niger*,[27] so the need for it – and presumably the hope that it would have the desired result – had continued into the 1470s.

A more important suppression of minstrel activity was issued for political purposes in a statute of 30 September 1402. Itinerant minstrels and others were fomenting dissent in Wales by expressing and disseminating Welsh nationalism through their performances and giving of news, and the king announced that[28]

> ... to avoid many troubles and misfortunes [*pluseurs diseases & meschiefs*] that have come about before now in the land of Wales on account of many jongleurs, rhymers, minstrels, and other vagabonds [*westours Rymours Ministralx & autres vacabondes*], it is ordained and established that no jongleur, rhymer, minstrel nor vagabond shall be supported in any way in the land of Wales by imposing comorthas or a collection upon the commen people there ...

Such treasonous activity was probably very hard to pin down, and the statute might have been difficult to enforce. Framed as a comprehensive ban on all aid for minstrels in Wales, it aimed to conduct a war of attrition on any who might engage in subversive activity. In late 1401 the pitched battles of 1400–1 arising from Owen Glyn Dwr's uprising partly gave way to guerrilla tactics on the part of the Welsh. In early 1402 this was fuelled by the arrival of a spectacular comet[29] and, in February, of unusually stormy weather. These were generally seen as portents, and the bards used them to rally support for Glyn Dwr's cause. This was a rather specific use of bardic propaganda, and quite different from any minstrel's usual activity of disseminating news. There is no evidence that the king's statute had the desired effect, but it remained in force until the mid-sixteenth century, and it led straight to the vagrancy laws of Elizabeth's reign.[30]

In contrast to this highly-charged threat to national security, the problems faced by Henry VI's minstrels in 1449 were local and personal, and yet the king took action on their behalf. As we saw in Chapter 9, this was a policing control, but it took the form of a potentially permanent administration, by which Henry gave his own

---

[27] Myers, *Household of Edward IV*, 132.

[28] Hen IV, c. 27: TNA C 74/5, m. 15*: see *REED Wales*, 28 (original) and 327 (translation). The editor notes (p. 399) that 'kymorthas' were 'originally a form of community assistance intended to aid those in economic difficulty': the meaning here is a little broader than that. On the political background, see D. Helen Allday, *Insurrection in Wales* (Lavenham, 1981), especially 78–80.

[29] Not Halley's comet, which had appeared in 1378 and next arrived in 1456.

[30] J.J. Jusserand, *English Wayfaring Life in the Middle Ages*, trans. Lucy Toulmin Smith (1889; University paperback edn, London and New York, 1961), 128.

minstrels the same powers as the minstrel-king at Tutbury had possessed, extended now to include the whole country except Chester.[31] Copies of this commission were sent to sheriffs throughout the country, with a request that assistance be given to the minstrels to carry out the inquisition.[32]

Although there seems to be no documentary evidence of fraudulent activity, it would not be surprising if a few independent minstrels sometimes earned their living less than honestly, nor that some should take advantage of the high status of the liveried minstrel. The distinction between 'minstrels of honour' and other minstrels grew more acute as time went on. The poverty and high prices of the first half of the fourteenth century, with an actual famine in 1315 and again in 1322 and 1346, cannot have helped independent minstrels to make a living. Nor did the second half of the century improve the situation, with five minor outbreaks of the Black Death by 1391, following the major plague of 1348–9. After the Black Death the rich were, generally speaking, better-off than before, and this may have helped to increase the difference in status between the liveried and the independent minstrels. The sharp decrease in population may also have reduced the opportunities for minstrels working independently.

The control of minstrelsy: the kings of heralds and of minstrels

John of Gaunt's king of minstrels, given the authority in 1380 to license minstrels at Tutbury, held a rare title. Very few kings of minstrels are known: but in fact, they seem to have been an offshoot of the kings of heralds, which was the more normal designation, and it seems almost certain that the kings of heralds and the kings of minstrels were the same men.[33]

Kings of heralds

The first king of heralds for whom we have any real information is King Robert. He is first recorded in a livery-list for 13 Ed I (1284/5), appearing as 'Robertus parvus rex haraldorum'.[34] Bullock-Davies has charted his career,[35] noting that there is virtually

---

[31] On the exemption of Chester, see below.

[32] The copy sent to Norwich survives. Hudson, *Norwich*, II, 328, gives the date as 17 Jan. 7 Henry VI, surely a misreading for 17 Jun. 27 Henry VI. Wykes and Cliff do not appear as king's minstrels before 25–6 Henry VI: see SM II, 127. William Langton was in fact dead by May 1449: CPR, Henry VI, vol. 5 (1446–52), 250 (17 May 1449).

[33] This was always Conklin's view: see 'Medieval English Minstrels', 28 f. I was cautious in SM I, 29 f, perhaps unnecessarily. The herald-kings were also known as Kings at Arms, a title still in use.

[34] BL Add roll 6710, cited in Conklin, 'Medieval English Minstrels', 28. Bullock-Davies (*Menestrellorum Multitudo*, 160, and *Register*, 139) gives 1277 as the date at which Robert was first mentioned, but this is almost certainly wrong. The relevant British Library catalogue offers 1277? or [1312] as the date of this section of the badly-damaged Cotton MS Vespasian C.xvi, but implies that 5 Ed I is a misreading for 5 Ed II. Robert was certainly in the garrison of Berwick-on-Tweed in 5 Ed II (TNA E101.374.16, p. 4, cal. SM II, 72), and it seems most likely that the Vespasian C.xvi entry concerning Robert on fol. 3r refers to this occasion.

[35] Bullock-Davies, *Menestrellorum Multitudo*, 159–62, and *Register*, 139–44.

no information about Robert's personal life, other than his long illness at York in 10 and 11 Ed II (1317/8). Even here we have no detail: he lay ill at York for a whole year, but the nature of his illness is not stated. He evidently recovered, as he was working in 1319 and 1320: but one suspects that health problems forced his retirement, or perhaps led to his death, in late 1320, when he must have been at least 60 years old. We do have one additional piece of information, however, for we know that Robert was married. On 24 May 14 Ed I (1286) the king gave a cup or goblet 'to the wife of Master Robert Parvus, King of Heralds'.[36]

Robert's career of 35 years or so was very distinguished, as we can see from the story of his judgment before Edward II (see Chapter 13), which probably occurred between 1308 and 1313. As noted there, Robert was considered both discreet and intelligent. While these are attributes that could be expected in a herald-king, Robert's reputation must have been considerable for the story still to be related around 1440, some 120 years after we last hear of him. Robert attended many notable occasions at Court, and also experienced hostilities on the Scottish borders. He was probably the main organiser of the ceremonies of the Pentecost feast in 1306; he was in charge of the ceremonies for the purification of the Countess of Hereford (probably at Knaresborough) on 11 October 32 Ed I (1304), and again for the Countess of Cornwall at York on 20 February 5 Ed II (1312);[37] and at his last appearance in the records, on 8 July 14 Ed II (1320), he was taking part in the king's accession-day celebrations at Amiens.[38]

Robert ranked as a squire and a serjeant-at-arms of the king's household, but his heraldic duties as King were at a national level. There is a potential anomaly here for all the herald-kings: but although the Wardrobe scribes referred to him as 'trumpator regis' they never called him 'rex haraldorum regis'. As a trumpeter, he was a member of the king's household only: as a King at Arms, his authority extended to all heralds and minstrels in the country. Although payments and rewards to minstrel-kings were generous, they were high enough only to place the Kings at the top of the hierarchy of heralds and liveried minstrels. The first five Kings on the 1306 Pentecost list, for example, each received 5 marks (£3 6s 8d), which is the highest payment: but the sixth, King Druet (the earl of Gloucester's herald), received only 40s 0d (£2), which puts him equal with Norfolk, who was probably not a King.[39]

---

[36] TNA E101.352.4, m. 1, printed in B.F. Byerly and C.R. Byerly, eds, *Records of the Wardrobe and Household, 1285–1286* (London, 1977), 197 (item 1987).

[37] TNA E101.365.20 (roll, 32 Ed I); BL Cotton MS Nero C viii (5 Ed II), fol. 84v (cal. SM II, 71).

[38] BL Cotton MS Vespasian C xvi, fol. 3r, cited in Bullock-Davies, *Register*, 144; BL Add MS 9951 (14 Ed II), fol. 19r (cal. SM II, 79).

[39] TNA E101.369.6 (34 Ed I). Hayes, *King's Music*, 31, mistranslated an item from the accounts of Queen Eleanor's executors, 1291, implying that a gold cup worth 39s 0d was a special gift to a minstrel-king. The recipient was not a King, in fact, but a minstrel *of* the King of Champagne. Botfield, *Manners*, 110, reads: 'Item, pro uno cypho empto, cum pede, de auro, et dato per executores Reginae cuidam menestrallo Regis Campanie, qui venit cum nunciis Francie, xxxix s.'. This gift was not unusual: items taken as presents on the queen's visit to France in 30 Ed I include 'lx Fermaux dor por donier as menestraus, messagiers et autre gentz' (TNA E101.361.27, cal. SM II, 29).

Robert was usually referred to as King Robert ('Robertus rex') or more fully as 'Robertus parvus rex haraldorum'. This is ambiguous: although he was clearly not one of those 'young' servants who appear in the king's and prince's households,[40] Parvus could be his surname, Little or Small, or a personal description of him. There is no firm evidence in either direction, but the likelihood that he was a small person is discussed below.

Robert is the only king of heralds in the records for 14 Ed I (1285/6), but by the following year he was joined by Colin Morel. Morel is described simply as a squire in the accounts for 15 Ed I (1286/7), but this is certainly Nicholas Morel, who was a herald-king in 18 Ed I and appears as such in the accounts until 23 Ed I.[41] Colin was a diminutive of Nicholas in England, and the accounts name King Morel variously as Colinus or Nicholas.[42] So for eight years or so, 15–23 Ed I, there were at least two herald-kings at Court. The herald-king Walter le Marchis may be a third, although it is possible that he was employed by Henry Percy, not by the king.[43] King Marchis is first heard of in 27 Ed I (1298/9) and last recorded at the Pentecost feast of 1306 (34 Ed I).

It is not clear how many herald-kings were employed at Court at any one time, and the picture is blurred by the appearance in the records of visiting herald-kings coming from abroad. In the accounts where Colin Morel first appears there are also three herald-kings: Greyhead, Maynanus of Champagne and Robert le Neim. The first two of these were certainly visitors: 'Greyhid rex haraldorum' was rewarded on 5 May 15 Ed I (1287), having come to Court with his master, Sir Robert de Audenard, whom the king knighted that day;[44] and Maynanus was presumably the herald-king of the Count of Champagne.[45] 'Robertus le Neim rex haraldorum' was given summer robes that year, and so was apparently a royal servant: the marginal heading reads *Menstrallus*.[46] 'Le Neim' is probably the French version of 'parvus', for two common letter-substitutions between old and modern French give us the word *nain* (from Latin *nanus*), a dwarf. King Robert was perhaps small enough in his person to be distinguished on one occasion as *nain* and otherwise known as 'little'.[47]

---

[40] Conklin took the opposite view, however, in 'Medieval English Minstrels', 29.

[41] TNA E36.201 (15 Ed I), fol. 43v (Byerly and Byerly, *Records 1286–1289*, 163; E101.352.31 (18 Ed I), m. 1 (*Ibid.*, 344); E36.202 (23 Ed I), *passim*.

[42] *The Oxford Names Dictionary*, ed. Patrick Hanks, Flavia Hodges, A.D. Mills and Adrian Room (Oxford, 2002), 729. For the naming of Morel in TNA E36.202, *passim*, see Fryde, *Book of Prests*, *passim* (Index, p. 251).

[43] See Bullock-Davies, *Register*, 109.

[44] TNA E36.201, fol. 29r, printed in Byerly and Byerly, *Records 1286–89*, 98 (items 870, 871).

[45] Rewarded by the king on 12 May (1287): TNA E36.201, fol. 29v, printed in Byerly and Byerly, *Records 1286–89*, 99 (item 878).

[46] E36.201, fol. 45v, printed in Byerly and Byerly, *Records 1286–89*, 99 (item 1522).

[47] In the transcript of the payment record dated 2 February 16 Ed I (1288), for £6 13s 4d (10 marks: TNA E101.352.12, f. 15v), Byerly and Byerly, *Records 1286–89*, 264, item 2422, say that the payment was made by the hands of Robert Pin, king of heralds. 'Pin' is however the abbreviated genitive 'Parvi' (Pui), the superscript a (also implying a following r) over the P being missing or obscured.

Several other herald-kings appear in the records late in Edward I's reign, at celebrations where herald-kings were responsible for distributing rewards to others. King Grey was at the marriage of the king's daughter Joan of Acre to the earl of Gloucester in 1290: Wagner says that he was 'Rex Haraldorum in partibus Francie',[48] a matter to which we shall return. Those rewarded at the marriage of the king's daughter Elizabeth to the Count of Holland in 1296 (25 Ed I) include the herald-kings Page, Morellus, Druet, Monthaut and Jakettus de Scocia.[49] Of Page I know nothing more;[50] Nicholas Morel was attached to the English Court; Druet was a string-player and herald-king to the earl of Gloucester (Gilbert de Clare, the king's son-in-law). John de Monthaut was apparently a royal minstrel in 1290, and he took a payment for daily wages on 17 July 23 Ed I (1295): he is listed as a *rex haraldorum* at Princess Elizabeth's wedding, but there is no subsequent record of him.[51] Jakettus de Scocia was otherwise known as Capiny, Capenny or similar, and sometimes by his full name, James de Cowpen. Cowpen is near Blyth, Northumberland, in what later became the English Middle March: the appellation 'de Scocia' implies an origin or authority in the border lands, not necessarily in Scotland itself.[52] Capenny was certainly a member of the king's household, and perhaps had authority in the Scottish borders. Bullock-Davies cites a fragmentary Chamber account as showing that he was a harper.[53]

Six herald-kings were present at the Pentecost feast on 22 May 34 Ed I (1306), the summary accounts for which refer to 'King Robert and other herald-kings, and … other minstrels'.[54] The full list of minstrels and heralds rewarded begins with the King of Champagne and the Kings Capenny, Baisescue, Marchis and Robert.[55] King Robert, as the senior English herald-king, may have been in overall charge, although that is not clear. The money, a gift of 200 marks (£133 6s 8d) from the Prince, was given out by a small group of heralds and minstrels, the largest sums to the most

---

[48] Anthony Richard Wagner, *Heralds and Heraldry in the Middle Ages: An Inquiry into the Growth of the Armorial Function of Heralds.* 2nd edn (Oxford, 1956), 36, n. 4.

[49] See above, Chapter 4, for the list of rewards.

[50] Bullock-Davies, *Register*, 138, correctly speculated that Page was the herald-king of the Count of Holland. The next item in the account (also on fol. 15v) is for the cost of a habergeon for Pagus Rex de Hollandia.

[51] Bullock-Davies, *Register*, 122: TNA E101.352.12, fol. 11v; E36.202 (23 Ed I), fol. 40r, printed in Fryde, *Book of Prests*, 156; BL Add. 7965 (25 Ed I), fol. 52r, cal. SM II, 16–17.

[52] Edward I's *vigilis* Adam de Skirewith, who presumably came from Skirwith, near Penrith, was known as Adam de Scocia Parva ('of Little Scotland'): Byerly and Byerly, *Records 1285–86*, 167 (item 1694).

[53] TNA E101.371.8, no. 152: Bullock-Davies, *Menestrellorum Multitudo*, 78.

[54] TNA E101.369.11 (34 Ed I), fol. 96r.

[55] The list also includes the heralds Carlton, Norfolk (probably William Taillant de Norfolk), Bruant (probably John le Boteler, or Bruiant, a herald-king by 1322), and Robert de Boistous (probably Bois Robert, King of the Heralds of France in 1318). For Bruiant and Bois Robert, see Wagner, *Heralds and Heraldry*, 29 and 32. The list of minstrels is TNA E101.369.6 (34 Ed I), cal. SM II, 53–8.

important performers being distributed by King Capenny.[56] Robert and Capenny, then, were the herald-kings of the English Court. Walter le Roy Marchis was a third, unless he was a servant of Henry Percy (Warden of the Scottish Marches).[57]

The King of Champagne was a foreign visitor: Baisescue was probably another, as were Master Conrad (apparently from Germany), the king of heralds of Sprus and Ludekin, king of heralds of Germany (all in 12 Ed III, 1338/9).[58] Both Conrad and Ludekin were rewarded for minstrelsy. Another foreign minstrel-king was Myttok, King of the Minstrels of Brabant: he and his companions (probably all minstrels of the duke of Brabant) were given safe conduct and expenses when they left the Court at Westminster in 1368.[59]

Duties

By the thirteenth century heralds had a variety of functions, as explained in Chapter 4: arranging and managing tournaments and indoor festivities, and distributing the rewards afterwards; acting as diplomatic messengers; and issuing the king's proclamations. Like many minstrels and heralds, King Robert also saw active service at Berwick-on-Tweed and elsewhere, and it was probably the heralds' business, ultimately the responsibility of the herald-kings, to count and identify casualties. During the course of the fourteenth century, and especially during the Hundred Years' War (1340–1453), the study and regulation of arms became increasingly necessary, so that allies could be identified in battle and the dead and wounded recovered afterwards. Heralds had started to make lists of armorial bearings, as an aid to this work, by the thirteenth century. It was important to ensure that no two knights bore the same arms, and therefore to settle disputes between rival claimants. The regulation of arms and the settling of disputes was often best done *in situ*, and the herald-kings therefore travelled through the country carrying out visitations in their own territories.[60]

Territories

John of Gaunt's minstrel-king, enforcing the duke's claim on minstrels in the Honour of Tutbury, held authority over a large area. This is probably typical of the herald-kings earlier, but while there is evidence that they were responsible

---

[56] Bullock-Davies, *Menestrellorum Multitudo*, 3–6, prints the list, showing who distributed rewards to whom.

[57] Bullock-Davies, *Register*, 109.

[58] TNA E36.201, fol. 29v (12 May 1287), printed in Byerly and Byerly, *Records 1286–1289*, 99; E36.203, fols 100r, 100v and 102r (28 August, 1 September and 25 December 1338), cal. SM II, 100.

[59] TNA Chancery, Warrants (Privy Seal bills) 918/2 (42 Ed III), translated in Rickert, *Chaucer's World*, 232. The minstrel-king Midach, no doubt the same man, headed a group of minstrels for Juan I of Spain in 1378: Richard Barber, *Magnificence and Princely Splendour in the Middle Ages* (Woodbridge, 2020), 127. I am not aware of any research on minstrel-kings in continental Europe.

[60] For heraldic visitations, see Wagner, *Heralds and Heraldry*, Chapters I, X and XI, *passim*.

for particular territories, assigning geographical areas to specific herald-kings is largely guesswork.

According to Wagner, a herald-king was given a 'kingdom', or area for which he was especially responsible, at his coronation. Wagner cites the case of one Peter, who in 1276 was King of the Heralds north of the Trent.[61] Peter's 'kingdom' may have stretched northwards as far as the Tweed, then considered the border between England and Scotland. Not until thirty years later was King Capenny King of the Heralds of Scotland, probably with authority in the border country. If Peter's territory in 1276 was the northern half of England,[62] it was the area later administered by herald-kings known as 'King of the North'. The first of these is William de Morle, who served Edward I and Edward II as a harper: he became a herald-king by 28 October 1322, with the title *Roi du North*. This apparently indicates an arrangement by which two herald-kings divided England between them, using the river Trent as the boundary between north and south. This northern territory, as already noted, was the area claimed by the Beverley administration, between Trent and Tweed.[63] This king was later known as Norroy (i.e. North-Roy), as he still is. The title of the herald-king responsible for the southern half of England is unknown until the mid-fourteenth century, since when he has been known as Clarenceux.[64]

The name of the herald-king Walter le Marchis raises the possibility that the herald-kings were given territorial authority as early as Edward I's reign. Marchis was a surname found elsewhere in the royal households: but his attendance on Henry Percy at Falkirk suggests that the Scottish marches were his heraldic territory and/or that he was employed by Percy. Another possibility is the Welsh marches. No other English herald-king is known to have administered a territory at this time, however: the livery-list for 1290 that includes both Robert and Morel lists the latter simply as 'the other king of heralds' (*alter rex haraldorum*).[65]

At what stage in their history did the kings of heralds acquire territorial responsibilities? It is generally considered that by 1279 England had been divided into northern and southern territories for heraldic purposes,[66] perhaps as the heralds' work increased. They certainly had to learn and remember the armorial insignia of those who would fight in a battle, and perhaps it was more practicable to verify and collect the information in two main areas, with heralds specifically assigned to each. Regulation – ensuring that arms were borne only by those entitled to them and that

---

[61] Wagner, *Heralds and Heraldry*, 39. D'Arcy J.D. Boulton, 'Heralds and Heraldry'. Szarmach et al., *Medieval England*, 354, gives 1276 as the date at which England was divided into the north and south marches, divided by the Trent, for heraldic purposes.

[62] Chappell, *Popular Music*, 28, refers to Capenny as King of the Heralds of Scotland in 1290: my first reference to this title is in E101.369.16, fol. 26r (25 Ed I).

[63] This would perhaps suggest that Norroy's authority covered only the north-east, but it seems likely that he also administered the geographically less accessible north-west of the country.

[64] H.W.C. Davis, *Mediaeval England* (Oxford, 1924), 225, and Boulton, 'Heralds and Heraldry', 354. It is doubtful if the title of 'Surroy' (i.e. South-Roy) ever existed.

[65] TNA E101.352.24, cited in Bullock-Davies, *Register*, 123.

[66] Boulton, 'Heralds and Heraldry', 354.

they bore them correctly – would be an off-shoot of the heralds' task of collecting, sharing and remembering the information. Probably by 1300 or so the whole process had grown in complexity and importance to the nation's security.

King Grey, who was at the marriage of Joan of Acre in 1290, was 'Rex Haraldorum in partibus Francie', according to Wagner.[67] This may mean that his authority was over the English possessions in France, and that he should therefore not be confused with the French Kings of Arms.[68] It is possible, therefore, that at the beginning of our period there were at least four English herald-kings, having authority over the Scottish marches (or just possibly Wales), northern England, southern England and English possessions in France, respectively.[69]

Herald-kings and their employment outside Court

The description of the Tutbury minstrel-king of 1380 as *nostre bien ame le roy des ministralx deinz nostre honour de Tuttebury* not only states the geographical area of his jurisdiction but implies at the same time that he was a retainer of John of Gaunt. To what extent did magnates other than the king employ a King of Heralds or Minstrels to supervise minstrelsy on their own lands? And did the area of such a king's jurisdiction overlap with that of a king appointed from Court, or was it separate?

To the first question we can cite King Druet (working for the earl of Gloucester), and perhaps Walter Marchis in the employ of Henry Percy; John of Gaunt's minstrel-king, Chandos Herald, employed by Sir John Chandos (see Chapter 13) and the herald of Sir Rhys ap Thomas (above, p. 83). There is also very slight evidence to suggest the identity of an earlier Lancaster herald-king. On 28 October 1322, Edward II granted to his minstrel William de Morle, *Roi du North*, certain houses in

---

[67] Wagner, *Heralds and Heraldry*, 36, n. 4. According to Bullock-Davies, *Register*, 64, TNA C47.4.5, fol. 45v, does not say this, so there may be another extant record concerning Grey.

[68] For King Grey, see Wagner, *Heralds and Heraldry*, 36, n. 4. The accounts for Joan of Acre's marriage to the earl of Gloucester (30 April 18 Ed I [1290]) are discussed in Chappell, *Popular Music*, 28 f: Chappell tentatively identified King Grey with King Robert and Poveret, minstrel of the Marshal of Champagne, with the Roy de Champagne of the 1306 Pentecost list (TNA E101/369/6: 34 Ed I). The first of these identifications is certainly wrong, and the second doubtful. Foreign herald- and minstrel-kings appearing in the English records are referred to by territory. The fact that kings travelled a great deal in company with liveried minstrels led Gerald Hayes to think of them as 'leaders of professional companies of minstrels' (Hayes *King's Music*, 31) – which they were, of course, although not quite in the sense that he implied. The use of a royal title was apparently French originally: Davis, *Mediaeval England*, 225, refers to several kingships in the French royal household, no precise date being given; Duncan, *Minstrelsy*, 74, n. 1, mentions the *Rex Juglatorum*, *Roy des Violins* and *Roy des Ménéstriers*. This last was apparently the head of a fraternity of *jongleurs* incorporated in 1321 (Vidal (A), *La Chapelle St-Julien*, 35).

[69] In the late fifteenth century, March King of Arms was responsible for Wales, Cornwall, and the West of England: Wagner, *Heralds and Heraldry*, 108. As Walter Marchis and James Cowpen were kings at the same time (both present at the Pentecost feast of 1306), Marchis could have overseen arms in a 'kingdom' including Wales.

Pontefract which had previously belonged to John le Botiler, known as *Roi Bruant*.[70] He was described as 'late a rebel', and the houses had been forfeited to the king. Pontefract was Lancaster territory: Thomas, Earl of Lancaster, had been executed seven months before and had forfeited his estates.[71] It is not possible at present to prove that King Bruant was a Lancaster retainer, but it is probable.

Herald-kings and minstrelsy

The connection between heralds and minstrels was close, as we saw in Chapter 4, and it was quite normal for a herald to perform 'minstrelsy' of some sort. The herald William Trenchant was rewarded for minstrelsy in 32 Ed I, but he is not known as an instrumentalist.[72] Heralds must often have performed by singing or telling stories, the kind of verbal entertainment discussed by Andrew Taylor in Chapter 13, and several surviving poems are known to have been written by heralds. A different situation can perhaps be seen in the Pentecost list of 1306, which includes several heralds not known to have performed minstrelsy: these were perhaps paid or rewarded only for overseeing the ceremonies rather than for entertaining the guests.

On the other hand some heralds are known to have been instrumentalists and therefore capable of purely musical entertainment. Robert Little, often referred to as 'Master' Robert from 14 Ed I (1285/6) onwards, was named at the head of six royal trumpeters that year: the others were John Leutor, Ranulph Folsank, Peter le Waffrur, John and Bertram.[73] This item is particularly interesting in showing that Master Robert was a king's minstrel – the marginal heading is *Menestrelli regis* – and the senior trumpeter, as well as King of Heralds. He appears again as the king's trumpeter in 29 Ed I and 32 Ed I, and as taborer in 5 Ed II.[74] There was no change of post here: it was probably convenient for a trumpeter to be also a competent taborer, the two functions being closely linked, and both associated with the work of a herald. A royal minstrel whose instrument is unknown was John Teysaunt, who was temporarily herald to Princess Eleanor in 1332 (see Chapter 8).

Herald-kings known to have been royal minstrels were William de Morle, a royal harper in the time of Edward II, and Andrew Norreys, minstrel for a few years in Edward III's reign.[75] These men continued to receive wages and liveries as squires of the household, but disappeared from 'the minstrels' once they were promoted as

---

[70] CPR, Edward II, vol. 4 (1321–4), 210.

[71] The earl was executed on 22 March 1322. His brother Henry was styled earl of Lancaster from 26 October 1326, and was formally restored to the earldom on 3 February 1327.

[72] BL Add MS 8835 (32 Ed I), fol. 42r, rewarded at the same time as King Robert, on 1 January 1304 (cal. SM II, 40).

[73] TNA E101.351.26, m. 1, printed in Byerly and Byerly, *Records 1285–1286*, 167 (item 1694). This item is also a warning against making assumptions that a man with a work-surname such as Leutor or Waffrer necessarily filled the post apparently referred to (although the man may have been competent in more than one capacity).

[74] TNA E101.359.6 (29 Ed I), fol. 11v and 12r; BL Add MS 35292 (32 Ed I), fol. 23r; TNA E101.374.16 (5 Ed II), pp. 3 and 4. Cal. SM II, 26, 31 and 72.

[75] 'Norreys' is apparently not cognate with 'Norroy', since Andrew Norreys was a royal minstrel under that name before he became a herald-king.

herald-kings: evidently they then could not undertake the day-to-day obligations of royal minstrels. King Robert seems to have stopped working as a household minstrel by around 32 Ed I (1303/4), and probably long before that; and William de Morle may have been replaced by Henry de Newsom.[76] A King who had been a household minstrel would sometimes perform when he was in Court, but apart from special occasions such as royal weddings, rewards to them for household minstrelsy are rare: King Robert, as far as I know, received such a reward only twice in the twenty years between 29 Ed I and 14 Ed II.[77] On the other hand William de Morle, as a harper, may well have been expert in the kind of verbal minstrelsy discussed in Chapter 13, a useful qualification for undertaking the ceremonial duties of a herald. James Cowpen, King Capenny, was once described as a harper (see above), but is not known to have been rewarded as an instrumentalist.

Minstrel-kings

Accounting scribes usually referred to herald-kings as 'Rex N' or 'N *rex haraldorum*', and this is how they were all known until 5 Ed II (1311/12). In that year King Robert was described as *rex ministrallorum* in the record of a prest on his wages dated 15 November (1311) at Berwick-on-Tweed.[78] That leaves at least a quarter-century of references to kings of heralds before any reference to a king of minstrels is found. The new title did not signal a change of post, since Robert and others continued to be known as kings of heralds. As the kings of heralds and the kings of minstrels were probably always the same men, it seems that authority over minstrels was a late addition to the herald-kings' work.

Why would minstrelsy be added to a herald-king's duties? For minstrels, the question of entitlement was secondary to that of regulation: and regulation, as we have seen, was carried out by a system of licensing that also provided entitlement. The earliest kings of minstrels that we know of were already kings of heralds: but since several herald-kings up to the middle of the fourteenth century were royal minstrels, one may suspect that the herald-kings had already been responsible for regulating minstrels for some time. What, then, were the duties of a herald-king in his capacity as a *minstrel*-king? Or, rather, what could be the duties of a minstrel-king who, as a King of Heralds, travelled through his 'kingdom' conducting heraldic visitations? There is some similarity between heraldic visitations and what I have previously called a 'travelling inquisition' of minstrelsy, and it is reasonable to suppose that a King of Arms, in his dual capacity as herald-king and minstrel-king, conducted the regulation of both armorial bearings and minstrelsy.

The Hundred Years' War and the Wars of the Roses ensured that the theory and practice of heraldry remained an important part of the national administration, and in 1484 Richard III strengthened and institutionalised it by founding the College of

---

[76] MERH, 12.

[77] BL Add MS 8835, fol. 42 (32 Ed I): BL Cotton MS Nero C viii, fol. 84v (5 Ed II): cal. SM II, 40 and 71. Even these were special days – New Year's Day and the purification of the Countess of Cornwall, respectively.

[78] TNA E101.374.16, p. 3: cal. SM II, 72.

Arms.[79] By this time the regulation of minstrelsy by Kings of Arms had long since ended: from Edward III's reign minstrel-kings are rarely heard of and are invariably elusive figures. John of Gaunt's anonymous minstrel-king in 1380 is not known to have been a minstrel, and there is no evidence that any of Gaunt's minstrels became a King. That may be due only to missing evidence, but it also suggests that Gaunt did not employ a minstrel-king for long. In fact, minstrel-kings died out before the end of the fourteenth century. Edward III's herald-king Andrew Norreys, who had been a royal minstrel, is the last minstrel known to hold the post, leaving office around 21 Ed III (1347/8). William Volaunt, king of heralds and minstrels in 33 Ed III, was apparently never rewarded for minstrelsy; Richard II's minstrel-king John Caumz is not known to have been rewarded for minstrelsy.[80]

Minstrel-kings and marshals

In the past the assumption was sometimes made that 'King' was the early title of the officer later known as 'Marshal of the king's minstrels'. One reason for this supposition was that the title of 'King of the Minstrels' seemed to have disappeared shortly before that of 'Marshal' was first used. As we have seen, however, the office and title of 'marshal' of the minstrels existed in the king's household in the time of Edward III,[81] while the last reference to a King of the Minstrels is dated 2 May 1387, in the time of Richard II.[82]

The other reason for the misunderstanding is that the marshal of the king's minstrels was thought to have exercised powers formerly held by a minstrel-king. The evidence for this is circumstantial, concerning the travelling inquisitions of the Tutbury minstrel-king and of Henry VI's minstrels. Henry's commission (noted above) was certainly an *ad hoc* arrangement by which the most pressing of the minstrel-king's duties were transferred to the king's minstrels (with the marshal at their head) because the office of King of the Minstrels had died out by 1449. True, the terms of the commission were repeated for a later administration: but that administration took the form not of an inquisition but of a fraternity.

The travelling inquisition of Henry VI's minstrels aimed to prevent two ways by which minstrels were defrauding the general public: the performance of minstrelsy by amateurs pretending to be professionals, and the wearing of the royal livery by

---

[79] The College was dissolved after Richard's death, but re-formed in 1555: it still regulates heraldry and the bearing of armorial insignia. The regulation of minstrelsy was never a part of the College's work.

[80] Norreys's last appearance is in TNA E101.391.9 (c. 21 Ed III), fol. 10r, cal. SM II, 107; for Volaunt, King of Heralds and Minstrels, see *REED Durham* (ed. John McKinnell, forthcoming), Cathedral Priory, Bursar's accounts for 1357/8; and Devon, *Issues of the Exchequer*, 169 (9 March 32 Ed III, 1358) and 171 (12 September 33 Ed III, 1359); for John Caumz, 'rex ministrallorum' of Richard II given a licence to go abroad in 1387, see Rymer, *Foedera*, VII, 555. Rymer gives his name as Caumz, perhaps a misreading for Camuz.

[81] Christmas 1364 or 1365: see above, Chapter 2. The grant to William Langton dated 14 October 1448 was formerly the first known use of the title: CPR, Henry VI, vol. 5 (1446–52), 200.

[82] Rymer, *Foedera*, VII, 555: John Caumz, as above.

those who were not royal servants. These were also acts of fraud against honest minstrels, whose standards and integrity were compromised. They particularly affected the royal minstrels, although the scam could have been used against any liveried minstrels. A minstrel's livery was more than a mark of his status: it gave a potential audience an indication of his professional competence, and could therefore affect the scale of his reward.[83] Hence, a minstrel wearing a livery to which he was not entitled could obtain a great deal of money by false pretences.[84] The different types of regulation discussed earlier in this chapter would largely have prevented this kind of fraud. Long before the demise of minstrel-kings and most of the minstrel courts, however, many minstrels resorted to a different type of protection – one that was more efficient and more sustainable, because more localised, and was also charitable in its aims: minstrel fraternities.

The protection of minstrelsy: the minstrel fraternities

Religious guilds and trade-guilds

Regulation by a feudal authority probably gave some security to liveried minstrels, but its benefits were rather uncertain. In the day-to-day disputes and injustices between minstrels, settlement had to wait for an annual gathering (as at Chester and Tutbury) or a travelling inquisition (Henry VI's minstrels and, presumably, the Tutbury minstrel-king). For the greater protection of their professional rights the best of the independent minstrels, and some liveried minstrels, as well, took other steps to maintain their status and to prevent less skilled players from taking their work and privileges.[85] They took advantage of the guild movement, especially in the fifteenth century, when the organisation of town waits threatened in some places to create a monopoly which could put other minstrels out of work. It would be hard to overestimate the importance of the guilds, or their effect on everyday life. The guilds were fraternities concerned with the work and maintenance of charitable endeavour (the religious guilds) or of the regulation of competition within a certain profession (the trade guilds). Both types of guild had their religious side, however, working for the welfare of members and their families. The trade guilds, too, were not exclusive to the particular trade, and they often admitted men working in trades other than that of the guild and the wives of members. It was through the guilds that

---

[83] Civic accounts of Kent, for example, show a scale of payments which is graduated more or less regularly (depending on the town) according to the livery of the minstrel concerned: see Table 21, for instance. The Canterbury accounts for 1477/8 are a good example, and quite typical (the original is in Latin): 'To minstrels of the king 6s 8d, and for wine given to them 8d. To minstrels of the queen 5s od, and for wine 8d. To minstrels of the Duke of Gloucester 5s od, and for wine 4d. (The kings' brother). To minstrels of the Duchess of York 3s 4d, and for wine 4d. (The king's mother). (*REED Kent: Diocese of Canterbury* I, 80: this is my calendar)'.

[84] It would be very difficult now to track down a case of such a fraud.

[85] Minstrels were among those exempted from the Acts of Apparel: see J. Payne Collier, *The History of English Dramatic Poetry to the Time of Shakespeare*. 3 vols (London, 1831), I, 36, and Stevens, *Music and Poetry*, 317 f.

a man became a freeman of his town. Life was altogether easier for a freeman, and the freemen's rolls contain the names of many minstrels.[86]

At first the king's minstrels probably felt no need of guild assistance, on account of their high status, although that changed in the mid-fifteenth century. Other minstrels, probably including liveried men, found it worthwhile to buy their freedom relatively early. One 'Hugo le Trumpeour' bought his freedom through the Merchants' Guild at Leicester in 18 Edward III; John Brothir, the Lancaster trumpeter, may be another case, to judge from his name; and civic minstrels eventually joined guilds.[87]

When minstrel fraternities were instituted, many of their characteristics were probably borrowed from the *puys* that existed in several places on the continent and led to one operating in London in the late thirteenth century.[88] The ordinances for the English branch were drawn up between 1306 and 1317.[89] The aims and effects of the brotherhood were too general for it to be called a guild. It was ruled by a prince and twelve companions, all of whom were elected at a yearly feast.[90]

Whatever the origin of particular features, the English fraternities were developed to provide charitable benefits, professional solidarity and protection from 'foreign' competition by minstrels coming from outside the town or immediate area covered by the fraternity. The earliest was that based in Cripplegate, London.

Minstrel-fraternities in London

The minstrel guild of 1350 at Cripplegate was not a trade guild in the sense that it tried to regulate minstrelsy itself. Indeed, it belongs to a form of social and religious guild that ante-dates the trade guilds proper.[91] The minstrels' most pressing need was to make their social situation both stable and secure, which would, *inter alia*, allow them to be better prepared to withstand professional competition. The Cripplegate fraternity was organised on the minstrels' own initiative, and existed by agreement between 'the minstrels of London and other good people in the same city dwelling'.[92]

The administration of the guild was simple, and was carried out by the wardens, who were responsible for the common box. Each member paid 13d into the common box each year: a member in need could borrow money against security, or could

---

[86] Westlake, *Parish Gilds*, 23, 109 and 118.

[87] For Hugo, see Kelly, *Notices*, 131: there is no evidence that Hugo was a minstrel of the earl of Leicester, as Kelly suggested. For John Brothir and for civic minstrels, see below. At least one royal minstrel was a member of the London fraternity, and all the London waits joined it in 1499/1500.

[88] See Nigel Wilkins, 'Puy', in Szarmach *et al.*, *Medieval England*, 625.

[89] George Unwin, *The Gilds and Companies of London*. 4th edn (London, 1963), 99 f.

[90] See below. The election bore some resemblance to the Tutbury election of 1680 – for instance, in the ceremonial cup of wine, handed to the Prince's successor in the case of the *puy* and used to drink the new King's health at Tutbury.

[91] For a useful overview of English fraternities, see Vanessa A. Harding, 'Guilds and Fraternities'. Szarmach *et al.*, *Medieval England*, 329–30.

[92] A translation of the 1350 ordinances is in H.F. Crewdson, *The Worshipful Company of Musicians* (London, 1950), 79–81, and in *REED Civic London* under that date.

be given help if through no fault of his own he suffered poverty, illness, robbery, maiming, old age, loss of property or wrongful imprisonment. A member who failed to contribute, if he was able to do so, or who persisted in malice towards another member, could be dismissed. In this case any money already paid in by him would remain in the common box, but his name would be included in the list of the fraternity's benefactors inscribed on the obituary roll of the Carmelite Friars. New members were admitted if deemed worthy and loyal: if they were required to be skilled in minstrelsy, the fact is not specifically stated. If a dispute arose which involved a member, the wardens were to attempt to settle the disagreement. On the death of a member, the guild paid for the burial and for thirty masses to be said for his soul.

The Cripplegate guild seems to have changed little between 1350 and 1389.[93] In the latter year its assets were 44s 5d in the common box, security for 8s 0d on loan, and a special garment for the company.[94] Nothing more is known of this guild, and it may not have survived for long. Almost certainly it would not be strong enough to coexist with the City of London waits when the latter were founded in the late fourteenth or early fifteenth century. For the next eighty years minstrels seem to have bought their protection through religious guilds or guilds of other trades, while specific area control over minstrelsy was exercised through the minstrel-courts already discussed.

When Henry VI organised the control of minstrelsy through his own minstrels he produced what was potentially a permanent administration. His successor, Edward IV, confirmed this administration in an ordinance of 24 April 1469. The new charter was based on that of 1449, as the wording of the preamble shows:[95]

> ... To our well-beloved Walter Haliday (marshal of our minstrels), John Cliff, Robert Marshall, Thomas Green, Thomas Calthorn, William Cliff, William Christian, and William Eynsham, ... because many uncultured husbandmen and craftsmen of various occupations [*rudes agricole et artifices diversarum misterarum*] of our realm of England, pretending to be minstrels, and some of them wearing our livery and so pretending to be our own minstrels, ... fraudulently collect and receive in certain parts of our said realm great exactions of money from our subjects ...

The king licensed these named royal minstrels, 'to establish, continue, and augment a fraternity or guild, which the brothers and sisters of the fraternity of minstrels of the realm erected in times past' in the chapel of the Blessed Virgin Mary in St Paul's cathedral, and in the king's free chapel of St Anthony.[96] The minstrels were to pray

---

[93] The copy of the 1350 ordinances is part of the return made in answer to the article of enquiry of 1389. See Westlake, *Parish Gilds*, 138–238, for a summary of these returns.

[94] Crewdson, *Worshipful Company*, 81. This probably does not mean a guild livery: it may refer to a single garment to distinguish the senior warden presiding over the guild.

[95] CPR, Edward IV and Henry VI (1467–77), 153: compare the wording of Henry VI's commission, Chapter 9, above. The administration was also confirmed by Henry VII, in 1496: see E.W.W. Veale, *The Great Red Book of Bristol* (Bristol, 1931–53), text, IV, 5–8.

[96] The hospital of St Anthony, with its free chapel, was in Threadneedle Street: Stowe, *Survey*, 164–6. It is shown in the 'Agas' map: see Adrian Prockter and Robert Taylor, *The*

for the good estate of the king and queen, and for their souls after death, and for the soul of the king's father, Richard, Duke of York. The fraternity was to admit others, both men and women, to form a perpetual corporation; they were to elect a marshal, who would hold office for life, and two wardens, to be elected annually, to govern the fraternity; they were to supervise the art of minstrels, except in the county of Chester; and they would nominate the king's minstrels, subject to the king's approval.

Since the county of Chester was excepted from the fraternity's authority, it may appear that the Dutton court flourished although the Tutbury court was at least dormant, but this is not necessarily the case. It may show only that the Duttons had justified their claim to the revenues from the Chester minstrels, thus effectively making their authority permanent; if the Lancaster claim at Tutbury still existed, on the other hand, it would have reverted to the crown in 1399.[97]

Surprisingly, the new administration not only gave the minstrels power to regulate minstrelsy over the whole country except Cheshire, but also tied the royal minstrels firmly to the fraternity.[98] There is however no evidence that either the royal minstrels or the fraternity made any use of these various powers: there is no record of a new minstrel body claiming national jurisdiction.

It has always been assumed that the earlier fraternity referred to was the Cripplegate one, no other eligible fraternity being known. That was a localised guild, however, and – in 1389, at least – was not a fraternity of minstrels 'of the realm'. There is in fact no evidence to connect them, and when a new fraternity came into being some time before 1500, the 'Fellowship of the Minstrels Freemen of the City of London' had no pretensions to control minstrelsy outside the city.

The first we hear of this fraternity is a petition in the year 1499/1500, asking the city to limit performance by 'foreyn' minstrels.[99] The ills of unregulated, often incompetent, minstrelsy are set out, in terms of annoyance to the citizens and financial loss to the fraternity's members. No mention is made of the civic minstrels, who worked in the city in the course of their duties, but the fraternity did in fact try to prevent them from performing.[100] The waits then petitioned the mayor and aldermen for the freedom of the city through the Fellowship of Minstrels without charge, saying that they could not afford the entrance-fee and that entry without charge had been the custom 'tyme out of mynde'. Whether it really was a well-established custom or

---

A to Z of Elizabethan London (London, 1979), 10, section Q4.

[97] For the general situation, see Stephen R. Morillo, 'Quo Warranto proceedings'. Szarmach et al., *Medieval England*, 629–30.

[98] It is not clear that the marshal of the fraternity and the marshal of the king's minstrels were the same man, but it seems likely: why, otherwise, use the term 'marshal' when 'warden' would be unambiguous? Both the old and the new fraternities admitted women, although it is not clear if non-minstrels could become members.

[99] REED *Civic London*, I, 258–61.

[100] Crewdson, *Worshipful Company*, 20 f.

not, the petition was granted, and the city waits became members of the minstrels' company without payment.[101]

The royal minstrels were another source of competition,[102] but the fraternity's petition specifically excluded all liveried minstrels. Apart from not wishing to cause trouble with powerful people, the fraternity perhaps realised that the presence of high-status minstrels at important events did not constitute damaging competition, since many professional minstrels of the city would be employed in any case. In 1509, however, the marshal of the king's minstrels, John Chamber, was admitted to the freedom of the city through the 'crafte of Mynstralx', for which he was charged 13s 4d (one mark).[103] As far as I know, no other royal minstrel was admitted at that time, and it would be interesting to know if Chamber's admission was for his personal work or stood for the royal minstrels as a group.

Despite the waits' appeal to a custom dating from 'tyme out of mynde', much of this sounds as if the fraternity was fairly new. The petition includes a request to the city to approve the fraternity's regulations, which may indicate this: but it could equally well be a codifying of regulations understood but not registered, or simply the restating of half-forgotten regulations after a period of time. The regulations are typical of contemporary guilds, setting out the procedure for electing two wardens (but no marshal, as in the 1469 charter) to keep the common box (i.e. the funds) and two members to hold the keys; specifying fines for non-members who perform in spite of the fraternity's proscriptions and for members who behave improperly or fail to pay their dues; and stating precise rules regulating apprenticeships, and penalties for contravening those rules.

Curiously, although the entry-fees, quarterly fees and fines are set out in detail, together with statements of what proportions go to the city and to the fraternity, there is no mention of administrative or charitable expenditure. One might not expect the costs of the fraternity's ceremonies and other social activities to be itemised, but a statement of charitable intentions could be expected, such as the relief of impoverished members, their burial, and the support of their families. The fraternity probably did fulfill such obligations, but the silence is a little puzzling.

Provincial minstrel-fraternities

While London was an obvious centre for such a fraternity, the need to protect themselves from itinerant competition was felt by local minstrels in the provinces, too. Little is known about these provincial fraternities, unfortunately, and the lack of records may suggest that they failed to survive for long. The guild returns of 1389 show that there was then a guild of minstrels and players at Lincoln. The members were to meet each year on the Wednesday in Whitsun week (the first of the Ember days), when they would process with a 'great candle' to the cathedral. There the

---

[101] *REED Civic London*, I, 267–8, and Woodfill, *Musicians*, 40. On the Fellowship's early history and its fight against professional competition, see Woodfill, *Musicians*, Chapter I, and especially pp. 10 f.

[102] Woodfill, *Musicians*, 6.

[103] *REED Civic London*, I, 294.

members (men and women) would each offer a penny. No other meetings were held, and no musical or dramatic activities are mentioned.[104] Another minstrel fraternity was at Launceston (Cornwall) in 1440, based on the church of St Mary Magdalene. The evidence does not indicate how old the fraternity then was, but it presumably did not exist in 1389. Like the Lincoln fraternity, it seems to have been in the nature of a religious guild rather than a professional trade-guild, as Bishop Edmund Lacy of Exeter offered indulgences to those who supported the 'confratria Ministrallorum beate Marie Magdalene Launceston' with alms.[105]

A fraternity at Shrewsbury in 1444 was said to date back to the reign of William I, instituted by a previous earl of Shrewsbury:[106] the reason for its foundation was religious, following a miracle, and the worship of the Blessed Virgin was a large part of the minstrels' obligations. Otherwise, the statutes clearly set out the same sort of requirements as seen in other fraternities, with some features of the courts. Every minstrel in Shropshire was to come to Shrewsbury annually on St Peter's day (Lammas day, 1 August) to honour Christ's mother. They were to elect a Master, answerable to the earl of Shrewsbury, the Master to rule the fraternity 'after the law of Armes'. A light was to burn before the statue of Our Lady, to the cost of which all minstrels would contribute 4d. Any 'foreign' minstrel coming into Shropshire would also pay 4d. If he refused, his instrument was to be taken from him (on the earl's authority) and placed before the statue of Our Lady for 40 days; and if he still refused to pay, his instrument would be forfeit. The light was to be taken in procession through the town, with the earl's banner before it, and it could then remain in either the church of St Alkmund (feast day 19 March) or the Abbey of Shrewsbury.

This organisation was very clear about protecting the professional rights of Shropshire minstrels but, surprisingly, seems to have had no charitable aim to support its members in illness, to pay for burial or to support dependents. It is unclear, however, in what respects the Master of the fraternity was to 'rule' the organisation, and it is possible that, having specified the religious and professional purposes of the fraternity, the earl allowed the fraternity and its Master to set up such charitable provisions as they wanted.

Later fraternities fall outside the chronological limits of this book and will not be discussed in detail here: but they deserve investigation as a part of the sixteenth-century history of music in England. A fraternity formed at Canterbury in about 1526 demonstrated a similar protectionism both against outsiders and in the way of regulating the activities of members. This was set up more in the way of a trade guild, however, with rules governing the seven-year-long training of apprentices.[107] In this, the Canterbury fraternity seems closely allied to the London one as it existed in the

---

[104] *REED Lincolnshire*, 107–8, translation 649–50.

[105] *REED Dorset* (ed. Rosalind Conklin Hays and C.E. McGee) *and Cornwall* (ed. Sally L.K. Joyce and Evelyn S. Newlyn), 491, and translation 582.

[106] *REED Shropshire*, II, 511–12. A document dated St Matthew's day, 23 Hen VI (21 September 1444) is the confirmation by John Talbot, earl of Shrewsbury, of a fraternity supposedly founded by a previous earl, Robert Belleme, in the reign of William I.

[107] The ordinances are quoted in John Brent, *Canterbury in the Olden Time*. 2nd edn (Canterbury and London, 1879), 154; see also Woodfill, *Musicians*, 18, and SM I, 18–19.

1550s. There was also a fraternity at York by 1561, since it presented the pageant of Herod in the mystery plays that year: its ordinances were detailed, but nothing more is known of the organisation.[108]

Of the later fraternities, those at Beverley and Tutbury were revivals of minstrel-courts that had survived and reconstituted themselves, as already noted. The main characteristics of the fraternities, which can be compared with those of the minstrel courts (above), are:

1. Local control of professional competition.
2. Control through a democratic fellowship.
3. Payment of entrance-fee and subscriptions, entitling the member to charitable and professional benefits.

The classification of minstrel administrations into court-licensing and guild-approval is, if useful, partly arbitrary. It is clear that to some extent the two types overlapped: the guilds levied fines and prevented non-members from playing, while the courts – at least in their later forms – attempted to settle disputes between members. The guild system implies a very much closer control over its members, however, and it is significant that during the late Middle Ages minstrel administration generally moved from court-control towards guild-organisation.

The mid-sixteenth-century fraternity at Beverley and the seventeenth-century Tutbury court both illustrate this change. As we have seen, the statutes of the Beverley administration as laid down in 1555 are those of a minstrel guild, showing a close parallel with the fraternities at London and Canterbury, but were clearly those of a court-administration in origin. Similarly, the Chester fraternity had originally been a minstrel-court that attempted to control minstrelsy over a wide area.[109]

The Tutbury court, too, acquired certain guild-like characteristics at some stage before 1680, when Dr Plot described it. John of Gaunt's organisation was not exempted from the statutes of Henry VI, Edward IV and Elizabeth I, perhaps because its authority had reverted to the crown in 1399, if not earlier. Dr Plot's description of 1680 certainly cannot be identified closely with the court as established by John of Gaunt. The court was held as before at the feast of the Assumption, and began with a procession in which the minstrels walked[110]

> two and two together, Musick playing before them, the King of the Minstrells for the year past walking between the Steward [of the Honour of Tutbury] and Bayliff, or their deputies; the four Stewards or under Officers of the said King of the Minstrells, each with a white wand in their hands, immediately following them; and then the rest of the company in order. Being come to the Church, the Vicar reads them divine service, chusing Psalms and Lessons suitable to the occasion. For which service every minstrel offered one penny, as a due always paid to the Vicar of the Church of Tutbury, upon this Solemnity.

---

[108] *REED York*, I, 334; the fraternity's ordinances are printed on pp. 334–8.

[109] Woodfill, *Musicians*, 116 f, discusses the Beverley fraternity, and comes to the conclusion that it was not a success.

[110] Plot, *Natural History of Stafford-shire*, 437 f, also 435 ff. This material is discussed in Mosley, *History of Tutbury*, 77 f.

The king by this time had no real administrative powers: the authority of such an officer was bound to wane as the need for guilds lessened during the sixteenth century, for fines and expulsion were then less effective as either punishment or deterrent. It was symptomatic of those circumstances that the 1555 Beverley statutes should rely ultimately on the authority of the king's officers.[111] In 1680 the Tutbury court was responsible to the Steward of the Honour.[112] The King's four assistants, although inherent in the original organisation, and seen in Henry VI's joint commission to a marshal and six other minstrels, was a product of the guild-movement: so, probably, was the religious dedication at the annual meeting.

According to Plot, the minstrels went to the castle after the service to elect the officers for the following year and to attend the court, which was held before the Steward of the Honour. The retiring king and his stewards then attended a banquet while their successors were elected.[113] The bull-running followed: this was in place by the late fifteenth century but was probably not part of the original organisation. What did belong originally were, probably, the King, the fines, and the hearing of complaints[114] – now before the Steward, but originally before the King. The election, the banquet, and the retention of money for a common fund[115] are typical of a guild.

The ordinances of 5 Charles I (1629–30) regulated the Tutbury court almost exactly as a trade guild,[116] and give us some idea of what affairs the court dealt with. No minstrel was allowed to take an apprentice for less than seven years: an apprentice was not allowed to play his instrument for money, and at the end of his apprenticeship he had to be examined by the court and passed as fit to do so. It was still obligatory at that date for every minstrel to attend the court annually: but behind the guild-regulations, little of the minstrel-king's travelling inquisition remained.

The chronology of the regulation and protection of minstrelsy is not straightforward. Elements of both can be seen soon after the Conquest, and in fact some elements of a fraternal organisation ante-date those of the regulatory ones. It seems that the herald-kings took on the regulation of minstrelsy late in the thirteenth century or soon after, but the more intense chivalric activity under Edward III may have caused an increase in the heralds' work and an inefficiency in the regulation of minstrelsy. The rise of minstrel-fraternities to some degree fostered regulation, at least locally, as well as providing charitable support. During the fifteenth century regulation on a national scale was the responsibility of the monarch, but almost certainly without the means formerly provided by the Kings of Arms. Attempts in 1449 and 1469 to regulate minstrelsy through the royal minstrels cannot have had much success, even when this was formulated as a new fraternity before 1499/1500.

---

[111] BL MS Lansdowne 896, fol. 154r: '... and if any Person ... shewe him selfe obstynate ... Then the Kings Officers be sent for to cary the Offenders to the gaile ...'.

[112] As at Newcastle under Lyme.

[113] Mosley, *History of Tutbury*, 78.

[114] This probably took place before the election.

[115] This money in fact went to the five officers: I count it as a common fund because they must have used it to defray the expenses of the banquet, etc.

[116] Mosley, *History of Tutbury*, 78.

The fraternities of the sixteenth century, which broadly speaking were successful as charitable organisations, regulated the profession locally as far as its members were concerned – mainly liveried minstrels – but could not be effective nationally. The monarch's solution to this, almost throughout the sixteenth century, was to leave local control of liveried minstrels to the fraternities and to place blanket prohibitions on independent minstrels who were not members of a fraternity: hence the acts concerning vagrants from the middle of the century onwards.[117]

---

[117] Much has been written about the vagrancy statutes, particularly in Elizabethan times. See, for example, A.L. Beier, *Masterless Men: The Vagrancy Problem in England, 1560–1640* (London, 1985), especially 97–8.

Part IV

Minstrel Performance

Introduction to Part IV

Consideration of minstrel performance is the ultimate goal of the study of minstrelsy: for the exploration of the circumstances of their lives and work concerns social history, whereas the more desirable end-product is the recovery of the minstrels' artistic achievement. For both vocal and instrumental minstrelsy the main evidence of this would seem to be the written literary and musical remains of the minstrels' repertory. The problem is to identify the precise relationship between the surviving written material – which apparently contains elements typical of the minstrels' performances – and the entertainment that the minstrels actually performed, as suggested by the relevant iconography, the very rare eye-witness statements and items of domestic documentation. Andrew Taylor and I have approached this problem independently, via the evidence concerned with our own disciplines. Firm conclusions seem impossible, but the directions in which this approach has led us are similar. The crux of the problem, in both cases, is the relationship between creation, performance and written text. One can guess at creative processes in the notated dance-music that may be echoed in the written *gestes* and romances: but only in the case of music do we have theoretical works that describe how a singer should improvise a new piece over existing material (in this case, a tune). We cannot be sure that all of these techniques were used by instrumentalists, although there is evidence that the simpler ones were. We here assess the possibilities in our own disciplines: the resulting conclusions are simply statements of our current understanding, which are not at odds with one another.

In these chapters the evidence is presented and assessed mainly in the course of the relevant chapters, rather than in this introduction: for, apart from the primary evidence of the written remains, the different types of evidence illuminate different aspects of the problem. Study of the literary remains relies heavily on close analysis and explication of the texts; knowledge of the musical instruments comes mainly from iconographic sources; understanding the nature of concerted instrumental music depends on iconographic and documentary sources. For some of this evidence, however, a general introduction is needed here.

The evidence

Literature

Some of the greatest works of medieval vernacular literature have been confidently assigned to the minstrels' repertory, conceived by modern scholars as works that were composed, recited or sung by professional entertainers (*scops, joglars, jongleurs*, and the like) rather than being read aloud from a book. Among the works performed before English men and women, it has been suggested, are the Old English *Beowulf*,[1] often considered to be a seventh- or eighth-century poem although copied much later; many of the Old French *chansons de geste*, epic poems from 2,000 to 10,000 lines long, which include the famous *Chanson de Roland*, surviving in a twelfth-century Anglo-Norman manuscript; many Middle English romances dating

---

[1] Further on *Beowulf*, see pp. 279–80.

from the thirteenth, fourteenth, and fifteenth centuries; and various saints' lives, *fabliaux*, short comic and satirical pieces, and of course love songs, in both English and French.

Of eighteenth- and nineteenth-century fantasies about primitive oral poetry, briefly mentioned at the start of our Introduction, one in particular underlies much modern discussion of medieval minstrel performance. Léon Gautier, who promoted the *Chanson de Roland* as expressing the true spirit of Christian France at the time of the Franco-Prussian War (1870–1), offered a detailed but entirely fictitious account of a single minstrel who visits a castle and chants the highlights of a number of *chansons de geste* in the course of a long afternoon.[2] Gautier coined a term for this performance: the *séance épique*. For Gautier, the sustained and dignified performance of the minstrel had both bardic and Christian overtones: the minstrel regarded his profession 'as a kind of lesser priesthood' ('une sorte de prêtrise de second ordre') and his song appealed to the crusading spirit.[3] The minstrel's power to hold his audience's attention echoed that of Homer. As an antidote to the enfeebling secularism of his own day, Gautier specifically evoked André Chenier's *L'aveugle*, where the blind Homer, passing unrecognized through a village, holds his peasant listeners enthralled as he sings of the creation of the world and the great moments of Greek history.[4]

Gautier's nostalgic vision has left a powerful legacy. The idea of the *séance épique* reappears at numerous places in discussions of the orality of the *chanson de geste*. Jean Rychner imagined a performance that might extend from dinner to nightfall, perhaps two hours or so, and covering 1,000 to 2,000 lines.[5] While Rychner allowed that on many occasions the *jongleur* would have had a far less attentive audience and that he could not necessarily count on resuming his performance the next day, he envisaged a situation in which some *jongleurs* did manage to do so, their linked performances being reflected in texts.[6] As we shall see in Chapter 11, however, the evidence does not support Gautier's theory: and if we discard this vision of sustained and linked performances, there is an alarming consequence. Texts such as the *Chanson de Roland* are cast in the voice of a minstrel who asks for silence and addresses the audience directly, but the actual poem is far too long for any minstrel to deliver, so it cannot actually have been sung or recited.[7] To abandon the theory, then (as the evidence requires), is to call into question everything that we thought we knew about the texts of vocal entertainment by minstrels, and about the nature

---

[2] Léon Gautier, *La Chevalerie* (Paris, 1884; new edn Paris, 1895), 656–69.

[3] Ibid., 656.

[4] André Chenier, *Oeuvres complètes*, ed. Gérard Walter (Paris, 1950), 46; Andrew Taylor, *Textual Situations: Three Medieval Manuscripts and Their Readers* (Philadelphia PA, 2002), 34–5.

[5] Jean Rychner, *La chanson de geste: essai sur l'art épique des jongleurs* (Geneva, 1955), 49.

[6] Ibid., 54. Rychner's model was in turn adopted by Zumthor in his influential account of *mouvance*, the flow and shifting of anonymous medieval poetry from one telling to another: Paul Zumthor, *Essai de poétique médiéval* (Paris, 1972), 73, 457.

[7] There are records of minstrels singing what would be a single section of a longer work, but these are among the titles transmitted by Warton and cannot be considered reliable.

and extent of the performances – in short, the whole relationship between surviving texts and the performance of *chansons de geste* and romances.

To step sideways for a moment, the obviously dramatic texts do not present the same problem, or else present it in a much-modified form. A speech of welcome in a royal entry, for instance, was clearly a composed text that had to be learned and recited accurately, with no scope for creative variation. Even if the performer was not very well educated, this was a text-based performance, not one in the aural tradition of the minstrels. Professional players, too, seem to have started with a script, which may however have acted only as a basic text against which the performers could improvise. We do not know how pervasive this process could be: theoretically, it would be possible to create a play without ever writing a text down, in the same way as, I suggest in Chapter 15, a piece of music could be created. There is no evidence of any kind for this, however. The performance of ceremonial recitation, such as welcome speeches, seems to have no connection to the tradition of oral minstrelsy, while in professional drama this possible connection cannot be demonstrated.

The performance of instrumental minstrelsy presents similar problems. Literary descriptions of minstrelsy may have their own purposes, and these affect both the form and the content of the work. To what extent does a fictional account of minstrelsy – or even what purports to be an eye-witness account – approach 'reality'? In such descriptions there is often a 'reality' that is other than the one we now recognise: a symbolic reality or conceptual imperative that could take precedence over real life. An obvious example is minstrelsy at a great banquet, where both the number and the visual splendour of minstrels and their instruments may be inflated in order to cast more glory on the host and the occasion. In literature, as in iconography, 'conspicuous consumption' was often a more important principle than factual accuracy.

In verbal accounts, as in depictions of instrumental minstrelsy, these fictional purposes need to be known before one can understand why an instrumental performance took the form it did – what type of instruments were used, how they were played, and in what circumstances the performance took place. Iconography is an important type of evidence for this.

Iconography

Iconographic evidence is most helpful in providing information about the physical features of the instruments and the manner in which they were held and played. One can usually assume that these are depicted correctly, although the assumption can be modified by two main factors: first, that only two dimensions can be shown, so that much of the instrument is hidden from view; and second, that the illustrator's knowledge, his competence, or both, may be limited. As in the case of the literary sources, it is the majority view of a large quantity of evidence that helps one to see what is normal. This is discussed further in Chapter 14.

One source of iconographic evidence that we might assume to be accurate is the personal seals of minstrels, which sometimes depict their instrument. For this statement of identity it seems unlikely that a minstrel would accept an inaccurate depiction. Whenever a household servant received a payment or his livery allowance he would sign for it, not with his written signature but with his seal, impressed on hot wax. In theory these would all be retained with other departmental documents after audit, but as far as is known only three have survived for minstrels, with another three still attached to other types of financial document. These are listed in Table 16 (Chapter 14). In all cases there is considerable deterioration of the wax, to the extent that any wording around the perimeter of the seal is illegible and the central picture is difficult to make out. Three of them, however, have proved helpful in identifying the instrument played by the individual concerned.

There remains a body of evidence that defies interpretation. Depictions of harps, for instance, do not show whether they are strung with gut, wire, silk or horse-hair. A different kind of example, where there is no doubt what is depicted, is the reverse bowing of stringed instruments shown in some paintings, the best-known being Matthias Grünewald's Isenheim altarpiece. This seems an aberration, whether deliberate or mistaken, but as a playing position it is not, in fact, impossible, although physically rather awkward. Moreover, it appears also in other circumstances – in the Unton memorial picture of c. 1596, bowed thus by the bass-violist of the 'English' consort accompanying a masque, and in a sixteenth-century German engraving.[8]

The list of what we do not know is a daunting one: to what extent trumpets were used for signalling or for music, and how these related to one another; precisely what constituted a loud band, and whether bagpipes could be part of it; whether the citole was gut-strung or wire-strung – or for that matter strung with silk or horse-hair – and how this affected the kind of playing techniques used; and a host of further questions. Perhaps we shall never know the answers, but we must approach them as closely as we can, settling for increased understanding when knowledge proves impossible.

Several other factors, well known to students of medieval art, must be considered when assessing iconographical evidence for its usefulness: these will surface in Chapter 14.

1. The physical limitations of the picture. The constraints of limited space, as in illuminated initials, misericords, or marginal illustrations in a manuscript, may result in an inaccurate depiction of a minstrel's playing-position or an incomplete illustration of the instrument itself. Typically, for instance, a harp may be depicted with too few strings.

2. More specifically, a particular instrumental shape can dictate aspects of the composition, especially in limited space. Some unusual bowing-styles may result from this, as does the one-handed hold on a *busine* (the long, straight trumpet) when a normal two-handed hold would take too much space and spoil the composition. In these modifications the compositional need over-rides the reality: the trumpeter's hold on the

---

[8] Mary Rasmussen, 'Viols, violists and Venus in Grünewald's Isenheim altar'. *Early Music* 29/1 (2001), 61–74, especially 66–8 and illustration 1, on the front cover; and in subsequent correspondence in *Early Music* 29/4 (2001), 667–9. The Unton painting is reproduced in Michael Fleming and John Bryan, *Early English Viols: Instruments, Makers and Music* (London and New York, 2016), Plate 4. Jonathan Wilkinson has suggested (in private correspondence) that the angel's bowing would allow easier access to the bottom string (although the angel is not in fact fingering that string); and one could also regard the bowing-technique of Grünewald's dark angel as a way of accessing the top string easily.

instrument in Plate 4 (p. 33), for instance, is physically impossible for any musical purpose.

3. In depicting any kind of narrative, a certain fluidity of space and time could be used. Typically, a medieval artist might conflate two elements of the narrative, so that two things are shown happening simultaneously that were actually separated in space and/or time. A good example of this is a fifteenth-century wall-painting in the chancel of Winchester Cathedral in which the image of a dead woman is superimposed on the picture of her when alive.

4. Formal patterns of foliage, flowers, insects, birds, animals and people were sometimes used as a solution to the *horror vacui* (the dislike of empty space), filling in and making use of a space that would otherwise be blank in the composition of the picture.[9] The dislike of empty space (and why should a patron pay for space that has not been used by the painter?) is responsible for much conventional decoration in manuscript illuminations and painted glass: and such scenes were not necessarily relevant to the text or main illustration.[10]

5. The purely visual needs of a depiction could result in a symmetrical or other arrangement of images that modifies what might be expected in a real performance. In laying out an illustrated page in a manuscript, for example, a painter could show instruments in pairs, one on each side of the page, resulting in a symmetrical arrangement. This principle might affect the main illustration: depictions of the Last Judgment often place the trumpets symmetrically in the upper corners; and a modified symmetry is common in depictions of the Blessed Virgin, where a lute or harp on one side may be balanced by a fiddle or portative organ on the other.

6. Artists sometimes depicted a greater number and variety of musical instruments than could ever be found in a real-life performance. This is usually for one of two reasons: to give a larger-than-life impression of wealth, extravagance and splendour, usually in the context of celebrations under the *aegis* of a noble who would thus be honoured; and to honour the Blessed Virgin, whose worship was normally accompanied by music – the more the better. Depictions of large consorts, often showing *haut* and *bas* instruments performing together in ways that certainly did not occur in real life, should be interpreted in this way, not as a sort of 'orchestra' of mixed instruments. The first of these has a precise parallel in literary descriptions of sumptuous feasts.

7. Related to this is the use of instruments as examples of a concept. In Plates 4 and 8, for instance, sacred music is symbolised by a liturgical singer and bells, while secular music is represented by instrumentalists; instrumental music is shown by plucked strings, bowed strings and wind; and brass and strings represent loud and still minstrelsy, respectively.

---

[9] For the *horror vacui*, see J. Huizinga, *The Waning of the Middle Ages* (1924; paperback edn, New York NY, 1954), 248.

[10] This difficult question is explored in Martine Clouzot, *Images de Musiciens (1350–1500)* (Turnhout, 2007).

Plate 8. The initial to Psalm 80, *Exultate Deo*, c. 1325. The Bromholm Psalter: Oxford, Bodleian Library, MS Ashmole 1523, fol. 99r.

8. The symbolic associations of instruments may result in the presence of a particular type of instrument, and may affect its number and disposition in the picture. The trumpet represented temporal authority and therefore judgment, and so appears in depictions of the Last Judgment: trumpets at a royal tournament carry both meanings, bringing symbolism and reality together. The origin of this symbolism is biblical, with the angels of the Apocalypse and the Last Judgment itself.[11] Other instruments carried different symbolisms: the bagpipe, of gluttony, but also of pilgrimage; and the harp, with its strings stretched over a wooden frame, of Christ's sinews nailed to the Cross.[12] These symbolisms underpinned the depiction of instruments, affecting the interpretation of the literary and iconographic evidence.

9. A special case of symbolic association concerns number. This is a difficult concept to demonstrate, and numerology is consequently viewed by many with deep suspicion: but it can suggest solutions for otherwise unanswerable questions.[13]

---

[11] See also Huizinga, *Waning*, 157.

[12] Bagpipe: Rastall, *The Heaven Singing*, 349–50; harp: Mannyng, *Handlyng Synne*, I, 158, lines 4755–6.

[13] Concerning the Wilton Diptych (temp. Richard II) and the Assumption of the Virgin by the Master of the St Lucy Legend (late fifteenth century), see Rastall, *The Heaven Singing*, 235.

10. Finally, we have to consider the effectiveness of certain activities from the depictor's point of view. Why, for instance, is reciting or singing, skills shown in other types of source, so rarely shown iconographically? Perhaps vocal minstrelsy was considered uninteresting visually: it is certainly not easy to depict as a distinct activity. This may be one reason why singers are shown with written music in front of them, the notation identifying them as singers rather than readers. It would perhaps be worth searching for further depictions of reciting or declaiming, but *prima facie* it seems that we lack illustrations of heraldic recitation and of improvised or memorised speaking or singing.

Notated music

One might expect the surviving written music to provide the best information about minstrel performance: but this presents the greatest challenge and, ultimately, the most intractable problem. The minstrels' art was aurally based, and no firm evidence has been brought forward that any minstrel in England could read notated music until well into the sixteenth century. What, then, is the relationship between whatever a minstrel performed and those pieces of written music that just might be part of his repertory? If the written remains are indeed 'frozen minstrelsy', a parallel to the putative 'captured performance' of some literary texts, who wrote them down and why? How do they relate to minstrels' actual performance, and can they tell us anything about those performances? These questions are discussed in Chapter 15.

Documentary evidence

In fictional accounts of performance, both vocal and instrumental, the author may be describing an unusual situation precisely because it *is* unusual – something that the medieval audience would recognise because they, unlike us, were conversant with the usual. Our task is to discover what was the norm, which is why, as explained earlier, so much of this book is concerned with the most nearly objective kind of evidence that we have, that of financial accounts. As will be obvious from examples given in earlier chapters, however, the financial details rarely tell us much about the types, styles or effects of performance. In these chapters, therefore, we have to rely mainly on the less objective forms of written description.

One of these is a resource not available to studies of medieval poetry: the theoretical writings that describe the methods – both written and improvised – by which polyphonic textures can be constructed. These will be considered at various points in Chapter 15, where we shall address the question of whether any notated medieval music might have originated as improvised composition that was then written down.

11

The enigma of the minstrels' songs

Andrew Taylor

From a literary perspective, the songs and recitation of the medieval minstrels are an enigma. In an age when reading was still a considerable social accomplishment, the minstrels must have played a crucial role in circulating all manner of stories and songs. One account describes them, not unreasonably, as 'the primary agents for the mass publication of narrative poetry' in medieval England.[1] In various tales, minstrels vaunt their range of amusements they could offer, including the instruments they could play and the songs they could sing, while preachers and moralists proclaim that they will tell of greater heroes than those praised by the minstrels, and proceed to list who these heroes are: Roland and Charlemagne, Octavian, Isumbras, Guy of Warwick, and Bevis of Southampton. It might seem, then, that it should be easy enough to establish the minstrel repertory: what songs they sang, what stories they told, how long they performed for, and in what languages. Yet it proves extraordinarily difficult to do so.

That minstrels sang or recited chivalric compositions of some kind seems clear, but just what these compositions were and how closely they resemble the surviving texts of *chansons de geste* or romances remain highly controversial questions. It is now widely (but not entirely) accepted that the oral tags and formulae in the surviving Middle English romances and Old English poems, notably *Beowulf*, are actually literary devices and that the surviving poems bear only a remote relation to any minstrel or *scop*'s performance.[2] Whether the same can be said for the *chansons de geste*, above all the *Chanson de Roland*, remains more hotly disputed.[3] The references to

---

[1] William Quinn and Audley Hall, *Jongleur: A Modified Theory of Oral Improvisation and Its Effects on the Performance and Transmission of Middle English Romance* (Washington DC, 1982), 1.

[2] See, for example, Carol Fewster, *Traditionality and Genre in Middle English Romance*. 2nd edn (Cambridge, 1993), 28; Harriet E. Hudson, 'Middle English popular romances'. Diss. (Ohio State University, 1982); Andrew Taylor, 'Fragmentation, corruption, and minstrel narration: the question of the Middle English romances', *Yearbook of English Studies* 22 (1992), 38–62. For opposing views, see Karl Reichl, 'From performance to text: a medievalist's perspective on the textualization of modern Turkic oral poetry'. *Western Folklore* 72/3 and 4 (2013), 252–71; and Linda Marie Zaerr, *Performance and the Middle English Romance* (Cambridge, 2012).

[3] Cf. Simon Gaunt, *Retelling the Tale: An Introduction to Medieval French Literature* (London, 2001), 95, on the 'fiction of orality', and more generally Chapters 1–3; Mark Chinca and Christopher Young, eds, *Orality and Literacy in the Middle Ages: Essays on*

minstrels singing cannot be dismissed. William the Conqueror's household minstrel was said to have sung of Roland and Oliver as he rode ahead of the Norman forces at Hastings. Preachers complained that a 'great deal is sung about Roland and Oliver' or that 'the voice of the minstrel sitting on the Petit Pont [leading to the Ile de la Cité in Paris] tells how the mighty soldiers of long ago, such as Roland, Oliver, and the rest, were slain in battle' and so moves the people to tears.[4] What is not clear is how close these songs were to the surviving texts of *La Chanson de Roland* or the other texts that have come down to us.

A crucial question is the normal length of a minstrel's performance. The belief that the *chansons de geste* and romances were once performed by minstrels more or less in their entirety depends upon the minstrels having been able to recite at length. If, as the bulk of the evidence suggests, minstrels rarely enjoyed such opportunities, then we must somehow explain how their shorter performances were related to the much longer texts. To tackle this question we will need to consider a wide range of evidence, much of it predating the chronological boundary of this history, much of it highly problematic, and a certain amount coming from outside England. Rather than offering a summary of the facts about what English minstrels were doing in late medieval England, this chapter offers a survey of conflicting theories, many of them reaching back to materials in Old English or Old Occitan.

The dearth of evidence is a large part of the problem. As Joseph Ritson remarked in his critique of Thomas Percy's *Reliques of Ancient English Poetry*, the 'misfortune is, that no historian or other writer who flourished in the time of the minstrels, has ever thought them worthy of much attention'.[5] Ritson was half right. There is little firm knowledge and, in its absence, fanciful speculation has proliferated. From the mid-eighteenth century on there have been innumerable efforts to imagine minstrel performances (efforts that have extended into lengthy and purely fictitious accounts) and to ascribe texts and manuscripts to minstrels, often on the basis of the flimsiest evidence. But Ritson was also half wrong. In fact, medieval writers, even though they rarely mention individual performances, have a good deal to say about minstrels. Often what they say takes the form of scornful references to minstrels' metrical incompetence, deceit, and general moral turpitude, but – puzzlingly – there

---

a Conjunction and its Consequences in Honour of D. H. Green (Turnhout, 2005); Philip E. Bennett, 'Orality and textuality: reading and/or hearing the *Song of Roland*'. William W. Kibler and Leslie Zarker Morgan, eds, *Approaches to Teaching the Song of Roland* (New York NY, 2006), 146–53; Evelyn Birge Vitz, *Orality and Performance in Early French Romance* (Cambridge, 1999); Evelyn Birge Vitz, Nancy Freeman Regalado and Marilyn Lawrence, eds, *Performing Medieval Narrative* (Cambridge, 2005).

4   Page, *Owl and Nightingale*, 11, 71 and 177, citing a sermon by the Dominican preacher Daniel of Paris of 1272 in BnF MS lat. 16481, f. 17v, and a thirteenth-century sermon preserved in two manuscripts: BnF lat. 14925, f. 132, and BnF lat. 3495, f. 192. For discussion of what these accounts suggest about performance conditions, see Page, *Owl and Nightingale*, 71–3 and 177–8, and Carol Symes, *A Common Stage: Theatre and Public Life in Medieval Arras* (Ithaca NY and London, 2007), 164.

5   Percy, *Reliques*, I, x; Joseph Ritson, *A Dissertation on Romance and Minstrelsy*. Vol. I of *Ancient English Metrical Romances*, new edn, rev. Edmund Goldsmid (Edinburgh, 1891), 85.

are also repeated evocations within literary texts of the voice of a professional entertainer, as he calls for attention and sets his listeners up to hear his story, casting the entire text as a minstrel performance. Partly because of the modern nostalgia for a purer and more oral culture, partly because medieval literature seems to have had a comparable nostalgia of its own, and partly because facts about real performances are so hard to come by, older visions of what minstrels did have proved very hard to displace. Anyone reading standard accounts of such works as *La Chanson de Roland*, or simply accepting unquestionably its title (a nineteenth-century invention), is likely to persist in the view that it is a sung epic, and that somehow, minstrels in the twelfth century regularly sang works of some 4000 lines or more (for many *chansons de geste* are much longer).[6]

External evidence

Administrative documents

As we have seen in previous chapters, pay records and other administrative documents allow us to reconstruct the professional organization of the more respectable full-time minstrels, including the patterns of their travels, for they travelled extensively and regularly across the land. Unfortunately, these documents almost never indicate what tunes minstrels sang or what stories they told. Over the centuries, antiquaries have also collected a number of passing references in sermons, chronicles, and other literary works, that do contain some information about performance.[7] Of these scholars, the most important for English minstrels was the eighteenth-century antiquary Thomas Warton, poet laureate and author of the *History of English Poetry* (1774–81), who supplied numerous new references of his own discovery. It was Warton, for instance, who first noted a passing reference to 'a certain minstrel named Herebert [who] sang the song of Colbrond, and the *geste* of 'Emma, freed from the ordeal by fire' at the cathedral priory of St Swithun in Winchester in 1338.[8] From such moments, E.K. Chambers traced out his account of the minstrel repertory in *The Mediaeval Stage* of 1903.[9]

---

[6] See, for example, the claim of Vitz, Regalado and Lawrence, in their introduction to *Performing Medieval Narrative*, that both *Beowulf* and the *Chanson de Roland* were 'sung epics' (1). Philip Bennett, in a volume on teaching *The Song of Roland*, asserts: 'That epic poems were sung in the twelfth century is not a matter of doubt, unless we wish to disregard every reference, both internal and external to the poems themselves, to such performances' ('Orality and textuality', 150).

[7] One of the first great sources was the dictionary often known simply as Du Cange, the *Glossarium mediae et infimae Latinitatis*, compiled by Charles du Fresne, Sieur du Cange, a noted antiquary and treasurer of France, and first published in 1678. Du Cange's entry for 'ministelli' (sic), 'quod vulgo *menestreux* vel *menestriers* appelamus' ('which in the vernacular we call *menestreux* or *menestriers*'), provided a point of departure for many later scholars: Du Cange, *Glossarium*, V, col. 393b.

[8] Warton, *History*, II, 97: 'Et cantabat Joculator quidam nomine Herebertus CANTICUM Colbrondi, necnon Gestum Emme regine a judicio ignis liberate, *in aula prioris*'.

[9] Chambers, *Mediaeval Stage*, I, 62.

It is alarming to realize just how dependent we have been on Warton's references. As Linda Marie Zaerr notes, there are all told only four 'explicit records of musical narrative performance' from post-Conquest England: 70 shillings for minstrels accompanying their songs with harps at the installation of the abbot of St Augustine's, Canterbury in 1309; the performance of the minstrel Herebert at St Swithun's in 1338; the performance of ten minstrels at St Swithun's in 1374; and the performance at Bicester Priory in 1432.[10] All four references come from Warton, and, alarmingly, not one of his sources has as yet been located. Warton's footnote strongly implies that he found the reference to Herebert's performance in 'the Prior's register of St Swithun's Winchester, [among the] parchment manuscripts in the archive of Wolvesey [the bishop's palace] at Winchester'.[11] Jane Cowling and Peter Greenfield, however, who have explored archives in Hampshire for Records of Early English Drama (REED), have been unable to locate any such document, and have questioned whether it ever existed. As they remark, 'some doubt attaches to these stories, as few of them appear in documents now extant, and scholars have challenged the reliability of some of Warton's non-Hampshire stories'.[12] Cowling and Greenfield conclude that while Warton may 'have had access to monastic records now lost, as he spent his summers in Winchester with his older brother Joseph, who was headmaster of Winchester College', the 'amount of detail [these references] contain is itself suspicious'.[13]

It has not been easy to find other references to English minstrels, especially ones offering any detail. The numerous volumes of the REED project published to date have yielded one substantial and previously largely unknown description of a performance by someone who appears to have been a professional entertainer: Humphrey Newton, a Cheshire gentleman, notes in a section of his diary dated between 1513 and 1521, that 'Christophar parkynston sang a song of Thomas Ersholedon & þe quene of ffeiree', that he also sang of several battles, and that he did 'rehersyn' various prophecies.[14] For Scotland, we have a reference to James IV paying nine shillings in 1497 to 'tua fithelaris that sang Graysteil to the King'.[15] As Linda Marie Zaerr notes, this is a reference to some version of the tale of *Gray Steel* or *Eger and Grime*, which

---

[10] Zaerr, *Performance*, 59.

[11] 'Registr. Priorat. S. Swithini Winton. MSS. pergamen. In Archiv. De Wolvesey Wint.'. Warton, *History*, I, 89, n. r; II, 174 adds the further information that 'The rest [of the entry] is much obliterated and the date is hardly discernible'.

[12] Jane Cowling and Peter Greenfield, 'Monks, minstrels and players: drama in Hampshire before 1642', *Hampshire Papers* 29 (Southampton, 2008), 1–28, at 2.

[13] *Ibid.* There are further reasons for doubt. Warton was something of a prankster, and he and his brother had composed and published poems which they attributed to their father: the so-called 'Warton forgeries'. The complex typography of the reference to Herebertus, with its block capitals and italics (see n. 8 above), looks very like that of the sixteenth-century black letter chapbooks on Guy of Warwick but very unlike any prior's register, and would have served to give the reference an 'olde Englande' look for Warton's readers.

[14] *REED Cheshire, including Chester*, II, 829. Further on this performance, see Deborah Youngs, *Humphrey Newton (1466–1536): An Early Tudor Gentleman* (Woodbridge, 2008), 162–4.

[15] Dickson and Paul, *Accounts*, I, 330. See p. 370.

survives in three early printed editions and the Percy Folio, along with a tune transcribed in 1839 from a seventeenth-century book of lute tablature, now lost.[16] Sources that one might hope would contain some reference to minstrels reciting the deeds of knights, such as the chronicles of Froissart or the lengthy depositions in the struggle between Sir John Scrope and Sir Richard Grosvenor over who had the right to the coat of arms *azure, a bend or*, at which more than four hundred witnesses testified to what they knew of the two knights' reputation, are strangely silent.[17] In this chivalric inquest, minstrels were apparently not considered a worthy source.

Identifiable minstrel authors

One obvious difficulty in trying to approach the question of the minstrel repertory is that the vast majority of the works that have been attributed to minstrel authors are anonymous. The 'Turoldus' whose name is mentioned at the end of *La Chanson de Roland* has never been further identified; the author of *Beowulf* is completely unknown, as are the authors of all but a handful of the *chansons de geste* and most of the Old French or Middle English romances. Earlier critics often speak casually of the authors of particular works as 'jongleurs' or 'minstrels' – the term has been applied to Chrétien de Troyes, for instance – but the list of specific minstrels that can be established with reasonable certainty as the authors of surviving works is short.

From the first years of the thirteenth century, we find French aristocrats commissioning vernacular histories, including the translation of the Pseudo-Turpin's account of Charlemagne and various dynastic histories.[18] The authors, mostly anonymous, were often attached to the household in some capacity. Robert VII, baron of Béthune, employed a household servant who composed two large chronicles, one on the dukes of Normandy and kings of England, the other on the kings of France.[19] Among these household servants was at least one minstrel, who worked for Alphonse de Poitiers, brother of Saint Louis, and translated the *Historia Regum Francorum* in about 1260.[20]

---

[16] Zaerr, *Performance*, 53–4.

[17] Sir Nicholas Harris Nicolas, ed., *The Controversy between Sir Richard Scrope and Sir Robert Grosvenor*. 2 vols (London, 1832). A good introduction to the depositions is R. Stewart-Brown, 'The Scrope and Grosvenor controversy, 1385–1391'. *Transactions of the Historic Society of Lancashire and Cheshire* 89 (1937), 1–22. See also N[oël] Denholm-Young, *The Country Gentry in the Fourteenth Century, with Special Reference to the Heraldic Rolls of Arms* (Oxford, 1969), 134; Joel T. Rosenthal, *Telling Tales: Sources and Narration in Late Medieval England* (University Park PA, 2003), 65–84; and further discussion below, pp. 309–10.

[18] Gillette Labory, 'Les débuts de la chronique en français (XIIe et XIIIe siècles)'. Erik Cooper, ed., *The Medieval Chronicle III: Proceedings of the 3rd International Conference on the Medieval Chronicle, Doorn/Utrecht 12–17 July 2002* (Amsterdam, 2004), 1–26.

[19] Edith Langlois Mace de Gastin, 'Chronique d'un anonyme de Bethune: histoire des ducs de Normandie et des rois d'Angleterre jusqu'en 1220'. PhD. diss. (Lille, 1990); Gabrielle M. Spiegel, *The Past as Text: The Theory and Practice of Medieval Historiography* (Baltimore MD and London, 1997), 197–200.

[20] Kathleen James-Teelucksingh, 'Critical edition of *La Chronique d'un ménestrel d'Alphonse de Poitiers* as contained in B.N. Fr. 570'. PhD. diss. (University of Maryland, 1984); Gaël

In northern France and the Low Countries there were, perhaps as early as the late thirteenth century, confraternities whose members included municipal musicians, some of them also writers.[21] Of these organizations, the best known is the *Carité de Notre Dame des Ardents d'Arras*, the confraternity of the *jongleurs* of Arras. According to its charter, the confraternity was established during a time of plague, when two *jongleurs*, sworn enemies, were both told by the Virgin in a dream to come to Arras and tell the bishop, Lambert de Guînes (1093–1115), that she would appear in the cathedral bearing a candle whose wax, mixed with water, would cure the people from the *feu d'enfer*.[22] Its members were respectable citizens, and included members of the clergy, bourgeois, and two famous trouvères: Jehan de Bodel (c. 1160–1210), known for his pastoral poetry, *fabliaux*, the *Jeu de Saint Nicholas*, and the *Chanson de Saisnes*, on Charlemagne's campaigns against the Saxons; and Adam de la Halle (d. c. 1288, or possibly later), who served Robert II, Count of Artois, and Charles d'Anjou, best known for the short pastoral comedy *Le Jeu de Robin et Marion*.[23]

Of these northern minstrel authors, one of the most copious and best documented is Adenet, who rose to be the king of minstrels for the Count of Flanders, and is generally known as Adenet le Roi. He wrote four lengthy romances, and from the autobiographical sketch that he inserts at the beginning of his last work, *Cleomadés*, and his occasional appearance in pay records it is possible to trace the outline of his career. He was born in about 1240, and educated in the court of Henry III, duke of Brabant, remaining there after his patron's death in 1261. In about 1265 he entered the service of Guy de Dampierre, who later became Count of Flanders. Adenet travelled widely, accompanying Guy de Dampierre to Tunisia on the short-lived Eighth Crusade, and also making numerous journeys to the Abbey of Saint Denis to consult their chronicles.[24] He composed four lengthy romances: the *Enfances Ogier*, on Charlemagne's hero Ogier the Dane, *Berte aus granspiés*, on Charlemagne's mother, *Bueves de Comarchis*, on Aimeri de Narbonne, and *Cleomadés*.[25] The frontispiece to one of the finest collections of these romances, MS Arsenal 3142, shows Adenet,

---

Chenard, *L'administration d'Alphonse de Poitiers (1241–1271)* (Paris, 2017); Ian Short, 'The Pseudo-Turpin Chronicle: some unnoticed versions and their sources'. *Medium Ævum* 38/1 (1969), 1–22, at 7–9.

[21] Peters, *Musical Sounds*, 153, notes the conditions that favoured this development, including 'a high concentration of large wealthy commercial centers based in trade that grew up at a cultural crossroads' and 'early independence [of these centres] from their overlords'.

[22] Symes, *Common Stage*, 85–92. The confraternity's necrology goes back to 1194, but as Symes notes, the legends of the miraculous cure are much older. The episcopate of Lambert de Guînes lasted from 1093 to 1115; an outbreak of ergotism was reported in Arras in 1129 and another between 1147 and 1151, by which time local monks of Saint-Vast clearly saw the stories of the Virgin as a threat (*Common Stage*, 95–6).

[23] Symes, *Common Stage*, 258–71.

[24] V[ictor Louis Marie] Gaillard, 'Expédition de Gui de Dampierre à Tunis, en 1270'. *Messager des sciences historiques ou archives des arts de la bibliographie de Belgique* (1853), 141–57.

[25] Adenet le Roi, *Les Œuvres d'Adenet le Roi*, ed. Albert Henry. 5 vols (Bruges and Brussels, 1951–71), I, 85–7.

vielle in hand and wearing his crown as a king of minstrels, in the presence of the two women who commissioned his romance *Cleomadés*, Marie, Queen of France, the dominant figure, who is reclining on a couch, and her sister-in-law, Blanche, daughter of St Louis and widow of the Infante of Castile, along with a young nobleman, probably Marie's nephew, Jean de Brabant (Plate 9).[26] Both Adenet and Blanche have their hands raised, as if speaking. Whether Adenet is meant to be reciting his romance, or Blanche telling him the story on which it is based, or whether both are speaking, in a fusion of two different moments, it is clear that Adenet is not playing his vielle. An illuminated initial below shows Adenet copying the romance into wax tablets. Echoing the prologues to his romances, these images insist on Adenet's status as a court poet and author, a trusted servant of his noble patrons holding a dignified position. For the artist, whom Adenet may have supervised, the position of king of minstrels contributed to this authorial status.[27] The images do not, however, tell us anything about how Adenet delivered *Cleomadés*, which runs to 18,698 lines.

In 1297 Adenet performed for Edward I in Ghent and was rewarded with a golden clasp worth sixty shillings, which was transmitted to him by the king's vielle-player Richard.[28] This generous reward may reflect the king's need to calm the anxieties of his knights and his allies. Adenet's performance came after Edward had been in Flanders for two and a half months in a lack-lustre and tardy campaign to drive back the French, who had invaded in June and taken Lille. Edward's ally the Count of Flanders reproached him for giving him so little financial assistance, while the citizens of Ghent were inclined to turn their allegiance to the French. Three months later the citizens actually rose against Edward, hoping to capture him and turn him over to the French.[29] Adenet's career provides some indication of the social status of a king of minstrels in the Low Countries, presumably not that different from the contemporary English kings of minstrels, the kings of minstrels of Edward I.

Alleged minstrel manuscripts

The problem of linking surviving texts with minstrel performance only grows worse when we turn to the manuscripts. Léon Gautier, one of the great champions of the *Chanson de Roland* as an expression of French national identity, confidently classified a number of manuscripts as 'manuscrits de jongleurs', and numerous Middle English scholars did much the same with the term 'minstrel manuscript'.[30] In the

---

[26] Adenet le Roi, *Œuvres*, I, 45, 96–7; V.2, 611, 797.

[27] Sylvia Huot, *From Song to Book*, 40–44; Silvère Menegaldo, 'Adenet le Roi tel qu'en ses prologues', *Cahiers de recherche médiévales et humanistes* 18 (2009), 309–28, at 324–6.

[28] 'Firmaculum aureum pretii lx. s. datur per Ricardum vidulatorem regis, nomine regis, Adae regi menestrallo comitis Flandriae, apud Gand., viii die. Novembris': BL Add MS 7965, f. 139r, cited in André Adnès, *Adenès, dernier grand trouvère: recherches historiques et anthroponymiques* (Paris, 1971), 20, n. 3.

[29] Michael Prestwich, *Edward I* (London, 1988, and New Haven CT, 1997), 392–3, 394 and 396.

[30] Léon Gautier, *Les épopées françaises: Étude sur les origines et l'histoire de la littérature nationale.* 3 vols (Paris, 1865–8), I, 186. For a fuller discussion of such manuscripts, see Andrew Taylor, 'The myth of the minstrel manuscript', *Speculum* 66/1 (1991), 43–73.

PLATE 9. Adenet le Roi in the presence of Marie, queen of France, Blanche of Castille, and Jean de Brabant. Paris, Arsenal MS 3142 (1275–1300), fol. 1r.

vast majority of cases such attributions have been based largely on the *contents* of the manuscript and at best a summary account of their codicological features. Gautier himself applied the term to six twelfth-century manuscripts, including Oxford, Bodleian Library, MS Digby 23, which contains the best-known version of the *Chanson de Roland*. The sole basis for these identifications, however, was that the manuscripts were early, plain, small, written in a single column, and often rather battered or soiled. When compared to the great decorated and illuminated copies of the romances or of texts such as *Le Roman de la Rose*, the manuscripts Gautier listed did indeed seem fit for the saddlebag of a poor wanderer. In fact, however, such plain volumes were used by all manner of people for all manner of purposes. Cheap, single-column manuscripts of the twelfth century contained a wide range of texts, many of them philosophical and theological, and clearly belonging to the schools, not the knightly halls.[31] Furthermore, in the case of Digby 23, there were a number of indications that the manuscript did not belong to a *jongleur*. Charles Samaran in his introduction to the facsimile questioned Gautier's classification, noting that both the original scribe and the corrector seemed unfamiliar with many of the heroes of the *chansons de geste* and that in the thirteenth century someone had copied verses by Juvenal on the flyleaf of the *Roland* (fol. 74r) and the word 'Chalcidius' under the last line of the text.[32] Admittedly, none of this evidence is conclusive. The mistakes in the names might be mere carelessness and the scribe also makes mistakes in naming Biblical characters.[33] The verses from Juvenal were copied perhaps a century after the text, so that they provide no information about the original owner, and the word 'Chalcidius' may not even be there.[34] On the other hand, there is no particular reason to associate the manuscript with a *jongleur* either, unless one is already convinced, as Gautier was, that such texts were generally performed by *jongleurs* and these *jongleurs* worked from written texts which they had learnt by heart.[35] Samaran's conclusions have often been ignored or misrepresented, however, since they disrupt the familiar understanding of the *chansons de geste* as a minstrel recitation.[36]

Turning to the manuscripts containing the Middle English romances provides evidence of similar wishful thinking. A particularly egregious example is London, Lincoln's Inn, MS 150. This is a tall volume copied shortly after 1400 that contains a copy of the A text of *Piers Plowman* and four romances: *Libeaus Desconus*, *Arthur and*

---

[31] M.B. Parkes, 'The date of the Oxford manuscript of *La Chanson de Roland* (Oxford, Bodleian Library, MS. Digby 23)'. *Medioevo Romanzo* 10 (1985), 161–75, at 165–6.

[32] C. Samaran, 'Étude historique et paléographique'. A. de Laborde, ed., *La Chanson de Roland: Reproduction phototypique du manuscrit Digby 23 de la Bodleian Library d'Oxford* (Paris, 1933), 1–50, at 24, 26–7 and 38–41.

[33] *Ibid.*, 39.

[34] Ian Short, 'L'avènement du texte vernaculaire: la mise en recueil'. Emmanuèle Baumgartner and Christiane Marchello-Nizia, eds, *Théories et pratiques de l'écriture au Moyen Age, Actes du colloque, Palais du Luxembourg-Sénat, 5–6 Mars 1987*, Special issue, *Littérales* 4 (1988), 11–24, at 11–12; and *Chanson de Roland, The Oxford Version*, ed. Ian Short. Volume 1 of *La Chanson de Roland/The Song of Roland: The French Corpus*, gen. ed. D. Joseph J. Dugan. 3 vols (Turnhout, 2005), I, 18.

[35] Gautier conceives this as the norm, although he does not explicitly say so: *Épopées françaises*, 41.

[36] Thus, whereas Samaran concludes by asking whether the *Satires* of Juvenal and the *Timaeus* would not be 'odd traveling companions for a wandering minstrel' ('singuliers compagnons de route pour un jongleur errant'), Brault concludes that '[a]fter reviewing all the available evidence in this regard, Charles Samaran was unable to resolve the issue': Gerard J. Brault, *The Song of Roland: An Analytical Edition*. 2 vols (London, 1978), I, 6. Paul Zumthor does not hesitate to claim these early manuscripts served as *aides mémoires* for professional singers (*Essai*, 457) and that he 'can distinguish without difficulty between a luxury manuscript, individualized by its dedication, and a quite ordinary minstrel manuscript': 'The text and the voice', trans. Marilyn C. Engelhardt. *New Literary History* 16/1 (1984), 67–92, at 69.

Merlin, Kyng Alisaunder, and *The Batayle of Troye.*³⁷ Perhaps because it contained such suitable material, perhaps because it was battered and stained, scholars have been ready to associate this manuscript with minstrels on the most tenuous grounds. Joseph Hunter noted that a document from the hospital of St John of Beverley had been used in its binding and 'connecting this with the fact that at Beverley there was in the time when this MS was written a noted fraternity of minstrels' concluded that 'a probability is raised that the contents of this book were originally transcribed for this use and that the MS may, without much hazard of misleading, be called hereafter the Book of the Minstrels of Beverley'.³⁸ M.E. Barnicle rejected Beverley in favour of Shrewsbury, another famous centre for minstrels: 'The peculiar format of the book, 5 inches wide by 12 inches long, and the fact that except for a version of *Piers Plowman* it contains only romances argue in favour of its being a minstrel book. Moreover, this later assumption gains greater credence from the fact that the town of Shrewsbury during the Middle Ages was a well-known centre for minstrels, music, and monarchs'.³⁹

Barnicle is the first to link explicitly the long narrow format of a manuscript with the possibility that it was used by a minstrel. Although she does not elaborate, two reasons have often been given for making the association. The first is that the long, narrow format is well suited to writing a single column of text, which can be easily scanned and reduces the number of times the page has to be turned.⁴⁰ For this reason, it is the format most often used for Tudor prompt books.⁴¹ The second reason is that such volumes could easily be stored in holster-shaped saddle-bags. G.S. Ivy may be the earliest to make the identification, when he refers to Cambridge, Trinity College, MS O.9.38, a fifteenth-century English and Latin miscellany, as 'a suitable shape for carrying in a holster'.⁴² This term, however, turns an interesting possibility into an established fact, since no one has actually produced an example of saddle-bags of this shape. There are actually a number of other reasons why this

---

37 The date is that proposed by Ralph Hanna, *London Literature, 1300–1380* (Cambridge, 2005), 16.

38 Joseph Hunter, *Three Catalogues Describing the Contents of the Red Book of the Exchequer, of the Dodsworth Manuscripts in the Bodleian Library, and of the Manuscripts in the Library of the Honourable Society of Lincoln's Inn* (London, 1838), 399, cited by Barnicle in *The Seege or Batayle of Troye*, ed. Mary Elizabeth Barnicle, EETS o.s. 172 (Oxford, 1927), xi.

39 *Seege or Batayle of Troye*, xiv. The grounds for associating the manuscript with Shrewsbury are also tenuous. See further Taylor 'Minstrel Manuscript', 56.

40 Gisela Guddat-Figge, *Catalogue of Manuscripts Containing Middle English Romances* (Munich, 1976), 31, citing the *Bodleian Library Record* 3 (1950–1), 50, anonymous note on Bodleian, MS Eng. Poet, e. 5.

41 W[alter] W[ilson] Greg, ed., *Dramatic Documents from the Elizabethan Playhouses: Stage Plots: Actors' Parts: Prompt Books*, 2 vols (Oxford, 1913), I, 204–5.

42 G.S. Ivy, 'The bibliography of the manuscript-book'. Francis Wormald and C. E. Wright, eds, *The English Library before 1700* (London, 1958), 32–65, at 64, n. 71. On this manuscript, see A.G. Rigg, *A Glastonbury Miscellany of the Fifteenth Century: A Descriptive Index of Trinity College, Cambridge, MS O.9.38* (Oxford, 1968); and A.G. Rigg, 'An edition of a fifteenth-century commonplace book (Trinity College, Cambridge, MS O.9.38)'. DPhil. diss. (Oxford, 1966).

format might be convenient, such as keeping accounts.[43] Perhaps the most extreme misapplication of this dubious term is to Oxford, Bodleian Library, MS Ashmole 61, a massive collection of poetry that stands over sixteen inches tall, the size of a standard folio volume. If this book was designed for a saddle-bag, it must have been a very large one. Gisela Guddat-Figge judiciously observes that 'The mere variety of the holster books ... makes a connection between the format of holster books and the Middle English minstrels very doubtful indeed'.[44]

Earlier scholars, when employing the term 'minstrel manuscript', had little sense of how extensive the early commercial book trade was or of the kinds of volumes it could produce.[45] So confronting Bodleian, Laud Misc. 108, the manuscript that contained two famous early romances, *King Horn* and *Havelok*, along with the *South English Legendary*, Laura Hibbard quickly concluded that some minstrel 'probably once packed into his saddle-bags the small compact manuscript which still preserves the poem'.[46] Others, recognizing that this elegant book with its numerous decorated initials did not quite fit this vision, suggested that the manuscript might have been copied *from* a minstrel's text.[47] In fact, Laud Misc. 108, a collaborative project involving two main scribes and three decorators, has all the indications of being a commercial product from a scriveners' quarter, possibly that of Catte Street in Oxford.[48]

Even when a book can definitely be identified as the property of a minstrel it is not clear how much this tells us. An instance is Cambridge University Library, MS

---

[43] This actually appears to have been the case with Cambridge, Trinity College, O.9.38, which began as an account book for Glastonbury Abbey. See Rigg, *Glastonbury Miscellany*, 1 and 40. On the practice of preparing long narrow booklets for keeping accounts, see D.F. Foxon, 'Some notes on agenda format'. *The Library* 8/3 (1953), 163–73; and, for earlier use on the Continent and for different reasons, Erik Kwakkel, 'Decoding the material book: cultural residue in medieval manuscripts'. Michael Johnston and Michael Van Dussen, eds, *The Medieval Manuscript Book: Cultural Approaches* (Cambridge, 2015), 60–76, at 72–3.

[44] Guddat-Figge, *Catalogue*, 32.

[45] Influential studies of the manuscripts containing the Middle English romances include Guddat-Figge, *Catalogue*, 32–6; Hudson, 'Middle English Popular Romances'; Carol Meale, '"gode men / Wiues maydnes and alle men": romance and its audiences'. Carol Meale, ed., *Readings in Medieval English Romance* (Woodbridge, 1994), 209–25; J. J. Thompson, 'Collecting Middle English romances and some related book-production activities in the later Middle Ages'. Maldwyn Mills, Jennifer Fellows and Carol M. Meale, eds, *Romance in Medieval England* (Newtown, 1988), 17–38; Michael Johnston, *Romance and the Gentry in Late Medieval England* (Oxford, 2014).

[46] Laura A. Hibbard, *Medieval Romance in England: A Study of the Sources and Analogues of the Non-Cyclic Metrical Romances* (New York NY, 1960), 106.

[47] J. Zupitza, 'Zum Havelok'. *Anglia* (1884), 145–55, at 155; Walter W. Skeat, ed., *The Lay of Havelok the Dane*. ed. 2nd edn, rev. K. Sisam (Oxford, 1915), vii; *King Horn: A Middle-English Romance*, ed. Joseph Hall (Oxford, 1901), ix.

[48] Orietta Da Rold concludes it is 'not unlikely that some of the scribes and shops' in Catte Street 'contributed to the copying, compilation, and finishing of MS Laud Misc. 108': 'Codicology, localization and Oxford, Bodleian Library, MS. Laud. Misc. 108'. Carol Meale and Derek Pearsall, eds, *The Makers and Users of Medieval Books* (Cambridge, 2014), 48–59, at 58.

Add. 5943, a late fourteenth-century collection of sermons and religious texts. The last pages, folios 161 to 172, were ruled for notation and contain fourteen songs in English, French, and Latin. This manuscript was initially attributed to a minstrel on the basis of two inscriptions: on the recto of the penultimate flyleaf, f. 184r, is the signature 'Wi*lli*am henny*n*g*is* harp*er*'. On the same page is a more detailed note of provenance, which E.J. Dobson read as a reference to a 'Master John [Morton. A joc]ulator' buying the book, assuming this *joculator* to be the harper.[49] In fact, the inscription indicates that the book belonged to Master John Morton *Senior* and that it was compiled by Thomas Turke, formerly perpetual vicar of Bere (i.e. Bere Regis, Dorset), who gave it to him in 1418 (although he probably actually copied the work much earlier, during the period 1395–1401 when he was at Winchester).[50] Morton was an official in the Salisbury diocesan administration, and Turke was one of the inaugural fellows of the College before he became a Carthusian monk.[51] The manuscript served partly as a collection of religious material, partly as a place to jot down personal memoranda, and partly as a place to copy down a small collection of polyphonic carols, exactly the kind of repertory that the Winchester College scholars might perform after dinner. Yet at some point, if 'Harper' was here still functioning as a professional designation and not as a surname, the manuscript belonged to a minstrel. It would be hazardous to construct too elaborate a hypothesis on this single example, but it does suggest how far the interests of an actual minstrel might diverge from the stereotype of the poor wandering *jongleur*.

Other candidates for minstrel ownership have been proposed, but rarely on convincing grounds. Thomas Wright classified two songbooks as minstrel collections: British Library MS Sloane 2593 and Bodleian MS Eng. Poet. E. 1; and Rossell Hope Robbins added a third, Cambridge, St John's College, MS 54.[52] All three are small, unadorned paper manuscripts of the fifteenth century and contain a variety of English lyrics, many of which might be classified as carols, that is, to use the definition of R.L. Greene, songs 'on any subject, composed of uniform stanzas and provided with a burden'.[53] In some cases, the titles of other songs are given at the beginning of a piece as a way of indicating the tune, but none of the manuscripts contain any notation.

---

[49] E.J. Dobson and Frank Ll. Harrison, *Medieval English Songs* (London, 1979), 23 and 25; Richard L. Greene, *The Early English Carols* (Oxford, 1935), 323.

[50] Rastall, *Two Fifteenth-Century Songbooks*, xi–xv.

[51] Iain Fenlon, ed., *Cambridge Music Manuscripts, 900–1700* (Cambridge, 1982), 85; Rastall, *Two Fifteenth-Century Songbooks*, vii–xv.

[52] Thomas Wright, *Songs and Carols Printed from a Manuscript in the Sloane Collection* (London, 1836); for Sloane MS 2593, *Songs and Carols from a Manuscript in the British Museum of the Fifteenth Century* (London, 1856); for Eng. Poet. E. 1, *Songs and Carols Now First Printed from a Manuscript of the Fifteenth Century* (London, 1847); and Rossell Hope Robbins, *Secular Lyrics of the XIVth and XVth Centuries*. 2nd edn (Oxford, 1955), xxvii (S.54); the full contents are edited in M.R. James and G.C. Macaulay, 'Fifteenth-century carols and other pieces'. *The Modern Language Review* 8/1 (1913), 68–87.

[53] Greene, *Early English Carols*, xxxii–xxxiii.

Sloane 2593 is copied in a single neat hand dating from around 1450. The original page numbering indicates that some 47 folios have been lost, but the 37 that remain contain one of the richest collections of Middle English songs, as well as three in Latin. One of these songs is a humorous refusal to sing, which begins 'If I synge ye wyl me lakke' (that is, you will blame or disparage me). Robbins went so far as to title this piece 'An Unwilling Minstrel'.[54] Another song is a plea for a drink, ending with the demand to give the singer or singers drink before they leave, while a third begins with a list of wares that a travelling pedlar might sell, including purses, pearls, and silver pins, but quickly shifts to a series of *double entendres*, as the singer boasts of the two precious stones in his pocket and a powder which makes 'maydenys wombys to swelle'. Such material might well suit a travelling entertainer and it is easy to understand why Wright and Robbins concluded that this was a minstrel's songbook. As Richard Greene has shown, however, the manuscript seems to be closely associated with the Abbey of Bury St Edmunds. The English is that of East Anglia, and the manuscript contains a rare carol in honour of St Edmund (indeed, the only carol in his honour to survive) and two carols in honour of St Nicholas, who was celebrated at Bury, with his own chapel. A truncated inscription on folio 36 notes that 'Johannes bardel debet istum librum ...' and Greene suggests that this owner may be one of the monks of Bury, whose name was John Berdwell.[55]

Bodleian MS Eng. Poet E.1 is a slightly later manuscript, from the second half of the fifteenth century, with three Latin and 73 English songs. Here too, Greene makes a strong case for associating the manuscript with a religious house, in this case Beverley minster in Yorkshire. It contains two carols and a processional hymn in the honour of St John the Evangelist. As Greene argues, even the worldlier Goliardic items, such as 'Bonum vinum cum sapore' would match the life of the secular canons of Beverley.[56]

On the basis of its appearance alone, the last collection, St John's College MS S.54, seems the most promising. It consists of a single quire of fourteen paper leaves which is stitched loosely into a soft leather cover, which has then been folded and seen hard use. The manuscript is the work of four hands and is extensively corrected.[57] Here too the twenty songs, two of which are also found in Sloane 2593 and one in Bodleian Eng. Poet. E. 1, range from carols on the Nativity and Annunciation to more worldly ones, such as praise for the singer's purse and a maiden's lament for her seduction by a wily clerk. The Latin of the refrains in the macaronic hymns 'Mary

---

[54] Robbins, *Secular Lyrics*, 4–5.

[55] Greene, *Early English Carols*, 306–7; John C. Hirsh, *Medieval Lyric: Middle English Lyrics, Ballads, and Carols* (Oxford, 2005), 7–8 and nos 9, 13, 16 and 39; Karin Boklund-Lagopoulou, '*I have a yong suster*': *Folksong, Ballad and the Middle English Lyric* (Dublin, 2001), 63–86.

[56] Greene, *Early English Carols*, 318. This Goliardic piece is also found in the Glogauer Liederbuch (Kraków, Biblioteka Jagiellońska, Mus. MS 40098), a part-book of *c.* 1480. See Pawel Gancarczyk, 'Abbot Martin Rinkenberg and the origins of the "Glogauer Liederbuch"'. *Early Music* 37/1 (2009), 27–36.

[57] Greene, *Early English Carols*, 325–6.

myld, for loue of the' and 'This world is falce', however, is complex and correct.[58] Once again, the codicological evidence does not match the stereotype of the penniless, wandering minstrel.

The collections of Middle English lyrics must have belonged to people who prided themselves on their abilities as singers and wanted to maintain a large and diverse repertory, and who knew what songs others were singing. The collections do have implications for the social history of music: they suggest something of the ceremonial role of popular vernacular song in celebrating particular saints and their feast days and they show that pious songs and bawdy songs could appeal to the same people. The collections cannot, however, be assigned to minstrels; they could equally well have belonged to any of the numerous lay people who worked for the monasteries or even, as Greene suggests, to the monks themselves.

One collection of songs and ballads that does have a strong association with a minstrel is Bodleian Ashmole 48, which appears to have belonged to, and was probably in large part copied by, Richard Sheale, a harper from Tamworth, with a multifaceted career. Sheale's wife was a peddler and he helped her in her business, and he composed a poem explaining how he was robbed of the money, no less than sixty pounds, that he was taking to London to pay off her debts. He himself, however, worked under the patronage of Edward Stanley, third Earl of Derby, and his son Henry, Lord Strange, and with the earl's support, he was admitted to the London Company of Minstrels in 1555.[59] Sheale is also probably the author of the verse history glorifying the family known as the *Stanley Poem*, which is found in two other manuscripts.[60] Ashmole 48 contains only a few items directly related to the Stanleys, notably an elegy for the earl's wife, Lady Catherine, but it does contain a certain number of items with a northern connection, including a song in praise of the northern lords who defeated the Scots at Berwick in 1558 and the famous *Hunting of the Cheviot*. Most of Ashmole 48, however, is devoted to songs and ballads of a general interest that might have been popular anywhere in England. Since several of these ballads are grouped together by author (which would have been extremely difficult to do once the ballads had been printed), it appears that Sheale was gathering this material for a London print shop.[61] The manuscript offers a rare glimpse into how popular poetry found its way into print. It cannot be taken as a direct reflection of a minstrel's repertory, and it falls outside the period covered by this study, but it does offer a significant challenge to any simple narrative of the decline of minstrelsy.

In short, on codicological grounds alone one cannot distinguish a manuscript designed to serve as an *aide-mémoire* for professional recitation from a manuscript to be read aloud by almost anyone. Many people in the Middle Ages travelled widely, many used cheap books and used them heavily, and many enjoyed singing and

---

[58] Ibid., nos 232 and 366; Stevens, *Music and Poetry*, 118.
[59] *REED Civic London*, II, 800.
[60] Taylor, *Songs and Travels*, 61–74.
[61] On the case for seeing Ashmole 48 not as a collection of handwritten copies of printed ballads but a collection of material for a printshop, see Taylor, *Songs and Travels*, xiv–xv and 94–5; and on the manuscript's relation to Sheale, *ibid.*, 99–107.

telling stories. The very category 'manuscrit de jongleur' or 'minstrel manuscript' is a sustained exercise in begging the question: too often a minstrel manuscript turns out to be simply a manuscript containing a text of the kind that is thought to have been recited by minstrels.

Fictional depictions of reciting or singing minstrels

In the absence of detailed reports of actual performances or of manuscripts that bear any clear and direct connection to a specific minstrel one has to turn to literary descriptions of minstrel activity that may be partially or entirely fictitious but contain verisimilitudinous detail. If one wants a picture of a medieval English minstrel, a man of many talents, one who can sing and play an instrument but also juggle and crack jokes, someone who knows how to work an audience and live by his wits, perhaps the most vivid of them all is offered by the character Haukyn, whom William Langland introduces into his complex allegory *Piers Plowman* (*c.* 1370–90) as a symbol of the busy but spiritually bereft active life. Haukyn is a minstrel, but not a very successful one. He cannot do all these things himself and he envies those who can:[62]

> 'I am a mynstrall', quod that man, 'my name is *Activa Vita*.
> Al ydel ich hatie, for of Actif is my name,
> A wafrer, wol ye wite, and serve manye lordes –
> And fewe robes I fonge or furrede gownes.
> Couthe I lye and do men laughe, thane lacchen I sholde
> Outher mantel or moneie amonges lordes mynstrals.
> Ac for I kan neither taboure ne trompe ne telle no gestes,
> Farten ne fithelen at festes, ne harpen,
> Jape ne jogele ne gentilliche pipe,
> Ne neither saille ne saute ne synge with the gyterne,
> I have no goode giftes of thise grete lordes
> For no breed that I brynge forth – save a benyson on the Sonday,
> Whan the preest preieth the peple hir *Paternoster* to bidde
> For Piers the Plowman and that hym profit waiten –
> And that am I, Actif, that ydelnesse hatie;
> For alle trewe travaillours and tiliers of the erthe,
> From Mighelmesse to Mighelemesse I fynde hem with wafres'.

> ('I am a minstrel', said that man, 'my name is *Activa Vita*.
> I hate everything idle, for from "active" is my name.
> A wafer-seller, if you want to know, and I work for many lords,
> But I've few robes as my fee from them, or fur-lined gowns.
> If I could lie to make men laugh, then I might look to get
> Either mantel or money among lords' minstrels.
> But because I can neither play a tabor nor a trumpet nor tell any stories

---

[62] William Langland, *The Vision of Piers Plowman*, ed. A.V.C. Schmidt. 2nd edn (London, 1995), XIII, lines 225–41; William Langland, *Will's Vision of Piers Plowman*, ed. Elizabeth D. Kirk and Judith H. Anderson, trans. E. Talbot Donaldson (New York NY, 1990), 139.

Nor fart nor fiddle at feasts, nor play the harp,
Joke nor juggle, nor gently pipe,
Nor dance nor strum the psaltery, nor sing to the guitar,
I have no good gifts from these great lords,
For any bread I bring forth, except a blessing on Sundays
When the priest prays the people to say their Paternoster
For Piers the Plowman and those who promote his profit.
And that is I, Active, who hate idleness.
For all true toilers and tillers of the earth
From Michaelmas to Michaelmas I feed them with wafers'.)

Haukyn's lament offers a picture of the minstrel's profession in the 1370s. At the top of the hierarchy, instantly recognizable by their livery, are those minstrels who serve great lords. These fortunate men can hope for great largesse, including fancy gowns that the nobles strip from their own shoulders when moved by a performance. Yet to maintain the interest of fickle listeners, these lords' minstrels are forced to offer a panoply of diversions, including singing and playing music but also telling jokes, juggling, and even farting. Haukyn practises one of the more puzzling forms of minstrelsy: he is a waferer, cooking and distributing small cakes or waffles at the end of feasts. Presumably the waferers offered some kind of entertainment as they did so – else why rank them among the minstrels? – but what this entertainment was remains a mystery.[63]

Much of what Haukyn tells us matches the little we know about what real minstrels actually did. There actually were minstrels who amused by farting, for example, as the name of Henry II's minstrel, Roland le Fartere or Roland le Pettour, suggests.[64] Waferers were a well-established group. They distributed their wafers at the end of feasts and the accounts for the butter, eggs, and sugar survive.[65] Minstrels were generally rewarded according to their patron's social status, so there is nothing surprising in an independent minstrel, such as Haukyn, expressing his jealousy of lords' minstrels. But what about the robes he says they were given? Those minstrels fortunate enough to be part of a lord's household normally received, in addition to their wages, a gown or livery of some kind, so that they might reflect credit on their

---

[63] See p. 350 (1334) for waferers with dancers, pp. 79–81 on banquets and pp. 84–5 on major feasts.

[64] Roland le Fartere is mentioned as holding forty acres in Hemmyngton (Hemingstone), Assh (Ashboking) and Gossbek, all just north of Ipswich in the hundred of Bosemere and Claydon, from a grant originally made by Henry II, in CCR, Edward III (1330–3), 187, cited in Constance Bullock-Davies, *A Register of Royal and Baronial Domestic Minstrels, 1272–1327* (Woodbridge, 1986), 174; Rollandus le Pettus is mentioned in a survey taken between 1226 and 1228 recorded in the *Liber Feodorum: The Book of Fees Commonly Called Testa de Nevill, Part I. A.D. 1198–1241*, ed. H.C. Maxwell Lyte. 3 vols (London, 1920–31), I, 386, as holding land worth a hundred shillings a year in the town of Langam, which is some thirteen miles to the north. In each case the annual service is to perform 'a leap, a whistle, and a fart'. An entry in the *Rotuli de Dominabus et Pueris et Puellis de Donatione Regis* (London, 1830), 33, notes that Herbert, a 'joculator', son of Roland, holds thirty acres in the hundred of Bosemere (Bosemere and Claydon).

[65] See p. 349.

patron. Did the lords they visited, moved by an especially beautiful lyric or astute song of praise and anxious to display their magnanimity, actually jump up from the table to place their own gowns upon a minstrel's shoulders? Romances and even some chronicles say that they did. According to the rhymed history of his life, the great twelfth-century jouster Sir William Marshall, who rose to become regent of England because of his chivalric reputation, went even further, once rewarding a minstrel who sang a song before him with the refrain 'Mareschal, / Kar me donez un boen cheval' (Marshal, come on, give me good horse), by unhorsing a passing knight to provide the desired reward.[66] The pay records of English households, however, suggest that such *beaux gestes* were rare. Already, Haukyn's account is shifting into the realm of literary convention.

This shift calls into question Haukyn's central claim, the one where he might be most valuable as a historical witness if only he could be trusted, that minstrels actually did offer a wide range of diverse entertainments, many of them vulgar, and that they succeeded through crass pliability and deception, lying to make men laugh. Perhaps this was the case; the accusation was certainly common. But the minstrel was a convenient figure. For the medieval church, the minstrel was 'a symbol of turpitude, immorality, and transgression', as Maria Dobozy argues.[67] The shameful speech of minstrels, or *turpiloquium*, was the inverse of the divine logos, their histrionic gestures a mockery of creation, one possible explanation of their frequent depiction in the pages of Psalters and Books of Hours.[68] These associations extend to both the deceitful minstrels Haukyn envies and to Haukyn himself. His *vita activa* is really just worldly busyness and his wafers are morally dubious luxuries that stand in symbolic opposition not just to the hard agricultural labour supervised by Piers but also to the bread of life, the word of God spread by true preachers. The symbolic structure of the poem dictates the qualities assigned to him. There is, therefore, no certainty that Haukyn's description of how minstrels made their living corresponds to actual practice. Haukyn is an extreme case, but the challenge of separating literary convention or symbolic function from historical information is one that we shall encounter repeatedly.

---

[66] *History of William Marshal*, ed. A.J. Holden, S. Gregory, and D. Crouch. 3 vols (London, 2002–6), I, lines 3483–520. The editors argue that while the rhymed life of William Marshal was commissioned by his son to celebrate his father's life and shapes it accordingly, it is often accurate in its depiction of chivalric life, especially the violent early tournaments (III, 4–8, 40–1).

[67] Dobozy, *Re-Membering*, 27. See also above, p. 198.

[68] Michael Camille, *Image on the Edge: The Margins of Medieval Art* (London, 1992), and *Mirror in Parchment: The Luttrell Psalter and the Making of Medieval England* (Chicago IL, 1998); Taylor, *Textual Situations*, 151–67.

Internal evidence

Stylistic features suggesting performance by minstrels

If we approach the question of minstrel performance from the surviving literary texts rather than from the surviving records, we suddenly face a wealth of evidence, but evidence of a very uncertain kind. While the historical record of specific minstrel performances is extremely scanty, many medieval texts present themselves as if they were minstrel recitations and many literary scholars have taken them at their word. As Jean Rychner notes, six of the best-known early *chansons de geste* begin with such a prologue. The *Couronnement de Louis* is a case in point:[69]

> Oiez, seignor, que Dieu vos seit adanz!
> Plaist vos oïr d'une histoire vaillant
> Bone chançon, corteise et avenant?
> Vilains joglere ne sai por quei se vant:
> Nul mot en die tresque on li comant.
> De Looïs ne lairai ne vos chant
> Et de Guillelme al Cort Nés le vaillant,
> Qui tant sofri sor sarrazine gent;
> De meillor ome ne cuit que nuls vos chant.
>
>> (Listen Lords, may God give you his aid! Do you wish to hear a story of bravery, a good song that is courteous and agreeable? The miserable jongleur has no reason to boast for he says no word unless one commands him. I will not stop from singing about Louis and Guillaume of the Short Nose, who suffered so from the Saracens – I do not believe anyone has ever sung of a better man.)

For many, such prologues speak for themselves. Rychner, for one, begins his analysis of the formulaic style of the *chansons de geste*: 'But first let us establish the facts: our *chansons de geste* were sung by *jongleurs*. We will not have to go far to find proof: many ... actually have a prologue that proves they were recited publically'.[70]

Numerous Middle-English and Old French romances offer similar prologues. The late fourteenth-century *Emaré*, for example, provides a two-stanza introduction in a minstrel's voice. This narrator begins with an opening prayer for aid, then says that such prayers are the appropriate way for minstrels to begin their stories, calls for the audience to tarry while he tells his story, and finally specifies his subject, the lady Emaré, of whom he will sing:[71]

> Jhesu, that ys kyng in trone,

---

[69] Ernest Langlois, ed., *Le Couronnement de Louis: chanson de geste du XIIe siècle*. 2nd edn (Paris, 1925), lines 1–9, my translation. For discussions of this passage, see Rychner, *Chanson de geste*, 10; Gaunt, *Retelling*, 34–5; Vitz, *Orality and Performance*, 91–2.

[70] Rychner, *Chanson de Geste*, 10, my translation.

[71] Anne Laskaya and Eve Salisbury, eds, *The Middle English Breton Lays* (Kalamazoo MI, 1995), lines 1–24.

> As Thou shoope bothe sonne and mone,
> And all that shalle dele and dyghte,　　[order and rule]
> Now lene us grace such dedus to done,　　[lend]
> In Thy blys that we may wone –　　[dwell]
> Men calle hyt heven lyghte;
> And Thy modur Mary, hevyn qwene,
> Bere our arunde so bytwene,　　[prayer]
> That semely ys of syght,
> To thy Sone that ys so fre,
> In heven wyth Hym that we may be,
> That lord ys most of myght.
>
> Menstrelles that walken fer and wyde,
> Her and ther in every a syde,
> In mony a dyverse londe,
> Sholde, at her bygynnyng,
> Speke of that ryghtwes kyng
> That made both see and sonde.
> Whoso wyll a stounde dwelle,　　[stay for a moment]
> Of mykyll myrght y may you telle,
> And mornyng ther amonge;
> Of a lady fayr and fre,
> Her name was called Emaré,
> As I here synge in songe.

Havelok (c. 1280–90) combines the same crucial elements: the call to the listening audience to tarry, the specification of the hero, and the prayer for help, and even adds a request for a cup of ale:[72]

> Herkneth to me, gode men –
> Wives, maydnes, and alle men –
> Of a tale that ich you wile telle,
> Wo so it wile here and therto dwelle.　　[stay]
> The tale is of Havelok imaked:
> While he was litel, he yede ful naked.　　[went around]
> Havelok was a ful god gome;　　[man]
> He was ful god in everi trome;　　[company]
> He was the wicteste man at nede　　[bravest]
> That thurte riden on ani stede.　　[might ride]
> That ye mowen now yhere,
> And the tale ye mowen ylere,
> At the biginnig of ure tale
> Fil me a cuppe of ful god ale.

---

[72] Ronald B. Herzman, Graham Drake and Eve Salisbury, eds, *Four Romances of England: King Horn, Havelok the Dane, Bevis of Hampton, Athelston* (Kalamazoo MI, 1999), 1–26.

The mid-thirteenth-century Anglo-Norman version of *Boeve de Haumtone* presents itself as an oral performance by a minstrel who knows many stories about the hero and will tell them 'if you wish to hear' ('Si vus volez oyer').[73] The Middle English version, *Bevis of Hampton* (c. 1324), does much the same:[74]

> Lordinges, herkneth to me tale!
> Is merrier than the nightingale,
> That I schel singe:
> Of a kynght ich wil yow roune,   [speak]
> Beves a highte of Hamtoune,
> Withouten lesing.

One Continental version of *Boeve de Haumtone*, of the first half of the thirteenth century, follows a more complicated path, offering itself as a song that is better than any jongleur could sing and insisting that this song is based on a written version composed by a cleric and found in a book from an ancient abbey.[75] Similar calls to listening lords begin many saints' lives and fabliaux, both Continental and Anglo-Norman.[76]

One of the fullest evocations of sustained recitation in any romance comes in the thirteenth-century *Huon de Bordeaux*, which devotes a full sixteen lines to a call for the listeners to return after dinner the next day:[77]

> Segnor preudomme, certes, bien le veés,
> Pres est de vespre et je sui moult lassé.
> Or vous proi tous, si cier com vous m'avés
> Ni Auberon, ne Huon le membré,
> Vous revenés demain aprés disner
> Et s'alons boire, car je l'ai desiré.
> Je ne puis, certes, mon coraige celer
> Que jou ne die çou que j'ai empensé :
> Moult sui joians quant je voi avesprer
> Car je desire que je m'en puise aler.
> Si revenés demain aprés disner.
> Et si vous proi cascuns m'ait aporté
> U pan de sa chemise une maille noué,
> Car en ces poitevins a poi de largeté;

---

[73] Albert Stimming, ed., *Der anglonormannische Boeve de Haumtone* (Halle, 1899), 4, lines 1–6; Judith E. Weiss, trans., *Boeve de Haumtone and Gui de Warewic: Two Anglo-Norman Romances* (Tempe AZ, 2008), 25.

[74] Herzman et al., *Four Romances*, 200.

[75] Albert Stimming, ed., *Der festländische Bueve de Hantone*. 3 vols (Halle, 1911–14), Fassung II, lines 1–15.

[76] A list of Anglo-Norman examples can easily be compiled by consulting Ruth J. Dean and Maureen Boulton's invaluable *Anglo-Norman Literature: A Guide to Texts and Manuscripts* (London, 1999).

[77] Pierre Ruelle, ed., *Huon de Bordeaux* (Brussels and Paris, 1960), lines 4976–4901, my translation.

Avers fu et escars qui les fist estorer
Ne qui ains les donna a cortois menestrel.

> (My lords, you can clearly see that it is almost evening and I am very tired. Therefore, I beg you, as you love me, or Auberon or the renowned Hugh, to return tomorrow after dinner, and that we go to drink, for that's what I desire. Indeed, I cannot hide my thought and not say what I think, that I'm overjoyed when I see evening coming because I want to be able to go. And I pray you come tomorrow after dinner, and each one bring a penny tied up in his shirt, because giving these small Poitevin farthings is hardly generosity – he was a stingy scoundrel who created them; no one should give them to a courteous minstrel.)

There are, in short, numerous instances in which *chansons de geste* and romances present themselves as if they were being delivered by a minstrel.

For those who wish to regard these appeals to the audience as direct reflections of minstrel performance, it is disconcerting to see how widely they are used. One of the earliest attempts to argue that such stylistic features assisted performers when they delivered romances, that of Ruth Crosby, foundered when she found almost as extensive use was being made by Chaucer.[78] The assurance that such prologues are clear proof that a twelfth-century *chanson de geste* was recited publicly tends to weaken when the prologues occur in a fourteenth- or fifteenth-century English romance and lapses altogether when they occur in a seventeenth-century collection such as the famous Percy Folio.[79] There is, moreover, a very strong reason not to take such prologues literally. Anyone who has ever tried to call for the attention of an unruly crowd will recognize that set phrases or standardized calls for attention must be modified to suit the crowd's response. Whether the call is 'Order, order' or 'Listen lordings', it may have to be repeated once or half a dozen times, and if the audience is unruly, improvisation will be required. The opening lines are where a minstrel would most need to be flexible. A minstrel might model his delivery on that displayed in *Boeve de Hamtoune* or *Havelok*, but he could not simply reproduce the fixed text as his personal introduction. Even if we were to accept that the prologues and the call for a pause in *Huon de Bordeaux* were based on direct transcriptions of specific performances, which seems highly unlikely, on all subsequent occasions these passages would have been evocations, like the appeal to the gentle reader in an eighteenth-century novel.

---

[78] Compare Ruth Crosby, 'Oral Delivery in the Middle Ages'. *Speculum* 11/1 (1936), 88–110, with her 'Chaucer and the Custom of Oral Delivery'. *Speculum* 13/4 (1938), 413–32, published just two years later.

[79] Andrew Taylor, 'Performing the Percy Folio'. Jacqueline Jenkins and Julie Sanders, eds, *Editing, Performance, Texts: New Practices in Medieval and Early Modern English Drama* (New York NY, 2015), 70–89.

Modern nostalgia and the myth of the *séance épique*: the harper in the hall

Driven by the nostalgia for pre-literate simplicity, there is, from the mid-eighteenth century and the days of Macpherson's *Ossian*, a drive to evoke the figure we might call 'the harper in the hall' – a single chanting minstrel, accompanying himself, usually on a harp, who offers to the entire assembly, a band of warriors, a sustained performance that compels their full attention (see Plate 1, p. xxiii). This drive to recapture lost bardic performance accounts for the repeated attempts to associate a surviving *chanson de geste* or romance, or the manuscripts that contain them, with a minstrel's performance. More surprisingly, what the introduction to *Havelok* (or *Boeve of Hamtoune* or innumerable other medieval texts) shows is that this nostalgia is not an exclusively modern phenomenon. This nostalgia may help explain the repeated evocation of dignified minstrel performance, even when minstrels were so often reviled in moralizing commentary. Medieval people too hankered for a simpler and nobler time and frequently evoked a golden age of true chivalry, the days of Roland and Oliver or of Arthur.[80]

A particularly compelling instance is provided by the Chandos Herald's *La Vie du Prince Noir* (1385). Like many before him, the herald begins by alluding to an earlier age that was more generous ('temps jadis', line 1), when those who made fine literary compositions ('beaux ditz') were regarded as authors. He then alludes to a general loss of vigour in the world, for there is nothing that does not dry up ('qui ne delzeche', line 9). By implication, chivalry itself is one of these things and this view is reinforced by the poem as a whole, in which the Black Prince is betrayed by those close to him and his noble nature is too fine for the corrupt world.[81] For the herald, as for Langland, the popularity of vulgar oral entertainers is a further sign of this general decline:[82]

> Ci ne serra plus arestans.
> Car combien qe homme n'en face compte
> Et qe homme tiendroit plus grant acompte
> D'un jangelour ou d'un faux menteur,
> D'un jogelour ou d'un bourdeur
> Qui voudroit faire une grimache
> Ou contreferoit le lymache
> Dount home purroit faire un risée
> Qe home ne ferroit sanz demoerée,

---

[80] Joachim Bumke, *Courtly Culture: Literature and Society in the High Middle Ages*, trans. Thomas Dunlap (Berkeley CA, 1991), 14–6; Sylvia Huot, 'Troubadour lyric and Old French narrative'. Simon Gaunt and Sarah Kay, eds, *The Troubadours: An Introduction* (Cambridge, 1999), 263–78 at 273; Renée R. Trilling, *The Aesthetics of Nostalgia: Historical Representation in Old English Verse* (Toronto, 2009), especially 3–4, 12.

[81] Hanna, *London Literature*, 230; Daisy Delogu, *Theorizing the Ideal Sovereign: The Rise of French Vernacular Royal Biography* (Toronto, 2008), 142.

[82] Chandos Herald, *La vie du Prince Noir by Chandos Herald*, ed. Diana B. Tyson (Tübingen, 1975), lines 14–30.

D'un autre qui saveroit bien dire!
Car cils ne sont saunz contredire
Mie bien venuz a la court
En le monde q'ore court.
Mais coment qe homme ne tiegne rien
De ceux qui demoustrent le bien,
Si ne se doit homme pas tenir
De beaux ditz faire et retenir.

> (On this I will dwell no longer, for although such writers are held of no account and a chatterer, a liar, a juggler, or a buffoon who, to raise a laugh, would grimace and make antics, is more esteemed than one who had the skill to indite – for, without gainsaying, such a one is ill received at court nowadays – but albeit they who set forth the good are held in no estimation, yet men ought not to refrain from making and remembering fair poems.)

It is part of the sad wisdom of age to accept that life and chivalric glory are transitory. As the Black Prince, himself gravely ill, says, when he hears of the death of Sir John Chandos, 'All will have its day' ('Tut avera son lieu', line 3964). What the Chandos Herald does not express is any sense that chivalric warfare, feudal hierarchy, or traditional minstrelsy is becoming obsolete in the face of technological or social change.[83]

The decline of true chivalry, then, is like aging, a perpetual process rather than a historical transition to some new period. In contrast, minstrel recitation could serve as a symbol of aristocratic life, of feasting, joy, and celebration, of the essential chivalric virtue of largesse, and of youthful vitality. Furthermore, the distinctive traditional phrases of heroic poetry, whether these were linked assonances, standard rhymes, or alliterative couplets, were often associated with regional identity and regional lineage, the old language which preserved the memory of the deeds of one's ancestors or of great local families. Those listening to a young man or woman reading aloud from a book and hearing themselves addressed as 'seigneurs' or 'lordings' could imagine themselves part of this idealized aristocratic society. When *chansons de geste* and romances allude to traditions of minstrel performance, they evoke a legendary past; they do not necessarily reflect contemporary practice.

The rogue at the door

There is another image of the minstrel, however, almost antithetical to that of the harper in the hall, but one that has also exercised a powerful fascination: that of the minstrel as a glib-tongued and manipulative rogue who shapes his words to suit his listeners, flattering them or threatening them with ridicule. The *fabliau* known

---

[83] The Herald's accusations against vulgar oral performers are a *topos* (see below, pp. 260–1) and there is no reason to take them as a reference to contemporary English poets or an indication that Anglo-Norman, or Picard, or Anglo/Gascon cultures are losing prestige, *pace* Hanna, *London Literature*, 232 and 238.

as *Jongleur of Ely* offers one of the most powerful surviving depictions of such a figure, although this time the word-play serves the higher purpose of teaching the king wisdom. The poem is preserved in the famous trilingual anthology Harley 2253 in the British Library, which dates from roughly 1330.[84] In the *fabliau*, a minstrel ('menestrel') or *jongleur* ('joglour'), who 'travels to seek marvels and adventures' ('passa la terre/ Pur merveille e aventure quere'), comes to the king in London. When the king begins to interrogate him, asking him who he is, 'qy este vus, sire joglour?', he deflects each of the king's questions with a series of deliberate misunderstandings: he is his lord's man, his lord is his lady's husband, he is called by the name of the one who raised him, he comes from his own town, and so forth. But when the king asks him what kind of man he is ('Diez de quel maner tu es') he replies more fully, describing an entire social order of idle ribalds:[85]

> Je vus dirroi, par seint Pere,
> Volenters de ma manere:
> Nous sumes compaignouns plusours;
> E de tiele manere sumes nous
> Qe nus mangeroms plus volenters
> La ou nus sumez priez,
> E plus volenters e plus tost
> Qe la ou nus payoms nostre escot.
> E bevoms plus volenters en seaunt
> Qe nus ne fesoms en esteaunt,
> E aprés manger qe devant,
> Pleyn hanap gros e grant.
> E si vodroms assez aver,
> Mais nus ne avoms cure de travyler,
> E purroms moult bien deporter
> D'aler matyn a mostier.
> E ce est le nostre us
> De gysyr longement en nos lys
> E a noune sus lever,
> E pus aler a manger.
>
> (By St Peter I'll gladly tell you about my kind. We are a numerous company and it is our nature to eat most willingly where we are invited, and with more pleasure and more eagerly than we do when we are paying the bill ourselves, and we drink more willingly when we are sitting down than when we are standing and enjoy a full flagon more willingly after we have eaten than before. We would like to have plenty but we don't want

---

[84] On BL Harley MS 2253 see the essays in Susanna Fein, *Studies in the Harley Manuscript: The Scribes, Contents, and Social Contexts of British Library MS Harley 2253* (Kalamazoo MI, 2000), especially Barbara Nolan, 'Anthologizing ribaldry: five Anglo-Norman fabliaux', 289–327.

[85] Willelm Noomen, *Le jongleur par lui-même* (Louvain, 2003), 96, lines 143–62, my translation.

to work and will gladly dispense with going to church in the morning. It is our custom to lie late abed, to rise at noon and then go to eat.)

The *jongleur* adds that he must tell no more of their ribaldry, for fear of speaking villainy ('Plus ne pus pur vileynye / Counter de nostre rybaudie', line 179–80).

The *Jongleur of Ely* draws on the recurring image of the minstrel as a disruptive parasite, the marginal figure who breaks all social and moral norms, and displays the minstrel's proverbial linguistic trickery or *jonglerie*, trickery which in his case also has a strong ethical dimension as a critique of hypocrisy. Of course, such word play was not limited to professional minstrels, either in literary convention or in reality. Throughout much of medieval Europe, the fool who can subvert the wisdom of the wise was exemplified by the wily peasant Marcolf, the hero of a widespread and enduring Latin and vernacular tradition, who plays similar verbal tricks on Solomon, in a series of exchanges that also begins with the king asking the rogue's identity. Although he plays no instrument, tells no stories, and is never described as a professional entertainer, Marcolf has many of the qualities of the stereotypical minstrel. A marginal figure who lives by his wits, Marcolf is a mouthpiece for scatology and satire; 'valde turpissimum et deformem sed eloquentissimum' ('most exceedingly ugly and misshapen but most eloquent'); he twists his body into obscene positions, repeatedly seeks access to a king's palace, and ends his story wandering, for having been granted by Solomon the right to choose the tree on which he is to be hanged, he journeys throughout the Holy Land and all of Arabia with the alleged intention of finding the right tree.[86] Although the earliest Latin manuscript to preserve his story dates from about 1410, and the earliest English version is found in a printing of 1492, Marcolf was well-known in England much earlier. He appears in the margins of several fourteenth-century Psalters and Henry III had his image painted in Westminster palace in what came to be known as the Marcolf Chamber.[87] Apparently, the king recognized a higher purpose in Marcolf's mocking critique of royal authority. Together, the jongleur of Ely, now known only through a single manuscript, and the almost ubiquitous Marcolf illustrate a broad medieval admiration for word play and trickery, especially when directed against authority. Such figures draw upon powerful and somewhat contradictory iconographic conventions. While the fool was sometimes associated with disbelief, as in the fool who says in his heart there is no God (Psalm 14, v. 1), he could also indicate a higher truth defying worldly wisdom. The tumbler, who literally subverts natural order by standing upside down, can serve as a symbol of the monk or wandering preacher, or ultimately Christ himself, casting

---

[86] Jan M. Ziolkowski, ed., *Solomon and Marcolf* (Cambridge MA, 2008), 52–3. On the possibility that versions of these dialogues were performed orally, see Nancy Mason Bradbury and Scott Bradbury, eds, *The Dialogue of Solomon and Marcolf: A Dual-Language Edition from Latin and Middle English Printed editions* (Kalamazoo MI, 2012), 5–6.

[87] Richard Firth Green, 'Marcolf the Fool and blind John Audelay'. R.F. Yeager and Charlotte C. Morse, eds, *Speaking Images: Essays in Honor of V.A. Kolve* (Asheville NC, 2001), 559–76; Camille, *Image on the Edge*, 26–8; Bradbury and Bradbury, *Dialogue of Solomon and Marcolf*, 6.

off power and enduring humiliation in order to bring others to salvation.[88] These associations my help explain part of the medieval fascination with the figure of the minstrel as fool or ribald.

Corruption, fragmentation and conversation

The two images, that of the harper in the hall and that of the rogue at the door, frame the question of minstrel performance of poetry, suggesting both what so many want these performances to have been and how difficult it is to recapture them. We must recognize how the longstanding desire to establish a connection to a lost tradition of bardic performance has driven efforts to classify the surviving texts of the *chansons de geste* and the romances as more or less direct transcriptions of a minstrel's performance. The second image of the minstrel, that of the linguistic trickster seeking to make a living, although it is in part a literary convention, may nonetheless help illustrate the kinds of violence that professional entertainers could do to a text, casting some light on the gap between real minstrels and their literary depiction. If we imagine a reciter as quick-tongued as the *jongleur* of Ely, and as foul-mouthed as Marcolf, we would have an example of the kind of lying farter that Langland so deplores, the rogue at the door, who must improvise and pander to gain admission and then shapes his performance to suit his audience's pleasure.

In part, such figures reflect the agonistic relationship between the performer and the more respectable writer, between the *literatus*, the troubadour or trouvère who had something of the status of a cleric or even author, and the *joglar* or *jongleur*, a mere popular entertainer, who might profit by using the words or tunes of others. The hostility is well captured by Chrétien de Troyes, who begins *Érec et Énide* by distinguishing his art, which offers a true version of the story, from the practice of the storytellers (the *conteurs*) who break the story apart and corrupt it:[89]

> d'Erec, le fil Lac, est li contes,
> que devant rois et devant contes
> depecier et corronpre suelent
> cil qui de conter vivre vuelent.
>
> > (The story is about Erec, the son of Lac, and it is one which those who
> > make their living telling stories before kings and nobles are in the habit of
> > breaking apart and corrupting.)

The accusation that lesser minstrels corrupt a story is echoed by many other writers. A number of these condemnations come from well-established minstrel-trouvères, men of letters who were also professional musicians and as such respectable

---

[88] Jean Leclercq, '"Ioculator et saltator": S. Bernard et l'image du jongleur dans les manuscrits'. Julian G. Plante, ed., *Translatio Studii: Manuscript and Library Studies Honoring Oliver L. Kapsner, O. S. B.* (Collegeville MN, 1973), 124–48; Jean Leclercq, 'L'idiot à la lumière de la tradition chrétienne'. *Revue histoire de la spiritualité* (1973), 288–304.

[89] Chrétien de Troyes, *Les Romans de Chrétien de Troyes, I: Éric et Énide*, ed. Mario Roques (Paris, 1963), lines 19–22, my translation.

gildsmen, like Adenet le Roi. Adenet begins his romance of the knight Ogier by condemning the lowly *jongleurs*, 'who do not know how to rhyme' ('qui ne sorent rimer'), for falsifying both the content and the meter of the work and says he no longer wants to hear the story of Ogier 'corrupted' ('corrompue').[90]

Similar comments can be found in the writings of other trouvères, such as Jean Bodel, in the introductions to Middle English works such as William of Nassington's *Speculum Vitae*, and, as we have seen, in Chandos Herald's *Vie du Prince Noir*. Froissart too is scornful in the introduction to his completion of Jehan le Bel: 'Pluiseur gongleour et enchanteour en place ont chanté et rimet lez guerres de Bretaigne et corumput, par leurs chançons et rimes controuvees, le juste et vraie histoire' (Many a jongleur or public singer have sung or made verses about the wars in Brittany and have corrupted the true and proper history with their verses and invented rhymes).[91]

These derogatory accounts should not be taken as direct historical reportage. Vernacular poets are scarcely unbiased witnesses and their criticisms are clearly a *topos*. For some vernacular writers, attaching oral performers was a means of promoting their own identity, allowing them something of the status of an author even while employing the humble mother tongue.[92] Conventionalized as they may be, however, these references to popular entertainers snatching up the works of others and then breaking them or distorting them to suit their audience do offer a kind of inverted tribute to the minstrel's art: they evoke a mental dexterity or ingenuity that allows the common man to 'surmount life's obstacles by manipulation and circumnavigation rather than by brute force or irresistible goodness', just as Marcolf and the *jongleur* of Ely did so well.[93] Here we have a further possible explanation for the fascination medieval people had for the figure of the minstrel, whether as a folk hero who bandies words with great lords or as a dangerous parasite who toadies to them.

---

[90] Adenet, *Œuvres*, III, *Les Enfances d'Ogier*, 59–60, lines 13–26. For further examples of the denigration of the oral performer by minstrel-authors, see Edmond Faral, *Les jongleurs en France au moyen âge* (Paris, 1910), 155–7, and Silvère Menegaldo, *Le jongleur dans la littérature narrative des XIIe et XIIIe siècles: du personage au masque* (Paris, 2005), 221–3. As Menegaldo notes, however, not all accounts are so derogatory (82–3, 264–75 *et passim*) and the reciting minstrel could also act as a representation of the writer (81).

[91] 953 Jean Froissart, *Chroniques, Livre I, Le Manuscrit d'Amiens*, ed. George T. Diller. 5 vols (Geneva, 1991–8), II, 96, my translation.

[92] On the construction of the medieval vernacular author, see Alastair Minnis, *Medieval Theory of Authorship: Scholastic Literary Attitudes in the Later Middle Ages*. 2nd edn (Philadelphia PA, 2010). For ways in which the figure of the oral performer could be used to enhance vernacular authorship, see Sylvia Huot, *From Song to Book: The Poetics of Writing in Old French Lyric and Lyrical Narrative Poetry* (Ithaca NY and London, 1987), 60–4. For the case of Chaucer and his depiction of minstrelsy in the *House of Fame*, see below, pp. 291–2.

[93] Robert W. Hanning, *The Individual in Twelfth-Century Romance* (New Haven CT and London, 1977), 106, defining the quality of 'engin' in twelfth-century romances, where it is associated with ingenious heroes such as Paris and Aeneas but also comes to represent the artifice of the 'trickster-poet' (109). Nancy Mason Bradbury draws the connection to Marcolf and his cleverness or 'ingenium', in 'Rival wisdom in the Latin dialogue of Solomon and Marcolf'. *Speculum* 83/2 (2008), 331–65, at 341.

Chrétien's two terms, *corronpre* (corrupt) and *depecier* (break apart) capture just what many a minstrel must have done on numerous occasions, modifying the story to flatter his listeners and appeal to their allegiances, thus corrupting the true version, and selecting from a long narrative tradition (which may never have coalesced into any fixed text, oral or written) the pieces that would most grip his audience.

Chrétien's term *depecier* is particularly suggestive because minstrel performances were probably generally fairly short. Writers such as Walter Scott and Léon Gautier drew freely on their imagination in their accounts of sustained recitation, and Gautier's concept of the sustained *séance épique* must be regarded at best as an unproven hypothesis inspired by bardic nostalgia. Of course, since so little evidence of minstrel performance survives, the hypothesis cannot simply be rejected. Perhaps on occasion minstrels did command their audience's attention for half an hour or more, or even an entire afternoon or evening.[94] Perhaps on some occasions they were even able to command attention over several days and work through a series of performances. After all, sequential readings of romances or other text were not unknown. Froissart, for one, possibly with some degree of self-serving aggrandizement, claims to have worked through a series of linked readings of his *Méliador*, night after night, for twelve weeks, at the court of Gaston Phoebus, Count of Foix.[95]

Of these two possibilities, sustained recitation on a single occasion and linked recitation over several days (the model of the *séance épique*), the former seems more likely. There are no historical records of such performances, but there are some vivid fictional accounts that do suggest how, on rare occasions, an especially bold and persuasive minstrel might engage the attention of the reigning lord and thus of his entire hall. One example occurs in *L'estoire de Merlin* (c. 1230), where a harper recites an entire Breton lay before Arthur's court:[96]

> Et li harperes aloit del .j. renc al autre & lor harpoit seriement & cler si le regarderent a merueilles li vn & li autre car il nauoient onques oi harper a cel guise. Si lor plot plus & enbelli le deduit del harpeor que de nule cose que li autre menestrel fisent.

---

[94] According to a charter of 1372, at Christmas, Easter, and Pentecost, and on feast days, the minstrel of Beauvais had the opportunity to 'chanter de geste' in the main square and no *jongleur* could sing there without his permission. See Faral, *Jongleurs*, 126. John W. Baldwin provides some examples of fictional accounts of short performances of parts of longer works in 'The image of the jongleur in northern France'. *Speculum* 72/3 (1997), 635–63, at 650.

[95] Jean Froissart, *Chroniques*, ed. Siméon Luce. 13 vols (Paris, 1869–99), III, cap. 13, 173–4 and *Dits et Debats*, ed. Anthime Fourrier (Geneva, 1979), 'Le Dit dou florin', 175–90, 186. Commentary on this highly self-reflexive scene is extensive. See, in particular, Peter F. Dembwoski, *Jean Froissart and His 'Méliador': Context, Craft and Sense* (Lexington KY, 1983); and Peter F. Ainsworth, *Jean Froissart and the Fabric of History* (Oxford, 1990), 154–5. On the tradition of sustained reading at court, see Joyce Coleman, *Public Reading and the Reading Public in Late Medieval England and France* (Cambridge, 1996).

[96] *The Vulgate Version of the Arthurian Romances*, ed. H. Oskar Sommer, Vol. II *Lestoire de Merlin* (Washington, 1908), 413; *The Old French Arthurian Vulgate and Post Vulgate in Translation*, gen. ed. Norris J. Lacy, Vol. II: *The Story of Merlin*, trans. Rupert T. Pickens (Cambridge, 2010), II, 441.

(And the harper went from one row to the next and played soothingly to everyone, and they all looked at him in wonder because they had never heard such harp-playing. And they found greater delight in the harper's playing than in anything the other minstrels did.)

While the harper goes from one row to the next, he appears to still the entire room and command some attention from all, including the king. Suggestively, however, this harper is none other than Merlin in disguise, and we may reasonably wonder how often any normal minstrel would have exercised such power.

A more extensive and complicated account of the performance of an entire work occurs in the late twelfth-century *Castia Gilos* (or *Castle of the Jealous*) of Raimon Vidal. This short poem of 450 lines is part cautionary tale, part *fabliau*, and part court satire. It begins with the narrator saying that he will retell a story that he heard a *joglar* deliver at the court of King Alfonso of Castille, a monarch on whom the narrator heaps praise:[97]

> Unas novas vos vuelh comtar
> que auzi dir a .I. joglar
> en la cort del pus savi rey
> que anc fos de neguna ley,
> del rey de Castela, n'Amfos,
> e qui era condutz e dos,
> sens e valors e cortezia
> e engenh de cavalayria;
> qu'el ne era onhs ni sagratz,
> mas de pretz era coronatz
> e de sen de lialeza
> e de valor e de proeza.
>
> (I wish to tell you a new story that I heard from a joglar at the court of the most wise king of any faith, the King of Castille, Alfonso, who has hospitality, good judgment, and valour, and courtesy, and the art of true chivalry, and who was never anointed or consecrated, but crowned for his good judgment, loyalty, valour, and prowess.)

After his queen, Eleanor, daughter of Henry II and Eleanor of Aquitaine, has taken her seat, a *joglar* enters and requests that he be heard (lines 26–31):

> Ab tan ve.us .I. joglar, ses bruy,
> denan lo rey franc, de bon aire,
> e.l. dis : 'Re, de pretz, emperaire,
> ieu soi vengut aisi a vos,
> e prec, sieus platz, que ma razos
> s'azuida e entenduda'.

---

[97] Raimon Vidal, *L'École des jaloux (Castia Gilos). Fabliau du XIIIe siècle par le troubadour catalan Raimon de Vidal de Bezalu*, ed. Irénée Cluzel (Paris, 1958), 21–2, line 13, drawing on Cluzel's translation. Cluzel suggests that the claim that Alfonso was never anointed or consecrated is a satirical allusion to the pretensions of the emperor (35, n. 3).

(At that moment, a *joglar* quietly approached the noble king, and said: 'Worthy king, emperor, I have come thus before you, and I ask you, if it please you, that my words be heard and given attention'.)

The king agrees to hear him and warns all those assembled that they must be silent, telling the court 'Whoever speaks before this man has expressed all he wishes has lost my love' ('M'amor a perduda / qui parlara d'aisi avan / tro aia dig tot son talan', lines 32–4). The *joglar* proceeds to tell the story of a jealous husband, Alfonso de Barbastre, who is warned by his knights that his wife is cuckolding him with one of them, a knight who is indeed desperately in love with her. The *joglar* says only that in all Aragon the knight is unrivalled for his chivalry ('car de bona cavalaria / non ac sa par en Arago', lines 62–3), but the king, the only one who interrupts the *joglar* as he tells his story, immediately identifies this perfect knight as Bascol de Cotando. At the suggestion of one of the other knights, who is 'villainous, churlish, and irresponsible' ('fel e vilan e leugier', line 90), the husband pretends that he is about to leave to assist the King of Léon in his wars, hoping to test his wife, and comes back at night pretending to be her supposed lover. His outraged wife pretends to be fooled, denounces the supposed Bascol as a traitor, beats him, and locks him in the room, and then proceeds to accept the real Bascol as her lover. Her husband rejoices in his injuries, convinced of his wife's fidelity. The *joglar* concludes by drawing the moral lessons: that women can always deceive men and that jealousy is a shameful sickness. King Alfonso then praises the *joglar* for his tale and rewards him generously. The *Castia Gilos* ends a mere ten lines later, saying that all the court enjoyed the story. The poem, in short, consists almost entirely of the story that the narrator claims he heard the *jongleur* tell.

The naming of both the lover and the jealous husband and a number of other current references suggest that the poem was designed to appeal to a specific and well-informed audience, who would get the joke. In fact, it may even have been delivered before King Alfonso himself, possibly at a great banquet that he gave in 1188, which marked a high point in his political maneuvers. On this occasion Alfonso knighted his cousin, the young King of Léon, Alfonso IX, and one of the younger sons of Emperor Frederick Barbarossa, and then announced their betrothal to his daughters, assigning his cousin the younger, Berengaria, thus crushing his cousin's political hopes to eventually succeed to the throne.[98] If Vidal himself read the poem at the ceremony, then there would have been an elaborate mirroring between the presentation by the fictional *joglar* in the poem, Vidal's own performance of this poem at the feast, and the subsequent circulation of the poem, either by other *joglars* or in manuscript.[99] If this ceremony was designed to humiliate Alfonso of Léon, as has been suggested (and the two cousins remained extremely hostile throughout their lives), then the poem, with its allusion to the need to help him in his wars, would have added to the sting. A public performance in 1188, whether by Vidal or his *joglar*, would have been highly charged, deriding the king's cousin, one of the two

---

[98] Linda M. Paterson, *The World of Troubadours: Medieval Occitan Society, c. 1100–c. 1300* (Cambridge and New York NY, 1993), 116–7.

[99] Ibid., 117, drawing on a suggestion of W.H.W. Field.

principal guests, and calling into question the chastity of all women in front of the young queen. Such a performance could only have been possible with the collusion of either the king himself or a handful of his barons brave enough to anticipate the king's desires. The *Castia Gilos*, then, suggests the kind of conditions under which a single *joglar* might command the attention of the entire hall, above all because he was not simply entertaining the court but delivering a message on the king's behalf, acting as a licensed conduit for royal displeasure.

The Middle English romance *Sir Cleges* (of the late fourteenth or early fifteenth century) offers a very different instance of a minstrel commanding the attention of the king and delivering a charged message, but this time in the relative privacy of his chamber. Here the minstrel's role is partly to provide solace and partly to provide advice. Cleges is a perfect knight: brave, loyal, and extremely generous to minstrels, so much so, indeed, that he ruins himself, and can only come to court disguised and in the poorest clothing. The king, however, receives him graciously, and thus Cleges is there in the king's chamber, when a harper sings his praises:[100]

The kynge was sett in hys parlore	
Wyth myrth, solas and onor;	
Sir Cleges thedyr went.	
An harpor sange a gest be mowth	
Of a knight ther be sowth,	
Hymeselffe [i.e., Cleges], werament.	[truly]
Than seyd the kynge to the harpor;	
'Were ys knyght Cleges, tell me here;	
For thou has wyde iwent.	
Telle me trewth, if thou can:	
Knowyste thou of that man?'	
The harpor seyd, 'Yee, iwysse'.	
Sum tyme forsooth I hym knewe;	
He was a kyght of youris full trewe	
And comly of gesture.	
We mynsetrellys mysse hym sekyrly,	[certainly]
Seth he went out of cunntré;	
He was fayre of stature'.	
The kyng sayd, 'Be myn hede,	
I trowe that Sir Cleges be dede.	
That I loved paramour.	
Wold God he were alyfe;	
I had hym levere than other five	
For he was stronge in stowre'.	[battle]

As does the *Castia Gilos*, *Sir Cleges* evokes a plausible set of performance conditions. The harper attends the king personally to provide solace in his more private

---

[100] *Middle English Metrical Romances*, ed. Walter H. French and Charles B. Hale. 2 vols (New York NY, 1930; repr. 1964), II, 892–3, lines 481–504. The spelling has been modernized slightly.

moments, as many harpers did in real life, for example when the king was being bled.[101] The harper knows the king's sympathies and chooses a hero for his *gest* who will appeal to him (and whose reputation is widespread because of his generosity to minstrels). When called upon, the minstrel can expand on his *gest*, telling the king what else he knows about the hero's recent doings, admittedly not very much. In doing so, his activity resembles what has sometimes been called 'urskyring', the prefixing of a ballad with a spoken account of the individuals involved.[102] There is no indication of how long the harper sang, but the situation suggests a relatively short performance, as if the harper limited himself to one or two of the most telling episodes in Cleges's life.

The *joglar* in *Castia Gilos* is described as if he were just a wanderer who happened to have dropped by, quite unknown to anyone there, but any such performance would have required precise knowledge of the court's undercurrents and the king's desires. The harper in *Sir Cleges*, who appears to be a household minstrel in regular attendance on the king, draws upon similar knowledge when he chooses to sing of a knight whose absence is already troubling the king. In each case, the performer anticipates or guesses his patron's feelings and then gives them expression. A rival knight or a humiliated guest would describe such performances very differently, however, and might well echo the accusations, from Chrétien de Troyes, Adenet le Roi, Langland, Froissart, the Chandos Herald and so many others, that minstrels are liars and toadies by profession.

The performance scenario that is most often mentioned, however, both in medieval works themselves and in modern criticism, is that of the great feast, where a host of minstrels contributes to the overall splendour of the occasion. The most copious literary account of such a feast comes from the Old Occitan romance *Flamenca*, composed around 1300, which describes a staggering multitude of diverse performers. When the table is cleared,[103]

> Apres se levon li juglar:
> Cascus se volc faire auzir.
> Adonc auziras retentir
> Cordas de manta tempradura.
> Qui saup novella violadura,
> Ni canzo ni descort ni lais,
> Al plus que poc avan si trais.
> L'uns viola[l] lais de Cabrefoil,

---

[101] On minstrelsy in the chamber, see pp. 5, 50–3, and on minstrelsy during blood-letting p. 75.

[102] One of the few scholars to address the phenomenon directly is William Motherwell, in *Minstrelsy, Ancient and Modern* (Glasgow, 1827): '[w]hen the singing or recitation of [these ballads] was the business of Minstrels, they were prefaced with some account of the previous history of the several individuals whom they respectively commemorate' (xiv). Motherwell was informed that this was also an Icelandic practice called *urskyring* (xvi).

[103] *The Romance of Flamenca: A Provençal Poem of the Thirteenth Century*, ed. Marion E. Porter, trans. Merton Jerome Hubert (Princeton NJ, 1962), lines 593–603, my translation.

E l'autre de Tintagoil;
L'us cantet dels Fins Amanz
E l'autre cel que fes Ivans.

> (Afterwards the *jongleurs* arose. Each one wished to make himself heard. Therefore, you could hear resounding chords tuned in many ways. Whoever knew a new piece for the viol, or a song, or a *descort*, or a *lai*, pushed himself forward as best as he could. One played on the viol the *lai* of the Honeysuckle, another one about Tintagel, and another sang of the Noble Lovers, and another the *lai* that was made about (or by) Yvain.)

The *jongleurs* sing and play over a dozen different instruments; they also offer lighter entertainment: juggling knives, tumbling, and jumping through hoops. They tell stories of Classical and Biblical heroes and of famous lovers, of Priamus, Piramus, Helen and Paris, Ulysses, Hector and Achilles, Aeneas and Dido, Alexander, Samson and Delilah, David and Goliath, Gawain, Lancelot, and Perceval, Arthur, Mordred, and Merlin. Only one author is mentioned specifically, Marcabru, but many of the heroes can be found either in the Bible, Ovid's *Metamorphoses*, or the romances of Chrétien de Troyes and his continuators, while the 'lais de Cabrefoil' has sometimes been associated with the lai *Chevrefeuil* of Marie de France, and the work 'que fes Ivans' (that Ivan made or that was made about Ivan) with the romance *Yvain* of Chrétien de Troyes.

Similar scenes can be found in innumerable romances, where the sound of a large number of minstrels playing on diverse instruments is an essential part of any feast.[104] The large number of minstrels at the feast is yet another *topos*; indeed, Geoffrey of Vinsauf, in his famous rhetorical manual the *Poetria nova*, actually suggests including references to musicians and entertainers as a form of *amplificatio* when describing feasts.[105] As we have seen, the pay records for minstrels tend to suggest that diverse and simultaneous performances were actually part of real courtly ceremonial: no medieval celebration ever attracted 1500 minstrels, but many attracted scores, even a hundred or more, and they appear to have performed individually (rather than being arranged into ensembles) and simultaneously, just like those in *Flamenca*.[106]

These literary depictions of minstrel performance at feasts illustrate in its most acute form the challenge of trying to reconstruct what minstrels actually did when they sang or recited. On the one hand, the figure of the minstrel is so highly conventionalized and symbolically charged that no account can be regarded

---

[104] See, among others, Chrétien de Troyes, *Les Romans I: Éric et Énide*, lines 1983–2000; Jean Renard, *L'Escoufle: roman d'aventure*, ed. Franklin P. Sweetser (Geneva, 1974), lines 8987–9005; *Floriant et Florete*, ed. Harry F. Williams (Ann Arbor MI, 1947), lines 5962–80; Adenet le Roi, *Œuvres V: Cleomadés*, lines 17281–302 and discussions in Faral, *Jongleurs*, 97–102, and Menegaldo, *Jongleur*, 229–33 and 617–29.

[105] Geoffrey of Vinsauf, *Poetria nova*, trans. Margaret F. Nims, rev. edn, with an intro by Martin Camargo (Toronto, 2010), 38; Jean-Pierre Martin, *Les motifs dans la chanson de geste: définition et utilisation: (discours de l'épopée médiévale 1)* (Paris, 2017), 36; Menegaldo, *Jongleur*, 87–8.

[106] On minstrels at banquets, see pp. 79–81.

as straightforward reporting. On the other, if we credit these references with any degree of historical accuracy, they suggest that there must have been a profound gap between the texts that survive, often running to thousands of lines, and the lost performances, most of which must have normally been far shorter. The great chivalric feasts, often thought of as the pre-eminent occasion for minstrel performance, provided especially challenging conditions that would have made fragmenting a story an absolute necessity. The surviving texts, many of which present themselves as if they were minstrel recitations, and many of which praise the same core heroes or tell the same stories that are said to have been the minstrels' standard fare, thus bear a problematic relation to the lost oral practice. The two were not the same but they were connected, and the nature of this connection is not easy to determine.

12

Professional recitation before the fourteenth century

Andrew Taylor

The *joglars* as wanderers or travellers

The one substantial body of medieval poetry that almost everyone agrees was regularly performed by professionals is that of the troubadours, the poets who composed love lyrics and satires in Old Occitan (or, as it is still sometimes called, Old Provençal) from the eleventh to the thirteenth centuries, and sometimes later, and their professional reciters, the *joglars*. On the whole, poets working in English seem to have drawn more heavily on Northern French traditions, often transmitted through Anglo-Norman works, but England maintained extensive ties to the south, above all in Aquitaine, which remained an English possession until 1453. The practice of the *joglars* may, therefore, provide insights into the later practice of the English minstrels.

The distinction between troubadour and *joglar* was never a firm one. An impecunious troubadour might act as his own *joglar*, a gifted *joglar* compose his own material.[1] It also seems likely that during their own lives many a *joglar* and many a troubadour would have performed a variety of functions at the court; the categories impose an artificial clarity.[2] The *vidas*, or short life stories, of the troubadours provide numerous examples of less fortunate troubadours who travelled the country reciting their own verse. The more desirable pattern, however, at least for the more prosperous, was to entrust the performance to a professional singer, the *joglar*. Many of the *joglars* are identified in the final lines of the poems, as when Bertran de Born concludes his plaint *Dompna, puois de mi no'us cal* ('Lady, since you don't care for me') by calling on his *joglar* Papiol to visit the lady.[3]

---

[1] Faral, *Jongleurs*, 79; Ruth E. Harvey, '*Joglars* and the professional status of the early troubadours'. *Medium Aevum* 62/2 (1993), 221–41, at 222–3; Elizabeth Aubrey, *The Music of the Troubadours* (Bloomington IN, 1996), xix.

[2] Harvey, '*Joglars*', 232.

[3] Bertran de Born, *The Poems of Bertran de Born*, ed. William D. Paden, Tilde Sankovitch and Patricia H. Stäblein (Berkeley CA, 1986), 158–9.

The other rich source of information about these singers is found in the *sirventes joglaresc* and *enshamen-sirventes* (satires against *joglars* and satires to teach *joglars*), in which a troubadour heaps abuse, often in the guise of instruction, on his own performer. Thus we hear, for example, the Catalan nobleman Guera de Cabrera complaining that his *joglar* Cabra (Goat) cannot play the *veille* properly, nor sing well, nor leap like the Gascon *joglars*, and is ignorant of a long list of songs, including those on famous heroes such as Augier (Ogier the Dane), Olivier (Roland's companion), and Girart de Rossillon (the hero of a famous *chanson de geste*).[4] Such texts were no doubt elaborately ironical, and the suggested repertory at least in part a joke, but they do suggest a well-established practice of using a professional to circulate one's songs.

Drawing on the *vidas* and the references to particular *joglars* in the poems themselves, it is possible to reconstruct something of the *joglar*'s trade as practised in Occitania. William Paden Jr has managed to identify eighty-one *joglars* in all, of whom sixty-seven are mentioned by one poet alone. He concludes:[5]

> It appears that the typical joglar performed the songs of a single poet, and was rewarded by the individual to whom the troubadour sent him. For this reason a joglar would approach a troubadour and ask him for a song. The typical joglar seems to have been no vagabond but a skilled messenger who was sent on a specific mission and encouraged to complete it by the prospect of a specific reward.

Occitan, therefore, provides both an early example, perhaps even one of the sources, for the literary image of the wandering minstrel and a certain amount of evidence for a significantly different professional practice, which entailed well-calculated journeys between patrons who knew each other – travelling, not wandering.

The fullest depiction of a *joglar*'s movements, one which falls somewhere between travelling and wandering, is that in *Abril issia* of Raimon Vidal, the author of the *Castia Gilos*. Once again, Vidal begins by having the narrator meet a *joglar* and the poem is made up almost entirely of that *joglar*'s story. One spring, as April was leaving and May was coming in, and he was walking in the main square of his hometown, Besalú in north-east Catalonia, the narrator was greeted by a *joglar* dressed and shod after the fashion 'of the time in which valour and worth were both found in the barons' ('a fort del temps / on hom trobava totz essems/ justa·ls baros valor

---

[4] Manuel Mila y Fontanals, *De los Trovatores en España: Estudio lengua y poesia provenzal* (Barcelona, 1861), 265–77. A more recent (but partial) edition is provided by Rita Lejeune, 'La forme de l'*Ensenhamen au jongleur* du troubadour Guiraut de Cabrera'. *Estudis Romànics* 9 (1961), 171–81. François Pirot concludes that the poet was Viscount Guerau III, who is mentioned in documents from 1145 to 1159, and that the poem must have been written no later than 1165: *Recherches sur les connaissances littéraires des troubadours occitans et catalans des XIIe et XIIIe siècles* (Barcelona, 1972), 196. Stefano M. Cingolani has argued that he is more likely to have been Guerau's grandson, Guerau IV, who might have composed the work around 1196–8: 'The *Sirventes-ensenhamen* of Guerau de Cabrera: a proposal for a new interpretation'. *Journal of Hispanic Research* 1 (1992–3), 191–201.

[5] William D. Paden, 'The role of the joglar in Troubadour lyric poetry'. Peter S. Noble and Linda M. Paterson, eds, *Chrétien de Troyes and the Troubadour: Essays in Memory of the Late Leslie Topsfield* (Cambridge, 1984), 90–111, at 94.

e pretz').⁶ The *joglar*, who has been on a quest to find true generosity worthy of the golden age of patronage, describes with great verisimilitude his journey, which begins in Riom, in the Auvergne, at Christmastime. He then journeys ten kilometres south, to the palace of the great troubadour and patron of troubadours Count Dalfi d'Alvernhe, at Montferrand (now a suburb of Clermont-Ferrand). The count welcomes him, brings him to sit by the fire, and, after most of the company has retired, inquires about his quest and explains to him the true nature of *saber*, the combination of self-control, good manners, social sophistication, and poetic knowledge that a minstrel must practise to be at home at court.⁷ Generously rewarded, the minstrel then journeys south-east to Le Puy and south into Provence, turns westward to find the Count of Toulouse, and then turns south once more, to Foix, where he finds the Count of Foix has already left. The minstrel then continues across the Pyrenees, arriving at last at Besalú. All told he has covered over six hundred kilometres in a period of about four months. The anonymous minstrel and his conversation with Dalfi d'Alvernhe may simply be a literary device, allowing Raimon Vidal to advance his own theories of the poetic art indirectly, but this journey sounds plausible enough.⁸

Of course, one cannot take the account offered by the *vidas* or by works such as *Abril issia* entirely at face value. The earliest of the *vidas* were probably not composed before about 1250, and the anonymous biographers would have had only partial information available to them. In many cases, the *vidas* simply extrapolate from the poem, reading their literary conventions, with their accounts of lovelorn troubadours forced into exile by jealous husbands, literally. When they use the term *joglar* they may be doing so only to 'plug a gap in the biographer's knowledge'.⁹ Furthermore, the *vidas* were arguably highly nostalgic, and offer an idealized vision of Occitanian court life, in part as a form of cultural resistance to the northern French in the wake of the Albigensian crusade.¹⁰ This sense of nostalgia is strong in Raimon Vidal, who evokes an image of himself as 'a poet who had come too late', after the age of the great patrons was past.¹¹ In their depiction of troubadour and *joglar*, the *vidas* may provide one of the earliest examples of how the figure of the man who gives his

---

6 Raimon Vidal, *Poetry and Prose, Volume II: Abril Issia*, ed. W.H.W. Field (Chapel Hill NC, 1971), lines 23–5, Field's translation.

7 Elizabeth Wilson Poe, 'The meaning of Saber in Raimon Vidal's *Abril Issia*'. *Studia Occitanica in Memoriam Paul Remy. Vol II. The Narrative-Philology*, ed. Hans-Erich Keller (Kalamazoo MI, 1986), 169–78.

8 Drawing on the poem and other sources, including a fifteenth-century sketch of the palace at Montferrand, Page describes the journey, which he characterizes as a 'fiction, but a realistic one', in detail: *Owl and Nightingale*, 53.

9 Harvey, 'Joglars', 232.

10 Eliza Miruna Ghil, *L'Age de parage: Essai sur le poétique et le politique en Occitanie au xiiie siècle* (New York NY, 1989), 38–56; Harvey, 'Joglars', 224. The *vidas* were probably written by Occitan exiles living in northern Italy. See Christian J.M. Anatole, 'Le souvenir de Muret et de la dépossession des comtes de Toulouse dans les vidas et les razos'. *Annales de l'Institut d'Études occitanes, Actes du colloque de Toulouse (9, 10 et 11 septembre 1963)* (1962–3), 11–22, at 18.

11 Page, *Owl and Nightingale*, 46.

life to poetry, either as composer, or as a performer, or both, and who wanders from castle to castle, celebrating the exalted love of the aristocracy, becomes part of an imaginary Middle Ages.

Given the powerful nostalgia in these accounts, it is hard to know how far we can accept the standard view that the troubadour movement was largely confined to the lands that spoke Occitan, that it ran only until about 1300, and that its golden age was already over by about 1210. The troubadours came from the area where some version of the *langue d'oc*, either Occitan or the related Catalan, was actually spoken, an area which stretched north almost as far as Poitiers, and there has been a longstanding tendency to claim their poetry for the region.[12] According to the thirteenth-century chronicler Philippe Mouskes, Charlemagne ceded the land to the minstrels:[13]

> Quar quant li buens rois Charlemainne
> Ot toute mise à son demainne
> Provence qui mult iert plentive
> De vins, de bois, d'aigüe, de rive
> As léceours, as manestreus [menestreux],
> Qui sunt auques luxurieus
> Le donna toute & départi.
>
> (For when the good king Charlemagne had taking control, he gave all of Provence, which is most plentiful in wine, woods, banks and rivers, to the lechers and minstrels, who are so lascivious, and then left.)

So, as Du Cange concluded, 'Indeque postea tantum in hac regione Poëtarum numerum excrevisse' ('And therefore, in this region of Provence, the number of poets [is said] to have grown').[14] While the passage denigrates minstrels it nonetheless claims that they have a special association with this fertile and sensuous land; the vision was widespread in the Middle Ages and has endured.[15] The Occitan of the troubadours, however, was a literary language, a *koine*.[16] It was used by court society in a much wider swathe of Europe, indeed wherever the patrons of the troubadours,

---

[12] See, for example, Gérard Zauchetto, *Terre des Troubadours: XIIIe et XIIIe siècles*, preface by Max Roquette (Paris, 1996), which reinforces this sense of geographical identity with photographs of the countryside from which each troubadour originally came. On Zauchetto's approach to Occitan identity, see John Haines, *Eight Centuries of Troubadours and Trouvères: The Changing Identity of Medieval Music* (Cambridge, 2004), 285–6.

[13] Philippe Mouskes, *Chronique rimée de Philippe Mouskes, évêque de Tournay au treizième siècle*, ed. Baron de Reiffenberg, 3 vols (Brussels 1836–45), II, 383, lines 2249–35. Eliza Zingesser discusses this gift in *Stolen Song: How the Troubadours Became French* (Ithaca NY, 2020), 6–7, 196–7.

[14] *Ibid.*, 383, lines 22429–35, and Du Cange, *Glossarium*, sub 'Ministelli' (*sic*), 772.

[15] For one influential statement, see C.S. Lewis, *The Allegory of Love: A Study in a Medieval Tradition* (London, 1936), p. 2: 'Every one has heard of courtly love, and every one knows that it appears quite suddenly at the end of the eleventh century in Languedoc'.

[16] Max Pfister, 'La langue de Guilhem IX, comte de Poitiers'. *Cahiers de Civilisation Médiévale* 19 (1976), 91–113; Sarah Kay, *Parrots and Nightingales: Troubadour Quotations and the Development of European Poetry* (Philadelphia PA, 2013), 9–10.

peripatetic aristocrats, might find themselves. Thus, the *vida* of the famous Bernart de Ventadorn, who came from north-east Perigord, tells us that he was forced into exile when he fell in love with his lord's wife, that he was then at the court of Eleanor of Aquitaine and fell in love with her, and that when Henry married her and took her to England, 'Lord Bernart remained here [on this side of the sea], sad and grieving' ('En Bernartz si remas de sai tristz e dolentz').[17] One of his own poems, however, makes it clear that Bernart actually did travel to England.[18]

Contact between the troubadours and *joglars* and the English court

Whatever connections there may have been between the troubadours and the royal or baronial courts in England, they have certainly not left many traces. It is sometimes suggested that one of the earliest troubadours, Marcabru, who composed in the 1130s and visited the courts at Toulouse and Poitiers, also visited England.[19] The story is based on an episode in the thirteenth-century romance *Joufroi de Poitiers* in which the Poitevins, under siege from the Count of Toulouse, send out a minstrel/troubadour named Marchabruns to find their lord, Jofroi, who has come to the court of Henry II in disguise.[20] Even assuming this Marchabruns is based on the historical Marcabru, there seems no particular reason to credit the story.

The one troubadour (apart from Richard I) who is definitely known to have spent time in England was Savaric de Mauléon, a minor baron whose home estate was about a hundred kilometres north-west of Poitiers. Savaric first came to England as a prisoner of King John in 1202, who imprisoned him in Corfe castle in Dorset. Savaric managed to get his guards drunk and took over the castle. He was allowed to return to France, and then entered John's service as seneschal of Poitou. He returned to England ten years later to fight on John's behalf against his rebellious English barons, and was rewarded with extensive English holdings. After John's death, Savaric, who was named as one of his executors, returned to France, this time to serve Henry III as seneschal of both Poitou and Gascony, although eventually surrendering La Rochelle to King Louis.[21]

---

[17] Jean Boutière, A.H. Schutz, and I.M. Cluzel, *Biographies des Troubadours: Textes Provençaux des XIIe et XIVe siècles*. 2nd edn (Paris, 1964), 21; Margarita Egan, trans., *The Vidas of the Troubadours* (New York NY, 1984), 12.

[18] 'Lancan vei per me landa'. See discussion in Ruth E. Harvey, 'Eleanor of Aquitaine and the troubadours'. Marcus Bull and Catherine Léglu, eds, *The World of Eleanor of Aquitaine: Literature and Society in Southern France between the Eleventh and the Twelfth Centuries* (Woodbridge, 2005), 101–14, at 104–5.

[19] Boutière et al., *Biographies*, 13, n. 3. Gaunt, Harvey and Paterson find no evidence of such a visit, although allowing that 'Marcabru's attachment to the dynastic interests of the house of Poitou seems more profound than has hitherto been suspected': Simon Gaunt, Ruth Harvey and Linda M. Paterson, eds, *Marcabru: A Critical Edition* (Cambridge, 2000), 4.

[20] *Joufroi de Poitiers: Roman d'aventure du XIIIe siècle*, ed. Percival B. Fay and John L. Grigsby (Geneva, 1972), line 3603.

[21] H.J. Chaytor, *Savaric de Mauléon, Baron and Troubadour* (Cambridge, 1939), 77; W.L. Warren, *King John*. 3rd edn (New Haven CT, 1997), 255.

Savaric was both a troubadour and a patron of other troubadours, including Jausbert de Puycibot, whom he first set up as a *joglar*, providing him a horse and costume, and Uc de Saint Circ, who became a friend.[22] One *tenso*, or poetic dialogue, between Savaric and two other troubadours concerns the question of whether a lady, Guilhelma, who has to meet all three of her admirers at the same time, shows the greatest favour to the one she gives a gentle look, the one whose hand she squeezes, or the one whose foot she presses.[23] According to the accompanying *razo*, which may have been composed by Uc, Savaric raised the question after discovering that he himself had been in that very situation, fondly believing that Guilhelma inclined to him alone until his two rivals undeceived him.[24] A second *razo*, in which Uc explicitly mentions himself as the author, describes how Savaric, long scorned by the same Guilhelma, abandons her for another and is rewarded with a promise of an assignation, only to have Guilhelma, who somehow manages to hear of this, offer an assignation herself, but for the very same day. Savaric accordingly writes to the Provost of Limoges asking him to participate in a *tenso* on the question of which assignation he should keep.[25]

These poems can scarcely be taken as an accurate account of Savaric's love-life, but they do suggest a great deal about the literary circle in which he moved during his years as seneschal of Poitou for King John and that this literary circle actually was limited to the Continent. The two *tensos* and their accompanying *razos* are filled with the names of the troubadours and nobles from Limousin, Poitou, and Gascony. The cruel fair herself is identified as a Gascon, Guilhelma of Benauges (just south of Bordeaux), wife of Sir Peire de Gavaret.[26] Chaytor, an admirer, suggests that 'possibly the only centre in the province at which troubadour or jongleur could find a welcome and obtain a hearing was the court of Savaric de Mauléon'.[27] The numerous references to noble patrons, however, create the impression of a series of small courts of enthusiasts, whose love poems are as much insider jokes as anything. Not a single English name is mentioned.

On the other hand, there is no doubt that many troubadours and *joglars* performed before English rulers when they were on the Continent. Eleanor's patronage has perhaps been exaggerated, in keeping with the romantic conventions of the *vidas*, in which the troubadour's song arises from his frustrated love for a great lady.[28] Given the evidence of Bernart de Ventadorn's close connection with the English

---

[22] Boutière *et al.*, *Biographies*, 239; Egan, *Vidas*, 110; W.P. Shephard, *Jausbert de Puycibot* (Paris, 1924).

[23] Chaytor, *Savaric de Mauléon*, 87–90, using the edition of Erhrad Lommatzsch, *Provenzalisches Liederbuch, Lieder der Troubadours mit einer Auswahl biographischer Zeugnisse, Nachdichtungen und Singweisen* (Berlin, 1917).

[24] Chaytor, *Savaric de Mauléon*, 67–8; Boutière *et al.*, *Biographies*, 227–8.

[25] Boutière *et al.*, *Biographies*, 223–6; Chaytor, *Savaric de Mauléon*, 71–5.

[26] For efforts to identify the ladies see Boutière *et al.*, *Biographies*, 225, n. 1; and Fritz Bergert, *Die von den Trobadors gennanten oder gefeierten Damen* (Halle, 1913), 29–30.

[27] Chaytor, *Savaric de Mauléon*, 65.

[28] Retto R. Bezzola, *Les origines et la formation de la littérature courtoise en occident (500–1200)*. 2 vols (vol. 2 in 2 parts) (Paris, 1958–63), III, part 1, 259, and Harvey, 'Eleanor of

court, however, it would seem that if he was not working under Eleanor's patronage, he must have been working under the patronage of her husband. He was probably not alone, although no other known troubadour or *joglar* can be positively identified as a member of Henry's household. Literary criticism has focussed, not unreasonably, 'on the known Occitan exponents of the art of *trobar* whose works have survived, rather than obscure *ioculatores*'.[29] It is these obscure practitioners, however, who would have passed the poetic and cultural traditions of the troubadours and *joglars* to England.

Of course, one famous Angevin king was himself a poet. Richard I was renowned for his love of music and poetry, his taste for the chivalric *beau geste*, and his generosity to minstrels. A number of poems are attributed to him, the best known being the plaint he allegedly composed while a prisoner in Austria, 'Ja nuls hom pres' ('No man who is a prisoner'), which is in the *langue d'oil*, the language he spoke most often.[30] Richard is also credited with a *sirventes* in the *langue d'oc* directed against Dalfi d'Alvernhe, the patron who welcomed Raimon Vidal.[31]

The *razo* of the poems of Arnaut Daniel, the man Dante praised as a 'better craftsman' (*miglior fabbro*), tells how once, at the court of Richard, Arnaut bet his palfrey against another *joglar*, who claimed he could produce 'more precious rhymes' ('pus caras rimas').[32] The king duly locked both up for ten days so they could prepare. Arnaut, so bored that he could not compose, eavesdropped on his competitor in the next chamber, who sang his song all night so that he would know it well ('per so que be la saubes'). When both appeared before the king, Arnaut sang his competitor's song, and then revealed the trick. Richard rewarded both generously. The story follows a common folkloric pattern, but it does indicate something of Richard's reputation as a patron; it seems entirely likely that he enjoyed the songs of Arnaut Daniel and welcomed him, but there is no proof. Perhaps all we can say is that the report is in keeping with Richard's fame as a patron, 'tant larcs, tant rics, tant arditz, tals donaire' ('so generous, so powerful, so ardent, so giving') as Gauclem Faidit said in his *planh* for Richard's death.[33]

There is, then, some evidence that the Angevins were generous patrons of the troubadours and *joglars*, and they were certainly cast as great patrons by their early chroniclers. But the case of Bertran de Born, a poor knight from the Limousin who

---

Aquitaine', reject the more enthusiastic picture offered by Rita Lejeune, 'Le rôle littéraire d'Aliénor d'Aquitane'. *Cultura Neolatina* 14 (1954), 5–57.

[29] Harvey, 'Eleanor of Aquitaine', 102, n. 5.

[30] F.J.M. Raynouard, *Choix des poésies originales des troubadours*. 6 vols (Paris, 1816), IV, 183–4. A version in Occitan also survives, but this was probably a translation. See H.J. Chaytor, *The Troubadours and England* (Cambridge, 1923), 56, n. 2.

[31] C.A.F. Mahn, *Die Werke der Troubadours*, 2 vols (Berlin, 1846–86), I, 129.

[32] *Purgatorio*, XXVI, 117. Boutière et al., *Biographies*, 62–3; Arnaut Daniel, *The Poetry of Arnaut Daniel*, ed. and trans. James J. Wilhelm (New York and London, 1981), xv–xvi; *Les poésies d'Arnaut Daniel*, ed. René Lavaud (Geneva, 1910), 119, n. 2; and *Canzoni: nuova edizione*, ed. Maurizio Perugi (Florence, 2015).

[33] 1001 Gaucelm Faidit, *Les poèmes de Gaucelm Faidit*, ed. Jean Mouzat (Paris, 1965), poem 50, line 13, my translation.

was known for his biting *sirventes*, illustrates some of the challenges of determining how close the relation between troubadour and patron really was. Bertran was initially an enthusiastic supporter of the Young King (Henry, heir apparent to the Angevin throne, whom his father, Henry II, crowned king of England in 1170). Bertran supported the Young King in his revolt against his father in 1183 and mocked him as the 'king of knaves' (*reis dels malvatz*) when he made peace.[34] After the Young King's death, Bertran supported his brothers, first Geoffrey and then Richard. How much contact this minor knight actually had with the princes, and how influential his *sirventes* were in inciting conflict is debatable. Bertran presented himself as a man who loved war and was valued by great patrons for his propaganda. His earliest datable poem begins by claiming great influence:[35]

> Lo coms m'a mandat e mogut
> per n'Araimon Luc d'Esparo
> q'ieu fassa per lui tal chansso
> on sion trencat mil escut,
> elm et auberc et alcoto,
> e perpoing falst e romput.
>
> > (The count [Raimon V of Tolouse] has asked and urged me through Sir Araimon Luc d'Esparo to make him a song that will chop a thousand shields, helmets, and hauberks and coats of mail and pierce doublets and tear them.)

W.L. Warren, however, judges that Bertran's fame as a poet has 'beguiled' historians into accepting his claims, and that 'it is extremely doubtful if his name-dropping and assertions of familiarity with the great are anything more than absurd pretensions'.[36]

The court of Henry II and Eleanor of Aquitaine, which welcomed Bernart de Ventadorn, or that of their son Richard, may represent the highpoint of Occitan poetry in England, but probably not its conclusion. Henry III's marriage to Eleanor of Provence in 1236 brought a flood of nobles from the area of the *langue d'oc*. As Matthew Paris commented, even London 'was full to overflowing, not only of Poitevins, Romans, and Provençals, but also of Spaniards, who did great injury to the English'.[37] There may have been *joglars* in the train of these lords, or in those of Simon de Montfort, whom Henry III appointed as his lieutenant in Gascony in 1248, or in that of Peter des Roches, bishop of Winchester, who was from Touraine.[38] How long such patronage might have continued is not clear. The one minstrel who

---

[34] Bertran de Born, *Poems*, poem 11, line 8.

[35] *Ibid.*, poem 1, lines 1–6.

[36] W.L. Warren, *Henry II* (Berkeley CA, 1973), 577.

[37] Giles, J.A., trans., *Mathew Paris's English History from the Year 1235 to 1273*. 3 vols (London, 1852–4), III, 151, cited in Albert C. Baugh and Thomas Cable, *A History of the English Language*. 5th edn (Upper Saddle River NJ, 2002), 132.

[38] J.R. Maddicott, *Simon de Montfort* (Cambridge, 1994), 107; Chaytor, *The Troubadours and England*, 79.

can be identified is Richard le Harpeur, who served Henry in Gascony.[39] In 1242 he was retained *ad solacium puerorum* ('to entertain the boys'). Chaytor suggests that 'the boys in question were Prince Edward and the eldest son of Nicolas de Molis, a Gascon who was brought up with him'.[40] In 1255 Henry ordered that Richard and his wife be given fur cloaks. The future Edward I had extensive dealings with Poitivin and Savoyard lords, but no reference to their *jongleurs* survives.[41]

While there is little evidence of known troubadours or *joglars* at the Angevin courts, let alone of them visiting England, their literary influence was still significant. As Peter Dronke notes, 'Northern France, so rich in narrative love-poetry, has no tradition of love-lyric comparable in range and stature to the Provençal'.[42] It is possible, therefore, that it was the tradition of Occitan that inspired the composers of early Anglo-Norman and English love lyrics.[43] Derek Pearsall has suggested that the lyrics found in BL MS Harley 2253, the manuscript that contains the *Jongleur of Ely*, which was copied perhaps as late as 1340, shows this influence, albeit 'largely through the medium of Anglo-Norman'.[44] Whether through direct contact with *joglars* working in the Occitanian tradition, or indirectly, through contact with northern French and Anglo-Norman *jongleurs*, England would inherit the image of the wandering *joglar* and transform it into the image of the wandering minstrel. So in the Anglo-Norman *Horn*, probably composed in the 1170s, the eponymous hero, returning to seek his beloved Rigmel, disguises himself and his hundred companions as wandering *jongleurs*:[45]

> Cent compaignuns menat, ke mult sunt de valor.
> Harpes portent asquanz, vieles li plusor:
> Ço volt sire Horn k'il seint jugleor.

---

[39] Chaytor, *The Troubadours and England*, 79, n. 2, citing Charles Bémont, *Rôles Gascons, transcrits et publiés par Francisque Michel*. 3 vols (Paris, 1885–1906), I, 22, no. 149 and I, 433, no. 3508. See also François Mugnier, *Les Savoyards en Angleterre au xiiie siècle, et Pierre d'Aigueblanche, évêque d'Hereford* (Paris, 1891), 208, referring to no. 3508 only.

[40] Chaytor, *The Troubadours and England*, 79, n. 2.

[41] Prestwich, *Edward I*, 21, drawing on Michael Clanchy, *England and Its Rulers, 1066–1272*. 3rd edn (Oxford, 2006), 210–40, and W.H. Ridgeway, 'The politics of the English royal court, 1247–65, with special reference to the role of the aliens'. DPhil. diss. (Oxford, 1983). See also W.H. Ridgeway, 'Foreign favourites and Henry III's problems of patronage, 1247–1258'. EHR 104/412 (1989), 590–610.

[42] Peter Dronke, *The Medieval Lyric*. 2nd edn (London, 1978), 126.

[43] See, for example, for Marie de France and Northern French writers, Huot, 'Troubadour Lyric and Old French Narrative'; for Chrétien de Troyes, Maria Luisa Meneghetti, *Il pubblico dei trovatori: ricezione e riuso dei testi lirici cortesi fino al XIV secolo*. 2nd edn (Turin, 1992), 138–44; and for Jean Renart and Gerbert de Montreuil, William D. Paden, 'Old Occitan as a lyric language: the insertions from Occitan in three thirteenth-century French romances'. *Speculum* 68/1 (1993), 36–53.

[44] Derek Pearsall, *Old English and Middle English Poetry* (London, 1977), 127.

[45] Thomas, *The Romance of Horn by Thomas*, ed. Mildred K. Pope, rev. T.B.W. Reid (Oxford, 1964), lines 5164–6.

(He brought a hundred companions, who were of great valour. Some
carried harps, most veilles. Lord Horn wanted them to seem like *jongleurs*.)

In the Middle English version, however, when Horn and his companions, who call themselves simply, 'harpurs' and 'gigours', that is fiddlers, appear before the castle what they perform is their 'gleowinge' or glee, a term that is rooted in the Old English tradition.[46] So an image of the wandering minstrel who turns up, unannounced and unrecognized at a castle, moves from the Continental into the English tradition.

Epic recitation before the fourteenth century

The English tradition

Middle English inherited from Old English two terms for an oral performer: *gleeman* and *scop*. La3amon, in his translation and reworking of Wace's *Brut*, employs both on several occasions. In his description of the feast that the British king Belyn holds for his brother Brenne, for example, La3amon says that 'Bemes [trumpets] þar bleuwen; blisse was on folke./ þar was gleomenne songe; þar was piping among'.[47] Similarly, after Arthur returns from accepting the allegiance of King Rumared of Winetland (possibly Gwynedd), he holds a feast, with fiddlers, song, harping, piping, and trumpeting, and 'Scopes þer sungen of Arðure þan kingen'.[48] These are the last uses of the term recorded by the *Middle English Dictionary*, and they are not easy to date. La3amon may have composed the *Brut* as early as 1189 and as late as the end of the thirteenth century.[49] It should also be noted that La3amon's style is deliberately archaic. Eric Stanley goes so far as to describe his use of alliterative poetic compounds as 'tokens of a past recreated by re-animating fossils of an extinct art form', as if advertising 'the English past by putting up *ye olde* signs'.[50] Perhaps all we can conclude from La3amon's use of the term *scop* is that some memory of the

---

[46] *King Horn: An Edition Based on Cambridge University Library MS. Gg. 4.27(2)*, ed. Rosamund Allen (New York NY, 1984), lines 1505–6, 1502.

[47] La3amon, *La3amon: Brut*, ed. G.L. Brooke and R.F. Leslie. 2 vols EETS o.s. 250, 277 (London, 1963–78), I, lines 2547–8 (Otho text). The version in BL Cotton MS Caligula A ix, often preferred as closer to La3amon's original, uses the phrase 'þer weore segge songe'.

[48] La3amon *Brut*, I, line 11330 (Caligula text).

[49] The range of the dating is set by a reference to the death of Henry II, offering a *terminus a quo* of 1189, and the palaeographical dating of the two manuscripts, in the second half of the thirteenth century. See Neil Cartlidge, 'The composition and social context of Oxford, Jesus College MS 29 (II) and London, British Library, MS Cotton Caligula A.IX'. *Medium Ævum* 66/2 (1997), 250–69, at 250. On the relation between the two versions see Lucy Perry, 'Origins and originality: reading Lawman's "Brut" and the rejection of British Library MS Cotton Otho C.xiii', *Arthuriana* 10/2 (2000), 66–84.

[50] Eric G. Stanley, 'La3amon's antiquarian sentiments'. *Medium Ævum* 38 (1969), 23–37, at 30. For a more sympathetic reading of La3amon's style, which still acknowledges elements of archaizing, see Daniel G. Donoghue, 'La3amon's ambivalence'. *Speculum* 65/3 (1990), 537–63; and Mark Amodio, *Writing the Oral Tradition* (Notre Dame IN, 2004), 101–6.

tradition of Old English recitation survived at least as late as the end of the twelfth century.

For a full sense of the power of the word *scop* we must return to *Beowulf*, which offers the most extensive description of a medieval European oral performance by a minstrel or his equivalent. The poem is preserved in a single manuscript, which may be as late as the early eleventh century, but may have originally been composed three or more centuries earlier and reflect still earlier social practice.[51] After Beowulf has killed Grendel, Hrothgar, King of the Danes, hosts a celebratory banquet at which his *scop* sings:[52]

> Þær wæs sang ond sweg   samod ætgædere
> for Healfdenes   hildewisan,
> gomenwudu greted,   gid oft wrecen,
> ðonne healgamen   Hroþgares scop
> æftere medobence   mænan scolde,
> Finnes eaferan: ða hie se fær begeat,
> hæleð Healf-Dena,   Hnæf Scyldinga,
> in Freswæle   feallan scolde.
>
> (There was song and music together
> before the leader of Healfdene's forces,   [Hrothgar]
> the wooden harp was touched, tales often told,
> when Hrothgar's *scop* was set to recite
> among the mead tables his hall-entertainment   [healgamen]
> about the sons of Finn, surprised in ambush,
> when the hero of the Half-Danes, Hnæf the Scylding,
> had to fall in a Frisian slaughter.)

There follow ninety lines evoking this grim feud. The presentation is obscure, but as far as scholars can tell, partly by referring to another anonymous poetic fragment, the Frisian Prince Finn has married the Danish princess Hildeburh in an effort to overcome an old feud. When her brother Hnæf visits, the feud resumes, and both Hildeburh's son and Hnæf are killed. The survivors are then trapped together by the onset of winter, but in the spring the Danes take their revenge, killing Finn and bringing Hildeburh home with them. The passage in *Beowulf* dwells on the elaborate

---

[51] On the date of the poem, see Colin Chase, ed., *The Dating of Beowulf* (Toronto, 1981; repr. with an afterward by Nicholas Howe, 1997); Roberta Frank, 'A scandal in Toronto: the dating of "*Beowulf*" a quarter century on'. *Speculum* 82/4 (2007), 843–64; and Leonard Neidorf, ed., *The Dating of Beowulf: A Reassessment* (Cambridge, 2014). On the date of the manuscript and the role of the later scribe, see Kevin S. Kiernan, *Beowulf and the Beowulf Manuscript*. 2nd edn, with a forward by Katherine O'Brien O'Keeffe (Ann Arbor MI, 1996).

[52] *Klaeber's Beowulf and the Fight at Finnsburg*, ed. R.D. Fulk, Robert E. Bjork and John D. Niles. 4th edn (Toronto, 2008), lines 1063–70; *Beowulf*, trans. R.M. Liuzza (Peterborough, 2000), with some minor modifications. In their re-edition of Klaeber, Fulk, Bjork and Niles capitalize 'Healgamen', taking this to be the scop's nickname.

funeral Hildeburh arranges and on the angry words of an old retainer that renew the feud in the spring. Then, the song ends and the merriment resumes:

> Leoð wæs asungen,
> gleomannes gyd.   Gamen eft astah,
> beorhtode bencsweg.
>
> (The lay was sung,
> the entertainer's words. Glad sounds rose again,
> the bench-noise glittered.) (lines 1159b–61a)

It seems the Danes in Hrothgar's hall have not understood the tale's grim implications.

This passage depicts the *scop* as an honoured retainer, a thane, who preserves the community's history and values, and who sings, alone, at important ritual moments in feasts, while the assembled warriors listen. The *scop* offers but a fragment of a longer story, and his listeners must supply this context to follow his lines. If we regard this scene as a reflection of actual social practice, then it shows that oral recitation was a powerful ritual, binding a community together and providing vital instruction, and consequently, that even if such recitation was largely confined to special occasions such as feasts or celebrations, it must have occurred with some regularity. Such socially sanctioned recitation could have allowed for the transmission of substantial bodies of material, perhaps even of poems not unlike *Beowulf* itself – at least so it has sometimes been suggested. John D. Niles, for one, hypothesizes that *Beowulf* must have derived 'from the recitation of a scop, from the writing of an ecclesiastic who remembered the singing of a scop and imitated it more or less accurately, or from the writing of an ecclesiastic who was himself a scop'.[53]

For a long time, the possibility that a poem of this length could be transmitted orally hinged upon the possibility that it was memorized. There is no doubt that such feats of memorization were, if not commonplace, by no means unusual in the Middle Ages, or for that matter in more recent times. The memorizing of a mere three thousand lines would pale in comparison to the accomplishment of the Kirghiz bard Jusup Mamay, who started training himself in the 1920s and after eight years had memorized over 200,000 lines.[54] But the oral performer does not necessarily memorize a fixed text and may equally well rely on a system of pre-established verbal units (formulae) that allow improvisation.

A second passage from *Beowulf* has often been taken as an illustration of how a *scop* might have improvised. As Hrothgar's men ride joyfully along the sands after Beowulf has defeated Grendel, a warrior bursts into song:

---

[53] John D. Niles, *Beowulf: The Poem and its Tradition* (Cambridge MA, 1983), 65.

[54] Lang Ying, 'The bard Jusup Mamay', *Oral Tradition* 16/2 (2001), 222–39. H.J. Chaytor provides several examples of medieval feats of memory in *From Script to Print: An Introduction to Medieval Vernacular Literature* (London, 1966), 116–7, as does Mary Carruthers, *The Book of Memory: A Study of Memory in Medieval Culture* (Cambridge, 1990), 2–7, 12–13 and 61. Minna Skafte Jensen offers further examples of extensive modern performances in 'Performance'. John Miles Foley, ed., *A Companion to Ancient Epic* (London, 2008), 45–54 at 46.

>   Hwilum cyninges þegn,
> guma gilhlæden,   gidda gemyndig,
> se ðe eal fela   ealdgesegena
> worn gemunde,   word oþer fand
> soðe gebunden;   secg eft ongan
> sið Beowulfes   snyttrum styrian
> ond on sped wrecan   spel gerade
> wordum wrixlan;   welhwylc gecwæð
> þæt he fram Sigemunde[s]   secgan hyrde
> ellendædum,   uncuþes fela,
> Wælsinges gewin,   wide siðas,
> þara þe gumena bearn   gearwe ne wiston,
> fæhðe ond fyrena.
>
> (At times the king's thane,
> full of grand stories, mindful of songs,
> who remembered much, a great many
> of the old tales, found other words
> truly bound together; he began again
> to recite with skill the adventure of Beowulf
> adeptly tell an apt tale,
> and weave his words. He said nearly all
> that he had heard said of Sigemund's
> stirring deeds, many strange things,
> the Volsung's strife, his distant voyages
> obscure, unknown to all the sons of men,
> his feuds and crimes ...) (lines 867b–879a)

Here the thane praises Beowulf by equating him with the great Sigemund, the dragon-slayer, whose deeds are told in the Old Norse *Volsunga Saga* and the Middle High German *Nibelungenlied* (although both works attribute the deed to his son, Sigurðr or Siegfried).[55] The thane, who has a repertoire of old stories, 'found other words' ('word oþer fand') for the occasion; he has the ability to weave together words, possibly phrases from old poems, so as to produce something new. He is improvising.[56]

The explanation of how a performer might manage to improvise in this fashion was first proposed by Milman Parry and then by his pupil Albert Bates Lord. Parry had studied Serbo-Croatian *guslars* in the former Yugoslavia in the 1930s and

---

[55] Andy Orchard, *A Critical Companion to Beowulf* (Cambridge, 2003), 105–14, noting the parallels to Sigemund are 'not necessarily wholly to [Beowulf's] credit' (p. 109).

[56] See further Jeff Opland, 'From horseback to monastic cell: the impact on English literature of the introduction of writing'. John D. Niles, ed., *Old English Literature in Context: Ten Essays* (Cambridge, 1980), 30–43; and John D. Niles, *Old English Heroic Poems and the Social Life of Texts* (Turnhout, 2007), 148–50. See, however, Norman E. Eliason, 'The "Improvised Lay" in *Beowulf*. *Philological Quarterly* 31/2 (1952), 171–9, who argues that 'word oþer fand' might mean 'found more words' (174). and Steven J.A. Breeze, *Performance in Beowulf and Other Old English Poems* (Cambridge, 2022), 77–84.

then used their practice as a model to explain the works of Homer. Drawing on a repertory of short metrical phrases (formulae) and standardized type scenes, Avdo Mededović, the most talented of the singers they recorded, could recite poetry by the hour, modifying his texts as he did so, depending on the interests of the audience. On one occasion, Parry arranged for Mededović to hear another singer, Mumin, who delivered several thousand lines, and then asked Mededović whether he could sing it himself:[57]

> He replied that it was a good song and that Mumin had sung it well, but that he thought that he might sing it better. The song was a long one of several thousand lines. Avdo began and as he sang, the song lengthened, the ornamentation and richness accumulated, and the human touches of character, touches that distinguished Avdo from other singers, imparted a depth of feeling that had been missing in Mumin's version.

A singer like Mededović, or, Lord would claim, Homer, was employing not merely a few stock epithets but rather a fully-developed formulaic system that covered everything he might wish to say and did so in appropriate metrical patterns. Hence, as Lord concluded, 'There is nothing in the poem that is not formulaic'.[58] The implication was that formulaic density allowed one to determine 'with a high degree of certainty' whether any text 'was formed by a traditional bard in the crucible of oral composition'.[59]

According to Parry's model, the poem's structure and form, from the smallest to the largest units, are inextricably linked to its oral composition, a composition that is never the same twice. What the poet performs is the tradition. The oral-formulaic theory thus heightens the meaning of the term 'oral performance', raising it above any mere recitation of a memorized text and thus distinguishing it clearly from early accounts, such as those of Léon Gautier. This interaction with the audience and capacity to modify a text to suit the occasion will remain something of a holy grail for modern scholars, trying to grasp a lost moment when 'the tradition is alive in the mouth of the singer'.[60] Ironically, as we have seen, one of the few guides to what this oral art may have entailed is provided by the minstrels' harshest critics, literate poets seeking to establish the dignity of their written art.

---

[57] Albert B. Lord, *The Singer of Tales*. 2nd edn, ed. Stephen Mitchell and Gregory Nagy (Cambridge MA, 2000), 78. The 2nd edition included a DVD containing some of Parry's audio and video recordings of a number of the *guslars*. A short film of Mededović performing eighteen lines can be seen on the DVD and also at the website of The Milman Parry Collection of Oral Literature. The Parry Collection is in the process of digitizing both Parry's transcriptions and his recordings.

[58] Lord, *Singer of Tales*, 47.

[59] Ibid., 45.

[60] Mark Amodio, discussing Benjamin Bagby's performance of *Beowulf*: Mark Amodio, Benjamin Bagby, Thomas Cable and John Miles Foley, 'Roundtable Discussion'. *Benjamin Bagby's Beowulf*. DVD (Paris, 2006), minute 18:45. The impossibility of recapturing what an original performance of *Beowulf* would have been like and the value of allowing the modern performer to break from the prison of the book and convey the poem's force in performance are two recurring themes in the discussion.

The initial attempts to apply the oral-formulaic theory to Old English poetry laid claim confidently to entire surviving poems as near-transcriptions. In 1953, Francis P. Magoun Jr. demonstrated the high formulaic density in *Beowulf* and *Christ and Satan*, and concluded that 'a *Béowulf* song in form fairly close to the preserved performance had come into being' by the early eighth century, the time when Cædmon was composing at Whitby.[61] Following Parry, Magoun maintained that 'the recurrence in a given poem of an appreciable number of formulas or formulaic phrases brands the latter as oral', in part because, or so he believed, metrical formulas do not occur 'in the poetry of lettered authors'.[62] The theory was also applied to Middle English romances, although somewhat less widely, since these texts belonged to a period of significantly broader literacy. *King Horn* and *Arthour and Merlin* were proposed as minstrel texts on the basis of Parry's model.[63]

One enormous problem with this theory is the question of how such oral performances ever got written down. The idea of a scribe frantically scribbling notes as a minstrel let forth a flood of improvised verse or carefully working with the minstrel as he delivered a command performance implies a very high level of respect for the minstrel's text, as if medieval scribes were ethnomusicologists.[64] The transcription of the *Cantigas de Santa Maria* of King Alfonso X provides one possible model. A busy scene in the Toldeo manuscript shows the king surrounded by musicians and scribes, all working under his supervision.[65] In this case the poet was a king and the subject Marian miracles. A more representative attitude towards popular lore is that expressed by Robert Mannyng of Brunne, a canon from Lincolnshire with a strong interest in regional history. In his *Chronicle* or *Story of England*, completed in 1338, he finds it a great wonder ('grete ferly') that nobody has told the story of Havelok, and lists the various chroniclers he has consulted in vain. He is aware that

---

[61] Francis P. Magoun, 'The oral-formulaic character of Anglo-Saxon narrative poetry'. *Speculum* 28/3 (1953), 446–67, at 455. Magoun explores the possibility that Cædmon was an oral-formulaic poet further in 'Bede's story of Cædman: the case-history of an Anglo-Saxon singer'. *Speculum* 30/1 (1955), 49–63.

[62] Magoun, 'Oral-formulaic character', 446–7, 449.

[63] William E. Holland, 'Formulaic diction and the descent of a Middle English romance'. *Speculum* 48/1 (1973), 89–109, for *Arthur and Merlin*; Quinn and Hall, *Jongleur*, for *Horn*. For other examples, see Ward Parks, 'The oral-formulaic theory in Middle English studies'. *Oral Tradition* 1/3 (1986), 636–94. Ronald A. Waldron provides a wide survey of formulaic language in the Middle English romances: 'Oral formulaic technique and Middle English alliterative poetry'. *Speculum* 32/4 (1957), 792–804. Despite his title, however, he insists that it 'would be rash to go on to say that this poetry itself must therefore be of oral origin' (800).

[64] Robert P. Creed, for example, describes Beowulf as 'a copy of a recording': 'The Beowulf-poet: master of sound pattern'. John Miles Foley, ed., *Oral Traditional Literature: A Festschrift for Albert Bates Lord* (Columbus OH, 1981), 194–216, at 194. Lord recognized that such a transcription would strike a purely oral poet as bizarre: *Singer of Tales*, 124 ff. For further discussion of textualization, see Karl Reichl, 'Plotting the map of medieval oral literature'. Karl Reichl, ed., *Medieval Oral Literature* (Berlin, 2012), 3–67, at 8–10.

[65] Vitz, *Orality and Performance*, 124. On the transcription of the *Cantigas*, see further Israel J. Katz and John E. Keller, eds, *Studies on the 'Cantigas de Santa Maria': Art, Music, and Poetry* (Madison WI, 1987).

the uneducated ('lowed men') tell stories about Havelok, pointing out in Lincoln the very stone he threw to prove his strength and the chapel where he married Goldeburh, but Mannyng is not sure these stories are true, and says again that he has found no compiler, that is, no writer who has collected the tales.[66] Despite his interest in local legends, it does not occur to Mannyng that he might interview the local story-tellers, still less attempt to reproduce their words. Orderic Vitalis (d. c. 1143) says that he was delighted when a monk from Winchester brought him a copy of the story of William Courtnez, for while 'jongleurs sing a popular song about him, an authentic account is rightly to be preferred' ('Vulgo canitur a ioculatoribus de illo cantilena, sed iure preferenda est relatio autentica').[67] For an example of high medieval culture treasuring popular oral culture and transcribing it with care, one must go back to Charlemagne, who, according to Einhart 'wrote down and committed to memory the barbarous and ancient songs which were sung of the deeds and wars of the old kings' ('Barbara et antiquissima carmina, quibus veterum regum actus et bella canebantur, scripsit et memoriaeque mandavit').[68]

Another problem with the oral-formulaic theory, as Larry Benson demonstrated in 1966, is that equal formulaic density can be found in works such as the verse translation of Boethius, which clearly is the work of a lettered author.[69] Oral-formulaic theory, at least in Old English, has been in continual retreat ever since. As Ann Chalmers Watts wrote over fifty years ago, 'The formulaic analysis of Old English texts may characterize what is on the page but not the means by which it got there'.[70] Subsequent efforts to refine the analysis of the formula have contributed much to our understanding of it as an artistic form, but never managed to establish

[66] Robert Manning de Brunne, *Robert Mannyng of Brunne: The Chronicle*, ed. Idelle Sullens (Binghamton NY, 1996), II, lines 519–38.

[67] Orderic Vitalis, *The Ecclesiastical History of Orderic Vitalis*, ed. Marjorie Chibnall. 6 vols (Oxford, 1969–78), Bk. VI, 218–9.

[68] Einhart, *Einhart's Life of Charlemagne*, ed. H.W. Garrod and R.B. Mowat (Oxford, 1915), 30.

[69] Larry D. Benson, 'The literary character of Anglo-Saxon formulaic poetry'. *PMLA* 81/5 (1966), 334–41. Others who have argued for the possibility of literate poets adopting a formulaic style include Stanley B. Greenfield, 'The formulaic expression of the theme of "Exile" in Anglo-Saxon poetry'. *Speculum* 30/2 (1955), 200–6; Waldron, 'Oral-formulaic technique'; Valerie Krishna, 'Parataxis, formulaic destiny, and thrift in the *Alliterative Morte Arthure*'. *Speculum* 57/1 (1982), 63–83; Michael Curschmann, 'The Concept of the oral formula as an impediment to our understanding of medieval oral poetry'. *Medievalia et Humanistica*, n.s. 8 (1977), 63–76; Susan Wittig, *Stylistic and Narrative Structures in the Middle English Romances* (Austin TX and London, 1978), 53–4; and Franz H. Bäuml, 'Varieties and consequences of medieval literacy and illiteracy'. *Speculum* 55/2 (1980), 237–65. For a demonstration of the density and literary effect of formulae being employed by literate poets, see Andy Orchard, *The Poetic Art of Aldhelm* (Cambridge, 1994), esp. 112–19, and Thomas A. Bredehoft, *Authors, Audiences, and Old English Verse* (Toronto, 2009).

[70] Ann Chalmers Watts, *The Lyre and the Harp: A Comparative Reconsideration of Oral Tradition in Homer and Old English Epic Poetry* (New Haven CT and London, 1969), 197.

oral provenance.[71] At the same time, accepting that a literate poet can deploy formulae explains how formulaic poems came to be written down. Among scholars of Old and Middle English, the notion that *Beowulf* itself, or even an earlier poem more or less like it, was performed by a *scop* has now been almost entirely abandoned, and the formulaic style and representations of performance by *scops* or minstrels recognized as 'the fictionalized and romanticized products of highly literate sensibilities'.[72] This does not mean, of course, that the poetry is not formulaic, or that the formulaic systems may not have *originated* as a means of allowing *scops* to improvise, merely that formulaic density is no guide to how any of the surviving poems was composed.

The implication for our understanding of minstrels working in Middle English is three-fold. First, there seems no reason to believe that the highly formulaic language of the kind the romances employ so heavily necessarily tells us anything about how a poem was composed or delivered. Second, the formulaic language would certainly permit improvisation. The descriptions of how contemporary oral poets, especially the south Slavic *guslars*, modify their works to suit the audience's interest provide suggestive examples of just how medieval minstrels might have been able to modify and break apart, or 'corronpre et depecier' as Chrétien de Troyes scornful puts it, a longer work. Third, the preservation of formulae shows that the writers who composed or copied the romances valued the tradition. As Ronald Waldron concluded, such romances were 'written by poets who were familiar with a body of formulas which probably originated in a tradition of oral composition and for readers who still retained a taste for the conventions of an oral style'.[73] People wanted to hear the familiar verbal patterns, which they associated with time-honoured chivalry and local lineage. A heavily-standardized alliterative vocabulary was still being employed by northern gentlemen in the sixteenth century to celebrate the deeds of their ancestors.[74] The patron who commissioned Bodleian Library, MS Laud Misc. 108, with its strong interest in Norfolk traditions, presumably valued the tag-lines and standardized rhyme schemes of *Horn* and *Havelok* for similar reasons.

The French tradition

The debate on Old French *chansons de geste* and their possible oral composition has followed a pattern similar to that for Old English. Only two years after the

---

[71] Lord himself eventually conceded that a writer who wishes to compose rapidly and has come in contact with oral traditional poetry 'not only can write formulas, or something very like them, but normally does so': Albert B. Lord, 'Perspectives in recent work on oral literature'. *Forum for Modern Language Studies* 10/3 (1974), 187–210, at 18. John Miles Foley concedes, in *Traditional Oral Epic: The Odyssey, Beowulf, and the Serbo-Croatian Return Song* (Berkeley CA, 1990), 4, that '[t]he formulaic test *as it has generally been carried out* cannot prove oral provenance' (italics in original). There seems no reason, however, to imagine that a formulaic test could ever be developed that would be able to prove oral provenance.

[72] Amodio, *Writing the Oral Tradition*, 98.

[73] Waldron, 'Oral-formulaic technique', 800.

[74] The poem *Scotish Feilde*, an account of the battle of Flodden, provides an example, discussed in Taylor, *Songs and Travels*, 53–6.

appearance of Magoun's first article on oral-formulaic composition, Jean Rychner published an extensive study of formulas in the *chansons de geste*, concluding that they too must have been oral compositions, in Parry's sense of the term, that is, the products of sustained improvisation, as opposed to mere memorization. Rychner first noted that numerous *chansons de geste* begin by addressing a listening audience with such phrases as 'Oiez seignor' and concluded, taking this evidence at face value, that these works must have been sung by *jongleurs*.[75] A number of scholars pursued Rychner's approach, most notably Joseph J. Duggan, who offered a detailed analysis of the formulaic passages in the *Chanson de Roland*.[76] Rychner argued that the *chansons de geste* were composed of a series of episodes that *jongleurs* would sing separately and which were subsequently linked together by a writer.[77] The examples he offers, including the episode of Baligant, often seen as an interruption in the *Song of Roland*, run from roughly 500 to 1500 lines.

While the scholarly debates on the implications of the formulaic density of Old English and Old French poetry turn on similar methodological principles, there is a crucial distinction between the two fields. In the case of Old English poetry, the formulaic systems might well have originated during an earlier period, before the Christianisation of the Angles and Saxons in the seventh century brought with it the use of Latin and of writing. How far the portrait of the *scop*'s performance in *Beowulf* actually corresponds to social practice is impossible to say. It served the poet's purpose to evoke a past that was, in Tolkien's famous formulation, 'heathen, noble, and hopeless', and the actual customs of the pre-Christian Danes, Saxons, or other Germanic peoples may have borne as much similarity to those depicted in *Beowulf* as the customs depicted in *The Magnificent Seven* bear to actual life in the American west.[78] Nevertheless, Anglo-Saxon England did have a powerful image of full epic recitation in an oral culture. Post-Conquest England did not: nowhere in Latin, Anglo-Norman, or Middle English is there a comparable evocation of such dignified and sustained recitation. Numerous *chansons de geste* and romances present themselves as if they were oral performances, and they often contain references to minstrels playing and telling stories at feasts. But with rare exceptions, such as the performances of the *joglar* in the *Castia Gilos* or of Merlin in *Le Roman de Merlin*, the *chansons de geste* and romances do not offer a detailed account of a single minstrel commanding the attention of the hall for a single sustained performance, as the *scop* in *Beowulf* does.

The differences between the cultural traditions west and east of the Rhine help explain the difference. The Anglo-Saxons were the descendants of peoples that, as late as Tacitus' *Germania*, composed *c.* 98 AD, preserved an almost purely oral culture. As Tacitus noted of the Germanic tribes, 'Celebrant carminibus antiquis, quod

---

[75] Rychner, *Chanson de geste*, 12.

[76] Joseph J. Duggan, *The Song of Roland: Formulaic Style and Poetic Craft* (Berkeley CA, 1973).

[77] Rychner, *Chanson de geste*, 46.

[78] J.R.R. Tolkien, '*Beowulf*: The monsters and the critics'. *Proceedings of the British Academy* 22 (1936), 245–95, at 264.

unum apud illos memoriae et annualium genus est, Tuistonem deum terra editum' ('They relate in ancient songs, which is the only kind of historical tradition among them, that the god Tuisto was born from earth').[79] By the time the Saxons who had taken over England were finally converted to Christianity, Gaul had been subject to Roman colonization for six and a half centuries. Textual habits of thought, however, which as Brian Stock has shown were diffused far more widely than actual literacy, were naturally more pervasive in Romance-speaking areas, where record-keeping had long been entrusted to professional literates, monks. Increasingly, from around the turn of the millennium, it was the authority of written texts that governed theological debate.[80] What *Beowulf* appears to preserve, then, is a memory of the status the *scop* might once have had in an entirely illiterate Germanic area.[81] Performers in other oral cultures have often had similar high status, which even the most respected performers in textual cultures can rarely command. The *menestrel* or *jongleur* and his English descendants worked in a culture that revolved around the book. It is not surprising, then, that the western Middle Ages offer numerous accounts of sustained reading, but almost none of sustained oral delivery. As we have seen, the performance of the satirical *Castia Gilos* depicted by Raimon Vidal is one of the most elaborate, and this work runs to only 450 lines; and while Vidal's *Abril Issia* depicts a *joglar* in extensive *conversation* with Dalfi d'Avernhe, it is Dalfi who does most of the talking. Minstrels played an important role in this culture but it was a marginalized and contested one – their performances were perforce shorter and subject to greater variation.

Taillefer at Hastings

The nearest we come to a performance that is given the high status of the *scop's* performance in *Beowulf* is that of Duke William's minstrel Taillefer at Hastings in 1066. The fullest account comes from Wace's *Roman de Rou*, a rhyming history of the Normans commissioned by Henry II. According to Wace, as the Normans approached the English line, Taillefer rode before them and sang:[82]

> Taillefer, qui mult bien chantout,
> sor un cheval qui tost alout,
> devant le duc alout chantant

---

[79] Tacitus, *Germany/Germania*, ed. and trans. Herbert W. Benario (Oxford, 1999), 14–15 (Benario's translation).

[80] Brian Stock, *The Implications of Literacy: Written Language and Models of Interpretation in the Eleventh and Twelfth Centuries* (Princeton NJ, 1983), 3, 91 and 522–31. Michelle Brown, however, argues that textual habits were much more widely disseminated in Anglo-Saxon society than has often been supposed: *The Book and the Transformation of Britain, c. 550–1050: A Study in Written and Visual Literacy and Orality* (London, 2011).

[81] The nostalgia for oral traditions may also reflect the relatively recent encroachment of writing in the Germanic areas. See Niles, *Old English Heroic Poems*, 185–6.

[82] Wace, *Le Roman de Rou de Wace*, ed. A.J. Holden. 3 vols (Paris, 1970–3), II, 8013–18; Wace, *The History of the Norman People: Wace's Roman de Rou*, trans. Glyn S. Burgess, with notes by Glyn S. Burgess and Elisabeth M.C. Van Houts (Woodbridge, 2004), 181.

de Karlemaigne e de Rollant,
e d'Oliver e des vassals
qui morurent en Rencevals.

> (Taillefer, a very good singer, rode before the duke on a swift horse, singing of Charlemagne and of Roland, and of Oliver and of the vassals who died at Rencesvals.)

Some version of the story of Roland had become the Norman battle-anthem.[83]

A number of references suggests that knights were on occasion preceded into battle by singers and that minstrels sometimes joined in battles.[84] Wace's account should not be taken as an anthropological report, however, and needs to be read in the context of his poem as a whole. Wace refers to the deeds of Charlemagne and Roland some thousand lines later, when William has his tent pitched on the field itself, among the dead, and then disarms. When his men see his battered shield and helmet, they all agree:[85]

'Tel bier ne fu,
qui si poinsist ne si ferist
ne qui d'armes tel soffrist;
pois Rollant ne pois Olivier
n'out en terre tel chevalier'.

> ('No man was ever so brave when spurring his horse or striking blows in such a way or supported such a weight of arms. Since Roland and Oliver there was never such a knight on earth'.)

The episode might equally be taken as an echo of a passage in *La Chanson de Roland* where Charlemagne surveys the dead, actually going so far as to lie down among them.[86] It seems, then, that the deeds of Charlemagne, Roland, and Oliver frame Wace's account of the Battle of Hastings because they symbolize righteousness and courage, and thus legitimize William's reign.[87] These associations were still in force three centuries later, when the Chandos Herald compared the bravery of knights to

---

[83] Many have assumed, all too hastily, that what Taillefer sang must have been some version of the very poem found in the earliest manuscript, Oxford, Bodleian, MS Digby 23. See, for example, Faral, *Jongleurs*, 57.

[84] J. Győry, 'Réflexions sur le jongleur guerrier'. *Annales Universitatis Scientiarum Budapestinensis de Rolando Eötvös Nominatae, Sectio Philologica* 3 (1961), 47–60; Menegaldo, *Jongleur*, 101–10.

[85] Wace, *Roman de Rou*, II, 8932–6; Wace, *History of the Norman People*, 191.

[86] 'Le gentilz reis descendut est a piét, / Culchet s'a tere', lines 2479–80, and 'Li emperere s'est culcét en un prét', line 2496. I owe this suggestion to Laura Ashe. On the symbolic importance of Charlemagne's perusal of the dead, see Eugene Vance, 'Roland and the poetics of memory'. Josué V. Harari, ed., *Textual Strategies: Perspectives in Post-Structuralist Criticism* (Ithaca NY, 1979, and London, 1980), 374–403, esp. 394–6.

[87] See, for example, David Douglas, 'The "Song of Roland" and the Norman conquest of England'. *French Studies* 14/2 (1960), 99–116.

that of Roland and Oliver and described how after the battle of Poitiers the Black Prince had his tent pitched on the field and spent the night among the dead.[88]

Wace is not the only one to refer to Taillefer or the singing about Roland and Oliver at Hastings. There are no less than five independent, or largely independent, accounts of a performance, three of them mentioning Taillefer by name, one describing him juggling his sword, and two mentioning his singing.[89] The sharpest contrast to Wace's account comes in that of the Anglo-Norman cleric Gaimar, whose *Estoire des Engleis* or *History of the English*, written *c*. 1136–7, predates Wace's *Roman de Rou* by some thirty years, making him 'the very first vernacular French chronicler whose work has survived'.[90] In Gaimar's brief account, only one action is mentioned with any specificity, and that is Taillefer's performance. But Gaimar tells the story from the Anglo-Saxon perspective. He calls Taillefer a *joglere* but makes no mention of his singing; instead he says that Taillefer juggled his spear and sword, and that all who saw him considered that he was performing 'merveilles' and 'enchantement' (lines 5278, 5291).

From these two accounts it is possible to attempt to reconstruct a single performance. The most extensive effort in this line is by John Southworth, who notes the discrepancy between Wace's description of Taillefer's singing and Gaimar's description of Taillefer juggling his sword. He concludes that the difference reflects the Norman and English experiences of the battle: the Normans catch enough of the words to recognize their familiar battle anthem: 'it is his *singing* that these will remember'.[91] Those further away, the Normans on the wings or the English, can only see him as he juggles his sword, and his actions, as he tosses a sword in the air, 'cast an incomprehensible spell'.[92]

Given their strong literary shape, trying to use these accounts to reconstruct an actual performance may seem naive. As Short remarks, for example, 'Taillefer is an ubiquitous figure who belongs more to literature than to history'.[93] But even if we read Wace's account of Taillefer as part of a purely literary tradition, indicating only what clerics thought minstrels should do, it shows that in the twelfth century

---

[88] Chandos Herald, *Vie du Prince Noir*, lines 1436–40, 2796, 3382–3.

[89] The accounts are: Guy d'Amiens (attrib.), *The Carmen de Hastingae proelio of Guy, Bishop of Amiens*, ed. Catherine Morton and Hope Muntz (Oxford, 1972), which may be contemporary and which mentions a *histrio* or *mimus* who juggles a sword; William of Malmesbury, *Gesta regum Anglorum*, ed. R.A.B. Mynors, Rodney M. Thomson and Michael Winterbottom (Oxford, 1998), begun by 1125, which mentions a 'cantilena Rolandi' sung by the Normans; Henry of Huntingdon, *Historia Anglorum*, ed. Diana E. Greenway (Oxford, 1996), completed by 1129, which mentions Taillefer singing of ancient warriors; Geffrei Gaimar, *Estoire des Engleis/History of the English*, ed. and trans. Ian Short (Oxford, 2009), completed by 1140, in which Taillefer is described as a *joglere* who juggles a sword; and Wace's *Roman de Rou*, completed by 1170. See William Sayers, 'The jongleur Taillefer at Hastings: antecedents and literary fate'. *Viator* 14 (1983), 77–88.

[90] Gaimar, *Estoire des Engleis*, xv.

[91] Southworth, *English Medieval Minstrel*, 34, emphasis in the original.

[92] Ibid.

[93] Gaimar, *Estoire des Engleis*, 428, note to line 5269 ff.

a minstrel's song was widely regarded as a crucial part of chivalric tradition and was closely associated with bravery. As Roland tells his men in the *Chanson de Roland*,[94]

> Or guart chascuns que granz colps i empleit
> male cançun de nus chantét ne seit!
> Paien unt tort e chrestïens unt dreit.
> Malvaisse essample n'en serat ja de mei. AOI
>
>> (Let each one of us take care to strike hard blows, so that no-one will sing a bad song about us. The Pagans are wrong and the Christians are right. I will never be a bad example. AOI)

The episode, even if entirely fictitious, suggests how a minstrel might have worked within a chivalric tradition, a body of knowledge shared by all the knights, so that even a fragment would have been immensely evocative. The greater unity now frozen into a single written text reproduces what, in its oral condition, would have been a combination of innumerable conversations and occasional short performances, or what Lauri Honko terms 'a mental text'. As she argues, drawing on ethnographic evidence from a range of cultures, 'long oral epics are rarely, if ever, performed in full. There may not be any cultural locus for a performance lasting several days. ... What unites, then, the actual performances of the epic in its cultural context, is something we will never see, namely the mental text in the minds of the singers and, probably in simpler forms, their audiences'.[95] If we were to apply this model to the medieval *jongleur*, we might imagine not a harper in the hall offering a series of performances of hundreds of lines but just such a figure as Taillefer.

---

[94] *Chanson de Roland*, lines 1013–15. The meaning of the letters AOI, which appear 180 times in the poem, has generated much debate.

[95] Lauri Honko, 'Texts as process and practice: the textualization of oral epics'. Lauri Honko, ed., *Textualisation of Oral Epics* (Berlin, 2000), 3–54, at 22–3.

13
Minstrels and heralds and chivalric fame

Andrew Taylor

Fame and the *gestour*

In his comic meditation on fame and rumour, *The House of Fame* (c. 1380), Chaucer describes a dream in which he was seized by an eagle and brought to 'Fames Hous' a place 'full of tidynges, / Bothe of feir speche and chidynges, / And of fals and soth compouned'.[1] He sees a hill of ice, on which are carved 'famous folkes names' that are all but effaced on the southern side but still fresh on the northern one. On the top of the hill is perched a castle, whose outer walls are covered with niches filled not with statues but with living performers:

> In which [niches] stoden, al withoute –
> Ful the castel, al aboute –
> Of alle maner of mynstralles
> And gestiours that tellen tales
> Both of wepinge and of game,
> Of al that longeth unto Fame. (lines 1195–1200)

The list of minstrels begins with Orpheus and includes Orion (that is Arion of Corinth), Achille's tutor Chiron, the bard Glascurion, Marcia, flayed for daring to challenge Apollo, and a host of 'small harpers with her gleës'.[2] The panoply of minstrels includes players of shawms bagpipes, horns, and shepherd's pipes, trumpeters, Dutch pipers and Spanish trumpeters, and also a wide range of illusionists, jugglers, magicians, *tregetours* (experts in special effects), old witches, sorceresses, and astrologers, and such famous enchantresses as Medea and Circe. Here is minstrelsy as both music and enchantment, all contributing to the preservation of fame, deserved

---

[1] Geoffrey Chaucer, *The Riverside Chaucer*, ed. Larry Benson. 3rd edn (Boston MA, 1987), lines 1027–9.

[2] Benson provides helpful notes. On Arion, see Ovid, *Ovid's Fasti with an English Translation by Sir James Frazer*, ed. A.J. Boyle and Roger D. Woodard (London, 1931), I, 79–118. Glascurion may appear in Welsh oral traditions: see Andrew Breeze, 'The Bret Glascurion and Chaucer's *House of Fame*'. *Review of English Studies* 45/177 (1994), 63–9. He reappears in later Scottish oral traditions: see Richard Firth Green, 'Did Chaucer know the ballad of *Glen Kindy*?'. *Neophilologus* 92 (2008), 351–8.

or undeserved, sought or avoided. This activity, according to Chaucer, is led by the 'gestiours' who are tellers of tales.

Chaucer's use of the term *gestour* is not unusual. In England the most common terms for someone who sang of the deeds of great men, their *gesta*, was either *gestour* or *disour*, one who tells a *dit* or simply one who speaks, and both terms recur frequently in the Middle English romances. *Richard Coer de Lyon* promises us 'Noble jestes ... Off doughty knyghtes off Yngelonde'.³ *Guy of Warwick* refers to 'minstrels of mouthe and mani dysour' and *The Seege of Troye* to 'mony mury disur of mouth', while Mannyng says that he did not write his *Chronicle* 'for no disours, / ne for seggers [reciters], no harpours'.⁴ *The Laud Troy Book* provides a full list of the *gestours*' repertory:⁵

> Many speken of men that romaunces rede
> That were sumtyme doughti in deed,
> The while that god hem lyff lent   [lent them life]
> That now ben dede and hennes went:
> Off Bevis, Gy, and of Gauwayn,
> Off Kyng Rychard, and of Owayn,
> Off Tristram, and of Percyvale,
> Off Rouland Ris, and Aglavale,
> Off Archeroun, and of Octavian,
> Off Charles, and of Casibaldan,
> Off Havelok, Horne, and of Wade;--
> In romaunces that of hem ben made
> That gestours often dos of hem gestes
> At mangeres and at gret festes.   [meals]
> Here dedis ben in rembraunce
> In many fair romaunce.

The fourteenth-century *Libeaus Desconus* says that heralds and *disours* can proclaim the strokes of the knights at a tournament ('Heorudes and dissoures / Her strokes con discrye'), while the fifteenth-century *Dives et Pauper* compares the cross, Christ's token, to a knight's arms, the token by which he is recognized so that his deeds can be recounted by 'herawdys and golyardeys and iestourrys'.⁶

---

3   *Richard Löwenherz*. Karl Brunner, ed., *Der Mittelenglische Versroman über Richard Löwenherz* (Vienna and Leipzig, 1913), lines 27–8.

4   *Stanzaic Guy of Warwick*, ed. Alison Wiggins (Kalamazoo MI, 2004), line 197; *Seege of Troye*, line 806; Mannyng, *Chronicle*, lines 75–6. For further examples see Zaerr, *Performance*, Appendix A.

5   *The Laud Troy Book: A Romance of about 1400 A.D.*, ed. Ernest Wülfing. 2 vols EETS o.s. 121, 122 (London, 1902–3), lines 11–26. 'Roland Rise' is also mentioned in Thomas the Rhymer, *Sir Tristrem*, ed. George P. McNeil (London, 1886), lines 44 and 49, and may be a reference to the Welsh name Rhys. For references to Wade, see R.M. Wilson, *The Lost Literature of Medieval England*. 2nd edn (London, 1970), 14–16.

6   Priscilla Heath Barnum, ed., *Dives et Pauper*. 2 vols EETS o.s. 275, 280, 323 (London, New York NY and Oxford, 1976–2004), I, part 1, 88–9.

One of the best-known accounts of the telling of the *gesta* is that of Thomas Chobham, sub-dean of Salisbury Cathedral (d. *c.* 1233–6), who was one of the scholars who formed part of the circle, or at least fell under the influence, of Peter the Chanter. As chanter, Peter was the man responsible for the music in Notre Dame de Paris in the 1140s, one of the most important choir directors in Europe and a man who was at the forefront not just of musical innovation but also of social theory, seeking to reconcile religious principles with the complexities of urban existence and professional specialization.[7] Chobham divides *histriones*, entertainers, into those who distort their bodies through shameful gestures, those who follow the courts of great lords and speak shameful and opprobrious things of those who are absent to please others ('*opprobria et ignominia de absentibus ut placeant aliis*'), and those who play on musical instruments. This third category he then subdivides into those who sing songs which promote lasciviousness and those whom he calls *joculatores* 'who sing of the deeds of great men and the acts of saints' ('*qui cantant gesta principium et vitas sanctorum*').[8] Only this last category will be saved from damnation.

Locating real *gestours* outside literary conventions or theological abstractions is harder. The dearth of references to *gestours*, *rhymours*, *jongleurs*, or the like in the pay records of the first three Edwards has sometimes been taken as evidence of the decline of narrative minstrelsy in the fourteenth century, or at least its decline at the royal court.[9] But the records are misleading. References to *gestours* and such were never that common.[10] Not one of the *menestrellorum multitudo* who attended the knighting of the future Edward II in 1306 is listed as either a *gestour* or *disour*, although Reginaldus le Mentour was perhaps some kind of storyteller.[11] Nor do references to *gestours* cease altogether in the fourteenth century. The king's household included William Percival, *gestour*, between November 37 Ed III (1363) and some time in Richard II's reign (1377–99); the household of the Prince of Wales included Richard the Rymour in 1305, and John Alisaundre, *rymour*, was employed in the king's and Black Prince's households between about 1357 and 1365.[12] A century later Alexander Mason, *geyster*, served three monarchs, 1468–94, becoming Marshal of the Still Minstrels in 1482.[13] This is a paltry handful of reciters, particularly since the references are culled from a reasonably complete account of the royal household minstrels for more than two centuries, but this small number should not be surprising. The vast majority of royal minstrels, whatever else they may have done, always played instruments and a minstrel's favoured instrument provided the most convenient designation for the book-keepers. This does not preclude the possibility

---

[7] John W. Baldwin, *Masters, Princes and Merchants: The Social Views of Peter the Chanter and his Circle.* 2 vols (Princeton NJ, 1970); Page, *Owl and Nightingale*.

[8] For discussion, see Page, *Owl and Nightingale*, 23–4.

[9] Claire C. Olson, 'Minstrels at the court of Edward III'. *PMLA* 56/3 (1941), 601–12, has been particularly influential in this regard.

[10] See above, pp. 5–6.

[11] Bullock-Davies, *Menestrallorum Multitudo*, 153, but changed to '? juggler' in *Register*, 158.

[12] See below, p. 344; MERH, 17, 18, 21, 24.

[13] MERH, 33–4, 37.

that the instrumentalists also sang or recited stories. While the loud musicians, particularly the trumpeters, had a full range of ceremonial duties, the activities of the still musicians, the harpers, fiddlers, lutenists, and players of the *crwth*, gittern, and psaltery, are only partially known. It is highly unlikely that they were all exclusively instrumentalists. Any one of the minstrels identified as a still musician could well have included storytelling or chanting or singing in his repertory.[14] It seems likely that most harpers, in particular, played their instrument as an accompaniment to their voice. The English harpers' repertory of purely instrumental music was limited: little survives, and that which does suggests that the English harpers did not expand their repertory to include polyphonic compositions until the sixteenth century.[15] Whether the vocal repertory of the still minstrels, including those sometimes called *gestour* or *rymour*, was limited to short lyrics or also included extensive narrative pieces or fragments of longer stories the records do not tell. From the references in the royal pay records and other administrative documents it is difficult to determine much about the activities and status of the *gestours*, except that the term was recognized outside the realms of literature and theology.

Minstrels and heralds as chivalric memorialists

Minstrels were always closely allied to heralds; both attended battles and tournaments and celebrated feats of arms. Minstrels would have had ample opportunity to learn blazons, keep track of which knights performed well, and spread word of what they saw, while reciting or singing the stories of their patrons would have been a natural extension of the heralds' responsibilities as court historians. It is not surprising that in contemporary romance, minstrels and heralds often appear together in standardized tag lines. While there is evidence of rivalry between minstrels and heralds, this might reflect the ease with which their roles could be confused.[16] The professions became more clearly distinguished in the fourteenth century, however, and as they did so the heralds' status increased. By the fifteenth century heralds were specialists of a higher social standing than minstrels.[17] When Edward IV invaded France in 1475, he included the four Kings of Arms, Garter, Clarenceaux, Norroy, and March. As Dennys notes, 'Garter's pay on active service was 4s a day, the same as a baron and a banneret, while the three other kings of arms received 2s 4d a day; the herald's pay was 2s. a day, the same as the knight; and the pursuivants got 1s 6d a day, rather better than a squire or man-at-arms, who got 1s a day'.[18] In comparison, Edward normally paid his minstrels only 4½d per day during peace-time, and no

---

[14] For the duties of the still minstrels, see below p. 353.

[15] Timothy J. McGee, *Medieval and Renaissance Music: A Performer's Guide* (Toronto, 1985), 76, and see below, pp. 363–5, 368–70.

[16] See Baudoin de Condé, 'Li Contes des Hiraus'. *Dits et Contes de Baudoin de Condé et de son fils Jean de Condé*, ed. Aug[uste] Scheler. 3 vols (Brussels, 1866–7), I, 153–73; Wagner, *Heralds and Heraldry*, 30.

[17] Jackson W. Armstrong, 'The development of the office of arms in England, c. 1413–1485'. Katie Stevenson, ed., *The Herald in Late Medieval Europe* (Woodbridge, 2009), 9–28.

[18] Rodney Dennys, *The Heraldic Imagination* (London, 1975), 37.

more than 12d per day in war-time (as men-at-arms with the household rank of squire).[19] Denholm-Young thinks it likely that the profession of herald and minstrel were united until about 1300 but then split apart.[20] There is no reason to suppose that the distinction was always drawn rigorously during the later period, however, particularly outside a few great households that could support such intensive specialization, and many minstrels must have taken on some of the herald's duties. The fourteenth-century romance *Richard Coer de Lyon* contains a telling scene in which Richard, travelling back from the Crusades *incognito* and reluctant to call attention to himself, unwisely orders away a traveling minstrel, only to be warned that 'praise comes from the minstrel' ('los ryses off mynstrale').[21]

As their professional status solidified, heralds began to develop specialized professional literature. The earliest surviving Anglo-Norman rolls of arms date from the mid-thirteenth century, and the earliest surviving Anglo-Norman heraldic treatise, *De Heraudie*, from about 1300.[22] By the late fifteenth century, if not earlier, heralds had developed an elaborate system for keeping score of the blows in tournaments, noting them down on score cards, score cheques, which could later be compiled.[23] They were also compiling major collections of challenges and detailed accounts of tournaments, tilts, and individual feats of arms, such as the combat between Sir Anthony Woodville, Edward IV's brother-in-law, and the Bastard of Burgundy in 1467.[24] By the time Richard III granted the heralds a charter to become a corporation in 1484, a library was considered a crucial requirement. According to the ordinances, 'At convenient times the officers of arms were to apply themselves to the study of books of good manners and eloquence, chronicles and accounts of honourable and notable deeds of arms, and the properties of colours, plants and precious stones,

---

[19] See p. 4.

[20] N[oël] Denholm-Young, 'The Song of Carlaverock and the parliamentary roll of arms as found in Cott. MS. Calig. A. XVIII in the British Museum'. *Proceedings of the British Academy* 47 (1961), 251–62, at 256.

[21] *Richard Löwenherz*, line 676.

[22] Gerard J. Brault, *Eight Thirteenth-Century Rolls of Arms in French and Anglo-Norman Blazon* (University Park PA, 1973). De Heraudie is preserved in Cambridge University Library MS Ee.iv.20, ff. 160v–161v and is edited in Ruth J. Dean, 'An early treatise on heraldry in Anglo-Norman'. U.T. Holmes, ed., *Romance Studies in Memory of Edward Billings*. California State College Publications 2 (Hayward CA, 1967), 21–9.

[23] Sidney Anglo, 'Archives of the English tournament: score cheques and lists'. *Journal of the Society of Archivists* 2/4 (1961), 153–62; Roy C. Strong, 'Elizabethan jousting cheques in the possession of the College of Arms'. *The Coat of Arms* 5 (1958–9), 4–8 and 63–8. Anglo notes that while the earliest surviving cheques date from 1511, later copies survive for cheques from 1501, and that there is evidence for the use of cheques in the collection of William Ballard, March King of Arms, who was dead by 1490 (154).

[24] G.A. Lester, 'Fifteenth-century English heraldic narrative'. *Yearbook of English Studies* 22 (1992), 201–12; 'The Literary activities of the English Heralds'. *English Studies* 71 (1990), 222–9; and *Sir John Paston's 'Grete Boke': A Descriptive Catalogue, with an Introduction, of British Library MS Lansdowne 285* (Cambridge, 1984). Also Gordon Kipling, *The Triumph of Honour: Burgundian Origins of the Elizabethan Renaissance* (The Hague, 1977), 119.

so that they might be able most properly and appropriately to assign arms to each person'.²⁵

King Robert's judgment at the court of Edward II

One of the most forceful and puzzling evocations of a herald's powers occurs in Walter Bower's *Scotichronicon* of 1440. Bower, an Augustinian canon, describes a charged scene at the court of Edward II:²⁶

> Almost always empty pleasure and delight for the unbridled spirit accompanies royal feasts. For while the body is set free in the pleasures of eating, the heart is made desolate through empty enjoyment. This happened one day to the King of England Edward de Caernarfon, who, when he was holding a great feast for the magnates and army commanders of his land, while the wine was glistening in the bowls and had gladdened the hearts of the guests, as a way of amusing himself he asked his herald called Robert the King [*herello suo Le Roye Robert nuncupato*], a man who was undoubtedly discreet and intelligent, who had besides been nominated and appointed king of all the heralds of England [*tocius Anglie propterea hirellorum rege nominato et effecto*] who in his judgment were the three knights then living who were the most tested and worthy fighters.

The herald, with bowed head and bended knee, answered him respectfully that in his judgment they were the emperor Henry, Giles d'Argentan, who fought three times against the Saracens and killed two each time, and 'the noble Robert king of Scotland ... a fighter of invincible courage according to the common popular estimation' [*nobilis scilicet Scocie rex ... invicte virtutis bellator juxta commune et populare judicium*].²⁷ The knights were furious, and shouted loudly that no Scot, let alone Bruce, should ever be compared to them. King Robert replied that he would defend his judgment on his own body, for 'no herald with due care for his own interests ought to announce anything before the king unless at the end of his sworn statement he holds himself ready to prove it by maintaining and defending with his body his statement of this kind against those who try to refute it'.²⁸ He then defended his ranking, insisting that Robert the Bruce should be rated the highest of the three, since Henry could always draw on large forces and Argentan was not experienced in controlling a large army or commanding many troops.²⁹ Bower, whose purpose

---

²⁵ Dennys, *Heraldic Imagination*, 55, citing Sir Anthony Richard Wagner, *Heralds of England: A History of the Office and College of Arms* (London, 1967), 66–8. Dennys argues that despite some doubt as to the authenticity of the ordinances attributed to Thomas of Lancaster, Duke of Clarence, and drawn up between 1417 and 1421, this passage was probably 'based on genuine originals of the fifteenth century'.

²⁶ Walter Bower, *Scotichronicon*, ed. and trans. D.E.R. Watt *et al.*, 9 vols (Aberdeen, 1990–8), VII, 50.

²⁷ Bower, *Scotichronicon*, VII, 52. The three were Henry VII of Luxembourg, Edward's bodyguard Giles d'Argentan, and Robert Bruce.

²⁸ Bower, *Scotichronicon*, VII, 52.

²⁹ Ibid., VII, 54.

was to praise Robert the Bruce, says no more of the episode, leaving the impression that King Robert had silenced his critics.

Bower, writing over a century after Argentan's death at the battle of Bannockburn, offers an account that is in many ways highly implausible – no herald would call Bruce 'king' in Edward's presence – and conventional; it is an *exemplum* illustrating the Biblical theme of the foolish king humbled. Edward's feast echoes those of Belshazzar, where Daniel prophesies the king's doom, and of Herod, as portrayed on the medieval stage, where the drunken king is visited by Death.[30] There are echoes of folk tales as well, specifically the theme of the rash question. Edward is in effect asking 'who is the bravest of them all?'. Bower's purpose would seem to be to pay tribute to Robert the Bruce through the mouths of his enemy. With good reason, the editors of the *Scotichronicon* described the account as 'a work of imagination'.[31] It is, however, a work of imagination with some remarkably accurate moments.

Le Roye Robert, or King Robert, is no fiction. He was one of the two chief heralds or kings of heralds for both Edward I and Edward II and is mentioned on numerous occasions in the royal pay records.[32] We last hear of King Robert in 1320, organizing the entertainment for a banquet for the king at Amiens. Obviously if he had praised Bruce's reputation it had not cost him the king's favour.

Just as King Robert was a real herald, Argentan was a real knight. He was, moreover, a knight whose career centred around his reputation to an unusual degree. It seems likely that Argentan, the son of the king's seneschal, had risen to be Edward's companion and bodyguard by carefully cultivating his reputation as a tournament champion and paragon of chivalric courage.[33] The story of how he met his death at Bannockburn (1314) when, after escorting the king to safety, he rode back into the battle is preserved in three other sources, all apparently completely independent. One is the *Vita Edwardi Secundi* of c. 1324, probably composed by a retired lawyer connected to the Earl of Hereford, which tells us that Argentan rode out to support the Earl of Gloucester, who had charged rashly, 'thinking it more honourable to perish with so great a man than to escape death by flight'.[34] The second is the account of the Border warrior Sir Thomas Gray, warden of Norham castle, written while he was a prisoner in Edinburgh castle in 1355 and 1356. Gray actually provides Argentan's death speech, which he delivers to the king after he has escorted him from the field:[35]

---

[30] '*Baltassar rex fecit grande convivium optimatibus suis mille, et unusquisque secundum suam bibebat aetatem*' (Daniel, 5.1); 'The death of Herod' in Stephen Spector, ed., *The N-Town Play*. 2 vols. EETS s.s. 11, 12 (London, 1991), I, 192–7.

[31] Bower, *Scotichronicon*, VII, 191.

[32] See above, pp. 208–10.

[33] Andrew Taylor, 'From heraldry to history: the death of Gilles d'Argentan'. Nicole Royan, ed., *Langage Cleir Illumynate: Scottish Poetry from Barbour to Drummond, 1375–1630* (Amsterdam, 2007), 25–41, at 34–5.

[34] *Vita Edwardi Secundi*, ed. N. Denholm-Young, rev. Wendy R. Childs (Oxford, 2005), 54.

[35] Sir Thomas Gray, *Scalacronica, 1272–1363*, ed. and trans. Andy King (Woodbridge, 2005), 77.

'Sire, your rein was committed to me; you are now in safety, there is your castle where your person may be safe. I am not accustomed to fly, nor am I going to begin now. I commend you to God!'

Finally there is John Barbour's account in the *Bruce*, written about 1375, which again has Argentan leading the king to safety and then deliberately returning to certain death, saying to the king:[36]

> 'Hawys gud day for agayne will I,
> Yeyt fled I never sekyrly
> And I cheys her to bid and dey
> Than for to lyve schamly and fley'.

Bower's story associates this exemplary knight, whose last words had passed into chivalric record, with an exemplary herald, who is admirably informed and well-spoken and who cannot be intimidated.

It is not surprising that Bower should have heard of Argentan, then, but it is surprising that he should have heard of King Robert. Presumably heralds, both Scottish and English, were involved in preserving some version of his speech. The account certainly serves as a defence of the profession, showing a herald as a determined and impartial judge of knightly prowess while also indicating, at least by the time it reached Bower, that the heralds did have the power to preserve a knight's reputation long after his death. The story also suggests why heralds were feared. King Robert's judgment is a rebuke to an idle king and his courtiers, all sunk in 'empty pleasure' (*vana voluptas*), and one that offers them a model few would dare to emulate. As heralds so often did when they bore challenges from one knight to another, King Robert is not just preserving the memory of courage but actively demanding it.

The power held by a herald can be seen in a short account of the first Battle of St Albans of 1455 that was written as an official record of the future Edward IV's victory. It begins as a proclamation: 'Be yt knowen & hadde in mynde, that the xxj. day of May the xxxiij. yere of the Regne of Kyng Herry the sext, Oure Sovereyne lord Kyng toke his jurnay from Westmynster toward Seynt Albones, and rested at Watford all nyght'.[37] The account offers much precise military detail: the nobles who were present, when the troops were mustered and when the battle began; the number of those slain and wounded, many of their names and even where their wounds were; and the exact location of the Earl of Warwick's crucial attack, between 'the signe of the Keye, and the sygne of the Chekkere in Holwell strete', as well as mentioning that 'the Erle of Wyldsshyre, Thorpe, and many other fflede & left her harneys behynde hem cowardly'. Much of the short text, however, is given over to the words of the two rivals. The account quotes at length Edward's humble request to Henry 'to enclyne your

---

36 John Barbour, *Barbour's Bruce: A Fredome is a Noble Thing*, ed. Matthew P. McDiarmid and James A.C. Stevenson. 3 vols (Edinburgh, 1980–5), XIII, lines 305–8.

37 John Bayley, ed., 'An account of the first battle of St. Albans from a contemporary manuscript'. *Archaeologia* 20 (1824), 519–23, at 519. I have expanded the abbreviations and substituted y for z. Bayley's source, Chancery Miscellanea, 37, File iii, 4–11, is identified by C.A.J. Armstrong, 'Politics and the Battle of St. Alban's, 1455'. *Bulletin of the Institute of Historical Research* 23/87 (1960), 1–72, at 1.

wille to here & fele the rightwyse pyte of us youre sugettes & legemen', as well as Henry's intemperate response that he will have them all hanged, drawn, and quartered as traitors, 'every moder sone'. The account also gives Edward's reluctant and pious conclusion that the king 'will not be reformed at our beseching ne prayer', and ends with the victorious Edward's humble request for the king's grace and his merciful proclamation, in the king's name, that the fighting cease. The account seems to have been written in haste, since it refers to 'xxv. more which her names be not yet knowen'.[38] Whoever wrote it was clearly a professional witness, a herald or someone with a herald's training, providing both the basic facts about the battle and a narrative that would promote the Yorkist cause. Why he singled out the Earl of Wiltshire and Thomas Thorpe for his special disapprobation is not clear.[39]

Lawrence Minot and the Chandos Herald

Two fourteenth-century writers who specialized in preserving the fame of English knights can actually be identified: Laurence Minot, who celebrated the victories of Edward III in short English poems that are peppered with abuse of England's enemies, and the personal herald of Sir John Chandos, who wrote a biography of the Black Prince in the Picard dialect of Hainault that runs to over 4000 lines. Minot has never been properly identified, whereas the herald was a distinguished court official who left numerous traces in the records and is mentioned on numerous occasions by Froissart and other chroniclers. Together they suggest the range of poetry, both of praise and blame, that commemorated knightly deeds.

Minot is known only through his poems, which are all preserved in a single manuscript, BL Cotton MS Galba E.ix, dating from the early fifteenth century, but cover events from 1333 to 1352. While the manuscript groups the poems as one, running to 926 lines, most editors have divided them by battle, making a series of eleven separate poems, all relatively short, the longest being 172 lines. The verse form is undemanding, rhyming couplets grouped into six-line stanzas, aaaabb, with some variation.[40] The poems describe the battles against the Scots at Halidon Hill and Neville's Cross, against the French and the Flemings at Sluys, Cambrai, and Guisnes, and against the Spaniards at Winchelsea, with one poem lamenting the earlier English defeat at Bannockburn, by way of stressing Edward II's subsequent revenge. While a few errors suggest that Minot was not actually an eye-witness at the battles, several of the poems seem to have been written relatively shortly after them. Richard Osberg notes, for example, that poem VI, which describes the siege of Tournai in the summer of 1340 and threatens the inhabitants that Edward will

---

[38] Lester, 'Fifteenth-century English heraldic narrative', 202.

[39] Wiltshire had been a close associate of the Duke of York, but chose the Lancashire side and became Treasurer; Thomas Thorpe was Speaker of the Commons and Chancellor of the Exchequer, and one of York's strongest opponents.

[40] For a more detailed analysis of the verse forms, stressing their variation, see A.S.G. Edwards, 'The authorship of the poems of Laurence Minot: a reconsideration'. *Florilegium* 23/1 (2006), 145–53.

break down their walls, makes no reference to the siege being lifted in September.[41] For each battle the poems mention some of the key English leaders by name and heap alliterative abuse on the opposing nations: the Scots, who are full of guile, are bag-bearers (berebag) and false wretches and the Spaniards black boys with beards, while the French are humbled for all their 'fine fare' (airs) and the *fleur de lys* flees for fear.

The opening lines give some sense of the style, with its strong use of alliterative epithets.

> Lithes and I sall tell yow tyll
> the bataile of Halidon Hyll.
>
> Trew king that sittes in trone,
> unto The I tell my tale,
> and unto The I bid a bone,
> for Thou ert bute of all my bale.   [remedy for all my sorrow]
> Als Thou made midelerd and the mone
> and bestes and fowles grete and smale,
> unto me send Thi socore sone
> and dresce my dedes in this dale.   [guide]

Given this forceful address to the audience, it is easy to understand why it was sometimes assumed that Minot was a minstrel.[42] Other efforts to identify Minot precisely have not been persuasive either. The name was not uncommon and a few of the Minots of the period, including Sir John Minot of Yorkshire, might conceivably be related to the poet, but there is no certainty.[43] Thomas James and John Simons suggest that Minot was 'one amongst the increasingly large retinue of minor functionaries who thronged the later medieval courts and who decided to seek preferment through the production of laudatory poetry in a style which may have appealed to the king himself'.[44] Minstrels would have been included among such minor functionaries, but so would many others. Richard Osberg, noting the strong interest in chivalric history in alliterative verse among the northern gentry, suggests that Minot might equally have been a country squire.[45] A.S.G. Edwards adds a further complication when he suggests that the original poems may have been by several people,

---

[41] Laurence Minot, *The Poems of Laurence Minot*, ed. Richard H. Osberg (Kalamazoo MI, 1996), 1.

[42] Rossell Hope Robbins, *Historical Poems of the XIVth and XVth Centuries* (New York NY, 1959), xxviii; Laurence Minot, *The War Ballads of Laurence Minot*, ed. Douglas C. Stedman (Dublin and London, 1917), xi. Further references are provided in Minot, *Poems*, ed. Osberg, 3-8, and in David Matthews, 'Laurence Minot, Edward III, and nationalism'. *Viator* 38/1 (2007), 269-88, at 284.

[43] Minot, *War Ballads*, xv; *Poems*, ed. Osberg, 6-7.

[44] T.B. James and John Simons, eds, *The Poems of Laurence Minot, 1333-1352* (Exeter, 1989), 10.

[45] Minot, *Poems*, ed. Osberg, 7-8.

and then grouped together by a fifteenth-century compiler.[46] Whether the original poems were the work of one poet or several, the compiler played an important role in repackaging material. The praise of Edward III from the 1330s and 1340s could still inspire an English audience nearly a century later, offering a distinguished lineage for the conquering Henry V.

Chandos Herald was the title given to the personal herald of the renowned champion Sir John Chandos, a companion of the Black Prince who served as the king's lieutenant in Aquitaine and was Constable for the Black Prince's expedition to Spain in 1367. The Chandos Herald was probably appointed to the post when Sir John was raised to the rank of banneret in 1360.[47] According to Froissart, the Chandos Herald delivered formal reports from his lord to the Black Prince, and brought back letters in return. As one would expect, the Chandos Herald's *Vie du Prince Noir* has high praise for Sir John Chandos, but it also singles out Henry Duke of Lancaster. The herald was happy to serve other English nobles, including the earls of Cambridge, Pembroke and Buckingham (Thomas of Woodstock, later Duke of Gloucester). After Sir John Chandos's death in 1369, the herald appears to have become an English officer at arms in 1377, assuming the title of Ireland King of Arms but retaining Chandos as a surname. Froissart's accounts of what the Chandos Herald did and the Chandos Herald's own accounts of what other heralds did together provide a detailed, although possibly somewhat glamourized, picture of the profession. The heralds travelled widely, bearing messages, commands, and challenges. They had no licence to negotiate on major political issues and were in no sense ambassadors, but they were called upon to provide assessments of what they had seen. When delivering challenges, in particular, their personal dignity was vital and, as their master's emissary, they might be required to address great lords with defiance. So at the siege of Belleperche in 1370, the Chandos Herald, bearing the challenge of the earls of Cambridge and Pembroke to the Duke of Bourbon, demanded to know why they had been kept waiting for fifteen days without the duke coming forth to meet them, adding, when the duke refused the challenge, that, in three days' time, the duke would see his mother 'placed on horseback and carried away'.[48]

Anonymous songs of praise and blame

One good example of the combination of heraldic record and simple narrative is the Anglo-Norman *Song of the Barons* of c. 1263, which praises Simon de Montfort and lampoons his enemies. The song is preserved in a small and simple roll of the kind one might expect a performer to carry around with him – a performance script rather than a luxury memento.[49] On the reverse side of the roll there is a short comic

[46] Edwards, 'Authorship of the poems of Laurence Minot'.
[47] Chandos Herald, *Vie du Prince Noir*, 16.
[48] Froissart, *Chroniques*, ed. Luce, VII, 218; Jonathan Sumption, *The Hundred Years War*. 4 vols (London and Philadelphia PA, 1990–9), III, 49–50.
[49] The manuscript, missing from the British Library since October 1971, is described in Isabel S.T. Aspin, *Anglo-Norman Political Songs*. Anglo Norman Texts 11 (Oxford, 1953), 12–13; the *Interludium* is reproduced in facsimile in Norman Davis, *Non-Cycle Plays and*

interlude in English, the *Interludium de clerico et puella*, which traces the wooing of a reluctant maiden by an amorous cleric. Several other short interludes of this kind survived and have sometimes been suggested as likely candidates for a minstrel's repertory.[50] It seems in this case that we actually do have an *aide-mémoire* of a professional entertainer, someone whose repertory covered both the deeds of great men and comic entertainment.

The roll has been damaged, and the *Song of the Barons* now consists of thirteen complete stanzas of six lines each and a fragment of a fourteenth. Each stanza is devoted to one man, beginning with Simon's supporters:[51]

> Mes de Warenne ly [bo]ns quens,
> Que tant ad richesse et biens,
> Si ad apris d[e] guere,
> En Norrfolk, en cel pais,
> Vint conquerrant ses enemis;
> Mes ore ne ad que fere.
>
> > (But the good Earl Warenne who owns so much wealth and property, and has been trained in warfare, he was conquering his foes in Norfolk, in that country, but now there is nothing for him to do.) (lines 1–12)

After listing several other supporters, the poem turns to Montfort himself:

> Il est apelé de Montford;
> Il est el mond et si est fort,
> Si ad grant chevalerie;
> Ce [est] voir et je m'accort:
> Il eime dreit et het le tort,
> Si avera la mestrie.
>
> > (He is called Montfort: he is in the world and he is strong, and great is his prowess; this is the truth and I concur: he loves right and hates wrong and he will get the upper hand.) (lines 37–42)

Finally the poem turns to Montfort's enemies, beginning with the bishop of Norwich, a pastor who devours his sheep (lines 55–60). The poem is little more than a list, one stanza for each of the major aristocratic leaders on each side. Offering neither a full narrative nor vivid description, it makes its appeal to those who already know the figures and their story.

Another work that is structured in much the same way, and adds to it a strong heraldic interest in the knights' coats of arms, is the *Song of Caerlaverock*, an Anglo-Norman poem in praise of the English knights who in 1300 successfully besieged

---

Fragments. EETS s.s. 1 (London, 1970), 7–11. The text is reproduced in J.A.W. Bennett and G.V. Smithers, *Early Middle English Verse and Prose*. 2nd edn (Oxford, 1968), 196–200.

[50] W. Heuser, 'Das interludium de Clerico et Puella und das Fabliau von Dame Siriz'. *Anglia* 30 (1907), 306–19; Bennett and Smithers, *Early Middle English Verse and Prose*, 78, 196.

[51] Text and translation in Aspin, *Anglo-Norman Political Songs*, 16–20.

the castle of Caerlaverock, in the West March of Scotland, near Dumfries.⁵² The song runs to just under a thousand lines. The author calls the poem 'mon sirventois' (line 257), normally the Occitan term for a satire, usually directed against knights or military leaders but here apparently simply meaning a poem about knightly deeds. Like the *Song of the Barons*, the *Song of Caerlaverock* works through the knights in sequence, but the narrator makes this an explicit commitment, asserting 'I will not pass over one' ('Ke nulle ne en trespasserai', line 32) and paying close attention to the blazons of each:⁵³

> Henri le bons quens de Nicole,
> Ki prouesce enbrasce e acole,
> E en son cuer le a soveraine
> Menans le eschele premeraine,
> Baner out de un cendal safrin
> O un lïoun rampant purprin.
>
> (Henry the good earl of Lincoln,
> Who embraces and loves valour,
> And holds it sovereign in his heart,
> Leading the first squadron
> Had a banner of yellow silk
> With a purple lion rampant.)

The praise of Robert Cliffort, however, who was given the castle by Edward, is more extensive than that for any other. The poet tells how he is descended from the noble earl Marshall, and fought a unicorn in lands beyond Constantinople, and blazons his coat of arms, ending that if he were a maiden, he would give him 'quer e cors' (heart and body, lines 275–302).

Denholm-Young has suggested that the poem, with its strong Cliffort sympathy, may be the work of a Cliffort dependant, possibly a herald/minstrel of Sir Robert Cliffort himself.⁵⁴ Certainly the author is fulfilling the function of a domestic herald, commemorating the deeds of his lord and his lord's ancestors and linking them to his coat of arms, while providing a roll-call of honour for the other lords on his side.

A song of praise which takes us a step closer to a full story and seems to bridge the gap between a minimalistic heraldic account and a full-fledged romance is a poem of 460 lines in short mono-rhymed *laisses* commemorating the disastrous Crusader

---

⁵² The poem survives in a single early manuscript, as a section of a miscellany, BL Cotton MS Caligula A. xviii, which was then copied, with the addition of illustrations, by the fifteenth-century herald Glover. See Brault, *Eight Thirteenth-Century Rolls of Arms*, 11–12.

⁵³ Ibid., 102; translation in Thomas Wright, *The Roll of Arms of the Princes, Barons, and Knights ... [at] the Siege of Caerlaverock* (London, 1864), 2.

⁵⁴ Denholm-Young, 'Song of Carlaverock' further suggests that the author might have been Philippe de Cambrai, the king of France's Flemish vielle-player. See also Bullock-Davies, *Menestrellorum Multitudo*, 146. Gerard J. Brault considers the possibility that the author was a Flemish minstrel influenced by Adenet le Roi: 'Heraldic terminology and legendary material in the *Siege of Caerlaverock* (c. 1300)'. Urban T. Holmes, ed., *Romance Studies in Memory of Edward Billings Ham* (Hayward CA, 1967), 5–20, at 6–7.

assault of Mansurah in 1250.⁵⁵ Following Tony Hunt, we may call this poem *La chanson de bon William Longespee*, as it tells of the heroic death of William de Longespee and his English companions after they had been provoked into a rash attack by the taunts of the Count of Artois, a man possessed by overweening pride ('qe mult fust surquiders', line 97).⁵⁶ The poem begins:

> [K]y vodra de doel et de pité oier tresgraunt
> De bon William Longespee, ly hardy combatant,
> Ke fust oscis en Babilone a la qarame pernant,
> Ke od le Roi Louys alat, o son host mut graunt,
>
> A un chastel de Babilone, Musoire est nomee,
> Ke touzjours en peinime serra renomee
> Pur ly rois qe fust pris en cele chevachee
> Et les altres chivalers ke furent de sa meignee!
>
>> ([Listen], those who wish to hear, with great sorrow and pity, of the
>> valiant warrior William de Longespee, who was slain in Babylon at
>> Shrovetide, and who accompanied King Louis and his numerous host
>> against a castle in Babylon called Mansurah, which will ever be renowned
>> in Paynim lands because the king was captured there and the other
>> knights of his company.)

The account shows a strong national bias, having Artois insult Longespee as an Englishman, and itself insisting on the nationality of the French knights it denigrates, as when it notes that Sir John de Bretain, 'was of Bourbon and not of Normandy' ('esteit de Boban e nent de Normandi', line 237); and it is written with considerable dramatic flair, providing vivid dialogue for the central figure. In many ways, though, it offers a relatively plausible account of what may actually have happened, with precise accounts of the exact wounds the leading crusaders received and just when and how they finally died. After the success of their initial charge, where over 1350 Saracens were killed, the crusaders are resting and waiting for reinforcements, when the Count of Artois rashly insists on attacking the castle immediately. He insults first the Master of the Temple and then Longespee, whom the poem then champions:

> De le hardi chivaler, le meilur combatant,
> Qe pur la krestienté puis le temps Rolant
> Ne combati en armes chivaler [si] vaillant.
>
> Ceo fu le count Longespee, qui mult fort combati;
> Avant ceo q'il fu mort, mult cher se vendi.

---

⁵⁵ On the circulation of reports on the battle and the composition of *La chanson de bon William Longespee*, see Simon Lloyd, 'William Longespee II: the making of an English crusading hero'. *Nottingham Medieval Studies* 35 (1991), 41–69, and Simon Lloyd and Tony Hunt, 'William Longespee II: the making of an English crusading hero. Part II'. *Nottingham Medieval Studies* 36 (1992), 79–125.

⁵⁶ Tony Hunt's edition in Lloyd and Hunt, 'William Longespee II. Part II'.

([And now we speak] of the bold knight, the best combatant. There was not a better knight fighting in arms for Christianity since the time of Roland. This was the earl of Longespee, who fought most strongly, and sold himself dearly before he was killed.) (lines 216–20)

The author of *La chanson de bon William Longespee* writes as if he had either been at the battle himself or spoken to those who had and as a clear partisan of Longespee. There is no particular reason to assume that he was a minstrel, but his work illustrates the kind of material that might be called a *geste*.[57]

Another place where one might look for signs of the professional memorialist is in those stories of battles that take so marked an interest in one particular family that they seem likely to have been composed under, or at least with an eye to, the family's patronage. Around 1300 or perhaps a little later, an anonymous southern author, possibly from Kent, reworked an Anglo-Norman romance *Richard Coer de Lyon*, and, or so it would seem, inserting an interpolation of some three hundred and fifty lines describing a tournament at Salisbury where Richard meets two Lincolnshire knights, Thomas de Moulton and Fulke Doilly, whose powerful blows so impress the king that he enlists them to go on pilgrimage with him to the Holy Land disguised as palmers.[58] Since neither of the knights appears to have been particularly famous, it seems likely that the interpolation was composed by someone working for one of the two families (who were connected by marriage).[59]

The duties of the praise singer, whether amateur or professional, can also be seen in numerous elegies. A good example is an elegy for Edward I, which exists in both English and Anglo-Norman versions, an indication that it circulated widely. The poem begins with a call to the audience:[60]

> Seignurs oiez, pur Dieu le grant,
> Chançonete de dure pité,
> De la mort un rei vaillaunt;
> Homme fu de grant bounté,

---

[57] Because it is found in a manuscript that also contains his work, BL Cotton Julius A. v, *La chanson de bon William Longespee* has sometimes been attributed to Peter Langtoft, an Augustinian canon from Bridlington in Yorkshire, whose *Chronicle of England* runs to over 9000 lines, and survives in twenty-one manuscripts, more than any other Anglo-Norman verse chronicle. Langtoft certainly shares the taste for vivid dialogue and he uses a similar verse form, and similar phrases, but his style is easily imitated and his other works make no mention of Longespee. See Jean Claude Thiolier, *Édition critique et commentée de Pierre de Langtoft, Le Règne d'Édouard Ier* (Créteil, 1989), 55; and Lloyd and Hunt, 'William Longespee. II. Part II', 85, n. 157.

[58] *Richard Löwenherz*, 92–109 (lines 251–608). The episode occurs only in the later tradition, represented by the early fifteenth-century manuscript Cambridge, Caius College, MS 175. For discussion see Hibbard, *Romance in England*, 148–9; and John Finlayson, 'Richard, Coer de Lyon: romance, history or something in between'. *Studies in Philology* 87/2 (1990), 156–80, at 166.

[59] Roger S. Loomis, Review of *Der Mittelenglische Versroman über Richard Löwenherz*, ed. Karl Brunner. *Journal of English and German Philology* 15/3 (1916), 455–66, at 460.

[60] Aspin, *Anglo-Norman Political Songs*, 83.

> E que par sa leauté
> Mut grant encuntre ad sustenue,
> Ceste chose est bien prové,
> De sa tere n'ad rien perdue.
> Priom Die en dovocioun
> Qe de ses pecchez la face pardoun.
>
>> (Listen, my lords, for the sake of Almighty God, to a lay of exceeding grief, on the death of a valiant king. He was a man of great excellence, and one who by his faithfulness sustained a very mighty encounter. He lost none of his kingdom – this is well proved. Let us pray God devoutly to grant him forgiveness of his sins.)

The poem concentrates on one moment, telling how the news is brought to the Pope at Poitiers, who is overcome with grief and says that Edward was 'the flower of Holy Church' ('De seint eglise il fu la flour', line 50). The English version is provided in the famous trilingual anthology BL Harley MS 2253.[61] Here too the Pope is filled with sorrow at the news of Edward's death and praises him in almost identical terms, saying that 'of crisendome he ber the flour' (line 48).[62] The Middle English version makes use of the various tag lines and standard epithets that are so common in the romances:

> All that beoth of huerte trewe,
> a stounde herkneth to my song
> of duel, that deth hath diht us newe
> (that maketh me syke and sorewe among!)
> of a knyht, that was so strong,
> of wham god hath don ys wille;
> me thuncheth that deth hath don us wrong,
> that he so sone shall ligge stille. (lines 1–8)

Here the listener actually does pause only for a 'stounde' (a brief moment), for the poem runs to only seventy-two lines. Admittedly, we cannot be sure that this introduction is functional while that of *Havelok* or many other romances was conventional. Indeed, by the time the poem was copied down into Harley 2253 it had moved away from oral recitation and become part of a literary tradition. Nonetheless, these shorts poems of praise for contemporary heroes seem ideally suited to meet the *gestour*'s need for brief partisan recitation. They might provide the closest surviving, that is, written, equivalents of the lost '*gestes* of mouth'.

---

[61] BL Harley MS 2253, ff. 73–73v: see the discussion in David Matthews, *Writing to the King: Nation, Kingship and Literature in England, 1250–1350* (Cambridge, 2010), 91–3.
[62] Aspin, *Anglo-Norman Political Songs*, 90, with spelling modernized.

Songs of shame

Singing praise was only half the job. The other half, for which we have even less direct evidence, was delivering abuse. The promise that the traveling minstrel makes to King Richard contains an implied threat: if praise comes from the minstrel, so too does shame. As a fourteenth-century English satirist says in condemning King David of Scotland, 'just as minstrels were wont to tell the strenuous and warlike deeds of good warriors, so they must sing the shameful and licentious doings of this David'.[63] Some clearly made abuse a speciality. According to his *vita*, Marcabru[64]

> fo mout cridatz et austiz pel mon, e doptatz per sa lenga; car el fo tant maldizens que, a la fin, los desfeiron li castellan de Guina[a], de cui avia dich mout gran mal
>
> (was very well known and listened to throughout the world and feared because of his tongue, for he was so slanderous that the castellans of Aquitaine, of whom he sang so much evil, did away with him').

In the thirteenth-century prose *Tristan*, Sir Dinadan makes a slanderous song about King Mark and sends a *joglar* to sing it at his court, a passage that was echoed by Malory. The harper, Elyot, comes before the court:[65]

> and because he was a coryous harper, men harde him synge the same lay that Sir Dynadan made, whyche spake the most vylany by Kynge Marke and of his treson that ever man herde.
>
> And whan the harper had sunge his songe to the ende, Kynge Marke was wondirly wrothe and sayde, 'Harper, how durste thou be so bolde, on thy hede, to singe this songe afore me?' 'Sir,' seyde Elyot, 'wyte thou well I am a mynstrell, and I muste do as I am commaunded of thos lordis that I beare the armys of, and, sir, wyte you well that Sir Dynadan, a knight of the Table Rounde, made this songe and made me to synge hit afore you'.

The song is never quoted, however, and we are left to imagine its contents. The custom that Malory describes does seem to have been maintained to some degree in real life. Froissart tells of innumerable formal challenges delivered by heralds, but minstrels would have served to bear these challenges as well.[66] According to the chronicler Johannes of Trokelowe, at a Pentecost feast in 1317, 'a certain woman,

---

[63] '... quia sic solebant ministralli dicere opera strenua et bellicosa bonorum militum, de isto David facient gesta luxuriosa'. Thomas Wright, *The Political Songs of England, From the Reign of John to that of Edward II* (London, 1839), I, 143. The poem is attributed to 'John of Bridlington', although the author himself suggests this is a pseudonym. See A.G. Rigg, 'John of Bridlington's prophecy: a new look'. *Speculum* 63 (1988), 596–613.

[64] Botière *et al.*, *Biographies des troubadours*, 12; Laura Kendrick, 'Jongleur as propagandist: the ecclesiastical politics of Marcabru's poetry'. Thomas N. Bisson, ed., *Cultures of Power: Lordship, Status, and Process in Twelfth-Century Europe* (Philadelphia PA, 1995), 259–86, at 259. Kendrick suggests that the description might be understood as a commentary on a tradition rather than on a single man.

[65] Stephen H.A. Shepherd, ed., *Le Morte Darthur or The Hoole Book of Kyng Arthur and of His Noble Knyghtes of The Rounde Table* (New York NY, 2004), 378.

[66] See, for example, Froissart, *Chroniques*, ed. Luce, I (2), 65, 68, 175; VI, 111–12; VII, 218.

adorned like a minstrel (*ornatu histrionali redimita*) sitting on a great horse' entered the hall and delivered to the king a letter, which reproached him for not treating his knights with enough respect. The porters, when questioned as to why they let her in, replied that 'it was not the custom of the king to deny access to any minstrel wishing to enter the palace on such a great occasion'.[67]

Of course, much of the abuse was sung by soldiers, camp followers, and the people at large – it was in no way limited to heralds or minstrels – and by its very nature (occasional and often obscene) it was unlikely to be copied down. A few examples survive, probably of the tamer material.[68] After Bannockburn the Scots composed a song 'in derision of the Englishmen':[69]

> Maydens of Englonde, sore maye ye morne,
> For your lemmans ye have loste at Bannockisborne,
>   With heue a lowe.
> What wenyth the kynge of Englonde.
> So soone to haue wonne Scotlande
>   With rumbylowe.

According to Fabyan, this song was sung for many days in dances and 'carolis' (or round dances) by 'the maydens & mynstrellys of Scotland'.[70]

One of the most extensive examples of a song of abuse is a piece of sixty-six lines satirizing the Flemings for their defeats at Calais and Guysnes in 1426 that happened to attract the attention of the chronicler. The poem begins by addressing the Flemish men:

> When ye fflemyng wer fressh florisshid in your flouris
> And had weth at your will, ye wold be conquerouris,
> Of Caleis, that littil toun, as it come in your mynde.
> But ye to conquere Caleis it comeþ you not of kynde.

---

[67] John Stow, *The Survey of London*, rev. edn, with an introduction by H.B. Wheatley (London and New York NY, 1956), 414; and Chambers, *Mediaeval Stage*, I, 44, n. 6. Chambers quotes the passage from John de Trokelowe and Henry Blaneforde, *Chronica et Annales: Regnantibus Henrico Tertio, Edwardo Primo, Edwardo Secundo, Ricardo Secundo, et Henrico Quarto*, ed. H.T Riley (London, 1866): 'quaedam mulier ornatu histrionali redimita equum bonum histrionaliter phaleratum ascensa dictam aulam intravit, mensas more histrionum circuivit'. Riding a horse indoors was not unusual: for an illustration see Edmund A. Bowles, *Musikgeschichte in Bildern* III/8: *Musikleben im 15. Jahrhundert* (Leipzig, 1977), Plate 28 (from Paris, Bibliothèque nationale de France, MS fr. 9342, fol. 13r, fifteenth century, made for Philip the Good, duke of Burgundy). Anonymous challengers interrupt feasts in several Arthurian romances, including *Sir Gawain and the Green Knight*.

[68] For further examples, see Wilson, *Lost Literature*, 205–8.

[69] Robert Fabyan, *The New Chronicles of England and France*, ed. H. Ellis (London, 1811), 420.

[70] Ibid., 420.

The poem runs though the losses they suffered at English hands, singling out the men of Bruges, Ghent, and Picardy, and then offers a derogatory etymology based on the Middle English verb 'flemen' (to banish or outlaw):[71]

> Remembres now ye fflemmynges, vpon youre owne shame,
> When ye laide seege to Caleis ye wer right full to blame,
> ffor more of reputacioun ben englisshmen þen ye
> And comen of more gentill blode of olde antiquite;
> Ffor flemmynges com of flemmed men, ye shal wel vndirstand,
> For fflemed men & banshid men enhabit first youre land.

The chronicler adds that 'Such & many othir rimes were made amonges englisshmen, aftir the fflemymynges were thus shamefully fled from Caleis and þe picardis from Guisnes fledd & gon þeire way".[72]

Knightly suspicion of professional chivalric memorialists

In 1385 Sir Robert Grosvenor, a Cheshire knight, brought an action against Sir Richard Scrope, 1st baron Scrope of Bolton, Yorkshire, objecting to his bearing the arms *azure* with *bend d'or*, which he claimed as his own.[73] The case was not finally resolved until 1389, by which point over four hundred depositions had been taken, including that of Geoffrey Chaucer. Those questioned were 'abbots, priors, and others of Holy Church and ... lords, knights, and squires of honour, and gentlemen having knowledge of arms', while men 'of the commons or of any other estate' were specifically excluded.[74] As Denholm-Young observes, 'The most remarkable feature of this controversy to a modern eye is that no herald was asked to give evidence; neither the royal heralds nor any private herald, nor the rolls made and used by them, are ever mentioned'.[75] Instead the document repeatedly employs such phrases as 'heard said by many noble and valiant knights and squires' ('ad oie dire des plusours nobles & vailantz chivalers & esquiers') to confirm the knowledge of the deeds of either knight. Denholm-Young suggests the witnesses were coached, but it is equally possible that the scribes drawing up the document imposed the

---

[71] Robbins, *Historical Poems*, 85, citing the version of the *St Alban's Chronicle* in Lambeth Palace MS 6.

[72] Ibid., 86.

[73] The depositions are edited in Nicolas, *Controversy*, and partly translated in John Gough Nichols, *The Herald and Genealogist*, vol. 1 (London, 1863). The case is discussed by Stewart-Brown, 'Scrope and Grosvenor controversy'; Denholm-Young, *Country Gentry*, 133–5; Lee Patterson, *Chaucer and the Subject of History* (Madison WI, 1991), 180–6; Rosenthal, *Telling Tales*, 64–84; Robert W. Barrett, *Against all England: Regional Identity and Cheshire Writing, 1195–1656* (Notre Dame IN, 2009), 140–50; and Philip J. Caudrey, *Military Society and the Court of Chivalry in the Age of the Hundred Years War* (Woodbridge, 2019), 96–114, 134–43, 178–9.

[74] Nicolas, *Controversy*, I, 40.

[75] Denholm-Young, *Country Gentry*, 134.

standardized phrasing.⁷⁶ In either case, the depositions create the impression of a community of fighting men, preserving the memory of their collective deeds of arms in a cultivated oral tradition, father to son, knight to squire. It is just such a community that is imagined in the regulations that Edward IV had drawn up for his household half a century later, so that the squires could be schooled in noble and courageous behaviour.⁷⁷

Minstrels and heralds, on the other hand, were onlookers, in no danger themselves, and they worked for money. The astutely generous could arrange to have their reputations enhanced at the expense of worthier men. It was said of the immensely unpopular chancellor of Richard I, William de Longchamp, bishop of Ely, that 'in order to increase his fame and glorify his name, he was in the habit of tricking out verses and adulatory jingles that he had picked up by begging, and of enticing jesters and singers from the kingdom of France by his presents, that they might sing about him in the streets; and but lately it was everywhere said that there was not such a person in all the world'.⁷⁸ This was an extreme case, but it was common knowledge that rewarding minstrels generously would promote one's reputation. The fundamental anxiety at the heart of Chaucer's *House of Fame*, that fame has nothing to do with merit, was widely shared.

Minstrels and heralds, travelling widely, keeping records, exchanging news and informing themselves of all knightly doings, were also dangerously well informed. Potential spies, their testimony, either true or false, could be damaging or even dangerous. The fifteenth-century 'Oath of the Herald When He Is Made before his Sovereign Lord' indicates some of the tensions inherent in such activity:⁷⁹

> **First** you shall swear that you shall be true to the most high and mighty prince our sovereign lord the king. And if you have any knowledge or have any imagination of treason or any language or word that should move some to the derogation or hurt of his estate and highness (which God defend) ye shall in that case as hastily and as soon as is possible unto you discover and show it unto his highness or to his noble and discreet council and conceal it in no wise.
>
> **Also** ye shall promise and swear that ye shall be conversant and serviceable to all gentlemen to do their commandments to their worship [knightly reputation] by your good council that God hath sent to you, and [be] ever ready to offer your service unto them.
>
> **Also** you shall promise and swear to be secret and keep the secrets of knights, squires, ladies, and gentlewomen, as a confessor of arms and not to discover them in no wise except if [it] be treason, as is before said.

---

⁷⁶ Ibid., 135.
⁷⁷ Myers, *Household of Edward IV*, 129. See p. 53.
⁷⁸ Wilson, *Lost Literature*, 189.
⁷⁹ Elias Ashmole, 'The Oath of the Herald when He Is Made before his Sovereign Lord': Bodleian Library MS Ashmole 1116, fols 2–2v, text modernized. Travers Twiss provides examples of similar oaths in *Monumenta Juridica: The Black Book of the Admiralty: With an Appendix*. 4 vols (London, 1871–6), I, 295–9.

During a period when half the English aristocracy at any time could easily be accused of treason and survival often required hastily changing sides, the obligations imposed by the herald's oath could easily become contradictory. Even had a herald wished to restrict himself to this disinterested championing of knightly honour, it would not always have been possible to do so.

The pieces of occasional verse and the passing references to minstrels, heralds, *gestours* and *disours* that have been gathered over the years allow us to draw some very tentative conclusions about how praise and shame actually circulated in late medieval England. They suggest that professionals of various kinds played a significant role. The great subject of conversation among knights, squires, and men-at-arms was knightly prowess, but it was also a subject for any number of others who were not themselves combatants and not necessarily of the gentry, among them heralds, minstrels, and men who acted as both. All contributed to this vast field of chivalric lore, which included much that would now be regarded as literary fiction, above all stories of the deeds of the great knights of old, a great body of heraldic, genealogical, and local history, and much abusive satire. While the exact words of the *gestours* remain elusive, they were a force to be feared. This fear may help explain why so often sources that one might expect to refer to heralds and minstrels, such as the depositions in the Scrope-Grosvenor case, fail to do so.

Minstrel performance and literary history

Since the mid-eighteenth century and the rage for Macpherson's *Ossian*, the minstrel has played a central role in sweeping accounts of cultural change. In these accounts two ideas are crucial: primitivism and displacement. According to the first, poetry at some earlier period before it was consigned to writing was more closely integrated with society, and both poetry and society were less sophisticated. Léon Gautier's evocation of the simple faith of the twelfth-century knights who listened to the *chansons de geste* is perhaps the most influential expression of this view, but it is widespread.[80] According to the second idea, each period and its characteristic art will be displaced by the one that follows: primitive oral poetry displaced by writing, epic displaced by romance, the oral entertainment of the hall first displaced by private or intimate reading in the chamber and finally by the advent of print.

Allowing for a cultural lag between France, or the French-speaking nobility, and the provincial English gentry, the view that earlier vernacular works, especially the *chansons de geste* of the twelfth and thirteenth centuries or the Middle English romances of the thirteenth and early fourteenth, normally circulated as oral performances fits easily into a standard literary history. According to this history, the *chansons de geste* were an earlier and more public genre well suited for recitation in the hall, and romance a more private or individualistic genre better suited for reading in the chamber. In this view, as far as French literature is concerned, the *chansons de geste* found their primary audience among the illiterate knights of the twelfth or thirteenth centuries, while the romances appealed to a more refined group of

---

[80] See, for example, Richard W. Southern, *The Making of the Middle Ages* (New Haven CT, 1953), 242.

listeners, many of them women.[81] Romance as a literary genre would displace the oral *chansons de geste* in France in the thirteenth century, but survived in England in a less sophisticated form until the end of the fourteenth century. So the editors of the early fourteenth-century *Yvain and Gawain* could refer to it as 'clearly the work of a minstrel catering to the sober, realistic audience of a provincial baron's court'.[82] In such a history, Warton's dubious reference to the minstrel who sang of Colbrond and Emma and the ploughshares at St Swithuns' abbey in 1338 would provide an example of the kind of full oral performance that would already have become somewhat *passé* among aristocratic audiences and two generations later would no longer find a place at the royal court.[83] The age of the reciting minstrel had given way to that of the court poet, and a 'literature of performance' had given way to 'a literature of participation'.[84] The minstrel ceased to be a jack-of-all-trades and became a professional musician or a jester. By the fourteenth century, the art of the minstrel, at least as poet or reciter, was in decline.

Admittedly, the late fourteenth century witnessed not just a major increase in the reputation of the English court poet, but also significant changes in court ceremonial, as the king began to take his meals in his chamber rather than the great hall. Richard Firth Green notes that the custom of the king dining in his chamber was well established by the reign of Edward II and had become common enough among the gentry at large to attract the condemnation of William Langland by the late fourteenth century.[85] Another possible indication of an apparent decline in oral recitation that has sometimes been suggested is the gradual eclipse of harpers at the royal court from the reign of Edward II onwards.[86] The implications of this change are not clear, however, since our knowledge of the instrumental and vocal repertoire is so limited. Recitation may have been part of the repertoire of the fiddlers and crowders. This was certainly the case at a lower social level. Above all, however, the view that there was a broad decline in narrative minstrelsy in the late fourteenth century turns in part on the assumption that in earlier times minstrels recited at length, and here, as we have seen, the evidence is far less compelling than is often supposed.

It is worth considering the case of one of the great book collectors of the period, Richard's uncle Thomas of Woodstock, Duke of Gloucester, one of the Lords Appellant, who defied Richard in 1388. When the king took his revenge in 1397, he confiscated his uncle's estate and an inventory of his possessions was drawn up, among them eighty-four books in English, French, and Latin.[87] These included a

---

[81] See, for example, Faral, *Jongleurs*, 255–6.

[82] Albert B. Friedman and Norman T. Harrington, eds, *Ywain and Gawain*, EETS o.s. 254 (London and New York NY, 1964), xvii.

[83] On the reliability of this reference, see above, p. 238.

[84] Richard Firth Green, *Poets and Princepleasers: Literature and the English Court in the Late Middle Ages* (Toronto, 1980), 111.

[85] Ibid., 35–6.

[86] Southworth, *English Medieval Minstrel*, 97.

[87] Viscount Dillon and W.H. St John Hope, eds, 'Inventory of the goods and chattels belonging to Thomas, Duke of Gloucester, and seized in his castle at Pleshy, co. Essex, 21

copy of the Wycliffite translation of the Bible, the *Romance de la rose, Ector de Troie, le Romance de Launcelot, la gest de Fouke filtz Waryn*, other romances and histories, a French translation of Livy, and Giles of Rome's *De regimine principum*. Gloucester had a reputation as a bibliophile and Froissart may have presented him with a copy of his collected poems, just as he did the king.[88] As Constable, Gloucester also took an interest in chivalric ceremonial, and wrote a small treatise in Anglo-Norman, 'un petit livret des ordnances et manières de combattre dedent lices'.[89] In short, Gloucester provides a fine example of the bookish, if somewhat conservative, aristocratic reader of Ricardian England. Yet the duke maintained a blind harper in his employ at Pleshey.

At the other end of the period, there is the case of Richard Sheale, the minstrel of Tamworth who around the year 1558 served the household of the Stanleys, earls of Derby, while maintaining close ties with the London ballad market. The poems in Bodleian Library, Ashmole MS 48, a manuscript that was closely associated with him, and poems in similar style, such as the Stanley Poem, show that as late as the mid-sixteenth century a harper could find employment singing the praises of a great family, as minstrel-heralds had been doing for centuries.[90] Neither wider literacy nor the advent of the printing press spelled the end of the minstrel as a singer of praise and teller of tales.

There was clearly a large gap between the poems that the minstrels sang or chanted, the lost *gestes*, and the much longer texts that have survived, even when these texts treat of the same heroes. Trying to see the oral tradition through the various literary and artistic representations of minstrels or to connect this tradition to the surviving literary texts or to the relatively respectable and stable lives of professional musicians, the minstrels of the records, is very difficult and allows for little certainty. The effort does, however, call into question some longstanding assumptions about the history of medieval literature. The tendency has been to cast the oral tradition as a precursor of the written one, and so to suggest that a poem like *King Horn*, with its extensive use of standard rhymes, or the *Chanson de Roland*, with its formulae, reflects an earlier period, when minstrels actually would have rapped out some version of such a poem from start to finish.

The evidence of performance history, however, tentative as it is, suggests a very different picture. Based on this evidence, we might include something like the following. There was already, by the time the *Chanson de Roland* was copied down, if not before, a medieval nostalgia for an age of purer chivalry when knights were

---

Richard II (1397), with their values as shown in the escheator's accounts'. *Archaeological Journal* 54 (1897), 275–303.

[88] Godfried Croenen, Kristen M. Figg, and Andrew Taylor, 'Authorship, patronage, and literary gifts: the books Froissart brought to England in 1395'. *Journal of the Early Book Society* 11 (2008), 1–42, at 10–11.

[89] The work is also known by the title of the Middle English translation, The Ordenaunce and Forme of Fightyng within Listes. See Twiss, *Monumenta Juridica*, I, xxxix–xl and 300–29; and Anthony Goodman, *The Loyal Conspiracy: The Lords Appellant under Richard II* (London, 1971), 77.

[90] Taylor, *Songs and Travels*.

united by a minstrel's song. The *chansons de geste* were more sophisticated and more literary than many early critics supposed and fully capable of misrepresenting themselves as part of this legendary past. The listeners too were more sophisticated than was once supposed. There were a significant number of people in England who enjoyed listening to heroic poems being read aloud and imagining that they were part of a nobler world.

There was, however, also a concurrent oral tradition; the heroic poems offered a fictional version of what was contemporary, not ancient, practice, and this too continued throughout the period.[91] This oral tradition was preserved by people called variously *jongleurs, gestours, disours* and minstrels; their duties and art often overlapped with those of the heralds, and they probably included a number of amateur performers as well as professional musicians. The group was loosely defined (unlike the minstrels proper, with their clear institutional identity), and could be so because the stories they were telling were really the property of society at large. The same heroes, the same key episodes, the same standardized descriptions, and possibly even the same tunes were used again and again, in a tradition whose complexity we can scarcely grasp. This tradition bridged what might now be considered fiction and what we might now consider history. So Roland provides a role model for the knights at Hastings and, three centuries later, for the knights at Nájera, who would have placed the *Vie du Prince Noir* and the *Chanson de Roland* in the same basic category. The people who told stories about these heroes were not just entertainers; they were historians, genealogists and publicity agents, and they retained this role throughout the Middle Ages. Their listeners' knowledge of the history they were telling allowed the minstrels to perform short fragments, just as Taillefer is said to have done, and gave these fragments immense emotional power. To these fragments, minstrels would add commentary and explanations, often to draw connections between the heroes of the past and their audience. These performers did indeed tell stories about knights, both old and contemporary, and their ability to make or break a knight's reputation could inspire knights but also provoked fear and suspicion. Minstrels and heralds, as a group, had long memories and could pass on accounts of notable deeds and even alleged death speeches for many years. They could also satirize enemies. Because they were feared and distrusted, their role as custodians of chivalric history was sometimes overlooked or erased, as in the case of the Scrope-Grosvenor depositions. In at least some cases, the silence of the writers about the oral performers is deliberate suppression.

---

[91] On the relation of this oral tradition to fourteenth-century English literary works, see Nancy Mason Bradbury, *Writing Aloud: Storytelling in Late Medieval England* (Urbana IL, 1998) and George Shuffelton, 'Is there a minstrel in the house?: domestic entertainment in late medieval England'. *Philological Quarterly* 87/1 (2008), 51–76.

14

Instruments and Performers

A few medieval instruments survive, and although most are very damaged and fragmentary it is still possible, given the necessary study, to learn about their original forms.[1] Of those found and apparently made in England, there is a fourteenth-century straight trumpet in the Museum of London and a citole from the same century in the British Museum.[2] Three late medieval celtic harps also survive, examples of the *clarsach* found in the Scottish royal accounts.[3] The instruments recovered from the wreck of the *Mary Rose*, which sank in 1545, are probably later than the period discussed in this book but late medieval in form: two fiddles, a *dulcina*, three three-hole pipes (two showing evidence of continental manufacture) and fragments of a tabor.[4]

Documentary evidence can sometimes support other kinds of information although it is not often helpful on its own. Much more useful is contemporary iconography, including illustrations of instruments in psalters and manuscripts of various literary works; several magnificent series of wood and stone carvings surviving in major churches at Beverley, Exeter, Lincoln, Manchester and Norwich, among

---

[1] For most types of instrument, updated information is available in *New Grove* (hereafter NG); and see also the very useful sections on various instruments in Ross W. Duffin, ed., *A Performer's Guide to Medieval Music* (Bloomington IN, 2000), and Chapter 6 of Victor Coelho and Keith Polk, *Instrumentalists and Renaissance Culture, 1420–1600* (Cambridge, 2016). In the current chapter particularly, though also elsewhere in this book, I am aware that Keith Polk's work on continental minstrelsy and my own on English minstrelsy run in parallel (see also Polk, *German Instrumental Music*). I have not drawn firm conclusions from continental evidence, but further work will provide a fuller picture of minstrelsy Europe-wide.

[2] For the Billingsgate trumpet, see <http://collections.museumoflondon.org.uk> under item BWB83[335]<225> (accessed 22 June 2022); John Webb, 'The Billingsgate trumpet'. *The Galpin Society Journal* 41 (October 1988), 59–67; and Graeme Lawson and Geoff Egan, 'Medieval trumpet from the city of London'. *The Galpin Society Journal* 41 (1988), 63–6. For the citole, see Crane, *Extant Medieval Instruments*, 14 f (catalogued as a gittern); and James Robinson, Naomi Speakman and Kathryn Buehler-McWilliams, eds, *The British Museum Citole: New Perspectives* (London, 2015).

[3] Crane, *Extant Medieval Instruments*, 17–18; Roslyn Rensch, *Harps and Harpists* (London, 1989), 114–20; SM II, 162–87, *passim*. The English royal accounts, as far as I know, never specify a *clarsach* in this period.

[4] Frances Palmer, 'Musical instruments from the Mary Rose: a report on work in progress'. *Early Music* 11 (1983), 53–60; and Herbert W. Myers, 'The Mary Rose "shawm"'. *Early Music* 11 (1983), 358–60.

others;⁵ and depictions of instrumentalists in the painted glass of some churches, such as the famous series in the Beauchamp Chapel in St Mary's, Warwick.

Such depictions may be accurately drawn, but one should not assume that they can be taken at face value. Did the illustrator really know what an instrument looked like, and how accurately did he depict it?⁶ There are few criteria for this: the level of detail can be considered, and how consistent the depiction is with other illustrations, both by that artist and by others; and one can see how realistic is the depiction of the minstrel's hands on the instrument, whether the method of bowing or plucking strings is likely to be physically possible and comfortable, and so on. This builds up a general impression of the picture's trustworthiness or otherwise, and this in turn enables comparison with other depictions, similarly assessed. The impression gained is always subjective, but, given enough illustrations of a particular type of instrument, it may be strong enough to stand as evidence and be tested against surviving instruments.

The circumstances of the depiction also demand careful interpretation. Some affect the way in which the artist has constructed the picture (Introduction to Part IV, items 2–4), some affect his decision about what instruments to include and the accuracy of their depiction (items 1, 5–7), and some affect the way instruments are brought together in consorts that may or may not reflect real-life practice (items 4–6 – literary evidence, too, is subject to this consideration, and should be assessed accordingly). One circumstance that argues for accuracy in depicting individual instruments is when a minstrel ordered the matrix for his personal seal, a matter discussed in the Introduction to Part IV. The six surviving minstrels' seals are listed in Table 16: three of them – those of Walter le Vyelur, Roger Wade (crowder) and John Harding (*vigilis*) – depict the instrument concerned and add to our knowledge of it.

The study of iconographic sources has led to another very useful type of evidence, the reconstruction and playing of medieval instruments. If enough is known about the physical form of an instrument and the materials used in its construction, a replica can be made which is then available for testing in performance. Playing such an instrument demands many subjective decisions, but can be helpful in showing what techniques do and do not work.

---

5   See Montagu, 'Beverley minster reconsidered', 401–15; W.C.B. Smith, *St Mary's Church Beverley: An Account of Its Building over 400 Years from 1120 to 1524* (Beverley, 2001); Martial Rose and Julia Hedgecoe, *Stories in Stone: The Medieval Roof Carvings of Norwich Cathedral* (London, 1997); Edith K. Prideaux, *The Carvings of Mediaeval Musical Instruments in Exeter Cathedral Church* (Exeter, 1915); and, more generally, Montagu, *Minstrels and Angels*, and other works by Montagu, Bowles, Remnant and others. Many individual churches now have informative booklets on the building's iconography, such as Simon Pickard and Richard Cann, *Christ in Majesty and the Angel Musicians in the Quire Vault of Gloucester Cathedral*. 2 vols (Gloucester, 2015).

6   The problems and limitations of iconographical evidence are discussed in SM I, xxviii–xxxv, and in Herbert W. Myers, 'Evidence of the emerging trombone in the late fifteenth century'. *Historic Brass Society Journal* 17 (2005), 7–35, at p. 7, cited in Stewart Carter, 'A tale of bells and bows: stalking the U-slide trumpet'. Timothy J. McGee and Stewart Carter, eds, *Instruments, Ensembles, and Repertory, 1300–1600: Essays in Honour of Keith Polk* (Turnhout, 2013), 13–30, at p. 15. See also Mary Remnant, *Musical Instruments of the West* (London, 1978), 15 ff.

Table 16. Minstrels' Seals.

Walter le Vyelur, fiddler, *fl. c. 1256–7*.	
Call-no.	TNA seal no. P 832.
Image	Three rebecs.
Illustration	Remnant, *English Bowed Instruments*, Plate 42.
References	Remnant, *English Bowed Instruments*, 31, 81.
Guillotus de Psalterio (le Sautreour), psaltery-player, *fl. before 1298–1319*.	
Call-no.	TNA E101.684.62, no. 3, attached to a quitclaim dated 3 April (Easter Monday) 29 Ed I (1301).
Image	A head (portrait of Guillotus?).
Illustration	Bullock-Davies, *Menestrellorum Multitudo*, frontispiece.
References	Bullock-Davies, *Menestrellorum Multitudo*, 98–104; Bullock-Davies, *Register*, 179–83; Rastall, SM II, Appendix A, *passim*.
Roger Wade, crowder, *fl. 10–16 Ed II. Died ?April 1323*.	
Call-no.	BL Seal 87 (formerly in Berkeley Castle), attached to the defeasance of a bond dated 29 August 10 Ed II (1316).
Image	Crowd and bow.
Illustrations	Heron-Allen, 10; Remnant, *English Bowed Instruments*, Plate 62.
References	Heron-Allen, *The Seal of Roger Wade* (transcription and translation of text); Remnant, *English Bowed Instruments*, 43, 46–9 and 55.
Ivo Vala, citoler, *fl. 1313–34. Died probably by Christmas 1334*.	
Call-no.	TNA E101.385.4, attached to a receipt for robes for Thomas Citoler and himself, dated 12 July 4 Ed III (1330).
Image	Foliage and birds, perhaps a visual pun on *ivus* (yew wood), from which Ivo's name is probably derived.
Illustration	Rastall, 'Citolers in the household', 48.
References	Margerum, *Situating the Citole*, 107–8; Bullock-Davies, *Register*, 212; Rastall, 'Citolers in the household'; Rastall, SM II, Appendix A, *passim*.
	NB Various given names beginning with J in the literature are apparently misreadings of the abbreviated dative case, Juonj (i.e. Ivoni).
Richard Bottore, gitterner, *fl. 4–14 Ed III*.	
Call-no.	TNA E101.385.4, attached to a receipt for his robe, dated 2 August 4 Ed III (1310).
Image	A cross potent and a flying insect (honey bee?).
Illustration	Plate 10.
Reference	Rastall, SM II, Appendix A, *passim*, especially 86.
John Harding, piper and *vigilis*, *fl. 16 Ed II–12 Ed III*.	
Call-no.	TNA E101.385.4, attached to a receipt for winter tunics for himself and his two companions, *vigilatores*, dated 10 December 4 Ed III (1310).
Image	Crossed shawms.
Illustration	Rastall, NG article 'Wait'.
References	Rastall, SM II, 86; Rastall, NG article 'Wait'.

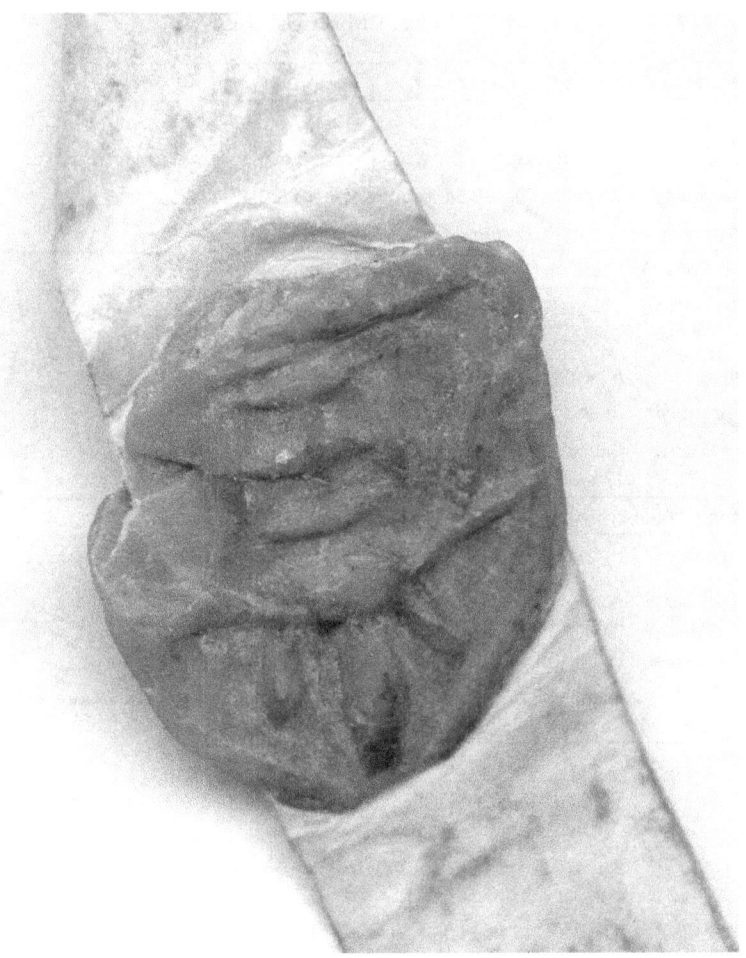

PLATE 10. The seal of Richard Bottore, the king's gitterner, on a receipt for his robe, 2 August 4 Ed III (1330), kept with a livery list. Kew, The National Archives, E101.385.4.

Putting all of the available types of evidence together, studies of medieval musical instruments in the last twenty years or so have greatly increased our knowledge and understanding of the instruments and their uses. In addition to the works already cited, many others have contributed enormously to a subject that is too large to be addressed effectively here and is still expanding.[7] In this chapter the instruments encountered here are briefly discussed and relevant information on their players given; and finally the matter of instrumental and vocal consorts is considered.

[7] In particular, see works by Timothy J. McGee, especially *Instruments and their Music in the Middle Ages* and McGee and Carter, *Instruments, Ensembles, and Repertory*; and by Christopher Page, especially *Voices and Instruments of the Middle Ages* (London, 1987).

Wind Instruments

Lip-reed instruments

Trumpets and sackbut

All forms of trumpet are lip-reed instruments, in which the air in a tube is vibrated by the player's lips against a mouthpiece. The oldest type of medieval trumpet in England was the straight **buisine**, between three and six feet long: the player took the instrument's weight in the palm of one hand under the shaft, holding the mouthpiece against the lips in the 'cigarette' hold with the other.[8] The tube was usually made in three sections, cylindrical except for the flared bell, and with a separate mouthpiece. Where a join occurred, with one tube fitting inside the other, the connection was not soldered but made airtight with a removable seal such as beeswax: the tube was strengthened at the join with a raised ring, easily visible in most depictions. This instrument had a restricted range, perhaps of only the first four harmonics.[9] Reconstructions based on the Billingsgate instrument that I have heard were about 6 feet long and pitched in G: they gave the notes g d' g' b' and d" (and, presumably, the fundamental G).[10]

The trumpet's range could be extended by lengthening its tube, thus lowering the pitch of the fundamental note:[11] but this increased the instrument's weight, and would take its centre of gravity further from the player, making it more difficult to hold. This problem was solved c. 1360, when metal-smiths learned how to bend a tube without flattening it and losing the round cross-section. The double bend produced an **S-shaped trumpet**, first depicted c. 1379 on a stall in Worcester cathedral.[12] The S-trumpet seems to have been much the same length as a *buisine*, but its closer centre of gravity allowed it to be held with one hand and therefore playable on horseback, the trumpeter controlling the horse with his other hand.[13]

Further improved techniques in bending tubes resulted in the **folded trumpet**, a more compact form allowing the parallel tubes to be bound with cord or connected with a metal brace. Increased rigidity allowed the instrument to be even longer and heavier than the S-trumpet. The folded trumpets shown in Hans Memling's Najera

---

[8] The mid-fourteenth-century 'Billingsgate' trumpet in the Museum of London (not listed in Crane, *Extant medieval Instruments*) is about 5' 3" long – slightly longer than Crane's measured examples of *buisines*.

[9] Several commentators cite Johannes de Grocheio's *De Musica* (c. 1300) for this, but Grocheio did not discuss the matter.

[10] Instruments made by Frank Tomes, played in Gloucester Cathedral, 28 October 2016, during celebrations for the 800th anniversary of Henry III's coronation.

[11] Tube-lengths and available notes are discussed in Jeremy Montagu, *The World of Medieval and Renaissance Musical Instruments* (Newton Abbot, London and Vancouver, 1976), 76–9.

[12] Misericord S9, illustrated in Galpin, *Old English Instruments*, Plate 49, facing p. 196; and in Montagu, *World*, 72. Galpin called this instrument a clarion, which is probably incorrect.

[13] See the front cover for one of the depictions of Henry VIII's mounted trumpeters on the Westminster Tournament Roll (1511) at the College of Arms in London.

panels of c. 1492 are long enough to demand a hold with two hands.[14] The three parallel yards were best gripped in the right-hand hold shown by Memling. The left hand held the mouthpiece in either the 'cigarette' hold or the 'dart' hold: Memling painted both. These would theoretically enable the player to slide the whole instrument along a shank attached to the mouthpiece, thus lengthening and shortening the tube to change the fundamental note and increase the repertory of notes available. This putative instrument is what we now call a **slide-trumpet**. It is generally accepted that the instrument must have existed, but there is no firm evidence for it and there are strongly-held views on both sides.[15] Questions concern the accuracy of Memling's apparently realistic paintings, the assessment of reconstructions made from these and other paintings, the musical necessity of an increased note-vocabulary, and the need for an improved instrument to match the style and content of written contratenors before and after its development by c. 1420. All the iconographic evidence for the folded trumpet, and therefore for the slide-trumpet, is continental.[16]

If the slide-trumpet existed it could be the instrument known as the *trompette des menestrels* in French-speaking regions from about 1410, apparently distinguished from the *trompette de guerre*, which would be the natural instrument with fixed mouthpiece.[17] This terminology does not require a slide-trumpet, but the minstrels' trumpet certainly provided more notes than the war-trumpet, since on the continent it functioned in a musical capacity with shawms. The war-trumpet would be suitable for fanfares and signals, and so could be a shorter instrument such as a herald's trumpet, or **clarion**, essentially a short, straight trumpet capable of being played with one hand. An instrument perhaps two feet long, or less, would have a limited and high note-range, hardly useful for music but ideal for making signals or for gaining attention before making an announcement. It is not certain that this is what 'clarion' meant – trumpet terminology is still problematic – but it would explain why some trumpeters were also known as clarioners: they were very useful minstrels, capable of both musical and signalling functions.[18]

By the 1480s there is evidence of an instrument now known as the **sackbut**: the name was used by Tinctoris (see below), and this may be the 'draucht trumpet' of the

---

[14] See Montagu, *World*, 78.

[15] There is apparently no evidence that the folded trumpet existed in England, and therefore none for the slide-trumpet: the (pictorial) evidence seems entirely continental.

[16] These matters are thoroughly discussed in three articles that appeared together in 1989: Ross W. Duffin, 'The *trompette des menestrels* in the 15th-century *alta capella*'. *Early Music* 17 (1989), 397–402, repr. McGee, *Instruments and their Music*, 409–14; Herbert W. Myers, 'Slide trumpet madness: fact or fiction?'. *Early Music* 17 (1989), 382–9, repr. McGee, *Instruments and their Music*, 391–8; and Keith Polk, 'The trombone, the slide trumpet and the ensemble tradition of the early Renaissance'. *Early Music* 17 (1989), 389–97, repr. McGee, *Instruments and their Music*, 399–408.

[17] Duffin, '*Trompette des menestrels*', 400.

[18] The identity of the one-hand clarion and the *trompette de guerre* neatly leaves a hand free to hold a herald's baton or (for military signals on the battlefield) a horse's reins. The other one-hand trumpet, the S-shaped instrument, seems to have been a more ceremonial instrument and was perhaps not included in the term 'war-trumpet'.

Scottish royal accounts in 1504.[19] 'Sackbut' could have been used for the slide-trumpet, but it is unlikely that a name would be coined for an instrument that had existed for decades. These names are much more likely to indicate the double-slide instrument (sackbut or trombone). The principle of changing the overall tube-length by sliding one tube inside another came into its own with a mechanism that used two parallel sliding tubes in a U shape, a more robust arrangement mechanically than any single slide could be. It was also more efficient musically, because a sliding U-tube had to be moved only about half the distance of a single tube to effect the same change in the instrument's overall length. The mechanical development of the sackbut from any slideless instrument was a large step that is one argument for the slide-trumpet's existence, as a mid-way invention: but whether the sackbut arrived as a single development from the folded trumpet or in stages, it was a game-changing innovation that must have caused a musical revolution. This is not easily discernible now, although stylistic traces of it might be visible in the music around 1480–1520 if we could identify them.

As already noted, heralds and trumpeters worked closely together. Trumpeters attended heralds, and in certain circumstances could probably make announcements themselves.[20] Their attendance was important aurally and visually, both in war and in peace-time. Trumpeters were given new banners before embarking for war, but also when preparing for peace-time missions.[21] Their signalling duties in war-time were extensive, and included instructions for troop movements as well as assisting when a truce was proclaimed.[22] Possibly they also assisted at the most unpleasant of the heralds' tasks in war-time, counting and identifying the dead after a battle, but this is not known.

A chronological survey of trumpeters shows that during the late Middle Ages their numbers increased. Late in Edward I's reign the king employed two pairs of trumpeters, while other nobles employed one pair or a single player.[23] These numbers remained general in peace-time until late in the fourteenth century: in 1392 the earl of Derby (Henry Bolingbroke) went abroad with two pairs of trumpeters, although an earlier expedition had employed only one pair. This number may still have been exceptional for an earl: the king's trumpeters do not seem to have increased until the reign of Henry VI, who inherited two pairs of trumpeters from his

---

[19] Dickson and Paul, *Accounts*, II, 449. (My suggestion of 'war-trumpet' in SM II, 184, was incorrect.)

[20] One of the King of Scots' trumpeters may have ranked as a pursuivant: see p. 84. An early sixteenth-century treatise on the apparel to be worn by a baron in the field deals with heralds, pursuivants and trumpeters together: see Frederic Madden, 'Remembrances for the Apparel ... of Henry Algernon Percy, Earl of Northumberland, 1513'. *Archaeologia* 26 (1836), 395–405.

[21] SM II, 154 f.

[22] Rickert, *Chaucer's World*, 232 (a translation of Baker's chronicle); *ibid.* 311 f (a translation of Froissart); and J.H. Wylie and W.T. Waugh, *The Reign of Henry the Fifth*. 3 vols (Cambridge, 1914–29), I, 156, n. 8.

[23] See SM II, 53–8, *passim*, for instance.

father and added another three players by 1447.[24] By the 6th or 7th year of Edward IV's reign the king had increased his trumpeters to nine, headed by a Marshal of the Trumpets. The duke of Clarence now had six trumpeters, which was also the standard number for an earl.[25] A baron, Lord Howard, apparently employed four in 1481, augmented by a fifth player at half pay for military purposes. The king's trumpeters remained at nine until Henry VIII's accession in 1509, when he added the six that he had employed as duke of York.[26]

This general increase in the number of trumpeters indicates a growing preoccupation with display and ceremonial, especially in war-time. Edward III's trumpeters were sometimes increased from four to five or six for military purposes. Sometimes one of the augmented band is named as a clarioner, and the war-time ordinances of 18–21 Ed III (1344–7) list five trumpeters and two clarioners among his minstrels.[27] The increase also suggests that the custom of employing trumpeters in pairs gradually died out, at least in the larger households. This was a slow process, and the minstrelsy of one or two trumpeters did not completely disappear during the fifteenth century.[28] The decline in such minstrelsy is evident as early as the reign of Edward III, when the Wardrobe books still recorded enough *Dona* for a comparison with earlier reigns to be made. The king's personal preference is clearly seen in the ordinances of 1455: although the saintly Henry VI had recently increased the number of his trumpeters from four to seven, the four minstrels in constant attendance did not include a trumpeter.[29] When we do hear of domestic trumpet-playing in the early sixteenth century – that which greeted the earl of Northumberland at his chamber door on New Year's Day – all six of his trumpeters were involved, and the music was presumably sophisticated ceremonial fanfares.[30]

Cornett

The cornett is a lip-reed instrument with finger-holes. It is made of a single piece of wood, split lengthways for the bore to be cut out, then glued together and covered in leather. A separate mouth-piece is fitted to the narrower end. Sometimes straight, but more often curved in imitation of an animal horn, it usually had a conical bore. A version with cylindrical bore is quieter, and is usually referred to as a 'mute' cornett: this normally had the mouth-piece cut into the top end of the instrument itself.

---

[24] MERH, 30. John Payte was probably dead by September 1451, however.

[25] *Ords & Regs*, 98: for the six trumpeters of an earl or duke, c. 1512, see Percy, *Regulations and Establishment*, 339.

[26] MERH, 40.

[27] For Edward III's trumpeters see SM II, 91–117, *passim* (the last *temp.* Ric II); for the war-time ordinances of 18–21 Ed III see *Ords & Regs*, 9, and above, pp. 5–6; for the augmented trumpeters of the Howard and Scottish households, see below. See also the trumpeters and taborers at Richard III's coronation, listed in MERH, 34 f.

[28] See SM II, 133 and 139. For gifts to single trumpeters, see SM II, 137 and Appendix D, *passim*.

[29] *Ords & Regs*, 18: Radcliff, Wykes and Cliff were all still minstrels, while More was a *wayt*.

[30] Percy, *Regulations and Establishment*, 342.

It has been suggested that rewards to 'one that bloweth in a horne' (13s 4d on 18 April 1498) and 'hym that pleyeth on the horne' (6s 8d on 26 April 1498, and again on 15 May) relate to the cornett-player Bontemps.[31] These sums are more than large enough to suggest musical performance, and might therefore relate to a horn with finger-holes (see below): but in the king's household at so late a date the instrument was more likely to be a cornett. Faced with this instrument, and not knowing its name, a scribe might well opt for the nearest equivalent that he knew. The instrument is virtually absent from English records until the sixteenth century, although it had appeared on the continent earlier (see Plate 11).

Bontemps appears as a cornett-player in the Scottish royal accounts for 1503, when he accompanied Princess Margaret to Edinburgh for her marriage to James IV on 8 August and remained at the Scottish court until at least 26 October. First described as 'Cornut', he appears later in the accounts as 'Bountas that played (or "plays") on the cornett' or simply as 'cornett-player'.[32] It is not known what kind of music Bountas might have performed, but he could have joined with a fiddle or plucked instrument, or supported voices in vocal music. He was also capable of solo minstrelsy, since he alone was rewarded for playing to Margaret in her chamber in late September 1503.[33]

Horns

The horn was not originally a musical instrument. At its simplest it was an animal horn with the tip cut to form a mouthpiece, making it a lip-reed instrument. Artificial horns were made from various materials, but most commonly from pottery, which was the cheapest material. It would be fair to assume that on any occasion where many horns were heard the majority were ceramic ones.[34]

In addition to the simple ceramic cow-horn instrument, a coiled form was made. This had a longer tube and therefore a lower fundamental note, so that a larger range of notes was available: but this too had no finger-holes,[35] and it appears that no surviving English horn does have them. There are many illustrations showing finger-holes cut into animal horns, however, providing the kind of instrument on which minstrelsy could be made. No medieval example is known to have survived, but entries in the royal records point towards such an instrument. On 9 June 17 Ed I (1289) the queen paid for a horn for Nicholas, *cornator*, which was presumably not

---

[31] Also Bonitamps, Bountaines and other variants. Ashbee and Lasocki, *Biographical Dictionary*, I, 169.

[32] Dickson and Paul, *Accounts*, II, 316, 398, 399, 400 and 403, cal. SM II, 179–81, *passim*.

[33] Dickson and Paul, *Accounts*, II, 398, cal. SM II, 180. It is possible that Margaret herself accompanied him, on lute or clavichord, which she was quite capable of doing: Stevens, *Music and Poetry*, 269.

[34] Further on horns, see above pp. 34–6.

[35] But see Natascha Mehler, Steinunn Kristjánsdóttir and Ralf Kluttig-Altmann, 'The sound of silence – a ceramic horn and its role in monasticism in late medieval Iceland'. *Early Music* 46/4 (2018), 551–60.

PLATE 11. King John of Portugal entertaining John of Gaunt in 1397: Jean de Wavrin, *Chroniques d'Angleterre*. Bruges, late 15th century. London, British Library, Royal MS 14 E iv, fol. 244v.

just a noise-maker.[36] Minstrels named *le Cornour* in the Wardrobe books also suggest a musical instrument: Laurence le Cornour received his livery-allowance and wages with the king's minstrels in 13–20 Ed II, and was clearly one of their number; and Walter le Cornour, minstrel of the Bishop of Exeter, was rewarded with 20s 0d on 19 January 14 Ed II (1321) for his minstrelsy in the king's chamber at Westminster.[37] A woodcut of *c*. 1500 by Israel van Meckenem provides a clear illustration of a large horn with finger-holes being played in consort for dancing.[38]

[36] Byerly and Byerly, *Records 1286–1289*, 391. Unfortunately the sum paid for this purchase is not specified.

[37] Laurence (13–20 Ed II), SM II, 79–83; Walter (14 Ed II), SM II, 79. The £1 reward to Walter is several times that expected for a bishop's minstrel. These dates are too early for the instrument to have been a cornett, so some sort of horn with finger-holes is probable. Other men named le Cornour or Horner cannot be identified as minstrels: John Horner (2–3 Ed III: a servant of the Marshalsea); Henry Cornour de Vise (45 Ed III); Picard Horner (37–8 Ed III and 1 Ric II) appears only in livery-lists of hunters; Robert Horner (16–17 Ric II) appears in a livery list but not among minstrels; John Horner (1 Hen V), a groom of the household, is not known as a minstrel. See SM II, Appendix A, under those dates.

[38] The horn is being played from the side of the mouth, like a cornett, and is part of the rather unlikely consort-grouping of horn, pipe-and-tabor, and trumpet. See Myers, 'Slide

Music-making apart, the horn had two main functions, for which finger-holes were not required. The first was to make noise, most commonly in raising animals and wild-fowl when hunting, but occasionally on the field of battle to disconcert the enemy. The second function, which required some skill, was as a signalling instrument. The chief huntsmen could inform the whole company of what stage the hunt had reached and where: for this there was a set of commonly-understood signals. On the field of battle signals were sent to deploy troops and to order their movements.[39] In the civic context, horns were used by the watch and by citizens to raise the hue-and-cry following the discovery of a felony; and in both towns and castles by the external watchmen to signal the arrival of someone for whom the gate must be opened, or the approach of a noble or an enemy force.[40]

Reed instruments

Shawms

The shawm was the loud double-reed instrument used both out-of-doors and in large indoor spaces. It had a conical bore, and finger-holes that varied the effective length of the body (as in all woodwind instruments) to give different pitches. It eventually came in several sizes – Praetorius shows five[41] – but in the fourteenth and fifteenth centuries we are mainly concerned with only two, treble and tenor. The treble shawm was probably the instrument used by the household *vigiles*, as depicted on John Harding's seal,[42] as well as providing the upper voice of the civic ensembles and other shawm bands. The tenor must originally have been small enough for the player's hands to encompass it, but a larger (and therefore deeper) instrument was made possible by the addition of a key for the lowest hole, this being covered with a wooden barrel, the *fontanelle*.[43] This improved tenor shawm is the *bombard*.

The *dulcina* is a type of shawm, but with a cylindrical bore. It is therefore quieter than a shawm of the same size: it could probably be heard with pleasure in quite a small room. It is rarely mentioned in literature or documentation, and because it is also difficult to distinguish visually from a shawm or recorder, its incidence is difficult to quantify from the iconographical evidence: its history is therefore uncertain. The only obvious distinguishing feature, apart from its cylindrical bore, is that it was sometimes made without a pirouette, the wooden ring against which a shawm-player could support his lips.

---

trumpet madness', 386.

[39] For hunting, see above, pp. 34–6; for the battlefield, see Rickert, *Chaucer's World*, 313.

[40] See Rastall, 'Civic minstrels', summarised in Chapter 7. In continental towns the civic watchmen-musicians used a range of instruments.

[41] Michael Praetorius, *Syntagma Musicum*. 3 vols (Wolfenbüttel, 1614–19; repr. Kassel, 1958–78), II, illustration XI.

[42] See Table 16.

[43] The bombard was known in England by 1380 (see p. 107), but a payment of 1390/1 (p. 136) suggests that there were two larger sizes of shawm. The 'large shawm' presumably did not have the key that distinguished the bombard.

It is possible that some shawmists played the *dulcina* as a second instrument, giving them a flexibility in their post that would have been quite useful, but there is no evidence. It is also possible that an ensemble of *dulcine* was what became known as the 'still shawms' in the early sixteenth century.[44] However, the status of the *dulcina* in the late medieval world remains speculative, and the only surviving example is the sixteenth-century one recovered from the *Mary Rose*.[45]

Bagpipes

The bagpipe, too, came in different sizes, and with different numbers of drones disposed in various ways. The bag, made from the skin of a goat or sheep, acts as a reservoir for the air supply, blown into it by the player through a pipe fitted with a valve that prevents the air from escaping. Under pressure, regulated by the player's arm, the air enters the drone-pipes and the chanter. Only this last is fingered in order to play tunes: different types of bagpipe have either single or double reeds.

The chanter can be either conical or cylindrical in bore, as can the drones, although the latter are more often cylindrical. In general, if a bagpipe is large, has multiple drones, and has a conical-bore chanter, it is likely to be a loud out-door instrument; if it is small, with only one or two drones (or none at all), and has a cylindrical-bore chanter, it is more likely to be for indoor use.

Bagpipes of various sizes were probably more common at Court than the incidence of the terms 'bagpiper' and 'cornemuser' would suggest: sometimes we know that a royal minstrel was a bagpiper only through a single entry amongst many referring to him as a 'piper'.[46] Other than a distinction between these two terms there is no information about the type of bagpipe played. It is possible that the smallest variety could be played with one hand, leaving the other free to strike a tabor.[47]

Some royal pipers were players of the **cornemuse**, a French bagpipe that had a single drone set parallel to the chanter. This is a relatively quiet instrument, and was perhaps suitable for indoor performance. In Edward III's reign the king employed the cornemusers John de Morleyns and John Perrot together for several years starting in 8 Ed III. Both were often known as 'piper', but they were also distinguished from the bagpiper Barberus in 8 Ed III. Probably there were other cornemusers at Court in other reigns, obscured by the more general terms 'piper' and 'bagpiper'.

Hornpipe

The hornpipe is identified by a variety of characteristics which do not distinguish it as a 'loud' or a 'still' instrument. It was normally a cylindrical pipe with a single reed and an animal horn as a bell, giving the instrument its name. Sometimes there was another horn at the top of the instrument that acted as a wind-cap and prevented the

---

[44] Ashbee, *Records*, VII, 28–9. Further on this ensemble, see below. The instrument was known by various names cognate with *dulcina*, for which see Duffin, *Performer's Guide*, 393.

[45] Palmer, 'Musical instruments from the *Mary Rose*' and Myers, 'Mary Rose "shawm"'.

[46] For instance, John Perrot in Edward III's reign and Pudsey in Henry VII's.

[47] See pp. 31–2, and SM II, 94. As Robert de Farebourn had been making minstrelsy to the king, and had presumably played pipe-and-tabor, John Perrot may have done the same.

player from taking the reed into his mouth; sometimes the air supply was provided from a bag. In the records there is no indication of the type of hornpipe in use, and in any case it is likely that a hornpiper might be referred to as 'piper' or 'bagpiper', thus disguising the identity of his instrument. In consequence, only a single player of the hornpipe can be identified in the royal records: Little Alain, who was probably not a permanent member of the household, is identified as a hornpiper in 17–18 Ed II (1323–5).[48]

Some hornpipes had two parallel pipes, each with a bell made from horn, and sometimes with two horns at the top end. A double pipe is mentioned by Tinctoris, who stated that a player was thus able to play two tunes at once.[49] This particular skill may be a reason for distinguishing a hornpiper as such (although Tinctoris considered it not to be very useful). Certainly double pipes are depicted in several Italian illustrations, although not, as far as I know, in any English source.

Flutes

In a duct flute, the player blows air through a small aperture that directs the breath against a sharp edge: this causes regular vibrations in the instrument's body, which is a cylindrical tube. In a transverse flute the player directs his or her breath against the edge of a hole cut in the tube itself near one end. In both cases, finger-holes vary the effective length of the tube, resulting in notes of different pitches.

Duct flutes

The recorder and the tabor-pipe are both duct flutes. The royal minstrel Flagilet (1359–65) probably played a duct flute, but perhaps not a pipe and tabor, as he was not named as a taborer.[50] One cannot be sure about the earlier fifteenth century, because the instruments played by 'still' minstrels are mainly unknown, as is the identity of the Black Book's 'small pipes'. The lack of evidence suggests that the recorder had no regular place in royal and noble households until 1497/8, when Arnold, recorder-player, was (briefly, it seems) one of Prince Arthur's minstrels.[51] The instrument came into its own at the English Court in the reign of Henry VIII, where it was played by both professionals and courtly amateurs.

Although the recorder may have existed under that name from 1388, a use of the term from the 1430s seems to refer to pan-pipes. The first clear reference to the instrument as we know it is perhaps that in the *Promptorium parvulorum* (1440),

---

[48] TNA E101.380.4 (Chamber accounts, 17–18 Ed II) fol. 22v (cal. SM II, 82). Alein may have been related to minstrels named Aleyn in later reigns, but even the first of these – William Aleyn in 37–8 Ed III – could hardly be the same man.

[49] Johannes Tinctoris, *De inventione et usu musice* (c. 1485), III, viii. Edition and translation at <http://earlymusictheory.org/Tinctoris/>: see below.

[50] TNA E101.393.11 (33–4 Ed III), fols 71r, 73v, 116v; E101.393.15 (34–5 Ed III), m. 2; E101.394.16 (37–8 Ed III), m. 8. (Cal. SM II, 110–12, *passim*). Instruments of the 'flag***' type were not normally transverse flutes. Flagilet was apparently in a trio with the pipers John Badencore and Peter de Burgoigne.

[51] Ashbee, *Records*, VII, 159 and 162.

where *canula* is translated as 'recorder or lytyll pipe'.[52] Iconographic evidence is sparse, and possible illustrations of the recorder may actually be of the *dulcina*, mute cornett or treble shawm. A late fifteenth-century example shown by Remnant seems certain, however.[53]

Pipe-and-tabor was a useful instrument for festive occasions: it could provide music for the celebrations after a wedding, for a solo dancer, or for the ceremonies and entertainments aboard ship.[54] Even in an elite household, where other instruments would be provided for dancing, a taborer was ideal as a teacher and master of ceremonies for dancing. Pipe and tabor were played by a single minstrel holding the pipe in his left hand and striking the tabor with a stick held in his right. The tabor was a small drum, slung from the neck, shoulder or, more usually, the left wrist (see below, under Tympanum). The pipe was normally a three-hole flute (playable with one hand), although it seems that even a small bagpipe could be played in this way.

Transverse flute

The side-blown flute is an ancient instrument, but its appearances in medieval European iconography are rare, as are documentary references. In England, flutes were not regularly used by the royal minstrel-corps until the reign of Henry VIII, and uncertain nomenclature is, as so often, a barrier to identification. John de Kyngorn, 'the king's *flutar[ius]*', who received money for a robe on 14 March 32 Ed I (1304), may have played a transverse flute: if so, he is the only flautist that I have found in the royal records before Tudor times.[55]

Pipers in the royal households

A short diversion is needed here, for the constitution of the royal 'pipers' changed during the period covered by this book and, as noted above, the terminology is not certain. Any performer on one of the woodwind instruments just described might be named as a 'piper', but normally that term probably meant a shawmist, with 'bagpiper' and 'cornemuser' also possible; players of the pipe-and-tabor were usually referred to as taborers, although perhaps not exclusively; and players of the recorder may have been termed 'piper' by some writers. Terms for woodwind players also included *fistulator*, *flutarius*, cornemuser and hornpiper.[56] The last two of these are specific, the first two probably distinct. *Fistulator* was most often used for a shawmist, interchangeably with 'wait': Guy Middleton, *fistulator*, was

---

[52] 1206 See NG article 'Recorder', especially 37–8.

[53] Remnant, *English Bowed Instruments*, Plate 133: from BL MS Harley 2838 (late fifteenth century), fol. 45r.

[54] SM II, 152, 156, 169, 176 and 183.

[55] BL Add MS 35292 (31–4 Ed I), fol. 33r (cal. SM II, 33). Despite the description as the king's *flutarius*, John was a local man (Edward was in Fife at the time) and evidently was not a king's minstrel for long.

[56] See SM II, 33, 82, 112, 120 and 138.

also known as Guy Waite, and both terms were used for civic minstrels.[57] *Flutarius* seems to have implied the player of a duct flute.[58] In a household context *vigilis* and *vigilator*, which are descriptive of the post rather than the instrument played, probably implied a shawm-player:[59] certainly several of the *vigiles* and *vigilatores* were referred to as 'piper', and John Harding's seal shows that his instrument was a shawm, apparently a treble.

Efforts to put specific instruments to the royal pipers are not wholly successful, therefore.[60] Despite the evident ubiquity of the shawm (if the iconography can be believed), there was apparently no word for that instrument until 'shawm' itself is found in the late fifteenth century.[61] A fifteenth-century gloss of *colomaula* (i.e. *chalemie*, shawm) as 'wayte-pipe' seems to identify the wait – common enough as a surname – with the shawm: but evidence of an instrument called a 'wait-pipe' depends entirely on that one source, which has not been identified.[62] The Leckingfield Proverbs, although late for our purposes (*temp.* Henry VIII), show a shawm to be low-pitched: 'A Shawme makithe a swete sounde, for he tunythe basse …'.[63] The pipe of a domestic watchman would have to be high-pitched (rather than merely noisy) in order to penetrate the thick walls and doors of a castle, and probably of small size to be handy for carrying around the building. The *Liber Niger* states that of Edward IV's minstrels 'sume use trumpettes, sume shalmuse and small pipes, and sume as strengmen …'.[64] 'Small pipes' may mean the small bagpipe here, although there is little evidence of it in the late fifteenth century; it could mean the *dulcina*; or perhaps this is an early indication of the growing use of the recorder at Court (players of the pipe and tabor appear to have been known as taborers rather than

---

[57] See SM II, 124, and Rastall, 'Civic minstrels', *passim*. For the derivation *of wayt* from the Old French *guet*, see p. 150. From this eventually came the designation 'waits' for a group of players making up a shawm band, including town minstrels.

[58] The phrase 'fistula nomine Ricordo' suggests that *fistula* could be as general a term as 'pipe', however: J.H. Wylie, *The History of England under Henry IV* (London, 1884–98), Appendix A. See also Remnant's article 'Recorder' in NG, vol. 21, p. 38. But if the scribe had not encountered the instrument before, *fistula* plus a qualifying phrase might have been the only description open to him.

[59] As noted in Chapter 7, a town wait who had a time-telling or tide-telling function was sometimes called *vigilis*, *vigilator* or, very rarely, *spiculator* or *speculator*: but in some places this was a horn-blowing watchman rather than a minstrel.

[60] It is likely, too, that pipers played more than one instrument, as they certainly did on the Continent. There is no firm English evidence for this, although there are several hints in what follows here.

[61] In the *Liber Niger*: see below.

[62] Galpin, *Old English Instruments*, 119–20, reiterated several misunderstandings, and did not name the fifteenth-century *nominale* that he quoted. A search through some obvious vocabularies has not brought it to light. Caution is now advised over definition 3 (the instrument played by a household *vigilis*) in my NG article 'Wait', therefore: but this does not invalidate the view that the household wait played a small shawm.

[63] Galpin, *Old English Instruments*, 117; Frances M.C. Cooper, 'The Leckingfield Proverbs'. *The Musical Times* 1552 (June 1972), 547–50, at 548.

[64] *Ords & Regs*, 48; Myers, *Household of Edward IV*.

pipers). Minstrels taking their description from a duct-flute are rare, however, and only Flagilet, Edward III's piper, might have played the instrument. The meaning of 'small pipes', therefore, remains in doubt.

The *Liber Niger* implies that the shawms and small pipes were played by the same men, and in this situation it is helpful to identify minstrels referred to in more than one way. The first royal household pipers of our period, late in Edward I's reign, were the household watchmen (*vigiles*) whose responsibility was the security of personnel and buildings at night. The twelfth-century *Dialogus de Scaccario* defines the duty of the royal *vigiles* as being to guard the very considerable treasures in the Exchequer.[65] This function need not detain us long, as there is no known connection with minstrelsy: but the use of the term 'wait' for one such *vigilis* must be followed up in order to clarify this point. A *vigilis* working at the palace of Westminster, including the treasury in the chapter-house of the abbey, appears in a list of prisoners held after the breaking of the Treasury in June 31 Ed I (1303):[66]

> Item Gilbertus le Wayte de Westmonasterio captus et detentus in eadem propter suspicinonem quia stetit Custos vigilie tempore quo Thesauraria illa fracta fuit.
>
> (Also, Gilbert the wait of Westminster, taken and detained in the same [Newgate Gaol] on suspicion because he was in charge of the watch at the time the Treasury there was broken into.)

Those who guarded the royal buildings, whether the king was resident or not, were apparently not connected with minstrelsy: but by the late thirteenth century there was a second group of *vigiles*, who provided security to the king's household, whether in a royal building or elsewhere. As the Wardrobe became an important repository of clothes and jewels no doubt more *vigiles* had to be allocated to the king's household, which was often on the move.

We have seen that the king's *vigiles* sometimes received extra liveries because they were required to keep watch during the night.[67] It seems reasonable to suppose that this duty remained unchanged throughout our period, and that the wait's regular duties as set down in the *Liber Niger* of 1471–2 were those of Edward I's *vigiles*.[68] There is a difference, however, that is not set out in the *Liber Niger*: Edward I's household *vigiles* were minstrels. Four of them received gifts for minstrelsy at the marriage of the king's daughter Elizabeth in 25 Ed I (1296/7),[69] and again at the

---

[65] Charles Johnson, ed., *Dialogus de Scaccario* (Edinburgh, 1950), 12 f.

[66] Sir Francis Palgrave, *The Antient Kalendars and Inventories of the Exchequer* (London, 1836), I, 269; T.F. Tout, 'A medieval burglary'. *Bulletin of the John Rylands Library* (October 1915), 1–24; and Paul Doherty, *The Great Crown Jewels Robbery of 1303* (London, 2005). Gilbert probably always worked in Westminster Palace, and he was not a member of the king's household. At this time the king was in Scotland, with a household that included his four *vigiles* (Alexander and Geoffrey de Windsor, Adam de Skirewith and Robert de Finchesle).

[67] SM II, 44 and 82.

[68] *Ords & Regs*, 48; Myers, *Household of Edward IV*, 132–3.

[69] Cal. SM II, 17.

Pentecost celebrations of 1306.⁷⁰ This situation obtained also in other households: in 31 Ed I the *vigilis* of the Prince of Wales apparently entertained his master *solo*.⁷¹ This *vigilis* may be the fourth member of the group just mentioned, for the records for 25 Ed I otherwise show only three *vigiles* in the king's household: John de Windsor, Adam de Skirewith and Alexander de Windsor, a trio also rewarded as a group for minstrelsy. John was replaced by Geoffrey de Windsor around *anno* 31, and Robert de Finchesle joined the group then as a fourth member. Alexander was replaced by Hugo de Lincoln *anno* 33; and the appearance of John de Staunton *anno* 34 (from 8 February 1306) brought the strength of the group to five.

This increase in the number of *vigiles* was no doubt for security reasons. The king's problems in Scotland, demanding protracted visits and long journeys, perhaps required a larger travelling security group: and if the *vigiles* were the only pipers in the king's household at that time (as was apparently the case), they would have fulfilled all the functions – ceremonial, military and social – required of a loud band. The presence of bagpipers in this band is not demonstrable.⁷² In short, while Edward I's household late in the reign included a variable number of *vigiles*, who were rewarded for minstrelsy as a group, no other pipers can be identified there; nor can pipers be identified in the dependent households, other than the one or two *vigiles* in each.

At the start of his reign (1307) Edward II employed only his father's two junior *vigiles*, Hugo de Lincoln and John de Staunton, and the available evidence is that two *vigiles* were normal for much of his reign.⁷³ In the 4th or 5th year the *vigilis* Geoffrey de Merton appears in the records, but only briefly.⁷⁴ When *vigiles* reappear in the king's household, *annis* 13–17 Ed II, they are named as John de Petrestre and Robert Chaunceler: Chaunceler had been a *vigilis* in the queen's household. These two were joined by John Harding *annis* 16–17, increasing the number of *vigiles* (reduced from five at the start of the reign) to three.

Early in the reign there were two *vigiles* in the queen's household: Robert Chaunceler and Richard de Burwardsle *anno* 5, and Robert Chaunceler and Robert de Baumburgh *anno* 9. Chaunceler's later transfer to the king's household was not an unusual move. One John, given money for robes *anno* 5, was the household *vigilis* of Thomas and Edmund, the king's brothers: he may or may not be John Mauprine, piper or *vigilis* in the following reign.

---

70 Cal. SM II, 57.

71 Cal. SM II, 38.

72 As noted earlier, the bagpiper Hamon *Lestivour*, who appears in the records several times, was employed by the Keeper of the Wardrobe.

73 Adam de Skirewith, Geoffrey de Windsor and Robert de Finchesle may have died, but the list of royal minstrels (MERH) suggests that minstrels sometimes used the change of monarch as an opportunity to retire, or that the king himself initiated a change of personnel.

74 SM II, 70 (two entries).

Little Alain, hornpiper, appears in the records *anno* 18,[75] but the only other identifiable piper in Edward II's household is John Mauprine. Records for 18–20 Ed II are particularly sparse, however, perhaps because of the situation that resulted in a sticky end to Edward's reign. John de Petrestre seems still to have been a *vigilis* in the king's household in the incomplete 20th year (1326/7), but no other pipers or *vigiles* can be identified. The rather negative evidence for Edward II's reign, if we can believe it, apparently shows that Edward probably employed fewer pipers than his father, and that not all of them were *vigiles*.

The records show various royal pipers and *vigiles* at the start of Edward III's 50-year reign (1327–77). Edward was often absent from England, sometimes for extended periods, and record-keeping was clearly disrupted in war-time. Of the various pipers, John Mauprine was described as 'king's minstrel' *anno* 5; Nicholas de Wycombe is not known as a *vigilis* until the 10th year; and Walter Gayt, who appears in the records only briefly at the opening of the reign, may not have been capable of minstrelsy.[76] The constitution of the *vigiles* becomes clearer in 4 Ed III, when three *vigiles* in the king's household were apparently a regular group: John Harding, William Harding and Radulphus le Gayte.[77] It was John Harding who, on 10 December 4 Ed III (1330), took delivery of fur and cloth for the winter tunics of himself and his two companions, the *vigilatores*, and set his seal to the receipt. This receipt survives: it is badly worn, but clearly shows two crossed shawms of conical bore.[78]

In the 11th and 12th years the *vigiles* were William Harding, John Harding and Nicholas de Wycombe; and in years 34 and 35 there were four *vigilatores*, named as Edmund Wayt, William Wayt, Walter Wayt and William Lamport or Langport. By this time in the reign other groups of pipers can also be seen in the records. John Mauprine, John Morleyns (known as a cornemuser) and Godscalk, piper, were transferred to the Black Prince's household for a while during 11 and 12 Ed III.[79] Around the 21st year there was a group of pipers headed by Lybkin and including his son Hankin fitzLybkin.[80] Another group that seems to have worked together in around 33–5 Ed III consisted of the pipers Flagilet, John Badencore and Peter de Burgoigne.

Some important trends can be seen, then, in the reign of Edward III. The *vigiles*, who gradually became known as *vigilatores*, probably worked less than at the end of Edward I's reign as a discrete group of minstrels. Another group of pipers was

---

[75] He may then have left royal service. Little Alain's hornpipe could have been either a shawm or a bagpipe.

[76] Several types of royal servant seem to have used a shawm, including huntsmen and falconers.

[77] Radulphus had been a servant of the kitchen in 2 or 3 Ed III. Perhaps he had been responsible for seeing that the kitchen fires were under control at night; or perhaps, when there were enough of them not to be on duty all night and every night, the *vigiles* had time for a second, part-time job in the household.

[78] Receipts collected with TNA E101.385.4 (4 Ed III). The seal is shown in my NG article 'Wait'.

[79] SM II, 97.

[80] Later perhaps the group's leader: see Chapter 2.

apparently formed to take over much of their minstrel duties – and this in addition to pipers, at least some of whom were bagpipers, who perhaps had a soloistic role in more intimate surroundings. An increase in the number of men called Wayt may reflect the larger number of pipers employed in this general increase.

For some of this reign the increase in pipers may reflect the constitution of a military expeditionary force. The household ordinances in war-time, drawn up some time in the years 18–21 Ed III, describe a minstrel-group that was not typical for peace-time, at least in its provision of *bas* (quiet) minstrelsy: five trumpeters, two clarioners, five pipers, a nakerer, a taborer, three waits, and only a fiddler and a citoler to make *bas* music. The group of three waits presumably consisted of William Harding, William de Hedele and Richard:[81] but one of the pipers, Ralph, was probably the *vigilator* of that name, which suggests again that there was some flexibility or overlap in the functions of those called pipers and *vigilatores*.

Records for Richard II's reign (1377–99) are sparse, but at the start of the reign there were four pipers: William Harding, Henry, David Welshman and Conute. Of these, William Harding was also a *vigilator*, apparently fulfilling a dual role, and Conute was perhaps a *vigilator* also at this time (as he was in the 17th year); William Lamport was a fellow *vigilator*, and so perhaps was one John Wayt, but neither of these is known to have been a minstrel. In the 17th year there were four *vigilatores*, Henry and Conute being joined by Nusselyn and William de Bingley. The pipers apparently consisted of a band of four, therefore, two of whom doubled as *vigilatores*, with another two *vigilatores* who were not minstrels.

Records of the reign of Henry IV (1399–1413) show three pipers. William Bingley, in service in the previous reign, was transferred (perhaps briefly) to the queen's household around the 8th year and is last heard of in the 14th. Guy Middleton appears first in 3 or 4 Hen IV, described as a *fistulator* 'formerly of the king's household': he remained in service, apparently as a minstrel, but is known as a *vigilator* in the following reign. Lastly, John Melton, first heard of in 7 or 8 Hen IV and apparently linked with William Bingley, may have been a *vigilator* at some time, although the evidence is not firm. The lack of *vigilatores* in this reign is probably due to incomplete records.

William Bingley's appearance in the queen's household in 8 Hen IV puts him together with William Algood, piper. It seems unlikely that the queen would require two shawmists, so perhaps these two also played an indoor instrument such as the *dulcina* or a small bagpipe.

Records early in Henry V's reign (1413–22) list three pipers among the minstrels: John Aleyn, Guy Middleton and John Melton. Middleton and Melton were certainly *vigilatores* by the time of the Agincourt campaign in 1415, for they are listed in the king's retinue as 'the king's guides by night'.[82] The fifteen minstrels at Agincourt are listed separately, and include a group of three pipers called Richard, Meysham and Broune. These three – Richard Geffrey, William Maisham and John Brown – appear together in a livery-list of 9 Hen V, for a coronation, presumably that of the queen

---

[81] See Table 1 and MERH, 16 and 19.

[82] See pp. 6–7.

(Katherine of Valois), whom Henry married on 2 June 8 Hen V (1420). I know nothing more about Geffrey and Brown, but William Maisham was later described as a still minstrel. He may have played a 'still' instrument in addition to a shawm, or perhaps he was a player of the *dulcina*.

Henry VI's household (1422–61) included no more than three pipers at any time; the dual minstrel/*vigilator* role is to be seen in the person of Guy Middleton. (The Lancastrian records tend not to specify the pipers, simply including them in lists of minstrels, while the *vigilatores* are so specified.) The other pipers at the start of the reign were William Maisham and perhaps Richard Geffrey. Middleton had apparently died or left service by 17 Hen VI, when the *vigilatores* of the king's household were named as Richard More and William Wodeford. Geffrey had died or left service by 22 Hen VI. In that year Robert More is first found among the minstrels, in the livery-lists covering the period 26–30 Hen VI: but he is named a *vigilator*, together with Hugo Joye and John Spolly, in the list of 35–6 Hen VI. Richard More continued in service until 22–3 Hen VI, when Robert More first appears. It is possible that Richard was written in error for Robert, or *vice versa*, but these are more likely two (presumably related) men. A John Wayt who appears in the accounts for a while between the 26th and the 31st years may be John Spolly.[83]

Robert More remained in place until the 5th or 6th year of Edward IV's reign (1461–83), apparently as a minstrel and thus probably fulfilling the dual role of minstrel and *vigilator*. Occasional references in the records to a man named Wayt (Thomas *anno* 8, John *anno* 22) are unhelpful, and the undifferentiated lists of minstrels in this reign do not show who were the pipers.

There is firm information on the duties of the minstrels and *vigilator* in the *Liber Niger* of 1471–2, as already noted. The minstrels are categorised as trumpeters, players of shawms and small pipes, and players of stringed instruments.[84] Leaving aside the trumpeters, who were always an exclusive group, this wording is interesting. The phrase 'sume use shalmuse and small pipes' suggests that pipers played more than one instrument, perhaps including bagpipe or *dulcina*, but perhaps also quieter instruments such as cornett or recorder. Those described as 'strengmen' would then be the rest of the 'still' minstrels, playing bowed or plucked strings.

The 'wayte' has a separate section, immediately following the minstrels, so he did not belong to the group of pipers. He was, nevertheless, directed to eat with the minstrels. His job was to pipe the watch four times each night in winter and three times in summer, checking for fire and other dangers. He had an assistant, who ranked as a groom but could perhaps carry out his master's duties in his absence (an arrangement that might have appeared as two *vigilatores* in previous decades). Despite his proximity to the minstrels, both on paper and in everyday life, the wait had no musical duties specified in the *Liber Niger*: but by implication, work as a minstrel was still open to him. As we have seen, Robert More could have fulfilled this dual role in the mid-1460s, only five years or so before the Black Book was compiled. In the ordinary way, one can imagine that a sole *vigilator*, piping the watch every night, might well

---

[83] See SM II, 124–6, *passim*.
[84] Myers, *Household of Edward IV*, 131–2.

spend much of his day asleep: but he would still have time for some minstrelsy, if the minstrels would have him, and his time would be much more his own if his assistant were capable.

Keyboards and percussion

Organ

The smallest type of organ depicted was hung from a neck-strap, the player using one hand to work the bellows and the other to play the keyboard. This is known as a 'portative' organ, and was perhaps exclusively a minstrel's instrument. The larger ones, 'positive' organs, were placed on a table or (the largest) were free-standing, with the player using both hands on the keyboard and an assistant working a pair of bellows. The largest would normally be placed permanently in a church or domestic chapel for liturgical use, although it probably had secular uses too. There was such an organ at the Prince of Wales's palace at King's Langley: this was repaired by the organist of Earl Warenne, Master John, against the arrival of the king and queen in February 1303. He must have been a skilled craftsman, for he and his apprentice worked there for nine days in January or February (see Plate 5, p. 35). The time spent and the 15 lbs of tin paid for suggest extensive repairs on a large instrument.[85]

An organist coming with certain Flemish nobles, Janinus de Rodes, was rewarded for his minstrelsy before the king and queen at Ogerston on 25 March 1303, apparently as a soloist (no other minstrels were rewarded then).[86] Earl Warenne's organist, presumably Master John, was later rewarded by the king for minstrelsy, with 20s 0d on 21 February 32 Ed I (1304) at Dunfermline.[87] Little William, the organist of the Countess of Hereford (the king's daughter Elizabeth), and Janin the organist, whose affiliation is not given, were rewarded for minstrelsy at the 1306 Pentecost feast.[88] Given the large number of minstrels present on that occasion, one assumes that these played the neck-slung portative organ, perhaps in consort with other minstrels, but it is possible that a positive organ had been installed in Westminster Hall.

Janin is likely to be the man employed first by Edward I and then by Edward II.[89] Organists appear in royal households in later reigns, but only briefly: they do not seem to be regular components of the royal minstrels, and there is no information about them or their work.[90] Unless they were specifically rewarded for minstrelsy

---

[85] TNA E101.363.18 (31 Ed I, household of the Prince of Wales), fol. 5v, cal. SM II, 38. See also above, pp. 33–4.

[86] TNA E101.363.10 (31 Ed I), fol. 11v, cal. SM II, 37. This was presumably at Hoggeston, Buckinghamshire, some 25 miles from King's Langley.

[87] BL Add. MS 35292 (journal, 31–4 Ed I), fol. 30v, cal. SM II, 32; and BL Add. MS 8835 (32 Ed I), fol. 42r, cal. SM II, 40–1.

[88] Bullock-Davies, *Menestrellorum Multitudo*, 1, 5, 115–6 and 144–5.

[89] MERH, 8 and 13. These various organists named John may not all be separate individuals.

[90] MERH, 17, 21 and 37–8; Bullock-Davies, *Menestrellorum Multitudo*, 116 (where John *Gallicus* seems to be a different man, the queen's French organist).

or were recorded as minstrels they may have performed in the liturgy, a skilled role that included improvisation on plainsong tunes.

The Chekker

Scholars debate the identity of the chekker (*eschequier* in French), which seems most likely to have been some form of clavichord. The minstrel John Perrot (or Perot – both spellings are used) is known to have presented an *eschequier* as a gift to the King of France from Edward III in 1360. Jean II of France had been in England for four years following his capture by the Black Prince at the battle of Poitiers, and was about to be released after successful negotiations for a ransom. The entry in the French royal accounts that records this gift, and Jean's reward to Perrot of 20 nobles (10 marks, or £6 13s 4d), also shows that Perrot had made the instrument himself. There can be no doubt that he would need considerable skill and experience to make such an instrument.[91]

Although there is no evidence that Perrot played any keyboard instrument it is convenient to discuss here what we know of his life. Perrot, piper, appears in the records over a period of 45 years. He is first recorded at Court on 22 October 5 Ed III (1331) in the queen's household, when he was paid for a saddle bought by him (at the queen's request) for a fellow-minstrel. In 9 Ed III (1335/6) he was paid for the replacement of a horse, and on 3 July and 5 August 1336 (10 Ed III) are the payments at St Johnstone concerning Robert de Farebourn's tympanum (related on pp. 31–2, above). For the last of these payments Perrot is described as John Perot, cornemuser de montvaleur. Perrot was French, then, perhaps from Montvalent, just south of the Limousin-Lot border, possibly coming to England with either Isabella, the dowager queen, or Philippa of Hainault (whose marriage to Edward III had been instigated by Isabella). In 11 Ed III (1337–8) the king was indebted to John Perot for £4 5s 4d, but Perrot is absent from the intervening livery-lists of the king's household, and was apparently still a minstrel of the queen: on 12 June 1337 (11 Ed III) the king rewarded Perotus and Janynus, minstrels of Queen Philippa, for performing before him. The following year, on 4 September 1338 (12 Ed III), at Sensk, John cornemuser, minstrel of Queen Philippa, was one of two royal minstrels rewarded for meeting the king there.[92]

There is then a ten-year gap in the English evidence. Possibly Perrot remained on the Continent, for a certain 'Perrot l'Estuveur' (i.e. bagpiper) was a member of the Confrérie de St-Julien des Menestriers in Paris in 1341.[93] Be that as it may, the name

---

[91] 'Jehan Perott qui apporta au Roy I instrument appelle leschequier quil avoit fait le Roy dangleterre avoit donne au Roy et li envoioit par le dit Jehan pour don a li fait a la relation M. J. le Royer xx nobles': Paris, Bibliothèque Nationale, MS fr. 11205, fol. 91v. See Edwin M. Ripin, 'Towards an identification of the chekker'. *Galpin Society Journal* 28 (1975), 11–25, repr. McGee, *Instruments and their Music*, 105–22: see at 108–9, where the nature of the instrument is discussed.

[92] Ed III (Rylands 235, queen's h/hd, 1331); 9 Ed III (Nero C viii, k's h/hd); 10 Ed III 3 July 1336, 5 Aug.; 11 Ed III (Nero C viii, k's h/hd): debts; 4 September 12 Ed III (1338), at Sensk: meeting the king (E36.203, k's h/hd).

[93] Vidal, *La Chapelle St-Julien*, 39; Kay Brainerd Slocum, '*Confrérie, Bruderschaft* and guild: the formation of musicians' fraternal organisations in thirteenth- and fourteenth-century

returned to the English records in *c.* 21 Ed III (*c.* 1347/8) when there is a record of Edward's debt of 12d to John Perat of the Chamber, apparently a member of the king's household.[94] A longer hiatus is broken by the French accounts of Edward's gift to Jean II in 1360, noted above, of a chekker made by Perrot.

Livery-lists for the king's household show that Christmas robes were delivered to Perrot, piper, in either 1363 or 1364, and then in 48, 49 and 50 Ed III, this last (1376) being the final Christmas of the reign.[95] The first livery-list of Richard II's reign (1 Ric II) does not include Perrot, who disappears completely from the record.

How many men feature in these records? If it is the same John Perrot throughout he can hardly have been born later than 1312 or so, entering Edward III's service at the age of 20 and leaving it (by retirement or death) at 65 or more. This is not at all impossible, and argues for a busy and fulfilled life in royal service (which could include earlier service with Isabella or Philippa). There are serious lacunae in his biography, however, and no conclusion can be reached. What is certain is that any of the possible John Perrots would probably be French: the first perhaps from Montvalent; the second a member of the Paris minstrels' guild; and the third a useful craftsman and emissary between Jean II and Edward III. Another piece of circumstantial evidence for the Perrots being one man is that they were described as piper, cornemuser or bagpiper (l'estuveur) – perhaps too great a coincidence to be set aside easily, even if the first was also a tympanistra (which is not, in fact, stated). John Perrot's biography invites further investigation.

Tympanum (tabor)

Used in Latin records, 'tympanum' is probably the term for a tabor, as in 'pipe and tabor' (see above, under Duct flutes). The story concerning Edward III and his piper who played the *tympanum* (pp. 31–2, above) may indicate a distinction between a *fistulator* or 'piper', playing a shawm or bagpipe, and a *tympanistra*, playing a pipe and tabor.

The tabor was a small cylindrical drum, with a head at each end: it usually had a gut snare on one or both heads. Most were shallow, in the manner of the tambourine, but some were as long as the diameter of the heads, or even longer. The tabor could be used for noise-making, especially in hunting and fowling, but musically its principal use was with the three-holed pipe.

In the late fifteenth century, if not earlier, the tabor seems to have taken over from nakers as the rhythmic backing to trumpets. In this case, and when used as a noise-maker, the tabor would be slung from the player's belt.

Nakers

Nakers were small bowl-shaped drums, slung in pairs from the player's belt. They were tunable, presumably to two different pitches, by means of cords attached to the

---

Europe'. *Early Music History* 14 (1995), 257–74, at 263–4 and n. 19.

[94] C. 21 Ed III: E101.391.9 (k's h/hd). Debt of 12d to John Perat of the Chamber.

[95] 1363 or 1364: E101.394.16 (k's h/hd, 37–8 Ed III), m. 8; 1374: E101.397.20 (k's h/hd, 48 Ed III), m. 23; 1375: (49 Ed III), *ibid.*, m. 25; 1376: (50 Ed III), *ibid.*, m. 27. These are cal. SM II, 112–16, *passim*.

head. While the nakers could perhaps be used for solo minstrelsy, their main use was in consort with a pair of trumpets.

No nakerer appears in the royal accounts later than Claux in 7 or 8 Hen IV, apparently leaving the drumming field open to the taborers. However, this coincides with a different naming of minstrels, in which the instrument is less often specified: taborers are apparently absent from the records for several decades, so the negative evidence must be treated with caution.[96]

Bells

A minstrel at the Pentecost celebrations in 1306, *le menestral ove les cloches* (the minstrel with the bells), is one of many puzzles. What sort of bells did the minstrel have, and what did he do with them? He appears to be an independent minstrel, yet he is surrounded by minstrels of royalty and the nobility, and his reward of half a mark (6s 8d) is more than enough to confirm his place among them. Moreover, he is the only player of bells that I have found in the royal accounts, and must be reckoned as special by reason of his rarity. Even allowing for the fact that many royal minstrels do not have instruments assigned to them in the Wardrobe books, it seems unlikely that no reference would be made to the instrument if a player of bells had been employed at Court or in any noble household. One must therefore conclude that bells were not a normal household instrument.

References are rare in civic and institutional records, too. A certain Adam *cum Campanis* appears in a list of minstrels and players rewarded by the city of York in 1448:[97] the very brief entry does not say whether Adam was regarded as a minstrel or a player, and so gives no indication of the sort of entertainment he offered. King's College Cambridge rewarded *tres cymbatores* in 1455/6, who presumably played *cymbala*, whatever sort of bells those might have been.[98] In all these cases the bells were presumably portable. At Henry VII's reception into Bristol in late May 1486, on the other hand, a pageant of the Resurrection included 'certeyne Imagerye smyting bellis'. Here, as in other pageants that used bells, the superior robustness and stability of bells suspended on a frame built into the waggon and 'smitten' would suggest chime-bells played with hammers.[99]

The dearth of documentary evidence is belied by the contemporary iconography. English illuminated psalters of the thirteenth and early fourteenth centuries show many depictions of bells, and these are consistent both in the appearance of the

---

[96] MERH, 26–7 and *passim*. However, the conjunction of tabors with trumpets, at Richard III's coronation, for instance, seems inherently unlikely. Noting that on the Continent the large kettle-drums 'came into vogue certainly by the 1480s', Keith Polk has suggested (in a private communication) that the term 'tabor' became used for them. A transfer of name to the kettle-drums would be for want of any other nomenclature. There is in fact no evidence of kettle-drums in England before Henry VIII's reign, as far as I know, but equally the use of 'tabor' at this date is difficult to explain.

[97] REED York, I, 72.

[98] SM II, 55, and Bullock-Davies, *Menestrellorum Multitudo*, 5; for 1455/6, see REED Cambridge, 36.

[99] REED Bristol, ed. Mark C. Pilkinton (1997), 13. For bells in the Towneley and Coventry mystery plays, see Rastall, 'Minstrelsy, church and clergy', 94–5.

bells[100] and in the method of playing them. The instrument consists of a number of bells suspended from a beam or rod and struck with two metal-headed hammers. The player sits or, less commonly, stands beneath them. Unfortunately, the bells are usually depicted within the limited space of an illuminated initial, and although the beam is normally shown, we rarely find out what supported it. In one illustration the beam is supported on pillars, and seems to be a fixture; in another, the unsteady-looking side-pieces must be a portable frame;[101] there is also a case of the frame being suspended from above.[102]

The number of bells depicted varies, but eight were usual. Where there are fewer than this, the available space is usually limited:[103] in one such case the illuminator appears to have solved his problem by arranging the bells in a rather impractical double row, by means of which he has just managed to fit in all eight.[104] A late twelfth-century psalter in the Hunterian Library[105] is exceptional in showing fifteen bells: two players, with two hammers each, stand on a raised platform (reached by ladders). The solmisation names of the notes are written on the beam from which the bells hang, giving a scale in each case from the end of the row upwards to the middle.[106] This arrangement gives the instrument a total range of a 10th: each player would have a large enough range to play most plainsong tunes, so that the two men playing together could perform a chant in strict organum at the 4th or 5th, or even polyphony.

It is however difficult to see what use might be made of a set of chime-bells. There are joyful liturgical pieces in which they would be appropriate, but no firm evidence that they were so used. It is an expensive instrument to use in teaching that could

---

[100] Their casting and tuning are discussed in J. Smits van Waesberghe, *Cymbala – Bells in the Middle Ages* (Rome, 1951).

[101] BL Harley MS 2804 (twelfth-century German Bible), fols 3v, 4r, reproduced in Eric G. Millar, *Reproductions from Illuminated Manuscripts*, series IV (London, 1928), 4, Plate XI; Bibliothèque de Dijon, Bible of St Stephen Harding (eleventh century), reproduced in *The New Oxford History of Music*. 10 vols (Oxford, 1954–75) (hereafter NOHM), III, Plate V.

[102] See Plate 6. Suspension from above suggests a permanent fixture, and should perhaps be treated with caution.

[103] See Eric G. Millar, *The York Psalter* (London, 1952), for the *Exultate Deo* initial of the York Psalter (c. 1250), where there are six; M.R. James, *The Peterborough Psalter and Bestiary* (London, 1921), for the Peterborough Psalter, where there are five; and BL Royal MS 3.E.VII (a thirteenth-century psalter), where there are four. See also the five in a corner-roundel of the Beatus page of the Evesham Psalter (BL Add MS 44874, c. 1250–60), reproduced in Derek Turner, *English Gothic Illuminated Manuscripts* (London, 1965), coloured Plate II. For an exception, see NOHM II, frontispiece (St John's College, Cambridge, MS B.18, twelfth century), where there are only seven bells, although there is no shortage of space.

[104] See Plate 6.

[105] Glasgow, Hunterian Library, MS 229 (press-mark U.32, Sect. 6), fol. lv: c. 1270, reproduced in NOHM III, Plate VII.

[106] Rastall, 'Minstrelsy, Church and Clergy', 95–7.

be accomplished with a monochord.[107] Some depictions are clearly of a temporary set-up, implying a portable instrument that could be moved around, but a set of bells and a wooden frame would not be easily manageable by one man. The work involved implies at least a mounted minstrel with one or more mounted servants. Such an instrument, too, would represent a lot of capital tied up, perhaps more than a minstrel would risk, even if he could afford it.

The frequent representation of chime-bells in illuminated psalters is undoubtedly due to its visual function in illustrating the Psalmist's *cymbala*, part of the joyful praise advocated in Psalm 150 and elsewhere. Robert Manning's translation (see p. 117) lists 'bellys ryngyng' in precisely this context.[108] The reference could be to the main bells of a church, of course (as in the reception of Adam Orleton at Winchester), which is not easy to illustrate in a psalter initial. The consistent use of chime-bells in illuminated psalters suggests more than a simple translation from the main ring of bells to a pictorially more manageable set, however. Chime-bells were probably used in pageants and plays,[109] and they seem likely to belong to an institutional context rather than to itinerant minstrelsy.

Chime-bells are almost always shown being played by one man, so they are a clear candidate for the instrument of the 'minstrel with the bells' (1306) and Adam *cum Campanis* (1448). A possible alternative is shown in the *Cantigas de Santa Maria*: a case, standing on wooden legs, containing seven small bells sounded by pull-down ribbons or cords, and played by one man. It is not clear whether this device moves the bell concerned or only the clapper.[110]

Chime-bells are shown in one illustration being played by two men, as noted above, but never, as far as I know, by three. For the three *cymbatores* (1455/6), handbells are perhaps the obvious alternative. One can imagine a small group of skilled players entertaining an audience not only musically but with a mimetic presentation based on the act of sounding the bells and the necessary movement between them: but that is pure speculation.

Stringed instruments

Plucked strings

Citole

The back, neck and sides of the citole were carved from a single piece of wood, so that there was no join between body and neck. The back was almost certainly flat

---

[107] The possible use of chime-bells liturgically and in teaching is briefly discussed in Waesberghe, *Cymbala*, 17–20; and see my 'Minstrelsy, Church and Clergy', 97–8. However, I can no longer confidently support all the conclusions that I reached in the 1960s.

[108] Mannyng, *Handlyng Synne*, I, 153.

[109] Rastall, *The Heaven Singing*, 263–4.

[110] See Zoltán Falvy, *Mediterranean Culture and Troubadour Music* (Budapest, 1986), 51, Plate 36.

or only slightly ridged. The table was flat and made from a separate piece of wood. The outline shape of the body varied considerably, but the balance of evidence suggests a close relationship with the fiddle. Most of the evidence for the citole's history, organology and playing technique is iconographic, with all the limitations and uncertainties that such evidence brings. To give an obvious example, illustrations of citolers performing do not show the back of the instrument, so that a citole is not always easily identifiable unless it is one of the waisted or holly-leaf types. Only one medieval citole has survived, and that mainly because of its wonderful carved decoration. Despite its reworking as a fiddle in the late sixteenth century, the British Museum citole (formerly known as the Warwick gittern)[111] allows us to see a good deal of the original instrument and has been subjected to an examination using the latest technology: this in turn has led to the manufacture of reconstructions for performance. A conference on the instrument in 2010 released much information about its organology and possible playing techniques.[112]

The citole is usually depicted with four strings, although both three and five are sometimes shown. Documentary sources suggest that it was gut-strung, but evidence for wire stringing also exists and the question remains unresolved. Other possible materials are silk and horse-hair, both known to have been used on stringed instruments. While the citole's tuning is unknown, Molina suggests that a tuning structure using perfect intervals (unison, 4th, 5th, octave) would facilitate an accompanimental role, a distinction first made by Jerome of Moravia.[113]

Other features suggest the same role. The citole's longitudinal cross-section is wedge shaped, with the deepest part at the neck end and the shallowest at the tail. This is a characteristic that seems designed for an easy plucking position, and especially for ease of strumming.[114] Iconographic evidence shows that the citole was normally played with a plectrum, that the neck was fretted, and that the player stood, holding the instrument across his chest: these are all features that would support incisive rhythmic playing, good projection, and textural clarity. Illustrations usually show the citole being used to accompany dancers, when this kind of performance would be appropriate.[115]

Demonstrations and performances during the British Museum conference and the associated concert showed that although the citole is a versatile instrument capable of a stylistic range from quiet reflection to very rhythmic percussive music, it is this last to which it is probably most suited. Different types of stringing would affect this playing-style, but in view of the other factors mentioned the stringing is perhaps not critical. The fact that the citole appears in the king's household but not in the

---

[111] On the terminology, see Alice C. Margerum, '"Alioquin Deficeret Hic Instrumentum Illud Multum Vulgare": a brief overview of citoles in art and literature c. 1200–1400'. Robinson et al., British Museum Citole, 15–38, at 15–18.

[112] Reports and papers from this conference are published in Robinson et al., British Museum Citole.

[113] Mauricio Molina, 'Li autres la citole mainne: towards a reconstruction of the citole's performance practice'. Robinson et al., British Museum Citole, 104–10, at 106.

[114] Ibid., 104.

[115] Ibid., 104 and 107.

queen's suggests, however, that it was suited to loud and rhythmic performance rather than for a lady's relaxation.

The citole originated in either Italy or Spain: the earliest useful depictions of it are in the Cantigas manuscripts of the late thirteenth century. It certainly worked its way northwards via France to England, where it arrived probably in the early fourteenth century. It seems to have been favoured at Court during the reigns of Edward II and Edward III, when four royal citolers can be identified in the king's household.[116] Records of apparently independent citolers in England can be found over a longer period of time, starting with an otherwise unidentified citoler named Janyn at the Pentecost feast of 1306.[117]

Gittern

Information on the gittern, too, largely relies on iconographical evidence: as with the citole, accurate identification is often uncertain. The instrument came to western Europe from Arab countries in the late thirteenth century. It resembled a small lute in having a rounded back, originally a single piece of wood with the neck and peg-box: there was no obvious division between body and neck, which merged without corners. Late fifteenth-century examples sometimes had the back made up from several ribs, as in a lute.

Some peg-boxes show a distinctive semicircular curve or sickle shape, not seen on other instruments. The gittern carried three or four strings, sometimes paired courses: these were probably of gut, suggested by the use of the gittern in literary sources for love-songs and serenades. The use of plectra leaves open the possibility of wire stringing, however, perhaps also suggested by the instrument's popularity for playing in taverns. The two surviving fifteenth-century gitterns – one at Eisenach in the Wartburg Collection, and one at Elblag – do not resolve this question.[118] Tinctoris stated that the gittern was tuned like a four-course lute, two fourths with a third in the middle.[119]

Gitterners are found occasionally in the royal accounts from Edward II's reign until Henry V's, only one player apparently being employed at Court at any one time. With a lack of more precise descriptions of the 'still minstrels' later in the fifteenth century, it is impossible to tell if the instrument continued at Court. It seems to have lost favour by Henry VII's reign, although in less exalted spheres it retained its popularity well into the sixteenth century.

Harps

Until the late fifteenth century the harp was the most prestigious courtly instrument. After that time the lute took its place: but for most of the later Middle Ages,

---

[116] Richard Rastall, 'Citolers in the household of the king of England'. Robinson *et al.*, *British Museum Citole*, 45–50, at 46–9.

[117] Alice Margerum, 'Situating the citole, circa 1200–1400'. PhD. diss. (London Metropolitan University, 2010), *passim*; Rastall, 'Citolers in the household', 50; Bullock-Davies, *Menestrellorum Multitudo*, 6, and SM II, 55.

[118] NG article 'Gittern', 907.

[119] *Ibid.*, 909.

when a man of rank was accompanied by a solitary minstrel, that minstrel was more often than not a harper.[120] Even when a noble employed many minstrels, his harper seems usually to have been the closest to him. Sometimes a payment was made to a man of standing by the hand of his harper:[121] and on one occasion a harper took letters.[122]

It is rare for the generic term 'harper' to be defined more closely. The harp most often played in England during the fourteenth century was probably the small frame-harp sometimes known as the *cythara anglica*.[123] This instrument, seen in many illuminated psalters, had anything from 8 to 23 strings (depictions in psalter initials being limited for space), but typically 12.[124] The strings were most often of gut, although materials such as leather and horse-hair are known to have been used.[125] The taller renaissance (or 'gothic') harp, common on the Continent and illustrated by Memling and others in the fifteenth century, was available in England also. Its longer strings allowed lower bass notes and made it suitable for playing slow-moving tenor parts in ensemble.[126]

One distinction sometimes made among harpers is the player of a clarsach, the Celtic harp, which accounting scribes no doubt found useful in identifying a performer: an obvious example is in the naming of Pate Harper and Pate Clarsach-player in the Scottish accounts, where the identical names are a potential source of confusion.[127] It is unlikely that any harper played both types, for the clarsach was strung with brass and played with long tapered nails – one played gut-strung harps with the finger-tips – and demanded a specialised skill. The clarsach was probably less common than the gut-strung harps, and it may be that the generic term 'harper' rarely if ever hides a clarsach-player.

Three late medieval Celtic harps survive, probably from the fifteenth century, or perhaps the late fourteenth: the Lamont and Queen Mary harps now in the National Museum, Edinburgh, and the so-called 'Brian Boru' harp in Trinity College Dublin. All are high-status instruments. They are typical in having a large triangular sound-box, and the more substantial neck and pillar required by wire stringing. The Lamont harp had 32 strings, the other two either 29 or 30. They are heavy instruments compared with English harps, and instead of being played in the harpist's lap were placed

---

[120] SM II, Appendix A, supplies examples to support the point.

[121] *Ibid.*, 17, 22 and 27 (three times): cf. also *ibid.*, 157.

[122] *Ibid.*, 104.

[123] See Hortense Panum, *The Stringed Instruments of the Middle Ages*, rev. and ed. Jeffrey Pulver (London, 1940), 102.

[124] Curt Sachs, *Real-Lexicon der Musikinstrumente*. 2nd, rev. and enlarged edn (New York NY, 1964), 84, *sub* 'Cithara anglica'. See Plate 6: the majority of illustrations are in illuminated initials in psalters.

[125] NG article 'Harp', 896.

[126] *Ibid.*, 898. For an illustration of a continental 'gothic' harp, see Rensch, *Harps & Harpists*, 121.

[127] SM II, Appendix D, *passim*.

on the floor, the harpist sitting on a low stool and perhaps gripping the harp with his crossed legs.[128]

The first two Edwards employed many harpers, and evidently thought well of them. Of those employed by Edward II, two were styled 'Master' and a third became *Roy de North*. No later monarch employed so many, however, and as far as one can tell from minstrel-lists a single harper became normal in the king's household, and remained so until the sixteenth century.

It is likely that at least one of the king's harpers was usually a *gestour*, singing songs of praise and the tales of saints and other great men of the past to his own accompaniment. The words *gestour* and *rymour* have appeared very rarely in the records searched for the present work, however, and amongst royal minstrels only three can be identified, each on a single reference: John Alisaundre is described as the *rymour* of the Prince of Wales in 1358, William Percival appears as *gestour* in a list of household servants in Richard II's reign, and Alexander Mason is described as *geyster* in a list of grants dated 22 Ed IV (1482/3).[129] We also know that Edward II, as Prince of Wales, had a *rhymer*, a matter which will be discussed below, in connection with the *crwth*.

Lute

The European lute is a gut-strung plucked instrument derived from the Arabian *'ūd*.[130] Its soundboard is a flat wooden table, and it has an arched back made of several ribs, making the instrument more or less in the shape of a half-pear. The strings are attached at one end to a bridge in the form of a bar glued to the table, and at the other to pegs in a peg-box fixed almost at right-angles to the neck, which is usually fretted. The lute is strung in pairs, and in the thirteenth century there were four such courses; a fifth course was added from quite early in the fifteenth century, and a sixth (and possibly a seventh) by about 1500: the top course was a single string. A plectrum was used throughout the late Middle Ages, which would make the lute principally a melodic instrument, though with the possibility of playing spread chords: but in the mid-fifteenth century players began to pluck the strings with their fingers, allowing both simultaneous chords and polyphonic strands to be played. The two methods – with a plectrum and with the fingers – co-existed into the early sixteenth century.

No lute survives from this period: the evidence for its organology is mainly iconographic. It is clear that lutes were made in several sizes, and therefore at different pitches, but all seem to have been tuned in fourths with a third in the middle. This gave the six-course lute an open-string range of two octaves which, with the possibility of playing chords and polyphonic strands, made it a very versatile instrument.

Luters may appear in the Wardrobe books as early as 17 Ed I (1288/9), when the queen gave 40s od to Gracius, *lutator*: but it is far from certain that that is what the

---

[128] Rensch, *Harps & Harpists*, 116; all three are illustrated on 115–19.

[129] Alisaundre: Lodge and Somerville, *John of Gaunt's Register*, III, 317; Percival: TNA E101.403.25 (cal. SM II, 117); Mason: BL Harley MS 433, fol. 311v (cal. SM II, 131).

[130] The NG article 'Lute', gives a very full account, on which this section is largely based.

word means, 'plasterer' being just as likely.[131] Men described as Le Leutor appear regularly from 25 Ed I amongst the royal minstrels, usually in the king's household, until Henry V's reign.[132] Identifying luters on the basis of this name is unsafe, even when the man is clearly a minstrel (for instance, the trumpeter John Leutor, named in Chapter 10): and for much of the fifteenth century luters are probably subsumed in the general designation 'still minstrel'. It seems probable that there were some luters in the English Court throughout the fourteenth century, but proof is currently impossible. Only in the late fifteenth century, with the records written in English, can luters be firmly identified, first in the Scottish court and then in the English.[133]

A livery-warrant of 2 November 1501 is for Giles Duwes, luter of the Duke of York (Prince Henry), who continued in service until his master became king as Henry VIII in 1509; Prince Arthur also employed a luter, William, in 14 Hen VII (1498/9); the king's luter in 1504 was Watt, about whom I know nothing more; and Kenner was luter to the Queen of Scots from 1503 onwards (see Chapter 8).[134] By this time the lute was clearly a common instrument considered suitable for ladies.[135]

Psaltery

The Wardrobe books record the psaltery only in the households of the queen and queen mother. It is an instrument of the zither type consisting of a flat-backed trapezoid or pig-snout shaped box with the strings stretched over two bridges. It was wire-strung and plucked with either fingers or quill plectra.[136] Evidently the psaltery was considered the most suitable plucked instrument for a lady's entertainment throughout the fourteenth century, and we do not find a harper in the queen's or queen mother's household until the reign of Henry VI.[137] The psaltery-players seem to have worked closely with the household fiddlers, to an extent that makes performance of fiddle and psaltery together very likely.

---

[131] Ed I (1294–5): see Byerly and Byerly, *Records 1286–1289*, 397.

[132] My first calendared entry is in SM II, 16 (Janinus le Leutor, rewarded for minstrelsy in early 1297 (25 Ed I)). Fryde, *Book of Prests*, 31 and 32, transcribed Janin's name as 'Lentour', which illustrates a common problem in identifying luters. For other possible royal luters, see the calendars in SM II, 35, 40, 42, 47, 49, 54, 66, 72, 86 and 122.

[133] For the Scottish entries, see Dickson and Paul, *Accounts*, I, *passim* (cal. SM II, Appendix D, 162–87, *passim*).

[134] Ashbee, *Records*, VII, 16; TNA E101.414.16, fol. 52r (cal. SM II, 140); Ashbee, *Records*, VII, 176; ibid., 20, and Dickson and Paul, *Accounts*, II, 316, 399–472, *passim* (cal. SM II, 179–87, *passim*).

[135] SM II, 179 ff.

[136] Remnant, *Musical Instruments of the West*, 28.

[137] See MERH, *passim*, for the queens' and queen mothers' households. The list of queen's minstrels at the marriage of Princess Philippa in 8 Hen IV does include a harper, but these minstrels were not usually members of the queen's household and were apparently loaned to her for the occasion (cal. SM II, 122).

Bowed strings

The players of bowed instruments are most often referred to as 'fitheler' or 'fiddler', for which the Latin version is *vidulator* and the French *vieller*. These are generic terms, but they normally apply to the large fiddle discussed by Jerome of Moravia.[138] This instrument was usually carved out of a single piece of hardwood to form the back, neck and peg-holder, with a softer wood for the belly.

Fiddles

The fiddle came in several shapes, including oval, rectangular and slightly waisted, and had a flat or near-flat back. It was gut-strung, with four or (more usually) five strings or double-string courses, the lowest of which could be a drone. Jerome of Moravia gives several alternative tunings, to be chosen by the player according to the music to be performed. Pictorial sources show that the neck was sometimes fretted.

The fiddle was most often held against the player's chest, shoulder or neck: but the largest instruments could be held horizontally across the chest, supported by a cord round the player's neck. Alternatively, it could be held in the lap, neck upwards in the manner of the later viol. There is no indication that this was a different instrument, and no separate name is known for it: it appears to be simply a waisted fiddle played in a different way.[139] This question was discussed at length by Woodfield in his Introduction, and picked up immediately at the start of his first chapter: '... the term "medieval viol" is now used to refer to a large, waisted fiddle, much used in twelfth- and thirteenth-century Europe, which was played with the instrument held downwards and the bow supported above the palm'.[140]

A smaller type of medieval fiddle was the spade-shaped instrument of which examples were found in the *Mary Rose*.[141] A wood-carving contemporary with the *Mary Rose*, in St Nonna's church, Altarnun (Cornwall), shows a minstrel playing such a fiddle (Plate 3, p. 27).

In the first three reigns of our period two fiddlers seem standard for the king's household, while dependent households sometimes included a single player. During the fifteenth century the fiddle may have suffered a temporary eclipse at Court: there was only a single player in the households of Henry IV and his two successors. Our information is insufficient for the reigns of the Yorkist kings,[142] but fiddlers may well be hidden among the 'still minstrels' of fifteenth-century records and the 'stringmen' itemized in the *Liber Niger* of 1471–2. The three string-players that feature in the wage-lists of Henry VII's household probably included a fiddler, and the queen

---

[138] See Page, *Voices and Instruments*, 126–36.

[139] My attempt in SM to translate *vidulator* as a viol-player was wrong-headed and should be ignored. Clearly, these were not regarded as different instruments.

[140] Ian Woodfield, *The Early History of the Viol* (Cambridge, 1984), 2–3 and 9.

[141] Palmer, 'Musical instruments from the *Mary Rose*', 55 and 58–9; NG article 'Fiddle'.

[142] Edward IV's *Liber Niger* refers to string-minstrels, as do the accounts of Henry VII's reign: see *Ords & Regs*, 48, Ashbee, *Records*, VII, *passim*, and SM II, 133–41, *passim*. This description, of course, includes plucked instruments.

certainly employed one: on 17 February 12 Hen VII (1497) he was rewarded with 26s 8d (i.e. 2 marks).[143]

The small spade-shaped fiddle was probably suitable for dance-music, and its players were possibly the *gigatores* or *gigours* to whom there is occasional reference in the royal accounts. Dance-music was more obviously the province of the **rebec**, however, a small half-pear-shaped instrument (that is, with a rounded back), usually with three strings. The rebec was held against the chest, shoulder or neck.

The terms *gigator* (Latin) and *gigour* (French) may be an attempt by the Wardrobe and Chamber scribes to render into those languages the German minstrels' description of themselves as players of the *Geige*. Gerald Hayes' conclusion that they were rebec-players, performing sharply-accented dance-music, is probably correct.[144] The issue is slightly confused by an entry (not known to Hayes) in which a *gigator* is described as *vidulator*,[145] which may be a scribal error caused by unfamiliarity with the terms: but it suggests that *vidulator* (i.e. 'fiddler') was used generically to encompass players on the small fiddles as well as the larger ones.

The three *gigatores* of Edward I were only temporarily at Court, although two of them remained there for several years. Named as Conrad, Henry and Conrad le Peper, they are identified as German minstrels. Conrad and Henry were at Court for about five years (29–34 Ed I), while Conrad le Peper joined them in the last year of their stay 'by the order of the king of Germany' (*ex mandato Regis Aleman'*).[146] Three groom *gigatores* who were at Court in 31 Ed I and, with two groom harpers, were governed by the royal harper John de Newenton, were perhaps being trained to replace the Germans: but they apparently did not become king's minstrels.[147]

Crowd

Another bowed instrument heard at Court was the crowd, the Welsh *crwth*. This is an instrument of the lyre type, its strings being stretched over a bridge across the sound-board. The crowd had originally been a plucked instrument, but during the fourteenth century it seems usually to have been bowed, this change roughly coinciding with it being given a finger-board. In the Welsh bardic *crwth* four of the six strings ran along the finger-board, while the remaining two were off the finger-board and could be plucked with the thumb as open strings. Panum gives the re-entrant tuning as g g' c' c' d' d'.[148] The seal of the crowder Roger Wade shows the instrument and its bow.[149]

---

[143] Cal. SM II, 135. See also Stevens, *Music & Poetry*, 277.

[144] Hayes, *King's Music*, 31.

[145] Cal. SM II, 88.

[146] E101.369.11 (34 Ed I), fol. 100v: cal. SM II, 46. Albrecht I was king of Germany 1298–1308.

[147] Cal. SM II, 31.

[148] Panum, *Stringed Instruments*, 240–1. Mary Remnant, 'Rebec, fiddle and crowd in England'. *Proceedings of the Royal Musical Association* 95 (1968–9), 15–28, repr. in McGee, *Instruments and their Music*, 315–29, at 325, also gives this tuning, together with a a' e' e' b' b'.

[149] For an illustration, see Remnant, 'Rebec, fiddle and crowd', 322. The seal dates from 1316 or earlier. For an angelic crowder of 1447 (using a bow) in the Beauchamp Chapel at

We noted in Chapter 3 that Edward II, as Prince of Wales, wished his *rymour* to learn to play the crowd. Edward apparently developed a taste for the crowd, for whereas there is no evidence that crowders were employed by Edward I, the prince employed three of them before the end of that reign and continued to do so after he came to the throne in 1307.[150] Edward III and his successors perhaps did not employ crowders, although, as with other instruments, the performers may be hidden by their general description as 'minstrel' or, in later reigns, 'still minstrel'.

Minstrelsy by those not known as 'minstrel'

Earlier discussions have shown that some royal servants who were not known as minstrels were nevertheless rewarded for minstrelsy. To some extent this demonstrates changes in the structure of the king's household, or at least in the duties required of some members of it; a certain range of abilities in some servants who had a second competence in addition to their main function; and a possible appointment pathway for the minstrels to be recruited from other departments, especially from the Chamber. It is difficult to demonstrate that anyone made the progression from a non-musical post, *via* the Chamber (using musical skills) to a post with the household minstrels, and there is only tenuous circumstantial evidence for it. As a professional career pathway, this would require professional training.

We saw in Chapter 3 that the Black Book of Edward IV (1471–2) required members of the king's household to acquire some competency in music and other activities in order to entertain themselves and any visitors to the Court. While it does not imply formal education in music, and therefore only amateur status, it shows members of the household being encouraged in the musical and other social skills required by, and helpful to the life of, a gentleman.

Heralds

The minstrelsy of heralds is discussed in Chapters 4 and 13. Some heralds are known to have been royal minstrels earlier in their careers, and these were no doubt capable of instrumental minstrelsy. All heralds, however, including those who had been instrumentalists, probably provided the kind of vocal minstrelsy discussed in Chapter 13. The duties of the heralds included managing the proceedings at banquets and other celebrations (Chapter 4). It is clear that there was a close relationship between heralds and trumpeters, and there is circumstantial evidence of trumpeters acting as pursuivants.

Waferers

Waferers were often associated with minstrels, by implication regarded as following a related profession. In a household, this is not surprising, but it happens that the relationship with minstrels occurs also among the itinerant minstrelsy. Liveried waferers, like the minstrels, may have been itinerant for some of the year: but in a

---

Warwick, see Remnant, *Musical Instruments*, 48 and Plate 36.
[150] MERH, 8–13, *passim*.

set of accounts which normally names the households to which visiting minstrels are attached, the entry[151]

Item, diversis ministrallis cum Wafirs, xxxj s.

(Also, various minstrels with wafers, 31s 0d)

almost certainly refers to a mixed bag of independent entertainers. So, too, does an entry recording a gift to 'Richard, *oblator* of Oxford, and other waferers and minstrels' in the accounts of Bishop Richard de Swinfield for 1289/90; and two similar gifts to waferers in the company of minstrels are found in the Derby accounts for 1391.[152] The fictional minstrel Haukyn, discussed in Chapter 11, mentions his function as waferer essentially as a sub-section of minstrelsy. The rewards to waferers for performing confirm the closeness, and perhaps the identity, of the waferer's profession and the minstrel's, without showing the precise nature of their entertainment. To make progress on that subject requires an examination of waferers at Court.

The waferer was responsible for making and serving sweet wafers at the end of a banquet, or perhaps at the end of any formal dinner at which the king was present. The royal household ordinances of 1318 show that he was to be lodged with the wayts; and the ordinances of 33 Hen VI name William Overton, yeoman, as the waferer, assisted by Thomas Caldwell, groom. A staff of one senior waferer assisted by a groom seems standard in the fourteenth and fifteenth centuries. The Black Book (1471–2) of Edward IV's reign states the quantities of eggs, butter, flour and sugar allowed to the wafery every day, but the duties of the waferer himself are not defined.[153] They were certainly considerable in the fourteenth century, when a waferer might be found in any dependent household, too. Although the wafery was only a sub-department of the Pantry, two king's waferers were styled 'Master': John Drake in Edward I's reign, and another John who served both Edward III and Richard II. John Drake must have been one of the senior servants of the Pantry, probably with considerable responsibilities: he held squire's rank and took the more generous livery-allowance. A payment of 20s 0d for shoes for his grooms suggests that he had six or seven of them in his care:[154] and as we noted earlier, he spent much time in Court.

The waferer's duties seem to have declined during the fifteenth century, when wafers were for the king alone except on such occasions as the principal feasts, when they were served to a very few nobles. The *Liber Niger* stated that the waferer's wages were lower at that time than in Edward III's reign because then 'his busynesse was muche more'. Despite this decline in the royal households, however, we should notice that the Duchess of Clarence had a yeoman waferer in her standing

---

[151] At Durham, 1402/3: cal. SM II, 148.

[152] See John Webb, ed., *A Roll of the Household Expenses of Richard de Swinfield, Bishop of Hereford, 1289–90* (London, 1854–5; repr. New York NY, 1968), I, 148.

[153] For the ordinances of *c.* 1136, see Johnson, *Dialogus*, 131; for those of Edward II, see Tout, *Place of the Reign*, 286; for those of Edward III, Henry VI and Edward IV, see *Ords & Regs*, 9, 18 and 72, respectively.

[154] Cal. SM II, 30.

household in 8 Ed IV, and that the Duke of Norfolk employed a waferer in 1481, when he was still Lord Howard.[155] In the fourteenth and early fifteenth centuries any household of importance – from barons and abbots upwards – probably employed a waferer, and the waferers will have served their wafers not only at the principal feasts, but also at other celebrations.

The waferer's dual capacity as maker and server of wafers probably made it desirable that he should be an entertainer. Towards the end of a banquet, with the main business of eating finished, the serving of wafers and other sweetmeats signalled the move towards entertainments of various sorts, starting with that of the waferer himself. It is hardly likely that he solemnly handed out the wafers and did nothing more: rather, he must surely have been adept at repartee and perhaps at stand-up comedy. The information that we have on the minstrelsy of waferers indicates that its nature was appropriate to this context, which also depended on the nature of the company. On one occasion in 5 Ed III Queen Philippa was entertained by two female dancers or tumblers (the marginal heading is *Quedam saltatrices*), one of whom was a waferer;[156] and some years later, on 21 August 12 Ed III (1338) her husband made a gift to two waferers who were probably a piper (*sifre*) and a dancer or tumbler (*sautour*).[157] One would like to know what entertainment was offered by the king's waferer Richard Pilke and his wife Helen on 24 June 5 Ed II (1312), but no information is given. Female minstrels were usually dancers, and indeed Matilda Makejoie, *saltatrix*, seems to have performed on the same occasion.[158]

As the royal waferers were sometimes capable of making minstrelsy, they were occasionally rewarded for it: and some attained the rank of squire. The waferer Peter de Normard was probably identical with the minstrel Peter Gaffrer (i.e. waferer), and Robert de Bosham was known as both waferer and minstrel in Edward III's reign; Henry Waufrer, minstrel of Henry IV, must also have been capable in both spheres. John de Bria, queen's waferer, may be identical with Edward II's minstrel John Briays.[159] At the marriage of Princess Margaret in 1290, one Boneurge, minstrel-waferer of William de Fenes, was rewarded for minstrelsy; when her sister Elizabeth was married seven years later, the waferer of the Prince of Wales and the king's waferer, John Drake, received similar gifts; and the list of those making minstrelsy at the Pentecost feast in 1306 included the waferers of the king (the same John Drake), the Earl of Lancaster and *Dominus* R. de Monte Alto.[160] The act of handing the wafers to the king was important, but there was special significance attached to it that had nothing to do with the day-to-day business of the waferer. One way of rewarding the king's supporters was land-tenure, and some tenures were wafer-serjeanties held by those who had handed wafers to the king on such ceremonial

---

[155] *Ords & Regs*, 100 (Clarence); Collier, *Norfolk*, 48 (Howard).

[156] Cal. SM II, 87 and n. 49: on or soon after 14 July 1331.

[157] Cal. SM II, 99. Medieval iconography and account-books both show that dancing could be of a very acrobatic nature, hardly to be distinguished from tumbling.

[158] See SM II, 74 f.

[159] MERH, 13–14.

[160] TNA C47.4.5, fol. 48 (not calendared); for 1297 and 1306, see SM II, 16 f, 55, 57 and 58.

occasions as coronations.¹⁶¹ In the early case of the manor of Liston Overhall, in Essex, the holder was bound in 1185 to make wafers when summoned to the king's feast: a holder of the same tenure in 1367 did so by virtue of having placed five wafers before Edward III at his coronation, and in 1377 a dispute arose between the Liston tenant and a rival claimant over the right to perform this service for Richard II.¹⁶² Presumably by this time the Liston tenant did not actually make the wafers.

Solo and concerted minstrelsy

Throughout this book there have been indications of the range and nature of solo and concerted music. This section summarises the conclusions originally published in 1974,¹⁶³ with some minor revisions due to further consideration of the evidence. Although these revisions do not always lead to clearer conclusions, they may help towards a better understanding of the issues involved.

The evidence for performance, as earlier chapters show, is notable for its silences rather than for the information it gives. The Wardrobe books never state that certain minstrels performed together – there is no reason why they should – although they show that groups of minstrels performing on the same occasion were often rewarded with a single sum to be distributed among them. On such occasions the minstrels may have performed either concurrently or consecutively. A gift may be recorded as made for 'minstrelsy' or for 'minstrelsies', the singular or plural form apparently being the choice of the recording scribe. One entry shows that a fiddler, two trumpeters and a nakerer received a gift for making *menestralciam suam*, although one cannot imagine the fiddler playing in consort with the other three.¹⁶⁴ This may be an error for *menestralcias suas*, with the fiddler and the trumpet group performing separately. The singular and plural forms probably do normally indicate one or more separate performances, although the use of one or the other is clearly not critical: 'minstrelsy' might cover several separate performances on any one occasion, and 'minstrelsies' could indicate either separate performances or performances of different types, such as instrumental and vocal items, by one minstrel. There is also the very common problem of the endings being abbreviated by scribal contractions (*menestralc' s'*), which leaves the number indeterminate.

Solo minstrelsy

There are nevertheless many certain instances of solo minstrelsy, with single minstrels being rewarded either on a day when no other minstrels were or, more commonly, being rewarded with a separate sum from others. The items of identifiable

---

¹⁶¹ Round, *Serjeants*, 227 ff, takes no account of the household wafery at Court prior to the late fifteenth century, so his comparison of Edward IV's waferer with the tenants of the earlier wafer-serjeanties is invalid.

¹⁶² Round, *Serjeants*, 229.

¹⁶³ Rastall, 'Some English consort groupings'.

¹⁶⁴ Cal. SM II, 39. Both the exclusivity of trumpeters and the broad division into 'loud' and 'still' argue against a fiddle joining the standard consort of trumpets and nakers.

solo minstrelsy in the royal households show that harpers, fiddlers, pipers, taborers, trumpeters and others could all produce acceptable entertainment – often well rewarded – on their own.[165] Some of the instruments concerned had features that made them particularly suitable for solo work, such as a drum (pipe and tabor), a drone (bagpipe), or the drone strings of the larger fiddles. These shaped the instrument's normal playing-techniques, and were therefore major factors in a minstrel's ability to hold his listeners' attention in what was basically monophonic music,[166] as were the ability of a capable performer to decorate and improvise.

The accompaniment of the voice

Rewards specifically for vocal entertainment are rare in the records, and usually identifiable only when the man concerned is described as *gestour, disour, rymer* or, possibly, *joculator*. These did not necessarily require musical accompaniment, and their entertainment is not invariably described as 'minstrelsy': but, even discounting Thomas Warton's evidence, there are clear indications that the singing of songs and the telling of tales could be accompanied by 'still' instruments, usually fiddle, rebec, crowd, harp, clarsach, gittern, psaltery or lute.[167] Conversely, it is likely that royal harpers and players of other stringed instruments, both plucked and bowed, sometimes performed vocal minstrelsy when the records do not specifically say so. Probably at least one of the king's harpers was usually a *gestour*, singing songs of praise and the tales of saints and other great men of the past.[168]

The use of a bowed instrument to accompany a song may still be surprising to a modern audience, but the use of the fiddle (of whatever type) to accompany singing is widespread enough over a long period to show that using a bowed instrument was nothing unusual.[169] This sometimes involved two people, but it could be a solo performance: in early November 11 Hen VII (1495) the king rewarded a woman 'that sings with a fiddle'.[170]

---

[165] See SM II, especially the *Dona* sections of Appendix A, and Appendices B, C and D, *passim*.

[166] Anthony Baines, ed., *Musical Instruments Through the Ages* (London, 1961), 227 f; also R. Thurston Dart, *The Interpretation of Early Music* (London, 1954), 154.

[167] For Warton, see Chapter 11. Literary evidence is useful in this respect: there is no reason to doubt that the 'gay sautrye' was used to accompany the voice, for instance, as Chaucer relates in *The Miller's Tale*: see Nigel Wilkins, *Music in the Age of Chaucer* (Cambridge, 1979), 119–20 and 114–21, *passim*.

[168] It is reasonable to suppose that a *gestour* sang *gestes* (which would presumably include *Grey Steil* as well as any extract from the *Chanson de Roland*), but the demarcation from other types of text is not certain. One might equally suppose that a *disour* told stories and a *rymer* was a poet: for these, too, specific evidence is lacking. *Joculator* seems to have been a more general term, with vocal minstrelsy implied.

[169] Rastall, 'Some English consort-groupings', 184–6; for instruments in the *Canterbury Tales*, see Franz Montgomery, 'The musical instruments in the *Canterbury Tales*'. *Musical Quarterly* 17 (1931), 439–48; and Chappell, *Popular Music*, 33 f. See also SM II, 133, 144, 170 and 174.

[170] TNA E101.414.6, fol. 6r (cal. SM II, 133).

'Still' consorts

In the fourteenth century the king employed players of bowed instruments in pairs. A gift to the king's two *vidulatores* at Easter, 29 Ed I, may be for minstrelsy when the king was making his offering:[171] no gifts were made to other minstrels that day, and we have examples of fiddlers making minstrelsy on such occasions. Later accounts suggest that fiddles were still played in pairs at the end of the fifteenth century: the two fiddlers who sang *Grey Steil* to the King of Scots on 19 April 1497 presumably played as well, and the Scottish accounts hint at several other occasions on which fiddlers may have played together.[172] A special case of this in the English accounts is the two German *gigatores* (noted above) working at Court at the end of Edward I's reign. They obviously worked very closely together, and surely played in concert: when the third *gigator* joined them they could have rung the changes on duos or, perhaps, formed a trio.[173]

In the late fifteenth century a rebec-player was one of what seems like a standard grouping to provide the basic minimum of minstrelsy needed in a household: rebec, lute (or harp) and tabor (with or without a pipe), providing dance instruction (tabor), social dancing (rebec, tabor), the accompaniment to a voice (lute/harp, rebec), and 'still' instrumental music (rebec, lute/harp).[174] This grouping is seen in the earl of Northumberland's household *c.* 1511 (see Chapter 5) and, probably, in the household of Prince Henry, since one of his minstrels was a rebec-player.[175]

Another combination that occurs in the royal households is that of one bowed and one plucked instrument, and in fact this is frequently found in the iconography of the time. In the king's household there was plenty of opportunity for this, and it seems likely that the fiddle was sometimes heard in concert with harp, lute or perhaps citole. In the reigns of Edward I, Edward II and Edward III, successive queens seem to have preferred the psaltery in their households: the psaltery-players seem to have worked closely with the household fiddlers, to an extent that makes performance of fiddle and psaltery together very likely. The gittern may have been used in this way, too;[176] and depictions of the citole paired in performance with a fiddle suggest that it would provide a more robust rhythmic and harmonic accompaniment to a melody instrument.

---

[171] SM II, 22 and 23.

[172] See SM II, 170 and 178. *Grey Steil* is a romance along rather Arthurian lines.

[173] There appears to be no evidence for three fiddles playing together, nor of techniques that they might have used. They could presumably have improvised a3 in a similar way to shawms.

[174] The tabor was also useful for military purposes, probably joining the trumpets.

[175] See SM II, 135; and Hugh Baillie, 'Some biographical notes on English church musicians, chiefly working in London (1485–1569)'. Royal Musical Association *Research Chronicle* 2 (1962), 18–57, under 'Savernake'. The rebec-player Pety John Savernake (or Cokeren) was teamed up with Stephen Delalaunde and Hakenett de Lewys, but it is not known what these two played.

[176] The description of Andrew Destrer as a citoler in 1363 (MERH, 20) is an error for gitterner.

Two trumpets, with nakers

An almost certain performance-grouping in the late thirteenth and early fourteenth centuries is that of two trumpeters, usually with a nakerer.[177] Trumpeters frequently appear in pairs in the records, often being rewarded together for minstrelsy and collecting payments for each other as *socii*.[178] The grouping of two trumpets and nakers is capable of exciting and complex ceremonial fanfares.

The king employed trumpeters *qui non sunt* in pairs, too – Doncaster and Crakestreng in 32 Ed I, and Yvan and Ithel in 1 Ed II.[179] As we noted in Chapter 1, the ordinances of 1318 required two trumpeters to be permanently in Court to perform at the king's pleasure, and two other minstrels if the king wished it.[180] There is no suggestion that these four minstrels played in consort, nor that one of them was a nakerer. It seems more likely that the additional pair were normally 'still' minstrels, and that the four men worked in two groups of two in supplying both loud ceremonial music and (if required) 'still' music.

Trumpets and drums

As the numbers of household trumpeters increased, so did the size of any potential trumpet-consort.[181] Any such group is usually referred to simply as 'the trumpets', and the Westminster Tournament Roll shows that the king's trumpeters formed homogeneous groups in procession as late as 1511. The music of all six of the earl of Northumberland's trumpets that greeted him at his chamber door on New Year's Day also seems to have been from a homogeneous consort, perhaps playing ceremonial fanfares of some intricacy.[182]

It would certainly be unwise to rule out the use of trumpets alone in any group, but rewards to 'trumpets' may sometimes have been scribal shorthand for a grouping of trumpets and tabors. Such a combination is made explicit in the list of 'Taborets and Trumpets' at the coronation of Richard III; and we should also remember that King Robert was known as both trumpeter and taborer. While there were taborers in the royal households throughout the fourteenth and fifteenth centuries, the employment of nakerers seems to have died out during the fourteenth, leaving taborers as the normal associates of trumpeters.[183]

Shawms

Four royal *vigiles* were among those who received gifts for minstrelsy at the marriage of the king's daughter Elizabeth in 25 Ed I (1296/7),[184] while the king's four *vigiles*

---

[177] Rastall, 'Some English consort-groupings', 187–9.
[178] SM II, 46, 65 and 99.
[179] SM II, Appendix A, for those dates.
[180] Tout, *Place of the Reign*, 303.
[181] Rastall, 'Some English consort groupings', 187–92.
[182] Percy, *Regulations and Establishment*, 342.
[183] But see the note on p. 338, n. 96, above.
[184] Cal. SM II, 17.

received a similar gift at the Pentecost celebrations of 1306.[185] Their minstrelsy was perhaps as acceptable as that of the minstrels proper, and in 31 Ed I the *vigilis* of the Prince of Wales apparently entertained his master *solo*.[186]

The kind of shawm band apparently formed by Edward I's *vigiles* was already known in England. John de Hertford, abbot-elect of St Albans, had been presented at the high altar in the abbey in 1235 *pulsato classico sonantibus chalamis quos burdones appelamus cum horologio* ('with the bells ringing and the shawms (which we call *burdones*) sounding with the clock').[187]

The bells would be those in the tower, sounding externally, but the clock would be inside the building, providing further chimes adding to the joyful noise of the shawms. *Calamus* is a reed or reed-instrument. *Burdo* (plural *burdones*) is a staff or wand of office, which suggests an instrument of some length and therefore of low pitch; but it could also mean the drone of an insect and therefore, perhaps, a buzzing or whining sound.[188] The description seems to imply that all the *calami* were *burdones*.

Royal pipers in later records include John Mauprine, John Morleyns (known as a cornemuser) and Godscalk, piper. These were all transferred to the Black Prince's household for a while during 11 and 12 Ed III,[189] perhaps as a coherent group, in which case we must consider shawms and a bagpipe as a possible performance grouping. Around the 21st year there was a group of pipers headed by Lybkin and including his son Hankin fitzLybkin.[190] Another group that seems to have worked together in around 33–5 Ed III consisted of the pipers Flagilet, John Badencore and Peter de Burgoigne.

A group of three pipers seems standard throughout the fourteenth and fifteenth centuries, as evidenced by some (mainly continental) iconography and the records of civic minstrels in various towns.[191] Towns began to employ four minstrels before the end of the fourteenth century. With certain exceptions these were probably all shawms, but with two sizes operating: although items specifying the bombard (tenor shawm) are rare, it is likely, for musical reasons, that a bombard was used for the lowest voice. By the late fifteenth century a large band of 'waits' might consist of six pipers.[192]

---

[185] Cal. SM II, 57.

[186] Cal. SM II, 38.

[187] H.T. Riley, ed., *Gesta Abbatum Monasterii Sancti Albani*. Rolls Series (London, 1867–9), I, 520, quoted in Frank Ll. Harrison, *Music in Medieval Britain* (London, 1958), 206, n. 3.

[188] R.E. Latham, *Revised Medieval Latin Word List* (Oxford, 1965), also lists a musical drone played by a wind instrument: but the date of this (c. 1255) suggests a speculative interpretation of this same passage.

[189] SM II, 97.

[190] Later perhaps the group's leader: see Chapter 2.

[191] Chapter 7 and Rastall, 'Civic minstrels', *passim*. The common continental grouping of two shawms (the second sometimes a bombarde) and trumpet does not appear in English sources.

[192] As we shall see below, however, Henry VII's 'waits' were probably the sackbuts and shawms.

The king's *vigiles* had become a regular band of three or four pipers by the end of the thirteenth century. Although the fourteenth saw a fluid relationship between the *vigiles* and the group of pipers that took over their musical role, that grouping clearly remained in place until the sixteenth century. To the consort of pipers was sometimes added a trumpeter from the later fourteenth century onwards. The earliest evidence for this appears to be the indentures of John of Gaunt's three pipers and clarioner in 1373. There is no direct evidence that these four performed as a group (and if they did the clarioner perhaps played a longer trumpet), but the group of three pipers and a trumpeter occurs as a consort in the Coventry records for 1423. It seems that a group of two or three shawms could function with or without a trumpeter, the implication being that the repertory and performance-style concerned were not determined by the presence or otherwise of a trumpet.

This element of variable presence is found in Johannes Tinctoris's famous comment in his unfinished work *De inventione et usu musice* of c. 1485.[193] It is worth giving the passage in full, because it is usually quoted only as a translated *prècis*:[194]

> Et quoniam tibia simplex vocem imitatur humanam, unicam scilicet partem cantuum edere potens, ut quemadmodum ex vocibus humanis gravitate et acumine disparibus cantores diversarum partium cantus pronuntiant, ita et tibicines inequalibus tibiis personarent, tibiarum alias acutas, alias graves, illas supremis partibus, istas mediocribus et imis adaptabiles excogitarunt. Unde tibiarum (ut cantus partium) alii nomen est 'suprema', alii 'tenor', quem vulgo 'bombardam' vocant, et alii 'contratenor'. Imos tamen contratenores semper, ac sepe reliquos, tibicinibus adiuncti tubicines ea tuba quam superius 'tromponem' ab Italis et 'sacqueboute' a Gallicis appellari diximus melodiosissime clangunt. Quorum omnium omnia instrumenta simul aggregata communiter dicuntur 'alta'. Et quamvis solus tibicen nonnullorum cantuum duas partes duplici tibia personare possit, quia tamen hec paucis aut pene nullis sufficit cantilenis imperfecta plurimum est.

> (And since the simple pipe imitates the human voice, namely being able to give out a single part of pieces of music, so that just as singers perform various parts of a song out of human voices that are unequal with respect to low and high, so also pipers play unequal pipes, contriving some pipes high, some low, the former adaptable to the highest parts, the latter to the middling and the lowest. Whence the name of some pipes (like the parts of a song) is 'soprano', others 'tenor', which they commonly call a 'bombard', and others 'contratenor'. Trumpeters added to the pipers always most melodiously play the lowest contratenors, and often the rest, on the trumpet that we have said above is called 'trombone' by the

---

[193] At the wedding of Philip of Austria a year later, in 1488, a motet was performed on three shawms and a *trompette-saicqueboute*: Olivier de la Marche, *Mémoires*, ed. H. Beaune and J. d'Arbaumont (Paris, 1883–8), III, 152.

[194] Tinctoris, *De inventione et usu musice*, III, viii, 44–8: edition and translation of this passage by Jeffrey Dean. See <https://earlymusictheory.org/Tinctoris/texts/deinventioneetusumusice> (accessed 15 April 2021). The NG article 'Sackbut' (Keith McGowan) derives the name from French *sacquer*, to move violently, and *bouter*, to shove. Tinctoris mentions the double pipe here, but dismisses it as not very useful (see Hornpipe, above).

Italians and 'sacqueboute' by the French. When all of all these instruments are added together they are commonly called an 'alta'. And although a single piper can play two parts of some songs on a double pipe, because however this suffices for few or almost no songs, it is extremely imperfect.)

Tinctoris states that the pipes come in two sizes and can cover the whole pitch-range needed, and he implies that the brass instrument, although desirable, is dispensable.[195] This dispensability is not just that the bombard has the range to perform anything that the sackbut can play (so that the music can be performed by four pipers), but that the second contratenor part, like the first, is not necessary to the texture. Indeed, he discusses the musical texture in terms of two principal voices (soprano and tenor) with optional contratenor parts.

Tinctoris's terms *trompone* (large trumpet) and *sacqueboute* could mean the double-slide instrument that was probably in use by the late fifteenth century, but the iconography shows that it was the folded trumpet that appeared in the shawms-and-trumpet band in the middle of that century. Whether this instrument did or did not have a single slide remains a burning question, of course: if it did, then Tinctoris's terms would be appropriate for that, too.

While an all-shawms band remained a norm, the consort of three shawms with a trumpet may be included in loud bands that appear in records as 'four minstrels'. This is not just enumerating them: phrases such as 'the four French minstrels' or the note of a reward 'to four minstrels' is apparently a specific description.[196] There is little evidence for such a grouping before the fifteenth century, however, although an earlier occasion for it is sometimes cited: a German dance, performed on board Sir John Chandos's ship in 1350 before the sea-battle of Winchelsea.[197] It is said that the music was of shawms and a trumpet, but Froissart says only that Chandos 'faisoit ses menestrelz corner devant lui une danse d'Alemagne'. The verb *courner* was a general term for musical performance on wind instruments, and did not necessarily refer to any lip-reed instrument.[198]

---

[195] The contratenor parts are those voices immediately above and below (or inhabiting the same range as) the tenor, which was originally the lowest voice. One of the *tromponi*, therefore, would be expected to play what had become the bass part by Tinctoris's time (the lower contratenor, or *contratenor bassus*). The interpretation of this passage is not indisputable.

[196] Rastall, 'Some English consort-groupings', 192.

[197] See Daniel Leech-Wilkinson, '*Le Voir Dit*: a reconstruction and a guide for musicians'. *Plainsong and Medieval Music* 2/1 (April 1993), 43–73 at 51–2, and his Examples 1a and 1b on p. 65. The lower parts of these examples should be compared both to Downey's examples and the tenors in BL Cotton MS Titus A xxvi, fols 3v–8v.

[198] John Harvey, *The Plantagenets* (London, 1959), 143, quotes Froissart's chronicle but seems to have added the phrase 'on their trumpets': Leech-Wilkinson, '*Le Voir Dit*', 51–2. For the original, see Froissart, *Chroniques*, 671.

Henry VII's reorganisation of his minstrels

As the foregoing shows, the evidence for identifiable performance-groups in England is not easy to interpret. Only at the very end of our period, in the *Liber Niger* and the records of Henry VII's reign, do we find clearly-labelled categories. In the latter we also find the minstrels' names, starting with a journal for 11 Hen VII (1495/6) recording wages paid to nine trumpets, four sackbuts and three string minstrels, corresponding to the trumpets, 'shawms and small pipes' and 'stringmen' of the *Liber Niger*. The four sackbuts soon became three, perhaps because of retirement, death or long-term absence of one minstrel, and the trumpets too, fluctuated a little in the next two years, but the overall pattern seems clear. Livery-lists later in the reign name the minstrels under specific group-headings. The most useful lists are those dated 23 February 1503 for the queen's funeral (here identified as 1503/1), 15 June 1503 for summer liveries (1503/2), 11 May 1509 for the funeral of Henry VII (1509/1), and 24 June 1509 for Henry VIII's coronation (1509/2).[199]

The trumpets

1503/1 names *the king's trumpets* as Peter de Casa Nova, Thomas Freman, John Gece, Jaket, William Freman, Domonys, Adryan, Pring and John Decessid (i.e. de Cecile). The summer list 1503/2 names only five: Peter de Casa Nova, Thomas Freman, Adrian, Dominic Justinian and the newcomer Francc Bocard. The other five might have been absent for a variety of reasons. Nine trumpeters appear on the list 1509/1, as Jakett, Petir (who does not head the list although he had long been marshal of the trumpets), Domynyk, John Cecile, Frank, Christopher, Adryan, John Broun and John Blank(e). This last has become relatively well known in recent years as the trumpeter of African descent identifiable on the Westminster Tournament Roll.[200]

Also in the list 1509/1 is a group of six 'Trumpettes', different from the nine just listed: these were Henry's trumpeters as Duke of York: John Hert, Thomas Wrey, John Scarlet, John Frere, John Strutt and Robert Wrey. In the list 1509/2 these six are added to the king's nine to make a total of fifteen king's trumpets, this remaining, broadly, the number of royal trumpeters for the rest of the sixteenth century. The two groups did function separately for a time, however, as the Westminster Tournament Roll of 1511 shows.

The Sackbuts and shawms

Another group appearing in these livery-lists is the sackbuts and shawms (in a variety of spellings). This too was a stable group. In 1503/1 they are named as John de Peler, William Burgh, Hans Naille, Edward Peler and Adrian Wilmorth (not Adrian the trumpeter, but a pupil of William Burgh). 1503/2 names the same men as the 'lowde mynstrelles'. John de Peler is here 'Maister Johannes de Peler' and William is 'Maister Guyllame vander Bourgh', while Naille is listed as Hans Nagle. Scribes often had different views as to how individuals should be named, but perhaps more

---

[199] Ashbee, *Records*, VII, 19–29, *passim*.
[200] See front cover. Blanke has an entry in ODNB.

often with foreigners, whose names were taken from dictation and could also be anglicised. The style Master is notable here, suggesting that John and William were in charge of apprentices, perhaps for groups other than their own. In 1509/1 the Sackbuts and Shawms were down to four, named as Johannes, Guyllam Borrow, Edward Johannes and Alex Massu (*recte* Manseno); the same four, named as Johannes, William, Alexander and Edward, appear as Sackbuts and Shawms of the Privy Chamber in the coronation list, 1509/2. This is something of a surprise: it may signal a change of function, but there is no reason to think so.[201]

John de Peler had been a king's trumpeter from 1482: he may have taken up the sackbut for service under Henry VII, but it is more likely that some years elapsed before 'sackbut' supplanted 'trumpet' as the term for the double-slide instrument. Edward de Peler was his son, and it was these two sackbuts who joined the five trumpeters in the journey to Scotland with Margaret Tudor in 1503.

Still minstrels

The summer livery-list 1503/2 includes a group of 'Still minstrels' who did not appear at all in 1503/1: Henry Glasebury (the marshal), John Farness, William Grene, Thomas Grennyng, Henry Swanne, John Raffe, Thomas Spence and Thomas Mayow. The list 1509/1 names John Chamber as marshal, with John Furnes, Thomas Spencer, Thomas Grening, Thomas Mayue, John Abys, Richard Waren and Thomas Peion (*sic* – read as Pejon). Clearly there had been some changes of personnel in the intervening years. The list 1509/2 then calls them 'The Still Shawms': John Chamber (marshal), John Furneys, Thomas Spence, Thomas Grening, Thomas Mayow, John Abys, Richard Waren and Thomas Pegion. The consistency of this group of eight minstrels suggests that they were not just a loose collection of individuals but that they had a unified purpose or function. 'Still shawms' suggests that some or all of them played the cylindrical-bored *dulcina* (which may have existed in various sizes),[202] or perhaps recorder or cornett.

Undefined minstrels

These various groups still leave several minstrels unaccounted for – individuals who perhaps had functions that were separate from those of the named groups. On the other hand, it may simply be that the order of minstrels in the livery-lists reflects the order in which they presented themselves for payment. These are clearly far more than the 'stringmen' of the *Liber Niger*, however. The list 1503/1, of 23 February 1503 (liveries for the queen's funeral), includes, interspersed among groups already noted,

---

[201] At Court, the sackbuts and shawms were known as the sackbuts or as the shawms, according to the scribe's point of view. In other contexts, later, they were sometimes referred to as the King's waits: REED *Ecclesiastical London*, 48, for example (1513/14). 'Edward Johannes' is Edward de Peler, Johannes de Peler's son. For further information on all these men see Ashbee *et al., Biographical Dictionary*.

[202] Ashbee, *Records*, VII, 28–9. Further on this ensemble, see below.

> Minstrel John Buntance (an error by contamination for Possant Bonitemps or Bountaine, cornett-player? John Buntyng was a yeoman or epistoler of the Chapel Royal).
> Schoolmaster at pipes Guillam. Perhaps Master William de Burgh, in charge of apprentices and not in this livery-list as a sackbut.
> Minstrel for the French lute Giles or Gilles Dewes.
> The prince's minstrels Stephen Delalaund, Pety John and Hakenet de Liners. Pety John Cokeren, or Savernake, is known as a rebec-player, but the instruments of the other two are not known.
> Queen of Scots's minstrels Gabriell, Kenner. Kenner is known as a luter; Gabriell's instrument is unknown.

The list 1503/2, of 17 June 1505 (summer liveries) includes

> [Minstrels] Markas Loriden, Bonntayns, Jenyn Markassyn, John de Haspere, Richard Denosse and John Potweye.
> This is an incomplete and unclassified list of the king's minstrels only. Loriden and Markassen had been two of the queen's minstrels, the other being John Fawkes (in 1495) and Richard Anows or Denows (in 1504, but see below).

The list 1509/1, of 11 May 1509 (liveries for the king's funeral) includes

> Minstrels Hakenett de Lewys and Stephen Delalaunde (presumably the prince's minstrels, but Pety John is absent).
> Minstrels of the Chamber[203] Giles [Dewes] (the luter), Buntanes (cornettist) and Barbram (that is, Bartram Brouard, instrument unknown).
> Tabrets with others Marquesse Loreden, Janyn Marquesyn and Richard Annos. These (see above) had been the queen's minstrels, and one wonders what this heading implies: perhaps that at least one of them played pipe-and-tabor?

The list 1509/2, of 24 June 1509 (liveries at the king's coronation) includes

> [Minstrel] Bartram Brewer, minstrel (the 'Barbram' of the previous list).
> [Minstrel] Bountaunce (cornettist).

Despite biographical details from Ashbee *et al.*, set into context by Dumitrescu, these lists leave questions unanswered.[204] In particular, the instrument played by each 'minstrel' remains unknown, and the information we do have is sometimes confusing. Why did the accounting scribes so rarely say what these minstrels played? The obvious answer is that the scribes did not know, although the heading 'Tabrets with others' in 1509/1 might suggest that some minstrels were proficient on more than one instrument. Sorting through the 'still minstrels' of previous reigns, no fixed group can be seen. On the other hand, one cannot even be sure that all the still minstrels are accurately identified.

---

[203] Further on musicians in the Privy Chamber in early Tudor times, see Ashbee, 'Groomed for service'.

[204] Ashbee *et al.*, *Biographical Dictionary*, *passim*; Theodor Dumitrescu, *The Early Tudor Court and International Musical Relations* (Aldershot, 2007), especially 63–106, *passim*.

Henry V (from a date unknown): Walter Haliday, William Maisham, Thomas Haliday, John Wilde.

Henry VI: Walter Haliday, William Maisham, Thomas Haliday, John Wilde, Thomas Radcliff, Robert Marshal, John Cliff (III), William Wykes, Thomas Green.

(Thomas Green appears in the records in 1459: he could have been a replacement for Maisham, Thomas Haliday, Wilde or Radcliff, all of whom had probably retired or died by then. This was nevertheless an eight-strong group up to the early or mid-1450s.)

Edward IV: Walter Haliday, Robert Marshal, John Cliff (III), William Wykes, Thomas Green.

It is impossible to guess how far back beyond the *Liber Niger* one might extrapolate any of the groups of Henry VII's time into pre-Tudor reigns: and extrapolating backwards is always dangerous. On the face of it, Henry VII's formation of instrumental groups was probably an innovation that radically changed the shape of minstrelsy at Court.

15

The instrumental repertory in England

In 1958, Frank Harrison noted that

> [Pre-Tudor] examples of secular music are few and of minor importance, and I have not dealt with them here. Nothing identifiable as minstrel music has survived, and the history of minstrelsy belongs to the study of social life and customs rather than of actual music. The history of musical instruments other than the organ is in much the same case, for there is no evidence that any instruments but the organ were normally played in church, and the musical remains are restricted to a small group of instrumental dances.

Thus secular music was dismissed from the authoritative work on music in medieval Britain.[1] One can hardly blame Harrison, for surviving examples of medieval English secular music are not only few in number, but so enigmatic that the precise problems are elusive, let alone the solutions. Some intriguing questions are raised by his remarks, nevertheless. It may be true that 'nothing identifiable as minstrel music has survived', but it is also true that we should probably not recognise a piece of minstrel music if we saw it. For this reason the surviving examples of secular music, few and enigmatic as they are, become of prime importance to any study of minstrelsy. Could any of these survivals be minstrels' music? – and, if so, could the minstrels have read the written music or performed from it?

Harrison also restricted himself to English sources, a pragmatic if rather limiting decision. At the time he wrote, it was sensible not to rely on continental evidence, because it was by no means clear that such evidence would be relevant to English music. Sixty years on, it is certain that the British Isles were not culturally isolated from the continent of Europe, and that minstrel practices in England and Scotland were likely to be influenced by those in continental Europe. There were opportunities for exchange of information during the visits of continental nobles to the English Court, and in the travels of the English abroad. As we have seen, some foreign minstrels remained in Court for weeks or even months at a time, and we should expect them to share their repertories and methods with their English colleagues, and *vice versa*. That was, after all, the purpose of the minstrel schools, to which English minstrels travelled. Yet humans are conservative creatures – not the minstrels themselves, perhaps, but their patrons, who may have seen no reason

---

[1] Harrison, *Music in Medieval Britain*, xiii–xiv. Harrison later took up the matter of instrumental performance, but only in very broad terms: Frank Ll. Harrison, 'Tradition and innovation in instrumental usage, 1100–1450'. Jan LaRue, ed., *Aspects of Medieval and Renaissance Music: A Birthday Offering to Gustave Reese* (London, 1967), 319–35.

to accept new-fangled ideas and methods for which they might be expected to pay higher fees and rewards.

While it is not unreasonable to take account of minstrel activity in Europe when reviewing the evidence of minstrelsy in England, then, it must be remembered that European influence on English minstrelsy relies on an important assumption. The evidence, such as it is, offers no indication of England keeping up with its continental neighbours, and on the contrary suggests that England may have lagged behind the continent in matters of technique and practice.[2] It may be simply that the evidence is missing, and that England only appears to have lagged behind its neighbours. Since we cannot currently know the answer, it is necessary to ask the right questions: To what extent could the minstrels use musical notation? What techniques did they use to improvise music? And can any manuscript sources of music be identified as belonging to, and used by, minstrels?

Literacy

At first sight it seems clear that minstrels in England did not, and presumably could not, use written music. English iconography of the late Middle Ages shows instrumentalists performing from memory, whereas secular and liturgical singers read from a book or scroll:[3] and this is true of continental sources too. This apparently clear distinction is supported by the fact that the Norwich waits were encouraged in 1533 to learn musical notation.[4] If they, some of the best minstrels in the country, were musically illiterate at such a late date, it seems unlikely that other minstrels could read music, at least in the difficult late medieval rhythmic notation that liturgical singers had to learn. It is true that they might have read songs, dance-tunes and liturgical pieces from non-rhythmic notation: but what (very limited) purpose would this have if they normally worked in the aural tradition, as the iconography shows?

As evidence this seems incontrovertible, but it leaves some important questions open. What is the purpose of simplified notation (in various forms of 'stroke' notation), examples of which are of both secular and sacred music?[5] Why are there collections of dance-tunes, that would surely be useful to minstrels rather than anyone

---

[2] See the various works by Keith Polk listed in the bibliography, Peters, *Musical Sounds*, and Dumitrescu, *Early Tudor Court*, *passim*. For earlier examples of foreign minstrels in the English Court and some English minstrels abroad, see later in this chapter and SM II, Appendix A, *passim*.

[3] See, for instance, Plate 7.

[4] SM I, 241–2, citing Stephen, 'Waits of the City of Norwich', 7 f.

[5] See Margaret Bent, 'New and little-known fragments of English medieval polyphony'. *Journal of the American Musicological Society* 21/2 (1968), 137–56, at 149–53; Hugh Benham, '"Salve Regina" (Power or Dunstable): a simplified version'. *Music & Letters* 59/1 (1978), 28–32. For an overview of these notations see Richard Rastall, *The Notation of Western Music*. 2nd edn (Leeds, 1998, and London, 2008), 112–15.

else, and who wrote them down?[6] And how should one perform those notated secular songs that apparently require instrumental accompaniment?

The question of singers reading while minstrels improvised by ear or played from memory assumes a situation that could not, in practice, have been so simple. If we accept that minstrels performed from memory – a proposition that is hard to deny – we need not assume that they also learned the tunes entirely by ear and rehearsed them from memory. No doubt they were capable of doing both, but it would be unsafe to assume that they never started the process with the notated tunes in front of them. Conversely, the importance of liturgical singers always reading from notation may be misleading, for they were trained to perform most chants by heart, even if the notation acted as an *aide mémoire*. Those who performed the liturgy – priests, readers, singers – read from a book primarily because of the words. The texts were too important to be recited from memory, which would carry the risk of error. Music in the most difficult rhythmic notation certainly did need to be read from the book, because that music was often too complex to perform from memory: and the continental evidence of minstrels joining singers in liturgical performances argues that by the late fifteenth century at least some minstrels could read the same notation as the singers did. Even so, we should not underestimate the ability of the trained medieval singer to memorise much of what had been rehearsed; simplified notation may have been used by the minstrels in such cases; and liturgical singers, in any case, often created polyphony by improvising around a known (notated or only memorised) chant. But, whatever the case on the continent, there is in fact no English evidence that minstrels joined with the singers in liturgical performances before the mid-sixteenth century.[7]

The musical sources show a general lack of corrections, and this has always been seen as an indication that comprehensive annotation was unnecessary. Secular songs such as were performed by amateur singers – gentlemen, ladies and students, performing for their own entertainment – were also rehearsed and performed using memory a great deal. But here the texts were less vital, and it seems that singers might fit an already-known text to imperfectly underlaid music, or might even supply text from another source to a song without underlay.

All this demands a different view of the relationships between improvisation, performance and the use of musical notation. As we shall see, Hendrik van der Werf and others have shown that the distinction between musical composition and the improvisation practised by trained singers must sometimes have been non-existent. The iconographical evidence of a dichotomy between singers reading and minstrels improvising, therefore, cannot be interpreted as simply as might be assumed. In music, as in poetry (discussed in Chapter 12), a case could be made for oral-formulaic (and aural-formulaic) construction. This would include both vocal and instrumental

---

[6] Written dance-tunes with choreographies would of course be useful to those who performed the dances, and to those in charge of the social events concerned: but the questions concerning the tunes remain.

[7] Other than in such well-known liturgical pieces as *Te Deum*, which both singers and instrumentalists could probably perform from memory.

music, with the same uncertainty in the conclusions. Is formulaic construction in written music indicative of improvised, notationless composition?

Instrumental performance 1: dances in one and two voices

In order to identify music that could have originated from minstrels' performances some important questions must be considered. What methods of improvisation were open to minstrels? Do any features of the surviving repertory suggest an origin in instrumental improvisation? And, most importantly, can a specifically instrumental repertory be distinguished from that for voices?

This last, crucial, question has occasioned much thought in the past. For our present purposes we can dispense with a discussion of music written in tablature and clearly intended specifically for solo instrumental performance. Such a discussion would not be without interest, but it is unlikely that the relationship between minstrels' performances and the written tablatures could be identified in music originating before the late fifteenth century. In any case there are almost no tablature sources of English origin from the late Middle Ages. Moreover, the discussion would necessarily be about the nature of the performer – whether he could be thought of as a 'minstrel' or something else – at different times and in different places. Fascinating as such an exploration would be, its results would not greatly affect the contents of this book. For the present, therefore, we shall accept the broad division of medieval written instrumental music into solo music notated in tablature (not discussed here) and music for instrumental (or vocal-instrumental) consort presented in staff notation and usually in separate voices.

When instrumental music has been considered in the past some obvious criteria have been brought to bear. There has been, first, an understanding that it was composed by those whose main compositional tasks were with vocal music: and as the style was likely to be much the same for both, untexted music was probably for instruments. Further, it was assumed that any 'unvocal' intervals – of a kind not unusual in fifteenth-century contratenor parts – signalled the use of an instrument. It was soon recognised, however, that these criteria cannot support a firm distinction. The texting or non-texting of a line was not as simple a matter to a medieval musician as it would be to a modern one, whose general rule has been 'if it's texted, sing it; if it isn't, play it'. On the question of vocal style, too, examination of the wider repertory has disposed of the notion that there is a boundary between what can be sung and what cannot.[8] Sarah Fuller proposed a number of *genres* that might have been intended for instrumental performance from the outset, her list being modified by Warwick Edwards and Louise Litterick: we shall return to these.[9] Edwards

---

[8] See Lloyd Hibberd, 'On "instrumental style" in early melody'. McGee, *Instruments and their Music*, 455–78; and the comments in Warwick Edwards, 'Songs without words by Josquin and his contemporaries'. Iain Fenlon, ed., *Music in Medieval & Early Modern Europe* (Cambridge, 1981), 79–92, at 80–1.

[9] Sarah Fuller, 'Additional notes on the 15th-century chansonnier Bologna Q16'. *Musica Disciplina* 23 (1969), 81; Edwards, 'Songs without words'; Louise Litterick, 'On Italian instrumental ensemble music in the late fifteenth century'. Fenlon, *Music in Medieval*

argued for an examination of the traditions of instrumental usage, an all-embracing approach which moved the discussion forward, although not to a conclusion.[10] This larger discussion is still a complex one: there is little agreement about what features of late medieval polyphony might signal instrumental usage or composition through improvisation, or how those features should be interpreted. The discussion, too, is mainly concerned with what appears to be polyphony composed by named composers using notation, a situation that does not greatly help in identifying how minstrels worked. The rest of this chapter will explore the subject by starting with what we might understand the minstrels to have been capable of doing.

What follows does not deal comprehensively with English sources, although I hope that all relevant issues are discussed. On the other hand, while continental sources cannot be assumed to belong to the same circumstances as English ones, it is occasionally helpful to take account of them.

Monophonic dances

If there is one type of music more likely than others to be minstrels' music, it is dance tunes. Although the *carole* is known to have been sung by the dancers themselves,[11] there is no evidence that other types of dance were accompanied vocally: the iconography shows that the music was supplied by minstrels playing instruments. We can begin with dances notated monophonically, the earliest in English sources being an *estampie* dating from the thirteenth century. Although this dance-tune is monophonic there are two extra voices in the final section.[12] Timothy McGee interprets one of these as a melodic line and the other as an unpitched line perhaps for percussion. The tune exhibits the features common to *estampies*, in which each section is repeated, usually with *ouvert* and *clos* endings. This gives a structure that can be represented as

AA' BB' CC' DD' EE' ...

and so on, where the letters represent structural sections, usually of one or two melodic phrases, while A', B' etc. are the same sections with variant endings. (Normally, the first ending is 'open', ending on a note other than the final, while the second is 'closed', ending on the final of the piece.) In this piece, successive sections are effectively repetitions with – unusually – varied beginnings, starting on successively higher notes going up the arpeggio. The openings of sections 1, 2 and 3 (McGee's numbering, = A, B and C above) illustrate this (Example 1). Section 4 presents a new tune that is similarly varied (although in the middle of the section) in section 5. Thus sections 1–3 and 4–5 form two larger units of varied material. The

---

& Early Modern Europe, 117–30. See also the summary in Jon Banks, *The Instrumental Consort Repertory of the Late Fifteenth Century* (Aldershot, 2006), 2–3.

[10] Edwards, 'Songs without words', 81 ff.

[11] See the NG article 'Carole' (Robert Mullally).

[12] Oxford, Bodleian Library, MS Douce 139, fol. 5v: see Timothy J. McGee, *Medieval Instrumental Dances* (Bloomington and Indianapolis IN, 1989), no. 2.

EXAMPLE 1. Openings of sections 1, 2 and 3 of the Bodleian *estampie*

process is continued to the end of the tune, with a total of ten sections grouped into four larger units.

This is not the place for a detailed analysis of the Bodleian *estampie*, which has been discussed by Wulf Arlt;[13] but it is perhaps clear that the dance's musical structure could have been arrived at by a process of improvised variation. One can imagine a minstrel starting with a musical phrase in a limited range, and then varying it in ways that gradually extend the range; then taking up another phrase and going through a similar process, and so on until the dance ends. This seems a suitable and entirely logical way of providing music for a dance of indeterminate length.

In such a process there is no clear boundary between composition and improvisation: it is ultimately a form of composition in which nothing need ever be written down. That this dance was written is no doubt due to unusual circumstances, of which we shall probably never learn. Were the dance written in non-rhythmic notation the scribe might be anyone who had been taught to write and knew the purpose of a music staff; but as it is notated rhythmically the scribe was probably a well-educated man with musical training. Why he would want to write the music down is another matter, although the wish to record a successful tune, perhaps with the intention of teaching it to another minstrel, may be enough reason. *How* he did it is more difficult, for transcribing the tune in real time was perhaps not possible. All the same, the processes by which the minstrel created the dance-music would be an aid also to memorising it: and while the scribe could have asked the minstrel to repeat the music to him on a later occasion, it is possible that he remembered quite a lot of it after one hearing.

These questions arise for any example of written-down dance-music of the time. If the manuscript concerned comes from a courtly *milieu*, as is perhaps the case with the series of eight monophonic *estampies reals* found in the late thirteenth-century *Chansonnier du Roy*, we can expect that there were several capable musical scribes

---

[13] Wulf Arlt, 'The "reconstruction" of instrumental music'. Stanley Boorman, ed., *Studies in the Performance of Late Medieval Music* (Cambridge, 1983), 75–100, at 87 ff.

at hand.¹⁴ This manuscript, which contains mainly troubadour and *trouvère* songs, transmits a repertory dating from the second half of the thirteenth century. Such a collection of dances is perhaps the nearest to minstrels' music that we shall be able to identify. Among other possible candidates are certain fourteenth- and early fifteenth-century dances from Italy.¹⁵

In the case of a source from a lower social level the provenance is not always easy to see. Even with simpler musical notation, however, the writing-down of music presupposes a certain amount of education, and therefore a certain social standing. The late fifteenth-century Gresley dances came into being in a *milieu* at the other end of the possible range from the courtly. David Fallows has located these dances near Ashbourne, Derbyshire, around the year 1500, and has ascribed the manuscript to one of two leading families in that area.¹⁶ The dances come, then, from a society of country gentry rather than from courtly or aristocratic circles, a relatively restricted society in an isolated location, in which there was nevertheless a certain amount of education and considerable administrative ability. (Of course, dance-tunes might be improvised at an even lower social level, but no-one there would be capable of writing them down.)

The Gresley manuscript is a pocket book containing memoranda and information on a variety of subjects. As it includes instructions for the various dances, as well as the tunes, it seems certain that its repertory was danced in those social circles.¹⁷ For all monophonic dances, both from the British Isles and from continental Europe, the notated tunes were presumably the basis for improvisation by one or more minstrels. In all cases a single fiddler would be enough for dancing in a relatively low-status society, or even for informal dancing in a higher-status household. There is also the possibility of using an instrument with a constant drone, such as a hurdy-gurdy or bagpipe. Beyond this, we know that two instruments might play together, two fiddles being the best-documented grouping. In this case we deal with a known tune, which is varied and decorated according to the minstrels' normal techniques and against which a second instrumentalist would add another melodic line. How would this be done?

Dances in two voices

The techniques that we know about for improvising a counter-tune against a given melodic line were used by trained liturgical singers to derive a polyphonic texture

---

[14] Paris, Bibliothèque National, f.fr. 844, fols 5r and 103v–104v: see McGee, *Medieval Instrumental Dances*, nos 3–13, and Pierre Aubry, *Estampies et Dances Royales* (Paris, 1907; repr. Geneva, 1975). Frederick Crane discussed the use of drones with these dance-tunes, but denied the need for an additional polyphonic voice: 'On performing the *Lo estampies*'. *Early Music* 7/1 (1979), 25–33, at 29.

[15] McGee, *Medieval Instrumental Dances*, nos 14–28 and 29.

[16] Matlock, Derbyshire CRO, D77 Box 38 (Gresley), 51–79: see David Fallows, 'The Gresley dance collection, *c.* 1500'. Royal Musical Association *Research Chronicle* 29 (1996), 1–20, *passim*.

[17] There are in fact choreographies for 26 dances and tunes for 13: but only 8 tunes match up with choreographies: Fallows, 'Gresley Dance Collection'.

from a liturgical chant. One of these techniques was also used instrumentally, however: it is described by Jerome of Moravia as a way of deriving a second, instrumental, line from the melody of a song. This is the technique of 'fifthing', which seems to have been used in Parisian circles in the late thirteenth century. As Christopher Page noted, it is Jerome's 'advanced' method for fiddlers although it is a very basic technique for singers.[18] Fifthing is a method by which a note-against-note countermelody is produced above a given line, largely at the interval of a fifth. The effect of plain consecutive fifths is avoided by introducing contrary motion between the beats, a process that is aided by the use of the octave (and occasionally the unison) as a secondary acceptable interval above the tune.

The two-voiced texture generated by this technique was referred to as 'note-against-note duophony' by Hendrik van der Werf: that is, a two-part texture in which the voices have the same rhythms. Although Van der Werf was discussing sacred vocal music, the characteristics of this style as he described them apply, with some exceptions, to the late thirteenth-century dances found in the same manuscript as *Sumer is icumen in*:[19]

1. 'Individual voices move by preference in seconds and thirds': as he noted, conjunct movement is the norm in music of this period.
2. 'In relation to one another, the voices stay in essentially the same range'. This is not true in these dances, however, in which the upper voice uses wider ranges than the lower voice: f-a', f-f' and g-g', as opposed to c-a, c-a and c-c'.
3. The voices 'are almost continuously in contrary motion'. The dances certainly contain more contrary motion than similar motion – a surprising amount, considering the basic movement in consecutive fifths or octaves. This argues for a well-practised strategy concerning decorative notes, especially passing-notes.
4. The voices 'frequently cross one another'. This is in fact untrue in these dances, where crossing of parts is rare and of very short duration, due to their inhabiting distinct ranges (see 2, above).
5. The composers 'had a strong predilection for octaves, fifths, and unisons' (chordally, not melodically).
6. 'Sequential patterns, especially descending ones, occur frequently in one or both voices'.

Van der Werf further noted that[20]

> the most noteworthy feature of passages in note-against-note style is the stylistic similarity of the two voices. Neither voice is obviously the more important or the more stable one.

---

[18] Page, *Voices and Instruments*, 69–73, esp. 73.

[19] The style is discussed in Hendrik van der Werf, *The Oldest Extant Part Music*. 2 vols (Rochester NY, 1993), I, 26. The dances are in London, British Library, MS Harley 978, fols 8v–9r, edited in McGee, *Medieval Instrumental Dances*, nos 39–41.

[20] Van der Werf, *Oldest Extant Part Music*, I, 28.

This is true also in the dances, although we shall return to the question of which of the voices was created first.

The Harley 978 dances not only show the features listed by Van der Werf, with the modifications noted: they also demonstrate considerable vitality in the melodic writing, disguising the fact that the texture hardly departs from a strict series of consecutive fifths, albeit with the occasional octave or unison. The openings of the second and third sections of the dance demonstrate this use of the alternative intervals (Example 2). The structure of this dance is not quite that of the Bodleian *estampie*, although varied repetition within each section features largely. The dance is effectively an *estampie* in which all the repeats are written out. More importantly, sections 4–6 are varied repeats of sections 1–3, with the upper voice usually taking the higher alternative note (normally the octave instead of the fifth, which can produce a series of consecutive octaves, as in section 5). Example 3 shows the openings of all six sections. In each case it is the *Cantus Superior*, the higher voice, that is varied, and this agrees with what we know of fifthing: it is the lower voice, the *Cantus Inferior*, which is the given tune (if there is one), and this is varied hardly at all, as we should expect. This also fits with the old story of Raimbaut de Vaqueiras hearing the tune of *Kalenda Maya* performed by two fiddlers.[21] Whether the story is true or not is immaterial, for it must have been based on a known possibility: and from extant written examples we know that the song-tune would be in the lower voice while the fiddler playing the upper voice improvised a part using the fifthing technique.[22]

Two things remain to be said at this stage. First, when we hear of such performances as the two fiddlers who sang *Graysteil* to the King of Scots in 1497 we can assume the kind of performance implied by these dances, whether the two minstrels both sang and played or each did one or the other.[23] The principle remains the same. Second, in the case of the dances, where the *Cantus Inferior* is apparently a made-up tune, not a pre-existent one, the question arises of composition in two parts by two performers. It will be useful to look at this in the light of Van der Werf's explanation.

Notation-free composition

Van der Werf envisaged a situation in which the composition of a chant was undertaken in a series of improvisations, without the use of notation. As the process continued, the singer amended and refined his work until he was satisfied with it. At that stage he had memorised a work that had been created and polished to the point at which it was ready for performance, a completed musical work that could be retrieved from the singer's memory at any time.[24] This situation could continue, the singer performing the work again as needed and teaching it to colleagues: should transmission to another institution be required, the composer or another singer

---

[21] See Werner Bachmann, *The Origins of Bowing* (London, 1969), 130, for this and other examples of two fiddlers performing together.

[22] Page, *Voices and Instruments*, 71.

[23] See p. 238.

[24] Van der Werf, *Oldest Extant Part Music*, I, 17–20, for the composition of chant.

EXAMPLE 2. Dance 1 from Harley 978, openings of sections 2 and 3

EXAMPLE 3. Dance 1 from Harley 978, openings of all sections

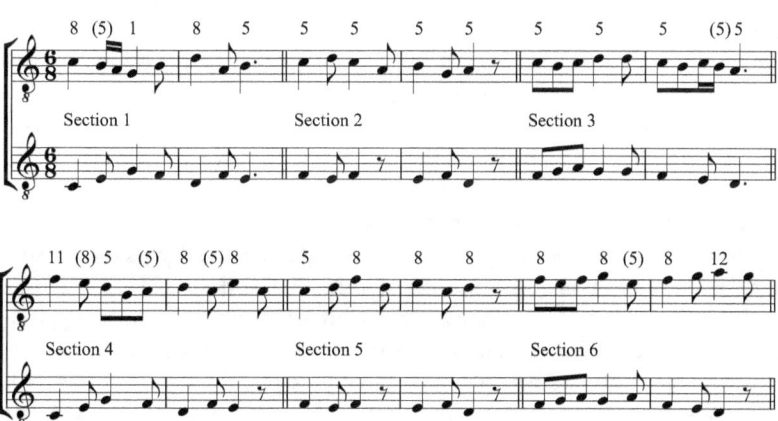

who had memorised the chant would visit the institution to teach the chant by ear. The chant might be written down as an *aide mémoire*, but it is unlikely that this was a normal means of transmission; and the aid was perhaps for the sake of the words as much as for the music, which in any case was at first written in unheighted neumes.

Van der Werf further envisaged the composition of sacred polyphony in two parts as an extension of this process.[25] He did not rule out the possibility of one singer composing both voices, and indeed this seems entirely sensible for music in sustained-pitch style, in which the lower voice carries a chant in long notes, with a more florid upper voice providing a counter-melody to it. Effectively this would be consecutive composition, a process that many commentators have taken for granted. Since the 1960s there has been a move towards the acceptance of simultaneous composition for two-voiced polyphony, however, especially for note-against-note works. Here, two singers improvise two voices and go through the same process of emendation and refinement as for monody. This would demand initial agreement on certain features of the music – a basic harmonic pattern and the basic rhythms – and no doubt the singers concentrated on developing each voice in turn over short musical periods. At first sight this may seem more complicated than consecutive composition, where the lower voice would be finalised before the upper voice was added to it, and in fact the composition might proceed that way: but simultaneous composition by two singers may ultimately have been simpler and quicker. Much would depend on how well-defined the outcome was initially, and how well the two singers co-operated.

Van der Werf's discussion of improvisation, composition and the relationship between them runs through much of his book,[26] building up a picture of a largely notation-free musical society in which very few people were at all fluent in reading either musical notation or written text; in which most singers found it easier to learn a piece of music by listening than by reading; and where the concepts that we understand as 'improvising' and 'composing' merged into a spectrum of activities that included elements of both. 'Composing' in this situation meant improvising – perhaps 'inventing' is a better word – a melodic line and, over a series of rehearsals in which the line was modified and memorised, honing the product until it was structurally acceptable and performable from memory.

This method of composing polyphony resulted in a musical work for two soloists, not for a choir, and there was a danger of losing the work should either of the two singers be incapacitated. There is a greater point in writing down the two-part repertory, therefore, than the monophonic repertory. Such writing could be undertaken by any musically-literate person, and in an ecclesiastical setting it is possible that either singer could have acted as scribe. It is also possible that a third person listened to the singers and copied the piece bit by bit from their performances, which could be geared toward that end. The two-part repertories are, in any case, examples of

---

[25] *Ibid.*, I, 26–8.
[26] *Ibid.*, especially I, 19–21 and 60–3.

rather special music that someone needed to record for some future purpose – most obviously, future performance by different singers.[27]

Although Van der Werf was writing about sacred vocal music, this method could have been applied also to the composition of secular pieces, including instrumental ones; and what he said about church singers could equally well apply to professional minstrels improvising a two-voiced work. In the performances of *Kalenda Maya* and *Greysteil* that we know about (although the first is apocryphal) we know that the piece was based on a pre-existent tune:[28] but two minstrels capable of that could also compose a piece not owing anything to such a tune. Indeed, the dance-tunes just discussed are in very much the same style as certain note-against-note sacred vocal pieces. The difference in process would be that, if the minstrels did not boast a knowledge of musical notation (other, perhaps than the ability to read the pitch of non-rhythmic notation), they had to belong to a household in which there was a trained singer to listen to their piece and write it down.

This presupposes a noble or royal household, or an ecclesiastical household in which minstrels were employed. The same must be true of non-English manuscripts of instrumental music if we assume that continental minstrels, too, did not read music. This is probably the case during the fourteenth century and much of the fifteenth, although it will be as well to keep an open mind. Even if a minstrel did not use notation in his everyday work, he may still have been able to read it and to use it for special purposes: the alternative is that in order for such music to be transmitted to a minstrel for performance, a trained chapel singer would have to sing the relevant line or play it on a keyboard instrument and teach it to the minstrel by ear. This would be a time-consuming activity, but perhaps worth doing if a reward were offered.[29] The question remains, therefore, to what extent the surviving notated sources impinged on the work of the minstrels, and what was the precise relationship between any source and the work of the minstrels concerned. We shall return to this, but meanwhile it will be useful to consider two dances in which the style on first acquaintance suggests notationless composition and the provenance seems to be royal or at least aristocratic.

---

[27] See n. 29, below.

[28] Bachmann, *Origins of Bowing*, 130; SM II, 170.

[29] There seems no reason for a chapel singer to spend time on it if the outcome would not be to his advantage. But chapel singers also performed in secular polyphonic music, and Keith Polk has pointed out that on 10 July 1478 a singer of Rene of Anjou's chapel was rewarded for demonstrating songs to his minstrels: 'A Villaige, chanteur, ledit jour, une canne et demye dudit gris [drap gris], à ladite raison, que le roy lui a donné pour avoir monstré des chansons aux menestrelz dudit seigneur'. Arnaud d'Agnel, Abbé Gustav, *Les comptes du roi René publiés d'après les originaux inédits conservés aux Archives des Bouches-du-Rhône*. 3 vols (Paris, 1908–10), III, 79. 'Demonstrating' is the best of several possible translations. Villaige presumably sang the songs to the minstrels, but 'monstrer' would normally indicate something visual, so he must also have shown them the notated tunes.

Instrumental performance 2: music in two and three voices

Later two-voiced dances

Two late fifteenth-century dances are based on tunes in relatively long notes in the tenor, in each case with a florid cantus part above. Both are given titles, and both bear composer ascriptions, which suggests to me a high-status environment in which individual musicians were valued. To what extent the composers concerned worked in notation is not clear: the cantus parts bear some of the stylistic features of improvised tunes, but not to the extent shown by the dances of two hundred years earlier.

The first is an Italian piece entitled *Falla con misuras*: it is ascribed to M[agister?] Gulielmus.[30] Bukofzer considered that this might be Guglielmo Ebreo da Pesaro (*c.* 1420–after 1484), Isabella d'Este's dancing teacher and the author of a dance treatise. The piece also survives in a source where it is unascribed but entitled *La bassa Castiglya*, the name of the *basse-danse* tune on which it is based.[31] This tune, more commonly known as *La Spagna*,[32] is given in breves (Gulielmus's double-length notes are two separate notes in the original tune), and at first hearing or sight the cantus seems a typical improvised line, with many scalic passages and syncopations. There is no longer the level of reliance on fifths and octaves above the tenor that we saw in the Harley 978 pieces, however, as Example 4 shows: the emphasis is more on thirds and sixths, and indeed the music seems often deliberately to avoid the fifth above the tenor note, as in bars 7, 9–10, 13, 16 and other places. The new emphasis on the sixth is partly because of the increased incidence of the 6–8 cadence, which occurred only through short passing-notes in the Harley dances, but in many places the third and sixth seem deliberate displacements of the fifth. Moreover, the parts sometimes cross (bars 18, 25, 30 and 37–8), which takes the piece outside of the normal circumstances in which fifthing would be practised.

Louise Litterick thought that this piece could 'confidently be interpreted as an improvisation frozen in written form',[33] but one should perhaps be more cautious. The features just discussed suggest that the piece is not wholly the result of notationless composition and that, even if it started out as an improvisation, some parts of it have been worked over and revised with the use of notation. If Guglielmo Ebreo da Pesaro was indeed the originator of the piece, this process will not be surprising, for he must have been literate in both words and music. Looking at it from the other direction, however, it might be fair to say that *Falla con misuras* shows that the

---

[30] Perugia, Bibl. Comunale, MS 431, ff. 105v–106r. See Manfred Bukofzer, 'A polyphonic basse dance of the Renaissance'. Manfred Bukofzer, *Studies in Medieval and Renaissance Music* (London, 1951), 190–216, at 195–6.

[31] Bologna, Liceo Musicale, MS 109, ff. 59v–60r. See Bukofzer, 'Polyphonic basse dance', 196–7.

[32] Bukofzer, 'Polyphonic basse dance': the transcription is on 199–200. On Guglielmo Ebreo da Pesaro, see the NG article on him (Ingrid Brainard).

[33] Litterick, 'On Italian instrumental ensemble music', 124.

EXAMPLE 4. *Falla con misuras*, opening

technique of fifthing was still alive and flourishing in the late fifteenth century, even if sometimes modified by the techniques of composition with notation.[34]

An apparently English piece, entitled *Quene note* and with the name Frank attached, perhaps as composer, survives on a manuscript leaf that contains three tenor parts copied in sequence. MS Digby 167 at the Bodleian Library, Oxford, is a compilation containing diverse materials: fol. 31v, shown as Plate 12, bears the only example in it of musical notation. All three tunes use stroke notation, which is mainly associated with Flemish sources of the second half of the fifteenth century although it is found also in several English sources. In consequence, this page of Digby 167 has been dated either to the third quarter or to the last quarter of the fifteenth century.[35]

---

[34] And perhaps by techniques of improvising over a tenor using the interval of the 6th, for which see below. Guglielmo's notation of a breve as two semibreves suggests the possibility that the tune was originally written in stroke notation, of which more below.

[35] See Anselm Hughes, *Medieval Polyphony in the Bodleian Library* (Oxford, 1951), 27; and Manfred Bukofzer, 'Changing aspects of medieval and renaissance music'.

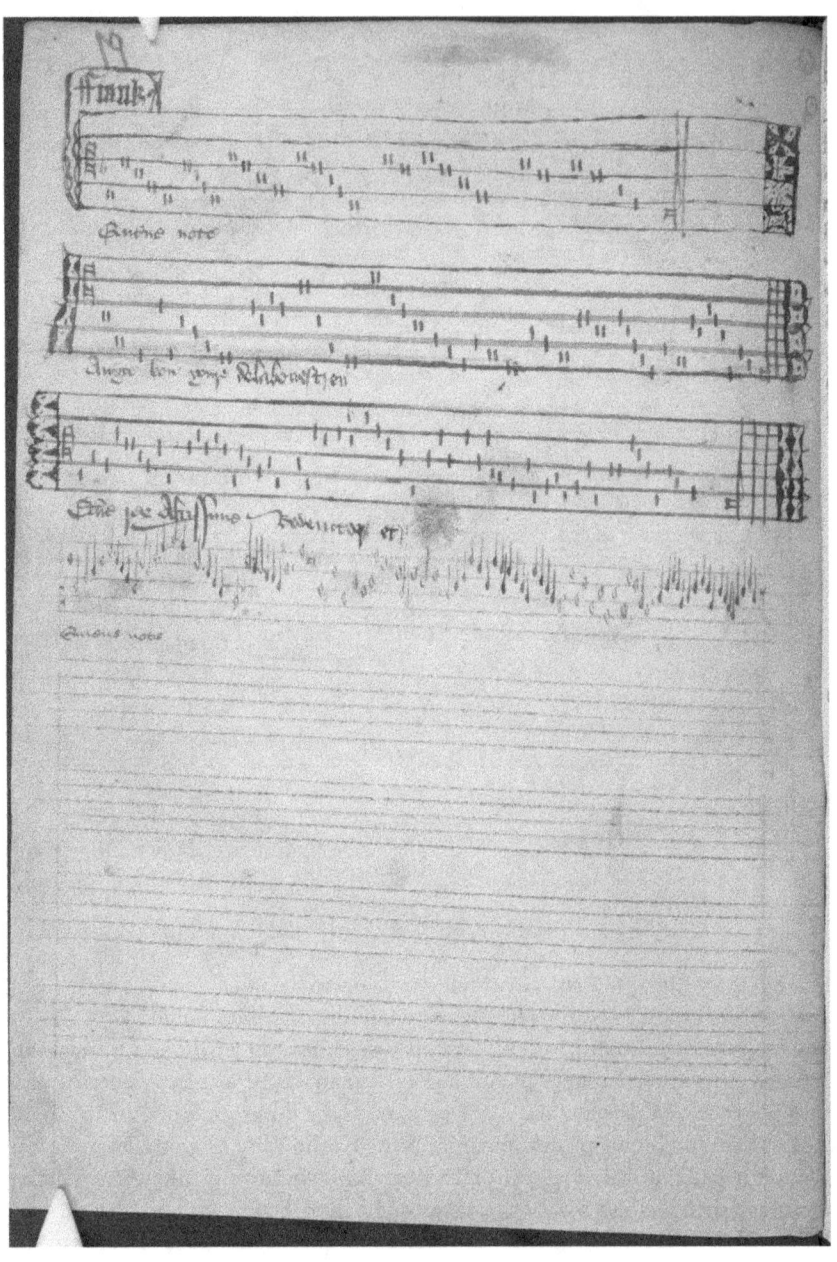

PLATE 12. *Quene Note* by Frank, with the tenors to *Anxce bon youre delabonestren* and *Eterne rex altissime*: late 15th or early 16th century.
Oxford, Bodleian Library, MS Digby 167, fol. 31v.

All three tunes seem to have existed originally in polyphonic settings, so the page seems to present a repertory of notated tenors on which a minstrel or a group of minstrels could improvise (on which more below).

These tenors bear the titles *Quene note*, *Anxce bon youre delabonestren* and *Eterne rex altissime Redemtor et ...*.[36] The last of these is not the chant *Eterne rex altissime* but a free counterpoint to it in the range of a contratenor altus: so while *Eterne rex* is not known as a polyphonic piece, it must in fact have existed at one time in a polyphonic version.[37] *Anxce bon youre* survives elsewhere as a polyphonic setting in three voices, and is considered below.

Quene note has an upper voice in Digby 167, on the same page as the tenor. Following the three tunes, below *Eterne rex*, is a cantus line entitled *Quene note*, written in a small, very different and less formal hand, in ordinary staff notation with round note-heads. The different C-clef suggests the possibility of a different scribe from the one who copied the three tenor tunes, but there is no positive reason to think that more than one scribe was involved. This line fits the *Quene note* tenor and works with it as a two-voiced piece. The different notation is explained by the difference in melodic style: the cantus is rhythmically too complex to be notated in stroke notation, and the scribe's evident wish to fit the notes of the cantus onto a single staff necessitated a much smaller musical script. It is tempting to speculate that this was necessary because he intended to copy upper parts for all three tenors on the five staves available below the tenor tunes.

This speculation has some support. The tenor of *Quene note* has thirty-one notes (double and single strokes), which are accommodated on the one staff with some space to spare; *Anxce bon youre* has forty-eight notes, fitted to the one staff but with noticeable lateral compression; and *Eterne rex* has fifty-six notes, again fitted to the single staff with noticeable compression. *Eterne rex* has far fewer double notes than *Anxce bon youre*, however, and takes up slightly less room. The cantus part of *Quene note* has ninety-four notes, and the scribe has used considerable lateral compression to keep the music within the one line.[38] If the cantus/tenor note-ratio is anything like the same for the other two tunes (3:1), their cantus lines would contain around 150 and 160 notes, respectively, both of which would require two staves. If this scenario is correct, then, it was very important for the 'cantus' scribe to use no more than the first of the available five staves (which he had set out) for the top line of

---

Musical Quarterly 44 (1954), 1–18, at 16. A facsimile is in J., J.F.R and C. Stainer and E. Nicholson, *Early Bodleian Music*. 3 vols (London, 1901; repr. Farnborough, 1967), I, Plate xcviii.

[36] The u and n of this page are largely indistinguishable: the second title actually reads *Auxce* and *yonre*, but these do not make sense.

[37] This tune, then, is a 'square' – a counterpoint removed from its polyphonic setting, and so separated from the tune to which it was originally added, and then used as a new tenor. A square was normally the lowest voice of the setting from which it was taken (i.e. the contratenor bassus), however. *Eterne rex altissime* is the Ascensiontide hymn at Vespers in the Sarum rite, for which see *Hymnarium Sarisburiense* (London, 1851), I, 101.

[38] I have ignored rests and accidentals in this discussion. They would slightly strengthen the argument put here.

Quene note. In fact, because the cantus part of *Anxce bon youre* surviving elsewhere is in triple mensuration, there are over 200 notes in that line: so if our 'cantus' scribe was intending to copy some version of that line he would have needed to use as much compression as for *Quene note* over both of the available staves.

While this is all speculative, the fact remains that the 'cantus' scribe did rule out five staves below the three tenor lines, presumably intending to use them; and since he did copy one cantus part it is fair to assume that he intended to copy the other two. The only alternative is that he was going to copy one or more contratenor parts (which admittedly would include fewer notes than the cantus lines).

The title and composer of *Quene note* have been a puzzle in the past, but a very tentative solution might be offered. Among the trumpeters given livery by Henry VII on 17 June 1503 was one Frannc Bocard; on 30 June 1503 he was one of five trumpeters given banners on being appointed to accompany two heralds in the train of Princess Margaret, about to travel to Scotland for her marriage to James IV. He was back in Court at the New Year 1506, and received his wages on 4 December that year; he received mourning livery on 11 May 1509 for the funeral of Henry VII; and on 24 June that year he received scarlet livery for the coronation of Henry VIII. On all occasions except the first he is listed simply as Frank or Franke.[39]

Although stroke notation is associated primarily with Flemish manuscripts, its use was certainly much wider than that. The presence in Digby 167 of the square to a Sarum chant suggests an English origin, while Frank's surname, Bocard, suggests that he came from a French-speaking area (as indeed did *Anxci bon jour*). None of this would run counter to the use of stroke notation in these tenors. If the trumpeter Frank Bocard was indeed the composer of *Quene note*, then his presence in the band of heralds and trumpeters accompanying the new Queen of Scots to her wedding may explain the title, 'The Queen's Tune'.[40] Perhaps it was composed especially for her during the journey, or for the celebrations when she had reached Edinburgh; or perhaps she herself gave Frank some of the tenor part (not all, since it is the tenor itself that is ascribed to Frank), which he then completed and furnished with a cantus. Such matters must remain speculative, however; and the very notion of a royal trumpeter being the composer of *Quene note* must also remain a speculation (albeit a pleasant one), for the evidence is entirely circumstantial.

1503 would be later than previous datings for Digby 167, fol. 31v, but the leaf has never been dated securely and Stainer's dating to the third quarter of the fifteenth century is almost certainly too early. The rather formal-looking writing of the three tenor parts could be of almost any date within twenty years or more on either side of 1500: and the hand of the cantus part of *Quene note* looks considerably later than c. 1450–75. If it was indeed copied around the same time as the tenors, this would tend to bring the copying of the tenors to a later date, too.

Whatever the origins of *Quene note*, the tenor is an artificially-constructed tune showing the old *estampie* form AA' BB' CC', with *ouvert* and *clos* endings to each

---

[39] Ashbee, *Records*, VII, 21, 22, 25, 29, 179 and 182; Ashbee et al., *Biographical Dictionary*, 166.

[40] 'Note' had several meanings, but the definition making the best sense here is 'tune' or 'melody': see H.H. Carter, *A Dictionary of Middle English Musical Terms* (Bloomington IN, 1961), 327, definition VI.

section – the same endings, as it happens, because A, B and C are very closely related (compare with examples earlier in this chapter). Sections C and C' actually incorporate sections B and B', shown as b and b' in Example 5, which presents the piece laid out to demonstrate this structure. The way in which the tenor line develops, through very simple variation from A to B and then to C, could certainly be the result of notation-free composition.

Coming to the cantus part, however, the situation looks rather different. The cantus line follows the same structure as the tenor: but while octaves and fifths above the tenor are fairly numerous, there are far fewer than in the Harley dances, and many of them are displaced from the strong beats. Moreover, the development from fifth to octave in the variant sections occurs hardly at all: compare bars 9–12 and 13–16, for example, or 19–22 and 25–8. On the other hand, there is some decoration in the variants, although it appears to go in both directions: bars 26–7 are certainly a decoration of 19–20, but in the same way 17–18 are a (pre-emptive) decoration of 23–4. As it stands, however, the cantus line is surprisingly devoid of rhythmic or melodic development in sections B and B' – one would expect a minstrel to fill in the rather uninventive syncopations of section B, although this does happen in sections C and C' – rather late in the day and with the curious pre-emptive decoration already noted.

Another question concerns the use of the sixth above the tenor note. This is sometimes a displacement of the fifth, as in bars 6 and 17, but is also used as a consonant note in its own right, as in bars 6–7 and 27. These are also approaches to a 6–8 cadence, as are the sixths in bar 15. The sixth also appears as a suspended note on the strong beat, which is a particular ploy of this improviser or composer. Instances of this are shown by * in Example 5. A method of improvising sixths above the tenor may have been in use here (see below), or perhaps it is due to the influence of written composition, as suggested by the two-part Burgundian cadence in bars 7–8.

It is difficult to say whether these features suggest notationless improvisation or notated composition.[41] The piece is by no means unsuccessful, but it does seem both too uninventive to be the result of considered improvisation and too inconsistent in the working-out of the material to be a composition using notation from the start. The repeated cantus decoration in bar 18 (marked with brackets) looks like an improviser free-wheeling, while the more interesting repeated material of bars 17 and 25–6 could well be the result of playful manipulation of a useful series of notes.

Quene note could have started out as an improvisation, being notated and tidied-up at a later stage, but without the full compositional process being brought to bear. The use of stroke notation in the tenor suggests a performer who was not used to reading mensural notation of any difficulty. Stroke notation avoids the problems of longer note-values, especially those concerned with triple mensuration: and while this is irrelevant for *Quene Note*, which is in duple mensuration, *Anxce bon youre* is not. Stroke notation is certainly easier to read than normal staff notation, and it is

---

[41] In this situation 'notationless improvisation' need not prohibit the cantus player from reading a written tenor line, although that procedure may have been less efficient than using his ears.

EXAMPLE 5. *Quene note*

also quicker to write than normal note-heads. Perhaps more importantly, it takes up less space, a matter discussed earlier.

The problem presented by this cantus part is essentially a musical one: why is it rhythmically 'sticky', and why are repetitions sometimes less interesting than the original presentations? These questions arise on the back of an assumption that we ought not to make: that notated instrumental polyphony is either 'frozen improvisation' (the record of a single actual performance) or a notated composition (the prescriptive record of what the composer requires the performers to do). In fact, these are the two ends of a spectrum of relationships between notation and performance that includes (among many other positions) a situation in which a written-out decoration may be followed by a plainer section in which the performer is expected to produce the kind of decoration already notated. This perhaps puts the *Quene note* cantus in perspective: the rather 'sticky' rhythms of bars 9–10 may be an invitation to decorate in a way that makes the music flow better, and the relatively plain passage at bars 23–5 an invitation to use the kind of decoration already presented in bars 17–19. The questions to be answered, then, are: (1) How would a medieval instrumentalist have interpreted this notation? and (2) What would he have played in consequence? The first is a question to which I have just tried to begin an answer; the second is answerable in detail only by the work of present-day instrumentalists versed in the art of improvisation and decoration.

A final question concerning *Quene note* is that of the instruments for which it was composed. The ranges of the two lines are so narrow that almost any combination of either loud or still instruments could have played it. For indoor performance, perhaps two lutes, or a fiddle and a lute, would be ideal; recorders would also be possible. For performance out of doors or in a large space such as a hall, one might expect treble and tenor shawms or a shawm and a sackbut. This latter ensemble (perhaps with a tabor added) seems most likely if, as it feels, the piece was intended as a *basse danse*.[42]

Other instrumental music in two voices

While dance music is an obvious contender for the status of minstrels' music, it is difficult to see how certain other pieces can be eliminated from that repertory. The music in the early fifteenth-century Faenza MS, for example, is generally thought to be for instruments: this is mainly on account of its style, which presents a florid top line over a slower-moving tenor derived from vocal music, both sacred and (mainly) secular.[43] McGee argued that these pieces would best be performed as lute duets or on lute and harp,[44] but this is not universally accepted. In English sources, there are instrumental pieces in the early fourteenth-century Robertsbridge manuscript: these are usually assumed to be for organ,[45] mainly because their mixed staff and letter notation (now called German organ tablature) was used for that instrument in the sixteenth century. This is hardly a good reason for assigning them to the organ, but the introduction of three-note chords into the two-voiced texture does suggest a keyboard instrument.

---

[42] At 31 notes *Quene note* is on the short side for a *basse danse* tenor: but of the tunes in the Toulouse print and the Brussels manuscript, nine are as short or shorter. See James L. Jackman, *Fifteenth Century Basse Dances* (Northampton MA, 1964); Michel Toulouze, *L'art et instruction de bien dancer* (Paris, c. 1496; repr. London, 1936; repr. with music ed. Richard Rastall and the text trans. A.E. Lequet. East Ardsley and New York NY, 1971); and Ernest Closson, *Le manuscrit dit les basses danses de la Bibliothèque de Bourgogne*. Societe des bibliophiles et iconophiles de Belgique (1912; repr. Geneva, 1976).

[43] Faenza, Biblioteca Comunale Manfrediana, Raccolte Musicali, MS 117.

[44] Timothy J. McGee, 'Instruments and the Faenza Codex'. *Early Music* 14 (1986), 480–90; repr. McGee, *Instruments and their Music*, 479–88.

[45] London, British Library, MS Arundel 28550 (the Robertsbridge MS, early fourteenth century), fol. 43r–43v. Transcriptions in McGee, *Medieval Instrumental Dances*, 130–41; fol. 43r shown as Plate LXI in Carl Parrish, *The Notation of Medieval Music* (New York NY, 1957, and London, 1958).

The other medieval piece of supposed English organ music does not show that feature, however, and may be for other instruments. In the music section of Oxford, Bodleian Library, Douce MS 381, which must date from around 1400 or soon after,[46] is a short two-voiced work notated in score. Example 6 shows the opening of the piece in Thurston Dart's transcription.[47] The other pieces in the manuscript are songs notated in separate parts. Dart had two reasons for treating this piece as organ music: first, it is in score, and he argued that vocal music would not be written in score unless the voices proceeded at the same speed, which these do not; and second, not all of the plainchant concerned is set. There is much to be said against this, however. The lower voice is completely underlaid with the text 'Felix namque ... sancta Maria', and the two voices are closely aligned, with the line-ends at the same place in the music. This is the usual arrangement for score-notated vocal music, where the text is written only once, below the lower voice. Moreover, the style of the top voice, with its frequent repeated notes, is very similar to that of the cantus parts of the songs in this manuscript and in Cambridge, University Library, Add MS 5943.

Although the setting would be incomplete as a liturgical piece, Dart was also wrong to say that it could not have been continued on another leaf. Some leaves from the manuscript have been turned round in rebinding, so that *recto* has become *verso* and *vice versa*. If the existing music, now on a *recto*, had in fact been originally on a *verso*, the piece could have been continued on the following leaf, now lost.

This could be organ music, therefore, although the texting and use of score layout suggest a vocal piece; but if it were indeed instrumental it could have been intended for a combination of melodic instruments. The top voice would go well on a large fiddle, and the lower voice would fit a harp or lute. In that case, is it likely to have been composed using notation, or as notation-free improvisation? The vertical intervals are almost all octaves and fifths, which points towards improvisation based on fifthing, and sixths are almost all passing-notes. There are two exceptions, however, at bars 2 and 5, where the sixth is used as a consonant interval in its own right. While these do not place the piece firmly in the realm of composed music using notation, they may point in that direction: but it is impossible to know how quickly a minstrel's aural sense might have followed stylistic changes in sacred vocal music, making the freer use of the sixth available for improvising.

In view of the many uncertainties about this piece, one cannot make a strong claim for it as music for two melody instruments, although it could have originated as improvisation by fifthing.

---

[46] Rastall, *Two Fifteenth-Century Song Books*, xv–xvi, and facsimile on fol. 23r; Dobson and Harrison, *Medieval English Songs*, 22.

[47] R. Thurston Dart, 'A new source of early English organ music'. *Music & Letters* 35/3 (1954), 201–5, at 205. Much of this piece is now illegible, but Dart read it under ultra-violet light. For facsimiles, see Rastall, *Two Fifteenth-Century Song Books*, fol. 23r, and Stainer *et al.*, *Early Bodleian Music*.

EXAMPLE 6. *Felix namque*, opening

Music in three voices

With music in two voices the question has been whether the piece could have been composed without the use of notation. The matter of simultaneous or consecutive composition has not been an issue: if a pre-existent tenor is in use then composition must be consecutive by definition; and if not, the possible working practices of the musician(s) involved make the question unanswerable. With music in three voices, however, the question immediately becomes relevant.

How might a group of minstrels have improvised a three-part texture? The important points about the technique of fifthing are (1) that the basic method is for the upper voice to play a fifth above the lower voice (which acts as a pre-existent tune, even if it is derived simultaneously), and (2) that the upper voice then deploys various techniques to disguise the resulting parallelism. The technique of fifthing might be extended into strict organum in three parts, producing a texture made entirely of consecutive fourths between voices I and II and consecutive fifths between voices II and III. With three voices, however, it would be harder to disguise the parallelism with interesting melodic variation, mainly because voices I and III progress in consecutive octaves. There were methods available, however, that improved this situation by modifying the consecutives with voice III. The first of these is the method generally known as faburden, a technique particularly associated with English music.

Faburden, originally used in liturgical music, starts with a pre-existent chant. Later it was applied to a secular tenor, which could be newly-composed. The given tune would be performed as a tenor part, with the treble part presenting the same tune exactly a fourth above the tenor. This treble line could however be decorated in whatever ways the singer knew, and the improvised decorations were a mark of his skill. Finally, the bass line would also be a version of the chant: the singer performed the notes at the start and end of each musical phrase a fifth below the tenor, but the notes between were pitched a third high: that is, most of the bass line was actually performed a third below the tenor. This made the texture into a series of first-inversion chords except for the first and last chords of each phrase.[48]

Much sacred vocal polyphony survives in this style, although decoration of the lines may partly disguise the simple origin of the texture. It is also a possible method for fleshing out a *basse danse* tune, and it is often assumed that the monophonic *basse danse* repertory was sometimes performed in this way. There is no evidence for this, though, and little if any English instrumental music in this style appears to have survived: a possible example will be discussed below.

Another way of producing a three-part texture from a given tune is closely related to the faburden method: the continental technique of fauxbourdon. This texture sounds very like faburden: the result is again a series of first-inversion chords, but the texture is arrived at by a different route. Here the chant or other tune is placed in the top part, transposed up an octave from the original written pitch. The middle voice performs exactly the same tune a fourth lower, so that the top and middle lines work in consecutive fourths. The bass would perform the tune an octave below the treble but, as in faburden, sings a third higher except at the start and end of a phrase. Again, any line can be decorated. The result of this process is that faburden and fauxbourdon sound the same, but fauxbourdon sounds at a higher pitch than faburden, with the tune in voice I rather than voice II.

Faburden and fauxbourdon both produce parallel chords, so that in their simplest forms there is no crossing of parts. In practice, the decoration of individual lines may result in parts crossing for very short periods. It is also worth noting that fauxbourdon is the only recognised method of top-down improvisation: that is, the pre-existent tune is in the top voice and it is the lower voices that are derived from it: most methods start with the tune in the tenor, so that the top voice is one of the improvised lines. There is apparently no surviving English instrumental music in fauxbourdon style, so that fauxbourdon, like faburden, must be reckoned only a potential method for performing a dance or song in three-part polyphony. There is at least one piece known in England, however, that originated from a very similar method, and perhaps other pieces will come to light.

In the three-voiced *Anxce bon youre delabonestren* a florid treble is underpinned by a relatively plain tenor and a more decorated contratenor (Example 7).[49] In the manuscript that contains *Quene Note* (see above) the tenor part is written in stroke notation. This would suggest that it was the tenor part that constituted the written basis for learning, improvising and performing the piece. This does not necessarily mean that the piece was composed otherwise without notation: the minstrels could have learned their individual parts by heart, using the written tenor part only as an *aide mémoire*. It probably does mean, however, that the tenor was used as the basis for yet another way of producing the first-inversion chords of faburden and

---

[48] Further on this process, see Jane Flynn, 'The education of choristers in England during the sixteenth century'. John Morehen, ed., *English Choral Practice, 1400–1650* (Cambridge, 1995), 180–99, at 184–8; and Rastall, *The Heaven Singing*, 95–7.

[49] Trent, Castello del Buon Consiglio, MS 87, fols 117v–118r. The cantus and tenor make good counterpoint without the contratenor.

EXAMPLE 7. *Anxce bon youre*, opening

fauxbourdon: a treble that starts and ends each phrase an octave above the tenor, with a contratenor that moves in parallel fourths below the treble.

At first sight *Anxce bon youre* looks like a 2+1 texture, for in the first bar the contratenor seems to show a typical filling-in process, leaping from one harmony note to another and crossing the tenor part in order to do so. It is certainly an example of a method producing first-inversion chords, as can be seen in the analysis in the lower system of Example 7: but the basic structure is disguised by the wealth of decoration in the upper parts. Whether this decoration could have been the result of directed and sustained improvisation or not, we have no means of knowing. Given competent minstrels and sufficient time there seems no reason why this piece should not have been composed by improvisation, mainly or wholly without the use of notation.

It will be useful at this stage to consider a three-part texture of the kind that was clearly derived from a different method of composition. Francisco de la Torre's three-voiced setting of *La Spagna* is a well-known piece, the voices of which were undoubtedly composed consecutively. Example 8 shows the opening.[50] First, the *basse danse* tune was set out with some rhythmicisation, as comparison with Example 4 will show: this version of the tune is slightly different, some notes being omitted and some extra notes added. These features suggest that the tenor was laid out as a deliberate act of composition, probably using notation.

The next step, almost certainly, was to add the treble part. This could have been accomplished as an improvisation: it seems likely that the notated version of the *basse danse* tune was available to the treble-player if so, although he could perhaps have memorised it first. It is also possible that the treble part was composed using notation: but in that case the composer would surely have eliminated the repeated melodic tritone of bars 17–18 and 19–20 (not shown in Example 8).

At this stage the piece consisted of a two-voiced setting, to which a contratenor was then added. This was the normal process for three-voiced music in the fifteenth century: much of the repertory works perfectly well as tenor-plus-treble and sometimes survives in that form, without the contratenor. The contratenor, then, is an add-on voice, even if the piece was conceived as being in three parts from the outset, and is not necessary to the musical sense and integrity of the piece. In fact, the contratenor often shows signs of having been composed against the tenor part without much reference to the treble.[51]

That does not happen in this setting of *La Spagna*, but there are examples in the song *Jeo hay en vos tote may fiance* (Example 9), which was apparently performed in Winchester College c. 1400 and is fairly typical of the repertory.[52] Although the contratenor part (the lowest voice in this score) is carefully composed to go with the tenor, it makes some dissonances against the treble (marked *) that show a lack of concern for what the treble is doing in those places. Perfect counterpoint in two parts, some clumsy dissonances in three. I do not suggest that *Jeo hay en vos* originated in improvisation, but that composition could adhere to the precepts of improvisation in this respect.

Two other three-part songs in this style, which also make perfectly good sense as treble-tenor duos, are known to have been performed to an accompaniment

---

[50] This piece has often been anthologised: Tess Knighton's transcription is in Lorenz Welker, 'Wind ensembles in the Renaissance'. Tess Knighton and David Fallows, eds, *Companion to Medieval and Renaissance Music* (London, 1992), 146–53, at 152–3; much of Higini Anglès's transcription is in Polk, *German Instrumental Music*, 202, with discussion on 201–5.

[51] Tinctoris, writing c. 1475, noted that all three voices should be consonant in compositions, but that in improvisation it was necessary only for cantus and contratenor to be individually consonant with the tenor: see Polk, *German Instrumental Music*, 172.

[52] Cambridge, University Library, Add MS 5943, fol. 164r; facsimile in Rastall, *Two Fifteenth-Century Songbooks*; edition in Richard Rastall, *Four French Songs from an English Songbook*. 2nd edn (Antico Edition, 2014), no. 2. *Esperanse*, in the same manuscript (fol. 165r), is in two parts there, although in three parts in continental sources (facsimile and edition as before).

EXAMPLE 8. Francisco de la Torre's *La Spagna*, opening

—(continued)

EXAMPLE 8—concluded

EXAMPLE 9. *Jeo hay en vos,* opening

of harp or lute. As discussed in Chapter 3, Thomas Rede's teaching of George Cely in 1473–5 included instruction in playing *O rosa bella* and *Go hert hurt with adversitie*, both songs that survive in 2+1 style. John Dunstable's *O rosa bella* is in Trent, Castello del Buon Consiglio, MS 90, together with alternative voices by Okeghem and Hert; *Go hert*, which is perhaps by the same Hert, survives only in MS Ashmole 191 in the Bodleian Library, Oxford. As they now exist they may not be the versions that Cely learned, of course, but it is fair to speculate that Cely's versions were not too far distant from the surviving songs.[53] If Cely were a beginner or very inexperienced, these songs in their two-voiced versions would have been useful teaching material; but if he were more capable, his abilities would be better stretched by the three-voiced versions. The opening of *Go hert* is shown in Example 10.

These songs survive in separate parts on the page, so that it would be difficult to learn them from the notation that we have. If notation were a part of the learning process, then Rede probably intabulated them: but, as already noted, Cely was probably taught entirely by ear, with no written material to hand. Perhaps Rede had himself learned the songs by ear, but it seems probable that at some stage in the teaching chain these songs had been intabulated. Unfortunately no such intabulation is known to have survived.

We should note in passing that instrumental tablatures mainly date from the fifteenth century. There are very rare earlier examples, such as the presumed organ pieces in the fourteenth-century Robertsbridge manuscript, mentioned above, and a possible example of lute-tablature from the same century.[54] The Faenza manuscript may present intabulations for keyboard (i.e. two-staff scores), although a keyboard score was ruled out by McGee, who considered the music to be for two melody instruments.[55]

By the time instrumental tablature was well established, in the late fifteenth century, it was accepted as the way of notating music for a solo instrument. This was in contradistinction to the use of staff notation for ensemble music, including notation in score for some vocal music. Instrumental ensemble music, it is generally agreed, used staff-notation in separate parts: and it is here that we must start our consideration of instrumental ensemble music in England.

---

[53] *O rosa bella* is edited in Manfred Bukofzer, ed., *John Dunstable: Complete Works*. Musica Britannica VIII. 2nd edn by Margaret Bent, Ian Bent and Brian Trowell (London, 1970), 133–4, and Brian Trowell, *Invitation to Medieval Music*, 4 (London, 1978), no. 1; and *Go hert* in R. Thurston Dart, ed., *Invitational to Medieval Music 1: Music of the Earlier Fifteenth Century* (London and New York NY, 1967), no. 9.

[54] Christopher Page, 'French lute tablature in the 14th century?'. *Early Music* 8/4 (1980), 488–92; and 'The 15th-century lute: new and neglected sources'. *Early Music* 9/1 (1981), 11–21.

[55] McGee, 'Instruments and the Faenza Codex', *passim*.

EXAMPLE 10. *Go hert hurt with adversitie*, opening

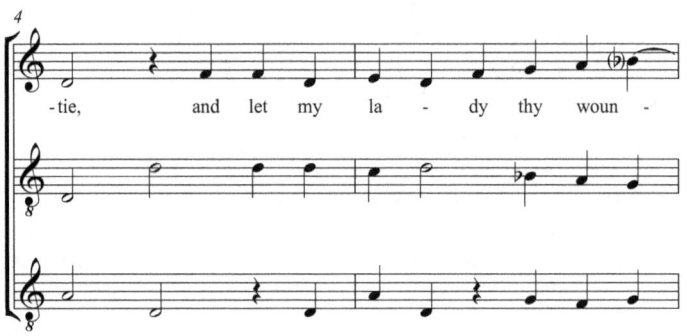

Minstrels' manuscripts?

At the start of this chapter I noted that no piece of minstrels' music had been identified in an English source, and that we did not really know what a minstrels' musical manuscript might look like. The problem has similarities with that of the textual sources discussed in Chapter 11. Digby 167, in fact, would be my answer to the implied question: What would a piece of minstrels' music look like? – or, rather, What would a minstrels' manuscript look like? A small collection of tenors (both sacred and secular, as it happens), tunes with small ranges, and written in a simplified notation such as stroke notation, would seem the most likely kind of source to be produced by a minstrel for his own use.[56] Tunes take much less room to copy than verbal texts, so for the music manuscript we look not for a book but for a fragment, perhaps only a single leaf, as Digby 167 is. A collection of three tunes may be regarded as an *aide mémoire* for performance rather than the record of something composed; but, more importantly, the use of stroke notation suggests something that could be written down by a minstrel, not merely read by one. The copying of tenors was perhaps occasional, but the tunes themselves certainly consumable, to be memorised and not necessarily saved for further use.

While the tenors of Digby 167 offer a possible example of a music manuscript produced by a minstrel, the cantus part presents a different problem, posed also by the Gresley manuscript and other sources: music associated with minstrel-performance, but written in notation that a minstrel might not be able to read. One possible solution, as already noted, is that a minstrel could work with a trained church singer; another, that there was always a range of musical literacy among minstrels and some were able to read standard mensural notation. The upper-voice tunes make use of smaller note-values than the tenors, and these do not raise the triple-mensuration problems that stroke-notation avoids. A necessary line of enquiry, therefore, is to examine the stroke-notation sources from a different point of view – not as teaching material (as they have usually been regarded) but as material for performance. Most stroke-notation appears in liturgical sources, or at least sources associated with liturgical singers: but this does not necessarily exclude minstrels, some of whom were taking part in liturgical performances on the continent by the late fifteenth century.[57] But it is also the case that minstrels included liturgical music in their repertories anyway, as Digby 167 shows. Identifying minstrels' manuscripts, therefore, should initially concentrate on sources containing secular music, whether or not they also contain sacred pieces.

It is worth looking to a continental source at this stage, for there is at least one that certainly belonged to, and was partly copied by, a minstrel. Zorzi Trombetta

---

[56] Stroke-notation sources are usually regarded as teaching material or a preliminary form of notation for those not yet versed in the difficult late medieval notation of sacred polyphony. It might now be worth reviewing these sources as potential minstrel-manuscripts – materials that are largely non-prescriptive, but available for appropriation and modification during performance.

[57] See, for example, Victor Coehlo and Keith Polk, *Instrumentalists and Renaissance Culture, 1420–1600* (Cambridge, 2016), 187.

da Modon was employed on a venetian galley in 1444, along with two pipers: he was therefore the trumpeter in a wind ensemble, as well as (presumably) sounding such signals as were needed on board the ship.[58] That year Zorzi started compiling a notebook on various subjects that interested him, including ten pages of music. Some of these had been copied a few years earlier by others; some Zorzi himself copied. Zorzi's section contains the tenors of both chansons and dance-pieces, while the rest consists of chansons in two or three voices. All of the tenors are copied in stroke notation, the other voices in mensural notation.

This is an example of what many stroke-notation sources offer: tenors in stroke-notation and other voices in mensural notation. The Digby and Zorzi manuscripts are unusual, however, in that they include secular pieces. Zorzi evidently compiled a small repertory of music suitable for the wind band in which he played, and that supports the possibility that Digby 167 was written out for a similar purpose.

Instrumental ensemble music in fifteenth-century England

Scholars who have discussed instrumental ensemble music in fifteenth-century Europe have accepted that the subject demands an examination of written, composed music, often by known and named composers, and of the instruments on which it might have been played.[59] Most have offered only a passing glance towards the improvised, notationless tradition of minstrelsy, together with some speculation on the use of memory and the minstrels' ability to improvise around, and to decorate, composed music. But, as we have seen, the tradition of improvised composition around a memorised tune, which was the staple fare of the earlier minstrel, was almost certainly alive and flourishing during the fifteenth century and into the sixteenth.

The newer tradition of composed polyphony for instruments, both vocal music performed instrumentally and ensemble music composed specifically for instruments, was strong in the Low Countries, Germany and Italy.[60] England had close connections with the Low Countries, and there was always a movement of minstrels from England to and from the Continent, so that it would be surprising if the tradition were not known in England. There is however no evidence that English minstrels took up the challenges of a written, composed, repertory before the beginning of Henry VII's reign (1485–1509), when an apparent reorganisation of the royal minstrels brought specialist bands into being, with foreign minstrels prominent at

---

[58] BL Cotton MS Titus A. xxvi, described in Coehlo and Polk, *Instrumentalists and Renaissance Culture*, 66–8. DIAMM provides images of the music at <www.diamm.ac.uk>. I have also made use of Linda Massey's undergraduate dissertation 'An edition of the music in Cotton MS Titus A xxvi' (Leeds University, 1976, but not generally available).

[59] See especially Banks, *Instrumental Consort Repertory*.

[60] See H. Colin Slim, 'Instrumental versions, c. 1515–1544, of a late-fifteenth-century Flemish chanson, *O waerde mont*'. Fenlon, *Music in Medieval & Early Modern Europe*, 131–61; Edwards, 'Songs without words'; Polk, *German Instrumental Music*; and Litterick, 'On Italian instrumental ensemble music'.

Court.⁶¹ More importantly, almost no instrumental music has survived in English sources from the pre-Tudor period. When a home-grown instrumental repertory eventually emerged, it was only after the appearance in England of manuscripts and prints of continental ensemble music, with which the new local repertory rubs shoulders. This is seen first in the songbook now known as Henry VIII's Manuscript (London, British Library, Add. MS 31922, c. 1510–13), where the impetus for local instrumental composition was the continental repertory of Petrucci's *Odhecaton* (1501) and other sources. Here the presence of such pieces as the famous *Benedictus* of Heinrich Isaac – the first item in the manuscript – is clearly linked to such works as the *Fa la sol* of William Cornish and the various untitled consort pieces.⁶²

Henry VIII's court certainly had the means to perform this repertory. Henry himself headed a group of noble amateurs capable of playing some of the instruments that he gathered together over the years, and they could apparently read the notation of the early Tudor song books, learning the music and committing it to memory. But that ability presupposes a literate and professional ability among his household servants. Such a culture could flourish only with the support of a professional band of musicians, and we must assume that the royal minstrels were involved, as well as the singers of the household chapel and other musician servants.

The point has been made before (and it is an important one) that the early Tudor royal households included specialist minstrel groups that were already part-way along the route from medieval minstrel to gentleman musician.⁶³ It is also true, however, that the new instrumental repertory, and the secular vocal repertory from which it sprang, was stylistically and notationally very different from the complex sacred music of the turn of the sixteenth century. This new, simpler style and the simpler notation that went with it allowed the reading of notation to be a major factor in learning new instrumental pieces. This is probably why the Norwich waits were encouraged to learn notation in 1533 – perhaps a late catching-up process by then. The new style also made it possible for minstrels to compose, and at least two minstrel-composers were active at Henry VIII's court: the king's blind harper William More (c. 1490–1565) and the Netherlander Philip Van Wilder (c. 1500–53).⁶⁴ If Frank Bocard indeed wrote *Quene note*, then there had been an earlier minstrel-composer at the Tudor Court.

There may have been an even earlier composer among the minstrels of the English aristocracy. In 1352 Elizabeth de Burgh paid her minstrel Roger 2s 6d for 'making 7

---

⁶¹ See pp. 358–61.

⁶² For the facsimiles and editions, respectively, see Ottaviano Petrucci, *Harmonice Musices Odhecaton* (Venice, 1501; repr. n.p., n.d.) and Helen Hewitt, ed., *Petrucci: Harmonice Musices Odhecaton A* (Cambridge MA, 1942; repr. New York NY, 1978); and David Fallows, intr., *The Henry VIII Book* (Oxford, 2014) and John Stevens, ed., *Music at the Court of Henry VIII*. Musica Britannica 18 (London, 1962). For the dating of the Henry VIII MS, see Fallows, *Henry VIII Book*, 25–6.

⁶³ Dumitrescu, *Early Tudor Court*, Chapter 3.

⁶⁴ The royal minstrel Possant Bontemps cannot be identified with the Bontemps of Pepys MS 1760 at Magdalene College Cambridge: see John T. Brobeck, 'A music book for Mary Tudor, Queen of France'. *Early Music History* 35 (2016), 1–93, at 6.

songs',[65] a wording usually associated with composition by chapel singers. It would be very interesting to know what sort of 'songs' these were, but we need not assume that they were polyphonic compositions. However we look at it, *Quene note* was at the start of a new era, the very rich musical history of the sixteenth century in England. If it was really composed by a royal minstrel, it represents social changes that were to have considerable effect on the musical scene. In the higher echelons of the profession the minstrels remained, as they had always been, respected servants, but now aspiring to the status of musician. This aspiration is clearly observable in the career of Thomas Whythorne (1528–96), struggling as an instrumentalist to attain the kind of status enjoyed by the 'gentlemen' of the Chapel Royal,[66] and perhaps also desired by William More (who was nevertheless regarded as the premier harper rather than as a composer). It is in Philip Van Wilder that we see the transition achieved, a royal minstrel known (and paid) as a composer. The minstrel as a *genre* did not disappear: but because of the changed status of the top practitioners the word 'minstrel' became a term of abuse, not just to the Church but to society in general, in the new order of Tudor England. The history of minstrelsy in the Tudor period (1485–1603) is a complex subject that largely remains to be explored in detail.

---

[65] Ward, *Elizabeth de Burgh*, 77.
[66] James M. Osborn, *The Autobiography of Thomas Whythorne*. Modern spelling edition (London, 1962), ix and *passim*.

Envoi

Studying the day-to-day activity of the minstrels, and thereby broadening the focus of enquiry outwards from special occasions into a wider field of study, offers no startling break-through but does help to increase our understanding. The current picture of minstrelsy and its place in late medieval English society is both broader and more detailed as a result.

Refocussing the picture allows a fuller understanding of the range of careers that minstrels followed. This includes the circumstances of their employment by magnates, towns and institutions, revealing the relatively stable and remunerative patterns of employment that were open to them, which of these they chose (when the choice was available) and which were imposed on them. The accumulation of day-to-day information, too, adds to our knowledge of individual lives, careers and even life-style, and sheds light on employment mobility, both within limited local areas and internationally. Among the careers illuminated are those of several interesting individuals, such as the trumpeter and herald-king Robert Little and the trumpeter and fixer Thomas Chatterton.[1]

It may also now be easier to see vocal and instrumental minstrelsy as parts of a single activity, if our work has fully dispelled the old romantic myths and replaced them by the historical facts of employment. Minstrelsy – all secular music – was no casual or occasional amusement: it was part of the under-lying structure of daily existence, fully integrated into the activities of all societies, from the established ceremonials of the king's household to the civic events normally available to dwellers in the most poverty-stricken urban slums.

Considering our ultimate reason for studying medieval minstrelsy, we have aimed for a better basic appreciation of how minstrels performed. One can never have all the information needed (that is so for the modern performance of any musical or dramatic work from a previous period) and so can never accurately reconstruct a medieval performance: but the more we know, the more we can understand both the work itself and those who performed and witnessed it. The problem is to uncover the relationship between written texts and notated music on the one hand and performance on the other.

On the musical side I have suggested that the stroke-notation sources may have provided minstrels with material that, being largely non-prescriptive, could be available for creative modification during performance. The means of modification were largely decorative. At the same time, some of the means of musical construction, such as 'fifthing' against an existing tune, could be used by minstrels to create a

---

[1] The work of a king of heralds and that of a fixer were at least partly similar, a matter that may bear further investigation.

texture of two or more parts. Other sources may be the result of writing down such work at some stage of creation and performance.

Concerning verbal performance, the evidence suggests that while medieval writers often cast long texts such as *chansons de geste* and romances as minstrel performances, in real life sustained recitation was rarely possible and that the gap between textual tradition and oral performance must have been wider than often acknowledged. Minstrel performances were relatively short and subject to interruption, and minstrels could not normally count on bringing their listeners back the following day. The evidence also suggests that minstrels often accompanied themselves on instruments during these short performances, and sang, rather than merely recited, when they did so. But how the long texts that have come down to us, often running to thousands of lines, were delivered is not clear. In many cases, the people who delivered these texts were not minstrels and presumably just read them aloud. Whether a minstrel such as Adenet le Roi ever delivered all 18,698 lines of his *Cleomadés*, and if so whether he accompanied himself on his vielle, remains an open question.

Such insights, however tentative, bring with them a raft of new and newly-refined questions to be answered, as all research should. What, therefore, remains to be done? What directions should now be taken by further research on minstrelsy in late medieval England?

The development of online resources, including the digitisation of record material, brings many benefits to research on minstrels. It is now easier to compile biographies of individual minstrels, as Constance Bullock-Davies started to do in her two books, and so to further our understanding of how minstrels fitted into society and how society was itself influenced by minstrels and others. One very interesting aspect of this is the presence of foreign minstrels, especially in the royal records. Such names as Ivo Vala, John de Depe and John de Bria show that foreign minstrels were employed at Court; and if we add in the occasions, both at Court and in the minstrel schools, when English and foreign minstrels could have met, listened to one another and exchanged techniques and repertory, it is clear that minstrels in England did not work in isolation from their colleagues in continental Europe.[2]

Quite how much these various connections affected the lives and working methods of English minstrels, and in what ways, is not yet clear. The influence of continental minstrelsy needs further exploration, especially because there certainly were situations (which we have tried to flag up) in which English and continental practices were not identical. The relationships between practices in England and on the continent, and between those in different parts of Europe, were dynamic and complex.

Minstrelsy is nothing if divorced from its context, whether that be international or local, and even some of the most obvious questions concerning the minstrels' lives in the royal households have yet to be answered. For instance, the two trumpeters and two other minstrels on permanent stand-by in the king's household could probably be identified through close analysis of sections of the Wardrobe accounts.

---

[2] This situation applies not only to the early Tudor period, as studied in detail by Dumitrescu and others, but to the whole of the fourteenth and fifteenth centuries. It also applies to minstrels in Scotland: see SM I, 208, for Scottish minstrels going abroad; and *ibid.*, 210, for the four Italian minstrels and the Moorish taborer.

In any year for which the principal records have survived – for both the Wardrobe and the Chamber, for preference – it will be possible to work out exactly who was in Court on which days.[3] The records have not been searched with that in mind, but they could be.

One obstacle to this process is the apparently irregular series of prests, or part-payments, that tend to obscure the expected patterns of wage payments: consequently, there are problems in identifying the exact range of dates for which any payment was made. Another is the practical difficulty of dating items. The recording scribes wrote down the payments made in order, day by day, noting the place at which each payment was made. The date and place were given for the first item: thereafter, 'the same day' was noted until the following day's payments were started, and 'the same place' was noted until the venue changed. These did not necessarily coincide: the king often transacted business at one place and then, after travelling onwards, transacted more business that evening at the next stopping-place. In order to ascertain the date and place of any payment, therefore, it might be necessary to search back quite a long way in the accounts, often a very time-consuming business.

The same difficulty arises with civic records: and here, while the place of a payment does not usually change, there is an added problem with precise dating. The royal records are always dated by the regnal year, but civic records are dated by the mayoral year, which may vary with the town concerned. As Chapter 9 showed, the lack of precise dating in the REED publications meant that it was impossible to date the visits of minstrels to the various ports on the south Kent coast and even to say in which direction the groups travelled. The various civic records concerned must be searched again in order to establish precise dates for these visits. The same is true, obviously, for the records of York and other places (see pp. 186–9).

The civic records have also shown that more detailed work is needed concerning the security arrangements at certain ports. In this case researchers must return to the records in order to search for items not directly concerned with entertainment and therefore not included in REED volumes. The relationships between minstrels, *vigilatores*, hornblowers and serjeants-at-arms cannot at present be elucidated in any of the towns concerned, and there are indications that such relationships differ from place to place.

Part III of this book shows that more work is needed, also, on the lives and work of independent minstrels. Apart from the records of the various courts of law, which largely remain to be searched for minstrels, a useful source of information will be the Patent Rolls, which record pardons, orders for the apprehension of felons, licences to travel, safe-conducts and much else. The fifteenth-century Patent Rolls have proved useful, for instance (and have not yet been used as fully as they might be), and the fourteenth-century and earlier Patent Rolls also need to be worked through.[4] The same applies to the Close Rolls, registers of wills and other types of document.

---

3   No minstrel was likely to be in Court for 365 days in any year (although the waferer Master John Drake apparently was in 31 Ed I: see p. 41): they must have taken it in turns to be on stand-by as one of the two trumpeters or other minstrels required.

4   This is an onerous task, even with the use of the indexes in the printed calendars. Grattan Flood undertook it for the fifteenth-century Patent Rolls, *via* the calendars – a huge and

On the performance side, we have tried to relate the work of minstrels to the remaining literary texts and the notated music, and to progress beyond the assumptions that (however credible in themselves) do not make the connection between these sources and actual performance practice. The minstrels' artistic achievement, to be understood, must first be described and assessed. For instrumentalists, one can go some way towards this by studying the written, composed music and the theoretical writings of the time, but ultimately these do not explain what minstrels did, only what singers were advised to do. In British sources the theory of improvisation for minstrels concerns the practice of fifthing, as described in Chapter 15. Can we go further and accept the simplest forms of 'sighting', faburden and fauxbourdon – techniques that imply improvisation over a written tune – as techniques actually used by late medieval minstrels? It is possible, as the notated tunes in MS Digby 167 suggest; it is even likely, since two of those tunes are secular pieces; and the two-voiced *Quene Note* does show features that suggest improvisation. The connection is certainly implied: but it is not proved, and at present one can only make assumptions on the basis of continental evidence.

Concerning vocal minstrelsy, direct references to what minstrels performed are rare, and most of those that survive have long been recognized; but further research has actually reduced their number by questioning their reliability. The possibility of finding a lost manuscript containing a detailed account of an actual performance seems remote. One body of material that has not been fully explored, however, is that of heraldic literature. As George Keiser noted in 1998, 'Manuscripts that preserve heraldic treatises ... exist in some abundance, and surprisingly few have been exploited for their historical, literary, or linguistic interest' and most of the manuscripts remain 'unedited and largely unnoticed'.[5] Several scholars have offered valuable studies of individual works,[6] but there is still no comprehensive survey of heraldic texts, whether in English, French, or Latin, that circulated in England. While minstrels and heralds had increasingly distinct roles, heraldic material may yet provide insights into their shared efforts to preserve a record of chivalric deeds.

If there seems much still to be done, it is because minstrelsy is indeed a very large subject. But further research will surely be worth the trouble: even if final answers are not easily found, we hope that we have posed the right questions, and that these will stimulate further research. Increasing our understanding of this complex subject in the future will be a real and exciting gain.

---

very useful task. See his 'Entries relating to Music'.

[5] George R. Keiser, 'Works of science and information'. Albert E. Hartung, ed., *A Manual of Writing in Middle English, 1050–1500*, vol. 10 (New Haven CT, c. 1998), 3594–967, at 3709.

[6] For instance, Gerard Brault, Noël Denholm-Young, Richard Moll, Jaclyn Rajsic and Craig Taylor. On the range of late medieval heraldic writing, see Jackson W. Armstrong, 'The development of the office of arms in England, c. 1413–1485'. Katie Stevenson, ed., *The Herald in Late Medieval Europe* (Woodbridge, 2009), 9–28.

Bibliography

This bibliography lists all works cited in this book, together with some useful reference works that do not necessarily receive citations, such as Latham's *Revised Medieval Latin Word-List*, the *Oxford Dictionary of National Biography* and works published by the Royal Historical Society – Cheney's *Handbook of Dates*, Mullins's *Texts and Calendars*, Powicke and Fryde's *Handbook of British Chronology*, and Spufford's *Handbook of Medieval Exchange*. Other works that have been in frequent use are cited by abbreviations: *The New Grove Dictionary of Music and Musicians* (NG), my 'Secular Musicians in Late Medieval England' (SM), the second volume of which includes calendars of many account-book entries cited and quoted here, and my 'The minstrels of the English royal households' (MERH).

Adenet le Roi, *Les Œuvres d'Adenet le Roi*, ed. Albert Henry. 5 vols (Bruges and Brussels, 1951–71)
Adnès, André, *Adenès, dernier grand trouvère: recherches historiques et anthroponymiques* (Paris, 1971)
d'Agnel, Arnaud, Abbé Gustav, *Les comptes du roi René / publiés d'après les originaux inédits conservés aux Archives des Bouches-du-Rhône*. 3 vols (Paris, 1908–10)
Ainsworth, Peter F., *Jean Froissart and the Fabric of History* (Oxford, 1990)
Allday, D. Helen, *Insurrection in Wales* (Lavenham, 1981)
Amodio, Mark, *Writing the Oral Tradition* (Notre Dame IN, 2004)
———, Benjamin Bagby, Thomas Cable and John Miles Foley, 'Roundtable Discussion'. *Benjamin Bagby's Beowulf*. DVD (Paris, 2006)
Anatole, Christian J.M., 'Le souvenir de Muret et de la dépossession des comtes de Toulouse dans les vidas et les razos'. *Annales de l'Institut d'Études occitanes, Actes du colloque de Toulouse (9, 10 et 11 septembre 1963)* (1962–3), 11–22
Anglo, Sidney, 'Archives of the English tournament: score cheques and lists'. *Journal of the Society of Archivists* 2/4 (1961), 153–62
Archaeologia. Society of Antiquaries (1770–)
Arlt, Wulf, 'The "reconstruction" of instrumental music'. Stanley Boorman, ed., *Studies in the Performance of Late Medieval Music* (Cambridge, 1983), 75–100
Armitage-Smith, Sydney, ed., *John of Gaunt's Register, 1371–75*. 2 vols. Camden Society, 20 and 21 (London, 1911). Vols I and II of the Register.
Armstrong, C.A.J., 'Politics and the Battle of St. Alban's, 1455'. *Bulletin of the Institute of Historical Research* 23/87 (1960), 1–72
Armstrong, Jackson W., 'The development of the office of arms in England, c. 1413–1485'. Katie Stevenson, ed., *The Herald in Late Medieval Europe* (Woodbridge, 2009), 9–28
Ashbee, Andrew, 'Groomed for service: musicians in the privy chamber at the English court, c. 1495–1558'. *Early Music* 25/2 (1997), 185–97
———, ed., *Records of English Court Music*. 9 vols (Aldershot, 1986–97)

——, and David Lasocki, assisted by Peter Holman and Fiona Kisby, *A Biographical Dictionary of English Court Musicians, 1485–1714*. 2 vols (Aldershot, 1998)
Aspin, Isabel S.T., *Anglo-Norman Political Songs*. Anglo-Norman Texts 11 (Oxford, 1953)
Aubrey, Elizabeth, *The Music of the Troubadours* (Bloomington IN, 1996)
Aubry, Pierre, *Estampies et Danses Royales* (Paris, 1907; repr. Geneva, 1975)
Bachmann, Werner, *The Origins of Bowing* (London, 1969)
Baillie, Hugh, 'Some biographical notes on English church musicians, chiefly working in London (1485–1569)'. Royal Musical Association *Research Chronicle* 2 (1962), 18–57
Baines, Anthony, 'Instruments from the *Mary Rose*'. *Galpin Society Journal* 35 (March 1982), 151
——, ed., *Musical Instruments through the Ages* (London, 1961)
Baldwin, John W., 'The image of the jongleur in northern France'. *Speculum* 72/3 (1997), 635–63
——, *Masters, Princes and Merchants: The Social Views of Peter the Chanter and his Circle*. 2 vols (Princeton NJ, 1970)
Banks, Jon, *The Instrumental Consort Repertory of the Late Fifteenth Century* (Aldershot, 2006)
Barber, Richard, *Magnificence and Princely Splendour in the Middle Ages* (Woodbridge, 2020)
——, and Juliet Barker, *Tournaments* (Woodbridge, 1989)
Barbour, John, *Barbour's Bruce: A Fredome is a Noble Thing*, ed. Matthew P. McDiarmid and James A.C. Stevenson. 3 vols (Edinburgh, 1980–5)
Barker, Juliet, *England, Arise!* (London, 2014)
Barnum, Priscilla Heath, ed., *Dives et Pauper*. 2 vols. EETS o.s. 275, 280, 323 (London, New York NY and Oxford, 1976–2004)
Barrett, Robert W., *Against all England: Regional Identity and Cheshire Writing, 1195–1656* (Notre Dame IN, 2009)
Bateson, Mary, *Records of the Borough of Leicester* (London and Cambridge, 1899)
Baudoin de Condé, 'Li Contes des Hiraus'. *Dits et Contes de Baudoin de Condé et de son fils Jean de Condé*, ed. Aug[uste] Scheler. 3 vols (Brussels, 1866–7)
Baugh, Albert C., and Thomas Cable, *A History of the English Language*. 5th edn (Upper Saddle River NJ, 2002)
Bäuml, Franz H., 'Varieties and consequences of medieval literacy and illiteracy'. *Speculum* 55/2 (1980), 237–65
Bayley, John, ed., 'An account of the first battle of St. Albans from a contemporary manuscript'. *Archaeologia* 20 (1824), 519–23
Beier, A.L., *Masterless Men: The Vagrancy Problem in England, 1560–1640* (London, 1985)
Bémont, Charles. *Rôles Gascons, transcrits et publiés par Francisque Michel*. 3 vols (Paris, 1885–1906)
Benham, Hugh, '"Salve Regina" (Power or Dunstable): a simplified version'. *Music & Letters* 59/1 (1978), 28–32
Bennett, Michael, *Richard II and the Revolution of 1399* (Stroud, 1999)

Bennett, Philip E., 'Orality and textuality: reading and/or hearing the *Song of Roland*'. William W. Kibler and Leslie Zarker Morgan, eds., *Approaches to Teaching the Song of Roland* (New York NY, 2006), 146–53

Bennett, J.A.W. and G.V. Smithers, *Early Middle English Verse and Prose*. 2nd edn (Oxford, 1968)

Benson, Larry D., 'The literary character of Anglo-Saxon formulaic poetry'. *PMLA* 81/5 (1966), 334–41

Bent, Margaret, 'New and little-known fragments of English medieval polyphony'. *Journal of the American Musicological Society* 21/2 (1968), 137–56

Beowulf, trans. R.M. Liuzza (Peterborough, 2000)

Bergert, Fritz, *Die von den Trobadors gennanten oder gefeierten Damen* (Halle, 1913)

Bertran de Born, *The Poems of Bertran de Born*, ed. William D. Paden, Tilde Sankovitch and Patricia H. Stäblein (Berkeley CA, 1986)

Bevan, Bryan, *Edward III: Monarch of Chivalry* (London, 1992)

Bezzola, Retto R., *Les origines et la formation de la littérature courtoise en occident (500–1200)*. 2 vols (vol. 2 in 2 parts) (Paris, 1958–63)

Black Prince, The Register of Edward (London, 1930–3)

Blount, Thomas, *Ancient Tenures of Land* (London, 1679)

Boklund-Lagopoulou, Karin, *'I have a yong suster': Folksong, Ballad and the Middle English Lyric* (Dublin, 2001)

Bolton, J.L., 'Prices and wages'. Szarmach *et al.*, *Medieval England*, 609–11

Bond, Edward A., 'Notices of the last days of Isabella'. *Archaeologia* 35 (1853), 453–69

Boorman, Stanley, ed., *Studies in the Performance of Late Medieval Music* (Cambridge, 1983)

Botfield, Beriah, ed., *Manners and Household Expenses of the 13th and 15th Centuries* (London, 1841)

Boulton, D'Arcy J.D., 'Heralds and heraldry'. Szarmach *et al.*, *Medieval England*, 354

Boutière, Jean, A.H. Schutz, and I.M. Cluzel, *Biographies des Troubadours: Textes Provençaux des XIIe et XIVe siècles*. 2nd edn (Paris, 1964)

Bower, Walter, *Scotichronicon*, ed. and trans. D.E.R. Watt *et al.*, 9 vols (Aberdeen, 1990–8)

Bowles, Edmund A., '*Haut* and *Bas*: the grouping of musical instruments in the Middle Ages'. *Musica Disciplina* 8 (1954), 115–40; repr. McGee, *Instruments and their Music*, 3–28

——, 'Musical Instruments in the Medieval Corpus Christi Procession'. *Journal of the American Musicological Society* 17 (1964), 251–60

——, *Musikgeschichte in Bildern* III/8: *Musikleben im 15. Jahrhundert* (Leipzig, 1977)

——, 'Were musical instruments used in the liturgical service during the Middle Ages?'. *Galpin Society Journal* 10 (1957), 40–56

Bradbury, Nancy Mason, 'Rival wisdom in the Latin dialogue of Solomon and Marcolf'. *Speculum* 83/2 (2008), 331–65

——, *Writing Aloud: Storytelling in Late Medieval England* (Urbana IL, 1998)

——, and Scott Bradbury, eds, *The Dialogue of Solomon and Marcolf: A Dual-Language Edition from Latin and Middle English Printed editions* (Kalamazoo MI, 2012)

Brault, Gerard J., *Eight Thirteenth-Century Rolls of Arms in French and Anglo-Norman Blazon* (University Park PA, 1973)
——, 'Heraldic terminology and legendary material in the *Siege of Caerlaverock* (c. 1300)'. Urban T. Holmes, ed., *Romance Studies in Memory of Edward Billings Ham* (Hayward CA, 1967), 5–20
——, *The Song of Roland: An Analytical Edition*. 2 vols (London, 1978)
Bredehoft, Thomas A., *Authors, Audiences, and Old English Verse* (Toronto, 2009)
Breeze, Andrew, 'The Bret Glascurion and Chaucer's *House of Fame*'. *Review of English Studies* 45/177 (1994), 63–9
Breeze, Steven J.A., *Performance in Beowulf and Other Old English Poems* (Cambridge, 2022)
Brent, John, *Canterbury in the Olden Time*. 2nd edn (Canterbury and London, 1879)
Bridge, Joseph C., 'Town waits and their tunes'. *Proceedings of the Musical Association* 54 (1927–8), 63–92
Brobeck, John T., 'A music book for Mary Tudor, Queen of France'. *Early Music History* 35 (2016), 1–93
Brown, Michelle P., *The Book and the Transformation of Britain, c. 550–1050: A Study in Written and Visual Literacy and Orality* (London, 2011)
Brunne, Robert Mannyng de. See under Manning.
Bukofzer, Manfred F., 'Changing aspects of medieval and renaissance music'. *Musical Quarterly* 44 (1954), 1–18
——, ed., *John Dunstable: Complete Works*. Musica Britannica VIII. 2nd edn by Margaret Bent, Ian Bent and Brian Trowell (London, 1970)
——, 'A polyphonic basse dance of the Renaissance'. Bukofzer, *Studies*, 190–216
——, *Studies in Medieval and Renaissance Music* (London, 1951)
Bullock-Davies, Constance, *Menestrellorum Multitudo* (Cardiff, 1978)
——, *A Register of Royal and Baronial Domestic Minstrels, 1272–1327* (Woodbridge, 1986)
Bumke, Joachim, *Courtly Culture: Literature and Society in the High Middle Ages*, trans. Thomas Dunlap (Berkeley CA, 1991)
Byerly, B.F., and C.R. Byerly, eds, *Records of the Wardrobe and Household, 1285–1286* (London, 1977)
——, eds, *Records of the Wardrobe and Household, 1286–1289* (London, 1986)
Calendar of the Patent Rolls Preserved in the Public Record Office (London, 1891–)
Camille, Michael, *Image on the Edge: The Margins of Medieval Art* (London, 1992)
——, *Mirror in Parchment: The Luttrell Psalter and the Making of Medieval England* (Chicago IL, 1998)
Carpenter, Nan Cooke, *Music in the Medieval and Renaissance Universities* (Norman OK, 1958; repr. New York NY, 1972)
Carruthers, Mary, *The Book of Memory: A Study of Memory in Medieval Culture* (Cambridge, 1990)
Carter, H.H., *A Dictionary of Middle English Musical Terms* (Bloomington IN, 1961)
Carter, Stewart, 'A tale of bells and bows: stalking the U-slide trumpet'. McGee and Carter, *Instruments, Ensembles, and Repertory*, 13–30

Cartlidge, Neil, 'The composition and social context of Oxford, Jesus College MS 29 (II) and London, British Library, MS Cotton Caligula A.IX'. *Medium Ævum* 66/2 (1997), 250–69

Caudrey, Philip J., *Military Society and the Court of Chivalry in the Age of the Hundred Years War* (Woodbridge, 2019)

Chambers, Edmund K., *The Mediaeval Stage*. 2 vols (Oxford, 1903)

Chandos Herald, *La vie du Prince Noir by Chandos Herald*, ed. Diana B. Tyson (Tübingen, 1975)

Chanson de Roland, The Oxford Version, ed. Ian Short. Volume 1 of *La Chanson de Roland/The Song of Roland: The French Corpus*, gen. ed. D. Joseph J. Dugan. 3 vols (Turnhout, 2005)

Chappell, William, *Popular Music of the Olden Time* (London, 1859; repr. 2 vols, with an introduction by Frederick W. Sternfeld. New York NY, 1965)

Chase, Colin, ed., *The Dating of Beowulf* (Toronto, 1981; repr. with an afterword by Nicholas Howe, 1997)

Chaucer, Geoffrey, *The Riverside Chaucer*, ed. Larry Benson. 3rd edn (Boston MA, 1987)

Chaytor, H. J., *From Script to Print: An Introduction to Medieval Vernacular Literature* (London, 1966)

——, *Savaric de Mauléon, Baron and Troubadour* (Cambridge, 1939)

——, *The Troubadours and England* (Cambridge, 1923)

Chenard, Gaël, *L'administration d'Alphonse de Poitiers (1241–1271)* (Paris, 2017)

Cheney, C.R., *Handbook of Dates for Students of English History*. Corrected repr. (London, 1978)

Chenier, André, *Oeuvres complètes*, ed. Gérard Walter (Paris, 1950)

Chinca, Mark, and Christopher Young, eds, *Orality and Literacy in the Middle Ages: Essays on a Conjunction and its Consequences in Honour of D. H. Green* (Turnhout, 2005)

Chrétien de Troyes, *Les Romans de Chrétien de Troyes, I: Éric et Énide*, ed. Mario Roques (Paris, 1958)

Chrimes, S.B., *An Introduction to the Administrative History of Medieval England* (Oxford, 1959)

Cingolani, Stefano M., 'The *Sirventes-ensenhamen* of Guerau de Cabrera: a proposal for a new interpretation'. *Journal of Hispanic Research* 1 (1992–3), 191–201

Clanchy, Michael, *England and Its Rulers, 1066–1272*. 3rd edn (Oxford, 2006)

Closson, Ernest, *Le manuscrit dit les basses danses de la Bibliothèque de Bourgogne*. Société des bibliophiles et iconophiles de Belgique (1912; repr. Geneva, 1976)

Clouzot, Martine, *Images de Musiciens (1350–1500)* (Turnhout, 2007)

Coehlo, Victor, and Keith Polk, *Instrumentalists and Renaissance Culture, 1420–1600* (Cambridge, 2016)

Coldewey, John, 'The Digby plays and the Chelmsford records'. *Research Opportunities in Renaissance Drama* 18 (1975), 103–21

Coleman, Joyce, *Public Reading and the Reading Public in Late Medieval England and France* (Cambridge, 1996)

A Collection of Ordinances and Regulations for … the Royal Household (London, 1790) (cited as *Ords & Regs*)

Collier, J. Payne, *The History of English Dramatic Poetry to the Time of Shakespeare* (London, 1831)

———, *Household Books of John, Duke of Norfolk, and Thomas, Earl of Surrey*. Roxburghe Club (London, 1844); repr. in Crawford, *Household Books*

Collins, Mark, Phillip Emery, Christopher Phillpotts, Mark Samuel and Christopher Thomas, 'The king's high table at the palace of Westminster'. *The Antiquaries Journal* 92 (2012), 197–243

Conklin, Rosalind, 'Medieval English Minstrels, 1216–1485'. PhD. diss. (University of Chicago, 1964)

Cook, Albert S., *Sir Eglamour, a Middle English Romance* (New York NY, 1911)

Cooper, C.H., *Annals of Cambridge*. 5 vols (Cambridge, 1842–1908)

Cooper, Francis M.C., 'The Leckingfield Proverbs'. *The Musical Times* 1552 (June 1972), 547–50

Couronnement de Louis. See under Langlois, Ernest

Cowling, Jane, and Peter Greenfield, 'Monks, minstrels and players: drama in Hampshire before 1642'. *Hampshire Papers* 29 (2008), 1–28

CPR, *Calendar of the Patent Rolls Preserved in the Public Record Office* (London, 1891–)

Crane, Frederick, *Extant Medieval Musical Instruments: A Provisional Catalogue by Types* (Iowa City IA, 1972)

———, 'On performing the *Lo estampies*'. *Early Music* 7/1 (1979), 25–33

Crawford, Anne, ed., *The Household Books of John Howard, Duke of Norfolk, 1462–1471, 1481–1483* (Stroud, 1992)

Creed, Robert P., 'The *Beowulf*-poet: master of sound pattern'. John Miles Foley, ed., *Oral Traditional Literature: A Festschrift for Albert Bates Lord* (Columbus OH, 1981), 194–216

Crewdson, H.F., *The Worshipful Company of Musicians* (London, 1950)

Croenen, Godfried, Kristen M. Figg, and Andrew Taylor, 'Authorship, patronage, and literary gifts: the books Froissart brought to England in 1395'. *Journal of the Early Book Society* 11 (2008), 1–42

Cronne, H.A., and R.H. Hilton, eds, 'The Beauchamp household book'. University of Birmingham *Historical Journal* 2 (1949–50), 208–18

Crosby, Ruth, 'Chaucer and the custom of oral delivery'. *Speculum* 13/4 (1938), 413–32

———, 'Oral delivery in the Middle Ages'. *Speculum* 11/1 (1936), 88–110

Curley, Thomas M., *Samuel Johnson, the Ossian Fraud, and the Celtic Revival in Great Britain and Ireland* (Cambridge and New York NY, 2009)

Curschmann, Michael, 'The Concept of the oral formula as an impediment to our understanding of medieval oral poetry'. *Medievalia et Humanistica*, n.s. 8 (1977), 63–76

Daniel, Arnaut, *Canzoni: nuova edizione*, ed. Maurizio Perugi (Florence, 2015)

———, *The Poetry of Arnaut Daniel*, ed. and trans. James J. Wilhelm (New York and London, 1981)

———, *Les poésies d'Arnaut Daniel*, ed. René Lavaud (Geneva, 1910)

Da Rold, Orietta, 'Codicology, localization and Oxford, Bodleian Library, MS. Laud. Misc. 108'. Carol Meale and Derek Pearsall, eds, *The Makers and Users of Medieval Books* (Cambridge, 2014), 48–59
Dart, R. Thurston, *The Interpretation of Early Music* (London, 1954)
——, ed., *Invitation to Medieval Music 1: Music of the Earlier Fifteenth Century* (London and New York NY, 1967)
——, 'A new source of early English organ music'. *Music and Letters* 35/3 (1954), 201–5
Davies, R., *Extracts from Municipal Records of York* (London, 1843)
Davis, H.W.C., ed., *Mediaeval England* (Oxford, 1924)
Davis, Norman, *Non-Cycle Plays and Fragments*. EETS s.s. 1 (London, 1970)
Dawson, Giles E., *Records of Plays and Players in Kent, 1450–1642*. Malone Society Collections 7 (Oxford, 1965)
Dean, Ruth J., 'An early treatise on heraldry in Anglo-Norman'. U.T. Holmes, ed., *Romance Studies in Memory of Edward Billings*. California State College Publications 2 (Hayward CA, 1967), 21–9
——, and Maureen B.M. Boulton, *Anglo-Norman Literature: A Guide to Texts and Manuscripts* (London, 1999)
Delogu, Daisy, *Theorizing the Ideal Sovereign: The Rise of the French Vernacular Royal Biography* (Toronto, 2008)
Dembowski, Peter F., *Jean Froissart and His 'Méliador': Context, Craft and Sense* (Lexington KY, 1983)
Denholm-Young, N[oël], *The Country Gentry in the Fourteenth Century, with Special Reference to the Heraldic Rolls of Arms* (Oxford, 1969)
——, 'The Song of Carlaverock and the parliamentary roll of arms as found in Cott. MS. Calig. A. XVIII in the British Museum'. *Proceedings of the British Academy* 47 (1961), 251–62
Dennys, Rodney, *The Heraldic Imagination* (London, 1975)
Devon, Frederick, ed., *Issue Roll of Thomas de Brantingham, Bishop of Exeter* (London, 1835)
——, *Issues of the Exchequer, Henry III–Henry VI* (London, 1837)
DIAMM, Digital Image Archive of Medieval Music. Online at <www.diamm.ac.uk>
Dickson, T., and J.B. Paul, eds, *Accounts of the Lord High Treasurer of Scotland*, I and II (Edinburgh, 1877 and 1900)
Dillon, Viscount, and W[illiam] H. St John Hope, eds., 'Inventory of the goods and chattels belonging to Thomas, Duke of Gloucester, and seized in his castle at Pleshy, co. Essex, 21 Richard II (1397), with their values as shown in the escheator's accounts'. *Archaeological Journal* 54 (1897), 275–303
Dobozy, Maria, *Re-Membering the Present: The Medieval German Poet-Minstrel in Cultural Context* (Turnhout, 2005)
Dobson, E.J., and Frank Ll. Harrison, *Medieval English Songs* (London, 1979)
Dobson, R.B., 'York, City of'. Szarmach et al., *Medieval England*, 828–9
Doherty, Paul, *The Great Crown Jewels Robbery of 1303* (London, 2005)
Donoghue, Daniel G., 'Laȝamon's ambivalence'. *Speculum* 65/3 (1990), 537–63
Douce, Francis, 'The Peaceable Jousts'. *Archaeologia* 17 (1814), 290–6

Douglas, David, 'The "Song of Roland" and the Norman conquest of England'. *French Studies* 14/2 (1960), 99–116

Downey, Peter, 'The renaissance slide trumpet: fact or fiction?'. *Early Music* 12 (1984), 26–33; repr. McGee, *Instruments and their Music*, 383–90

Dronke, Peter, *The Medieval Lyric*. 2nd edn (London, 1978)

Du Cange, Charles du Fresne, Seigneur, *Glossarium Mediae et Infimae Latinitatis*, ed. G.A.L. Henschel (Paris, 1882–7)

Duffin, Ross W., ed., *A Performer's Guide to Medieval Music* (Bloomington IN, 2000)

——, 'The *trompette des menestrels* in the 15th-century *alta capella*'. *Early Music* 17 (1989), 397–402; repr. McGee, *Instruments and their Music*, 409–14

Duggan, Joseph J., *The Song of Roland: Formulaic Style and Poetic Craft* (Berkeley CA, 1973)

Dumitrescu, Theodor, *The Early Tudor Court and International Musical Relations* (Aldershot, 2007)

Duncan, Edmondstoune, *The Story of Minstrelsy* (London, 1907)

Edwards, A.S.G., 'The authorship of the poems of Laurence Minot: a reconsideration'. *Florilegium* 23/1 (2006), 145–53

Edwards, Warwick, 'Songs without words by Josquin and his contemporaries'. Fenlon, *Music in Medieval & Early Modern Europe*, 79–92

Egan, Margarita, trans., *The Vidas of the Troubadours* (New York NY, 1984)

Einhart, *Einhart's Life of Charlemagne*, ed. H.W. Garrod and R.B. Mowat (Oxford, 1915)

Eliason, Norman E., 'The "Improvised Lay" in *Beowulf*'. *Philological Quarterly* 31/2 (1952), 171–9

Elmham, Thomas de, *Thomæ de Elmham Vita & Gesta Henrici Quinti, Anglorum Regis*, ed. Thomas Hearne (Oxford, 1727)

Epstein, R., 'Eating their words: food and text in the coronation banquet of Henry VI'. *Journal of Medieval and Early Modern Studies* 36/2 (2006), 355–78

Fabyan, Robert, *The New Chronicles of England and France*, ed. H. Ellis (London, 1811)

Faidit, Gaucelm, *Les poèmes de Gaucelm Faidit*, ed. Jean Mouzat (Paris, 1965)

Fallows, David, 'The Gresley dance collection, c. 1500'. *Royal Musical Association Research Chronicle* 29 (1996), 1–20

——, intr., *The Henry VIII Book* (Oxford, 2014)

Falvy, Zoltán, *Mediterranean Culture and Troubadour Music* (Budapest, 1986)

Faral, Edmond, *Les jongleurs en France au moyen âge* (Paris, 1910)

Fein, Susanna, *Studies in the Harley Manuscript: The Scribes, Contents, and Social Contexts of British Library MS Harley 2253* (Kalamazoo MI, 2000)

Fenlon, Iain, ed., *Cambridge Music Manuscripts, 900–1700* (Cambridge, 1982)

——, ed., *Music in Medieval & Early Modern Europe* (Cambridge, 1981)

Fewster, Carol, *Traditionality and Genre in Middle English Romance*. 2nd edn (Cambridge, 1993)

Finlayson, John, '*Richard, Coer de Lyon*: romance, history or something in between'. *Studies in Philology* 87/2 (1990), 156–80

Fleming, Michael, and John Bryan, *Early English Viols: Instruments, Makers and Music* (London and New York NY, 2016)

Floriant et Florete, ed. Harry F. Williams (Ann Arbor MI, 1947)
Flynn, Jane, 'The education of choristers in England during the sixteenth century'. Morehen, *English Choral Practice*, 180–99
Foley, John Miles, *Traditional Oral Epic: The Odyssey, Beowulf, and the Serbo-Croatian Return Song* (Berkeley CA, 1990)
Fowler, J.T., ed., *The Account-Rolls of Durham Priory*. Surtees Society 99, 100 and 103 (1898–1901)
Fox, E.T., 'Tudor bench ends of the West Country'. <https://benchends.wordpress.com> (accessed 14 January 2020)
Foxon, D.F., 'Some notes on agenda format'. *The Library* 8/3 (1953), 163–73
Frank, Roberta, 'A scandal in Toronto: the dating of "*Beowulf*" a quarter century on'. *Speculum* 82/4 (2007), 843–64
Friedman, Albert B., and Norman T. Harrington, *Ywain and Gawain*. EETS o.s. 254 (London and New York NY, 1964)
Froissart, Jean, *Chroniques*, ed. Peter F. Ainsworth, George T. Diller, and Alberto Varvaro. 2 vols (Paris, 2001–4)
——, *Chroniques, Livre I, Le Manuscrit d'Amiens*, ed. George T. Diller. 5 vols (Geneva, 1991–8)
——, *Chroniques*, ed. Siméon Luce. 13 vols (Paris, 1869–99)
——, *Dits et Debats*, ed. Anthime Fourrier (Geneva, 1979)
Fryde, E.B., ed., *A Book of Prests, 23 Ed I* (Oxford, 1962)
——, D.E. Greenway, S. Porter and I. Roy, eds, *Handbook of British Chronology*. 3rd edn (London, 1986)
Fuller, Sarah, 'Additional notes on the 15th-century chansonnier Bologna Q16'. *Musica Disciplina* 23 (1969), 81
——, 'Discant and the theory of fifthing'. *Acta Musicologica* 50 (1978), 241–75
Gage, John, 'Extracts from the Household Books of Edward Stafford, Duke of Buckingham'. *Archaeologia* 25 (1834), 311–41
Gaillard, V[ictor Louis Marie], 'Expédition de Gui de Dampierre à Tunis, en 1270', *Messager des sciences historiques ou archives des arts de la bibliographie de Belgique* (1853), 141–57
Gaimar, Geffrei, *Estoire des Engleis/History of the English*, ed. and trans. Ian Short (Oxford, 2009)
Gairdner, James, *History of the Life and Reign of Richard III*, rev. edn (1898; repr. Bath, 1972)
——, *The Paston Letters* (London, 1904; repr. Gloucester, 1986)
Galpin, Francis W., *Old English Instruments of Music*. 4th edn, rev. Thurston Dart (London, 1965)
Gancarczyk, Pawel, 'Abbot Martin Rinkenberg and the origins of the "Glogauer Liederbuch"'. *Early Music* 37/1 (2009), 27–36
Gardner, Arthur, *English Medieval Sculpture* (Cambridge, 1951)
Gaskell, Howard, ed., *The Reception of Ossian in Europe* (London, 2004)
Gaunt, Simon, *Retelling the Tale: An Introduction to Medieval French Literature* (London, 2001)
——, Ruth Harvey and Linda Paterson, *Marcabru: A Critical Edition* (Cambridge, 2000)

——, and Sarah Kay, eds, *The Troubadours: An Introduction* (Cambridge, 1999)
Gautier, Léon, *La Chevalerie* (Paris, 1884; new edn Paris, 1895)
——, *Les épopées françaises: Étude sur les origines et l'histoire de la littérature nationale*. 3 vols (Paris, 1865–8)
Geoffrey of Vinsauf, *Poetria nova*, trans. Margaret F. Nims, rev. edn, with an introduction by Martin Camargo (Toronto, 2010)
Ghil, Eliza Miruna, *L'Age de parage: Essai sur le poétique et la politique en Occitanie au XIIIe siècle* (New York NY, 1989)
Giles, J.A., trans., *Mathew Paris's English History from the Year 1235 to 1273*. 3 vols (London, 1852–4)
Given-Wilson, Chris, *The Royal Household and the King's Affinity* (New Haven CT and London, 1986)
Gomez, Maricarmen, 'Minstrel schools in the late Middle Ages'. *Early Music* 18/2 (1989), 213–16
Goodman, Anthony, *The Loyal Conspiracy: The Lords Appellant under Richard II* (London, 1971)
Gough, Henry, *Itinerary of King Edward the First* (Paisley, 1900, and London, 1976)
Grattan Flood, W.H., 'Entries relating to music in the English patent rolls of the 15th century'. *Musical Antiquary* 4 (1912–13), 225–35
Gray, Sir Thomas, *Scalacronica 1272–1363*, ed. and trans. Andy King (Woodbridge, 2005)
Green, Alice, *Town Life in the Fifteenth Century* (London, 1894)
Green, M.A.E., *Lives of the Princesses of England* (London, 1849)
Green, Richard Firth, 'Did Chaucer know the ballad of *Glen Kindy*?'. *Neophilologus* 92 (2008), 351–8
——, 'Marcolf the Fool and blind John Audelay'. R.F. Yeager and Charlotte C. Morse, eds, *Speaking Images: Essays in Honor of V.A. Kolve* (Asheville NC, 2001), 559–76
——, *Poets and Princepleasers: Literature and the English Court in the Late Middle Ages* (Toronto, 1980)
Greene, Richard L., *The Early English Carols* (Oxford, 1935)
Greenfield, Stanley B., 'The formulaic expression of the theme of "Exile" in Anglo-Saxon poetry'. *Speculum* 30/2 (1955), 200–6
Greg, W[alter] W[ilson], ed., *Dramatic Documents from the Elizabethan Playhouses: Stage Plots: Actors' Parts: Prompt Books*. 2 vols (Oxford, 1913)
Grenade, L., *The Singularities of London, 1578*, ed. Derek Keene and Ian W. Archer (London, 2014)
Guddat-Figge, Gisela, *Catalogue of Manuscripts Containing Middle English Romances* (Munich, 1976)
Guerrero Lovillo, José, *Las Cántigas: estudio arqueológico de sus miniaturas* (Madrid, 1949)
Gushee, Lawrence, 'Minstrel' in NG
Guy d'Amiens (attrib.), *The Carmen de Hastingae proelio of Guy, Bishop of Amiens*, ed. Catherine Morton and Hope Muntz (Oxford, 1972)
Győry, J., 'Réflexions sur le jongleur guerrier'. *Annales Universitatis Scientiarum Budapestinensis de Rolando Eötvös Nominatae, Sectio Philologica* 3 (1961), 47–60

Haberl, Franz Xaver, 'Die römische *Schola Cantorum* und die papstlichen Kapellsänger bis zur Mitte der 16. Jahrhundert'. *Vierteljahrsschrift für Musikwissenschaft*, III (1887)

Haines, John, *Eight Centuries of Troubadours and Trouvères: The Changing Identity of Medieval Music* (Cambridge, 2004)

Hallam, Elizabeth M., *Itinerary of Edward II and His Household, 1307-28* (London, 1984)

Hanham, Alison, 'The musical studies of a fifteenth-century wool merchant'. *Review of English Studies*, n.s. 8 (1957), 270–4

Hanna, Ralph, *London Literature, 1300–1380* (Cambridge, 2005)

Hanning, Robert W., *The Individual in Twelfth-Century Romance* (New Haven CT and London, 1977)

Harding, Vanessa A., 'Guilds and Fraternities'. Szarmach *et al.*, *Medieval England*, 329–30

——, 'London'. Szarmach *et al.*, *Medieval England*, 457–60

Harris, Mary Dormer, *The Coventry Leet Book*. EETS o.s. 134, 135, 138, 146 (London, 1907–13)

Harrison, Frank Ll., *Music in Medieval Britain* (London, 1958)

——, 'Tradition and innovation in instrumental usage, 1100–1450'. Jan LaRue, ed., *Aspects of Medieval and Renaissance Music: A Birthday Offering to Gustave Reese* (London, 1967), 319–35

Hartung, Albert E., ed., *A Manual of Writing in Middle English, 1050–1500*, vol. 10 (New Haven CT, *c.* 1998)

Harvey, John H., 'The last years of Thetford Cluniac priory'. *Norfolk Archaeology* 27 (1939), 1–2

——, *The Plantagenets* (London, 1959)

Harvey, Ruth E., 'Eleanor of Aquitaine and the troubadours'. Marcus Bull and Catherine Léglu, eds, *The World of Eleanor of Aquitaine: Literature and Society in Southern France between the Eleventh and the Twelfth Centuries* (Woodbridge, 2005), 101–14

——, '*Joglars* and the professional status of the early troubadours'. *Medium Aevum* 62/2 (1993), 221–41

Hayes, Gerald, *King's Music* (Oxford, 1937)

Hayward, Maria, *The Great Wardrobe Accounts of Henry VII and Henry VIII* (London, 2012)

Hearne, Thomas, *Liber Niger Scaccarii* (London, 1728; 2/1771)

Heartz, Daniel, 'A 15th-Century Ballo: *Rôti Bouilli Joyeux*'. Jan LaRue, ed., *Aspects of Medieval and Renaissance Music: A Birthday Offering to Gustave Reese* (New York NY, 1966; repr. 1978), 359–75

Henry of Huntingdon, *Historia Anglorum*, ed. Diana E. Greenway (Oxford, 1996)

Heron-Allen, Edward, *The Seal of Roger Wade* (London, 1895)

Herzman, Ronald B., Graham Drake and Eve Salisbury, eds, *Four Romances of England* (Kalamazoo MI, 1999)

Heuser, W., 'Das Interludium de Clerico et Puella und das Fabliau von Dame Siriz'. *Anglia* 30 (1907), 306–19

Hewitt, H.J., *Mediaeval Cheshire: An Economic and Social History of Cheshire in the Reigns of the Three Edwards* (Manchester, 1929)

Hewitt, Helen, ed., *Petrucci: Harmonice Musices Odhecaton A* (Cambridge MA, 1942; repr. New York NY, 1978)

Hibbard, Laura A., *Medieval Romance in England: A Study of the Sources and Analogues of the Non-Cyclic Metrical Romances* (New York NY, 1960)

Hibberd, Lloyd, 'On "instrumental style" in early melody'. McGee, *Instruments and their Music*, 455-78

Hibbert, Christopher, *Agincourt* (London, 1964)

Hill, Mary C., *The King's Messengers 1199-1377* (Stroud, 1994)

Hindle, Brian Paul, 'Roads and tracks'. Leonard Cantor, ed., *The English Medieval Landscape* (London, 1982), 193-217

Hirsh, John C., *Medieval Lyric: Middle English Lyrics, Ballads, and Carols* (Oxford, 2005)

History of William Marshal, ed. A.J. Holden, S. Gregory, and D. Crouch. 3 vols (London, 2002-6)

HMC, Royal Commission on Historical Manuscripts (Historical Manuscripts Commission) (London, 1870-)

Holland, William E., 'Formulaic diction and the descent of a Middle English romance'. *Speculum* 48/1 (1973), 89-109

Honko, Lauri, 'Texts as process and practice: the textualization of oral epics'. Lauri Honko, ed., *Textualization of Oral Epics* (Berlin, 2000), 3-54

Horrox, Rosemary, and P.W. Hammond, *British Library Harleian Manuscript 433* (Stroud, 1979)

Hudson, Harriet E., 'Middle English popular romances'. Diss. (Ohio State University, 1982)

Hudson, Henry A., *The Medieval Woodwork of Manchester Cathedral* (Manchester, 1924)

Hudson, W., and J.C. Tingey, *The Records of the City of Norwich* (Norwich and London, 1906-10)

Hughes, Andrew, 'Antiphons and acclamations'. *Journal of Musicology* 6/2 (1988), 150-68

Hughes, Anselm, *Medieval Polyphony in the Bodleian Library* (Oxford, 1951)

——, 'Music of the coronation over a thousand years'. *Proceedings of the Royal Musical Association* 79 (1952-3), 81-100

Huizinga, J., *The Waning of the Middle Ages* (1924; paperback edn, New York NY, 1954)

Hunter, Joseph, *Three Catalogues Describing the Contents of the Red Book of the Exchequer, of the Dodsworth Manuscripts in the Bodleian Library, and of the Manuscripts in the Library of the Honourable Society of Lincoln's Inn* (London, 1838)

Huot, Sylvia, *From Song to Book: The Poetics of Writing in Old French Lyric and Lyrical Narrative Poetry* (Ithaca NY and London, 1987)

——, 'Troubadour lyric and Old French narrative'. Simon Gaunt and Sarah Kay, eds, *The Troubadours: An Introduction* (Cambridge, 1999), 263-78

Hymnarium Sarisburiense (London, 1851)

Ives, John, *Select Papers Chiefly Relating to English Antiquities* (London, 1773)
Ivy, G.S., 'The bibliography of the manuscript-book'. Francis Wormald and C. E. Wright, eds, *The English Library before 1700* (London, 1958), 32–65
Jackman, James L., *Fifteenth Century Basse Dances* (Northampton MA, 1964)
James, M.R., *The Peterborough Psalter and Bestiary* (London, 1921)
——, and G.C. Macaulay, 'Fifteenth-century carols and other pieces'. *The Modern Language Review* 8/1 (1913), 68–87
James, T.B., and John Simons, eds, *The Poems of Laurence Minot, 1333–1352* (Exeter, 1989)
James-Teelucksingh, Kathleen, 'Critical edition of *La Chronique d'un ménestrel d'Alphonse de Poitiers* as contained in B.N. Fr. 570'. PhD. diss. (University of Maryland, 1984)
Janssen, Carole Ann, 'The waytes of Norwich in medieval and renaissance civic pageantry'. PhD. diss. (University of New Brunswick, 1978)
Jeffries, Helen Marsh, 'Job descriptions, nepotism, and part-time work: the minstrels and trumpeters of the court of Edward IV of England (1461–83)'. *Plainsong & Medieval Music* 12/2 (October 2003), 165–77
Jensen, Minna Skafte, 'Performance'. John Miles Foley, ed., *A Companion to Ancient Epic* (London, 2008), 45–54
Johnson, Charles, ed., *Dialogus de Scaccario* (Edinburgh, 1950)
Johnston, Michael, *Romance and the Gentry in Late Medieval England* (Oxford, 2014)
Joufroi de Poitiers: Roman d'aventure du XIIIe siècle, ed. Percival B. Fay and John L. Grigsby (Geneva, 1972)
Jusserand, J.J., *English Wayfaring Life in the Middle Ages*, trans. Lucy Toulmin Smith (1889; University paperback edn, London and New York, 1961)
Karkov, Catherine E., 'Metalwork, gothic', in Szarmach *et al.*, *Medieval England*, 506–11
Katz, Israel J., and John E. Keller, eds, *Studies on the 'Cantigas de Santa Maria': Art, Music, and Poetry* (Madison WI, 1987)
Kay, Sarah, *Parrots and Nightingales: Troubadour Quotations and the Development of European Poetry* (Philadelphia PA, 2013)
Keiser, George R., 'Works of science and information'. Albert E. Hartung, ed., *A Manual of Writing in Middle English, 1050–1500*, vol. 10 (New Haven CT, c. 1998), 3594–967
Kelly, W., *Notices Illustrative of the Drama at Leicester* (London, 1865)
Kendrick, Laura, 'Jongleur as propagandist: the ecclesiastical politics of Marcabru's poetry'. Thomas N. Bisson, ed., *Cultures of Power: Lordship, Status, and Process in Twelfth-Century Europe* (Philadelphia PA, 1995), 259–86
Kermode, Jennifer L., 'Lincoln'. Szarmach *et al.*, *Medieval England*, 419–20
Kiernan, Kevin S., *Beowulf and the Beowulf Manuscript*. 2nd edn, with a forward by Katherine O'Brien O'Keeffe (Ann Arbor MI, 1996)
King, Pamela, and Clifford Davidson, eds, *The Coventry Corpus Christi Plays* (Kalamazoo MI, 2000)
King Horn: A Middle-English Romance, ed. Joseph Hall (Oxford, 1901)
King Horn: An Edition Based on Cambridge University Library MS. Gg. 4.27(2), ed. Rosamund Allen (New York NY, 1984)

Kipling, Gordon, *The Triumph of Honour: Burgundian origins of the Elizabethan Renaissance* (The Hague, 1977)

Kirby, T.F., *Annals of Winchester College* (London, 1892)

Kirke, Henry, 'The Ancient Court of Minstrels at Tutbury'. *Journal of the Derbyshire Archaeological Society* (1910), 105–13

Kisby, Fiona, 'Royal minstrels in the city and suburbs of early Tudor London'. *Early Music* 25/2 (1997), 199–219

Klaeber's Beowulf and the Fight at Finnsburg, ed. R.D. Fulk, Robert E. Bjork, and John D. Niles. 4th edn (Toronto, 2008)

Knight, Alan E., *Aspects of Genre in Late Medieval French Drama* (Manchester, 1983)

Knighton, Tess, and David Fallows, eds, *Companion to Medieval and Renaissance Music* (London, 1992)

Krishna, Valerie, 'Parataxis, formulaic destiny, and thrift in the *Alliterative Morte Arthure*'. *Speculum* 57/1 (1982), 63–83

Kwakkel, Erik, 'Decoding the material book: cultural residue in medieval manuscripts'. Michael Johnston and Michael Van Dussen, eds, *The Medieval Manuscript Book: Cultural Approaches* (Cambridge, 2015), 60–76

Labory, Gillette, 'Les débuts de la chronique en français (XIIe et XIIIe siècles)'. Erik Cooper, ed., *The Medieval Chronicle III: Proceedings of the 3rd International Conference on the Medieval Chronicle, Doorn/Utrecht 12–17 July 2002* (Amsterdam, 2004), 1–26

Lafontaine, H.C. de, *The King's Musick* (London, 1909)

Lambert, J. Malet, *Two Thousand Years of Gild Life* (Hull, 1891)

Lambert, M.R., and M.S. Sprague, *Lincoln* (Oxford, 1933)

Langeron, M. Olivier, 'La Trompette d'argent'. *Mémoires de la Commission des antiquités de la Côte d'Or*, 2nd ser. 14 (1851), 91–102

Langland, William, *The Vision of Piers Plowman*, ed. A.V.C. Schmidt. 2nd edn (London, 1995)

——, *Will's Vision of Piers Plowman*, ed. Elizabeth D. Kirk and Judith H. Anderson, trans. E. Talbot Donaldson (New York NY, 1990)

Langlois, Ernest, ed., *Le Couronnement de Louis: chanson de geste du XIIe siècle*. 2nd edn (Paris, 1925)

Langlois Mace de Gastin, Edith, 'Chronique d'un anonyme de Bethune: histoire des ducs de Normandie et des rois d'Angleterre jusqu'en 1220'. PhD. diss. (Lille, 1990)

Langwill, Lyndesay G., 'The Waits: a short historical study'. *Hinrichsen's Musical Year Book* 7 (1950), 170–83

Laskaya, Anne, and Eve Salisbury, eds, *The Middle English Breton Lays* (Kalamazoo MI, 1995)

Latham, R.E., *Revised Medieval Latin Word-List* (Oxford, 1965)

The Laud Troy Book: A Romance of about 1400 A.D., ed. Ernst Wülfing. 2 vols. EETS o.s. 121, 122 (London, 1902–3)

Lawson, Graeme, and Geoff Egan, 'Medieval trumpet from the city of London'. *The Galpin Society Journal* 41 (1988), 63–6

Laȝamon, *Laȝamon: Brut*, ed. G.L. Brooke and R.F. Leslie. 2 vols. EETS o.s. 250, 277 (London, 1963–78)

Leach, A.F., *Beverley Town Documents* (London, 1900)
——, *Report on the Manuscripts of the Corporation of Beverley* (London, 1900)
Leclercq, Jean, '"Ioculator et saltator": S. Bernard et l'image du jongleur dans les manuscrits'. Julian G. Plante, ed., *Translatio Studii: Manuscript and Library Studies Honoring Oliver L. Kapsner, O. S. B.* (Collegeville MN, 1973), 124–48
——, 'L'idiot à la lumière de la tradition chrétienne'. *Revue histoire de la spiritualité* (1973), 288–304
Leech-Wilkinson, Daniel, 'Il libro di appunti di un suonatore di tromba del quindicesimo secolo'. *Rivista italiana di musicologia* 16 (1981), 16–39
——, '*Le Voir Dit*: a reconstruction and a guide for musicians'. *Plainsong and Medieval Music* 2/1 (April 1993), 43–73
Lejeune, Rita, 'La forme de l'*Ensenhamen au jongleur* du troubadour Guiraut de Cabrera'. *Estudis Romànics* 9 (1961), 171–81
——, 'Le rôle littéraire d'Aliénor d'Aquitane'. *Cultura Neolatina* 14 (1954), 5–57
Leland, John, *Joannis Lelandi antiquarii De rebus britannicis collectanea*, ed. Thomas Hearne (London, 1774)
Leo of Rozmital, *The Travels of Leo of Rozmital through Germany, Flanders, England, France, Spain, Portugal and Italy, 1465–1467*, ed. Gabriel Tetzel and Václav Šašek (Cambridge, 1957)
Le Patourel, Jean, 'Ceramic horns'. David Gaimster and Mark Redknap, eds, *Everyday and Exotic Pottery from Europe, c. 650–1900* (Oxford, 1992), 157–66
Lester, G.A., 'Fifteenth-century English heraldic narrative'. *Yearbook of English Studies* 22 (1992), 201–12
——, 'The literary activities of the English heralds'. *English Studies* 71 (1990), 222–9
——, *Sir John Paston's 'Grete Boke': A Descriptive Catalogue, with an Introduction, of British Library MS Lansdowne 285* (Cambridge, 1984)
Lewis, C.S., *The Allegory of Love: A Study in a Medieval Tradition* (London, 1936)
Leycester, Peter, *Historical Antiquities* (London, 1673)
Liber Feodorum: The Book of Fees Commonly Called Testa de Nevill, Part I. A.D. 1198–1241, ed. H. C. Maxwell Lyte. 3 vols (London, 1920–31)
List and Index of Warrants for Issues, 1399–1485. Public Record Office Lists and Indexes, no. 9, vol. II (repr. New York NY, 1964)
Litterick, Louise, 'On Italian instrumental ensemble music in the late fifteenth century'. Fenlon, *Music in Medieval & Early Modern Europe*, 117–30
Lloyd, Simon, 'William Longespee II: the making of an English crusading hero'. *Nottingham Medieval Studies* 35 (1991), 41–69
——, and Tony Hunt, 'William Longespee II: the making of an English crusading hero. Part II'. *Nottingham Medieval Studies* 36 (1992), 79–125
Lodge, E.C., and Sir Robert Somerville, eds, *John of Gaunt's Register, 1379–1383*. 2 vols. Camden Society, third series 56 and 57 (1937)
Lommatzsch, Erhrad, *Provenzalisches Liederbuch, Lieder der Troubadours mit einer Auswahl biographischer Zeugnisse, Nachdichtungen und Singweisen* (Berlin, 1917)
Loomis, Laura Hibbard. See under Hibbard
Loomis, Roger S., Review of *Der Mittelenglische Versroman über Richard Löwenherz*, ed. Karl Brunne. *Journal of English and German Philology* 15/3 (1916), 455–66

Lord, Albert B., *The Singer of Tales*. 2nd edn, ed. Stephen Mitchell and Gregory Nagy (Cambridge MA, 2000)

———, 'Perspectives in recent work on oral literature'. *Forum for Modern Language Studies* 10/3 (1974), 187–210

McGee, Timothy J., 'Instruments and the Faenza Codex'. *Early Music* 14 (1986), 480–90; repr. McGee, *Instruments and their Music*, 479–88

———, ed., *Instruments and their Music in the Middle Ages* (Farnham, 2009)

———, *Medieval Instrumental Dances* (Bloomington and Indianapolis IN, 1989)

———, *Medieval and Renaissance Music: A Performer's Guide* (Toronto, 1985)

———, and Stewart Carter, eds, *Instruments, Ensembles, and Repertory, 1300–1600: Essays in Honour of Keith Polk* (Turnhout, 2013)

MacGibbon, David, *Elizabeth Woodville*. 2nd edn (Stroud, 2013)

Macpherson, James, *The Poems of Ossian and Related Works*, ed. Howard Gaskill (Edinburgh, 2003)

Madden, Sir Frederic, 'Remembrances for the Apparel ... of Henry Algernon Percy, Earl of Northumberland, 1513'. *Archaeologia* 26 (1836), 395–405

Maddicott, J.R., *Simon de Montfort* (Cambridge, 1994)

Magoun, Francis P., 'The oral-formulaic character of Anglo-Saxon narrative poetry'. *Speculum* 28/3 (1953), 446–67

———, 'Bede's story of Cædman: the case-history of an Anglo-Saxon singer'. *Speculum* 30/1 (1955), 49–63

Mahn, C.A.F., *Die Werke der Troubadours*. 2 vols (Berlin, 1846–86)

Manly, John M., and Edith Rickert, *The Text of the Canterbury Tales* (Chicago, 1940)

Manning de Brunne, Robert, *Handlyng Synne*, ed. F.J. Furnivall. 2 vols. EETS o.s. 119, 123 (London, 1901 and 1903)

———, *Robert Mannyng of Brunne: The Chronicle*, ed. Idelle Sullens (Binghamton NY, 1996)

Manuale ad usum ecclesie Sarisburiensis, ed. A. Jefferies Collins (London, 1960)

Marche, Olivier de la, *Mémoires*, ed. H. Beaune and J. d'Arbaumont (Paris, 1883–8)

Margerum, Alice C., '"Alioquin Deficeret Hic Instrumentum Illud Multum Vulgare": a brief overview of citoles in art and literature c. 1200–1400'. Robinson et al., *British Museum Citole*, 15–38

———, 'Situating the citole, circa 1200–1400'. PhD. diss. (London Metropolitan University, 2010)

Martin, Jean-Pierre, *Les motifs dans la chanson de geste: définition et utilisation (discours de l'épopée médiévale 1)* (Paris, 2017)

Matthews, David, 'Laurence Minot, Edward III, and nationalism'. *Viator* 38/1 (2007), 269–88

———, *Writing to the King: Nation, Kingship and Literature in England, 1250–1350* (Cambridge, 2010)

Meale, Carol M., '"gode men / Wiues maydnes and alle men": romance and its audiences'. Carol Meale, ed., *Readings in Medieval English Romance* (Cambridge, 1994), 209–25

Mehler, Natascha, Steinunn Kristjánsdóttir and Ralf Kluttig-Altmann, 'The sound of silence – a ceramic horn and its role in monasticism in late medieval Iceland'. *Early Music* 46/4 (2018), 551–60

Menegaldo, Silvère, *Le jongleur dans la littérature narrative des XIIe et XIIIe siècles: du personage au masque* (Paris, 2005)

——, 'Adenet le Roi tel qu'en ses prologues', *Cahiers de recherche médiévales et humanistes* 18 (2009), 309–28

Meneghetti, Maria Luisa, *Il pubblico dei trovatori: ricezione e riuso dei testi lirici cortesi fino al XIV secolo*. 2nd edn (Turin, 1992)

Meredith, Peter, 'The professional travelling players of the fifteenth century: myth or reality?'. Sydney Higgins, ed., *European Medieval Drama 1997* (Camerino, 1997), 25–40

Merryweather, James, 'The minstrels' pillar in St Mary's church, Beverley: a Tudor portrait of the York waites?'. <http://www.townwaits.org.uk/essays_st-marys.shtml>

Middle English Metrical Romances, ed. Walter H. French and Charles B. Hale. 2 vols (New York NY, 1930; repr. 1964)

Milá y Fontanals, Manuel, *De los Trovadores en España: Estudio lengua y poesia provenzal* (Barcelona, 1861)

Millar, Eric G., *Reproductions from Illuminated Manuscripts*, series IV (London, 1928)

——, *The York Psalter* (London, 1952)

Minnis, Alastair, *Medieval Theory of Authorship: Scholastic Literary Attitudes in the Later Middle Ages*. 2nd edn (Philadelphia PA, 2010)

Minot, Laurence, *The Poems of Laurence Minot*, ed. Richard H. Osberg (Kalamazoo MI, 1996)

——, *The War Ballads of Laurence Minot*, ed. Douglas C. Stedman (Dublin and London, 1917)

Mitchell, R. J., *The Medieval Feast: The Story of the Coronation Banquet of King Henry IV in Westminster Hall, 13th October 1399* (London, 1958)

Molina, Mauricio, '*Li autres la citole mainne*: towards a reconstruction of the citole's performance practice'. Robinson *et al.*, *British Museum Citole*, 104–10

Montagu, Jeremy, *Shawms around the World* (2019). Online at <http://jeremymontagu.co.uk/Books.html#ebooks> (accessed 6 June 2019)

——, *The World of Medieval and Renaissance Musical Instruments* (Newton Abbot, London and Vancouver, 1976)

——, Gwen and Jeremy, 'Beverley minster reconsidered'. *Early Music* 6 (1978), 401–15

——, Gwen and Jeremy, *Minstrels and Angels: Carvings of Musicians in Medieval English Churches* (Berkeley CA, 1998)

Montgomery, Franz, 'The musical instruments in the *Canterbury Tales*'. *Musical Quarterly* 17 (1931), 439–48

Morehen, John, ed., *English Choral Practice, 1400–1650* (Cambridge, 1995)

Morillo, Stephen R., 'Quo Warranto proceedings'. Szarmach *et al.*, *Medieval England*, 629–30

Mortimer, Ian, *The Time Traveller's Guide to Medieval England* (London, 2008)

Mosley, Sir Oswald, *The History of the Castle, Priory, and Town of Tutbury, in the County of Stafford* (London, 1832)

Motherwell, William, *Minstrelsy, Ancient and Modern* (Glasgow, 1827)

Mouskes, Philippe, *Chronique rimée de Philippe Mouskes, évêque de Tournay au treizième siècle*, ed. Baron de Reiffenberg. 3 vols (Brussels 1836–45)

Mugnier, François, *Les Savoyards en Angleterre au xiiie siècle, et Pierre d'Aigueblanche, évêque d'Hereford* (Paris, 1891)

Mullins, E.L.C., *Texts and Calendars*. 2 vols (London, 1958 and 1983)

Munby, Julian, Richard Barber and Richard Brown, *Edward III's Round Table at Windsor: The House of the Round Table and the Windsor Festival of 1344* (Woodbridge, 2007)

Musik in Geschichte und Gegenwart, Die (Kassel, 1949–; 2nd edn 1994–)

Myers, A.R., *England in the Late Middle Ages*. 2nd edn (London, 1963)

——, *The Household of Edward IV* (Manchester, 1959)

Myers, Herbert W., 'Evidence of the emerging trombone in the late fifteenth century'. *Historic Brass Society Journal* 17 (2005), 7–35

——, 'The *Mary Rose* "shawm"'. *Early Music* 11 (1983), 358–60

——, 'Slide trumpet madness: fact or fiction?'. *Early Music* 17 (1989), 382–9; repr. McGee, *Instruments and their Music*, 391–8

Nagel, Wilibald, *Geschichte der Musik in England*. 2 vols (Strasbourg, 1894 and 1897)

Neidorf, Leonard, ed., *The Dating of Beowulf: A Reassessment* (Cambridge, 2014)

The New Grove Dictionary of Music and Musicians, ed. Stanley Sadie. 2nd edn (London, 2001). Available as Oxford Music Online

The New Oxford History of Music. 10 vols (Oxford, 1954–75) (NOHM)

Nichols, John Gough, *The Herald and Genealogist*, vol. 1 (London, 1863)

Nicolas, Nicholas Harris, *History of the Battle of Agincourt* (London, 1832)

——, ed., *The Controversy between Sir Richard Scrope and Sir Robert Grosvenor*. 2 vols (London, 1832)

Niles, John D., *Beowulf: The Poem and its Tradition* (Cambridge MA, 1983)

——, *Old English Heroic Poems and the Social Life of Texts* (Turnhout, 2007)

NOHM, *The New Oxford History of Music*

Nolan, Barbara, 'Anthologizing ribaldry: five Anglo-Norman fabliaux'. Fein, *Studies*, 289–327

Noomen, Willem, ed., *Le jongleur par lui-même* (Louvain, 2003)

'The oath of the herald when he is made before his sovereign lord'. Oxford, Bodleian Library, MS Ashmole 1117

ODNB, *The Oxford Dictionary of National Biography*. Online at <https://www.oxforddnb.com>

The Old French Arthurian Vulgate and Post Vulgate in Translation, gen. ed. Norris J. Lacy. Vol. II: *The Story of Merlin*, trans. Rupert T. Pickens (Cambridge, 2010)

Olson, Clair C., 'Minstrels at the court of Edward III'. *PMLA* 56/3 (1941), 601–12

Opland, Jeff, 'From horseback to monastic cell: the impact on English literature of the introduction of writing'. John D. Niles, ed., *Old English Literature in Context: Ten essays* (Cambridge, 1980), 30–43

Orchard, Andy, *A Critical Companion to Beowulf* (Cambridge, 2003)

——, *The Poetic Art of Aldhelm* (Cambridge, 1994)

Orderic Vitalis, *The Ecclesiastical History of Orderic Vitalis*, ed. Marjorie Chibnall. 6 vols (Oxford, 1969–78)

Ords & Regs, A Collection of Ordinances and Regulations for the Government of the Royal Household (London, 1790)

Osborn, James M., *The Autobiography of Thomas Whythorne*. Modern spelling edition (London, 1962)

Ovid, *Ovid's Fasti with an English Translation by Sir James George Frazer*, ed. A.J. Boyle and Roger D. Woodard (London, 1931)

Owen, A.E.B., 'A scrivener's notebook from Bury St Edmunds'. *Archives* (The Journal of the British Records Association) 14, no. 61 (Spring 1979), 16–22

Owen, Hugh, and John B. Blakeway, *The History of Shrewsbury* (London, 1825)

The Oxford Dictionary of National Biography. Online at <https://www.oxforddnb.com>

The Oxford Names Dictionary, ed. Patrick Hanks, Flavia Hodges, A.D. Mills and Adrian Room (Oxford, 2002)

Paden, William D., 'Old Occitan as a lyric language: the insertions from Occitan in three thirteenth-century French romances'. *Speculum* 68/1 (1993), 36–53

——, 'The role of the joglar in Troubadour lyric poetry'. Peter S. Noble and Linda M. Paterson, eds, *Chrétien de Troyes and the Troubadour: Essays in Memory of the Late Leslie Topsfield* (Cambridge, 1984), 90–111

Page, Christopher, 'The 15th-century lute: new and neglected sources'. *Early Music* 9/1 (1981), 11–21

——, 'French lute tablature in the 14th century?'. *Early Music* 8/4 (1980), 488–92

——, 'German musicians and their instruments: a 14th-century account by Konrad of Megenberg'. *Early Music* 10/2 (1982), 192–200; repr. McGee, *Instruments and their Music*, 29–37

——, *The Owl and the Nightingale: Musical Life and Ideas in France 1100–1300* (London, 1989)

——, *Voices and Instruments of the Middle Ages* (London, 1987)

Palgrave, Francis, *The Antient Kalendars and Inventories of the Exchequer* (London, 1836)

Palmer, Frances, 'Musical instruments from the *Mary Rose*: a report on work in progress'. *Early Music* 11 (1983), 53–60

Panum, Hortense, *The Stringed Instruments of the Middle Ages*, rev. and ed. Jeffrey Pulver (London, 1940)

Parkes, M.B., 'The date of the Oxford manuscript of *La Chanson de Roland* (Oxford, Bodleian Library, MS. Digby 23)'. *Medioevo Romanzo* 10 (1985), 161–75

Parks, Ward, 'The oral-formulaic theory in Middle English studies'. *Oral Tradition* 1/3 (1986), 636–94

Parrish, Carl, *The Notation of Medieval Music* (New York NY, 1957, and London, 1958)

Paterson, Linda M., *The World of Troubadours: Medieval Occitan Society, c. 1100–c.1300* (Cambridge and New York NY, 1993)

Patterson, Lee, *Chaucer and the Subject of History* (Madison WI, 1991)

Pearsall, Derek, *Old English and Middle English Poetry* (London, 1977)

Pegge, [ ], 'The bull-running, at Tutbury, in Staffordshire, considered. By the Reverend Mr Pegge'. *Archaeologia* 2 (1773), 86–91

Percy, Thomas, late bishop of Dromore, *Regulations and Establishment of Henry Algernon Percy, 5th Earl of Northumberland* (London, 1827)

——, *Reliques of Ancient English Poetry* (London, 1765); repr. with an introduction by Henry B. Wheatley. 3 vols (New York NY, 1966)

——, *Reliques of Ancient English Poetry Consisting of Old Heroic Ballads, Songs, and Other Pieces of Our Earlier Poets, Chiefly of the Lyric Kind*. 4 vols (Dublin, 1766)

Perry, Lucy, 'Origins and originality: reading Lawman's "Brut" and the rejection of British Library MS Cotton Otho C.xiii'. *Arthuriana* 10/2 (2000), 66–84

Peters, Gretchen, *The Musical Sounds of Medieval French Cities: Players, Patrons, and Politics* (Cambridge, 2012)

Petrucci, Ottaviano, *Harmonice Musices Odhecaton* (Venice, 1501; repr. n.p., n.d.)

Pfister, Max, 'La langue de Guilhem IX, comte de Poitiers'. *Cahiers de Civilisation Médiévale* 19 (1976), 91–113

Pickard, Simon, and Richard Cann, *Christ in Majesty and the Angel Musicians in the Quire Vault of Gloucester Cathedral*. 2 vols (Gloucester, 2015)

Pirot, François, *Recherches sur les conaissances littéraires des troubadours occitans et catalans des XIIe et XIIIe siècles* (Barcelona, 1972)

Pirro, André, *La Musique à Paris sous le regne de Charles VI* (Paris, 1930)

Plot, Robert, *The Natural History of Stafford-shire* (Oxford, 1686)

PMLA, Publications of the Modern Language Association of America (Cambridge [UK] and Baltimore MD, 1886–)

Poe, Elizabeth Wilson, 'The meaning of Saber in Raimon Vidal's *Abril Issia*'. *Studia Occitanica in Memoriam Paul Remy. Vol II. The Narrative-Philology*, ed. Hans-Erich Keller (Kalamazoo MI, 1986), 169–78

Polk, Keith, 'English instrumental music in the fifteenth century'. *Uno Gentile et Subtile Ingenio: Studies in Renaissance Music in Honour of Bonnie J. Blackburn*, ed. M. Jennifer Bloxam, Gioia Filocamo and Leofranc Holford-Strevens (Turnhout, 2009), 659–67

——, *German Instrumental Music of the Late Middle Ages: Players, Patrons and Performance Practice* (Cambridge, 1992)

——, 'The trombone, the slide trumpet and the ensemble tradition of the early Renaissance'. *Early Music* 17 (1989), 389–97; repr. McGee, *Instruments and their Music*, 399–408

Poulson, George, *Beverlac, or, The Antiquities and History of … Beverley* (London, 1829)

Praetorius, Michael, *Syntagma Musicum*. 3 vols (Wolfenbüttel, 1614–19; repr. Kassel, 1958–78)

Prestwich, Michael, *Edward I* (London, 1988, and New Haven CT, 1997)

Prideaux, Edith K., *The Carvings of Mediaeval Musical Instruments in Exeter Cathedral Church* (Exeter, 1915)

Prockter, Adrian, and Robert Taylor, *The A to Z of Elizabethan London* (London, 1979)

Quinn, William, and Audley Hall, *Jongleur: A Modified Theory of Oral Improvisation and Its Effects on the Performance and Transmission of Middle English Romance* (Washington DC, 1982)

Raine, A., ed., *York Civic Records*. 2 vols (York, 1939 and 1941)

Rasmussen, Mary, 'Viols, violists and Venus in Grünewald's Isenheim altar'. *Early Music* 29/1 (2001), 61–74. (See also correspondence in *Early Music* 29/4 (2001), 667–9)

Rastall, G. R[ichard], 'The minstrel court in late medieval England'. R.L. Thomson, ed., *A Medieval Miscellany in Honour of Professor John le Patourel*. Leeds Philosophical and Literary Society, Literary and Historical Section, *Proceedings* 18/1 (April 1982), 96–105

——, 'Secular Musicians in Late Medieval England'. 2 vols. PhD. diss. (Victoria University of Manchester, 1968). Online at <https://secureservercdn.net/160.153.138.177/e66.8db.myftpupload.com/wp-content/uploads/2022/02/richard_rastall_thesis-1.pdf>

Rastall, Richard, 'Citolers in the household of the king of England'. Robinson *et al.*, *British Museum Citole*, 45–50

——, 'Civic minstrels in late medieval England: new light on duties and careers'. Royal Musical Association *Research Chronicle* 52 (2021), 183–218

——, *Four French Songs from an English Songbook*. 2nd edn (Antico Edition, 2014)

——, *The Heaven Singing. Music in Early English Religious Drama*, I (Cambridge, 1996)

——, 'Minstrels and players: functions and terminology'. ROMARD 55 (2016), 81–92

——, 'The minstrels of the English royal households, 25 Ed I–1 Hen VIII: an inventory'. Royal Musical Association *Research Chronicle* 4 (1964), 1–41 (MERH)

——, *Minstrels Playing. Music in Early English Religious Drama*, II (Cambridge, 2001)

——, 'The minstrels and trumpeters of Edward IV: some further thoughts'. *Plainsong & Medieval Music* 13/2 (2004), 163–9

——, 'Minstrelsy, church and clergy in medieval England'. *Proceedings of the Royal Musical Association* 97 (1970–1), 83–98

——, 'Music for a royal entry, 1474'. *Musical Times* 1612 (June 1977), 463–6

——, 'Neckam: a mystery solved'. <http://www.townwaits.org.uk/essays_neckham.shtml> (posted December 2015)

——, *The Notation of Western Music*. 2nd edn (Leeds, 1998, and London, 2008)

——, 'The origin of the Town Waits, and the myth of the watchman-turned-musician'. <http://www.townwaits.org.uk/essays_index.shtml> (posted 19 June 2009)

——, 'Pipers and waits in the English royal households, c. 1290–1475: issues of identity and function'. <http://www.waits.org.uk/essays/index.htm> (posted 19 June 2009)

——, 'Some English consort-groupings of the late Middle Ages'. *Music & Letters* 55/2 (April 1974), 179–202; repr. McGee, *Instruments and their Music*, 61–84

——, *Two Fifteenth-Century Song Books* (Aberystwyth, 1990)

Raynouard, F.J.M., *Choix des poésies originales des troubadours*. 6 vols (Paris, 1816)

REED, Records of Early English Drama. University of Toronto Press:
Cambridge (Alan H. Nelson). 2 vols. 1989
Chester (Lawrence M. Clopper). 1979

Cheshire, including Chester (Elizabeth Baldwin, Lawrence M. Clopper and
    David Mills). 2 vols. 2007
Coventry (R.W. Ingram). 1981
Cumberland, Westmorland (Audrey Douglas) and Gloucestershire (Peter
    Greenfield). 1986
Devon (John M. Wasson). 1986
Dorset (Rosalind Conklin Hays and C.E. McGee) and Cornwall (Sally L.K.
    Joyce and Evelyn S. Newlyn). 1999
Hampshire (Peter Greenfield and Jane Cowling). Online, 2019
Herefordshire and Worcestershire (David N. Klausner). 1990
Kent: Diocese of Canterbury (James M. Gibson). 3 vols. 2002
Lancashire (David George). 1991
Lincolnshire (James Stokes). 2 vols. 2009
Civic London to 1558 (Anne B. Lancashire). 3 vols. 2015
Ecclesiastical London (Mary C. Erler). 2008
Newcastle upon Tyne (J.J. Anderson). 1982
Oxford (John R. Elliott Jr, Alan H. Nelson, Alexandra F. Johnston and
    Diana Wyatt). 2 vols. 2004
Shropshire (J. Alan B. Somerset). 2 vols. 1994
Sussex (Cameron Louis). 2000
Wales (David N. Klausner). 2005
York (Alexandra F. Johnston and Margaret Rogerson). 2 vols. 1979
REED online, *Berkshire and Staffordshire*. <https://ereed.library.utoronto.ca/search/> (accessed November 2019)
Reichl, Karl, 'From performance to text: a medievalist's perspective on the textualization of modern Turkic oral poetry'. *Western Folklore* 72/3 and 4 (2013), 252–71
——, 'Plotting the map of medieval oral literature'. Karl Reichl, ed., *Medieval Oral Literature* (Berlin, 2012), 3–67
Remnant, Mary, *English Bowed Instruments from Anglo-Saxon to Tudor Times* (Oxford, 1986)
——, *Musical Instruments of the West* (London, 1978)
——, 'Rebec, fiddle and crowd in England'. *Proceedings of the Royal Musical Association* 95 (1968–9), 15–28
——, and Richard Marks, 'A medieval "gittern"'. *The British Museum Yearbook 4: Music and Civilisation* (London, 1980), 83–134
Renard, Jean, *l'Escoufle: roman d'aventure*, ed. Franklin P. Sweetser (Geneva, 1974)
Rensch, Roslyn, *Harps and Harpists* (London, 1989)
Richard Löwenherz. Karl Brunner, ed., *Der Mittelenglische Versroman über Richard Löwenherz* (Vienna and Leipzig, 1913)
Rickert, Edith, *Chaucer's World* (New York NY and London, 1948)
Ridgeway, W.H., 'Foreign favourites and Henry III's problems of patronage, 1247–1258'. *English Historical Review* 104/412 (1989), 590–610
——, 'The politics of the English royal court, 1247–65, with special reference to the role of the aliens'. DPhil. diss. (Oxford, 1983)
Rigg, A.G., 'An edition of a fifteenth-century commonplace book (Trinity College, Cambridge, MS O.9.38)'. DPhil. diss. (Oxford, 1966)

——, *A Glastonbury Miscellany of the Fifteenth Century: A Descriptive Index of Trinity College, Cambridge, MS O.9.38* (Oxford, 1968)
——, 'John of Bridlington's prophecy: a new look'. *Speculum* 63 (1988), 596–613
Riley, H.T., ed., *Gesta Abbatum Monasterii Sancti Albani*. Rolls Series (London, 1867–9)
Ripin, Edwin M., 'Towards an identification of the chekker'. *Galpin Society Journal* 28 (1975), 11–25; repr. McGee, *Instruments and their Music*, 105–22
Ritson, Joseph, *A Dissertation on Romance and Minstrelsy*. Vol. I of *Ancient English Metrical Romances*, new edn, rev. Edmund Goldsmid (Edinburgh, 1891)
Robbins, Rossell Hope, *Secular Lyrics of the XIVth and XVth Centuries*. 2nd edn (Oxford, 1955)
——, *Historical Poems of the XIVth and XVth Centuries* (New York NY, 1959)
Robinson, James, Naomi Speakman and Kathryn Buehler-McWilliams, eds, *The British Museum Citole: New Perspectives* (London, 2015)
The Romance of Flamenca: A Provençal Poem of the Thirteenth Century, ed. Marion E. Porter, trans. Merton Jerome Hubert (Princeton NJ, 1962)
ROMARD, *Research on Medieval and Renaissance Drama* (London, Ontario)
Rose, Martial, and Julia Hedgecoe, *Stories in Stone: The Medieval Roof Carvings of Norwich Cathedral* (London, 1997)
Rosenthal, Joel T., *Telling Tales: Sources and Narration in Late Medieval England* (University Park PA, 2003)
Rotuli de Dominabus et Pueris et Puellis de Donatione Regis in XII Comitatibus (London, 1830)
Round, J.H., *The King's Serjeants* (London, 1911)
Ruelle, Pierre, ed., *Huon de Bordeaux* (Brussels and Paris, 1960)
Rychner, Jean, *La chanson de geste: essai sur l'art épique des jongleurs* (Geneva, 1955)
Rymer, Thomas, *Foedera conventiones, literae et cujuscunque generis acta publica*. 20 vols (London, 1704–35)
Sachs, Curt, *Real-Lexicon der Musikinstrumente*. 2nd, rev. and enlarged edn (New York NY, 1964)
Safford, E.W., 'An account of the expenses of Eleanor, sister of Edward III, on the occasion of her marriage to Reynald, Count of Guelders'. *Archaeologia* 67 (1927), 111–20
Salmen, Walter, *Der Spielmann im Mittelalter* (Innsbruck, 1983)
Salzman, L.F., *English Industries of the Middle Ages* (London, 1970)
Samaran, C., 'Étude historique et paléographique'. A. de Laborde, ed., *La Chanson de Roland: Reproduction phototypique du manuscrit Digby 23 de la Bodleian Library d'Oxford* (Paris, 1933), 1–50
Sayers, William, 'The jongleur Taillefer at Hastings: antecedents and literary fate'. *Viator* 14 (1983), 77–88
The Seege or Batayle of Troye, ed. Mary Elizabeth Barnicle. EETS o.s. 172 (Oxford, 1927)
Sharp, Thomas, *A Dissertation on the Pageants ... at Coventry* (Coventry, 1825; repr. with a new foreword by A.C. Cawley, East Ardsley, 1973)
Shephard, W.P., *Jausbert de Puycibot* (Paris, 1924)

Shepherd, Stephen H.A., *Le Morte Darthur or The Hoole Book of Kyng Arthur and of His Noble Knyghtes of The Rounde Table* (New York NY, 2004)

Short, Ian, 'L'avènement du texte vernaculaire: la mise en recueil'. Emmanuèle Baumgartner and Christiane Marchello-Nizia, eds, *Théories et pratiques de l'écriture au Moyen Age, Actes du colloque, Palais du Luxembourg-Sénat, 5–6 Mars 1987*. Special issue, *Littérales* 4 (1988), 11–24

——, 'The *Pseudo-Turpin Chronicle*: some unnoticed versions and their sources'. *Medium Ævum* 38/1 (1969), 1–22

Shuffelton, George, 'Is there a minstrel in the house?: domestic entertainment in late medieval England'. *Philological Quarterly* 87/1 (2008), 51–76

Skeat, Walter W., *The Lay of Havelok the Dane*. 2nd edn, rev. K. Sisam (Oxford, 1915)

Slim, H. Colin, 'Instrumental versions, c. 1515–1544, of a late-fifteenth-century Flemish chanson, *O waerde mont*'. Fenlon, *Music in Medieval & Early Modern Europe*, 131–61

Slocum, Kay Brainerd, '*Confrérie, Bruderschaft* and guild: the formation of musicians' fraternal organisations in thirteenth- and fourteenth-century Europe'. *Early Music History* 14 (1995), 257–74

Smith, George, *The Coronation of Elizabeth Wydeville* (London, 1935)

Smith, Joshua Toulmin, *English Gilds* (London, 1870)

Smith, Lucy Toulmin, ed., *Expeditions to Prussia and the Holy Land made by Henry Earl of Derby* (London, 1894)

Smith, W.C.B., *St Mary's Church Beverley: An Account of Its Building over 400 Years from 1120 to 1524* (Beverley, 2001)

Southern, Richard W., *The Making of the Middle Ages* (New Haven CT, 1953)

Southworth, John, *The English Medieval Minstrel* (Woodbridge, 1989)

——, *Fools and Jesters at the English Court* (Stroud, 1998)

Spector, Stephen, ed., *The N-Town Play*. 2 vols. EETS s.s. 11, 12 (London, 1991)

Spiegel, Gabrielle M., *The Past as Text: The Theory and Practice of Medieval Historiography* (Baltimore MD and London, 1997)

Spufford, Peter, *Handbook of Medieval Exchange* (Woodbridge, 1986)

Stainer, J, J.F.R. and C., and E. Nicholson, *Early Bodleian Music*. 3 vols (London, 1901; repr. Farnborough, 1967)

Stanley, Eric G., 'Laʒamon's antiquarian sentiments'. *Medium Ævum* 38 (1969), 23–37

Stanzaic Guy of Warwick, ed. Alison Wiggins (Kalamzoo MI, 2004)

Starkey, David, Maria Hayward and Philip Ward, *The Inventory of King Henry VIII* (London, 1998)

Stephen, G.A., 'The waits of the city of Norwich'. *Norfolk Archaeology* 25 (1933), 1–70

Stevens, John, 'Carols and Court Songs of the Early Tudor Period'. *Proceedings of the Royal Musical Association* 77 (1950), 51–62

——, ed., *Music at the Court of Henry VIII*. Musica Britannica 18 (London, 1962)

——, 'Music in mediaeval drama'. *Proceedings of the Royal Musical Association* 84 (1958), 81–95

——, *Music and Poetry in the Early Tudor Court* (London, 1961)

Stevenson, Katie, ed., *The Herald in Late Medieval Europe* (Woodbridge, 2009)

Stevenson, W.H., and W.T. Baker, eds, *Records of the Borough of Nottingham* (London and Nottingham, 1882–1900)
Stewart-Brown, R., 'The Scrope and Grosvenor controversy, 1385–1391'. *Transactions of the Historic Society of Lancashire and Cheshire* 89 (1937), 1–22
Stimming, Albert, *Der anglonormannische Boeve de Haumtone* (Halle, 1899)
———, ed., *Der festländische Bueve de Hantone*. 3 vols (Halle, 1911–14)
Stock, Brian, *The Implications of Literacy: Written Language and Models of Interpretation in the Eleventh and Twelfth Centuries* (Princeton NJ, 1983)
Stow, John, *A Survey of London*, rev. edn, with an introduction by H.B. Wheatley (London and New York NY, 1956)
Strong, Roy C., 'Elizabethan jousting cheques in the possession of the College of Arms'. *The Coat of Arms* 5 (1958–9), 4–8, 63–8
Sumption, Jonathan, *The Hundred Years War*. 4 vols (London and Philadelphia PA, 1990–9)
Sutton, Anne, and Peter Hammond, *The Coronation of Richard III: The Extant Documents* (Gloucester, 1982)
Symes, Carol, *A Common Stage: Theatre and Public Life in Medieval Arras* (Ithaca NY and London, 2007)
Szarmach, Paul, M. Teresa Tavormina and Joel T. Rosenthal, eds, *Medieval England: An Encyclopedia* (New York NY and London, 1998)
Tacitus, *Germany/Germania*, ed. and trans. Herbert W. Benario (Oxford, 1999)
Taylor, Andrew, 'Fragmentation, corruption, and minstrel narration: the question of the Middle English romances'. *Yearbook of English Studies* 22 (1992), 38–62
———, 'From heraldry to history: the death of Gilles d'Argentan'. Nicole Royan, ed., *Langage Cleir Illumynate: Scottish Poetry from Barbour to Drummond, 1375–1630* (Amsterdam, 2007), 25–41
———, 'The myth of the minstrel manuscript', *Speculum* 66/1 (1991), 43–73
———, 'Performing the Percy Folio'. Jacqueline Jenkins and Julie Sanders, eds, *Editing, Performance, Texts: New Practices in Medieval and Early Modern English Drama* (New York NY, 2015), 70–89
———, *The Songs and Travels of a Tudor Minstrel: Richard Sheale of Tamworth* (York, 2012)
———, *Textual Situations: Three Medieval Manuscripts and their Readers* (Philadelphia PA, 2002)
———, 'Were minstrels actors in waiting?'. ROMARD 55 (2016), 57–68
Taylor, Arthur, *The Glory of Regality* (London, 1820)
Thiolier, Jean Claude, ed., *Édition critique et commentée de Pierre de Langtoft, Le Règne d'Édouard Ier* (Créteil, 1989)
Thomas, *The Romance of Horn by Thomas*, ed. Mildred K. Pope, rev. T.B.W. Reid (Oxford, 1964)
Thomas the Rhymer, *Sir Tristrem*, ed. George P. McNeil (London, 1886)
Thompson, J.J., 'Collecting Middle English romances and some related book-production activities in the later Middle Ages'. Maldwyn Mills, Jennifer Fellows and Carol M. Meale, eds, *Romance in Medieval England* (Newtown, 1988), 17–38
Tinctoris, Johannes, *De inventione et usu musice (c. 1485)*. Edition and translation at <http://earlymusictheory.org/Tinctoris/>

Tittler, Robert, 'Coventry'. Szarmach et al., Medieval England, 219
——, 'Towns and urban life'. Szarmach et al., Medieval England, 736–7
Tolkien, J.R.R., 'Beowulf: The monsters and the critics'. Proceedings of the British Academy 22 (1936), 245–95
Toulouze, Michel, L'art et instruction de bien dancer (Paris, c. 1496; repr. London, 1936; repr. with music ed. Richard Rastall and the text trans. A.E. Lequet. East Ardsley and New York NY, 1971)
Tout, T.F., Chapters in the Administrative History of Medieval England. 6 vols (Manchester, 1920–33)
——, 'A medieval burglary'. Bulletin of the John Rylands Library (October 1915), 1–24
——, The Place of the Reign of Edward II in English History. 2nd edn (Manchester, 1936)
Trilling, Renée R., The Aesthetics of Nostalgia: Historical Representation in Old English Verse (Toronto, 2009)
Tringham, Nigel, 'Honor of Tutbury'. A History of the County of Stafford, X: Tutbury and Needwood Forest (London, 2007)
Trokelowe, John de, and Henry Blaneforde, Chronica et Annales: Regnantibus Henrico Tertio, Edwardo Primo, Edwardo Secundo, Ricardo Secundo, et Henrico Quarto, ed. H.T Riley (London, 1866)
Trowell, Brian, ed., Invitation to Medieval Music, 4 (London, 1978)
Turner, Derek, English Gothic Illuminated Manuscripts (London, 1965)
Twiss, Travers, ed., Monumenta Juridica: The Black Book of the Admiralty: With an Appendix. 4 vols (London, 1871–6)
Twiti, William, The Middle English Text of The Art of Hunting, ed. David Scott-Macnab (Universitätverlag Winter, 2009)
Unwin, George, The Gilds and Companies of London. 4th edn (London, 1963)
Van der Werf, Hendrik, The Oldest Extant Part Music. 2 vols (Rochester NY, 1993)
Vance, Eugene, 'Roland and the poetics of memory'. Josué V. Harari, ed., Textual Strategies: Perspectives in Post-Structuralist Criticism (Ithaca NY, 1979, and London, 1980), 374–403
VCH East Riding, The Victoria County History of England: East Riding of Yorkshire (Folkestone, 1974)
Veale, E.W.W., The Great Red Book of Bristol (Bristol, 1931–53)
Vidal, Antoine, La Chapelle St-Julien-des-Ménestriers (Paris, 1878)
Vidal, Raimon, L'École des jaloux (Castia Gilos). Fabliau du XIIIe siècle par le troubadour catalan Raimon de Vidal de Bezalu, ed. Irénée Cluzel (Paris, 1958)
——, Poetry and Prose, ed. W.H.W. Field (Chapel Hill NC, 1971)
Virgoe, Roger, 'Norwich'. Szarmach et al., Medieval England, 549
Vita Edwardi Secundi, ed. N. Denholm-Young, rev. Wendy R. Childs (Oxford, 2005)
Vitz, Evelyn Birge, Orality and Performance in Early French Romance (Cambridge, 1999)
——, Nancy Freeman Regalado and Marilyn Lawrence, eds., Performing Medieval Narrative (Cambridge, 2005)
The Vulgate Version of the Arthurian Romances, ed. H. Oskar Sommer, Vol. II Lestoire de Merlin (Washington, 1908)

Wace, *Le Roman de Rou de Wace*, ed. A.J. Holden. 3 vols (Paris, 1970–3)
——, *The History of the Norman People: Wace's Roman de Rou*, trans. Glyn S. Burgess, with notes by Glyn S. Burgess and Elisabeth M.C. Van Houts (Woodbridge, 2004)
Waesberghe, J. Smits van, *Cymbala – Bells in the Middle Ages* (Rome, 1951)
Wagner, Anthony R., *Heralds and Heraldry in the Middle Ages: An Inquiry into the Growth of the Armorial Function of Heralds*. 2nd edn (Oxford, 1956)
——, *Heralds of England: A History of the Office and College of Arms* (London, 1967)
Waldron, Ronald A., 'Oral-formulaic technique and Middle English alliterative poetry'. *Speculum* 32/4 (1957), 792–804
Ward, Jennifer, *Elizabeth de Burgh, Lady of Clare (1295–1360)* (Woodbridge, 2014)
Ward, Matthew, *The Livery Collar in Late Medieval England and Wales: Politics, Identity and Affinity* (Woodbridge, 2016)
Warren, W.L., *Henry II* (Berkeley CA, 1973)
——, *King John*. 3rd edn (New Haven CT, 1997)
Warton, Thomas, *The History of English Poetry*. 3 vols (London, 1774; edn of 1871)
Wathey, Andrew, 'The peace of 1360–1369 and Anglo-French musical relations'. *Early Music History* 9 (1990), 129–74
Watts, Ann Chalmers, *The Lyre and the Harp: A Comparative Reconsideration of Oral Tradition in Homer and Old English Epic Poetry* (New Haven CT and London, 1969)
Webb, John, 'The Billingsgate trumpet'. *The Galpin Society Journal* 41 (October 1988), 59–67
Webb, John, ed., *A Roll of the Household Expenses of Richard de Swinfield, Bishop of Hereford, 1289–90* (London, 1854–5; repr. New York NY, 1968)
Wegman, Rob C., 'The minstrel school in the late Middle Ages'. *Historic Brass Society Journal* 14 (2002), 11–30
Weiss, Judith E., trans., *Boeve de Haumtone and Gui de Warewic: Two Anglo-Norman Romances* (Tempe AZ, 2008)
Welker, Lorenz, 'Wind ensembles in the Renaissance'. Knighton and Fallows, *Companion*, 146–53
Westlake, H.F., *The Parish Gilds of Medieval England* (London, 1919)
Wilkins, Nigel, *Music in the Age of Chaucer* (Cambridge, 1979)
——, 'Music and poetry at court: England and France in the late Middle Ages'. V.J. Scattergood and J.W. Sherborne, eds, *English Court Culture in the Later Middle Ages* (London, 1983), 183–204
——, 'Puy'. Szarmach et al., *Medieval England*, 625
William of Malmesbury, *Gesta regum Anglorum*, ed. R.A.B. Mynors, Rodney M. Thomson and Michael Winterbottom (Oxford, 1998)
Wilson, R.M., *The Lost Literature of Medieval England*. 2nd edn (London, 1970)
Winternitz, Emanuel, *Musical Instruments and their Symbolism in Western Art* (London, 1967)
Wittig, Susan, *Stylistic and Narrative Structures in the Middle English Romances* (Austin TX and London, 1978)
Woodfield, Ian, *The Early History of the Viol* (Cambridge, 1984)
Woodfill, Walter L., *Musicians in English Society* (Princeton NJ, 1953)

Woolgar, Christopher M., *The Great Household in Late Medieval England* (New Haven and London, 1999)
——, ed., *The Elite Household in Medieval England, 1100–1550* (Donington, 2018)
Wright, Thomas, *The Political Songs of England, From the Reign of John to that of Edward II* (London, 1839)
——, *The Roll of Arms of the Princes, Barons, and Knights … [at] the Siege of Caerlaverock* (London, 1864)
——, *Songs and Carols from a Manuscript in the British Museum of the Fifteenth Century* (London, 1856)
——, *Songs and Carols Now First Printed from a Manuscript of the Fifteenth Century* (London, 1847)
——, *Songs and Carols Printed from a Manuscript in the Sloane Collection* (London, 1836)
——, ed., *A Volume of Vocabularies Illustrating the Condition and Manners of our Forefathers … from the Tenth Century to the Fifteenth*. 2 vols (Liverpool, 1857 and 1873)
Wylie, J.H., *The History of England under Henry IV*. 4 vols (London, 1884–98)
——, and W.T. Waugh, *The Reign of Henry the Fifth*. 3 vols (Cambridge, 1914–29)
Ying, Lang, 'The bard Jusup Mamay'. *Oral Tradition* 16/2 (2001), 222–39
Young, Abigail Ann, 'Plays and players: the Latin terms for performance'. *REED Newsletter* 9/2 (1984), 56–62
——, 'Plays and players: the Latin terms for performance (part ii)'. *REED Newsletter* 10/1 (1985), 9–16
Youngs, Deborah, *Humphrey Newton (1466–1536): An Early Tudor Gentleman* (Woodbridge, 2008)
Zaerr, Linda Marie, *Performance and the Middle English Romance* (Cambridge, 2012)
Zauchetto, Gérard, *Terre des Troubadours: XIIe et XIIIe siècles*, preface by Max Roquette (Paris, 1996)
Zingesser, Eliza, *Stolen Song: How the Troubadours Became French* (Ithaca NY, 2020)
Ziolkowski, Jan M., ed., *Solomon and Marcolf* (Cambridge MA, 2008)
Zumthor, Paul, *Essai de poétique médiéval* (Paris, 1972)
——, 'The text and the voice', trans. Marilyn C. Engelhardt. *New Literary History* 16/1 (1984), 67–92
Zupitza, J., 'Zum Havelok'. *Anglia* (1884), 145–55

Index

Aberdeen 70
Abergavenny, Lady, wife of William Beauchamp 112
Abingdon 38
  Abbot of 119
Absolon, John, minstrel of Edward III 16
Abys, John, minstrel of Henry VII 359
Adam *cum Campanis*, minstrel 338, 340
Adam de la Halle, *Le Jeu de Robin et Marion* 240
Adam le Boscu, minstrel 47
Adenet le Roi, 376
  Berte aus granspiés 240
  Bueves de Comarchis 240
  Cleomadés 240–1, 396
  Enfances Ogier 240, 261
Adrian, trumpeter of Henry VII 182, 358
Agincourt, battle of 84, 143
  minstrels at 6–7, 20, 24, 142, 151, 333
Aleyn, John, piper of Henry IV and Henry V 111, 333
Aleyn, Thomas, trumpeter of Henry IV 111
Aleyn, Walter, minstrel of Henry IV 10, 93
Alfonso VIII, King of Castile 263
Alfonso IX, King of León 264
Alfonso X, King of Castile and León, *Cantigas de Santa Maria* 283, 340
Algode, William, piper of Henry IV 10, 93
Algood, John, piper of Henry IV 111, 333
Alice, wife of Robert Crudworth, harper 133
Alisaundre, John, *rymour* of Edward III 103, 293, 344
Alphonse de Poitiers 239
Altarnun, Cornwall 25, 26, 27, 346
Alverton, Notts. 118
Alwyn, Bishop of Winchester 97
Amiens 24, 88, 297
Ancelinus, minstrel of Archbishop of Cologne 76
Andrew, minstrel 54
Andrew, organist 55
Anne of Bohemia, Queen, wife of Richard II 68, 95, 110
Anows (Denows), Richard, minstrel of Henry VII 360
Antwerp 56, 96
Anxce bon youre delabonestren 384–5
Aragon, John of 61, 103 n.23
Argentan, Giles d' 296–8

Arnald le Pyper, minstrel of Edward III 16
Arnhem 177
Arnold, trumpeter of Edward II 5
Arras 240
Arthur, Prince 22, 140, 145, 179, 327, 345
Arthur (Arthour) and Merlin 243–4, 283
Arundel, Earl of 38, 195
Ashbourne, Derbs. 368
Ashford 190, 196
Athelstan, King of Wessex and Mercia 205
Audenard, Sir Robert de 210

Baath, Richard, minstrel of Edward III 16
Badencore, John, piper of Edward III 332, 355
bagpipers/bagpipes *see* pipers/pipes/bagpipes
Baldwin, William, minstrel of Henry V 7
Bannockburn, battle of 297, 299, 308
Barberus, bagpiper of Edward III 67, 326
Barbour, John, *Bruce* 298
Barley, William, minstrel of Edward IV and Henry VII 17, 49
Barley, William, minstrel of George, Duke of Clarence 15 n.12
Barlings 94
Barnebroke, William, minstrel 133–4
Barnstaple 140, 170 n.10
Barton (Burton), Richard, wait 160
Barwyck, Thomas, wait 161
Bassingbourn, Cambs. 158
Batayle of Troye, The 244
Battle 194
Baudettus, taborer of Edward I 91
Baumburgh, Robert de, *vigilis* of Queen Isabelle 5 n.9
bearwards xxv, 140–1, 177, 191, 193, 195, 197
Beauchamp, John, minstrel of Henry IV 10, 93
Beauchamp, Richard, Earl of Warwick 112
Beaumanoir, Sir Robert, of Brittany 109
Beaumunt, Philip, minstrel 140
Beaurepaire 125
Belleperche 301
bells 33, 117, 146–7, 338–40, 355
Beowulf 228, 235, 239, 279–81, 282 n.60, 283, 285–7
Bere Regis, Dorset 246
Berkeley 112

Berkhamstead 94
Bernart de Ventadorn 273–6
Bertram, trumpeter of Edward I 215
Bertrand de Born 269, 275–6
Bertruchus, minstrel of Geneva 28 n.65
Berwick-on-Tweed 216, 248
Besalú 270–1
Bestruche, minstrel of Geneva 28 n.65
Bestulphus, minstrel of Geneva 28 n.65
Beverley 25, 60, 100, 117–18, 135, 187, 213, 244, 247
   carvings of instruments 315
   civic minstrels 147, 152–3, 155–6, 158–60, 162
   minstrel-court 205–6
   minstrel-fraternity 224–5
Bevis of Hampton 254
Bicester 122–3, 238
Bingley (Byngeley), William de, *vigilator* of Richard II, piper of Henry IV 10, 14, 93, 333
Bisshop, John, minstrel of Bishop of Ely, and of Edward II 37, 50, 119
Bisshop, William, minstrel of Edward III 119
Blache, trumpeter 114
Black Book *see Liber Niger*
Black Death 129–30, 208
Blanche, daughter of Louis IX of France 241, 242
Blanche of Lancaster, wife of John of Gaunt 11, 95, 104
Blanche, wife of Ludwig, son of Ruprecht, King of the Romans 93
Blank, John, trumpeter of Henry VII 358
Blewet, wait of London 152
Blewit, John, wait 159
Blewit, William, wait 159
Blida (Blyda), Richard de, trumpeter of Edward I and Edward II 5, 24 n.50, 31, 37, 40, 58, 60–1
Blyth, Notts. 40, 58, 60–1, 211
Blyton, Richard de, Carmelite friar 174
Bocard, Frannc, trumpeter of Henry VII 182, 358, 378, 393
Bodel, Jean 261
Boethius 284
Boeve de Haumtone 254–6
Boneurge, minstrel-waferer of William de Fenes 350
Bonetemps, minstrel of Henry VII 22, 41, 360
Bontemps, cornett-player 323
Borrow, Guyllam, sackbut player of Henry VII 359

Bosham, Robert de, waferer of Edward III 350
Bosworth 113
Bottore, Richard, gittener 317, 318
Boulogne 175
Bountaine, cornett-player 360
Bountas, cornett-player 182
Bourg-en-Bresse, minstrel school 66–7
Bourne, Thomas, member of London Grocers 141
Bower, Walter, *Scotichronicon* 296–8
Braburne, Northumb. 63
Bradstrete, trumpeter 62
Braybrok, Roger de, minstrel of Edward III 55
Breese, William, wait of Shrewsbury 159
Brese, wait of Coventry 159
Bretain, Sir John de 304
Brewer, Bartram, minstrel of Henry VII and Henry VIII 51–52
Bria (Briays), John de, waferer of Queen Isabella 5 n.9, 350, 396
Bristol 129, 148, 158, 338
Broden, John, minstrel of Edward IV 134
Brompton, William de, burgess of Newcastle under Lyme 203
Brotherton, Thomas de 70
Brothir, John, trumpeter of Henry IV 111, 134, 219
Brouard, Bartram, minstrel of Henry VII 360
Broun, John, trumpeter of Henry VII 358
Broune (Brown), John, piper of Henry V 7, 333–4
Brown, John, lute-player of James III of Scotland 69
Brown, trumpeter 142
Bruges 88, 102, 176–7, 179, 309
   minstrel-school 66, 69
Brussels 66
buisines 88, 231, 319
Bukyngham, John de, trumpeter of Edward III, clarioner of John of Gaunt 16, 49, 105–6
Bulson, John, wait 159–60, 162
Bumbepiper, Jacob, piper of John of Gaunt 107
Buntance, John, minstrel 360
Buntyng, John, yeoman of Chapel Royal 360
Burdegala, Bernard de, minstrel of Lord Ufford 36
Burdwardsle, Richard de, *vigilis* of Queen Isabella 331

Burgh, William, sackbut of Henry VII 22 n.34, 358–60
Burgoigne, Peter de, piper of Edward III 332, 355
Burton-on-Trent 120
Bury St Edmunds 63, 71, 247
Buxnell, Thomas 187

Cædmon 283
Calais 64, 74, 114, 176, 308
Caldwell, Thomas, groom of Henry VI 349
Calthorn, Thomas, minstrel of Edward IV 220
Cambridge 148, 155, 158
   King's College 338
Canterbury 36, 38, 50, 76–8, 97–8, 175, 178, 190–2, 194–6
   Archbishop of 120
   civic minstrels 153, 159–60, 162
   minstrel-fraternity 223–4
   St Augustine's 238
Capiny (Jakettus de Scocia, James de Cowpen), King of Heralds of Edward I 36, 91–2, 211–13, 216
Cardinal, Walter 55
Cardinal, William, minstrel of Edward III 55, 175, 177–8
Carité de Notre Dame des Ardents d'Arras 240
Carlisle 125
Cary, Thomas 67
Casa Nova (Casanova), Peter de, Marshal of Trumpets of Henry VIII 25, 45, 182, 194, 197, 358
Cateloyne, Janin de, trumpeter of Edward II 30–1, 74, 101
Caumz, John, minstrel-king of Richard II 217
Cawthorn, Thomas, minstrel of Edward IV 17–18
Cecile, John de (Decessid), trumpeter of Henry VII 358
Cely, George, merchant, amateur harper 64–5, 389
Chamber, John, Marshal of Minstrels of Henry VII and Henry VIII 25, 45, 222, 359
Chandos, Sir John 214, 257, 357
Chandos Herald, minstrel of John of Gaunt 214, 266, 299
   La Vie du Prince Noir 256–7, 261, 301, 314
Chanson de bon William Longespee 304–5
Chanson de Roland xxviii, 228–9, 235–7, 239, 241–3, 286, 288, 290, 313–14
Chanson de Saisnes 240

Chansonnier du Roy 367
chansons de geste xxiv, 228–30, 235–7, 239, 243, 252–7, 260, 270, 285–6, 311–14, 396; *see also Chanson de bon William Longespee*; *Chanson de Roland*; *Chanson de Saisnes*
Charlemagne, Frankish emperor 200 n.7, 235, 239–40, 272, 284, 288
Charles I, King of England 225
Charles VI, King of France 31, 88, 89
Charles d'Anjou 240
Chatterton (Chalkton, Chateron, Chatirton), Thomas, trumpeter 46, 62, 141, 395
Chaucer, Geoffrey 255, 309
   Canterbury Tales 81
   House of Fame 291–2, 310
Chaunceler, Robert, *vigilis* of Queen Isabella and of Edward II 5 n.9, 41, 331
Chelmsford 110
chekkers 336–7
Chester 152, 161
   minstrel courts 199–205, 208, 218, 221
Chesterton, Warks. 14
Chichester 77–8
Chobham, Thomas 121, 293
Chrétien de Troyes 239, 266–7, 285
   Érec et Énide 260, 262
   Yvain 267
Christ and Satan 283
Christian, William, minstrel of Edward IV 15 n.12, 220
Christopher, harper of Lord Clifford 187
Christopher, trumpeter of Henry VII 358
citolers/citoles 5–6, 10, 42–3, 231, 317, 333, 353
   description of 340–2
   surviving citoles 315
civic minstrels 146–7
   appointment and conditions 151–4
   duties 155–7
   employment mobility 157–60
   independent work 157–8
   institution of 148–9
   instruments 160–1
   liveries 148–9, 153–5, 157
   pay 152–4
   pensions 161
   status and standards 161–2
   'wait', meaning of 148–51
Clarenceaux, King of Arms of Edward IV 294
clarioners/clarions *see under* trumpeters/trumpets
Claus, nakerer of John of Gaunt 106
Clay, Lambyn, minstrel 28 n.65, 74, 91

Cliderhou, Adam de, harper of Edward I   39, 57
Cliff (I), John, trumpeter of Black Prince   20, 101, 108
Cliff(e) (II), John, of Coventry, nakerer of John of Gaunt and minstrel of Henry V   6 n.13, 7, 20–1, 61– 2, 106–8
Cliff (Clyff) (III), John, Marshal of minstrels of Henry VI and Edward IV   7–8, 20, 44–7, 108, 184, 208 n.32, 220
Cliff, William, minstrel of Edward IV   220
Clifford, Lord   187
Cliffort, Sir Robert   303
Clifton, William, trumpeter of Edward IV   15, 17–18, 51–3
Clipstone   58, 61
Clitheroe, Lancs.   57
Clough, Robert de, minstrel of Edward II   39, 47
Colchester   63, 115, 148
Cole, trumpeter of Howards   113
Colet, John, of Colchester   63–4
Cologne, Hanekin de, German *gigator*   37
Comgilton, Robert, wait   159–60
composition *see* repertory, instrumental
Comyn, John   91
Congilton, Robert, wait   159–60
Conrad, *gigator* of Edward I   347
Conrad, Master, King of Heralds of Sprus   212
Conrad, minstrel of Archbishop of Cologne   76
Conrad, piper of Edward I   347
Constance of Castile, wife of John of Gaunt   204
Constitutio Domus Regis   4
Conute, piper of Richard II   333
Conute, son of John, fiddler (*vidulator*)   56, 91
Conutz, piper of Edward the Black Prince   103
Conway   124
Cook, Hugh, trumpeter of Lord Beaumont   14
Cook, Piers, trumpeter of John of Gaunt   105, 107
Corff, William, harper   24 n.53
cornemusers   31, 101, 326, 328, 332, 336–7, 355
cornetts   80, 182, 322–3, 324 nn.37–8, 328, 334, 359–60
Cornish, William, *Fa la sol*   393
Couronnement de Louis   252
courts, minstrel *see* regulation and protection
Coventry   81, 97, 106–8, 122, 128–9, 131, 172 n.19, 356

civic ceremonies   133–4, 136–9
civic minstrels   148, 154–5, 158–9, 161
mystery plays   137
reception of royalty   143–5
Cowpen, James de *see* Capiny
Crakestreng, John, trumpeter of Earl Warenne   19, 36, 54 n.30, 57, 354
Crakill, Robert, trumpeter of Henry IV   111
Crécy, battle of   85, 101
Cremeryak, minstrel of Duke William   104
Cressy (Cressin), John de, minstrel   91–2
crowders/crowds/*crwth*   43, 65, 119, 123, 312, 316–17, 352
description of   347–8
Crowland, John, minstrel of Edward IV, and Marshal of Trumpeters of Richard III   17–18, 45–6
Crudworth, Robert, harper   133–4, 137
crwth see crowders/crowds/*crwth*

Dalfi d'Alvernhe, Count of Clermont and Montferrand, troubadour   275, 287
Damme   66
dancing   xxv–xxvi, 6, 53, 64, 79, 81, 86 n.52, 96, 98, 110, 115m 117–18, 123–4, 139, 177, 179, 181, 250, 308, 324, 328, 341, 347, 350, 357, 362, 365, 391
banning of   120
instruction in   353
notation of dance-music   228, 363, 364 n.6, 365, 371, 375, 376, 380, 383
monophonic   366–8
in two voices   365, 368–70, 374–81
in three voices   384
Daniel, Arnaut   275
Dante Alighieri   275
David II, King of Scots   104, 307
Davy, William, minstrel of Henry VII   9
De Heraudie   295
Decessid, John *see* Cecile, John de
definitions and terminology   xxiv–xxvi, 121, 148–51, 328–9
Delalaunde, Stephen, minstrel   353 n.175, 360
Dengaigne, John, yeoman of Edward II   34
Denosse, Richard, minstrel of Henry VII   360
Denys, Thomas, minstrel of Edward II   37
Depe, John de, trumpeter of Edward I   30–2, 57, 74, 167, 396
Derby, Earl of *see* Henry IV, King of England
Dewes, Giles, lute-player of Henry VII   345, 360
Dexestre, Ralph, trumpeter of Edward the Black Prince   101–2

Dieppe 57
Docking, Thomas 121
Dominic, gitterner of Queen Isabella 5 n.9
Dominic, trumpeter of Henry VII 358
Doncaster 58
Doncaster, Nicholas de, trumpeter of Earl Warenne 19, 36, 54 n.30, 57, 354
Dorre (Dore), Richard, string-player of Edward II 47, 174–5
Dosenill, Robert de, constable of Pontefract castle 31
Dovayn 171
Dover 38, 66, 100, 120, 148, 156–7, 175–6, 190, 192, 194–6
Drake, John, waferer of Edward I 9, 20–1, 23, 41, 47–8, 91, 349–50
Draper, Thomas, minstrel of Edward IV 15 n.12
Druet, minstrel-king of Gilbert de Clare, earl of Gloucester 204, 209, 211, 214
Druettus, minstrel 91
Ducheman, William, trumpeter of Edward IV 17–18
dulcina 9, 63, 315, 325–6, 328–9, 333–4, 359
Dunfermline 31, 335
Dunkirk 176
Dunrine, minstrel of Edward I 91
Dunstable, John 389
Dunwich, Robert, trumpeter of Howards 113
Durham 2, 71, 120–5, 158, 169–70
  Bishop of 118–19
  itineraries of minstrels 188–90
duties of minstrels 73–4, 212
  alms-giving 76–8
  ceremonial occasions 78–84, 82, 95, 110
  civic minstrels 155–7
  coronations 85–90, 89
  feasts, major 5, 7–8, 84–5, 105, 108, 122–3, 349
  prelates, installation of 97–8
  private entertainment 74–6
  purifications 95–7, 209
  weddings 90–5, 110, 164
Dutton, Hugh de, steward of the constable of Chester 200–1
Dutton, Laurence 201
Duwes, Giles, lute-player of Henry VIII *see* Dewes

East Grimstead 194
Edinburgh 165, 182, 297, 323
Edmund, Earl of Kent 33
Edmund, Earl of Lancaster 67
Edward of Woodstock, the Black Prince 11, 20, 25, 32–3, 56–7, 61, 71, 74–5
  Crécy, victory at 85
  death of 104
  in fiction 256–7
  household of 100–4, 293, 355
  Poitiers, victory at 289, 336
Edward I, King of England 4, 12, 33–4, 47, 51, 74, 78, 85, 151, 170–1, 210–11, 213, 241, 277, 297, 299, 305, 321, 323, 353–4
  elegy for 305–6
  gifts to minstrels 28–9, 31, 54, 67, 75, 77, 91
  itinerary of 58, 59, 60
  liveries of minstrels 23
  personnel, minstrel 43, 47, 54–5, 57–8, 60–1, 65, 330–2, 335, 344, 347
  residence of minstrels 39–41
  wages of minstrels 14, 19–20, 103
  war on Scots 21
Edward II, King of England xxv, 5, 10, 30–1, 33, 61, 65, 67, 151, 167, 174, 177, 204, 206–7, 209, 214–15, 312, 324, 326, 342, 350, 353–4
  accession of 85
  knighting of 29, 93, 293
  liveries of minstrels 24–5
  personnel, minstrel 43, 47, 56, 331–2, 335, 344–5, 348
  residence of minstrels 39–41
  and Robert I the Bruce 296–9
  Vita Edwardi Secundi 298
  wages of minstrels 17, 19, 37, 58, 74, 94
Edward III, King of England 5, 8–10, 32, 49, 51, 68, 70, 76, 85, 92, 100, 151, 215–17, 225, 299, 301, 322, 342, 349–51, 353, 355
  birth of 118
  death of 104
  gifts to minstrels 28, 31, 67, 73, 93–5
  liveries of minstrels 23–4, 99
  marriage of 94
  personnel, minstrel 43–5, 47, 50, 55–7, 293, 326, 331–3, 336–7, 348
  residence of minstrels 40
  wages of minstrels 14–16, 19–20, 103
Edward IV, King of England 8, 36, 44, 62, 86, 95, 162, 190, 207, 220, 224, 294, 310, 322, 348–50
  gifts to minstrels 29
  liveries of minstrels 22–3, 38
  personnel, minstrels 43, 49, 52, 329, 334
  residence of minstrels 38
  and St Albans, Battle of 298
  wages to minstrels 15, 17–18, 22, 37
Edward V, King of England 143–5
Egremont, Lord 187
Einhart 284

432 Index

Eland, Nicholas de, harper of Edward I   32, 57, 74
Elder, William, minstrel of Henry VII   9
Eleanor, Princess, Countess of Guelders   77, 92, 165, 173–9, 215
Eleanor, Queen, wife of Alfonso VIII of Castile   263
Eleanor of Castile, Queen, wife of Edward I   95
Eleanor of Aquitaine, Queen, wife of Henry II   263, 273–6
Eleanor of Provence, Queen, wife of Henry III   276
Eleanor, wife of Hugh le Despenser   29, 93
Elias, piper of Edward III   19
Elizabeth, daughter of John of Gaunt   109
Elizabeth, Princess, wife of John, Count of Holland, and of Humphrey de Bohun, Earl of Hereford   29, 56, 91, 95, 18, 211, 330, 335, 350, 354
Elizabeth I, Queen of England   207, 224
Elizabeth Woodville, Queen, wife of Edward IV   86–7, 89–90, 96, 143
Elizabeth of York, Queen, wife of Henry VII   87, 89–90, 96
Elizabeth de Burgh, wife of Lionel of Antwerp   92, 113, 168, 393
Elizabeth Berkeley, wife of Richard Beauchamp, Earl of Warwick   112
Elland, Yorks.   57
Ely   259–61
   Bishop of   119
Emaré   252–3
Enguerrand de Coucy   93
Estoire de Merline, L'   262–3
Eston   37
Eu   32
Everlin, shawmist of John of Aragon   103 n.23
Exeter   129, 140, 148, 155, 315
Eynsham, William, minstrel of Edward IV   220

fabliaux   229, 240, 254, 257–8, 263; *see also* Vidal, Raimon, *Castia Gilos*
faburden and fauxbourdon   383–5, 398
Faidit, Gaucelm   275
Falla con misuras   374–5
fame
   and Chandos Herald   299
   and the *gestour*   291–4
   and literary history   311–14
   memorialists, knightly suspicion of   309–11
   memorialists, minstrels as

   chivalric   294–6
   and Minot, Lawrence   299
   praise or blame, anonymous songs of   301–6
   shame, songs of   307–9
Farebourn, Robert de, *tympanista* of constable of Pontefract castle   31–2, 326 n.47, 336
Farness, John, minstrel of Henry VII   359
Fawkes, John, minstrel of Henry VII   360
Faxfleet   60
fees and wages   14–22, 40, 51, 89, 97, 99, 103, 105–9, 111–13, 116, 122–4, 141–2, 152–4, 168–9, 188, 192, 196, 209, 215, 238, 294–5, 324, 397; *see also* gifts and grants
Felix namque   382–3
Fenes, William de   350
fiddlers/fiddles   xxvii, 5–7, 10, 14, 40, 43, 51, 56, 64–5, 67, 78 n.22, 101, 111, 121, 123, 139, 171, 200–1, 250, 278, 294, 312, 323, 333, 341, 345, 351–3, 368–70, 381–2
   description of   346–7
   in fiction   250
   iconography   25, 27, 77, 232, 233, 317
   liveries of   25, 26
   residence of   45
   surviving fiddles   315
   travelling   171
Finchesle, Robert de, *vigilis* of Edward I   20–1, 41, 330 n.66, 331
fistulators   156, 328, 333, 337
Fitz Lybkyn (FitzLibkin), Hanekin (Hankin), minstrel and marshal of Edward III   16, 44–5, 55, 332, 355 *and see under* Hankyn
FitzHugh, Lord   187
Flagilet, piper of Edward III   332, 355
Flamenca   266–7
Flint   14
Florence   31
flutists/flutes   42, 329–30, 337
   description of   327–8
Foix   271
Folkestone   190, 196
Folsank, Ranulph, trumpeter of Edward I   215
Fotheringay   14
Foxlee, Gilbert, clerk of Oxford   139
Francekinus, nakerer   28 n.65, 37, 54–5
Francis, John, minstrel of Edward III   16
Frank, trumpeter of Henry VII *see* Bocard, Frannc
fraternities, minstrel   199
   guilds, religious and trade   218–19
   in London   219–24

provincial 222–6
Frederick I Barbarossa, Holy Roman Emperor 264
Freman, Thomas, trumpeter of Henry VII 182, 358
Freman, William, trumpeter of Henry VII 358
Frente, Edmund, trumpeter of John, Lord Howard 115
Frere, John, trumpeter of Henry VII 358
Freville, Sir Baldwin 109
Frith, John, wait of London 152
Froissart, Jean, 239, 261, 266, 301, 307, 313, 357
  Meliador 262
Frysh, Hankyn, minstrel of John of Gaunt 106
Fulham 107
Furnes, John, minstrel of Henry VII 359

Gabriell, minstrel of Margaret Tudor 182
Gaimar, *Estoire des Engleis* 289
Gainsborough 60
Garceon, John, trumpeter of Edward I 48, 54
Garsie, John, trumpeter of Edward II 47, 74
Garsynton, Elias de, minstrel of Edward II 39, 47–8
Garter, King of Arms of Edward IV 294
Gaveston, Piers, Earl of Cornwall 94, 97
Gayt, Walter, *vigilis* of Edward III 332
Gece, John, trumpeter of Henry VII 358
Geffrey, Richard, piper of Henry V 333–4
Geneva 66
Geoffrey of Vinsauf, *Poetria nova* 267
Geoffrey, Duke of Brittany 276
George, Duke of Clarence 15 n.12, 49
Gerard le Wayte, *vigilator* of Edward III 19
Gerard, *vigilis* of Queen Philippa 168
Gest de Fouke filtz Waryn 313
Gestour (Reymer), Thomas, minstrel 142
gestours 43, 46, 100 n.3, 101, 121 n.106, 124, 132, 142, 291–4, 306, 311, 314, 344, 352
Ghent 177–8, 241, 309
Gibson, John, minstrel of John of Gaunt 109
gifts and grants 28–9, 54–5, 99, 101–4, 107–10, 116, 125
  horses 36–8, 102, 111
  retirement 70–2, 124–5, 161
  weddings 91–5
gigatores 37, 48, 54, 347, 353
Gilbert de Clare, Earl of Gloucester 204
Gilbert, harper of Edward I 14
Gilbert, trumpeter of Edward I 10
Gilbert, wait of Westminster 330
Gildesburgh, trumpeter 62
Giles, Peter 71 n.83

Giles of Rome, *De regimine principum* 313
Gillotus, harper of Hugo of Cressingham 28 n.63
gitterners/gitterns 5 n.9, 10, 43, 55, 294, 317, 318, 341, 352–3
  description of 342
  surviving gitterns 342
Glasebury, Henry, minstrel of Marshal of Minstrels of Edward IV and Henry VII 45, 51 n.12, 52, 359
gleeman 278
Glyn Dwr, Owen, Prince of Wales 207
Go hert hurt with adversitie 389–90
Goddislond, John, minstrel 153
Godscalk, piper of Edward III and of Edward the Black Prince 36, 332, 355
Goldfynch, William, minstrel 153
Goodyere, John, groom of Chamber of Henry VII 52–3, 62
Gough, Hans, piper of John of Gaunt 105–7
Gravelines 176
Gray, Sir Thomas, warden of Norham Castle 297–8
Green, Thomas, minstrel of Henry VI 54, 220
Grene (Green), Robert, minstrel of Edward IV and Richard III 17–18, 52–3
Grene, Robert, minstrel of Henry VII 9
Grene, William, minstrel of Henry VII 9, 359
Grennyng, Thomas, minstrel of Henry VII 359
Grevyll, William, minstrel 140
Grey, King of Heralds 211, 214
Grey, Robert, minstrel of Edward IV 15 n.12
Greyhead, herald-king 210
Greyndon, John de, minstrel of Bishop of Durham 118
'Graysteil' 370, 373
Grimsby 148, 157
Grisecote, mime or actor 91–2
grooms (*garciones*) 4, 8, 22, 24, 29, 34, 41, 48, 51–2, 54–6, 63, 71, 105, 107–8, 114, 324 n.37, 334, 347, 349
  training 55, 62
Grosvenor, Sir Richard 239
Grosvenor, Sir Robert 309, 311, 314
guets 146, 150
Guildford, Richard, minstrel of Richard II 70
Guilhelma of Benauges, wife of Peire de Gavaret 274
Guillotus, harper of Bishop of Durham 118–19
Guillotus, queen's psaltery-player 37, 317

Gunradus, German *gigator* 37
guslars 281–2, 285
Guy de Dampierre, Count of Flanders 240
Guy of Warwick 292
Guysnes 308–9

Haich, John, trumpeter of Edward IV 18
Haliday, Thomas, minstrel of Henry V 7, 62
Haliday, Walter, minstrel of Henry V, Marshal of Minstrels of Henry VI 7, 45–6, 54, 61, 89, 220
Haliday (Halliday), William, minstrel of Henry V and Henry VI 7, 14, 184
Halidon Hill, battle of 299–300
Hampton, John de, minstrel of Edward III 16
Hankyn, piper of Edward the Black Prince 103
Hankyn, piper of John of Gaunt 105–6, 109
Hanneye, minstrel of Edward III 16
Hans, minstrel of Edward the Black Prince 74, 103
Harbledown 178
Harden, John, harper 72
Hardiberd, Thomas, minstrel of Henry V 7
Harding, John, minstrel of Edward II and Edward III 20, 316–17, 325, 329, 331–3
Harding, William, *vigilator* of Edward III and Richard II 16, 19–20, 332–3
Harper, Barry 125
Harper, Heliseus, minstrel 125
Harper, John, mason 125
Harper, John, provisioner 125
Harper, John, squire of Chamber of Edward IV 52
Harper, Thomas, groom and valet of the Chamber of Henry VI 52, 54
Harper, William, minstrel 125
harpers/harps xxii, xxiv, 5, 7, 10, 24 n.53, 28 n.63, 42–3, 47–8, 51–4, 56–7, 62, 71, 78, 100, 112–13, 115, 118–19, 121–5, 144, 197, 211, 213, 215–16, 246, 248, 273, 290, 294, 312–13, 345, 347, 352–3, 381–2, 389, 393–4
  and Church 97, 117–19, 238
  description of 342–4
  fees, wages, and gifts 14, 32, 70, 72, 74–5, 77 n.18, 91, 132, 193, 238
  in fiction 249–50, 262–3, 265–6, 277–9, 291–2, 307
  iconography xxiii, 32, 33, 231–3
  and nostalgia 256–7, 260
  residence of 39–40
  royal persons as owners of 29
  surviving harps 315, 343
  of towns and guilds 133–4, 137–9, 160

n.59, 187
  training 63–4
  travelling 170–1, 187
  at weddings 91, 93
Harpour, Thomas 125
Haspere, John de, minstrel of Henry VII 360
Hastings, battle of 236, 287–9, 314
Hatche (Hache), minstrel of Edward IV and Richard III 17–18
Hatfield 96
Haukyn 349, 249-51
Havelock/Havelok 245, 253, 255–6, 285, 306
Hawking, Thomas, minstrel of Edward IV 17–18
Hawkyns (Hawkins), John, minstrel of Richard III and Henry VII 9, 18
Hedele, William de, wait of Edward III 333
Helen, wife of Richard Pilke, waferer xxv, 350
Helen, wife of Robert de Maule 94
Hennyngis, William, harper 246
Henry III, Duke of Brabant 240
Henry, Duke of Lancaster 301
Henry, Earl of Derby *see* Henry IV (Bolingbroke), King of England
Henry of Grosmont, Earl and Duke of Lancaster 104
Henry, fiddler of Queen Philippa 77
Henry, German *gigator* 37, 347
Henry, harper 91
Henry VII, Holy Roman Emperor 296
Henry II, King of England 250, 263, 273, 275–6, 287
Henry III, King of England 259, 273, 276–7
Henry IV (Bolingbroke), King of England (Earl of Derby) 29, 47, 50, 81, 93, 95, 321, 333, 338, 350
  coronation of 135–6
  household of 111
  marriage of 110
  Prussia, expedition to 111
  wages of minstrels 20
Henry V, King of England 6–7, 42, 47, 84, 112, 143, 151, 301, 342
  harp playing of 29
  liveries of minstrels 25
  marriage of 95
  personnel, minstrel 43–4, 54, 108, 333–4, 345
  wages of minstrels 15, 20–1
Henry VI, King of England 7–8, 95, 112, 142, 207, 217, 220, 224–5, 298–9, 321–2, 349
  gifts to minstrels 29
  liveries of minstrels 23–4
  mental illness of 62

personnel, minstrel   43, 52, 61–2, 108, 184–5, 197, 334, 345–6
wages of minstrels   15, 21–2, 38
Henry VII, King of England   9, 29, 95, 338, 342, 392
  coronation of   86–7
  funeral of   51
  gifts to minstrels   29, 71, 352
  personnel, minstrel   43–4, 50, 345–7, 378
  reorganisation of minstrels   358–61
  residence of minstrels   41
  wages to minstrels   22
Henry VIII, King of England   95, 140, 179, 322, 327–8, 345, 393
  coronation of   80, 194, 358 378
  liveries of minstrels   25
  musical instruments of   30
Henry, the Young King, of England   276
Henry, Lord Strange   248
Henry, piper   67
Henry, piper of John of Gaunt   105–7
Henry, piper and marshal of Richard II   45, 333
Herald, Somerset   182
heralds/heraldry   xxv, 31, 95, 106, 141–2, 149, 174, 176–9, 182, 206, 320–1, 348, 378, 398
  banquets   80
  and chivalry   301, 303, 307–11, 313–14; see also Chandos Herald
  coronations   86–90
  duties   212, 214, 225, 296–8, 314
  feasts   85
  iconography   82, 234
  in literature   256–7, 261, 266, 292, 298, 311
  king of   12, 23, 44, 164–5, 208–17, 225, 395
  marshal of   44
  as memorialists, chivalric   294–6
  as messengers   113, 167–8
  processions   79, 86–8, 96
  purifications   96
  territories   212–14
  tournaments and jousts   81, 82, 83–4, 102, 104
  wages and gifts   89, 93, 102, 104, 108–10, 177
  weddings   93
  at York   186, 189
Herebert, minstrel   123, 237–8
Heroune, clerk of royal chapel (Scotland)   69–70
Hert, John, trumpeter of Henry VII   358
Hert, Walter, *vigilis* of Queen Isabella   67–8
Hertford   110
'sHertogenbosch   175, 177
Hills, Richard, trumpeter of Edward IV and Richard III   17–18
Hills, Simon de, groom of John de Newenton   54

Historia Regum Francorum   239
historiography   xxvi, 128
Hoggeston (Ogerston)   335 n.86
Homer   229, 282
Horn   277–8, 285
horns *see* trumpeters/trumpets
Hotham, John, Bishop of Ely   50
households, royal and elite   xxvi–xxvii
  of Church   116–25
  clergy, personal minstrels of   118–20
  dependent   10–11
  domestic context   99–100
  of Edward the Black Prince   100–4
  of Eleanor, Princess   173–5
  of Howards   113–15
  of Lancaster   104–11
  of Northumberland   115–16
  ranks   4–5
  of religious houses   120–5
  royal   3–9, 50–3, 99, 184, 328–35
  sources   2–9, 11–12
  transfers between   49–50, 58
  Wardrobe and Chamber   11–12, 17, 50–3, 348
  of Warwick   112–14, 183
  see also fees and wages; recruitment
Howard, John, Lord Howard, Duke of Norfolk   63–4, 350
  household of   113, 115
Hugo le Despenser   29, 93–4
Hugo le Trumpeour   219
Hull   153, 155, 159
Hultescrane, Henry, piper of John of Gaunt   105–7
Humberston   72
Humphrey, Duke of Gloucester   15 n.12
Hunting of the Cheviot   248
Huon de Bordeaux   254–5
Hyde   124
Hythe   100, 190, 192, 194–6

iconography   xxii, *xxiii*, xxiv, xxvii, 26, 27, 33, 82, 89, 117, 228, 233, 241, 242, 324
  of instruments   230, 315–18, 320, 324, 328, 338–40, 343, 346–7
  limitations of   231–4
  seals of minstrels   230–1, 316–17, 318, 325, 347
instruments
  civic minstrels   160–1
  cost of   101–2, 115, 136
  coverings for   32–3
  iconography of   230, 315–18, 320, 324, 328, 338–40, 343, 346–7
  keyboards and percussion, descriptions of   335–40

instruments (cont'd)
   owned by minstrels 30–6
   reed instruments, descriptions of 319–28
   repairs to 33–4, 35, 48, 101, 115, 125, 136, 335
   of royal persons 29–30
   string instruments, bowed, descriptions of 346–8
   string instruments, plucked, descriptions of 340–5
   surviving 315, 342–3
   wind instruments, descriptions of 319–28
Interludium de clerico et puella 302
Isaac, Heinrich, *Benedictus* 393
Isabella of France, Queen, wife of Edward II 67–8, 70, 77, 118, 125, 173, 175, 336
Isabella, wife of Enguerrand de Coucy 93
Ithel, trumpeter of Edward II 19, 354
itineraries of minstrels
   circuits 183–6
   at Durham cathedral priory 188–90
   in Kent 184, 189–96
   as regular feature 196–7
   at York 183–9

Jakelot, piper of Edward the Black Prince 103
Jakelyn, piper of Edward the Black Prince 102–3
Jaket, minstrel of Henry VII 9, 358
Jaket, Marcus, minstrel of Elizabeth of York 9
James IV, King of Scots 76, 179, 238, 323, 378
James, minstrel of Howards 115
Janettus (Janotus), psaltery-player of Queen Isabella 5 n.9, 70, 125
Janin, organist 335
Janinus, nakerer of Edward the Black Prince 33
Janinus le Leutor, minstrel of Edward II 91
Janyn, citoler 342
Janotus, nakerer of Edward II 74
Januche, trumpeter of Edward I 74
Jausbert de Puycibot, *joglar* 274
Jean II, King of France 32, 104, 336–7
Jean de Brabant 241, 242
Jehan de Bodel, trouvère 240
Jeffrey, harper 70, 124
Jeffrey, Arnold, organ-player of Prince Arthur 22
Jeo hay en vos tote may fiance 386, 388
Jerome of Moravia 341, 346, 369
Jeu de Saint Nicholas 240
Joan of Acre, wife of Earl of Gloucester 211, 214

Joan, wife of Earl Warenne 29, 93
Joan of Navarre, wife of Henry IV 29
Joan, wife of John Cliff II 21
joculatores 121, 124, 246, 275
joglars see recitation
Johannes, Edward, sackbut player of Henry VII 359
Johannes of Trokelowe 307–8
John de Hertford, abbot-elect of St Albans 355
John of Tong, cleric of Princess Eleanor 174
John of Artois, Count of Eu 101–2
John Cokeren, Pety, rebec-player 353 n.175, 360
John, Count of Holland 29, 56, 91
John, crowder of Shrewsbury 119
John II, Duke of Brabant 67
John, Duke of Brittany 93
John of Gaunt, Earl and Duke of Lancaster 10–11, 49–50, 95, 212, 214, 217, 224, 324, 356
   household of 104–11
   and minstrel courts 202–5, 208
John, fiddler 56
John, harper of Henry IV 10, 93
John, King of England 273–4
John Balliol, King of Scots 171
John, lute-player of Edward I 40
John, messenger and minstrel of Count of Savoy 36
John, minstrel of Edward the Black Prince 102
John, Master, nakerer 67
John, nakerer of Edward II 5
John, nakerer of Henry IV 47
John, Master, organist of Earl Warenne 33–4, 35, 47–8, 335
John, Prior of Maxstoke 97
John, trumpeter of Edward I 167, 215
John le Trumpour 71 n.83
John, *vidulator* of Edward I 91
John, waferer of Edward the Black Prince 103
John, waferer of Edward III 47
John le Botiler, *Roi Bruant* 215
John of Aragon 103 n.23
John le Nakerer 71 n.83
Jongleur of Ely 258–61, 277
jongleurs 207, 214 n.68, 228–9, 239–41, 243, 248–9, 252, 286–7, 290, 293, 314
Joufroi de Poitiers 273
Joye, Hugh, *vigilator* of Edward III 16
Joye, Hugo, *vigilator* of Henry VI 334
Justinian, Dominic, trumpeter of Henry VII 182, 358
Juvenal 243

Kalenda Maya 370, 373
Kalfoort 178
Katherine of Valois, Queen, wife of Henry V 29, 95, 135, 334
Kenilworth 109
Kenner, lute-player of Margaret Tudor 182, 345, 360
Kennington 69
King Horn 245, 283, 313
King's Langley 335
Kingston, Dorset 70
Kingston-on-Hull 60
Kirkham 60
Knaresborough 209
Kyng Alisaunder 244
Kyngorn, John de, flutist of Edward I 328

La Rochelle 273
La Tour Landry 25
Lacy, Edmund, Bishop of Exeter 223
Lacy, Roger, constable of Chester 199–201
Lambert de Guînes, Bishop of Arras 240
Lambekin, taborer 16
Lamport (Langport), William, watchman of Edward III and Richard II 16, 332–3
Langland, William, *Piers Plowman* xxiv, 243–4, 249–51, 256, 260, 266, 312
Langley 33, 35, 48
Langton, William, minstrel and marshal of Henry V and Henry VI 7, 44–5, 62, 184, 208 n.32
Laud Troy Book 292
Launceston 223
Laurence, harper 91
Laurence le Cornour 324
Laȝamon, *Brut* 278–9
Le Puy 271
Leicester 130, 133–4, 154–5, 158, 219
Lenton priory 58, 60
Lescluses 176, 178–9
Lestivour, Hamon, bagpiper of Keeper of Wardrobe 91
Leutor, John, trumpeter of Edward I 215, 345
Lewes 194
Lewys *see* Liners
Leyland, Richard de, harper 93
Libekin (Lubkin, Lybkin), piper of Earl of Northampton and of Edward III 50, 55, 332, 355
Libeaus Desconus 243, 292
Liber Niger (Black Book) 8–9, 22, 28, 37–8, 43–4, 46–7, 53, 73, 79, 90, 151, 207, 327, 329–30, 334, 346, 348–9, 358–9, 361
Limebrook, Herefordshire 120

Lincoln 61, 115, 117, 130, 147–8, 155, 158, 222–3, 284
  carvings of instruments 315
Lincoln, Hugo, *vigilis* of Edward I and Edward II 331
Liners (Lewys), Hakenet de, minstrel 353 n.175, 360
Lionel of Antwerp 92, 96
Liston Overhaul 351
literature, minstrels in 228–30, 234, 235–7, 239–41, 242, 249
  corruption and fragmentation 260–8
  and literary history 311–14
  and nostalgia for chivalry 256–7, 260, 262, 313–14
  rogue, minstrel as 257–60
  stylistic features 252–5
  see also heralds, in literature
Little, Robert, trumpeter and herald-king *see* Robert Little
Little Alein (Alain) 55, 327, 332
Little Andrew 28 n.65, 55
Little William, organist of Countess of Hereford 55, 335
liveries xxv, xxvii, 2, 63, 105, 107, 115, 120, 197, 208, 218, 226, 230, 250, 324, 333, 345
  categories of 22–3, 28
  civic minstrels 148–9, 153–5, 157, 161–2
  Pentecost 24–5
  royal 3, 10, 12, 22–8, 56–7, 74, 99, 184–5, 215, 358–60, 378
  of towns 130, 134–5
  and travelling 164, 167, 169
  weddings and coronations 25, 93
Livy 313
London 40, 57, 63–4, 92, 115, 131, 143, 171, 194, 248
  civic ceremonies 135, 138–9
  civic minstrels 147, 149–50, 152–3, 155–6, 159, 161
  coronations 86–90
  fraternities, minstrel 219–24
  guilds, minstrels employed by 132, 138, 141–2
  minstrel-schools 66–8
  population 129
  processions 79, 84, 86–8, 96
  St Paul's 77–8, 84, 118, 120, 122, 143, 175, 178
  see also Southwark; Westminster
London, John de, trumpeter of Edward I 30–2, 40, 47–8, 54–5, 57
Longespee, William de 304–5
Lorydon, Marcus, minstrel of Elizabeth of York 9, 360

Lorymer, Thomas, harper 63–4
Louis, Duke of Touraine 68
Louis VIII, King of France 273
Louis IX, King of France 88
Loyter, Hugo, minstrel 189
Ludkin, King of Heralds of Germany 212
Ludkin, piper 96
Ludwig, son of Ruprecht, King of the
    Romans 93
Lund, Walter, harper of Chichester 78
lute-players/lutes xxii, 40, 43, 64, 69, 91,
    115–16, 119, 123, 133, 137–8, 140, 144, 182,
    189, 239, 294, 323 n.23, 342, 352–5, 360,
    381–2, 389
  description of 344–5
  iconography 232
Luter, Thomas 140
Lydd 38, 100, 120, 190, 194, 196
Lynn 153, 155–6, 158
Lynne, Walter, minstrel of Henry IV 10, 93

Magote, mime or actor 91–2
Maisham (Meysham), William, minstrel and
    serjeant of Henry VI 7, 47, 62, 333–4
Makejoie, Matilda, *saltatrix* 350
Malhard, John, minstrel of Edward III 55
Malines 177–8
Malory, Sir Thomas 307
Mamay, Jusup, Kirghiz bard 280
Manchester 117, 315
Manning (Mannyng) de Brunne,
    Robert 117, 283–4, 292
Mantzt, Miemus de, minstrel of
    Gascony 28 n.63
manuscripts, alleged minstrel 241–9, 362,
    291–2
Marcabru, troubadour 273, 307
March, Cambs. 117
March, King of Arms of Edward IV 294
March, Richard, minstrel 153
Marchis, Walter le, King of Heralds of
    Edward I or of Henry Percy 210,
    212–14
Marchis, minstrel of Edward III 20
Margaret, Countess of Cornwall 97
Margaret of England, Princess, wife of John II
    of Brabant 67, 350
Margaret of Anjou, Queen, wife of Henry
    VI 143
Margaret Tudor, Queen, wife of James IV of
    Scotland 76, 144 n.66, 165, 179–82,
    323, 359, 378
Margery, wife of William, trumpeter xxv
Margery, wife of William de Brompton 203
Marie, Queen, wife of Philip III of
    France 241, 242
Marie de France, *Chevrefeuil* 267
Markassyn, Jenyn, minstrel of Henry
    VII 360
Marquis, minstrel of Henry VII 9
Marshal, Robert, minstrel of Henry VI 45,
    61–2, 184, 220
Marshall, Sir William 251
Marshall, William, groom of Chamber of
    Henry VI 52
marshals of minstrels 9, 15, 20, 44–7, 52, 89,
    108, 217–18, 220, 221 n.98, 222, 225, 293,
    359; *see also* trumpets, marshals of
Martin, John, trumpeter of Edward the Black
    Prince 101–2
Martinettus, taborer of Edward I 33, 91
Mary, daughter of John of Brittany 93
Mary Bohun, Queen, wife of Henry IV 110
Mason, Alexander, Marshal of Minstrels of
    Henry VII 9, 15, 17–18, 45–6, 293, 344
'Master', style of 47–8
Masu, Alex, sackbut player of Henry VII 359
Matilda of Lancaster, wife of William, Duke of
    Bavaria 104
Maule, Robert de 94
Mauprine (Maupryne), John, piper, minstrel
    of Edward II 5, 71, 71 n.83, 94, 331–2,
    355
Mautravers, Sir John 75
Maxstoke 122, 124
Mayanus of Champagne, herald-king 210
Mayho (Mayhue, Mayow), Thomas, minstrel
    of Henry VII 9, 17–18, 359
Maysham, William, minstrel of Henry
    VI 184
Mededović, Avdo, *guslar* 282
Meliorus, harper of Edward I 75
Melton 37
Melton, John, *vigilator* of Henry IV and Henry
    V 6, 333
Merlin, fiddler 67
Merlin, fiddler of Queen Philippa 40 n.118
Merlyn, Thomas, valet of Edward III 16
Merton, Geoffrey de, *vigilis* of Edward II 331
Metcalf, William, minstrel 133–4
Mézières, Philippe de 31
Michel, John, minstrel of Henry V 7
Middelton, John de, minstrel of Edward
    III 16
Middleton 60
Middleton, Guy (Guy Waite),
    fistulator 328–9
Middleton, Guy, *vigilator* of Henry V and
    Henry VI 6, 15 n.7, 333–4
Minot, Lawrence 299–301

minstrel-kings 216–18
Modon, Zorzi Trombetta da *see* Zorzi
Montferrand 271
Montfort, Simon de 276, 301–2
Monthaut, minstrel 91
Monthaut, John de, herald-king of Edward I 211
Montvalent 336
Moray, Bishop of 119
More, Richard, *vigilator* of Henry VI 334
More, Robert, wait and *vigilator* of Henry VI and Edward IV 8, 62, 334
More, William, harper of Henry VIII 393–4
Morel (Morellus), Nicholas (Colin), King of Heralds of Edward I 91, 210–11
Morlanus, bagpiper of Edward the Black Prince *see* Morleyns
Morle, William de, King of the North, herald-king of Edward II 5, 213–16
Morley, William de, minstrel of Edward I 14, 39
Morleyns, John de, cornemuser of Edward III 67, 101, 326, 332, 355
Mortimer, Robert 24
Morton, Master John (Senior) 246
Mouskes, Philippe 272
Mumin, *guslar* 282
Mylton, Thomas de 91
Myttok, King of Minstrels of Brabant 212

Naille, Hans, sackbut player of Henry VII 358
Nájera 314
nakerers/nakers xxvii, 5–6, 11, 28 n.65, 33, 42–3, 47, 54–5, 67, 71 n.83, 74, 88, 106–8, 110–11, 333, 351, 354
    description of 337–8
Naunton, Hugo de, harper of Edward II 5, 54
Neckam, Alexander 150
Neusom (Newsom), Henry de, harper of Edward II 40, 56, 216
Nevill, Richard, Earl of Salisbury 187
Neville, George, Archbishop of York 97
Neville's Cross, battle of 299
New Romney 38, 120, 157, 190, 192, 194–6
Newcastle under Lyme 111, 203–4
Newcastle upon Tyne 31, 156, 158, 181–2, 188
Newenton, John de, harper of Edward I 47–8, 54, 347
Nibelungenlied 281
Nicholas, *cornator* 323
Nicholas, organist of Edward the Black Prince 101

Nicholas Trompour, minstrel of Edward III 16
Nijmegen 173–5, 177
Normand, Peter de (Peter Gaffrer), waferer 350
Norreys, Andrew, King of Heralds of Edward III 23, 217
Norroy, King of Arms of Edward IV 294
Northampton 156
Northampton, Stephen de, *vigilis* 70
Northleigh, minstrel of Edward III 20
Norwich 122, 129, 132–3
    Bishop of 119
    carvings of instruments 315
    civic minstrels 148, 154–8, 161–2
Norys, Thomas, trumpeter of Henry V 7
notation *see* dancing, notation of dance-music; repertory, instrumental, literacy and notation
Nottingham 130, 155, 158
Nusselyn, *vigilator* of Richard II 333
Nytherton, minstrel 140

O rosa bella 389
'Oath of the Herald When He Is Made before his Sovereign Lord' 310–11
Ogerston 335
Orderic Vitalis 284
organists/organs 11 n.32, 22, 33–4, 35, 42–3, 47–8, 54–5, 101, 115, 117, 143, 145, 362, 381–2, 389
    description of 335–6
    iconography 232
Orleton, Adam, Bishop of Winchester 123, 340
Ospring 178
Ossian, legendary poet xxii, *xxiii*
Oswestry 41
Oundle 14
Overton, William, yeoman of Henry VI 349
Ovid, *Metamorphoses* 267
Oxford 139, 245

Page, King of Heralds 91, 211
page/*pagettus* 4, 83, 113–14
Palling, William, wait 159
Panel (Panell), John, trumpeter of Henry V 7, 46–7
Paris 168
    minstrel schools 66–7, 69, 336
    Notre Dame 293
Paris, Matthew 276
Paten, Richard, minstrel and Marshal of Trumpets 45–6

Patrick, trumpeter of Edward I 70
Paynell, John, minstrel of Edward IV, Henry V, and Richard III 17–18, 45, 54, 62
Paynell, William, minstrel of Henry VI 15, 62
Paynter (Payntour), Thomas, trumpeter of Edward IV and Richard III 17–18
Payte, John, trumpeter 62
Pejon, Thomas, minstrel of Henry VII 359
Peter, Edward de, sackbut player 182, 358–9
Peler, John de, trumpeter of Edward IV and Richard III, sackbut player of Henry VII 17–18, 182, 358–9
Perche, Earl of 114
Percival, William, *gestour* of Edward III and Richard II 293, 344
Percy, Henry 210, 213
Percy, Lord 122
performance xxiv, xxvi, xxviii, 65, 120, 228, 234, 398
　concerted 351, 353–7
　in literature *see* literature, minstrels in
　loud and still 42–3, 90, 174, 231–2, 353–4, 359
　solo 351–2, 355
　voice accompaniment 352
　see also iconography; recitation; repertory, instrumental
Perrot (Perot), John, *cornemuser de montvalour* 31–3, 326, 336–7
Perth 70, 171
Pesaro, Guglielmo Ebreo da 374
Peter des Roches, Bishop of Winchester 276
Peter, King of Heralds north of Trent 213
Peter le Waffrur, trumpeter of Edward I 215
Peter le crouder 14
Peter le fitheler 14
Peter the Chanter 293
Peterkin, piper 67
Petrekyn, piper of John of Gaunt 106
Petrestre, John de, *vigilis* of Edward II 331–2
Petrucci, *Odhecaton* 393
Peut, John, trumpeter of Henry V 7
Phoebus, Gaston, Count of Foix 262
Philip de Windsor, bearward 177
Philippa, Princess, daughter of Henry IV 10, 25
Philippa of Hainault, Queen, wife of Edward III 24–5, 40 n.118, 76–7, 94, 96, 104, 168, 174 n.22, 350, 336
Philippa, Queen, wife of Erik IX of Denmark 93
Pickering 106
Pigeon, Richard, minstrel of Edward III 16

Pilke, Richard, waferer of Edward II xxv, 5, 41, 350
pipers/pipes/bagpipes 5 n.9, 6–10, 14, 16, 19, 32–3, 36, 42–3, 45, 50, 55, 61, 67, 101–3, 105–6, 110–11, 123, 179, 328, 336–7, 350, 352–3, 355–7, 368, 393
　description of bagpipes 326
　description of hornpipe 326–7
　in fiction 250
　iconography 26, 231, 317
　liveries 25, 26, 130
　and purifications 93
　in royal households 328–35
　surviving pipes 315
　of towns 130–3, 136–7, 151
　and weddings 93
　see also dulcina; flutes; *vigiles/vigilatores*
Plymouth 102
Poitiers 272–3, 289, 306, 336
Polydod, John, minstrel of Edward III 55
Polydod, Robert, minstrel of Edward III, and of Bishop of Ely 37, 50, 55, 119
Pontefract 14, 31, 107, 215
Ponthieu 24
Poole 156
Porchester, Roger de, waferer 36
Potweye, John, minstrel of Henry VII 360
Praga (Prage), Nicholas, fiddler and valet of Edward III 16, 51
Prat, John, minstrel of Edward III 16
Promptorium parvulorum 327
psaltery-players/psalteries 5 n.9, 10, 37, 43, 70, 125, 250, 294, 317, 352–3
　description of psalteries 345
　in fiction 250
Pseudo-Turpin 239
Purchaceour, minstrel of Edward II 37
Purchaseour, Thomas, minstrel 71 n.83
Pursuivant, Bluemantle 182

Quene note 375–81, 384, 393–4, 398

Radcliff (Ratclyff), Thomas, minstrel of Henry VI 7–8, 15, 62, 184
Radulphus le Gayte, *vigilis* of Edward III 332
Raffe, John, wait 160, 359
Raimon V, Count of Toulouse 276
Ralph, Abbot of St Augustine's, Canterbury 97
Ralph, piper of Edward III 333
Ralph, trumpeter of Edward the Black Prince 102–3
Ralph le Wayte, valet of Edward III 16
Ramsey 70, 125

Randal, Earl of Chester   199, 202
Raumpayn, William, wait   159
rebec-players/rebecs   115–16, 317, 347, 352–3, 360
recitation
  joglars as wanderers   269–73
  oral-formulaic   280–6
  and Taillefer   287–90
  tradition, English   278–86
  tradition, French   285–7
  troubadours/*joglars* and English court   273–8
recorders   9, 62, 144, 325, 327–9, 334, 359, 381
recruitment
  in Chamber and other departments   50–3, 348
  civic minstrels   153
  independent minstrels   56–62
  king's household   50–3
  transfers between households   49–50, 58
  young minstrels   54–6
Rede, Thomas, harper   64, 389
Reginald II, Count of Guelders   173
Reginald, waferer of Edward II   91
Reginaldus le Mentour   293
regulation and protection   198–9
  kings of heralds   208–16
  marshals   217–18
  minstrel courts   199–208
  minstrel kings   199, 205–5, 208, 212, 216–18
  see also fraternities, minstrel
Rentry, Nicholas de, minstrel of Edward II   5
repertory, instrumental   362–3
  compostion, notation-free   xxviii, 370–3
  dances in one and two voices   365–81
  ensemble music of fifteenth century   389, 392–4
  literacy and notation   xxvii, xxviii, 234, 363–4, 366, 391–3, 395, 398
  manuscripts of minstrels   241–9, 362, 391–2
  music in three voices   382–90
  other instrumental in two voices   381–2
residence of minstrels   38–41
retirement *see under* gifts and grants
Reve, Adam de, minstrel   47
Reymund Arnald de Rycan, minstrel of Edward II   5
Reynolds, John, wait   161
Rhuddlan Castle   199–202
rhymer/*rymer*/*rymour*   54, 65, 103, 119, 207, 293–4, 344, 348, 352
Richard de Swinfield, Bishop of Hereford   349

Richard, Duke of York   221
Richard, gitterner of Edward III   55
Richard le Harpeur, harper of Henry III   277
Richard I, King of England   273, 275–6, 305, 307, 310
Richard II, King of England   20, 45, 47, 50, 68–71, 86 n.52, 105, 108, 133, 144, 169, 205, 217, 293, 333, 349, 351
  coronation of   88
  gifts to minstrels   29
  marriage of   95, 110
Richard III, King of England   9, 113, 154, 181n35, 295, 354
  and College of Arms   216
  coronation of   46, 54, 88–9, 122, 159–60, 162
  wages of minstrels   15, 17–18
Richard, piper of Henry V   7
Richard, *rymour* of Edward I   54, 65, 293
Richard, trumpeter of Henry IV   10, 93
Richard, *vidulator* of Princess Eleanor   177–8
Richard, waferer   349
Richard, wait of Edward III   333
Richard Coer de Lyon   292, 295, 305
Richardyn, fiddler of Edward II   40
Riom   271
Robert VII, Baron of Béthune   239
Robert II, Count of Artois   240
Robert, harper of Abbot of Abingdon   119
Robert le Neim, herald-king   210
Robert Little, King of Heralds   24, 85, 97, 208–12, 215, 216, 297–8, 354, 395
Robert I the Bruce, King of Scots   296–9
Robert, trumpeter   123
Robert, waferer   187
Robertsbridge   194
Rochester   175, 189, 194, 196
Roet, Paon de   176 n.28
Roger, harper of Bishop of Ely   119
Roger, minstrel of Elizabeth de Burgh   393
Roger, piper of John of Gaunt   105, 107
Roger, trumpeter of Edward II   5, 28 n.65, 54–5
Roger, trumpeter of Edward III   96
Roger, *vigilis* of Edward the Black Prince   101
Roland le Fartere (le Pettour)   250
Rollekyn, piper of John of Gaunt   106
Roman de la Rose, Le   242, 313
Roman de Merlin, Le   286
Romance de Launcelot   313
romances   xxiv, 80, 228–30, 235–6, 243–5, 251–7, 262, 267, 312–13, 396; *see also chansons de geste*
Roos, Peter, trumpeter, *scutifer*   51
Ros, Guillotus de, minstrel of Edward I   91

Rose, Hugo de la, minstrel of Edward I   39
Rosendaal   177
Roxborough   74
Ruardinus, *vidulator* of Edward I   91
Rye   117, 192, 194–6
rymer/rymour see rhymer/*rymer/rymour*
Ryppes, John, wait   159, 161
Ryppes, Nicholas, wait   159

Sabulones   171
sackbuts   9, 22, 41, 182, 320–1, 355 n.192, 356 n.194, 357–60, 381
St Albans   62, 71 n.83, 355
   Battle of   298
St Andrews   70, 171
St Johnstone   31, 171, 336
St Michael's Mount   71, 104
St Swithun's *see under* Winchester
Salisbury, Lord   189–90
Salisbury, William de, waferer   70
Sandal   58
Sandwich   100, 153, 156–7, 159, 190, 194–6
Sanford   171
Sauthe, James, clarioner of John of Gaunt   105–7
Sautreour, William, minstrel of queen   40
Savaric de Mauléon, troubadour   273–4
Savernake (Cokeren), Pety John, rebec-player *see under* John Cokeren
Scarlet, John, trumpeter of Henry VII   358
Scarlett, William, wait   159–60, 162
Schene, Robert, wait   159
Scocia, Jakettus de *see* Capiny
scops   228, 235, 278–80, 285–7
Scot, John, trumpeter of Edward II   5, 28 n.65, 54–5
Scot, Robert   125
Scrope, Sir John   239
Scrope, Sir Richard, 1st baron of Bolton   309, 311, 314
scutifer see squires/*scutiferi*
Seege of Troye, The   292
Sensk   336
serjeanties   14, 17 n.16, 45–7, 86, 209, 350, 397
Shareshill, Staffs.   56–7
Shareshull, John de, harper of Edward III   56–7
shawms   9, 42–3, 52, 105, 107, 110, 176, 197, 328–9, 332–4, 337, 354–7, 358–9, 381
   and banquets   80
   of civic minstrels   160–1
   and coronations   88
   description of   325–6
   of towns   136–8, 147, 151
   wages of   22
Sheale, Richard, minstrel   171–2, 184 n.2, 248, 313
Shepherd, John, Warwick official   112
Sheyne, Robert, wait   159–61
Shrewsbury   119, 148, 155, 159, 223, 244
Sir Cleges   265–6
Sir Eglamour   80
Skirewith, Adam, *vigilis* of Edward I   41, 330 n.66, 331
Smeltes, piper of John of Gaunt   105–7
Smethley, William, wait of Chester   152
Smith, John, piper of Henry IV   111
Smithfield   68, 110
Snayth, Conute, fiddler of Henry V   7
socii   12–13, 57–8, 109, 182, 354
Soerus of Valencenis, cleric of Princess Eleanor   174
Somerset, John, minstrel of Lord Clifford   187
Song of Caerlaverock   302–3
Song of the Barons   301–2
South English Legendary   245
Southampton   153, 158
Southwark   129
Soz, minstrel of Edward the Black Prince   74, 103
Speke, Robert, wait   159
Spence(r), Thomas, minstrel of Henry VII   9, 359
Spofford, Thomas, Bishop of Hereford   120
Spolly, John, *vigilator* of Henry VI   334
squires/*scutiferi*   xxvii, 4, 13, 25, 28, 38, 40–1, 47, 51–3, 55, 63, 105, 114, 165, 176, 209–10, 309–11, 349–50
   wages   14, 19–20, 23, 36, 51, 58, 103, 108, 215, 294–5
Stakford, Gilbert, trumpeter of Edward the Black Prince   71, 104
Stanley, Edward, third Earl of Derby   248
Stanley Poem   248
Staunton, John de, *vigilis* of Edward I and Edward II   31, 41, 331
Stephen, King of England   4
Stevenson, Thomas, of Brabune   63
Stevenson, William, harper   63–4
Stirling   36, 170–1
Stoke by Nayland   115
Stratfleur   124
string-minstrels   8–9, 22, 42–3, 73, 334
   and purification   96
   see also citolers/citoles; crowders/crowds/crwth; fiddlers/fiddles; harpers/harps; gitterners/gitterns; lute-players/lutes; psaltery-players/psalteries; rebec-players/rebecs
Strutt, John, trumpeter of Henry VII   358
Sturmyn, John, trumpeter   133

Sturton, Michael de, minstrel of Edward I 57
Sturton, Walter de, harper of Edward I 57
Swan, Henry, minstrel of Henry VII 9, 359
Symond, John, taboret of Howards 113, 115

Taborer, Lambekin, minstrel of Edward III *see under* Lambekin
taborers/tabors/tabretts 6, 9, 32–3, 42–3, 102, 110, 113, 115, 215, 328–9, 333, 352–4
  and coronations 89, 160
  description of 337
  for hunting/hawking 34–6
  iconography, 233
  wages of 16
  and weddings 91
  see also tympanum
Taburer, John le 51
Tacitus, *Germania* 286–7
Taillefer, minstrel of William I 287–90, 314
Taillour, Ranulphus, minstrel of Edward III 40
Talbot, Countess 10, 113–14
Tamworth 171, 184 n.2, 248, 313
Taysaunt, John, minstrel of Edward III 174, 176–8, 215
Thetford 122, 158
Thirsk 60
Thixendale 60
Thomas of Lancaster, Duke of Clarence 112
Thomas of Woodstock, Duke of Gloucester 301, 312–13
Thomas, Earl of Lancaster 215
Thomas, Earl of Norfolk 33
Thomas *fatuus*, fool 121
Thomas, fiddler of Edward II 5
Thomas, fiddler of Edward the Black Prince 101
Thomas, harper of John, Lord Howard 115
Thomas, harper of Durham cathedral priory 71, 124–5
Thomas le Barber, minstrel of Bishop of Ely 119
Thomas *le Fole*, minstrel of Edward I 91
Thomas, Sir Rhys ap 80, 83, 214
Thomas, trumpeter of Henry IV 111
Thomas, waferer of Edward the Black Prince 101–2
Thomas of Elmham 143
Thomelmus, *vidulator* of Edward I 91
Thornbury 158
Tickhill 60–1
Tiddersley Hay 14
Tinctoris, Johannes, *De inventione et usu musice* 356–7
Torre, Francisco de la, *La Spagna* 386–8

Touk, Nicholas, cleric of Princess Eleanor 174
Toulouse 273
Tournai 299
training xxviii, 55
  minstrel-schools 65–70
  personal instruction 63–5
travelling of minstrels 164, 169–72, 207, 239, 397
  as messengers/letter carriers 113, 167–8
  royal minstrels 172–82
  sources 165
  as wanderers 269–73
  see also itineraries of minstrels
Trenchant, William, minstrel of Edward I 215
Trentham, John de, harper 71 n.83
Trewennard, Roland 71
Tristan 307
Trompour, Nicholas, minstrel of Edward III *see* Nicholas Trompour
troubadours/*trouvères see* recitation
Trumellus, minstrel of King of France 24
Trumpere, Thomas, minstrel 141
Trumpeter, Thomas (Thomas the trumpeter), trumpeter of Edward III 51–2
trumpeters/trumpets xxv–xxvii, 5–7, 9–11, 32, 36, 42–4, 47, 50–2, 54–5, 57–8, 60–2, 70–1, 73–4, 100–6, 108, 110–16, 118, 170–1, 209, 215, 294, 333–4, 336, 345, 354, 356–8, 378, 396
  and banquets 80
  of civic minstrels 160–1
  clarioners/clarions 6, 80 n.28, 105–6, 110, 136, 319 n.12, 320, 322, 333, 356
  and coronations 86–90
  descriptions of instruments 319–20, 323–5
  iconography 33, 82, 89, 231, 233, 233, 242, 320, 324
  liturgical use of 30–1
  liveries of 25
  marshals of 25, 45–7, 182, 194, 322, 358
  as messengers 167–8
  number of trumpeters 321–2
  and processions 79
  and purifications 96
  residence of 39
  surviving instruments 315
  and tournaments and jousts 81, 82, 83–4
  of towns 131, 133–4, 136–8, 147
  travelling 167–8, 174, 176, 182, 194
  wages of 14, 16, 18–19, 22
  and weddings 91, 93–4
Trumpington, John, minstrel of Henry IV 10, 93

Trumpour, John le *see* John le Trumpour
Tunbridge Wells 194
Turges, John, harper of Queen Margaret 62
Turke, Thomas, vicar of Bere Regis 246
Tussetus, minstrel of King of France 24
Tutbury 111, 199, 203–5, 208, 212, 214, 217–18, 221
   minstrel-fraternity 224–5
Tyas (Tyes), John, minstrel of John of Gaunt 104–7
Tykhill, Richard de, trumpeter of Edward I 61
tympanum 31–2, 328, 336–7; *see also* taborers/tabors/tabretts

Uc de Saint Circ, troubadour 274
Ufford, Lord 36
Ulyn, piper of Edward the Black Prince 103
Unton, Adam, minstrel of Edward the Black Prince 103
urban minstrelsy xxvi, 355, 395
   ceremonies, civic 133–8
   expenditure, levels of 138–41
   guilds 130–9, 141–2
   hiring minstrels 141–2
   hosting royalty and nobility 142–5
   and REED project 128, 149, 151–2
   town life, daily 131
   towns, overview of 129–31
   see also civic minstrels

Vala, Ivo, citoler of Edward II 5, 37, 317, 396
valetti see yeoman/*valetti*
Van Wilder, Philip, minstrel-composer 393–4
veriger/verger 44, 46
Vidal, Raimon 275
   Abril issia 270–1, 287
   Castia Gilos (*Castle of the Jealous*) 263–6, 270, 286–7
vigiles/*vigilatores* 4–7, 36, 57, 70, 74, 80 n.26, 99, 101, 110, 150–1, 156, 325, 329–34, 347, 353–6
   instruments of 31
   liveries 232–4
   and processions 79
   residence of 41
   wages 16, 19–20
   and weddings 91
Visage, mime or actor 91–2
Volaunt, King of heralds and minstrels of Edward III 217
Volsunga Saga 281

Wace
   Brut 278
   Roman de Rou 287–9

Wade, Roger, crowder 65, 316–17, 347
waferers xxv, 4–5, 8–9, 36, 47, 62, 70, 99, 101, 103, 110, 114, 189
   duties 348–51
   in fiction 250, 349
   liveries 23–4, 348
   residence of 41
   wages 20
   and weddings 91, 350
Wafrer, Richard, *scutifer* 51
wages *see* fees and wages; gifts and grants
Wait, Roger, piper 133
Waite, Richard, of Coventry 161
waits 5–8, 50, 330, 332–4
   as civic minstrels 148–53, 155–61
   liveries 23, 130
   meaning of 'wait' 148–51
   of towns 130–1, 138, 355
   travelling 172
   wages 15–16, 22
Waleran of Luxembourg 68
Walter, groom of Hugo of Naunton 54
Walter le Cornour, minstrel of Bishop of Exeter 324
Walter le Vyelur 316–17
Wardlow, John, wait 158
Waren, Richard, minstrel of Henry VII 359
Warenne, Earl 19, 29, 33–4, 36, 47, 54, 58, 93–4, 302, 335
Warham, William, Archbishop of Canterbury 98
Warwick 316
Wastell, William, harper 63–4
Watson, John, wait 159
Watson, William, wait 159
Watt, lute-player of Henry VII 345
Waufrer, Henry, minstrel of Henry IV 350
Wayt, Edmund, *vigilis* of Edward III 332
Wayt, John, *vigilator* of Henry VI 334
Wayt, John, *vigilator* of Richard II 333
Wayt, William *vigilis* of Edward III 332
Wayte, John, groom of Chamber of Henry VI 52
Wayte, Walter, minstrel at Grimsby 157
Wayte, Walter, *vigilis* of Edward III 16, 332
Welshman, David, piper of Richard II 333
Wenceslas of Bohemia, King of the Romans 110
Wessington, John, Prior of Durham cathedral 121
Westminster 12, 20, 84, 86, 143, 165, 173, 175, 176, 180, 182, 183
   Abbey 79
   Hall/palace 25, 79, 87, 89, 93, 96, 212, 259, 324, 330, 335
   ordinance of 4

population 129
tournaments 90, 95, 319 n.13, 354, 358
Westmoreland, Lord 189–90
Whetlay, John, harper 187
Whissh, Henry, minstrel of Edward III 20–1, 37
Whitby 283
Whiteacre, Richard de, harper 93
Whithorn, Prior of 119
Whythorne, Thomas 394
Wild, trumpeter 114
Wilde, John, groom of the Chamber and minstrel of Henry VI 52–3, 62
Wilde, Thomas, squire of the Chamber of Edward IV 52
William de Longchamp, Bishop of Ely 310
William of Bavaria, Count of Ostrevant 69
William, Duke of Bavaria, Count of Holland and of Hainault 104
William I the Conqueror, King of England 236, 287–8
William, lute-player of Henry VII 345
William le Tauborer, minstrel 133
William, psaltery-player of Queen Isabella 5 n.9
William, trumpeter of Edward II xxv, 39
William of Hatfield 96
William of Nassington, *Speculum Vitae* 261
Williamson, Thomas, wait 158
Willyn, piper of Edward the Black Prince 103
Wilmorth, Adrian, sackbut player of Henry VII 358
Winchelsea 299, 357
Winchester 97, 148, 153, 158, 184, 246, 284
  Bishop of 119
  College 53, 119
  Hyde Abbey 70
  St Swithun's 123, 237–8, 312
Windsor 37, 70, 85, 95, 102, 104, 110
Windsor, Alexander de, *vigilis* of Edward I 57, 330 n. 66, 331
Windsor, Geoffrey de, *vigilis* of Edward I 57, 330 n.66, 331
Windsor, John de, *vigilis* of Edward I 56, 331

Wodeford, William *vigilator* of Henry VI 334
Wolston, William, trumpeter of Earl of Northumberland 14
women
  as minstrels xxv–xxvi, 179
  as wives of minstrels xxv, 21, 133, 350
Woodhouse, Hugh, minstrel and marshal 45
Woodstock, Edmund de 70
Woodville, Sir Anthony 295
Worcester 2, 123
Worsley, William, Dean of St Paul's 121
Wrey, Robert, trumpeter of Henry VII 358
Wrey, Thomas, trumpeter of Henry VII 358
Wycombe, minstrel of Edward III 20
Wycombe, Nicholas de, *vigilis* of Edward III 36, 332
Wykes, John, wait 161
Wykes, William, minstrel of Henry VI 7–8, 47, 61–2, 184, 208 n.32

yeoman/*valettus* xxvii, 4, 8, 13, 14, 22, 41, 54–5, 114, 116, 349, 360
  liveries 23–4
  wages 14, 16, 19, 51, 58, 116 n.78
Yetham 170
York 58, 60–1, 66, 71 n.83, 74, 97, 168, 179, 181–2, 209, 338, 397
  aldermen 130
  civic ceremonies 133, 135, 139–41
  civic minstrels 153–5, 158–61
  drama at 30
  itineraries of minstrels 183–9
  minstrel-fraternity 224
  population 129
York, Robert de, trumpeter of Edward I 31, 58, 60
Ypres 66
Yvain and Gawain 312
Yven, trumpeter of Edward II 19, 354

Zevlyn (Jevelyn, Yevelyn, Zeulyn), piper of Edward the Black Prince 102–3
Zorzi Trombetta da Modon 391–2

www.ingramcontent.com/pod-product-compliance
Lightning Source LLC
Chambersburg PA
CBHW070803300426
44111CB00014B/2414